UNEMPLOYMENT IN WESTERN COUNTRIES

INTERNATIONAL ECONOMIC ASSOCIATION PUBLICATIONS

Monopoly and Competition and their Regulation
The Economic Consequences of the Size of Nations
The Theory of Capital
Inflation
The Economics of Take-off into Sustained Growth
International Trade Theory in a Developing World
The Theory of Interest Rates
The Economics of Education
Problems in Economic Development
Price Formation in Various Economies
The Distribution of National Income
Risk and Uncertainty
Economic Problems of Agriculture in Industrial Societies
International Economic Relations
Backward Areas in Advanced Countries
Public Economics
Economic Development in South Asia
North American and Western European Economic Policies
Planning and Market Relations
The Gap Between Rich and Poor Nations
Latin America in the International Economy
Models of Economic Growth
Science and Technology in Economic Growth
Allocation under Uncertainty
Transport and the Urban Environment
The Economics of Health and Medical Care
The Management of Water Quality and the Environment
Agriculture Policy in Developing Countries
The Economic Development of Bangladesh
Economic Factors in Population Growth
Classics in the Theory of Public Finance
Methods of Long-term Planning and Forecasting
Economic Integration
The Economics of Public Services
The Organisation and Retrieval of Economic Knowledge
The Microeconomic Foundations of Macroeconomics
Economic Relations between East and West
Econometric Contributions to Public Policy
Appropriate Technologies for Third World Development
Economic Growth and Resources (5 volumes)
The Relevance of Economic Theories

Unemployment in Western Countries

Proceedings of a Conference held by the International Economic Association at Bischenberg, France

Edited by
EDMOND MALINVAUD
and
JEAN-PAUL FITOUSSI

St. Martin's Press   New York

ISBN 0–312–83268–0

Library of Congress Cataloging in Publication Data
Main entry under title:

Unemployment in Western countries.

Includes index.
1. Unemployed--Congresses. 2. Labor supply--
Congresses. I. Malinvaud, Edmond. II. Fitoussi, Jean
Paul. III. International Economic Association.
HD5707.U45 1980   331.13′79181′2   79–29710
ISBN 0–312–83268–0

Contents

PART THREE MACROECONOMIC ANALYSIS

PART FOUR THE LABOUR MARKET

Acknowledgements

The scientific planning of this Conference was carried through and completed by J.-P. Fitoussi and E. Malinvaud following preliminary work under the guidance of E. Emmerij. The Association owes its thanks to all three, as well as to the other members of the Programme Committee for the result. The Association is further indebted to E. Malinvaud and J.-P. Fitoussi who edited the volume.

Special gratitude goes again to J.-P. Fitoussi for all the excellent local arrangements, and to the three French institutions which financed the local costs and made a generous contribution to the travel — la Direction Générale à la Recherche Scientifique et Technique, le Ministère des Universités, and l'Université de Strasbourg.

The Association offers its thanks also to the Ford Foundation and to UNESCO whose grants were used to supplement the financing recorded above, and to Professor D. Hague, who undertook the responsible task of summarising the discussions.

Programme Committee

J.-P. Fitoussi (France)
E. Malinvaud (France)
B. van Arkadie (Netherlands)
E. Emmerij (Netherlands)
L. Frey (Italy)
H. Gerfin (FRG)
C. Kerr (US)
G. Rehn (Sweden)
E. Thorbecke (US)
T. Timofeev (USSR)

Rapporteur

D. Hague (UK)

List of Participants

Professor Barbara R. Bergmann, University of Maryland, USA.
M. Dos Santos, Université Louis Pasteur, Strasbourg, France.
Professor H. C. Eastman, University of Toronto, Canada.
Professor L. Emmerij, Institute of Social Studies, The Hague, Netherlands.
Professor Luc Fauvel (Secretary General, IEA), 54, Boulevard Raspail, Paris, France.
Professor J.-P. Fitoussi, Université Louis Pasteur, Strasbourg, France.
Mr L. Frey, University of Parma, Italy.
M. J.-L. Gaffard, Université Louis Pasteur, Strasbourg, France.
Professor N. Georgescu-Roegen, Université Louis Pasteur, Strasbourg, France.
Professor Dr H. Giersch (Treasurer, IEA), Institut für Weltwirtschaft, Kiel, FRG.
Dr Margaret S. Gordon, Carnegie Council on Policy Studies in Higher Education, Berkeley, California, USA.
Professor X. Greffe, Faculté des Sciences Economiques, Villetaneuse, France.
Professor E. Grinols, Cornell University, USA.
Professor D. Hague (Rapporteur), Manchester Business School, UK.
Professor P.-Y. Henin, University of Paris, France.
Professor A. G. Hines, Birkbeck College, University of London, UK.
Professor C. C. Holt, The University of Texas at Austin, USA.
Professor S. Honkapohja, Yrjö Jahnsson Foundation, Helsinki, Finland.
Professor Lord Kaldor, King's College, Cambridge, UK.
Mr M. Kaser, St Antony's College, Oxford, UK.
Professor R. T. Kaufman, Amherst College, USA.
Professor S. Khachaturov, Association of Soviet Economic Scientific Institutions, Moscow, USSR.
Professor Th. van de Klundert, Katholieke Hogeschool, Tilburg, Netherlands.
Mr. C Koellreuter, European Centre for Applied Economic Research, Basel, Switzerland.
Professor S. Kolm, Paris, France.
Professor A. Lukaszewicz, Polish Economic Society, Warsaw, Poland.
Professor P. Maillet, Lille, France.
Professor E. Malinvaud, Paris, France.
Professor F. Modigliani (Vice-President, IEA), Sloan School of Management, MIT, Cambridge, USA.

Professor K. Odaka, Hitotsubashi University, Japan.
Professor H. M. A. Onitiri, Nigerian Institute of Social and Economic Research, Ibadan, Nigeria.
Professor M. Parkin, University of Western Ontario, London, Canada.
Professor J. J. Paunio, University of Helsinki, Finland.
Professor Pollin, Université Louis Pasteur, Strasbourg, France.
Professor G. Rehn, Swedish Institute for Social Research, Stockholm, Sweden.
M. M. Richonnier, CEE, Brussels, Belgium.
Professor Sir Austin Robinson (IEA General Editor), The Marshall Library, Cambridge, UK.
M. R. Salais, Chef de la Division Salaires, INSEE, Paris, France.
Professor B. Södersten, Nationalekonomiska Institutionen, Lund, Sweden.
Professor E. Thorbecke, Cornell University, Ithaca, USA.
Professor T. Timofeev, Institute for International Labour Movement, Academy of Sciences, Moscow, USSR.
Professor S. Tsuru (President, IEA), The Asahi Shimbun, Tokyo, Japan.
Professor D. Vitry, Université Louis Pasteur, Strasbourg, France.

Interpreters

M. A. Naudeau, Boulogne/Billancourt, France.
Mrs Janine Yates, Geneva, Switzerland.

Secretariat

Miss Mary Crook, Administrative Secretary, IEA.
Mrs Elizabeth Majid, Assistant, IEA.
Mrs Brenda Hague, Wilmslow, UK.

Introduction

E. Malinvaud and J.-P. Fitoussi

Economists of western countries are faced with the pressing problem of unemployment. How could a conference of the International Economic Association help them better to take on the challenging task that confronts them in this respect? What contribution can these proceedings make? Answers have to remain modest and readers should not hope to find recipes with immediate practical usefulness in this volume.

People expect of economists that they should prepare more adequate government decisions and indeed this is probably the main duty of our profession. Moreover, since economic situations within various countries are largely interdependent, concerted action at the international level seems to be called for. But a scientific organisation can only have a very indirect impact on policies and fortunately many international meetings deal with unemployment problems from the intergovernmental point of view.

The conference that met in Bischenberg was therefore intended to stimulate mutual understanding between research workers and mainly concerned with the theoretical analysis of unemployment. The purpose was to identify the issues correctly, to confront and evaluate alternative approaches, to suggest new questions to be considered and to elucidate the exact domain of validity of various analytical tools.

The conference also wanted to propose a better understanding between labour economists and those general economists who pay special attention to unemployment. Preconditions for an improved understanding are met since each of the two groups feels it needs collaboration from the other one: labour economists know that explaining the level of unemployment requires consideration of the full macroeconomic set up; general economists know that unemployment has very important structural aspects requiring specific studies and that the actual working of the labour market is not well described in available general theories.

The organisation of this book reflects the purpose of the conference. Its two major parts respectively concern on the one hand the macroeconomic analysis to which general economists devote most of their attention, on the other hand the analysis of the labour market, which is the main field of interest of labour economists. But two shorter parts initiate the subsequent developments. The first one intends to pose the problems in the precise context that western countries now experience. The second one concerns the crucial issue of the interdependence between unemployment and international trade policy.

The conference was not intended to provide a complete description of current unemployment, nor to concentrate on the identification of its causes, nor to elaborate a programme for curing it. Participants were, of course, well informed of the prevailing situation, even if, as it appears in particular in the report of the discussions, they often differed somewhat as to their views concerning what was fundamentally new about it. However, three papers of a rather general nature and directly concerned with the current situation were considered as a background material and make up the first part of these proceedings.

Studying unemployment in North America, Western Europe and Japan, R. T. Kaufman first shows that changes in the demographic structure of the labour force can only explain at most a very small part of the recent surge, which is largely due to an increasing gap between potential and actual output. His analysis also shows that unemployment rates are more sensitive in America than elsewhere to macroeconomic disturbances, which implies that the firm's manpower policies significantly vary from one region to another.

T. Timofeev presents a survey of the unemployment problem in western countries and in Eastern Europe. He not only reviews the broad lines of argument used by theorists but also looks at the positions taken by trades unions, by politicians and by various international conferences. Concerning the scientific management of the labour force in socialist countries, he discusses some of the challenges it had to face.

Starting from the view that unemployment is going to be a long-term phenomenon, L. Emmerij dismisses as ineffective the conventional economic instruments of either private demand management or profit restoration. Although a worldwide Marshall Plan and the development of local public services could contribute somewhat to the solution of the present problem, he believes that new legislation that would reduce the labour supply is also required. He presents a definite proposal to this effect.

Among the policy measures that are considered for curing unemployment, those restricting international trade are particularly debated. Indeed, whereas many cases are known at the microeconomic level in which foreign competition is responsible for unemployment, the question arises whether international trade as a whole is a factor in aggregate unemployment. To this question the two papers of the second part are devoted.

N. Kaldor starts from a critique of the abstract theory of international trade. He thinks this theory overlooked that in some cases free trade will create unemployment and make the world worse off than it would be under some system of regulated trade. He finds reasons in economic history for believing this case to be significant. Unemployment effects are seen as particularly noteworthy in trade between manufacturing countries, sensitive as it is to economies of scale, polarisation processes and the resultant trade imbalance.

E. Grinols and E. Thorbecke use input-output techniques to examine the related but distinct question as to whether trade between the US and the developing countries has caused the US employment situation to deteriorate. A rigorous answer is difficult to get, as usual when one somehow compares an actual evolution with what might have been otherwise. But a careful discussion suggests that the net overall effect between 1962 and 1975 was small and that, if anything, it was rather favourable to American employment.

Macroeconomic analysis, which is the subject of the third part, is here mainly approached from the theoretical side, but the last of the five papers deals with an application to the study of trends and policies in one country. The first two are concerned with how analysis of unemployment can benefit from the theory of general equilibrium under sticky prices and rationing.

A. G. Hines scrutinises the notion of involuntary unemployment and argues that it can make sense only at the macro level. Indeed, according to him, that unemployment is involuntary which can only be cured by an expansion of aggregate demand by accepting that lower-wage labour would not get rid of this unemployment, which then does not depend on labour's actions. He then studies the consequences that the behaviour of prices and money wages may have, depending on the type of situation that prevails.

The main focus of the paper by E. Malinvaud is to discuss, from two points of view, the relevance of the concept of classical unemployment. When a disaggregated representation of production is considered, such unemployment may be recognised in some sectors and its occurrence significantly reduces the multiplier. A heuristic discussion of the dynamics of price and wage adjustments under classical unemployment also suggests that the latter may not vanish as quickly as one might have thought.

J.-P. Fitoussi and N. Georgescu-Roegen want first to point out that post-war technological progress has an important role in explaining present unemployment, which often appears as structural. Large changes in the structures of the productive sector have been required. The authors then analyse why asymmetries in agents' behaviour prevent quick adaptations to these changes.

No complete treatment of unemployment can ignore inflation. M. Parkin surveys the present state of knowledge about the so-called trade-off. He considers, systematically and often critically, the theoretical research of the past ten years and shows that it raises a number of puzzles to be clarified by empirical work. He sees no justification for activism in demand management or incomes policies but wonders whether the institutions ruling the money supply should not be reformed.

Two econometric models of Western Germany are used by C. Koellreuter who discusses in particular their representation of the demand for labour and the employment elasticities with respect to output and wages. *Ex post* analysis of the 1974–75 recession is followed by the examination of various scenarios for 1978–80, these being intended to help in the choice of a macroeconomic policy.

The fourth part of these proceedings begins with the observation that in a segmented labour market the unemployment rate is high where high wages are paid, so that a low 'job availability' compensates for the attraction of good wages. C. Holt presents a theoretical model for the phenomenon and argues that, when allocation is made by job availability as well as by wages, the market has a full spectrum of equilibria, which brings a new light on the rationale for, and nature of, the Phillips relation.

Dealing with employment discrimination in the US, B. Bergmann surveys a number of theoretical explanations. She then builds and applies a simulation model in which various race-sex groups are characterised by distinct transition probabilities as between different states with respect to employment or activity. The discrepancies between these probabilities provide measures of the segmentation of the labour market. The model shows what can be expected from actions that would remove some of these discrepancies.

B. Södersten scrutinises two major evolutions affecting the labour supply: the increasing participation of women and the trend towards new forms of organisation of work. He sees the first one as being partially explained by the modern theory of the household but also as due to the feedback of some other social changes. The appearance of new types of organisation within firms is a response to a new attitude of employees, who put higher weight than before on work satisfaction.

L. Frey argues along somewhat different lines. He considers that income inequality is a major factor explaining the present high labour supply. Due to the demonstration effect, strong incentives exist within families for high consumption spending, which leads to an increase of female participation in the labour force. Hence a policy aiming at income equalisation would make a significant contribution to the cure of unemployment.

The remarkably low level of unemployment in Japan and its lack of sensitivity to business fluctuations have often been related to special features of manpower management in that country. It is therefore fitting that K. Odaka provides a careful account of the working of the Japanese labour market. It turns out that flexibility exists both in the supply of and in the demand for labour.

This brief summary of the purpose of each of the fifteen papers leaves no room for the discussion of the ideas and results that were proposed. But the discussion was lively, as the reader will see from the reports presented in this book, reports that of course defy abridgement.

PART ONE

The Unemployment Problem

1 Patterns of Unemployment in North America, Western Europe and Japan*

Roger T. Kaufman
AMHERST COLLEGE, USA

I INTRODUCTION

With few exceptions, unemployment rates throughout the Western world have increased sharply during the past five years. Although they have begun to decline in several countries, especially the United States, it appears that they will remain at historically high levels for at least several more years. In this paper we shall present an overview of recent unemployment patterns in North America, Japan and several countries in western Europe.

We begin by illustrating the increases in unemployment rates and proceed to identify and isolate the structural causes of these increases. We then show how unemployment rates in North America are more sensitive to macro-economic disturbances in the short run than those in Europe and Japan, and we suggest several reasons for this phenomenon. Finally, we present evidence that indicates that the growth rate of potential output is lower in the post-1973 period, but the relationship between employment rates and potential output has remained constant. This suggests that the recent surge in unemployment rates is largely the result of output levels continuing to rise at rates substantially below the growth rates of potential output.

II RECENT TRENDS IN UNEMPLOYMENT RATES

In Table 1.1 we present annual unemployment rates from 1960 to 1977 as published by officials in the United States, Canada, Japan and several European nations. Although these rates differ substantially among countries, all of the countries listed except Sweden have experienced a sharp increase in unemployment during the past three to five years. In France, Germany, Italy

* The author wishes to thank Richard Spady, Peter Montiel and Frank Westhoff for their helpful suggestions and comments. Technical assistance by Constance Sorrentino and Joyanna Moy of the US Department of Labor is also gratefully acknowledged. Support for this research was provided by the Sloan Foundation through its grant to MIT on Public Control of Economic Activity.

TABLE 1.1 PUBLISHED UNEMPLOYMENT RATES IN VARIOUS ADVANCED COUNTRIES, 1960–77[a]
(percentages)

Year	United States	Canada	Japan	France	West Germany	Italy	Sweden	Great Britain
1960	5.5	7.0	1.7	1.3	1.3	4.0	NA	1.5
1961	6.7	7.2	1.4	1.1	0.8	3.4	1.4	1.4
1962	5.5	5.9	1.3	1.2	0.7	3.0	1.5	1.9
1963	5.7	5.5	1.3	1.4	0.8	2.5	1.7	2.3
1964	5.2	4.7	1.1	1.1	0.8	2.7	1.6	1.6
1965	4.5	3.9	1.2	1.4	0.7	3.6	1.2	1.4
1966	3.8	3.4	1.3	1.4	0.7	3.9	1.6	1.4
1967	3.8	3.8	1.3	1.8	2.1	3.5	2.1	2.2
1968	3.6	4.5	1.2	2.1	1.5	3.5	2.2	2.4
1969	3.5	4.4	1.1	1.7	0.9	3.4	1.9	2.4
1970	4.9	5.7	1.1	1.7	0.7	3.2	1.5	2.5
1971	5.9	6.2	1.2	2.1	0.8	3.2	2.5	3.4
1972	5.6	6.2	1.4	2.3	1.1	3.7	2.7	3.7
1973	4.9	5.6	1.3	2.1	1.2	3.5	2.5	2.6
1974	5.6	5.4	1.4	2.8	2.6	2.9	2.0	2.6
1975	8.5	6.9	1.9	4.1	4.7	3.3	1.6	4.1
1976	7.7	7.1	2.0	4.5	4.6	3.7	1.6	5.6
1977	7.0	8.1	2.0	5.2	4.5	7.2	1.8	6.2

[a] For the United States, Canada and France unemployment as a per cent of the civilian labour force; for Italy, Japan and Sweden, unemployment as a per cent of the civilian labour force plus career military personnel; for Great Britain and West Germany, registered unemployed as a per cent of employed wage and salary workers plus the unemployed. With the exception of France, which does not publish an unemployment rate, these are the usually published unemployment rates for each country.

SOURCE Private communication with Constance Sorrentino, US Bureau of Labor Statistics, May 1978.

and Great Britain unemployment rates have more than doubled. It should be noted, however, that the Italian survey was revised in 1977, and these revisions partially account for the large increase in the Italian unemployment rate for that year.

The national authorities in the various countries often use different definitions of unemployment and labour force participation, and they often employ different methods of obtaining these data. As a result, these published unemployment rates are usually incommensurable across nations. The US Department of Labor has resolved this problem by using labour force survey data in each country to calculate unemployment rates adjusted to US concepts. The adjusted unemployment definitions are essentially those recommended by the International Labour Office in 1954 and reaffirmed in 1973. A person is generally counted as unemployed in the adjusted data if he or she did not work at all for pay or profit during the survey week but has actively sought work within some pre-specified period. Workers on temporary layoff and people waiting to begin a new job within a specified period are counted among the unemployed even if they have not actively sought other employment.[1] Adjustments to published data on the labour force are also necessary to achieve conformity. These adjusted unemployment rates are displayed in Table 1.2.

Throughout the 1960s and part of the 1970s, the US and Canadian adjusted unemployment rates were more than twice those prevailing in most of the other countries listed in Table 1.2. Some of the reasons for these differences have been discussed elsewhere.[2] Excepting Sweden, the adjusted unemployment rates in all the countries listed in Table 1.2 have increased significantly in the past five years. At least one European country now has a higher adjusted unemployment rate than the United States.

III DEMOGRAPHIC FACTORS IN THE INCREASE OF UNEMPLOYMENT RATES

Several authors have attributed much of the increase in the unemployment rates of the mid-1970s to changes in demography and labour force participation rates. Inasmuch as women and youth typically have looser attachments to their jobs than adult men, *ceteris paribus* the aggregate unemployment rate may be expected to rise as the former groups increase their relative shares of the labour force. This increase in the unemployment

---

[1] For a detailed description of these adjustments see Constance Sorrentino, 'Methodological and Conceptual Problems of Measuring Unemployment in O.E.C.D. Countries' (Paper prepared for the OECD, January 1976).

[2] See, for example, Roger T. Kaufman, 'An International Comparison of Unemployment Rates: The Effects of Job Security and Job Continuity' (Ph.D. dissertation, Massachusetts Institute of Technology, 1978).

TABLE 1.2 UNEMPLOYMENT RATES ADJUSTED TO INTERNATIONAL CONCEPTS, 1960–77
(Unemployment as a Percentage of the Civilian Labour Force)

Year	United States	Canada	Japan	France	West Germany	Italy	Sweden	Great Britain
1960	5.5	7.0	1.7	1.8	1.1	3.8	NA	2.2
1961	6.7	7.1	1.5	1.6	0.6	3.2	1.4	2.0
1962	5.5	5.9	1.3	1.5	0.6	2.8	1.5	2.8
1963	5.7	5.5	1.3	1.3	0.5	2.4	1.7	3.4
1964	5.2	4.7	1.2	1.5	0.4	2.6	1.5	2.5
1965	4.5	3.9	1.2	1.6	0.3	3.5	1.2	2.2
1966	3.8	3.4	1.4	1.9	0.3	3.8	1.6	2.3
1967	3.8	3.8	1.3	2.0	1.3	3.4	2.1	3.4
1968	3.6	4.5	1.2	2.6	1.4	3.4	2.2	3.3
1969	3.5	4.4	1.1	2.4	0.9	3.3	1.9	3.0
1970	4.9	5.7	1.2	2.6	0.8	3.1	1.5	3.1
1971	5.9	6.2	1.3	2.8	0.8	3.1	2.6	3.9
1972	5.6	6.2	1.4	2.8	0.8	3.6	2.7	4.2
1973	4.9	5.6	1.3	2.7	0.8	3.4	2.5	3.2
1974	5.6	5.4	1.4	3.0	1.7	2.8	2.0	2.8
1975	8.5	6.9	1.9	4.2	3.7	3.2	1.6	4.7[a]
1976	7.7	7.1	2.0	4.6	3.6	3.6	1.6	6.4[a]
1977	7.0	8.1	2.0	5.2	3.6	3.3	1.8	6.9[a]

[a] Preliminary estimates based on incomplete data.

SOURCE Private communication with Constance Sorrentino, US Bureau of Labor Statistics, May 1978.

rate would not be the result of deficient aggregate demand but the result of increased 'search activity'.

In order to ascertain the magnitude of these effects on unemployment rates within the past decade, we divided the working-age population into four groups: males and females below the age of twenty-five and males and females twenty-five years and older. Clearly,

$$U = U_1 + U_2 + U_3 + U_4 = \sum_i U_i \tag{1}$$

$$L = L_1 + L_2 + L_3 + L_4 = \sum_i L_i \tag{2}$$

$$P = P_1 + P_2 + P_3 + P_4 = \sum_i P_i \tag{3}$$

where U, L and P equal aggregate unemployment, labour force, and working-age population and U_i, L_i and P_i equal unemployment, labour force and population in the ith group. Whereas we use upper case letters to denote absolute levels, we shall use lower case letters to denote rates. Thus, if u is equal to the aggregate unemployment rate, then

$$u = \frac{U}{L} = \frac{\sum_i U_i}{\sum_i L_i}. \tag{4}$$

Also note that

$$U_i = \frac{U_i}{L_i} \cdot \frac{L_i}{P_i} \cdot \frac{P_i}{P} \cdot P = u_i l_i \pi_i P \tag{5}$$

and

$$L_i = \frac{L_i}{P_i} \cdot \frac{P_i}{P} \cdot P = l_i \pi_i P \tag{6}$$

where u_i and l_i equal the unemployment rate and the labour force participation rate within the ith group and π_i equals the population within the ith group expressed as a fraction of the total working-age population, which we have taken to be the total population above the age of fifteen or sixteen, depending on the country.

Combining equations (1) through (6) we obtain

$$u = \frac{\sum_i u_1 l_i \pi_i}{\sum_i l_i \pi_i}. \tag{7}$$

Equation (7) reveals that the aggregate unemployment rate can be expressed as a weighted average of the unemployment rates in the four groups previously mentioned. The weights are merely combinations of the labour force participation rates and population shares of these same four groups. To view

the effects of the aforementioned changes in demography and labour force
participation rates, we made two sets of calculations. First, we held the
individual group unemployment and labour force participation rates constant
at the levels achieved in some 'typical' initial year in the late 1960s or 1970.
In choosing the particular year we tried to avoid years with abnormally high
or low unemployment. The choice was occasionally determined by the
availability of consistent data. We then calculated the hypothetical 1976 or
1977 aggregate unemployment rate that would have been achieved in each
country if only demographic changes had occurred during the period. In other
words, we computed equation (7) using the population shares in 1976 or
1977 and the group unemployment rates and labour force participation rates
that prevailed in the initial year. The resulting hypothetical unemployment
rates are listed in the third column of Table 1.3 (see pp. 10–11).

In the fourth column of Table 1.3 we show the results of our second set of
calculations. Here, we allowed both population shares and group labour force
participation rates to change during the period. Thus, these hypothetical
unemployment rates were computed using population shares and group
labour force participation rates from 1976 or 1977 and group unemployment
rates from the initial year in the 1960s.

Table 1.3 clearly indicates that the sharp increases in unemployment rates
in the past few years have *not* been the result of changes in demography and
labour force participation rates. Only in the United States has the net effect
been greater than 0.1 percentage points, and even here the effect has
accounted for only about 11 per cent of the total change in the unemployment rate. The unemployment rate increases have been caused primarily by
increases in the group unemployment rates. While these in turn may be
affected by labour force participation and demography, other factors are
undoubtedly present. Of course, we may not infer that these increases were
solely caused by deficiencies in aggregate demand or the demand for labour.
Increases in unemployment benefits and the number of secondary earners,
for instance, may increase search activity and possibly increase the unemployment rate independently of any changes in labour demand. We will, however,
return to this question in the last section of this paper.

It should be noted that we excluded Italy from these calculations. Even
before the Italians revised their labour force survey in 1977 several authors
questioned the comprehensiveness and the consistency of their data. The size
of the so-called 'black' or unofficial labour market has allegedly been growing
very rapidly in Italy. This renders historical comparisons of the data quite
unreliable.

IV SEPARATING THE DIFFERENT DEMOGRAPHIC FACTORS

In this section we attempt to answer a different question: What portions of
the increases in the unemployment rates may be attributed to changes
affecting each of the four previously mentioned demographic groups?

Reviewing equation (4), we note again that the aggregate unemployment rate u may be written as

$$u = \frac{U}{L} = \frac{\sum_i U_i}{\sum_i L_i}. \tag{4}$$

Totally differentiating equation (4), we obtain

$$du = \frac{L\sum_i dU_i - U\sum_i dL_i}{L^2}. \tag{8}$$

Each age and sex group obviously contributes to changes in the aggregate unemployment rate in two ways: through changes in the number of unemployed and through changes in the labour force. Equation (8) may be broken down more completely into changes in group unemployment rates, labour force participation rates and population shares, but this is unnecessary for our current purposes.

Let the change in the aggregate unemployment rate attributable to the ith group be designated by du^i. Assuming that any intergroup effects are minimal,

$$du^i = \frac{LdU_i - UdL_i}{L^2}. \tag{9}$$

Also note that

$$du = \sum_i du^i \tag{10}$$

For the periods given in Table 1.3 we estimated the fractions of the total change in the unemployment rate attributable to our four age and sex groups. These percentages, given in Table 1.4, reveal several noteworthy patterns. In all seven countries except Sweden, where the percentage contributions are rather meaningless because the total change in the aggregate unemployment rate is only 0.1 percentage point, the relative contribution of adult males is surprisingly high. This is especially true in Japan, where labour force and unemployment changes among males over the age of twenty-four accounted for 65.8 per cent of the increase in the aggregate unemployment rate between 1967 and 1976. In addition, the contributions of adult men in West Germany and the United States are also quite high. Changes among the female and younger groups clearly do not account for an overwhelming portion of the unemployment rate increases. This may be seen more easily in Table 1.5, where we have combined the results of Table 1.4 in two convenient ways.

Before concluding this section we should note that comparisons of the two French and British cases show the expected results. In Great Britain married women often exercise their option of withholding contributions from the otherwise compulsory national unemployment insurance fund. As a result, many have been unable to collect unemployment benefits and have

TABLE 1.3 ACTUAL AND HYPOTHETICAL UNEMPLOYMENT RATES

Country[a]	Actual unemployment rate in the late 1960s (exact date)	Actual unemployment rate in 1976 or 1977 (exact date)	Hypothetical unemployment rate in the later year assuming that only population shares had changed during the period	Hypothetical unemployment rate in the later year assuming that only population shares and group labour force participation rates had changed during the period
United States	4.9 (1970)	7.7 (1976)	5.0	5.2
Canada	4.4 (1969)	8.1 (1977)	4.4	4.5
Japan	1.3 (1967)	2.0 (1976)	1.3	1.3
France I[b]	2.7 (March 1969)	4.8 (March 1977)	2.7	2.7
France II[b]	1.7 (March 1969)	4.5 (March 1977)	1.7	1.7
West Germany	0.6 (April 1970)	3.6 (May 1976)	0.6	0.6
Sweden	1.5 (1970)	1.6 (1976)	1.5	1.5
Great Britain I[c]	2.3 (1966)	2.8 (1974)[d]	2.3	2.2
Great Britain II[c]	1.1 (July 1966)	6.0 (July 1977)	1.1	1.0

[a] Unless noted otherwise the data utilised in these calculations are labour force and unemployment data adjusted to US (international) concepts. Hence, the unemployment rates refer to the number of unemployed as a percentage of the civilian labour force. US and Canadian data require no adjustments, and the adjustments to the published Japanese and Swedish data are very small.

[b] In France I we use French data adjusted to BIT, or international concepts, which are very similar to US definitions. The March 1969 data have been adjusted by the author. In France II we use published French data on the unemployed population which is available to look for a job (*population disponible à la recherche d'un emploi* – PDRE), and published labour force and population data.

Note that the March 1969 unemployment rate is not equal to the 1969 figure presented in Table 1.2 because the former refers to one particular month in that year. The same comment is pertinent in viewing the German data.

[c] In Great Britain I we use British data which have been adjusted to US concepts by the US Department of Labor. These emanated from the 1966 Census and the 1974 General Household Survey. Additional adjustments to exclude 15-year-olds from the 1966 data have been made by the author. In Great Britain II we use unadjusted British data published by the Department of Employment. The unemployment data here refer to those registered as unemployed.

In both Great Britain I and II the total population figures included military personnel, and in Great Britain II the labour force included military personnel.

[d] 1974 was the latest year for which complete adjusted data were available to the author.

SOURCES US Department of Labor and individual country sources.

TABLE 1.4 PERCENTAGE CONTRIBUTIONS TO CHANGES IN THE AGGREGATE UNEMPLOYMENT RATE

Country	Total percentage point change in the aggregate unemployment rate during the period given in Table 1.3	Percentage of the total change in the unemployment rate attributable to changes among:			
		Males 15–24 years old	Males 25 years and older	Females 15–24 years old	Females 25 years and older
United States	2.8	24.5[a]	33.2	19.7[a]	22.6
Canada	3.7	32.9	17.7	27.6	21.8
Japan	0.7	20.6	65.8	9.6	4.1
France I[b]	2.1	21.4	15.8	32.6	30.2
France II[b]	2.8	20.0	22.5	32.5	25.0
West Germany	3.0	17.1	40.1	17.1	25.8
Sweden	0.1	33.3[a]	–77.8[c]	133.3[a]	11.1[c]
Great Britain I[b]	0.6	32.1[a]	23.2	23.2[a]	21.4
Great Britain II[b]	4.9	29.9[a]	41.3	22.6[a]	6.1

[a] Data for youths 16–24 years old were used for the United States, Sweden and Great Britain.
[b] See the notes to Table 1.3 for a description of the data and periods used in these cases.
[c] Swedish data refer to adults between the ages of 25 and 74.

SOURCES Calculated from data obtained from the US Department of Labor and individual country sources.

TABLE 1.5 SUMMARY OF THE PERCENTAGE CONTRIBUTIONS TO
CHANGES IN THE AGGREGATE UNEMPLOYMENT RATE AS SHOWN
IN TABLE 1.4

	Percentage[a] of the total change in the unemployment rate attributable to changes among:			
Country	Males	Females	Youths (under 25)	Adults (25 years and older)
United States	57.7	43.3	44.2	55.8
Canada	50.6	49.4	60.5	39.5
Japan	86.4	13.6	30.2	69.8
France I	37.2	62.8	54.0	46.0
France II	42.5	57.5	52.5	47.5
West Germany	57.2	42.9	34.2	65.9
Sweden	−44.5	144.4	166.6	−66.7
Great Britain I	55.3	44.6	55.3	44.6
Great Britain II	71.2	28.7	52.5	47.4

[a] Totals may not add to 100.0 per cent because of rounding errors.

not bothered to register. Compared with the General Household Surveys the
British registration data have significantly underestimated the level and the
change in the level of female unemployment. Similarly, the unadjusted French
unemployment data in Tables 1.3–1.5 exclude all the 'marginally unemployed'
(PMDRE), many of whom are adult women. In contrast, many of these
women are included in the unemployment data adjusted to international
definitions.

V. THE CYCLICAL SENSITIVITY OF UNEMPLOYMENT

In this section we estimate the cyclical sensitivity of unemployment in five
countries. We find that unemployment rates abroad are significantly less
sensitive to macroeconomic disturbances in the immediate and short run.
Except in the case of Japan, however, these differences diminish in the longer
run. We attribute the smaller short-run reactions in Western Europe and Japan
to the prevalence of legal and traditional sanctions against temporary and
permanent layoffs.

The basic model we utilise was first developed by Arthur Okun.[1] Okun

[1] Arthur M. Okun, 'Potential GNP: Its Measurement and Significance',
*Proceedings of the Business and Economic Statistics Section of the American
Statistical Association* (1962), pp. 98–104.

hypothesised a relationship between the unemployment (or employment) rate and the levels or growth rates of actual and 'potential' output. Potential output is defined as the level of output which could be produced if the economy were operating at some optimal level, in the sense that unemployment is minimised (and output is maximised) subject perhaps to the constraint that inflation be held to some acceptable level. Alternatively, potential output may be defined as the level of output associated with the 'natural rate of unemployment'.

Lacking rigorous measurement of either potential output or its growth rate, Okun and more recent authors employed linear and exponential time trends starting from some benchmark. Friedman and Wachter[1] show the simplicity involved in typical Okun's Law equations. If we postulate a two-input Cobb–Douglas aggregate production function with constant returns to scale and disembodied technological progress, we may express total output Y in period t as

$$Y_t = (Cap_t \cdot K_t)^\alpha [(POP_t \cdot Part_t)(1.00 - u_t)(H_t)]^{1-\alpha} \beta e^{\gamma t} \qquad (11)$$

where

Cap_t = capacity utilisation

K_t = capital stock

POP_t = total population

$Part_t$ = participation rate

u_t = unemployment rate

H_t = hours worked per employed worker

all measured at time t, and

$\alpha, \beta\ \gamma$ are parameters.

Okun's Law essentially collapses all the right-hand-side variables into u_t and a composite time trend, the latter representing the growth of potential output. Despite their simplicity, conventional Okun's Laws play an important role in recent macroeconomic models inasmuch as they provide a simple nexus between the goods market and the labour market, thereby establishing a relationship between output and wage and price inflation.

In Okun's original article he estimated three alternative specifications of

---

[1] Benjamin M. Friedman and Michael L. Wachter, 'Unemployment: Okun's Law, Labor Force, and Productivity', *Review of Economics and Statistics*, 56 (May 1974), 167–76.

his model (two of which can be shown to be mathematically equivalent)[1] and found that each additional percentage point increase in the measured US unemployment rate was associated with approximately a three percentage point reduction in real GNP. The three-to-one ratio resulted from changes in the labour force, employment, hours worked per worker and procyclical productivity changes. After experimenting with several specifications we chose Okun's third formulation, in which he posited the following constant elasticity relationship:

$$\frac{N_t}{N_t^P} = \left(\frac{Y_t}{Y_t^P}\right)^{\gamma}.$$

where

N_t = the employment rate (i.e., $1 - u_t$) in quarter t

N_t^P = the 'potential' employment rate in quarter t

Y_t = output, or real GNP, in quarter t, and

Y_t^P = potential output in quarter t.

Several authors have attempted to estimate potential output from aggregate production functions which incorporate estimates of the current

---

[1] Two of Okun's specifications were:

$$u_t - u_{t-1} = \alpha[(Y_t^P - Y_{t-1}^P)/Y_{t-1}^P - (Y_t - Y_{t-1})/Y_{t-1}]$$

and

$$u_t = \alpha + \beta[(Y_t^P - Y^t)/Y_t^P].$$

Note, however, that

$$\beta[(Y_t^P - Y_t)/Y_t^P] \simeq \beta[\ln Y_t^P - \ln Y_t]$$

for small percentage gaps between actual and potential output. Thus,

$$u_t = \alpha + \beta[(Y_t^P - Y_t)/Y_t^P] \simeq \alpha + \beta[\ln Y_t^P - \ln Y_t].$$

Similarly,

$$u_{t-1} \simeq \alpha + \beta[\ln Y_{t-1}^P - \ln Y_{t-1}].$$

Thus,

$$u_t - u_{t-1} \simeq \beta[\ln Y_t^P - \ln Y_{t-1}^P - (\ln Y_t - \ln Y_{t-1})]$$

and the two specifications are almost mathematically equivalent. It is therefore no surprise that estimations of the two yield similar results.

capital stock and the hypothetical size of the labour force at potential output.[1] The current capital stock is usually calculated as the cumulative addition of net investment to some historical benchmark estimate. Lacking comparable data across countries, we merely assumed that potential output grows at some constant exponential growth rate r such that

$$Y_t^P = Y_0^P e^{rt}. \tag{13}$$

Later, however, we test the hypothesis that this growth rate has changed.

Substituting equation (13) into equation (12), taking logarithms and rearranging yields

$$\log N_t = [\log N_t^P - \gamma \log Y_0^P] + \gamma \log Y_t - \gamma rt. \tag{14}$$

Direct estimation of this equation, treating the terms within the brackets as a constant,[2] yielded reasonable results for four of the five countries in our sample. The results were dramatically improved, however, when we accounted for the likelihood that changes in the employment rate will lag behind changes in output. These lags will occur for a variety of reasons. If firms have invested in specific training for their workers they will be reluctant to lay them off during temporary shortfalls of demand lest they be unable to rehire them as demand rebounds. Similarly, they may be cautious about hiring new workers and training them if they feel that increases in demand are temporary. If there are significant adjustment costs in altering the level of labour input, it may be optimal for firms to adjust only partially to the desired level of labour input in each period. The prevalence of job security and job continuity

---

[1] For estimates of potential output in the United States see Edwin Kuh, 'Measurement of Potential Output', *American Economic Review*, 56 (September 1966); 758–76; Stanley W. Black and R. Robert Russell, 'An Alternative Estimate of Potential GNP', *Review of Economics and Statistics*, 51 (February 1969), 70–6; Lester C. Thurow and L. Taylor, 'The Interaction between the Actual and Potential Rates of Growth', *Review of Economics and Statistics*, 48 (November 1966), 351–60; and George L. Perry, 'Potential Output and Productivity', *Brookings Papers on Economic Activity* (1977:1), pp. 11–47. Jacques Artus has recently made similar computations to estimate potential output in manufacturing for several countries. As we shall indicate, however, his assumption that the speed of factor adjustment is identical in all countries (save the current and preceding six month period) seems inappropriate. Jacques R. Artus, 'Measures of Potential Output in Manufacturing for Eight Industrial Countries', *I.M.F. Staff Papers* 24 (March 1977), 1–35. More sophisticated efforts have also been undertaken by the OECD. See, for instance, Annex II in OECD, *A Medium Term Strategy for Employment and Manpower Policies* (Paris: OECD, 1978).

[2] If the potential rate of employment N_t^P is not constant, this procedure is, of course, invalid and the estimates will be biased. Nevertheless, any quarterly percentage changes in N_t^P are probably very small compared with the percentage changes in actual and potential output. The estimates of γ and r will be biased but the biases are small.

provisions, especially outside the United States, makes it more difficult for firms to lay off workers and also makes them more wary about adding new employees.[1]

We suggest that the current employment rate will be dependent upon past as well as current output. Thus, our specification becomes:

$$\frac{N_t}{N_t^P} = \left[\frac{Y_t^{a_0} Y_{t-1}^{a_1} Y_{t-2}^{a_2} \cdots Y_{t-k}^{a_k}}{Y_t^P} \right]^{\gamma} \tag{15}$$

In order for γ to be identified in equation (15), we must make one restriction on the a_is. We choose to constrain the a_is such that $\Sigma_{i=0}^{k} a_i = 1$. Taking the logarithm of equation (15) yields

$$\log N_t - \log N_t^P = \gamma[a_0 \log Y_t + a_1 \log Y_{t-1} + \cdots + a_k \log Y_{t-k}] - \gamma \log Y_t^P. \tag{16}$$

We shall again assume that potential output grows at a constant exponential rate, i.e., $Y_t^P = Y_0^P e^{rt}$. Substituting into equation (16) and rearranging yields:

$$\log N_t = [\log N_t^P - \gamma \log Y_0^P] - \gamma rt + \gamma[a_0 \log Y_t + \cdots + a_k \log Y_{t-k}]. \tag{17}$$

Note that the log specification allows us to measure differences in the speed of adjustments among countries as well as the cumulative adjustment. *A priori* we expect the response of the US and Canadian unemployment rates to be quicker than those in other countries because of the relative dearth of job security and job continuity provisions in the former two countries. Over time, however, we might expect the cumulative responses to be less disparate.

Equation (17) can also be derived from a more structural model of the labour market. By definition,

$$\frac{N_t}{N_t^P} = \frac{E_t/L_t}{E_t^P/L_t^P} = \frac{E_t/E_t^P}{L_t/L_t^P} \tag{18}$$

where E_t and E_t^P equal the actual and 'potential' levels of employment in quarter t, respectively, and L_t and L_t^P equal the actual and 'potential' levels of the civilian labour force in quarter t. Assume that the employment ratio in the numerator is determined by

$$\frac{E_t}{E_t^P} = \left(\frac{Y_t}{Y_t^P} \right)^{a_0} \left(\frac{Y_{t-1}}{Y_t^P} \right)^{a_1} \left(\frac{Y_{t-2}}{Y_t^P} \right)^{a_2} \cdots \left(\frac{Y_{t-j}}{Y_t^P} \right)^{a_j}. \tag{19}$$

The coefficients $a_0, \ldots, a_j$ emanate from the inverse production function and the costs of adjusting employment. It is assumed that firms can change output without altering employment via adjusting hours and possibly

---

[1] Desired employment itself, as calculated from an inverse production function, will be a function of expected demand. This has also been typically modelled so a weighted average of previous output levels. Rational expectations theorists, however, have discouraged the practice.

productivity. Similarly, assume that the labour force ratio in the denominator is determined by:

$$\frac{L_t}{L_t^P} = \left(\frac{Y_t}{Y_t^P}\right)^{b_0} \left(\frac{Y_{t-1}}{Y_t^P}\right)^{b_1} \cdots \left(\frac{Y_{t-m}}{Y_t^P}\right)^{b_m} \tag{20}$$

where the coefficients $b_0, \ldots, b_m$ reflect technological requirements and current and lagged labour force responses.

Substituting equations (19) and (20) into equation (18), taking logarithms, and rearranging yields:

$$\log N_t = \left[\log N_t^P - \left(\sum_{i=0}^{n} a_i - b_i \right) \log Y_0^P \right]$$
$$- \left(\sum_{i=0}^{n} a_i - b_i \right) rt + \sum_{i=0}^{n} (a_i - b_i) \log Y_{t-1}, \tag{21}$$

where n is equal to the larger of j and m. As stated previously, the estimation of this equation is the same as that of equation (17) although in this case no limiting restrictions need to be made in order to identify $\Sigma(a_i - b_i)$. In this model, the individual coefficients on current and lagged output, $a_i - b_i$, indicate the excess of the employment ratio response over the labour force ratio response.[1]

We estimated this equation for five countries. Because we wanted to compare responses across countries, we were limited in our choice of countries by the availability of comparable data. International data collected on real Gross National Product (or real Gross Domestic Product) and adjusted by the OECD are generally considered to be comparable, but we have seen earlier that unemployment data are not. We therefore used the unemployment rates adjusted to US concepts by the US Department of Labor. Although the Department of Labor publishes adjustments to the annual data, the adjustments for Sweden and Japan primarily involve subtracting military personnel from both the labour force and the number employed. Therefore, we were able to make these adjustments on the quarterly data published by both of these countries. The adjustments to the British data are more complex.[2] We adjusted

---

[1] Although it might be argued that in a steady state $\sum_i (a_i - b_i) = 0$ in the long run, the sum may diverge from zero in the short run and even in the long run outside a steady state.

[2] Only in the past few years has Great Britain begun conducting annual household surveys. Nevertheless, the official data for the United Kingdom are unusually extensive inasmuch as they include registrants for unemployment benefits and registrants at youth employment offices. In collaboration with British demographers the US Department of Labor has compiled an adjusted series beginning in 1959.

the published quarterly data for the United Kingdom by applying the Labor Department's adjustment factor for Great Britain for that year.[1] We originally included Italy in our sample inasmuch as Italian unemployment data have been collected from household surveys for several decades. Several authors,[2] however, have questioned the comprehensiveness of these data. Indeed, the Italian labour force survey has recently been revised and the revised data are practically double those previously published. Therefore, the lack of comparable historical data forced us to drop Italy from our sample.

Although the Department of Labor also publishes adjusted data for France and West Germany, the French do not publish their own quarterly unemployment rates and the adjustment factors for Germany fluctuated significantly and seemed suspicious. Furthermore, the empirical regularities which make 'Okun's Laws' reliable involve certain *ceteris paribus* assumptions. The presence of large numbers of guest workers in both these countries may render some of these assumptions untenable inasmuch as each country is able to 'export' a portion of its unemployment, although not a majority, as some critics allege. In terms of equation (11), resident population and participation rates in France and Germany may be more erratic than in the other five countries and may be affected by unforeseen and unpredictable variables. Sweden also has large numbers of guest workers, but these workers come mainly from other countries in Scandinavia, and their attachment to the Swedish labour force appears to be stronger. Similarly, most of the immigrant workers in the United Kingdom have a strong attachment to that labour force.

Finally, the sample periods for our regressions were usually dictated by the availability of consistent data. Surprisingly, the lack of historical quarterly GNP data was one of the main restrictions. In the absence of any constraints we began with the post-Korean War year 1954 and ended with the third or fourth quarter of 1977.

We estimated our basic equation for these five countries using an unconstrained third-order polynomial distributed (Almon) lag on real GNP and utilising the Hildreth–Lu adjustment for first order serial correlation. Summaries of these equations are presented in Table 1.6, along with the estimated growth rates of potential output and the actual growth rates of real GNP within the sample period. We allowed the length of the lag to vary from

---

[1] We used data for the United Kingdom rather than Great Britain because the consistent historical time series published by the OECD relate to the former. The inclusion of Northern Ireland changes the overall unemployment rate by only 0.1–0.2 percentage points.

[2] Censis, 'L'occupazione Occulta: Caratieristiche della Partecipazione al Laboro in Italia' (Rome, 1976). This phenomenon is also referred to in Michael Piore, 'Dualism in the Labor Market: A Response to Uncertainty and Flux: The Case of France' (Cambridge, Mass., 1977) and various publications by the OECD and the US Department of Labor.

TABLE 1.6 DEPENDENT VARIABLE: $\log N_t$

Country (Sample period)[a]	United States (1955:IV –77:IV)	Canada (1956:II –77:IV)	United Kingdom (1961:IV –77:III)	Sweden (1970:IV –77:III)	Japan (1956:IV –77:III)
Constant term	0.167** (0.0475)[b]	0.980* (0.478)	-1.658** (0.366)	-1.105** (0.210)	0.631** (0.098)
Coefficient on time trend	-0.00442** (0.00028)	-0.00470** (0.00111)	-0.00335** (0.00040)	-0.00045 (0.00057)	-0.00109** (0.00017)
Sum of coefficients on the logarithms of current and lagged output[c]	0.484** (0.0315)	0.349** (0.0796)	0.487** (0.0680)	0.211* (0.0983)	0.047** (0.0074)
Number of quarters in lag (mean lag)	8 (0.8)	6 (0.6)	8 (3.0)	8 (2.3)	8 (1.9)
SE_E	0.0020	0.0033	0.0021	0.0019	0.00077
$\hat{\rho}$	0.81	0.96	0.90	0.69	0.87
$\hat{S}E_u$[d]	0.0035	0.0120	0.0048	0.0026	0.0016

Implied exponential growth rate of potential output[e]	0.0091	0.013	0.0069	0.0021	0.023
Actual growth rate of output within the sample period	0.0081	0.011	0.0056	0.0035	0.021

* Coefficient significantly different from zero with 95 per cent confidence.

** Coefficient significantly different from zero with 99 per cent confidence.

[a] The sample periods have been adjusted to conform with the first observation of the dependent variable.

[b] Henceforth, numbers in parentheses beneath coefficients are their estimated standard errors.

[c] Real Gross National Product was used for the US, Canada and Japan, and real Gross Domestic Product was used for Sweden and the United Kingdom.

[d] The standard error of the untransformed regression $\hat{SE}_u$ is estimated as follows:

$$\hat{SE}_u = SE_E / \sqrt{1 - \delta^2}$$

where SE_E is equal to the standard error of the transformed regression.

[e] The implied exponential growth rate of potential output is calculated by dividing the equivalent coefficient on the time trend by the estimated sum of the coefficients on current and added real output.

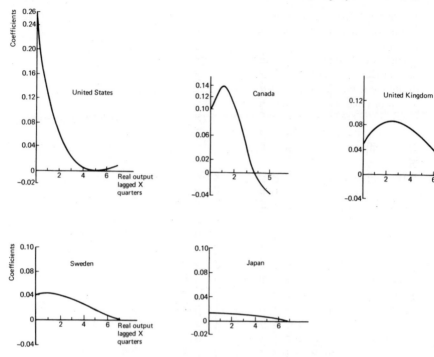

Fig. 1.1 Graphs of coefficients on current and lagged output

six to sixteen quarters. In most cases the effects were minimal; in making our final choices we eliminated the longer lags in which the coefficients were trivially different from zero and disregarded one or two equations in which the coefficients on output lagged eleven to fifteen quarters comprised a substantial portion of the total effect. The individual implicit coefficients on current and lagged output are graphed in Figure 1.1.

With the exception of the Swedish equation, where the implicit growth rate of potential output is severely underestimated,[1] the results are reasonable and illuminating. In particular, they confirm our prior expectations. In Canada and especially in the United States the unemployment rate rapidly responds to disturbances in real GNP. In terms of our alternative derivation, the immediate employment response appears to be much greater than the immediate labour force response for these two countries. We attribute this phenomenon largely to the dearth of job security and job continuity

---

[1] The actual growth rate of real GDP in Sweden may appear surprisingly small, but this is due to the particular sample period, which was restricted by the lack of quarterly GDP data prior to 1969.

provisions on the western side of the Atlantic. This is not conclusive, however, because we only observe that the *net* reaction $a_i - b_i$ is greater in North America.

The individual coefficients on current and lagged output in the US equation were remarkably stable as we varied the length of the lag. The elasticity of the employment rate with respect to real GNP in the current quarter is about 0.25, more than twice that in any of the other four countries. The Canadian equation suffers from a disturbingly high standard error, but again the results are reasonable and confirm our hypothesis. Note that the mean lag in both the United States and Canada is considerably smaller than in the other three countries.

The equation for the United Kingdom indicates that the total response of the unemployment rate is similar to that in the United States and Canada, but the adjustment process is markedly slower. The Swedish equation reveals both a smaller and slower response in that country. Confirming commonly held opinion, the measured Japanese unemployment rate is relatively impervious to macroeconomic disturbances. Until recently, many (but by no means all) Japanese firms guaranteed lifetime job security. It is estimated that between 25 and 40 per cent of the non-agricultural labour force was covered by such provisions.[1] Japanese employers also appear to have more flexibility in varying their work force. They can reduce the number of hours worked by their temporary and day labourers without creating new unemployment so long as each worker works some positive amount during the survey week. Nevertheless, Japanese employers tend to hoard labour during economic downturns, creating large swings in productivity. Although the unemployment rates in North America appear to be much more sensitive to macroeconomic disturbances in the short run, the welfare implications are unclear and require further analysis. One is not justified in asserting that labour hoarding and work sharing are more equitable than layoffs.

We tested these equations in several ways. First, we examined the stability of the entire set of coefficients over time for the United States, Canada, Japan and the United Kingdom. Inasmuch as our sample data for Sweden begin in 1969, it did not seem feasible to include it. We chose to test the equality of all the coefficients in the two periods separated by the first quarter of 1973 in order to observe the effects of the sharp rise in oil prices. The relevant F statistics were all less than 1.35 for the United States, Canada and Japan, compared with a critical F value of 3.1 required to reject the null hypothesis with 90 per cent confidence. Thus, we are unable to reject the null hypothesis in these three countries. In the United Kingdom, on the other hand, the

---

[1] Robert E. Cole, 'Permanent Employment in Japan: Facts and Fantasies', *Industrial and Labor Relations Review*, 26 (October 1972), 615–30; Hugh Patrick and Henry Rosovsky (eds), *Asia's New Giant* (Washington, DC: The Brookings Institution, 1976); and US Department of Labor, *Labor Law and Practice in Japan*, BLS Report 376 (Washington, DC, 1970).

computed F statistic was 7.2. The potential growth rate of output appears to have slowed significantly in the United Kingdom and unemployment now seems to be more responsive to macroeconomic disturbances.

We then tested the hypotheses that the growth rate of potential output (as measured by the coefficient on the time trend) and/or the 'potential' rate of employment N_t^P (as measured within the constant term) were different in the period beginning in 1973. It has been argued that the huge increase in the relative price of oil depressed the potential growth rate of output in several ways. Since many advanced technologies are very energy-intensive, the oil price rise may have acted as a brake on technological change. The great transfer of wealth to the OPEC countries may have had similar effects. Regarding the potential employment rate, it has been argued that a significant portion of the recent increase in unemployment rates is the result of changes in labour force patterns, unemployment compensation, and the like, and is not related to the apparent shortfalls in aggregate demand.

Only in the United States does it appear that the potential employment rate was lower in the period beginning in 1973, and even in this equation the relevant t statistic remained less than 1.0. The growth rate of potential output, however, appears to have fallen in the United States, the United Kingdom and Japan. The results to these three equations are summarised in Table 1.7. The coefficients on current and lagged output are only trivially different from those displayed in Figure 1.1.

The growth rate of potential output appears to have fallen most sharply in Japan. Although the coefficient on the time trend starting in 1973, which measures this shift, is not significantly different from zero at either the 99 or 95 per cent confidence level in either the United Kingdom or Japan, the t statistic in the Japanese equation is greater than 1.8. In the United Kingdom there is some evidence that the growth rate of potential output has also declined since 1970.

These three equations and the ones for Sweden and Canada presented in Table 1.6 have tracked the recent upsurge in unemployment rates remarkably well. This upsurge is primarily the result of slower growth. The responses of the employment (or unemployment) rate to current and previous macro-economic disturbances has not significantly changed since 1973. Indeed, inasmuch as the potential growth rate of GNP has now declined, new technologies may be relatively more labour-intensive and less labour-displacing, and the percentage increases in real output which are required to reduce the unemployment rate now appear to be smaller. Quicker employment responses in the United States both exacerbated the increase in US unemployment in 1974–75 and enabled us to reduce our unemployment rate since 1976, whereas the European labour markets have adjusted more slowly. Nevertheless, unemployment rates will remain high unless future increases in output exceed current expectations.

TABLE 1.7 DEPENDENT VARIABLE: $\log N_t$

Country	United States	United Kingdom	Japan
Constant term	0.367** (0.082)	-1.54** (0.316)	1.06** (0.262)
Coefficient on time trend Beginning at start of sample	-0.00528** (0.00037)	-0.00366** (0.00058)	-0.00170 (0.00040)
Coefficient on time trend starting in 1973 : I	0.00094** (0.00030)	0.00044 (0.00052)	0.00052 (0.00029)
Sum of the coefficients on the logarithms of current and lagged output	0.561** (0.038)	0.507** (0.077)	0.067** (0.015)
Number of quarters in lag (mean lag)	8 (1.1)	8 (2.9)	8 (2.2)
SE_E	0.0019	0.0021	0.00076
$\hat{\rho}$	0.84	0.87	0.93
$\widehat{SE}_u$	0.0036	0.0044	0.0021
Implied exponential growth rate of potential output through 1972	0.0094	0.0072	0.0255
Actual growth rate of output through 1972	0.0087	0.0072	0.024
Implied exponential growth rate of output since 1972 : IV	0.0077	0.0064	0.0176
Actual growth rate of output since 1972 : IV	0.0062	0.0020	0.0093

** Coefficient significantly different from zero with 99 per cent confidence.

BIBLIOGRAPHY

Akaoka, Isao, 'Control of Amount of Employment in Japanese Companies under the Life-Time Employment', *Kyoto University Economic Review*, 44 (April–October 1974), 59–78.

Barkin, Solomon (ed.), *Worker Militancy and Its Consequences 1965–75* (New York: Praeger, 1975).

Blaustein, Saul J. and Craig, Isabel, *An International Review of Unemployment Insurance Schemes* (Kalamazoo, Mich.: W. E. Upjohn Institute for Employment Research, 1977).

Bok, Derek, 'Reflections on the Distinctive Character of American Labor Laws', *Harvard Law Review*, 84 (April 1971), 1394–463.

Brechling, Frank and O'Brien, Peter, 'Short-Run Employment Functions in Manufacturing Industries: An International Comparison', *The Review of Economics and Statistics*, 49 (August 1967), 277–87.

Doeringer, Peter B. and Piore, Michael J., *Internal Labor Markets and Manpower Analysis* (Lexington, Mass.: Heath Lexington Books, 1971).

Evans, Robert, Jr., *The Labor Economics of Japan and the United States* (New York: Praeger, 1971).

Feldstein, Martin, 'The Economics of the New Unemployment', *Public Interest*, 33 (Fall 1973), 3–42.

Flanagan, Robert, 'A Study of International Differences in Phillips Curves', Ph.D. dissertation, University of California at Berkeley, 1970.

Great Britain Ministry of Labour, *Dismissal Procedures: Report of a Committee of the National Joint Advisory Council on Dismissal Procedures* (London: HMSO, 1967).

Hall, Robert E., 'The Rigidity of Wages and the Persistence of Unemployment', *Brookings Papers on Economic Activity* (1975:2), 301–35.

——, 'Turnover in the Labor Force', *Brookings Papers on Economic Activity* (1972:3), 709–56.

Hedberg, Magnus, *The Process of Labor Turnover* (Stockholm: Sweden Council for Personnel Administration, 1967).

International Labour Office, *Income Security in Europe in the Light of Structural Change* (Geneva: ILO, 1974).

——, *Termination of Employment*. International Labour Conference 59th Session Report III, Parts 2 and 4B (Geneva: ILO, 1974).

Kassalow, Everett M., *Trade Unions and Industrial Relations: An International Comparison* (New York: Random House, 1969).

Kaufman, Roger T., 'An International Comparison of Unemployment Rates: The Effects of Job Security and Job Continuity'. Ph.D. dissertation, Massachusetts Institute of Technology, 1978.

——, 'Why the U.S. Unemployment Rate Is So High', *Challenge* (May/June 1978), pp. 40–9.

Kerr, Clark, Dunlop, J. T., Harbison, F. H. and Myers, C. A., *Industrialism and Industrial Man* (New York: Oxford University Press, 1964).

Lal, Deepak, *Unemployment and Wage Inflation in Industrial Economies* (Paris: OECD, 1977).

Le Département de 'Population et Ménages', 'Croissance de l'emploi et du chômage de 1968 à 1974' (Paris, 22 January, 1975).

——, 'Les Liens Entre l'emploi et le chômage' (Paris, 26 May 1975).

Lucas, Robert E., Jr., 'Econometric Policy Evaluation: A Critique', in *The*

Phillips Curve and Labor Markets, ed. by Karl Brunner and Allen H. Meltzer (Rochester: North Holland, Vol. 1, 1976), pp. 19–46.

Marston, Stephen T., 'The Impact of Unemployment Insurance on Job Search', *Brookings Papers on Economic Activity* (1975:1), 13–48.

Meyers, Frederic, *Ownership of Jobs: A Comparative Study* (Los Angeles: Institute of Industrial Relations, University of California, Los Angeles, 1964).

Moy, Joyanna and Sorrentino, Constance, 'An Analysis of Unemployment in Nine Industrial Countries', *Monthly Labor Review*, 100 (April 1977), 12–24.

Mukherjee, Santosh, *Through No Fault of Their Own: Systems for Handling Redundancy in Britain, France, and Germany* (London: MacDonald & Co., 1973).

Myers, Robert J., 'Unemployment in Western Europe and the United States', in Arthur M. Ross (ed.), *Unemployment and the American Economy* (New York: Wiley, 1964), pp. 172–86.

Nadiri, M. Ishaq and Rosen, Sherwin, *A Disequilibrium Model of Demand for Factors of Production* (National Bureau of Economic Research: New York, 1973).

National Commission for Manpower Policy, *From School to Work: Improving the Transition* (Washington, DC: Government Printing Office, 1976).

———, *Reexamining European Manpower Policies*. Special Report #10 (Washington: August 1976).

Oi, W. Y., 'Labor as a Quasi-fixed Factor', *Journal of Political Economy*, 70 (December 1962), 538–55.

Organisation for Economic Cooperation and Development, *A Medium-Term Strategy for Employment and Manpower Policies* (Paris: OECD, 1978).

Parsons, D. O., 'Specific Human Capital: An Application to Quit Rates and Layoff Rates', *Journal of Political Economy*, 80 (November/December 1972), 1120–43.

Perry, George L., 'Changing Labor Markets and Inflation'. *Brookings Papers on Economic Activity* (1971:2), 411–41.

Phelps, Edmund S. *et al.*, *Microeconomic Foundations of Employment and Inflation Theory* (New York: W. W. Norton, 1970).

President's Committee to Appraise Employment and Unemployment Statistics, *Measuring Employment and Unemployment* (Washington, DC: Government Printing Office, 1962).

Reubens, Beatrice G., *The Hard-to-Employ: European Programs* (New York and London: Columbia University Press, 1970).

Sargent, Thomas J., 'Rational Expectations, the Real Rate of Interest, and the Natural Rate of Unemployment', *Brookings Papers on Economic Activity* (1973:2), 429–72.

——— and Wallace, Neil, *Rational Expectations and the Theory of Economic Policy* (Minneapolis: Federal Reserve Bank of Minneapolis, 1976).

Smith, Gary, 'Okun's Law Revisited', *Quarterly Review of Economics and Business*, 15 (Winter 1975), 37–53.

Sorrentino, Constance, 'Unemployment in the United States and Seven Foreign Countries', *Monthly Labor Review*, 93 (September 1970), 12–23.

———, 'Why Unemployment Rates Differ' (Bureau of Labor Statistics, 1977).

Theil, Henri, *Principles of Econometrics* (New York: Wiley, 1971).

Discussion of Professor Kaufman's Paper

Professor Hague introduced the discussion. This, he said, was a clear and
interesting paper which looked at some major questions about employment
in developed industrial countries. It concentrated on recent experience in
North America, Western Europe and Japan.
    Professor Kaufman began with unemployment rates since 1960. Table 1.1
gave the unadjusted figures and led to the conclusion that in the last three to
five years there had been a substantial increase in unemployment rates in all
the countries he studied except Sweden. Because of the way unemployment
statistics were compiled, national figures did not allow for comparison between
countries. Professor Kaufman had therefore obtained from the US Bureau of
Labor Statistics unemployment rates adjusted to US conventions. The result
was Table 1.2. This was interesting because economists did not always use
standardised figures.
    Professor Hague said that a quick study of Table 1.2 suggested Professor
Kaufman was right and that, apart from Sweden, there was a sharp break in
the series in 1974–5 following the oil crisis and the onset of world recession.
But perhaps one could go farther. Perhaps unemployment began to increase
before this, at least in the US, Canada and the UK. In the UK we knew that
unemployment began to worsen in the late 1960s. In the US and Canada it
appeared that unemployment was worse in the 1970 than it had been in the
late 1960s. If so, perhaps there was a less sharp break in economic circumstances in 1973–4 than Professor Kaufman implied. Perhaps things had begun
to deteriorate even before the oil crisis.
    Table 1.2 also suggested that in Italy, as in Sweden, unemployment was
much the same over the whole period since 1960. It seemed to Professor
Hague that we should find during the conference that Sweden and Italy were
often the exceptions to generalisations we might otherwise make.
    The paper went on to test several hypotheses. It first looked at the view
that the recent increase in unemployment was due to demographic changes
in participation rates. It had been suggested that since women and young
people had a looser attachment to jobs, an increase in the percentage of
women and young people in the population itself led to more unemployment.
This would mean that unemployment was a result not of deficient demand so
much as of a greater amount of time spent on 'search activity'. To test this
view, Kaufman divided up the population according to whether people were
under 25, or 25 and over, and whether they were men or women. This gave
him four groups. Kaufman calculated the effect of the changing demographic
pattern and of changing participation rates on unemployment for these groups.
The results, in Table 1.3, showed an increase in unemployment in recent years,
but not because of changes in demography or participation rates. Kaufman
emphasised, however, that one might not go on to say that unemployment was
solely a result of deficient aggregate demand. For example, higher unemploy-

ment benefits had perhaps led to increased search activity and therefore unemployment.

Italy was again excluded, because it now had a substantial 'black' labour market.

Professor Kaufman went on to estimate changes in unemployment rates for each of his four groups. Sweden apart, he was surprised at the size of the contribution made by males of 25 and over to increasing unemployment. That contribution was especially high in Japan, West Germany and the USA. Institutional factors might have helped. For example, the failure of many women in the UK to register as unemployed might overstate the increase in unemployment among men. It also appeared that the increase in unemployment was not so closely associated with young people as much popular discussion implied.

Professor Kaufman then went on to test for cyclical patterns. Here his basic model was that of Okun, who suggested that there was a relationship between unemployment and the growth of actual output relative to potential output. For brevity, potential output could be defined as that output which would maintain the natural rate of unemployment over time.

Professor Kaufman's analysis showed that for most countries the fit of equation (14) of his paper was improved significantly if lags were introduced. More precisely, results were improved if the change in the unemployment rate was lagged behind changes in output. We knew some of the reasons. In some countries, if output fell, firms did not at first lay off workers: later they did. Similarly, if output recovered, they did not at first increase employment. Professor Hague said he sometimes suggested that the reason was that no-one ever told the personnel department of any new development for at least six months! More seriously, in many countries there were significant costs in taking on or dismissing labour and, given Kaufman's findings, these seemed to be major causes of the lag in response. For example, Kaufman used his data to confirm, though not conclusively, his expectations for the USA and Canada. There, job security and continuity was less than in other countries, and unemployment seemed to respond more quickly to changes in output. Over a period, however, the total response of unemployment to changes in output was more similar between countries. For example, the USA and the UK showed much the same total response, but there was a different pattern, as Figure 1.1 showed.

In Japan, unemployment was apparently relatively unaffected by changes in output. This was because institution factors led Japanese employers to retain labour. The result was a big swing in labour productivity as output changed — the counterpart of swings in employment in the USA.

Finally, Professor Kaufman looked at the relationship between the rate of growth of potential output and the rate of growth of potential employment. His argument was that many economists would have expected the increase in oil prices and the world recession since 1973 to lead to a fall in the rate of growth of potential output. It had, however, been argued that the recent increase in unemployment was also a result of changes in patterns of the labour force, unemployment compensation etc.

Professor Kaufman suggested that only in the USA was the potential employment rate lower before 1973. He also concluded that the potential rate of output had fallen in the USA, the UK and Japan – especially Japan. The paper ended with the conclusion that the recent upsurge of unemployment was the result of a slower rate of growth of output, and that the response of unemployment to changing output had not significantly altered since 1973. However, Professor Kaufman suggested that new technology might be more labour-intensive and the increase in output needed to reduce unemployment now smaller. Nevertheless, his final observation was that there was no sign that unemployment would fall in future unless output would increase more rapidly in the next few years than most of us expected.

Professor Hague thought the conference should not spend very long discussing the interpretation and manipulation of basic labour statistics, where Professor Kaufman seemed to him to have avoided the pitfalls. Nor did he think that the conference should spend too much time discussing the econometrics in the paper. Having read the papers, he thought there was a danger that the conference would spend too much time in discussing symptoms and not enough on causes. The current methodology in economics pushed out in this direction. There was a danger that economists would concentrate too much on what he called the 'black box' approach, looking at the output resulting from inputs into the economic system and not at the way the system inside the black box worked. The reason was that to do so was not thought to be scientifically respectable. This, after all, lay at the root of much dispute between monetarists and Keynesians. The latter wanted to get inside the black box; the former were more reluctant to do so. Nevertheless, if we were to get to the causes rather than the symptoms of unemployment, we needed to go beyond regression analysis, even if that was risky for our scientific reputation. Economics today seemed to him to be too often in danger of promoting ignorance in the name of science.

He wanted the conference to spend some time discussing root causes. The big issue here was whether 1973–4 was a major turning point in world history to be followed for many years by slow rates of growth and rising unemployment. Or was it a major hiccup after which growth would soon be resumed?

There were good reasons for arguing that this was a hiccup. Professor Parkin had looked at the issue in what he called 'puzzles' in an interesting part of his own paper for the conference. Professor Hague would like to hear from him during the current discussion. One could suggest that we had 'all been here before'. In the 1930s the world took so long to recover from the world depression that economists began to talk of secular stagnation. There were suggestions in the 1930s that economic history had come to an end and that all we could do was to work to provide the last Chinese coolie with the contemporary standard of living of the USA. The implication was that major innovations – the introduction of television, for instance – would not happen.

Economists had been proved wrong then and perhaps might be proved wrong again now. However, in his paper Professor Parkin suggested that even if the world did resume something like its earlier course, it would do so slowly for the same reason that it took many years to recover from the great depression of the 1930s. Professor Parkin attributed the slowness of adjustment in both instances to the difficulty of adapting institutions, contractual arrangements and expectations. It was important to recognise that what we now called 'real' world economy could not have changed overnight in 1973. Our perceptions did. In other words, what could and did change overnight was expectations and, to a lesser degree, prices. On this view, the 1980s might be more like the 1960s than we now thought.

If we were to take a view on causes, what factors should we consider? Professor Hague suggested three issues as a start. First, was Professor Hicks right that the ceiling to growth in the world economy in recent years had been imposed by resource scarcity, or, as with oil, by producers behaving as if resources were scarce? Second, there were the world's monetary arrangements. Here one would need to look at the move to floating rather than fixed exchange rates in the early 1970s, the role of reserve currencies, and so on. Third, there was the fact that the short-run economic cycle in the major countries now seemed to be more synchronised. These were the kind of fundamental issues that this paper raised for him. He would like to hear them discussed.

Professor Kaufman wanted to point out that it was not his contention that a secular increase in unemployment rates began only in 1973. There appeared to have been some increase from the middle to late 1960s. His paper was primarily concerned with what happened between the late 1960s and 1976–7, including the period after 1973.

Lord Kaldor said there was no mention in the paper of induced migration. The period was one in which there had been large migratory movements in countries like Germany, which made interpretation of the figures difficult. The concept of potential output assumed that the labour force was given exogenously in each country. This was not so. Federal Germany and Switzerland had very large numbers of guest workers who increased their labour force. Statistically, countries like Italy provided some of these, and that reduced the Italian labour force. These movements needed taking into account.

There was no such large recorded migration into the USA. However, there were suggestions that there were now perhaps 12 million illegal immigrants from Mexico representing about 12 per cent of the American labour force. These factors needed taking into account before one drew far-reaching conclusions on the relation between potential and actual output.

Professor Khachaturov wondered how Kaufman estimated the trend of unemployment relative to technical progress.

Professor Giersch wanted to follow up Lord Kaldor. In the 1950s a permanent inflow of refugees from the East held wages down, increased profits and thus favoured high rates of capital accumulation. This process continued in the 1960s, now because of the inflow of guest workers.

The immigrants were members of what one might call the industrial reserve army and were recruited by German employers while still in their home countries. The employers were therefore able to be selective and to find labour which was complementary to the domestic labour force. Unemployment rates were very low and, relative to the German labour force, there was even an excess demand. In the early 1970s, economists, union leaders and politicians raised a discussion of whether wages were not too low, given the existing exchange rate. Should the trade unions rather follow a balance-of-payments oriented policy? This would, however, lead to a sharp rise of real wages, to the need for additional structural change and, closely related to this, frictional unemployment.

Professor Holt said that in general he agreed with Lord Kaldor but not on the estimate of 12 million illegal immigrants in the USA. Since these immigrants were illegal, it was difficult to know how much immigration there had been. For particular purposes, the highly inflated estimate of 12 million had been given. More recent research, which suggested the total might be five or six million, also showed that there was a seasonal pattern, with the immigrants staying for months rather than years.

Lord Kaldor replied that planners in Mexico assumed that two-thirds of those entering the labour force would work in the USA.

Professor Hines suggested that differences in unemployment between countries might reflect different policies with regard to guest workers. In the 1960s in Western Europe, when the demand for labour fell, the guest workers went home. However, in the UK attitudes were such that West Indians and Asians could not be sent home, so that unemployment increased when the demand for labour fell.

Professor Hines thought there was too little discussion of changes in female participation rates. Discussions of demand-deficient unemployment assumed that those unemployed were white males aged between 25 and 60. However, an increase in demand pulled more female labour into the market. There was no presumption that a fall in demand would then send them back home. He therefore doubted whether one could say much about search activity from figures for one country.

Professor Frey pointed out that in Table 1.1 the figures for Italy in 1977 were different from those for the year before. This resulted from a change in methodology in dealing with actual search for work. The new data gave a rather different trend, with more unemployment, especially for women and young people. So it was important to look at unemployment rates, recognising that unemployment problems might be larger than the figures suggested because of variation in labour participation rates, etc.

Professor Modigliani was surprised, looking at Table 1.3 of the paper, to see the small impact of the composition of the labour force on unemployment. Earlier work of his own had given a different result. Perhaps this was because

Professor Kaufman had based the analysis on 1970. Professor Modigliani calculated that if Kaufman had used 1963 as a base instead this would have made 0.6 per cent difference to his results. Thus, the natural rate for unemployment was 4.8 per cent in 1970 and 5.6 per cent now.

In Table 1.4, when Professor Kaufman looked at changes in unemployment rates for different components of the labour force, the analysis was misleading. Not surprisingly, Kaufman found that the group which comprised most of the labour force also accounted for most of the unemployment. To be meaningful, one should look at percentage changes.

Nevertheless, he sympathised with the general conclusion that lack of demand was the main problem. This was due to government policies and not to Kondratieff or Kitchen cycles. Governments did not know how to control inflation except through causing recession.

Professor Parkin did not think the paper actually said that. It said that slower growth was the cause of increased unemployment and left open the question of why growth was now slower. It was significant that Professor Kaufman admitted that there had been a secular trend towards higher unemployment before 1970. One needed to see honestly, objectively and with an open mind whether this resulted from demand deficiency or supply factors. There were several possible hypotheses. For example, in the early 1970s because of monetary variability and variations in exchange rates, there were some important supply responses which we did not yet understand in detail. Perhaps the greater flexibility in exchange rates provided signals to which people found it hard to respond. Again, the big increase in government expenditure and taxation led to an increasing wedge between wages and take-home pay. Unemployment compensation had also increased dramatically. So several supply-side factors as well as monetary variability were candidates to explain what had happened. There had certainly been some demand deficiency but it was hard to say how much. Certainly not everything had resulted from it.

Professor Bergmann thought that it had been useful to do what Professor Kaufman had done by studying group unemployment and changes in the composition of the labour force, but that Kaufman had overlooked some factors. If a particular group increased in size and there were large numbers unemployed, this meant unused resources and should lead to adjustments. There could be changes in the pattern of demand and use of resources. It was usual to attribute bad behaviour to the unemployed, but she did not agree.

Professor Södersten noted that the Swedish figures did not seem to fit Professor Kaufman's main thesis. It was true that Sweden had a low rate of open unemployment but there was also labour hoarding. With the existing labour force, one could probably increase output by 10 per cent. This situation resulted from government policy which had been to provide a subsidy to firms in order to increase inventories. Later, it had been discontinued as the recession lasted longer than had been expected. This raised an interesting structural point. Perhaps labour was now a fixed factor.

Whether this continued depended on various influences, but the signs were there, and if there were a pick-up, the situation might continue.

Professor Kolm said that the paper touched upon one of the most important and significant recent social changes in Western Europe, the most important and premonitory one resulting from the economic crisis initiated in 1974. This was labour retention or hoarding over what firms would have spontaneously chosen.

Normally, when demand turned down, firms did not at once dismiss an equivalent number of employees, because they were not sure that the decrease in demand was durable, and there were costs to them in firing and rehiring: firms might not be able to rehire the same employees, who might be valuable as workers, or for their special skills, or because they knew the particular firm. Firms waited and kept temporarily useless labour until the downturn had lasted long enough to appear likely to last longer. There was, of course, an analogous process for demand upturns. Labour hoarding was reinforced by laws requiring indemnities and advance warning of dismissal – a first step towards a new phenomenon.

During and since the 1974 crisis, labour retention had been greater than firms would spontaneously have chosen for economic reasons. The intensity of this phenomenon varied widely: negligible in the USA; somewhat important in England; very important in France; huge in Italy. This was not to mention Japan's special labour relations. The international comparison was well documented by Boyer and Mistral in 'Profit, emploi, inflation en 1975', *Revue économique*, January 1977. The cause of labour retention was pressure on firms from employees, unions and governments which themsleves acted under popular political pressures or threats.

One interpretation was to see this development as a change in the allocation of rights among members of society: the right to fire was partially withdrawn from the firms' directors (or capital owners). However, rights to terminate a relationship (to fire, to quit, etc.) were not like property rights. To remove them was to limit the set of possible bilateral voluntary agreements. It belonged to the category of constraints on contracts, like minimum wage laws etc. and thus impeded Pareto optimality. But the latter was a limited criterion in the absence of lump sum redistribution resulting from reasons of information and political power. The new situation might improve the position of some people. This was certainly the case for employees in the present case, especially if we considered the non-pecuniary value of work (social integration and relations, occupation, participation and involvement, sense of belonging etc.).

However, a change in one social parameter was likely to induce changes in others. With their right to fire more restricted, firms would be more hesitant about hiring. This might lead, in the future, to interference with the right to hire, to some obligation to recruit young people, local workers, etc. The long-run result could be sweeping changes in the relationship between labour and the owners of capital or their representatives.

Professor Kaufman replied to the discussion. On migration, he wanted to point out that he did mention this in his paper, including illegal immigration. Indeed, it was the impact of migration on the figures which influenced his decision to drop France, Germany and Italy from his econometric sample. One could analyse the situation, even with migration, using a Cobb—Douglas model. Perhaps the paper abstracted too much from factors like the increase in female participation rates. Nevertheless, he felt his analysis was useful and dispelled several 'myths' about unemployment in those countries.

Professor Kaufman felt that if what Professor Hines had said were true, the sensitivity of the measured unemployment rate to output should have decreased in the UK. The opposite seemed to have occurred. In addition, analysis suggested that the sudden rise in UK unemployment was due to an 'employment shake-out' rather than changes in labour force participation.

In response to Professor Modigliani's comments, he would agree that the results in parts II and III were sensitive to the chosen base date, but he had wanted to focus on the demographic and labour force participation changes that had or had not occurred during the past decade. Concerning Professor Modigliani's comments about his Table 1.4, Professor Kaufman remarked that he wanted to emphasise the important weight of adult male unemployment in determining aggregate unemployment rates. The large increases in aggregate unemployment rates experienced in the western world were *not* solely, or even primarily, the result of changes in female and youth labour force participation rates. He had not expected to agree so readily with Professor Parkin, but did feel that his (Kaufman's) paper showed the relationship between output and unemployment. Both aggregate demand and aggregate supply were important in determining output.

The fact that labour appeared to have become a quasi-fixed cost in France and Japan was the result of institutional arrangements. These were likely to make unemployment rates less sensitive to changes in output. Whether labour hoarding was good or bad relative to more unemployment was something he hoped the conference would discuss. However, if labour were a fixed cost, he wondered how countries would or should react in the future toward businesses which 'dumped' products abroad at less than full cost.

2 On Certain International Aspects of Employment Policy

T. Timofeev

INSTITUTE FOR INTERNATIONAL LABOUR MOVEMENT,
MOSCOW, USSR

I THE PROBLEMS

The problems of employment form one of the key problems of economic policy both at the national and international levels. The worsening of the employment situation in western countries late in the 1960s, and increasingly from the beginning of the 1970s, with mounting unemployment, made the problems extremely urgent.

What are the main causes of this recent worsening of the employment situation? In my view this results (apart from demographic and other factors affecting the growth of the labour supply) from factors that are predominantly structural in character, from changes in the general conditions of production, and from a new phase in the scientifico-technological revolution which has had the effect of decreasing the opportunities for employment of labour in the productive sectors as compared with the non-productive branches of the economy. There has emerged in the labour market in western countries during the 1970s a situation that is not the result of the traditional cyclical fluctuations of an economy.

It is relevant to compare the employment situation as it was, on the one hand, during the period in the 1960s before the adoption of the World Employment Programme, with the present situation in the labour market. Such an analysis shows considerable differences in the whole trend of employment, in the whole structure of the employed population, and in the scale of unemployment in the various countries and regions of the non-socialist world as between the first and second periods.

Figures for the industrially developed countries of the West show that there was an increase of employment during the first of the two periods, though at different rates. In this group of countries taken as a whole employment increased between 1960 and 1969 by approximately 27 million (11.2 per cent); for the United States the figure was 11.2 million (16.8 per cent); for Japan it was 5.8 million (13.0 per cent); while in the countries of western Europe it was only 4.9 million (3.8 per cent). Changes in the general economic situation (in 1957–58, in 1960–61, and in 1969–70) had different effects: in the USA and Japan employment continued to increase; in western Europe the growth rate fell from 3.8 per cent to no more than 1.0 per cent. The whole trend of employment from 1970 on was entirely different. Taken as a whole there was an increase of employment by 12.5 million (4.3 per cent). But during the period of 1974–75 employment actually diminished by 3.1 million (1.1 per cent). Thereafter the rate of growth fell to 1.2 per cent as compared to the 3.2 per cent of the first half of the 1970s. In the USA over the period 1970–77 employment in total increased by 13.5 per cent, but in 1974–75 it decreased, measured in numbers employed, by 1.2 million. Thus the trend of employment in the USA has shown, in the first place, a decrease in the rate of growth, and, in the second, periods of actual decline in the numbers employed. Such sharp fluctuations in the trends of employment have been accompanied by growth of unemployment and its stabilisation at a comparatively high level.

In Japan there was a similar tendency for the rate of the growth of employment to fall and for an increase in the amount of unemployment, which since 1975 has never fallen below the 1 million level.

So far as the west European countries are concerned, the decline in employment has been even more clearly evident. The virtual stagnation of the number employed during the 1970s at around 101–2 million was followed during the years of crisis in 1974–75 by a sharp drop in employment, to the extent of 2 million. Moreover, taking the whole period 1971–75 there was a drop in employment by 365,000. During the years 1975–78 the situation has deteriorated further. It need not be said that the situation was different in different countries. Thus the trend of employment in Italy was different from that of the other countries of the region; over the years 1961–65 there was a sharp fall in the number of employed (by 1.1 million), followed by another fall in 1966–70 (by 0.3 million).

It is interesting to find that in a number of the countries of this region (FRG, Belgium, Spain, the Netherlands, Ireland, Finland), even after the fall of production due to the 1974–75 crisis, the employment situation continued to deteriorate.

The trends of unemployment have been changing similarly. While at the beginning of the 1970s the total figure reached 2.6 million in the countries of western Europe, by 1973 it had increased to 3.1 million, and in 1977 exceeded 6.5 million (a two and a half times increase). During the last two years the number of unemployed in each of the largest industrial countries of western Europe – the FRG, France, UK and Italy – exceeded 1 million.

This growing scale of unemployment and the corresponding crisis of employment, in the conditions of instability of the economy of the West, are causing increasing anxiety to the broad masses of population and the organisations that represent them. This is aggravated by the fact that the majority of the western countries have found no effective way to decrease unemployment, while the existing systems determining the level of employ-ment fail at present to produce the required effects in the labour market.

A long time has passed since a number of countries of the West first passed legislation requiring their governments to maintain a high level of employment, or even full employment, of their populations, and since then similar obligations have been undertaken by governments of many countries in compliance with such well-known international acts as the UN Charter, the documents of the European Economic Community, and the ILO World Employment Programme.

But the practical implementation of these policies has everywhere remained remote. The 1970s have again witnessed a deterioration in employment and an increase in the scale of chronic unemployment throughout the West. The characteristic features of the present aggravation of the problems of unemployment have been an absolute as well as a relative increase in the proportion of young people among the total number of the 'superfluous' population, and an increase of unemployment among skilled workers and specialists.

Within the wide range of problems of modern employment and unemployment, I shall confine myself in the present paper to putting forward some observations on the following questions: (i) the characteristics of mass unemployment as a socio-economic phenomenon in relation to certain aspects of international employment policy; (ii) attempts to explain the causes of this phenomenon; (iii) some possible recommendations for international organisations in shaping their policies.

II THE CHARACTERISTICS OF MASS UNEMPLOYMENT

Many economists, statisticians and sociologists continue to debate whom one should consider to be unemployed — it is not by chance that national statistical data on unemployment are not always comparable.

Moreover, western economists continue to debate whether any special measures at all need to be taken for the solution of the problems of employment and unemployment. Extreme points of view are put forward, some of them denying the necessity for such measures[1] while others argue their vital significance for the development of the whole western economy.

Many theorists and politicians in the West recognise the different attitudes towards employment and unemployment on the part of hired labour and employers. Such contradictions in the interpretation of unemployment and its consequences are emphasised by the authors of some of the papers contributed to this conference, for instance, those of Emmerij and Malinvaud.

May I note, while discussing the causes of the emergence and existence of the current unemployment, that during the past few years a number of economists in the West have been re-examining certain earlier theoretical propositions (including the postulates of neo-Keynesian ideas) declaring them

[1] See P. Samuelson, 'Full Employment versus Progress and Other Economic Goals', *Income Stabilization*, Ch. XII, p. 547 (London, 1953).

to be unacceptable for the formulation of general employment policies by the state and for the reduction of unemployment in present conditions.[1]

The authors of a number of studies suggest various reasons for the aggravation of the problems of employment and unemployment: certain demographic factors; technological and structural changes resulting from scientifico-technological progress; changes in the forms of development.

In the labour market one can see both a quantitative disparity between supply and demand of labour, and at the same time a failure to match demand with supply in terms of professional skills, qualifications, specialisations and similar respects. Reasons explaining this quantitative lack of demand for manpower combined with a qualitative lag of labour supply as compared with the quality requirements are, in my view, at the bottom of the emergence and continued existence of mass unemployment.

Some of the recommendations of economists emphasise principally the demographic, technico-economic, technological and other factors mentioned above, and at best certain aspects of distribution and redistribution of national income and gross national product, such as levels of wages, prices and taxes. In the view of such economists, the most important instrument of a government is the budget and budgetary policy. They do not usually cover in their analysis the whole range of social relations, including the implications of ownership of the main means of mass production, the practical socio-economic conditions for training and retraining the existing manpower, so far as they concern in-family upbringing and education, general education and occupational training, public health, the physical provision for active holidays and relaxation in the form of sport, tourism and the like.

Since at present the immediate, or to be more precise the externally visible, causes of mass unemployment are not only the quantitative and qualitative requirements for manpower, but equally the quantitative and specially the qualitative characteristics of the labour force itself, it is only too clear that scientific research and practical proposals in the field of social relations towards the training or retraining of the working people are of vital importance. They are needed for the improvement of the quality of the labour force, so as to bring it into conformity with the requirements of the technological and scientific revolution.

Justice should be done to those economists in the West who during the last two decades have studied fairly thoroughly the technico-economic elements and the processes of shaping and developing mental and physical abilities of

[1] A. Okun, *The Political Economy of Prosperity* (Washington, 1970); J. Herron, *Labour Market in Crisis* (London, 1976); *The Concept and Measurement of Involuntary Unemployment,* ed. by G. Worswick (London, 1976); G. Moore, *How Full is Full Employment?* (Washington, 1973); E. Malinvaud, *The Theory of Unemployment Reconsidered* (Basil Blackwell, Oxford, 1977).

men to work, including those men who form the current manpower.[1] Those responsible for the 'consumption activity' conception (Lankaster and others) have analysed some of those elements and processes within the framework of the intrafamily economy of the working people,[2] while the advocates of the 'investments in man' theory (Thurow, Weisbrod, and others) and of the concept of the 'production of human capital' (Shultz, Becker, Ben-Yorath and others) have tackled the same problems on the level of family activities, systems of education, public health and in other fields taking part in the production and reproduction of manpower.[3]

What is valuable in those studies, in my view, is their approach to the problems of the training and retraining of manpower (in the terminology used by western economists – 'commodity labour' and 'human capital') as an element, but a relatively independent element, in the whole economy.

III MASS UNEMPLOYMENT AS A SOCIO-ECONOMIC PHENOMENON

In order to understand and explain the nature and essence of some of the fundamental problems of employment and unemployment, in terms of these concepts, and in particular to make practical proposals for the actual solution of these problems, it would be necessary to widen this analysis to include the study of contemporary socio-economic attitudes to the training of manpower. This need stems from the fact that technico-economic, technological, structural and similar factors can explain only to a certain extent some of the actual causes of dismissals while the reasons for the emergence and continuance of mass unemployment, as mentioned earlier, can only be discovered by the analysis of the relevant socio-economic phenomena and relationships.

[1] In detail see V. Goilo, *Modern Theories of the Reproduction of Manpower* (Moscow, 1975), in Russian. Also by the same author, 'Forming and Exploitation of Complex Manpower' in *Problems of Economics*, in Russian (1977), n12; and 'The Crisis of Western Conceptions of Reproduction of Labour Resources' in *Socialist Labour* in Russian (1977), n7, etc.

[2] See K. Lankaster, 'Change and Innovation in the Technology of Consumption', *The American Economic Review* (May 1966), 'A New Approach to Consumer Theory', *Journal of Political Economy* (April, 1966).

[3] See L. Thurow, *Investment in Human Capital* (Belmont, 1970); B. Weisbrod, 'Education and Investment in Human Capital', *Journal of Political Economy* (Suppl. Oct. 1962), and 'Investing in Human Capital', in *Education and the Economics of Human Capital* (New York, 1971); T. Shultz, 'Human Capital: Policy Issues and Research Opportunities', in *Human Resources* (New York, 1972); G. Becker, *Human Capital: A Theoretical and Empirical Analysis* (New York, 1964), and *Economic Theory* (New York, 1971); Y. Ben-Yorath, 'The Production of Human Capital and the Life Cycle of Earnings', *Journal of Political Economy* (Aug. 1967), and 'The Production of Human Capital Over Time', *Education, Income and Human Capital* (New York and London, 1970).

Before turning to the discussion of some of the problems of employment policy I will mention one significant trend. Recently one has seen attempts by certain western academics and politicians to explain the existing level of unemployment as 'normal for a dynamic economy' and even claim it as the state of 'complete employment'. For the sake of truth it must be noted that during the post-war period the absolute and relative figure for this 'normal level' has progressively been increased by one author after another. Instead of this so-called 'full employment' with a level of 4—6 per cent of chronic unemployment, it is vital, as is demonstrated by the accumulated international experience regarding the planning of the employment of a population and the elimination of unemployment, that all countries should enact laws that legally secure and economically guarantee to all working people the right to work.

IV IMPLEMENTING THE RIGHT TO WORK

This is a complicated task, involving the compulsory introduction of legal and collective bargaining norms governing all hiring, conditions of work and dismissal; on the one hand it must include, first and foremost, a ban on any kind of discrimination in hiring; it must provide for an increased network of employment agencies with a simultaneous ban on all private hiring offices and the like; at the same time the necessity for a considerable practical reorganisation and modification of the socio-economic goals of the economy will be needed to make it function in the interests of the whole society and not simply to increase the gross national product and national income. A declaration will be needed that one of the goals of the national economy is to ensure work and income for all those wishing to be gainfully employed, and in particular for the principal wage-earners in working families.

In a legal sense one of the principal requirements should be the establishment of effective control, with the participation of trade unions, over all hiring, conditions of work and dismissals. Practical economic guarantees of the right to work, as has been confirmed by experience, are ensured by simultaneously carrying into effect a large number of technico-economic and socio-economic reorganisations. The former includes the development of the national and to some extent the international division of labour; this covers the improvement of the industrial structures of the economies of some of the countries concerned; and also — and this is of special importance in the present period of scientifico-technological revolution — the expansion of international co-operation in the economic, cultural, scientific and other spheres.

It is of particular importance that all the physical and intellectual resources and capacities not only of individual firms, universities and governments shall be involved in the solution of the problems of unemployment, but also that working masses and their organisations shall be drawn into this task.

Some economists are inclined to reduce the role to be played in such activities by the working masses to that of passive acceptance of the employer's policy. But it is expedient to enlist a broader participation of the organisations representing the working masses, since these have a fundamental interest in the effective solution of the problems of employment and unemployment, and in improving the system of training and retraining of personnel, in order to achieve success both in national and in international efforts to stabilise employment and avoid unemployment.

One significant reserve for increasing employment and reducing unemployment is the shortening of the working day without reducing the level of real wages. Many experts, as well as trade union representatives, feel that contemporary economy has reserves and potentialities sufficient to permit the shortening of working time. At the same time that it restricts the tendency of employers to force and persuade workers and other employees to work overtime, such a measure would provide a practical way to reduce mass unemployment. In practice, in a number of western countries the length of the actual working week far exceeds the legally established working week.

The problems of leisure time are directly related to the shortening of working hours. Under conditions providing a rational organisation of useful human activities, an increase of free time would in the final analysis result in the growth and improvement of the structure of national employment and in a decrease of unemployment; this is due to the fact that during their leisure time the working people and the younger generation would acquire new general, cultural and professional knowledge and skills, and improve their physical and mental well-being.

Under the conditions of the present scientifico-technological revolution, the value to society of the general education and professional training of the working people is increasing immensely. This is an unquestionable fact. The labour movement is fighting for a qualitative improvement of the whole system of general education and professional training of workers and other employees, as well as for additional education, training and retraining.

As long ago as 1968 the International Trade Union Conference in Turin approved 'The Charter on Vocational Education'. But not enough has yet been done in this field.

In any study of the problems of maintaining and raising the present potentialities of working people it is necessary to take into account the activities of public health institutions, as well as other branches of the economy which directly contribute to the education and training of existing power. Such problems deserve a special study and it is natural that many authors have devoted time to them during the past few years.[1]

---

[1] See P. Coombs, *The World Educational Crisis* (New York and London, 1968); J. Vaizey, *The Political Economy of Education* (London, 1972); H. Klarman, *Empirical Studies in Health Economics* (Baltimore and London, 1971).

In the socialist countries an important step in any study of the employment problem is the question of the optimal utilisation of a man's capacity for socially useful work together with his requirement of such work, taking account both of the national economic requirements and of the personal needs of the individual man or woman and the population as a whole. In socialist countries the unemployment problem was overcome, as an element in the socio-economic system, at an early or initial stage of the socialist transformation. It is a significant fact that in the majority of such countries this aspect of employment has become almost entirely the province of historical research.[1]

Today the main emphasis of the work of the economists and sociologists of our countries is devoted to the studying of the socio-economic aspects of the employment problem, and to the questions of the more efficient utilisation of labour resources in some branches of the national economy.

V TEMPORARY AND LOCAL PROBLEMS OF LABOUR SUPPLY AND EMPLOYMENT

In any study of the problems of employment, that of temporary shortage of labour resources — particularly in major industrial centres — has to be taken into account. Such shortage of manpower is often felt in Siberia, in the Far East and in the North, as well as in some other regions of the country, where there are difficulties with housing, services, transportation and the like for workers. One of the most interesting and challenging problems for scientific planning and economics in the USSR is the improvement in the use of labour resources, eradicating mistakes in the planning of the training of the labour force, providing for its mobility and so on. One of the results of this, as Academician Khachaturov has noted, is the existence of hidden reserves of labour force in industrial enterprises.[2] There are also problems concerned with the more effective utilisation of labour resources in small as well as medium-sized towns and cities. A great deal of attention has been given to the solution of the problems of the economic and demographic development of whole regions of the country.[3]

---

[1] See L. Rogachevskaya, *Liquidation of Unemployment in the USSR. 1917–1930* (1973), in Russian.

[2] T. S. Khachaturov, *The Societ Economy at the Present Stage of Development* (Moscow, 1975), pp. 76–7, in Russian.

[3] See, for more detail, V. P. Korchagin, *Labour Resources Under Conditions of the Scientifico-technological Revolution* (Moscow, 1974), in Russian; L. E. Minz, *Labour Resources of the USSR* (Moscow, 1975), in Russian; *Labour Resources: A Socio-economic analysis*, ed. by V. G. Kostakov (Moscow, 1976), in Russian; B. D. Breev, *Mobility of Population and Labour Resources* (Moscow, 1977), in Russian.

Some of the yet unsolved problems are either a consequence of circumstances more or less external to the social system of the USSR or of imbalances that have emerged during the development of the system itself — imbalances that are capable of being overcome.

To take one instance, the unusual demographic situation in Poland that emerged in the 1960s as a result of a post-war rise in the birthrate has made it necessary to create a special set of measures to ensure work for all young people reaching the age when they become available for work. The following facts show convincingly the effectiveness of the measures taken in Poland: while at one time there were two persons for each vacant working place in the Polish economy, in the middle of the 1970s the demand for manpower considerably exceeded the supply.[1] This explains why the policy of industrialisation, carried out in practically all the countries that have taken the road of socialism, has to be regarded as a component part (and at certain stages even the most essential element) in both economic and social policy; its objective has been to overcome unemployment, as well as to absorb all population capable of working in the most rapidly expanding branches of national production.

The employment problem and that of overcoming the difficulties associated with it have an essentially different character in the socialist countries. In the USSR, some of the difficulties of this kind are associated with the overspecialisation of the economic development of certain cities that has not yet been overcome (they have a predominantly either 'female' or 'male' employment pattern). But on the whole it is essentially the shortage of labour resources in conditions of rapid economic development that characterises the socialist countries (this is certainly shown by the example of the European socialist countries, members of the Council on Mutual Economic Assistance). But above all it is this that primarily determines the chief direction both of practical policy and of scientific research in the field of employment in the USSR and the other socialist countries.[2]

VI IMPROVING THE CONDITIONS OF WORK

A subject of very close study both by academics and economic policy-makers has been the question of improving the conditions of labour, and particularly

---

[1] T. Rudolf, *Economic Policy in Socialist Countries* (Warsaw, 1978) p. 111, in.Polish.

[2] Among many studies of this subject the following are noteworthy: I. Yu. Pisarev, *Population and Labour in the USSR* (Moscow, 1966), in Russian; I. M. Musatov, *Social Problems of Labour Resources in the USSR* (the results of a concrete economico-sociological study) (Moscow, 1967), in Russian; *Labour Resources, their Formations and Utilisation*, ed. E. V. Kasimovsky (Moscow, 1975), in Russian; see also 'Socialism and Labour' in *The Communist*, No. 12 (Moscow, 1978).

the elimination of excessively heavy and exhausting forms of labour, with the help of automation and complete mechanisation of production processes, including all subsidiary operations. This concern has not been due wholly to difficulties caused by demographic factors. It has also been the result of the change taking place in the majority of socialist countries from predominantly extensive forms of economic development to intensive forms. Apart from the question of improving socio-economic conditions of labour, these are being re-examined both in economic terms and also as a most important element in social policy, contributing to the achievement of the ultimate goal of the complete socialist transformation of society.

One aspect of this question is the full utilisation of female labour resources. The complexity of this problem arises from the need to take account both of its physiological and social aspects, including the multiple roles played in any society by women. Its urgency has encouraged the development of research into many if not all of the important aspects of this problem.[1]

It is only natural that the solution of a number of the questions of the optimum employment of the population in a socialist country, and in particular those of increasing the skill and strengthening the creative element in work and at the same time enabling workers to find a greater interest in their work, depends on how young men and women start their working lives, and on the stock of knowledge and occupational skills with which they enter production. It is not by chance that such specific aspects of youth employment attract so much attention in socialist countries at present. A practical result of increasing interest in such problems is a significant improvement in the vocational education of young people.[2] This interest is reflected in the scientific field by the appearance of a number of studies, some of them very useful, of the problems of professional orientation and professional adaptation, particularly in the case of young people, resulting in a rapid improvement of their level of general education.[3]

This aspect of the problem of employment is not limited to the beginning of the working life of the youth. An important development of practical policies, and consequently of scientific research, has been the optimum

[1] See A. G. Kharchev and S. I. Golod, *Professional Employment of Women and the Family* (Leningrad, 1971), in Russian; A. E. Kotlar and S. Ya. Turchaninova, 'Employment of Women in Production', *Statistico-Sociological Review* (Moscow, 1975), in Russian.

[2] See, for more detail, A. A. Bulgakov, *Professional and Technical Training in the USSR at the Present Stage* (Moscow, 1977), in Russian.

[3] See V. S. Nemchenko and others, *Professional Adaptation of Youth* (Moscow, 1969), in Russian; E. K. Vasilyeva, *The Socio-professional Standards of Youth* (Leningrad, 1973), in Russian; M. H. Titma, *Choice of Profession as a Social Problem* (Moscow, 1975), in Russian; D. D. Konstantinovsky, *Dynamics of Professional Orientation of Youth* (Novosibirsk, 1977), in Russian; A. E. Kotlar and M. I. Talalai, *Youth Enters Production* (Moscow, 1977), in Russian.

utilisation of a man's capacity to work for the benefit of the nation during the whole of his working life. In particular, a problem of growing urgency is that of the functional and non-functional transfer of workers between various locations and various branches of the national economy, between enterprises and between occupations. The problems include the extent of the value of such transfers (from the point of view of the nation, the enterprise and the individual). Scientific studies and discussions (which have been reflected in the public media) have significantly contributed to the development of practical policy in this field.[1]

Mention should also be made of two very important features in the solution of the employment problem in the USSR and other socialist countries. First, its study is being conducted on a broad basis, involving the investigation of the whole complex of socio-economic processes under the conditions of socialism. In this context, for instance, the study of the changing elements in the composition of the national labour resources at different stages of a socialist transformation of society is of great interest. It is affected by the changes in the social and demographic sources, with a transition from mainly peasant sources from the countryside to urban sources, with a strengthening of the process of self-replacement of the working class.[2]

VII EMPLOYMENT CREATION AS A PLANNED PROCESS

It is very important to emphasise in connection with the attempts being made to solve the problems of employment in various parts of the world that the solution of this problem in socialist countries continues to become a more and more consciously-controlled and organised process. It is the concern of both governmental and economic organisations and central trade union organs on the one hand, and of local government organs, local enterprises, and local groups of working people in various public organisations on the other hand. Such an arrangement for the solution of the problem of employment has been included in the Constitution. For instance, the new constitution of the USSR (adopted in 1977) lays down, as the main goals of the State's activity, the improvement of labour conditions and labour protection, the creation of real opportunities for all citizens to employ their creative capacities, the development of a system of general and vocational education for young people, and in addition — as one of the most important rights of a Soviet citizen — the right to work: the right, that is, to obtain guaranteed work, with remuneration for it in accordance

---

[1] A series of studies of some of these problems have been made by, among others, scientists in the Siberian Branch of the USSR Academy of Sciences, for instance, E. G. Antosenkov and Z. V. Kuprianova, 'Trends in the Mobility of Working People' in *Dynamic Aspects of Analysis* (Novosibirsk, 1977), in Russian.

[2] See *Social Development of the Working Class of the USSR: Increase in Numbers, Skills, and Welfare of the Workers* (Moscow, 1977), in Russian.

with its quantity and quality, not below the minimum established by the State. This includes the right to choose one's occupation, one's kind of employment and work, having regard to one's vocation, one's abilities, one's vocational education and training, one's general education, and at the same time taking into account the requirements of the national economy. The implementation of these guarantees undertaken by the Soviet State to make the right to work effective determines the direction of the employment policy in the Soviet Union.

Among other important problems that are being tackled in the USSR one must mention the various measures aimed at improving the nature of work, taking account of its influence on the intellectual, mental and physical development of workers as well as preparing young people for independent life. Economic science is actively contributing to the solution of these problems. For instance, the Institute for International Labour Movement of the USSR Academy of Sciences is participating in an international comparative study of the lives of young workers, in which there are associated with scientists from the USSR and Hungary a number of colleagues from Bulgaria, the GDR and Poland.

The International Labour Organisation, as is well known, has announced that the problems of employment represent one of the main fields of its activities. The ILO has approved a number of international acts to give effect to this, such as the World Employment Programme and the documentation of the Geneva World Conference on Employment in 1976, with over 120 countries taking part. But the ILO activities in the field of employment are at present mostly in the developing countries, and the industrially developed countries of the West do not, in a sense, get their 'share' of attention from the ILO.

VIII THE NEED FOR ACTION

Programmes designed to deal with employment and unemployment put forward by different national and other trade union organisations are very similar in many important respects, and even identical. This creates conditions favourable for joint action, including action in the ILO. Thus it would seem advisable to concentrate for the moment on the following issues: the assurance of the actual right to work and to choice of occupation, covered and guaranteed by the constitution, and supported by measures aimed at giving effect by countries to socio-economic policy in the field of economics, and increasing the number of countries that have ratified the Employment Convention.

The major demand of working people is the removal of discrimination based on colour, race, nationality, sex or age of workers and employees, as enlarged recently into a condition of employment. In the USA, for instance, unemployment among the black population exceeds 12 per cent, while unemployment among young coloured people amounts to 37 per cent. In the countries belonging to the EEC, young people below the age of 25 years constitute 40 per cent of all unemployed.

In solving the problems of employment it is important to introduce measures aimed to make structural changes in the economy, and in particular, reforms in agriculture, democratic reforms in taxation, redistribution of the ownership of the means of production and so on.

Of considerable importance to the solution of problems of employment and unemployment are efforts aimed at limiting and stopping the arms race and further relaxation of international tensions. The Special Session of the UN General Assembly that took place in the summer of 1978, once again demonstrated the extent to which the consequences of the arms race are detrimental to economic and social development. It was emphasised in the report by the UN Secretary General that during the past 25 years military expenditures in the world have exceeded 1.8 thousand billion dollars (at current prices), at a time when enormous unsolved social problems have existed in the world.

Contrary to the views expressed by some western authors disarmament measures will not lead to the growth of unemployment, but will rather result in the creation of many new jobs in civil industries. In this respect, of considerable interest are conclusions contained in a recent study by US scientists, sponsored by the Public Interest Research Group in Michigan and released by Senator Edward M. Kennedy, indicating 'an *inverse* correlation between military spending and employment'. Senator Kennedy pointed out that 'the nation loses jobs each time we commit another billion dollars to the arms budget . . . Money spent on munitions puts jobs in danger'.[1]

The mitigation of unemployment could be achieved to a large degree through a further development of international economic, trade and scientific and technological exchanges, and of co-operation between states with different social systems.

IX THE NEED FOR JOINT RESEARCH

In this connection one must mention the subject of further scientific studies on the problems of employment. It is most important to achieve a complex all-sided analysis of the whole spectrum of the problems of employment and unemployment, including all the relevant questions of an economic, sociological and socio-political character; to study the extent of the actual influence of the technological and scientific revolution and the rationalisation of production upon the level of employment in various parts of economy; to conduct joint research projects on such subjects as 'Readaptation and the Employment Problem'.

---

[1] Edward M. Kennedy, 'Jobs and Defence Spending', *Wall Street Journal*, 27, IV, 1978.

It would be of considerable interest also to conduct a thorough comparative study and comparison of various concepts relating to employment, and of the interpretations of different organisations — governmental and non-governmental, national and international.

Soviet scientists and scholars would be ready to participate in further studies and discussions of these important problems.

Discussion of Professor Timofeev's Paper

Mr Kaser opened the discussion by suggesting that Professor Timofeev had interpreted his task of discussing international aspects of employment policy along two lines. The first was the causes of the coincidence of contemporary high unemployment in developed market economies, the second with a transnational comparison which included an analysis of employment problems and policy in industrialised planned economies (or, more precisely, in the European members of the Council of Mutual Economic Assistance, Comecon, and especially in his own country, the USSR).

In understanding Professor Timofeev's analysis of how international relationships had affected rates of employment in the western countries which were the focus of the present Round Table, Mr Kaser had been helped by a summary of the paper which the author had kindly sent to him in advance. This summary enlarged on some of the points in the text and had helped him to understand it.

The summary made clear that Professor Timofeev did not perceive the existing situation in the West as one of a traditional cyclical downturn. Mr Kaser took this to refer to the short cycle, but drew attention to the revival of interest in the West to the theory of long cycles put forward in the twenties by the Soviet economist Kondratiev, whose periodisation would forecast a recession at about the present time.

Professor Timofeev's analysis of the international nexus on the under-utilisation of the labour force was synchronic rather than causative, i.e. similar structural disequilibria had emerged at about the same time in these economies, and the policies which governments used during the 1960s had proved ineffective under the new conditions of the 1970s. The argument was of a coincidental phase of technological unemployment throughout the developed market economies. The fall in labour intensity of productive sectors, affected by what he and many others in his country termed the 'scientific-technological revolution', involved a sharp variation from the factor proportions prevailing in the 1960s, such that any unit of current output required less labour input. In addition, it inhibited the transfer of manpower from lower to higher productivity uses, because those higher productivity sectors required smaller incremental labour inputs. That supplementary feature of Professor Timofeev's analysis had something in common with the diagnosis put forward for Britain by Bacon and Eltis, in that they and Timofeev perceived an unwanted accumulation of manpower in the 'non-productive sectors'. Bacon and Eltis, of course, had a distinct theme in criticising western governments for fostering the growth of those non-productive absorptions of manpower, but the effect was the same as that which Timofeev suggested.

Whatever the underlying causes, the present crisis was serious because its effects were synchronous. Although Professor Timofeev appreciated that the experience of western countries was by no means identical, the crisis had assumed worldwide proportions because structural factors had affected the western economies at the same time and in the same direction of institutionalising substantial percentages of unemployment.

In looking at western government policies aimed at diminishing unemployment, Professor Timofeev rejected any which would postulate continuance of a level above 4 per cent of those seeking gainful employment. The ILO, he noted, had long been concerned with the structural unemployment endemic in developing countries, but had only recently had its attention turned to that of the developed west. The policy measures which Timofeev judged desirable to counter structural unemployment in those western countries fell into two parts – international and concerted national measures.

The international solution which the author particularly advocated was of freeing resources so that working hours could be shortened by a simultaneous cut in expenditure on armaments. By itself, a substantial diminution of arms spending would merely add to unemployment, as a view he quoted recognised, but he envisaged corresponding capital expenditure in civilian industries to absorb the manpower so released. Timofeev's reference to 'unsolved social problems' which could be solved by diverting defence expenditures suggested that some labour-intensive non-productive uses could also be embraced. His other solution was also one frequently discussed at the intergovernmental level, namely, the stimulation of domestic productive activity by external trade. The summary (but not the paper) pointed briefly to the dynamics of East–West trade over recent years and to its increasing component of technology transfer. As these were tradeables, the expansion of their output by the stimulation of international commerce favoured the productive rather than the non-productive sectors. Mr Kaser noted that Professor Timofeev entered into more detail on the national policies which would be more effective if taken by most western governments in concert with each other.

Unemployment brought about by a sharp increment in the capital intensity of production and by parallel demographic developments comprised, in Professor Timofeev's interpretation, a significant share of frictional unemployment. As he put it, there was 'a considerable number of vacancies alongside high unemployment' and an above-average incidence among young people. He advocated as solutions government programmes improving search and training facilities and legislative obstacles to dismissals. He did not explain how public services for job search in the West were currently deficient, nor why he would prohibit the corresponding private services. In a market economy, one would have expected such market-oriented agents to complement rather than hinder the work of government agencies.

The author devoted much attention to the need for appropriate education and retraining (he urged reform of the apprenticeship system) seeing these not only as the right responses to rapid technological change, but also as a means usefully to employ the time of the young unemployed. Non-vocational education was, he contended, better than idleness, and could bring long-run improvements in life-style. These two remedies, government provision of search services and investment in human capital, were scarcely controversial against Professor Timofeev's third role for the state, in establishing the legislative obstacles to dismissal for which he argued within an objective of constitutional guarantees of full employment. Professor Timofeev recognised that western parliaments had made legislative moves in that direction — the Employment Protection Act in the UK, for example — but he might also wish to consider effects which were undesirable, such as the generation of a non-contractual stratum of employment to escape the law (like the Italian black market in labour to which attention had earlier been paid) as counterproductive. This was because labour mobility should be actively promoted if manpower were to move as quickly as rapidly changing technology demanded.

This and the fourth policy instrument the author proposed — the limitation of working hours — were inspired by Soviet practice. Work-sharing with an unchanged real wage must, Professor Timofeev recognised, depend upon the scope for productivity gain from existing capital. Using the notation of Professor Malinvaud's paper, to which Professor Timofeev referred, the potential gain in the Keynesian model was where $\bar{y}$ (capacity) exceeded d (demand) and could be raised towards βL (full employment output). The two measures for work-sharing were the curtailment of the working day and the virtual prohibition of overtime. Both to some extent went together, because a statutory shortening of the working day could be offset by increasing overtime. The author might not, however, have fully appreciated that, as a permanent arrangement, overtime could be a technical bargaining procedure for increasing the wage: standard hours were cut while actual hours were not, the difference in hours being remunerated at a premium rate. As a temporary phenomenon, overtime could be used to adjust labour inputs to the level required by a rise in demand, when demand was expected to decline and as an alternative to the recruitment of more labour. Mr Kaser did not think it relevant to cite the virtual absence of overtime in the USSR — the last figure he had himself seen was that overtime payments constituted only 1½ per cent of the wage bill. This was because in a centrally-planned economy, production costs were planned as much as selling prices, and there was no mechanism to increase the latter to pay for the higher unit costs that overtime rates would entail.

In this paper, Professor Timofeev not only advanced Soviet policies as worthy of consideration for use in the West, but described quite extensively the circumstances of labour shortage and surplus that prevailed in the USSR. Mr Kaser did not want to diverge from the international theme of the sessions to repeat what the paper recounted, but drew attention to one of the causes of Soviet unemployment, viz. the availability in some localities of fewer job vacancies for women than the participation rate desired by local females and elsewhere, *mutatis mutandis*, for men. No-one would dissent from the closing words of the paper that the broadest research on unemployment in all industrialised countries could only be beneficial.

Professor Holt wondered about unemployment in the USSR. He remembered that the constitution said that not to work was illegal. One needed a sufficiently strong legal sanction to prevent unemployment. However, he suspected that what had happened was not that the problem had been solved, but that unemployment had been made invisible. If this was so, then the problems in the USSR and other countries were similar, and he would like to hear how the USSR responded to fluctuations, for example, in agricultural activity resulting from the weather. There must occasionally be raw material shortages, etc. There were also seasonal fluctuations in temperature. In a market economy, one would handle this by changes in the stocks, orders, and by hiring and lay-offs. How did one tackle forecast and non-forecast fluctuations? He wondered what data the USSR had which showed what was going on in the economy.

Professor Modigliani recalled that the USSR claimed to have solved the unemployment problem fifty years ago. However, in 1960 it had been said that 78 per cent of the population was in productive activities, and this had now increased to 92 per cent. Had the whole change been due to an increase in the participation rate, and if so, how had this come about?

Professor Tsuru had the impression that the USSR now suffered from a lack of labour rather than the opposite. There were many indications of this from both non-Soviet and Soviet sources. Why was this? Was it a demographic question? He did not think so. Moreover, in the 1980s perhaps, there would be an increase in the numbers of workers being transferred geographically between jobs; but this might lead to more loss of working days than in the West. He wondered whether this was true? Also perhaps, in some enterprises, there was not enough rationalisation of the labour force. So, for example, in iron and steel, labour productivity was probably low. He had seen statistics suggesting that the labour coefficient in the USSR in steel was greater than in Japan. So more rationalisation might save labour. It was a question of how to economise on labour. Since one knew how to do this, why was it not done?

Sir Austin Robinson wanted to go on to a puzzle over bottlenecks. Mr Kaser had said there was no overtime in the USSR. If this was so, how were bottlenecks dealt with? In the UK, overtime was in many cases not uniform, but enabled one to adjust an individual process to the needs of the whole operation. How did Russian enterprises operate? Was it necessary to reduce the whole output of the business to match that in the sector experiencing the bottleneck? In a world of advancing technology, was it possible to arrange training so that the skills available always matched the demand for them and no bottlenecks emerged?

Mr Kaser thought the answer was probably that there was a lot of underused time. Men hung around waiting for bottlenecks to be resolved.

Sir Austin Robinson asked, if there were excess demand, as there appeared to be, why one should reduce total supply instead of undertaking the simplest possible adjustment? He was unconvinced by what he was being told.

Professor Khachaturov replied that there were many interesting questions to be asked about the way employment was organised in the USSR and perhaps one needed a paper on that question alone. In the USSR, there was a shortage of labour and from a macroeconomic point of view the reasons were demographic. In the late 1980s there would be a greater shortage of labour than there was now. There was currently an increase in population of 0.8 per cent per annum which was only half that before the Second World War and after 1945. Another problem was great differences between regions. One would not transfer labour between Moscow and Leningrad because labour was short in both places, but there were acute problems in the eastern parts of the country, associated, for example, with the exploitation of oil resources. There was no unemployment in agriculture; there were fluctuations in output but not in the amount of labour needed from year to year. The main problem was bringing about a rise in labour productivity.

Professor Tsuru said that Professor Khachaturov had answered part of his question. He would like to clarify what he was asking. He was referring to a remark made by A. Z. Milov, Vice-Chairman of the Committee on Labour and Society, who was asking for a greater saving of time during the hiring and discharge of labour. He claimed that ten days were lost during, for example, medical checks before employment, and in obtaining documents at the end. Eliminating these delays would help to produce hundreds of thousands more days of work each year. In addition to this, was not the transfer of labour between geographical locations taking more time than is necessary?

Professor Khachaturov agreed that time was being lost, but workers needed to get used to the procedures.

Professor Malinvaud wanted to ask a question about capitalist countries. Professor Timofeev asked for effective control by governments and trade unions on recruitment, conditions of employment, etc. This was a demand that was often made, especially in France and was an example of social progress toward greater equality of employer and worker, which it was wrong to think did not exist. In France, there was already control on the conditions of work, and the employer could be prevented from dismissing employees. The 'rapport de force' was already an effective control.

Professor Malinvaud wanted to know if this helped to solve unemployment problems. He could give examples in France of where it appeared to be a *cause* of unemployment. From the point of view of the employer, there might be too much control over his activities, leading to an increase in the cost of labour. It was harder to use labour in a regulated régime than in a free one, so that there tended to be a reduction both in hiring and in firing. He would like to know what was the answer to this contradiction. The recent period had been a difficult one for social problems, but he thought labour economists needed to look at this aspect of unemployment.

Professor Modigliani suggested that the answer to Professor Malinvaud might be that the consequence of greater regulation was rigidity of employment. If one compared Italy and the USA, one saw that regulations – especially those limiting the ability of the firm to dismiss excess labour –

discouraged employment. It was important to recognise that this kind of regulation lay at the heart of the unemployment problem among young people. Those already in the work system were safe and protected, perhaps having two jobs. However, young people could not get into it. So, on balance, a policy of restrictive regulations was causing the unemployment problem to grow more severe.

Dr Gordon agreed with this. The major problem was that young people were not in the constituency of the trade unions.

Professor Holt referred Professor Malinvaud to an operational research study which indicated the importance of cost in hiring and firing.[1] What employers wanted was to avoid the penalties of fluctuation. The cost had to be traded off against a minimum of fluctuation in unemployment. There was no sign that this altered the average level of unemployment but it did affect fluctuations. This was only one mathematical model but it showed that it was not clear that there must be a bias. However, Professor Modigliani was right that regulation kept those outside the labour market outside it, and that social costs could easily be concealed.

Professor Malinvaud asked whether Professor Holt was saying that the average level of unemployment was independent of the costs incurred in hiring and firing?

Professor Holt replied that the cost of hiring and firing was likely to have no effect on the optimal average level of employment.

Professor Malinvaud asked whether the model Professor Holt had in mind recognised two factors. First, did it recognise that technology could be labour-saving? Second, did it take account of demand fluctuations and the element of risk? He suggested that even without an element of technological choice, a firm facing risk might aim at a lower output if there was a restriction on hiring and firing than if there was none.

Professor Holt replied that the model to which he was referring used quadratic equations with linear constraints and did not include risk. It could, however, take in technological progress if that were required.

Dr Kaufman wanted to ask several questions. First, what were the effects of various job security arrangements on productivity? If a worker felt that high production in the current week would increase the probability of his being laid off in a future week, how would he react?

Second, if labour costs were relatively fixed and an imperfectly competitive firm experienced a fall in the demand for its output, is it more likely to respond by reducing price rather than output?

In the USA existing constraints on hiring and firing are usually contained in collective bargaining agreements. In France and Italy they often resulted

[1] Holt, C. C., Modigliani, F., Mirrett, J. F. and Simon, H. A., *Planning Production, Instructions and Work Force* (Prentice Hall, 1960).

from government legislation. What political and sociological factors were responsible for these differences?

Finally, few neo-classical models included the effects of layoffs and firings on productivity and/or unemployment. Job security provisions and other institutional arrangements merited further investigation. We could not exclude all of these institutions from our economic models and yet expect to get meaningful and useful results.

Professor Bergmann referred to inflation in the West. One knew it was there and that it was a weakness. Her own training had been with Professor Haberler, who referred frequently to the trauma of the 1920s in Germany. He therefore emphasised the importance of inflation, and how, once it was started, one could not stop it. At the time, she and her fellow students had pooh-poohed this idea, but perhaps they now saw that Professor Haberler was right. What might be needed in the West was simply old-fashioned price control. There were problems in this, but they might be worth accepting. She also wondered whether there were inflationary problems in the East. Was there suppressed inflation leading to queues of customers with rationing of a formal or informal kind? The real problem was how to solve inflation in the West other than by creating slack.

Professor Timofeev replied to the discussion. He thought it might have been a mistake in his paper not to separate more clearly the part of the paper that looked at international questions and that which considered the USSR. He was sorry that some participants seemed to think that he had not recognised the problems of the USSR, especially those of unemployment. As Mr Kaser said, he looked at western problems with Soviet eyes but, similarly, many participants had discussed his paper from a western point of view.

In the first part of his paper when he discussed international aspects of unemployment he had recognised not only the causes of unemployment, but also interconnections between countries.

Professor Malinvaud's question showed that there was a correlation between social and economic problems. One had to look at the roles of trade unions, governments etc.

He agreed with Mr Kaser that one issue should be what was happening in different countries. Professor Modigliani compared experience in Italy and the USA. In Italy one had a left-wing government and trade unions had an important role. They could therefore bring about changes. A major need was to strengthen the role of labour and this was a major objective of the labour movement.

He thought that some economists in the West underestimated the importance of providing a dialectical linkage in their analysis. This was true, for example, both of the structural repercussions of science and technology and of the relationship between employment, the arms race, etc.

It had been suggested that there was an accumulation of manpower in the Soviet Union in non-productive activities and he thought there were similar conditions in other countries. This implied that one should analyse the long-run consequences of the contemporary stage of the technological revolution. He certainly thought one could say there was a new situation; for example, automation was becoming more complex and having repercussions on unemployment. He had seen a study by the West German Metal Workers trade union on unemployment resulting from computers, and some strong words about this. In West Germany, as the technological revolution spread, it led to new problems, including training and retraining.

He did not retreat from what he had said about the short cycle; but, on the long wave, one had to remember the ideas put forward by Schumpeter in his writings on the business cycle. No matter how many short-run cycles we had seen recently, there was a coincidence in the 1970s in the turning points of the short and the long cycle. Thirty years ago Varga had talked about desynchronisation. Now there was greater synchronisation because of the coincidence of various kinds of cycle. One reason for the pessimistic views seen in the West, for example those put forward by the ILO, was that there was this serious conjunction of problems which required further analysis.

Some people claimed that there could be full employment only if there were high military expenditure, but he noticed that Edward Kennedy now said that non-military expenditure would create more jobs than military expenditure.

Of course, he supported dialectical concepts and wanted to look in a dialectical way at the USSR where they were also used. There were real and unresolved difficulties in the USSR, certainly in the inter-mobility of labour. There were two extremes. First, there was a shortage of labour in some regions and cities. Second, an interesting book by Professor Khachaturov had talked about hidden manpower surpluses in enterprises. Perhaps he should have given more detail of this. If one could overcome them, then mobility of labour would be normal. In a socialist country one had uneven development with division of labour increasing in modern enterprises. But perhaps not enough was being done in the more backward ones. Plants in new industries had better-trained labour forces and were at the centre of policy-making. He had recently received a new issue of a magazine, half of which was devoted to the problems of labour. He had been surprised to see that this was a very honest and sharply self-critical view of how to make jobs more creative and attractive, and how to change the ratio between heavy manual and intellectual work.

3 The Social Economy of Today's Employment Problem in the Industrialised Countries

Louis Emmerij
INSTITUTE OF SOCIAL STUDIES, THE HAGUE, NETHERLANDS

I INTRODUCTION

In this paper I shall present two hypotheses regarding the duration of, and the remedies against, unemployment in the industrialised countries.

The first hypothesis is that unemployment — as defined today — is bound to be a long-term affair. The second is that traditional economic policy instruments are insufficient if we are to come closer to a solution of the employment problem.

This paper is divided into four parts:

(i) an explanation of why unemployment is a long-term phenomenon;
(ii) a discussion of available economic policy instruments with which the employment problem may be alleviated;
(iii) outlines of a global approach to the employment problem in industrialised countries;
(iv) main components of the approach on the supply side.

II WHY UNEMPLOYMENT IS A LONG-TERM PHENOMENON

In a nutshell, the reason is straightforward: the rates of economic growth which industrialised countries are most likely to be able to maintain over the next decade will be lower than the rates they have known in the twenty-five to thirty years since the Second World War.

On the other hand, the labour force is likely to continue to increase during the 1980s, not so much because of demographic reasons as because of the continued increase in female participation in the labour force.

If we put both sides of the equation together, the lower rate of economic growth and the growing labour force, we get the inescapable result that full employment as we understand it today is an almost unattainable goal.

Why would rates of economic growth be lower in the coming years than during the 1950–75 period? At least three reasons can be advanced to substantiate this assertion.

Firstly, economic growth in the industrialised countries during the period behind us was largely due to the manufacturing sector in which a considerable expansion of production was accompanied by high productivity and important direct and indirect employment creation. As has been the case for the agricultural sector in the past, the manufacturing base of our economy is now becoming smaller, both in relative and in absolute terms, in favour of the tertiary sector.

In other words, to maintain the same rate of overall economic growth, the manufacturing sector must expand faster and faster because its weight in the total economy is becoming smaller and smaller.

An escape from this arithmetical straightjacket is only possible if we identify alternative engines of economic growth in the tertiary sector, engines that would have the same radiating power on the total economy as that of manufacturing in the past. No such engines have been identified so far and to rely on them would therefore be an act of faith.

The second reason is that the days of cheap raw materials are over. Analogous trends are discernible with respect to access to cheap migrant labour. In other words, industrialised countries will have to pay higher prices for their economic inputs, and this is bound to affect their competitive position on the world market.

The third reason has to do with small but vocal groups in our societies, who are very much in favour of zero-growth for ecological and other reasons, even if it *were* possible to grow faster. These groups would take a dim view of anything that smacked of capital-intensive, polluting, large-scale economic expansion.

If the rate of economic growth is no longer what it used to be, it could be asked why this necessarily has implications for full employment. After all, more labour-intensive technologies could be used so that more labour is needed per unit of output as compared to a situation where capital-intensive technologies continue to be used.

Without dismissing such a proposition out of hand, it is highly unlikely, and probably highly undesirable, that we should move into such a direction, mainly because this would go against one of the few comparative advantages which the industrialised countries still have today. Any trend towards maintaining or even reinforcing the labour intensity of our economy would jeopardise our competitive situation in international trade. Not only that, but through its implications for labour productivity it would also have negative effects on wages and salaries of the workers, and on profits for the employers.

I would therefore like to agree with Professor Kaufman's conclusion in his paper to this conference that 'unemployment rates will remain high unless future increases in output exceed current expectations'.

III CONVENTIONAL ECONOMIC INSTRUMENTS

So far, two main employment policies have been implemented in the industrialised countries. First, the Keynesian policy of stimulating effective demand. In so far as this policy is aimed at stimulating private demand, the effects are insufficient. Part of the increased purchasing power is used for imports or for the production of 'nonsense' goods, neither of which contributes to a structural and long-term increase in employment. Moreover, there seems to be a structural decline in the growth rate of private consumption and also in the propensity to invest, which seemingly cannot be influenced by a policy of stimulating private demand.

Secondly, there is the neo-classical approach of the relative decrease in production costs, particularly labour costs. Insofar as this approach leads to higher business profits, it is becoming increasingly clear that there is no such thing as an automatic link between higher profits and increased employment. In a number of cases, high profits are not reinvested but consumed, or transferred abroad, or are only invested in labour-saving processes. Some therefore advocate provisions for social assessment of the allocation of business profits.

Not only do these policy instruments have intrinsic shortcomings, but in the economic situation described in the first section of this paper, it is obvious that even if they could be applied in optimum conditions and were effective to the full 100 per cent, they would still be insufficient to get us back to reasonable and acceptable levels of unemployment. A broader socio-economic policy package is needed for that.

I shall deal with these broader measures in the next and final sections of this paper. Here, I shall confine myself to stressing what could be done within the realm of economic policy instruments.

Two major efforts must be made, one relating to the international scene, the other to maximising employment opportunities through local efforts.

There is no doubt that part of the problem is the fall in aggregate demand. To boost this demand nationally through Keynesian measures entails a great risk of falling into the inflation trap. The industrialised countries have taken a long time to avoid the two horns of the dilemma, i.e. unemployment and inflation.

It is self-evident, therefore, that demand from abroad should be stimulated by initiating a sizeable transfer of capital to the developing countries. This would be good for the third world and also for tackling the stagflation and unemployment problems of the industrialised countries.

More and more often, from circles including the EEC and OECD, we hear suggestions that a worldwide Marshall Plan should be created. The political gesture that this would involve is extremely important and the economic consequences favourable, both for the developing countries and for giving an injection to a certain number of growth sectors in the developed countries.

However, when applying the latter policy, care must be taken that industries are not stimulated which have no long-term survival chances. The spectre of protectionism is always with us when we face a situation such as that described above. The temptation to initiate an inward-looking policy is much greater than the will to continue and even to stimulate further one that is outward-oriented.

Nothing can be gained by stifling the economic structures of the rich countries. They must evolve with the changes in the world economy. In such a situation, the political and economic appeal of a worldwide Marshall Plan is very important indeed. It implies, however, that industrialised countries must accelerate the economic restructuring of their societies, moving towards greater emphasis on economic activities that are more intensive in their use of capital and skills.

In this context, a worldwide Marshall Plan for development would boost the rate of economic growth of the industrialised countries, but not sufficiently to make full employment as now defined a realistic proposition.

The second main thrust that must take place is the creation of employment in the local sector of the economy, i.e. that part of the economy that is not, or very little dependent on international trade.

It will be clear that if that part of the economy that is integrated into the world economy is restructured along the lines indicated, resources will be available for investment in relatively more labour-intensive activities in the tertiary sector and especially in non-commercial services — a segment of our economy that is also called the quarternary sector.

Although this will be very important for the quality of life in our societies, it would be naïve to believe that it would create the necessary number of employment opportunities. At the end of the road, we are therefore left with a perplexing question: Is there an economically viable set of policy measures which will enable us to solve the dilemma before us in a humanly and socially constructive manner?

Such a set of policy instruments should also be sufficiently flexible to face a possible situation in the 1990s and beyond, when the labour force of the rich countries will possibly have stabilised itself, which could considerably ease the problem we are now facing. Such a set of policy instruments does exist and we shall present it in the next section.

IV OUTLINES OF A GLOBAL APPROACH TO THE EMPLOYMENT PROBLEM IN INDUSTRIALISED COUNTRIES

Summarising what we have said so far, it is our contention that nothing could be worse for the economic health of the industrialised countries than to be seduced by the spectre of protectionism. We are in favour of an outward-oriented economic policy in the framework of an equitable international division of labour.

This means that the rich countries should not resist moving away from uncompetitive lines of production. An economic restructuring is required towards economic activities in which we continue to have a comparative advantage. These activities are on the whole more capital-intensive and will secure a reasonable rate of economic growth, but will not be instrumental in creating many jobs. To encourage the economic expansion of rich countries we have argued, in addition to economic restructuring into capital-intensive and skill-intensive activities, in favour of a worldwide Marshall Plan that will stimulate aggregate demand in the richer countries and will improve the economic situation of the poorer countries.

To boost the creation of employment, the only real possibility seems to be situated in the tertiary sector, particularly in its non-commercial (so-called quarternary) part.

However, all these measures will not secure a rate of growth of the economy that is high enough to reach the objective of full employment in the conventional sense of the term. On the demand side, therefore, it is highly improbable that our economies will be able to create sufficient productive employment opportunities.

Consequently, something will have to be done on the supply side. In other words, we must influence the number of people who present themselves on the labour market in search of jobs.

The influence exercised today is a negative one in the sense that people are expelled from the labour force through unemployment or through the rich countries' way of hiding unemployment, i.e. declaring individuals unfit for work even though their physical condition does not warrant such an extreme measure.

Small wonder, therefore, that in recent years an important discussion has started on how to divide the available number of jobs over the total number of people willing and able to work. This is, therefore, another rationing of the labour supply than that dealt with by Professor Malinvaud in his paper before this conference.

Suggestions have been made by governments, trade unions and employers' organisations to decrease the retirement age, to increase the duration of compulsory schooling, to shorten the working day or working week, etc. etc. All these suggestions linearly follow the trend that we have witnessed over many decades of improvement of working conditions.

It is obvious that the concept and definition of 'full employment' are not static; they have changed considerably over time. For example, the definition of full employment in most industrialised societies today amounts to providing all those who are willing and able to work with a job at which they can work for 8 hours a day, 5 days a week, 48 weeks a year, for 45 or 50 years at a stretch.

It was different in the past when people had to work more hours a day, more days per week and more weeks per year. If we were to apply the concept and definition of full employment of, say, some fifty years ago to today's situation (in other words, if we were to attempt to reach full employment as defined some fifty years ago), it is clear that the rate of unemployment would be very much higher than it actually is at present.

We have dwelt at some length on this example in order to illustrate that most suggestions about redistribution of the available number of jobs are straightforward extrapolations of past trends. However, the question that must be raised is whether this is the best way to deal with the employment problem on the supply side in the present circumstances and, even more important, in the circumstances likely to exist in the 1990s and beyond.

We believe that a different and more comprehensive approach is required to reduce the amount of time which individuals spend on the labour market during their lifespans. Such an approach would not be limited to relatively unimportant measures of labour market policy, but would consist of a more global package, including educational policies, labour market policies, social policies, combined of course with the economic and development co-operation policies discussed in the third section of this paper.

We believe that a social and cultural policy package should be proposed, in addition to the economic proposals. The one characteristic of the new package is that it would combine a progressive policy with leaving the greatest possible initiative to the individual so that he has more control over the shaping of his career and life pattern than is the case at present. Such a global approach must also be able to deal with the rationing of labour, but as a by-product rather than as a major and unique objective.

What would be the contours of such a global approach to the employment problem in industrialised countries?

The life of an individual is divided into three parts, separated in most countries by watertight partitions:

(i) the period spent at school and, for the more fortunate, at university;
(ii) active life, whether spent on the labour market or not, whether remunerated or not;
(iii) the period spent after retirement.

These periods follow one another sequentially. We go to school at an early age and remain there until (depending on the country) 16 or 18 years and, in the case of university students, very often up to the age of 25 or even older.

Then we enter the period of so-called active life until the age of 60 to 65, when we are kindly but firmly asked to go out into retirement. It is very difficult – particularly in most European countries – to reverse the sequence of these three events. *The essence of our proposal is to transform this rigid sequential system into a more flexible recurrent system, in which it will be possible to combine or alternate periods of education, work and retirement throughout a person's adult life*

The idea of recurrent education which cuts through the first two periods of life mentioned above, was launched some ten years ago and has been discussed ever since. The complementary idea of retirement 'a la carte' has been discussed less frequently, but is the logical extension and the mirror image of recurrent education because it cuts across the second and third periods. Individuals could even be given an opportunity to combine all three periods by, for example, taking at age 30 a period of six months of anticipated retirement in order to continue or resume further education. Although this sounds extremely straightforward and simple, in reality it amounts to a social and cultural change of the first order.

Before going into somewhat more detail it is important to underline the advantages of such an approach for the various partners, social and individual, in our countries.

In the first place, this much more flexible approach would enable an equally flexible labour market policy to be introduced which would have advantages both for employers and for workers. The employers would obtain a labour force which could be more easily and more quickly retrained in line with technological changes. The workers would get easier and more frequent chances to reorient themselves.

The educational system as it exists at present is extremely rigid and has long-time lags. These were some of the reasons why in the 1950s and 60s forecasts of occupational and educational structures of the labour force became fashionable. These were long-term forecasts due to the long gestation periods inherent to the educational production process. Indeed, it takes approximately six years to complete each of the main levels of the educational system. Hence, the school will react very slowly to changes in technology which, in turn, have implications for the required skill structure of the labour force.

Experience has shown that it is nearly impossible to make more or less reliable long-term forecasts of the occupational and educational structures of the labour force. It is therefore much more realistic and desirable to shorten the gestation periods because, by doing so, the educational system will become more easily adaptable. In other words, the relationship between school and work will become closer, more effective, and more beneficial to all parties.

In the second place, there is a specific advantage to the individual in terms of self-fulfilment and of being able better to realise his full potential.

We all know that motivation occurs at very different moments in a person's life and not necessarily at those points in time required by the sequential educational system. Educational opportunities and achievements will definitely be enhanced if individuals can go back to school when they are motivated to do so instead of being pushed by parents or other persons in authority to remain in school. These people are right, of course, because in the present set-up it is difficult to return to school once you have dropped out.

What is true for educational opportunities is equally true for occupational and income opportunities. In the global approach which we favour, the individual has more than one opportunity to (re-)orient himself in the labour market. We go even further and offer individuals the possibility of taking a period of anticipatory retirement earlier in life, during which they do not necessarily have to return to school but can do other things for which they are strongly motivated at that particular time of their lives.

In the third place, and precisely because of its flexibility, our approach is also an effective anti-cyclical weapon. At times when a particularly strong but temporary storm approaches the economic coasts of our countries, it would be possible to stimulate more people to withdraw for a while from the labour force in order to benefit from either recurrent education or a sabbatical period.

In the fourth place, and this is among others an anti-structural weapon, we shall have on average fewer people on the labour market at each point in time than is presently the case because – and again on average – people will spend more time in the first and third blocks of their life as compared to the second. In this way, total labour supply will diminish.

Thus, the approach we advocate is on the one hand a generalisation of traditional trade union demands for shorter working hours, more holidays and earlier retirement and, on the other hand, of the more recent proposals with respect to part-time work, the sharing of jobs, and the rationing of labour supply in general.

Our global approach thus kills several birds with one stone: the economic structural limits for once will be consistent with the socio-cultural objectives of the individual. Instead of a diminishing majority which works harder and harder and an increasing minority which is expelled shamefully from the labour market, we are proposing that available work be rationed in a more intelligent and comprehensive fashion than has been suggested so far.

V MAIN COMPONENTS OF AN APPROACH ON THE SUPPLY SIDE

Let us look at the various magnitudes affecting the supply side of our approach in just a little more detail.

First, there is the necessity to introduce *a system of recurrent education* after the compulsory schooling period. There are almost as many definitions of recurrent education as there are people who believe they know what they are talking about. For many it is a second-chance parallel network next to the full-time formal educational system. This is definitely not the case. Recurrent education, as we understand it, is a comprehensive and flexible post-compulsory educational system which combines the present formal educational branches and the various types of adult education. Recurrent education, therefore, does not necessarily imply creating additional types of education and training, but the integration of the existing types into one harmonious whole.

In order to speak about recurrent education, four conditions must be met:

(i) it must be able to receive people from all age groups;
(ii) it must be one integrated education and training system, as indicated earlier;

(iii) it must offer 'educational units' of variable and flexible duration which can be used as building blocks for, and stepping stones towards, obtaining a diploma or degree; and

(iv) it must have exit possibilities at different levels which are all to be rewarded with a diploma or degree.

A few words on each of these four points.

On the first point, it is to be expected that most youngsters – who decide at the age of 17 or 18 to postpone the continuation of their studies for a while – will resume their schooling between their twentieth and thirtieth birthdays. This makes sense from an individual and therefore private rate-of-return point of view. It also makes sense from a macroeconomic and therefore social rate-of-return point of view.

Were people to decide to start their university education at, say 55, they could not expect to receive important material returns in terms of income during the rest of their lifetime – nor could society. It is to be expected that as people grow older, they will prefer to take up stretches of anticipatory retirement in order to do other things than to return to school.

The second point is important because in our approach individuals must be able to travel along alternative educational paths and still achieve the same educational goal. People must have the opportunity to obtain the same 'credits' by spending, say, 52 long weekends at school as by attending full-time education during a period of three to four months. This flexibility must be built into the recurrent system, otherwise it cannot cope with the much greater variety of students and circumstances as compared to today's situation.

This is much easier said than done – hence the third point, namely, to introduce educational units which in relatively short time periods can give a well-rounded part of a given educational career. Thus, the student or participant builds up credits in a flexible manner which he does not lose because they contribute to the total credits necessary to obtain a given diploma or degree.

The fourth and last point refers to the necessity for recurrent education to have exit possibilities at different levels so that we do not fall into the all-or-nothing trap of current educational systems.

In sum, the educational characteristics of our approach are the following:

(i) to hold as many options open for as long a period as possible;

(ii) to transfer the emphasis on pursuing higher levels of education to a later age in order to interrupt the rat race of spending more and more years of education in the existing sequential system, even when there is no real desire to do so;

(iii) to integrate formal and non-formal types of education.

Then we have the *labour market policy* component. Our proposals will have positive effects on the structural, cyclical and individual levels of labour market policy. These have been mentioned above and a brief reference will suffice here.

On the structural plane, our approach will be instrumental in creating a better linkage between the changing skills required on the one hand, and the educational and training supply delivered by our recurrent educational system on the other. There is no doubt that one of the more important structural problems we are facing in our industrialised countries, namely, the growing mismatch between skills required and qualifications supplied, will be effectively countered by our proposals.

On the cyclical plane the government, through appropriate incentives, can stimulate relatively more people to leave the labour force temporarily during an ebb tide of the economic situation. But more precise targets can be attained. For instance, the government could well direct such measures to a specific sector of the economy or to specific groups of workers in the labour force. This could be done by giving higher financial rewards to people working in that sector or in that specific group – higher rewards to withdraw for a given period of time into education or training. In other words, paid educational leave need not necessarily be the same from one group to another, from one sector to another, or from one period of time to another.

On the individual plane the advantages of our proposals for individuals to re-enter the labour market or to change within it are obvious and reflect those mentioned under the structural and cyclical components.

There is, however, one additional point which needs to be emphasised. This refers to the possibility for the individual to obtain an orientation-period on the labour market between terminating his compulsory schooling and before starting recurrent education and training. During this period youngsters who have not yet firmly decided on their professional career will have the chance to sniff at various job opportunities. This would replace the training periods of today – training periods which are very often neither education, nor training, nor work, but fall between all these stools.

A third dimension of our package is related to *income distribution*. What would be the implications of a system of recurrent education and leave for the income distribution of our countries? The 'perverse' tendencies of providing additional educational and other facilities on tertiary income distribution have been frequently noted. Indeed, in most cases education is provided at strongly reduced prices through government subsidies. The government expenditure involved comes from taxes paid by all. On the other hand, we know that those who attend higher levels of education come much more frequently from the higher social classes than from the lower ones. Such a situation is a clear example of how the poor subsidise the rich. This is one illustration of 'perverse' tendencies in providing not only education, but also health and other facilities at subsidised prices.

We must therefore take care that paid educational leave is granted as a matter of priority to those who have not been able to benefit optimally from educational facilities when young. In other words, a positive discrimination must be introduced in order to counter the perverse tendencies.

Still on the subject of income distribution, Jan Tinbergen has shown — drawing on time series from the Netherlands — that education has expanded faster than warranted on purely economic and technological grounds. This apparent educational oversupply has resulted, however, in a narrowing of income disparities between people with different levels of educational attainment.[1] If his conclusions are correct and can be generalised to situations in other countries, it would follow that our proposals could have further positive implications for income distribution while at the same time maintaining a somewhat better balance between the demand for skills and the supply of qualifications.

Another implication — and this is a fourth dimension of our proposal — would be to create a better *work climate*. The genuine opportunity which people would have occasionally to withdraw from the labour force is likely to diminish the number of those who declare themselves sick or otherwise unfit for work. Absenteeism due to sickness is a growing problem in most countries. Very often it is due to the fact that people work for too long a period under great stress. The safety valve provide by voluntary withdrawal could make a big difference.

Moreover, people who withdraw voluntarily from the labour force are in a very different psychological situation from those who are forcefully expelled from the labour market. It is obvious that, psychologically speaking, this makes all the difference. The pressure on health facilities can therefore be expected to diminish, meaning a considerable saving of money in the *health and welfare sectors* — money that can be used to contribute towards financing our proposals.

Finally, our policy package will almost necessarily imply the harmonisation of the entire *social security* system. This also means that the great variety of pension schemes now in existence must be integrated so that one no longer witnesses bureaucratic difficulties when moving from one firm to another, or from one job to another, with respect to the rights one has to retirement benefits.

Having arrived at this point, many will think that this approach is an interesting and perhaps highly positive and productive way of causing unemployment to disappear through a redefinition of the concept of full employment, but that the costs involved will be such that its realisation is highly unlikely.

This would be judging too fast, however. Part of the trick — and this is precisely where it ceases to *be* a trick — is to use the money now invested in social security schemes of all kinds to finance our proposal concerning recurrent education and leave.

---

[1] Jan Tinbergen, *Income Distribution: Analyses and Policies* (North-Holland Publishing Company, Amsterdam, 1975).

It is important in this connection to remember that those who benefit from our approach will consist of two groups. First, the youngsters who, after compulsory education, continue immediately with what will then be recurrent education. Second, those who – after having worked during a certain period of time – withdraw voluntarily into a period of paid leave.

The financing of these groups will come from different sources. The cost of the first group is borne by the Ministry of Education's budget combined with a certain number of tax and other facilities granted to the parents. In our approach the financial resources, inasfar as they come from different budgets, will have to be centralised. In practice, this will amount to the granting of a student salary and abolishing tax facilities and other regulations that are now in existence. During periods of paid leave, the incomes of those in the second category must come from the amounts that are now paid by social security facilities to people who are being involuntarily placed outside the labour market.

We refer to part of the unemployed, some of those declared unfit for work, and a fraction of those who are 'sick' and who, through health insurance schemes, can be viewed as disguised unemployed.

We have made concrete calculations about the magnitudes involved in the case of the Netherlands. We wanted to estimate the proportion of people who fall under unemployment benefits, unfit-for-work benefits, and sickness insurance respectively, but who should in reality be classified under the label 'structurally unemployed'. In other words, the groups that we tried to separate from the rest consist of people who are either openly unemployed or unemployed in a more or less disguised manner, who find themselves in those categories because of the structural unemployment problem in the industrialised world.

We found that out of a total of about 940,000 people in the Netherlands who live on social security benefits of one kind or another, 40 per cent fall into the category of 'structurally unemployed'. In other words, the cost involved in paying social security benefits to about 380,000 people could be used as the starting capital for our scheme for educational and other leave.

If we add to that number the total student body of 17 years and over, we come to the startling conclusion that at each point in time about 13 per cent of the (slightly redefined) labour force could be participating in recurrent education and leave schemes without the community paying one penny extra. This would also mean that in an active life of normal duration, one could go out into periods of educational leave up to a total duration of six to seven years. The details of these calculations can be found in a book published in October 1978.[1]

---

[1] By Publishing House Kluwer, Netherlands. The book is in Dutch and its title was still a matter of controversy at the time of writing this paper.

Discussion of Professor Emmerij's Paper

Professor Tsuru summarised the paper first, and then commented on it. He said there were two hypotheses in the paper. First, unemployment was bound to be a long-term affair. This was, because: (a) rates of economic growth over the coming decades were likely to be lower than those of 1950–73; and (b) the labour force was likely to continue to increase during the 1980s, largely because of the continued rise in female participation in the labour force.

The second hypothesis was that traditional economic policy instruments were insufficient if we were to come closer to a solution of the employment problem. The traditional policy instruments were: (a) the Keynesian policy of stimulating effective demand, especially private demand; and (b) the neo-classical approach of a relative reduction in costs of production, particularly labour costs, thus raising the marginal efficiency of capital.

Professor Emmerij went on to ask what could be done within the realm of economic policy instruments. He suggested that demand from abroad could be stimulated by initiating a sizeable transfer of capital to the developing countries – a worldwide Marshall Plan. This implied, however, that industrialised countries must accelerate the economic restructuring of their societies. Employment could be created or expanded in the local sector of the economy, i.e. in relatively more labour-intensive activities in the tertiary sector, and especially in non-commercial services (the quaternary sector). But these would not be enough. In other words, we could not do very much on the demand side. Consequently, something would have to be done on the supply side.

What, then, could be done about supply? First, one could continue present trends. This would:

    (a) lower the retirement age;
    (b) increase the duration of compulsory schooling; and
    (c) shorten the working day or week.

This, again, could not fully meet the requirement of the problem.

Second, therefore, a more comprehensive approach was proposed. This was 'a global package, including educational policies, labour market policies, social policies, combined with the economic and development co-operation policies'.

One important feature was that the greatest possible initiative to the individual was preserved, so that he had more control over the shaping of his career and life pattern than was the case at present. Rationing of labour could also be carried out, but more as a by-product.

Professor Emmerij saw the contours of the global approach as follows. There were three sequential parts of an individual's life:

    (a) schooling years,
    (b) working years,
    (c) years of retirement.

The essence of the proposal was 'to transform this rigid sequential system into a more flexible recurrent (and/or reversible) system, in which it will be possible to combine or alternate periods of education, work and retirement throughout a person's adult life'. It was important to be aware that 'in reality [this proposal] amounted to a social and cultural change of the first order'.

What were the advantages of this global approach?

(a) The gestation period of education became shorter;
(b) one could choose the particular stage when one was motivated;
(c) It was effective as an anti-cyclical device; and
(d) also as an anti-structural weapon by reducing, on average, the number of people on the labour market at each point in time.

The main components of the approach on the supply side were:

(1) A system of recurrent education had to be introduced. This was 'a comprehensive and flexible post-compulsory educational system which combined the present formal educational branches and the various types of adult education'.
(2) A labour market policy component. It had positive effects on the structural, cyclical and individual levels of labour market policy.
(3) Implications for income distribution. Thus: 'paid educational leave can be granted as a matter of priority to those who have not been able to benefit optimally from educational facilities when young'.
(4) A better work climate. A safety valve was provided by voluntary withdrawal, which was psychologically more conducive to better health and leading to 'considerable saving of money in the health and welfare sectors'.
(5) The harmonisation of the entire social security system. The great variety of pension schemes now in existence must be, and could be, integrated.
(6) The costs and the financing. The idea was 'to use the money now invested in social security schemes of all kinds to finance our proposal concerning recurrent education and leave'.

Estimates for the Netherlands were: out of 940,000 who lived on social security benefits of one kind or another, 40 per cent fell into the category of 'structurally unemployed'. The cost of paying social security benefits to these people (about 380,000) could be used as the starting capital for the scheme.

If we added to this the total number of students of 17 years and over, we could say that at each point of time about 13 per cent of the labour force (slightly redefined) could be participating in recurrent education and leave schemes without the community having to pay one penny extra.

Professor Tsuru added his own comments to the summary. (1) On the hypothesis that rates of economic growth for advanced countries would be lower in the coming decades, he agreed with Professor Emmerij completely, although his reasoning might be slightly different. He would put greater emphasis on (a) the encroachment of the newly industrialising countries on the market which developed countries used to dominate; and (b) the 'social limits to growth' as expounded by Fred Hirsch.

(2) To agree on the above did not necessarily mean that we had to conclude that 'unemployment is bound to be a long-term affair', even if the labour force continued to increase because of the rise in female participation.

Professor Tsuru thought Professor Emmerij should have said that the unemployment problem represented a major challenge which had to be met by a type of proposal which 'in reality amounts to a social and cultural change of the first order'. He was making such a proposal which, if actually implemented, would go a long way towards solving the unemployment problem.

(3) Professor Tsuru distinguished two basic types of approach; one from the demand side and the other from the supply side. He agreed with Professor Emmerij on the demand side. The economic policy instruments which could be used and which immediately sprang to mind would not be sufficient to bring about that sustained rate of growth which would maintain full employment. In fact, he was more pessimistic than Professor Emmerij about the long-run possibility of boosting the rate of economic growth of industrialised countries through 'a worldwide Marshall Plan for development'.

There was, however, a school of thought which maintained that, irrespective of whatever we might, or might not, be able to do on the supply side for employment, we should do our utmost in stimulating demand. We might then be able to maintain a stable rate of growth of something like 3 to 4 per cent per annum, incidentally easing the employment problem at the same time.

(4) Professor Tsuru was not in favour of such a position. For the 'expansion of effective demand by all means' school was prone to open its door to wasteful, and often dangerous, types of public expenditure, as exemplified typically by armament expenditure.

On the other hand, the zero growth prospect was no ground for pessimism. As J. S. Mill wrote: 'It is scarcely necessary to remark that a stationary condition of capital and population implies no stationary state of human improvement. There would be as much scope as ever for all kinds of mental culture, and moral and social progress; as much room for improving the Art of Living, and much more likelihood of its being improved, when minds ceased to be engrossed by the art of getting on'.[1]

Keynes also, in his lecture in Madrid in 1930, on the 'Economic Possibilities for our Grandchildren' concluded that the day might not be all that far off when everybody would be rich. We should then, he said, 'once more value ends above means and prefer the good to the useful. We shall honour those

[1] *Principles of Political Economy* (Longmans, Green, London, 1925), p. 751.

who can teach us how to pluck the hour and the day virtuously and well, the delightful people who are capable of taking direct enjoyment in things, the lilies of the field who toil not, neither do they spin. . . . I look forward, therefore, in days not so very remote, to the greatest change which has ever occurred in the material environment of life for human beings in the aggregate . . . .'[1]

Such idealistic prospects, however, would require, in the words of Professor Emmerij, 'a social and cultural change of the first order'. In fact, a new system of values would have to be developed gradually among us.

(5) Turning to the supply side, Professor Tsuru thought this became all the more important if we were to countenance the zero growth society with an expanding labour force. We had seen Professor Emmerij's 'global package' approach. It certainly merited careful scrutiny, especially as to how it could be implemented within the institutional constraints of each country, and also as regards its cost implications which could not be dissociated from the existing cost-sharing patterns of each country.

Although Professor Emmerij's proposal was an integrated one, Professor Tsuru thought we might examine its feasibility by dividing it into two parts: (a) recurrent education, and (b) anticipatory retirement. The former was in a way already practised, though not in a systematic fashion as Professor Emmerij envisaged. Two examples were the sabbatical system in the educational profession, and retraining leave for specialists in private firms. This was easier because the benefit of such recurrent education redounded to the employer by shortening the gestation periods, as Professor Emmerij said. The difficulty might remain if, in accordance with Emmerij's prescription, 'the greatest possible initiative to the individual is preserved' in choosing the particular timing of the recurrent education.

(6) Professor Emmerij emphasised 'voluntariness' and the 'motivation effect' in the 'global package'. He did so even to the extent of suggesting that there would be 'a considerable saving of money in the health and welfare sectors' if people were permitted to withdraw from the labour force voluntarily, and thus were able to feel psychologically better adjusted. However, to the extent that voluntariness was emphasised, his recurrent and reversible system, especially as regards the anticipatory retirement, would face resistance from employers.

Professor Tsuru said that taking a job was somewhat similar to getting married. Both acts were voluntarily undertaken between two parties and both could be terminated voluntarily, though occasionally under stress. But there were important differences. (a) Even with a strong trade union, the bargaining position of the employer was stronger at the point of an employing act, though in socialist countries things might be different; (b) after divorce, one might be able to find no less agreeable a partner than before. But returning to the same firm after anticipatory retirement might require a mandatory system,

[1] *Essays in Persuasion* (Macmillan, 1931), p. 372.

and taking a job in a new firm after anticipatory retirement might mean a retrogressive position. In a word, the institutional transformation required might be of a large order, depending on the conventions, the legal framework etc. of each country.

This aspect of the practical difficulties of Professor Emmerij's proposal could not be generalised. As for Japan, Professor Tsuru thought that her somewhat unique system of permanent employment and seniority pay would be a strong barrier to the proposal of anticipatory retirement, if not of recurrent education.

(7) If we were prepared to undergo 'a social and cultural change of the first order', as Professor Emmerij was, Professor Tsuru suggested that we might explore the possibility of what we could do by way of what Professor Emmerij called 'the extrapolation of past trends', and particularly 'the shortening of the working day and/or the work week'. Professor Tsuru thought, however, not simply in terms of the extensive aspect of the time involved, but also of the intensive aspect, both as regards the working time and the leisure time. We tended to emphasise too much the number of hours worked or the number of days taken as holidays. But All of of us knew that the question of alienation had been with us for more than a century. Also, there was a significant distinction in western languages between:

work	and	labour
ergazesthai	and	ponein
facere (or fabricari)	and	laborare
ouvrer	and	travailler (derived from 'tripalium' a kind of torture!)
werken	and	arbeiten

Economists had been accustomed to thinking of labour as disutility. But we knew that there was a range of 'disutilitiness' involved in different jobs and professions, and also that we could, in fact we must, improve the 'work climate' in many of the jobs in our society.

This was not a philosophical question, but one where a great many concrete steps could be taken. It seemed more important to Professor Tsuru for us to make our leisure time intensively of more positive value. Net National Welfare calculations by Tobin and Nordhaus and others had already treated the increase in leisure hours as a positive contribution to real welfare. If workers could be persuaded to regard one hour's increase in leisure as equivalent to receiving one hour's wage, it would certainly be easier to shorten the working day and implement a scheme of work-sharing.

At present, however, in most countries workers would resist any proposal which embodied a *quid pro quo* between one hour's wage and one hour's leisure. They could not simply be talked into such a *quid pro quo* scheme by exhortation. What could be done was for the government, local bodies and enterprises to provide various facilities and services which would enable the general public to make use of their leisure time in a rewarding way. This would give a sense of positive value to the leisure that was taken.

Finally, whether we were to follow Professor Emmerij's proposal or his own, Professor Tsuru thought the actual implementation might turn out to be faced with serious difficulties in the context of free trade. Even the rather lukewarm guideline for PPP by OECD, which was intended to equalise the additional cost burden of environmental protection among OECD countries, was having a hard time in making progress. International competition among industrialised countries was severe enough already; and in the coming decades the competition coming from the NICs would be still stronger in many industries.

Uneven development was a fact of life in this world. A country had to solve its employment problem in this context; and it was likely that we should have to resort more and more to policy instruments of the social engineering type. In other words, reliance on the Adam Smith type of Invisible Hand would become less and less adequate for the task at hand, and it might well be that we would have to put up with an enlightened protectionism in the future.

Professor Lukaszewicz found this a provocative and inspiring paper. He thought it relevant to all developed countries, and perhaps to less-developed countries too. He was convinced that developed countries would have un-employment if they continued their present policies, and was not sure that Lord Kaldor's optimism was right. He shared the opinion that one needed a global approach.

The concept of recurrent education and regulated labour supply was said to be radical. He hoped Professor Emmerij would study the issues with a dynamic simulation model. However, he thought that what Professor Emmerij was proposing had some important consequences..

He agreed on the importance of the concept of recurrent education in the paper. This existed here and there because of organisational and technical change. We needed more such education to keep abreast of change. We were concerned with the modification of human capital, which had become of unprecedented importance. Recurrent education could make a contribution to a changing labour market. Even at the aggregate level it could deal with a bias in the labour supply to the economy. However, the paper appeared to be dealing with a given labour force, and did not explicitly include technical progress.

Professor Emmerij accepted that what he was proposing would lead to changes in organisation and operation, but perhaps underestimated some points. His paper was strategic and long-run, and one must include all of the national economy and discussion between interested parties, because one needed the support of all. One had to have a coincidence between the needs of the group and of society. So perhaps one could achieve Professor Emmerij's results only through national planning. This seemed to be logically implied, and one could not escape it by using the tax system. As for finance, he thought of problems like bringing the pattern for demand and supply of labour into balance. How would employers and employees react?

Professor Lukaszewicz did not complain at the shortness of the paper, but he did want to emphasise that Professor Emmerij's inventive approach needed strong roots in a realistic appreciation of the true conditions of the market economy.

Professor Holt was largely in agreement with what the two previous speakers had said. There were two major points. First, there was the pessimism about unemployment growth in the future. Second, there was the question of structural reform. He wondered whether the case for pessimism had been overdone. One could argue that the lack of growth was a result of shortage of aggregate demand, of inflation, of pollution, and of congestion, but the paper did not deal deeply with this issue.

Whether one accepted this first point or not, the remedy seemed highly appropriate. Even in boom conditions, he would agree with the need to reform social security arrangements, education, manpower, etc. But the public sector of the economy did not run as well as the private one and we were here delegating to the public sector.

On growth, his concern was not quantitative but qualitative too. Factors like pollution were perhaps now out of hand. Population growth led to pollution and it was difficult to see what solution one could propose.

Professor Holt wondered whether Professor Emmerij recognised the implications of the structure he proposed. An improved labour supply would help growth, and Professor Emmerij seemed to have a one-way view of causality. His was a defensive response to a pessimistic situation, yet the same analysis might lead to an optimistic one. The idea of continuing education was linked to the putty/clay investment model. One could educate people for work but such human capital might not be appropriate for a rapidly changing technology. If one 'retreaded' people every five years, one would get a better supply of human capital and a better allocation of resources.

One long-run change needed in developed countries was an increase in worker participation. The problem was that most of us were not particularly keen to work. The strange conclusion was that people wanted to spend less time at work because this allowed them to do more at home, and the implication was that there was no work at home. One might end with women working more outside the home and men working more in it. This implied an important social change which had nothing to do with continuing education except that men would need to be taught a new role.

Professor Khachaturov thought this was a stimulating paper which made concrete proposals. He found some of them convincing. If the labour force was larger than the number of places, or if the number of man-hours needed at full employment was less than the man-hours available in the existing labour force, one could adapt by reducing working hours, reducing the age of retirement, or increasing the amount of schooling. It was important to see that this led not simply to more jobs but also to an increase in productivity. One could bring in more young workers, give a shorter working day etc.

In the USSR, when one looked at increasing productivity resulting from technical progress, the preference had been given to a reduction in working hours, a shorter working day, more holidays etc. This was possible in a planned economy but he did not see how the same thing could be achieved in a market economy or a mixed economy. How did one convince entrepreneurs what they ought to do? The government could create jobs but that led to an increase in taxation. No answer was given to this problem in the paper. One possibility might be to increase investment in order to stimulate technical progress and thereby to get new jobs.

Professor Henin looked at the relationship between Professor Emmerij's measures and more traditional ones. Theoretical analysis allowed a comparison.

First, policies designed to influence the scale of activity affected the level of employment. Second, policies could be organised to influence the process of rationing, as conceived by Professor Malinvaud. The author's propositions concerned only the second issue.

Professor dos Santos Ferreira wanted to ask a question. Professor Emmerij had said that part of the increase in unemployment was due to a fall in aggregate demand, adding that Keynesian measures to increase aggregate demand entailed a risk of higher inflation. This was the well-known dilemma of stagflation. So, Professor Emmerij recommended the stimulation of demand from abroad, through a transfer of capital to the developing countries. Professor dos Santos Ferreira could not see why such a stimulation of external demand should be less inflationary than a stimulation of internal demand.

Professor Eastman explained that he was inevitably influenced by what went on in his own country. Canada had high unemployment but it was recognised that, to some extent, the level of unemployment was affected by the current ability of the unemployed to spend longer in searching for new jobs. The change in the structure of unemployment insurance helped. He did not see that one necessarily wanted to try and resolve the issue by a change in aggregate demand.

Another factor in Canada was demographic change, with a lot of people entering the labour force and a lag in an adjustment of the capital stock to take them into jobs. To this extent, unemployment would disappear and one might run into a labour shortage.

Professor Eastman thought there might be too much pessimism in the paper. The real question was whether we had a real long-run problem or not. He suggested that in general people spent what they earned, and that new investment would be needed, for example in energy. He saw no reason to fear that there would be inadequate investment to use savings. But Professor Emmerij had made an important contribution to raising the quality of the labour force and so of life. Some of what was necessary was taking place, for example, through an enormous increase in the amount of in-work training. There was a good deal of training for specialists and for professional people, where what was aimed at was a honing of the skills of those who were already the most able.

The paper wanted to induce people to undertake general education at a later age. Since general education was the basis of productivity growth, a postponement of that education would reduce productivity at once, and the cost might perhaps be greater than the amount of social welfare provided. Taking paid holidays and bringing forward retirement was also expensive, and one had to take account of migration. How did one handle the situation where someone took his retirement when he was 30, emigrated, and never made any repayment?

Professor Malinvaud thought one should applaud Professor Emmerij's search for an organisation intended to allow people to choose career patterns, but one should still not be blind to the difficulties.

Two difficulties were worth mentioning, and perhaps the paper had deliberately neglected these. First, the proposed system could stimulate an increase of the labour supply as well as a reduction. The paper only discussed a reduction in the hours of work offered by the existing labour force, but Professor Emmerij's scheme might bring in more young people or women, who could find it possible to work under a more flexible system. Second, a social programme like this should be seen as irreversible. Whereas one had to admit that the current unemployment would last for some years, perhaps the paper was too pessimistic, and showed too little imagination, as if things would go on for ever as they currently were.

To evaluate a programme such as this one, consideration of a full employment society in which it would apply should have come first. If the programme then had looked attractive, there were indeed important reasons for introducing it now. However, it would not be easy to make a long-run choice from the paper itself. He thought, for example, that one ought to look at the question of financing the programme in a situation other than a very short-run one. Whereas he would like to see the development of such a system, even if in the long run there were more employment, perhaps not everyone would agree with him.

Professor van de Klundert did not think the argument early in the paper about the slowing of the rate of growth was correct in the sense of a shift between sectors. He thought Professor Emmerij was thinking of the working population rather than real output, which was reasonably constant in western countries. However, there might be a slower rate of growth. What did this mean, especially for labour productivity? If there were less labour saving, then perhaps the problem might be less serious. Even then, if potential labour productivity increased, then one had the kind of situation one knew from the past. For example, one could reduce working hours and arrange for substitution between capital and labour if there were flexibility in wage rates.

Like Professor Malinvaud, he had doubts about the standard of living.

Professor Emmerij expected it to fall. This was a problem, because one could perhaps push the participation rate up to 100 per cent. Everyone could participate if they did not do so much work but this would increase the financing problem. It would mean defining the retirement period in a new way, as well as the level of compensation allowed. One would then need a notion of the elasticity of compensation relative to retirement.

Professor Georgescu-Roegen wanted to speak about the ability of a capitalist economy to adjust its normal working hours. He would like to consider what Engels had said about the working conditions in the UK and what other literature said about working conditions in the USA during the nineteenth century. In 1850 (or thereabouts) the most politically advanced state in the USA, the Commonwealth of Massachussetts, had passed a law forbidding children from working for more than twelve hours a day. That meant that children actually worked longer than twelve hours a day. Mature people must have worked even longer. Now there was a 40-hour week and paid holidays. Moreover, in the USA the idea to adopt a six-hour day and 30-hour week was still being debated. He agreed that there were difficulties in such a move. But work-sharing had been possible in the past, so why not in the future?

Professor Tsuru had talked about a static economy and considered the problems like pollution. That static case had been viewed as the long-run final equilibrium situation of mankind's economy. However, the possibility of such a perpetual state was contradicted by the laws of physics. Economists did not often look at the laws of the natural world, but we lived in one and were constrained by its laws.

Professor Grinols thought it was important to consider groups of unemployed outside the labour force. Professor Emmerij's proposals were aimed only at those who benefited most from education; perhaps those who needed it most would not be benefited at all. He therefore wanted to know, first, how the proposals would help the unemployed; and second, how it would increase the quality of life, either for the whole population or part of it.

Professor Bergmann said that Professor Emmerij wrote off the 'nonsense output' of economic growth. She wondered what he was talking about. Perhaps he had in mind something like rock-music records. She would agree with Professor Emmerij here, but economists were not supposed to make such judgements.

We might here be too civilised to think of such questions but when we spoke of reducing the supply of labour by policy measures, we were likely to be pushed from advocating voluntary to advocating forced withdrawal. One might end not by sending workers in general home but by discriminating against women or by forcing early retirement. She thought this was of doubtful ethical value. She did not believe that we could afford Professor Emmerij's pessimism about demand. We always took the most recent movement as a permanent one, and in five years' time that often led to shortages.

Professor Bergmann wanted to agree with Professor Holt on the possible reorganisation of domestic work. In fact, there must be more equality within the home or women would refuse to be married and have children.

Professor Modigliani wanted to make two points. First, he agreed with Professor Holt and Bergmann that it was risky to talk of a great new economic change simply because there had been unemployment since 1974. The level of unemployment was a result of the way that we reacted to inflation, and did not represent a fundamental and rapid change. Fundamental movements were slow. The change in the oil price was a small structural change, not a large one. It was being suggested that a wiggle in the economy had become a trend.

In the 1960s when there had been relatively high unemployment up to 1964, this was seen as a basic new development. It was suggested that there was a mis-match of skills, and that problems were arising from the computer society. Many economists, however, said there was not enough increase in aggregate demand to reduce unemployment – and they were proven right! Indeed, the reduction in unemployment went too far. However, this resulted from complicated political mistakes, especially to do with Vietnam, and not to a failure by economists to give appropriate advice.

Professor Modigliani said strong evidence would be needed to show that there would be a reduction in the standard of living. There was a great deal of evidence of a new phenomenon, of people taking second or third jobs. In Italy this was happening on a gigantic scale, in part to evade legal restrictions. The trade unions were pressing for a reduction in hours of work, but those who were not willing to accept it were finding second or third jobs. This was one of the obvious dangers of an attempt to reduce working hours.

Professor Giersch said that when people talked about zero growth, they often talked about a zero rate of industrial growth. He thought that the income elasticity of demand for services was increasing and these were not subject to so much alienation at work. For example, librarians sometimes went on working after their retirement age of 65 and were unhappy to be separated from their jobs. There were no incentives to earlier retirement. One needed a flexible system to signal what was required and to take account also of individuals' preferences. Professor Emmerij had missed the point about self-employment, and perhaps in the service sector there was more self-employment.

Professor Giersch wondered whether the trade unions' system could cope with extra flexibility with prices affected by pressures in different directions. One had to ask how far wage systems resulting from collective bargaining would have to be overridden. The trade unions themselves would be endangered if the system became more flexible. Research into this was needed.

Professor Emmerij thanked participants for a constructive and generous discussion, especially Professor Tsuru. Proposals like his required considerable discussion, and he was glad the debate had been so helpful.

He thought that three main points emerged. First, there was the question of whether there was now a long-run change in prosperity, or whether the events of recent years were simply short-run phenomena. The question was whether long-run growth would be rapid enough to employ all those wishing to be employed. Why should one think this was the case? No-one had given quantified reasons showing that full employment was possible. In any case, his proposals would help on the supply side whatever the demand situation. This was an interesting feature of the proposals which would, of course, have to be adjusted to circumstances as they developed. If industrial growth fell back to zero, there would have to be more emphasis on qualitative rather than quantitative growth, and the proposals fitted in with this.

The second question was what alternative supply-side packages were available? Professor Tsuru argued that this depended on institutional arrangements. In Japan it was easier to make adjustments through a reduction in working hours rather than by more radical social and cultural changes. It was not just a question of a division between remunerated and unremunerated work. His proposals were opposed to any linear extrapolation of present trends. They got away from the imposition of a dictatorial régime and gave flexibility. He was not interested simply in a reduction of working hours, but felt one could kill several birds with the one stone. His proposals would give the individual greater freedom to shape his own life.

Third, on the detail of the paper, he was surprised that some feared that bureaucracy would increase, or that he was seeking an extension of national planning beyond what now existed. When he said that the implication was a harmonisation of social security and pension arrangements, he was certainly not calling for a strengthening of the bureaucracy. He was calling for the bureaucracy to be instructed to return decisions to individuals. The question was how the 'actors' would react. He had looked at this in a forthcoming book based on discussions with important groups. The aim was to bring into being a positive sum game, in which all actors gained. The employers appeared to see more benefit than the trade unions, which feared that the gains from collective bargaining would be substituted for something else. In particular, the use of social security funds for creative purposes was too much for the trade unions, though with higher unemployment they were now showing more flexibility in discussing this possibility. And perhaps the costs of the scheme would be greater than was suggested by the calculations at the end of his paper.

He thought everything depended on how developed countries worked out their social security systems. Detailed calculations showed that what was spent today on higher education and unemployment benefits and on health and sickness was not very different from the amount his paper required. He had not taken account of the cost of extra educational facilities, but there were other points here. For example, for demographic reasons in Holland, there were unemployed primary and secondary schoolteachers, and it was possible to use educational buildings more efficiently.

Participants had asked whether the scheme would increase or decrease the size of the labour force. It was true that his proposals could do either. There was an anti-cyclical problem here which he thought could be dealt with by differentiating the amount of pay to take account of whether there was a return or not. Elasticities had not been estimated but they could, and certainly should, be evaluated through survey techniques.

On the question of irreversibility, Professor Emmerij said that one of the major points of his proposal was its flexibility so that parts of the package were indeed reversible. In times of unemployment more people should be encouraged to leave the labour market temporarily, whilst in times of tight labour markets fewer people should be encouraged to step out.

Finally, he was surprised that nobody had mentioned explicitly the question of the rate of return of education. A possible criticism could be that higher education taken at an advanced age would give a lower return both to the individual and to society. He would therefore expect that rational people — which was what we were — would take the bulk of their recurrent education between the ages of 20 and 30 rather than between 45 and 55.

PART TWO

International Trade and Unemployment

4 The Foundations of Free Trade Theory and their Implications for the Current World Recession

Nicholas Kaldor
CAMBRIDGE UNIVERSITY

I THE TRADITIONAL THEORY

Traditional theory, both classical and neo-classical, asserts that free trade in goods between different regions is always to the advantage of *each* trading country, and is therefore the best arrangement from the point of view of the welfare of the trading world as a whole, as well as of each part of the world taken separately.[1] The purpose of this paper is to show that these propositions are only true under specific abstract assumptions which do not correspond to reality. I want to show that conditions *can* exist (and indeed are likely to exist) in which unrestricted trade may lead to a loss of welfare to particular regions or countries and even to the world as a whole — the world will be worse off under free trade than it could be under some system of regulated trade.

Traditional theory emanated from Ricardo's doctrine of comparative costs which says that even if one country is more efficient in everything — has a higher productivity all round — it pays for it to specialise in those things in which its comparative efficiency is greatest and to rely on the rest for supplies from the less efficient countries. His famous example was the exchange of cloth for wine between England and Portugal; he supposed that Portugal had a higher output per man both in the production of wine and cloth than England but its productivity-advantage was greater in wine production than in cloth-making; hence Portugal would be better off if it specialised in producing wine and obtained cloth by way of trade with England.

This theory went through further important stages of development; some of it was due to J. S. Mill, some to Marshall and later, more importantly, to two Swedish economists, Ely Hecksher and Professor Ohlin. The latter has shown that under certain assumptions differences in comparative costs can only exist if the 'resource endowment' or 'factor proportions' of the different regions are different; such differences must be reflected in differences in relative factor

[1] The latter part of this proposition abstracts from the possibility that a particular country possesses some degree of monopoly power and thereby can turn the terms of trade in its favour by means of a tariff even after retaliation by other countries is taken into account.

prices, and the effect of trade must be to bring relative factor prices into a closer relationship to one another (each country exports goods which require larger quantities of those resources in which it is relatively well endowed). Later Stolper and Samuelson in their well-known 'factor price equalisation theorem' carried this doctrine a stage further in showing that on certain assumptions as regards the production functions, the effect of free trade must be to *equalise factor prices* in the different participating areas.

The implications are very far-reaching. If true they show:

(1) that the free movement of goods can be a substitute to the movement of factors (and *vice versa*), and therefore

(2) trade brings about the same tendency to equalisation of factor prices (mainly wages and interest rates) as the free mobility of factors would cause (abstracting from the cost of movement in each case);

(3) from which it follows that trade must necessarily *reduce* the differences in real earnings per head between the different trading areas and in favourable circumstances (i.e. identical production functions which are suitably 'well behaved')[1] eliminate them altogether.

However all this rests on a number of artificial assumptions which are not always stated or even understood:

(1) that the 'production functions' for different goods are the same in different countries — i.e. technology and the efficiency of its exploitation are the same everywhere;

(2) perfect competition prevails throughout;

(3) constant returns to scale (homogeneous and linear production functions) for all processes of production.

It is these two latter assumptions — which are themselves closely involved in one another — which are critical from the point of view of the theory. (Perfect competition can normally obtain only when costs of production are the same, however small or however large is the rate of production.)

As soon as we allow either for diminishing returns (to transferable factors) and/or for increasing returns due to economies of scale, the above propositions will no longer hold.

II INTRODUCING DIMINISHING RETURNS

Take first the case of *diminishing returns*. Suppose the amount of wine produced in Portugal is limited by the amount of land suitable for viniculture (while only a limited amount of labour can be used with advantage on any one hectare of land). Production could then be limited by a *land constraint*,

---

[1] A production function is 'well-behaved' when, besides being linear and homogeneous, it also has a constant elasticity of substitution sufficiently near unity irrespective of factor proportions. This means, in geometric terms, that the isoquants of the function are convex to the origin throughout and are asymptotic to the two axes (which measure quantities of these factors of production).

not a *labour constraint*. If the maximum number of people who can be usefully employed on the land is smaller than the total number available to work, the remainder can only be employed in industry or services. In the absence of international trade, the people who are not wanted on the land will be engaged in making 'cloth', in the ratio, say, of 1 yard of cloth = 10 litres of wine. In England on the other hand 10 litres of wine cost the same as 10 yards of cloth. The opening of trade will mean that the price of *cloth* will fall so much, both in terms of money and in terms of wine, that it will no longer be profitable to produce cloth in Portugal – the Portugese textile trade will be ruined. (This is not just an imaginary example: according to Friedrich List this is what *actually* happened as a result of the Methuen Treaty with Portugal of 1704.) Now if all the workers freed from cloth-making could be employed in increasing the production of wine, in proportion to the increase in labour employed there, all would be well: the real income of Portugal would be greater than before. Portugal would have *more* cloth and *more* wine to consume than in the absence of trade. However if land is limited, this may not be possible. Nor will it be possible to save the cloth-trade by reducing wages. For there is a minimum wage (in terms of wine) below which the cloth-workers could not subsist. Hence the result might be that while Portugal will export more wine to England, the national real income of Portugal would shrink, since the addition to its wine output may not compensate for the loss of output of the cloth trade. Portugal could well end up by being a much poorer country than before – there would be less employment and less output.[1]

It will be readily seen that this could not have occurred under the rule of constant labour costs in both industries. But the same kind of conclusion emerges if one considers the existence not of diminishing returns in *agriculture* but that of increasing returns in *industry*.

III THE FURTHER DIFFICULTIES DUE TO INCREASING RETURNS

The case of increasing returns has never been properly explored in economic theory – beyond the famous statement of Marshall (and of Cournot and Walras before him) that increasing returns lead to monopoly because some producers get ahead of their rivals and gain a cumulative advantage over the others whom they will drive out of business – hence they could not exist under conditions which prevail in a *competitive market*. When in the 1930s

[1] The example involves that England can manufacture clothes much cheaper in terms of wine than Portugal and not solely on account of the unsuitability of the British climate for wine production. The example also supposes that England uses a superior technology in clothes' production, involving a smaller outlay of labour per unit of output, otherwise it could not sell clothes at a price which is below the *minimum* cost at which they can be produced in Portugal, even when wages are at the minimum quantity of wine on which workers can subsist (unless English workers can subsist on so much less wine than Portugese workers which is unlikely!).

the new theories concerning the imperfection of markets suggested that this need not be so — falling costs and competition can co-exist — economists in general shied away from exploring the consequences. Hicks, for example, recognised at an early stage that these doctrines of imperfect competition 'threaten the wreckage of the greater part of economic theory'[1] and all the post-war economists (particularly the US economists) followed his example in ignoring the phenomenon altogether.

However, business men could never ignore the existence of diminishing costs. It is on account of the economies of large-scale production that a rising market share means success and a falling market share spells trouble. And it is on that account that in a growing market a business *cannot* stand still: it must grow if it wishes to survive.[2]

Owing to increasing returns in processing activities (in manufactures) success breeds further success and failure begets more failure. Another Swedish economist, Gunnar Myrdal, called this 'the principle of circular and cumulative causation'.

It is as a result of this that free trade in the field of manufactured goods led to the concentration of manufacturing production in certain areas — to a *'polarisation process'* which inhibits the growth of such activities in some areas and concentrates them in others.

This is just what happened as a result of the Industrial Revolution and the transport revolution of the nineteenth century. Areas which were wholly isolated previously became drawn into the world economy. But one cannot say that the enlargement of markets brought about by these technological revolutions benefited *all* participating areas in the same way. The manufacturing industry of Britain (at first chiefly the cotton industry, later iron and steel and machinery) received an enormous stimulus through the opening of markets in Europe, in North and South America and then in India and China. But at the same time the arrival of cheap factory-made goods eliminated local producers (of hand-woven textiles and so on) who became uncompetitive in consequence, and it made these countries 'specialise' in the production of raw materials and minerals which however could only offer employment to limited numbers of workers. As a result of this the countries dependent on the exports of primary products remained comparatively poor — the poverty was a consequence, not of low productivity of labour in their export sectors, but of the limited employment capacity of their 'profitable' industries.

Britain's example in industrialisation was followed, with the assistance of protective tariffs, by Germany, France, the US and finally Japan (plus a number of smaller European countries). All these became producers, and

[1] *Value and Capital* (Oxford, 1939), pp. 83–5.

[2] The only economist of the nineteenth century who fully recognised this was Karl Marx. In neo-classical theory, each firm has an 'optimum size'; when the output of an industry grows, it is the *number* of firms, not the size of existing firms, which increases.

later exporters, of manufactured goods, both in exchange for raw materials and in exchanges with each other. But in the course of this development while the trade between the different regions of the globe was greatly intensified the differences in wealth and living standards became considerably larger and not smaller. The present division of the world between rich and poor countries is a relatively recent phenomenon: it is due to the fact that the countries which successfully industrialised accumulated a great deal of material and human capital in the course of industrialisation. All *developed* countries are invariably successful producers and exporters of manufactured goods. The phenomenon of 'polarisation' happens *within* as well as *between* countries – the classic example is that of the North and South of Italy which, following unification, have shown a strongly divergent development – unification served to enrich the North and to impoverish the South.

IV INTERNATIONAL TRADE AND LIVING STANDARDS

Thus international or interregional trade is capable of enlarging differences in living standards between areas, as well as diminishing them. Both forces operate, the important question is which of these two tendencies is likely to predominate?

We can distinguish between three types of trade:

(1) trade between manufacturing countries and primary producers;
(2) trade between manufacturing countries with each other;
(3) trade between primary producers with each other.

It is only in the case of the *third type of trade* that the classical theory of mutual advantage strictly applies. Depending on climate etc. it pays some countries to concentrate on producing wheat or potatoes and others on oranges and bananas. As regards the first type of trade – whether it is the exchange of wine against cloth or raw cotton against cotton shirts – the benefits from trade are likely to be disproportionately large for those countries which import raw materials and export manufactures.

The interesting case is *trade of the second type* – trade between manufacturing countries which has greatly intensified since the Second World War, thus reversing the trend of the previous fifty years which was towards more 'autarky' as between the leading powers.

In principle such trade is of great practical benefit since specialisation *between* the industries of different areas should enable the benefits of the economies of scale to be realised more fully. However the truth of this proposition depends on the trade being *balanced* in both directions – a state of affairs in which the exports of manufactures of each country increase *pari passu* with its imports of manufactures. But as past experience, both pre-war and post-war, has shown, this does not come about naturally. Growing imbalances of trade may arise which are not easily corrected. After the Second World War the successful countries like Germany and Japan acquired a cumulative advantage through their fast growth, whereas the slow-growing countries such as Britain (and to some extent also the United States of America) faced an increasing handicap due to their slow growth.[1] On account of the dynamic effects of fast growth it is possible that a particular country's products become qualitatively superior, and hence preferred to those of another country, in *all* branches of industry. It can be argued that Japan's growth (and to some extent also Germany's growth) in the post-Second World War period was enhanced at the expense of the two trade-losing countries, the US and the UK. These latter countries suffered from increasing import penetration in their domestic markets of manufactures which were not offset by higher exports, which meant in effect that their national output was reduced in consequence. (The labour released from manufacturing industry either remained unemployed or found employment in trades where its social marginal productivity is very low.)[2]

If one looks at the trade of the various industrialised countries in the last two decades there were some (such as Sweden, Belgium or Switzerland) whose exports and imports grew roughly in balance. But there were others which maintained a high level of production and employment by what used to be called 'beggar my neighbour' policies — by exporting goods but without importing the equivalent in return. At the moment both Germany and Japan refuse to expand their home demand to the extent that would be necessary to make their exports equal to their imports and thereby enable other countries to maintain reasonably full employment without being constrained by their balance of payments.

V THE NEED FOR NEW RULES OF THE GAME

The restoration of full employment and prosperity requires that these imbalances of trade be removed. What we need, as M. Barré, the French Prime Minister, said in an article in the *Journal de Geneve*,[3] is that there should be new 'rules of the game' (which should be collectively defined and applied) which assure conditions of growth, security and regularity of trade

---

[1] This is not meant to suggest that comparative success or failure in international trade was *caused* by comparatively fast or slow economic growth rates. The truth is more likely to be the other way round — in the same way in which a successful business achieves an exceptional growth rate as a result of marketing a successful product (as, for example, the Model T of Henry Ford, or the Volkswagen).

[2] It could be argued that there was an offsetting gain to the consumer in the form of quality improvements and a greater range of choice — e.g. Japanese cameras, television sets or electronic calculating machines may have been superior to anything the US could have produced if the choice of buying Japanese goods had not been present. However, though these things are by their nature not susceptible to measurement, it is difficult to believe that such short-term consumer gains can make up for the consequential loss of industrial development which brings not only lower output growth and productivity growth in its trail, but also less technical progress of the learning-by-doing type, and hence a lower rate of accrual of new products.

[3] 17 September 1977.

without which 'free trade is nothing more than a pretext for the strongest and least scrupulous as well as being a trap for the weakest'. I interpret this to mean (admittedly the sentence is capable of more than one interpretation) that trade must be mutual and that each country should strive to balance its export of manufactures to the other industrialised countries (taken as a group) by equivalent imports.

Most industrialised countries have an import requirement of primary products (food, raw materials and fuel) and therefore need a corresponding net export of manufactures to pay for them.[1] The natural way of securing such net exports is to export manufactures to those countries who do not produce (or export) manufactured goods in sufficient volume to cover their own requirements, and are therefore net importers of manufactured goods. It is quite possible however (or even probable, in the case of some of the smaller countries) that their manufactured exports are of a specialised kind and of a technical quality which find their natural market in other industrialised countries and not in the countries producing primary products. In these cases the overall balance of foreign trade involves a triangular relationship – their net imports from the primary producing countries are matched by net export of manufactures to the other industrialised countries who in turn earn sufficient surpluses in their trade with the primary producers to pay both for their own net imports and also for those of the 'specialised' group of manufacturing exporters.

But apart from such cases (which account for only a fraction of the imbalances of trade between industrialised countries) the existence of surpluses and deficits in the intra-trade of the developed industrialised countries is evidence of an asymmetrical relationship – some countries tend to export more (at the prevailing level of production and employment) than they wish to import, whereas others suffer from the insufficiency of exports relative to their import propensity which prevents them from utilising their own production potential fully. The evidence for this consists of overall surpluses and deficits in the foreign trade of the various industrial countries which are of a chronic nature – which tend to persist year after year despite variations in relative costs, exchange rates, etc.[2]

---

[1] In so far as such import needs are not financed by invisible items – i.e. income from past foreign investment, tourism, transport or financial services etc. But as the historical example of the UK shows, such 'service income' is not an effective substitute in the long run for the failure to maintain an adequate export potential in manufactures.

[2] Moreover, the actual surpluses and deficits are not a *proper* measure of the potential size of such imbalances (and of the deflationary force which they exert) since the countries who suffer from an excessive import propensity tend, on that account, to suffer from an insufficiency of domestic demand as well so that their aggregate output or income is demand-constrained; they may, in addition, be forced to follow a deflationary fiscal and monetary policy, and for both of these reasons, will import less from the surplus countries than they would do under full employment conditions.

In a recent article on the 'Causes of Growth and Recession in World Trade',[1] T. F. Cripps has demonstrated that a country is not 'balance of payments constrained' if its full employment imports, M^*, are less than its import capacity, $\overline{M}$ (as determined by its earnings from exports). Such a country is free to choose the level of domestic demand which it considers optimal for its own circumstances,[2] whereas the other countries for whom $M^* > \overline{M}$, must, under conditions of free trade, reduce their output and employment below the full employment level, and import only what they can afford to finance. He then shows that the sum of imports of the 'unconstrained' countries determine the attainable level of production and employment of the 'constrained' countries, and the remedy for this situation requires measures that increase the level of 'full-employment' imports, or else reduce the export share of the 'unconstrained' countries. The 'rules of the game' which would be capable of securing growth and stability in international trade, and of restoring the production of the 'constrained' countries to full employment levels, may require discriminatory measures of import control, of the type envisaged in the famous 'scarce currency clause' of the Bretton Woods agreement.

In the absence of such measures *all* countries may suffer a slower rate of growth and a lower level of output and employment, and not only the group of countries whose economic activity is 'balance-of-payments constrained'. This is because the 'surplus' countries' own exports will be lower with the shrinkage of world trade, and they may not offset this (or not adequately) by domestic reflationary measures so that their imports will also be lower. Provided that the import regulations introduced relate to *import propensities* (i.e. to the relation of imports to domestic output) and not to the absolute level of imports as such, the very fact that such measures will raise the trade, production and employment of the 'constrained' countries will mean that the volume of exports and domestic income of the 'unconstrained' countries will also be greater, despite the downward change in their *share* of world exports.[3]

[1] *Cambridge Economic Policy Review* (March 1978), pp. 37–43.

[2] Owing to the widespread view according to which a given increase in effective demand is more 'inflationary' in its consequences if brought about by budgetary measures than if it is the result of additional investment or exports (irrespective of any limitations of import capacity) the inequality or potential inequality in its payments balance may cause a surplus country to regard a lower level of domestic demand as 'optimal' in the first case than in the second case.

[3] In other words, if countries whose 'full employment' balance of payments shows a surplus because $M^* < \alpha W$ (where M^* is the level of full employment imports, α is the share of a particular country's exports in world trade, W) after a reduction of α to $\hat{\alpha}$ ($\hat{\alpha} < \alpha$) through the imposition of discriminatory measures, the country will still be better off if $\hat{\alpha} W^* > \alpha W$ where W^* is the volume of world trade generated under full employment conditions.

Discussion of Lord Kaldor's Paper

Professor Malinvaud introduced the paper by asking why Lord Kaldor had presented a paper entitled 'The Foundations of Free Trade Theory and their Implications for the current World Recession' to this conference on unemployment. Was it because Lord Kaldor thought the current world recession had to do with the organisation of international trade, and therefore that some appropriate changes were likely to reduce world unemployment? This idea was quite natural and fitted in with the purpose of this conference, so we should consider it closely.

Professor Malinvaud recalled that the paper by Thorbecke and Grinols, to be discussed later, showed that trade with developing countries had tended to create more jobs in the USA than it had destroyed. Similar results were obtained for France. This suggested that raising barriers to imports from developing countries would not be appropriate. But Lord Kaldor seemed essentially to consider trade in manufactured goods between industrial countries. Hence, there should be no conflict between Lord Kaldor and the Thorbeck−Grinols paper.

What was more surprising was that Lord Kaldor's paper should start with a discussion of the pure theory of international trade. This theory assumed a full employment equilibrium, and could not be directly useful for evaluating the comparative merits of situations in which unemployment occurred.

Professor Malinvaud did not dispute the brief and elegant review of the pure theory of international trade given early in the paper even though he disagreed with the second footnote. He wondered also whether the factor price equalisation theorem implied a reduction of the inequalities in living standards between various regions. The question was whether, for instance, Indian labour had the same quality as American labour? Lord Kaldor went on to discuss the artificial assumptions of the pure theory, and more particularly those concerning returns to scale. He reminded us that increasing returns were incompatible with competitive equilibrium, and that wherever they played an important role, we must rely for positive analysis on other theories, particularly development theory.

But Lord Kaldor seemed to argue also that under diminishing returns a competitive free-trade equilibrium might be more unfavourable for one of the trading countries than a no-trade equilibrium. Professor Malinvaud did not accept this argument.

Lord Kaldor considered the case in which Portugal would not have enough land to employ its full labour force in wine production. He then stated that under free competitive trade the excess Portuguese labour force would remain unemployed. But this was not the result to which the pure theory led. In this case, a solution appeared in which, even if England specialised in the production of cloth, cloth was also produced in Portugal with a lower wage rate; the factor price equalisation did not apply, but the free trade equilibrium was still better for Portugal than the no-trade equilibrium.

Professor Malinvaud reiterated that the pure theory was not really relevant to the present discussion, because it assumed full employment. He then turned to the development theory sketched in Lord Kaldor's paper.

This theory placed emphasis on increasing returns to scale in manufacturing, and on the polarisation process which that implied: increasing returns helped the first industrial countries to grow more and more easily, and protected them from potential competition by other countries.

From this point of view, Lord Kaldor distinguished three types of trade. Trade between primary producers would benefit all of them. Trade between manufacturing countries and primary producers would benefit mainly the first type of country, because such trade would destroy the manufacturing and handicraft sector of primary producing countries and drive a substantial part of the labour force into unemployment.

If we wanted to subject this statement to scientific scrutiny, we could look first at historical evidence and second to a logical model that would explain it. Professor Malinvaud disclaimed much knowledge of economic history or of primary producers, but the historians he had consulted agreed with Lord Kaldor's view on this point. Professor Malinvaud did not know of a model of the economic process. The Marxist theory of imperialism provided no logical model of this; it only brought forward the use of political power by industrial capitalism. His own guess was that a logical model that would explain the theory was feasible. As he saw it, this model would have to take explicit account of price rigidities. In particular, these rigidities might explain why the solution of the pure theory for the Portugal—England example did not easily come about, and why free trade might generate unemployment in non-industrial countries.

The third type of trade considered by Lord Kaldor was trade between manufacturing countries. He again saw the polarisation process bringing about increasing imbalances in trade; the fastest growing countries benefited from cumulative competitive advantages, which led them to accumulate ever-increasing surpluses as long as free trade prevailed. They therefore experienced full employment, whereas slow-growing countries suffered from ever-increasing unemployment.

Professor Malinvaud thought this vision of a cure for the current recession oversimplified because economic development was a much more complex phenomenon. In particular, reasons must be found why Britain, which should have been by far the main beneficiary of the polarisation process, lost in the late nineteenth century and in this century *vis-à-vis* USA and Germany. To attribute the responsibility to protective tariffs in those countries did not seem to suffice.

It must also be recognised that the tremendous increase in trade in manufactures between industrial countries from 1950 to 1975 should appear striking to us because it generated so little imbalance, and certainly much less than was forecast in the early 1950s in many countries, particularly France. Moreover, the difference in the present unemployment rates between deficit and surplus countries was rather small. Certainly present unemployment could not be explained solely by trade imbalances.

In the final part of his paper, Lord Kaldor argued convincingly that employment would be higher at present if deficit countries did not restrain their aggregate demand in order to limit the size of their deficit. He then suggested that discriminatory import control measures in deficit countries should be considered, possibly with the agreement of surplus countries.

Professor Malinvaud would like to have seen this last suggestion more thoroughly discussed. It was not a purely intellectual exercise today. Import controls were being spoken of, and even introduced in some countries. It was important to know under which conditions they would achieve their purpose, and under which conditions they would not induce detrimental effects worse than the beneficial effects in the short run on unemployment.

Economists must not stop after the statement that *some* system of regulated trade was likely to exist in the future that would increase welfare in the world. This might be understood as meaning that *any* system of import control was justified, whoever introduced it, whether it was reversible or not. We did not mean that, and should be much clearer on specific suggestions.

Professor Malinvaud ended his introduction by saying that if we accepted Lord Kaldor's analysis concerning the effect on employment of trade between primary producers and manufacturing countries, the first duty of any attempt at regulating international trade should be to improve employment in developing countries more than in the already affluent manufacturing countries.

In reply *Lord Kaldor* pointed out that 'full employment equilibrium' was a modern term. One might well ask whether the classical economists assumed full employment. He would say no, but the point was arguable. The result depended on how one interpreted the doctrine that capital accumulation determined the demand for labour while the growth of employment opportunities governed the increase in population. The kind of theory given in his paper was fully within the classical realm of discourse, and his results critically depended on the absence of constant costs in agriculture in terms of transferable factors. What made his interpretation of the Ricardian example yield the results the validity of which Professor Malinvaud claims to have denied was that labour had a minimum supply price, whether or not the demand and supply of labour were equal. A large excess supply did not make the wage of labour zero. This was why both the capital stock of Portugal and the amount of labour employed could be smaller under free trade than under protection, if the effective constraint on wine production was the amount of land, not labour or capital, while only the latter were involved in the production of clothes. He wished to draw attention to the footnote on p. 87 of his paper[1] (which Professor Malinvaud might not have seen).

As regards the trade in manufactures, there might only be a *small* imbalance of trade between 'surplus' and 'deficit' countries, but the size of that imbalance was not the proper measure of the real income loss that might be caused by asymmetrical relationships between import propensities and abilities to export. The imbalances actually observed were *ex post* and this obscured the underlying situation of disequilibrium, causing a loss of world income and trade. The results achieved reflected the fact that if imports were constrained by lack of exports, the exports of other countries would be smaller; and this in turn would adversely affect the exports of the first country. *Ex post* one need have no imbalance at all between imports and exports. Yet world production and employment might be seriously below potential owing to such asymmetries. If a particular country was hampered by an unfavourable competitive position, unemployment was not the sole, or even the proper measure of its disadvantage. The proper measure was a low rate of growth which would tend to counteract the unemployment effects. The most important point, he thought, was that, as the experience of the last ten years had shown, income elasticities were far more important for world trade than price elasticities. It was variations in levels of income and output which were the main cause of changes in imports relative to exports; the large exchange rate adjustments which were supposed to exert their influence through changes in relative prices had not been effective in changing the relative competitive position of industrial countries during the 1970s.

Mr Kaser said that while this was a conference about western countries, what Lord Kaldor had said also applied in eastern Europe. All socialist economies were oriented to full employment with job security. When eastern European countries traded, they arranged for imports of manufactures to equal exports. So any country could get more non-manufactures only if it imported more manufactures. This perhaps was because of low productivity in non-manufacturing. Certainly the Kaldor argument would be correct for a country like Romania. So what Lord Kaldor proposed was an eastern European practice with two-way trade.

The aim was to increase economies of scale and opportunities for development. In eastern Europe, a reason for the smaller amount of two-way trade was that this was adversely affected by pricing practice. It reflected the more general problem in socialist economies that prices did not reflect factor scarcities. They were borrowed, and then distorted, from the West. Difficulties arose because of fixed prices in Comecon. In the long run some products (manufactures) were in surplus. Hard goods, which were in deficit,

---

[1] A superficial critic could point out that this example violated one of Ricardo's conditions — *viz* that Portugal had a higher productivity in *both* sectors than England. But Ricardo only introduced this assumption in order to demonstrate the validity of his proposition in an *extreme* case; he would have said that if Portugal had superior productivity only in wine and inferior productivity in cloth, the proposition derived from the doctrine of comparative costs followed *à fortiori*.

were food, raw materials and energy. There was here a neat parallel with hard and soft currencies under fixed exchange rates. It was no coincidence that eastern Europe could pursue a Kaldorian policy because the countries there had controls over the allocation of production to both home and export markets.

Professor Khachaturov said it was possible to agree with much of the first part of Lord Kaldor's paper while noting that there were no practical proposals for policy measures on foreign trade. He thought it reasonable to go further. If free trade was undesirable for less-developed countries because of unemployment, what was the mechanism to overcome the difficulties? The suggestion was the use of protective tariffs and quotas, but such measures should lead to unemployment in exporting countries and increased employment in importing countries. The relationship depended on labour productivity in the two types of country. He thought the issue should be studied and that practical proposals should be made which did help.

Professor Giersch wondered whether, in Lord Kaldor's example, if the Portuguese wine producers had offered to compensate the textile workers, Portugal would be better off.

He found no references to the international capital market. Trade surpluses were often induced by capital outflows. Some of the surpluses of Germany, a country with high unit labour costs, were invested abroad in countries with low unit labour costs and created jobs there.

Professor Giersch wondered whether competition might not be favourable for growth, and whether a growth-biased social atmosphere might not stimulate active competition. This would also be a cumulative process.

Professor Parkin did not see what economic agents were doing in Lord Kaldor's model. Lord Kaldor said that income elasticities were more important than price elasticities. If there was a budget constraint on individual agents, then prices did matter. He wondered how Lord Kaldor reached the conclusion that there could be a balance of payments problem at all in such circumstances. If all private agents were free to make their own trading decisions, the capital account would enter in, to bring equilibrium. This was true both for the individual and for the aggregate of individuals.

Professor Parkin suggested that the problem lay in a different area. The fact was that one agent (or rather a collective of agents) was the central government and the central bank. These both avoided the normal budgetary constraints, printing money where necessary to balance expenditures, so the real issue was posed by countries with a large public sector deficit and a reluctance to allow the exchange rate to change. This was the source of payments imbalance. A fast-growing country would then be one with a big demand for money and so a smaller tendency to export, and *vice versa*. Perhaps one should integrate what Lord Kaldor said more with monetary theory. One could not have a purely real theory of international trade. It was a monetary phenomenon.

Professor Kolm said that Lord Kaldor's paper raised many questions. He wanted to focus on an essential one. The basic theorem of welfare economics on the superiority of free international trade could only be that, given the traditional classical assumptions (convexities, competition, etc.) an allocation was Pareto-optimal for individual welfares if and only if it was reachable by free trade. In general, and with relevant assumptions, given a situation not reachable by free trade, there were sets of lump sum transfers such that the freeing of trade accompanied by these transfers made someone better off and no-one worse off. There might be other kinds of transfers yielding this result. The situation might require some of these transfers to be international (i.e. between agents of different nationalities). For some partial freeing of trade, there might exist sets of transfers, with the possible requirement that some of these transfers were international, such that this change plus one of these sets of transfers made someone better off and no-one worse off.

For a given situation and a given liberalisation (worldwide or more limited), it might be that all the sets of transfers which would make it benefit somebody and hurt nobody were impossible to achieve. This might be for reasons of information or of politics (intranational or international). This move necessarily made some person worse off.

Professor Kolm asked the conference to consider, for instance, a dramatic application of these remarks, which was the present-day equivalent of the 1704 Anglo-Portuguese Methuen Treaties. Advised by faithful supporters of the liberal ideology, General Pinochet had dismantled the high tariff barriers which protected Chilean industry. The argument was that Chile must take advantage of the international division of labour and specialise in the types of production in which it had the greatest comparative advantage. These were copper-mining and large-scale export farming. It might be that Chile's national product had increased as a result. But we must see how this had happened. A large number of workers were driven out of work, and a large number of small firms had to close. Unemployment and severe poverty increased substantially. Of course, these losses might have been 'compensated' by the success of the 'advantageous' production activities, that is, by the rents of copper mines and of large farms. But the owners of these were not even Chilean – for the mines, and some of the land. The analytical ignorance of free trade ideologues did not hurt at random!

Professor Rehn noted that Professor Giersch wondered whether Portugal could compensate its textile workers. He would like to take this argument farther. Lord Kaldor seemed to be saying that it would be a good idea if one could protect deficit countries, but protection was not necessarily elegantly applied: there was a risk of a vicious circle of protection. However, he would like to underline that things could go the other way. One need not have a negative solution but could have an elegantly applied protective arrangement helping both types of country. So perhaps deficit countries should apply an incremental, or marginal, employment subsidy. This would enable Portugal to sell cloth at competitive prices and also to break the spiral of inflation. Expansion would be possible without a general increase in profit margins and so an unaccepted change in income distribution. Economists like Professor Parkin might not care for a change in income distribution but politicians had to take them seriously. He would like to point out that such a solution would not represent dumping because it would help to expand world trade.

Lord Kaldor replied to the discussion. His own view was that one should discriminate by import controls against countries whose imports were unconstrained by the balance of payments, but who, in turn, constrained the level of exports and employment of other countries. He was thinking of the situation where, for a given country, the chosen 'optimal' level of imports was less than its capacity to export, whether or not it had a positive balance of trade. The actual balance of payments surplus or deficit was not the proper measure of the disequilibrating effect of such asymmetries. Lord Kaldor agreed that it might be true for Federal Germany that the balance of payments surplus was offset by genuine (because employment-creating) capital flows; but these were not a measure of its potential surplus when other countries were constrained in their imports by balance of payments difficulties. The problem was the relationship of import propensities and export abilities to each other. If one country had a bigger import propensity, as a share of income, than the ratio of its exports to its full-employment output, then its production and employment would be restricted on account of the balance of payments. This might happen automatically via the Harrod multiplier, so that output and imports fell. The problem he was tackling was one of structural disproportions between the profile of import propensities and of export abilities. It was the cause of a good deal of depression in world trade and world production. Its removal would help every country.

To Professor Giersch, Lord Kaldor said that in his version of the Ricardian case, the Kaldor—Hicks compensation test would give a negative result for Portugal. The wine-growers would not be able to compensate the cloth manufacturers and remain better off. Free trade was bad on the Kaldor—Hicks criteria because, under free trade, cloth prices were below the lowest possible production costs in Portugal, governed by subsistence wages. This did not matter to Ricardo, Mill, or for that matter to Walras, because the production of wine could be increased, in their international trade models, at constant cost.

If one wanted both maximum growth and maximum trade, the situation was difficult. Structural disproportions resulting from differences in income elasticities could make this impossible. He would point out, in answer to Professor Parkin, that it was not possible to derive an assertion about reality solely from *a priori* reasoning. Whether price elasticities were important or not was a question of fact. Their magnitude did not follow from the assumption of utility-maximisation. One could imagine utility functions with no elasticities of substitution at all. For example, one could have a function based on a simple ranking of commodities. This was beyond the range of possibilities allowed for in neo-classical theory. As for the role of the central government or of the central bank, the ruin of Portugal, admirably described by Friedrich List, had not assumed the existence of paper money or of government expenditure. Portugal may simply have had a given amount of gold which was not increased or decreased (except as a result of imbalances of trade which may have been strictly temporary). Yet the same result followed. The situation had nothing to do with monetarism.

In answer to Professor Kolm, Lord Kaldor said that if one introduced technology as a separate factor of production, one reduced the theory of the production function to mere tautology. Factors of production must be genuine – i.e. alienable and exchangeable. As we all knew, any production function could be made linear and homogeneous by the simple device of adding an extra variable with the requisite co-efficient, but that meant nothing. This would not make a situation Pareto-optimal if it lacked optimality for other reasons.

Marx was indeed the first man to point out that if there were increasing returns, these *could* co-exist with competition. Competition would compel the firm to grow as rapidly as possible so as to keep pace with, or keep ahead of, its rivals. Marx saw intense competition and increasing returns existing side by side, but this was ruled out of court by the whole school of orthodox economics, based on Cournot and Walras. Economics was the poorer for it.

Lord Kaldor agreed with Professor Rehn's sentiments but was less optimistic than he had been some years ago about the effects of an employment subsidy. Using subsidies to reduce labour costs was like an indirect change in the exchange rate. This avoided some of the ill effects of devaluation but it was still dependent on the effectiveness of devaluation as an instrument. In practice, we could not accept the redistribution of income from labour to capital which a *large* devaluation implied. From that point of view, subsidisation of wages was a preferable alternative. But its effectiveness still depended on the existence of reasonably large price elasticities. Recent experience did not bear this out. Since the early 1970s, the price of the dollar had fallen beyond all limits that could reasonably have been foreseen. Even so, the pattern of world trade in manufactures had hardly changed. When the first discussion on an agreed devaluation of the dollar took place in 1971, the French had feared that US goods would overrun the markets of the rest of the world, if the dollar was devalued by as much as 10 per cent relative to the currencies of the other industrial countries. Since then the American dollar had fallen (in terms of comparative labour cost per unit of output) not by 10, but by 50 per cent – with no marked effect on relative trade flows. This criticism also held against the Rehn proposal.

5 The Effects of Trade between the US and Developing Countries on US Employment

Errol Grinols and Erik Thorbecke*
CORNELL UNIVERSITY, USA

INTRODUCTION

The major objective of this paper is to attempt to estimate the effects of trade between the US and the developing world on US employment over the recent past. The paper is divided into four sections.

The first section analyses the changes which occurred in the pattern of trade between the US and the developing countries[1] during the period 1962 to 1975. In this section an attempt is made at estimating the effects of the change in the US–Developing World trade on US employment for a sample of twenty-two most affected industries. Cumulative job gains and losses are measured for these industries, comparing the trade pattern prevailing in 1975 to the one prevailing in 1962.

Section II is devoted to an alternative procedure, which estimates the annual changes in US employment over the same period, 1962–75, resulting from US–Less-Developed-Countries (LDC) trade. In contrast with the simple cumulative estimates derived in the previous section, a structural demand model is built and used in Section II to yield these employment effects.

Section III describes some further characteristics of the trade pattern between the US and the developing countries during 1963–75. It is subdivided into four parts, analysing respectively:

(a) the sectors displaying the greatest positive or negative changes in US net trade balance with LDCs and the changes in actual US employment for these same sectors;

*We would like to acknowledge the valuable help of our Research Assistant, Joel Greer, whose work was essential to the completion of the present study.
[1] Developing countries are defined according to the UN classification for the period studied. These are referred to as 'developing countries' or 'Economic Classification II' in the UN Commodity Trade Statistics.

(b) the sectors displaying high growth of imports from LDCs and concomitant high export growth to LDCs;

(c) dissimilarities between the US–LDCs and US-Developing Countries trade pattern; and

(d) trade adjustment assistance as it relates to LDCs.

The final section of the paper is devoted to a brief summary of the findings and major conclusions.

I MAJOR CHANGES IN TRADE PATTERNS BETWEEN US AND DEVELOPING WORLD AND ESTIMATES OF CUMULATIVE EMPLOYMENT EFFECTS OF THE CHANGE IN US–LDC TRADE, 1963–75

The purpose of this paper is to estimate the effects of increasing trade between the US and the developing countries on US employment. However, before actually attempting to estimate these employment effects it is important to review briefly the changes which took place in the aggregate trade pattern between the US and the developing world over the recent past.

Tables 5.1 and 5.2 reveal the changes in US imports from, and exports to the lesser developed countries (LDCs) and the world as a whole. The major observations which are brought out by these tables are as follows. First, the growth in US trade with the world and with LDCs during the period 1962 to 1975 was considerably faster than that of US GNP. In nominal terms (i.e. at current prices), US imports from and exports to both the world and LDCs grew roughly twice as fast as GNP. In real terms (at 1972 prices), the growth of US imports from the developing world, relative to GNP growth – i.e. the income elasticity of demand for LDC imports[1] – is even more pronounced, amounting to 2.74 over the period 1962–75, compared to an elasticity of 1.95 where both imports and GNP are expressed at current prices. What is perhaps more interesting is that this high income elasticity of demand for LDC imports can not simply be accounted for by the phenomenal growth of oil and oil related imports from LDCs, which rose from $1.8 billion to $26.2 billion between 1962 and 1975, or at a cumulative annual rate of 22.8 per cent. Indeed, as column 7 in Table 5.1 indicates, US non-oil imports from LDCs rose at a rate only slightly lower than that of US imports from the world or US total imports from LDCs. In nominal terms the corresponding US income elasticity of demand for non-oil LDC imports was around 1.5 in 1962–75.

Secondly, Table 5.2 reveals clearly, in column 1, that the share of LDC imports in total US imports fell considerably from about 39 per cent in 1962

---

[1] By this, of course, we mean simply an *ex post* calculation based on historical values for GNP imports. Since the calculated figures represent a mix of supply factors as well as demand factors they are not meant to be income demand elasticities in the usual sense.

TABLE 5.1 AGGREGATE TRADE PATTERN BETWEEN THE US AND THE DEVELOPING WORLD, SELECTED YEARS 1962–75
(in dollars at current prices)

Year	(1) Total US imports $(M_T^{US}) \times 10^6$	(2) Total US exports $(X_T^{US}) \times 10^6$	(3) US imports from LDC countries $(M_{LDC}^{US}) \times 10^6$	(4) US exports to LDC countries $(X_{LOC}^{US}) \times 10^6$	(5) US GNP $(GNP^{US}) \times 10^6$	(6) Total US imports, excluding oil[a] $(M_{T-O}^{US}) \times 10^6$	(7) US imports from LDC countries, excluding oil[a] $(M_{LDC-O}^{US}) \times 10^6$
1962	15291	20254	5970	6960	563.8	13467	4460
1966	24340	27003	7751	9228	753.0	22093	5971
1971	43405	40587	10620	12393	1063.4	39712	8232
1974	96865	91430	39327	31688	1419.9	71763	19988
1975	92849	102575	39051	37920	1528.8	66648	18170
annual growth rate 1962–75	14.88	13.29	15.54	13.93	7.88	13.09	11.41

[a] Excluding crude petroleum and natural gas (SIC 1311 and 1321) and petroleum refining and related products (SIC 29).

TABLE 5.2 RELATIVE IMPORTANCE OF TRADE BETWEEN US AND DEVELOPING WORLD, SELECTED YEARS 1962–75
(in percentages based on figures in Table 5.1. All variables are defined in Table 5.1.

Year	(1) M_{LDC}^{US}/M_T^{US}	(2) $M_{LDC-O}^{US}/M_{T-O}^{US}$	(3) X_{LDC}^{US}/X_T^{US}	(4) M_{LDC}^{US}/GNP^{US}	(5) M_{LDC-O}^{US}/GNP^{US}	(6) X_{LDC}^{US}/GNP^{US}	(7) M_T^{US}/GNP^{US}	(8) X_T^{US}/GNP^{US}
1962	39.04	33.12	34.36	1.06	.79	1.24	2.71	3.59
1966	31.84	27.03	33.26	1.03	.79	1.23	3.23	3.68
1971	24.47	20.73	30.53	1.00	.77	1.17	4.08	3.82
1974	40.60	27.85	34.66	2.77	1.41	2.23	6.82	6.44
1975	42.06	27.26	36.97	2.55	1.19	2.48	6.11	6.71

to 24.5 per cent in 1971, before skyrocketing to 42.1 per cent in 1975, mainly because of the OPEC price rise. The corresponding share of non-oil imports (see column 2 of Table 5.2) declined from 33.1 per cent in 1962 to 20.7 per cent in 1971, subsequently to rise again to 27.3 per cent in 1975. It is relevant to note that this relative share had, by 1974–75, regained its 1966 level – i.e. between 27 and 28 per cent which was, however, still substantially below its 1962 level.

Thirdly, the relative importance of trade to GNP rose substantially in the US, from 2.71 per cent in 1962 to 6.11 per cent in 1975 with regard to total imports (see column 4 of Table 5.2) and from 3.59 to 6.71 per cent with regard to total exports (column 8 of Table 5.2). The corresponding share of US imports from LDCs to GNP rose from 1.06 to 2.55 per cent over the period under consideration, and that of exports to LDCs from 1.24 to 2.48 per cent. Again, the greater relative dependence of imports from the developing world cannot be attributed wholly to the growth of oil imports since the share of non-oil imports from LDCs to GNP rose from about 0.8 per cent in 1962, 1966 and 1971 to about 1.4 per cent in 1974 and 1.2 per cent in 1975 (see column 5 of Table 5.2).

Clearly, part of the rising dependence of the US economy on imports from the third world reflects the success which a number of the newly industrialised countries have enjoyed in exporting manufactured goods. In this connection a recent survey emphasised the fact that during the decade from the mid-sixties to the mid-seventies, the performance of developing countries with regard to the growth of manufacturing output and exports was significantly better than that of the developed countries.[1] The same survey showed that exports from developing countries had penetrated the market of industrialised countries in a number of products and particularly in textiles and clothing.

After having reviewed briefly the changes in the trade pattern between the US and the developing countries, we can now turn to the heart of our subject, namely, trying to estimate the employment effects resulting from the change in the pattern of trade between the US and LDCs. The first obvious point to make is that to the extent that the previously observed high growth of imports from LDCs into the US occurred jointly with an almost equally high growth of US exports to LDCs,[2] the net employment effects are not likely to have

---

[1] Over the period 1965–74, the real growth rate of manufacturing output in LDCs was 6.9 per cent compared to 4.8 per cent in DCs, while that of manufacturing exports was 13.1 per cent in LDCs and 10.6 per cent in DCs. (See Donald B. Keesing, 'World Trade and Output of Manufactures: Structural Trends and Developing Countries Exports', World Bank (February 1978), p. 9.)

[2] The imports from LDCs grew at 15.5 per cent while exports to LDCs grew at 13.9 per cent during this period. However, US non-oil imports from LDCs grew at 11.4 per cent (see Table 5.1).

been more than marginal. The proceeds of greater imports into the US from the third world permits these countries to purchase goods in the US, thereby stimulating US export growth. A second important observation is that a substantial part of the US imports from developing countries consists of non-competing goods such as crude oil, certain base metals and minerals, and tropical beverages which are either not produced domestically or are in short supply. Consequently, US imports of these products from developing countries cannot, by definition, substitute for domestic production and thereby displace American workers.

Thus, one problem which had to be faced in attempting to estimate the employment effects of the increasing and changing trade patterns between the US and the developing world over the period 1963–75, was to select those industries and sectors which were actually affected employment-wise. However, before specifying the criteria used in choosing these sectors, it is important to describe the data base which underlies this study.

It was decided to use an input-output table of the US economy for 1972, broken down into 157 sectors,[1] out of which 117 produce tradeable goods. The most time-consuming task of this study was to reclassify the trade and employment data into the same sectoral breakdown as the above input-output table. This entailed undertaking a tedious and often difficult process of concordance between different classification schemes, i.e. SITC, SIC, and the adopted I-O disaggregation. In a number of cases, somewhat arbitrary judgements had to be made in converting data from one classification system to another, which means that the estimates which were ultimately derived in this study should be considered, at best, as representing rough orders of magnitude.

Two major criteria were used in identifying those sectors most likely to have been affected in terms of employment as a result of the changes in the trade pattern between the US and the developing world. Sectors were selected if they produced competing products for which the US net trade balance (either positively or negatively) changed by at least 175 million dollars (at constant 1972 prices) over the period 1963–75. These criteria yielded 22 industries (or sectors) which are listed in Table 5.3.[2]

An attempt at estimating the employment effects in the US of the change in the trade pattern with the developing world was then undertaken for this sample of affected sectors. These employment effects were estimated on the

[1] This Input-Output table was provided by the US Department of Labour, Bureau of Economic Analysis.

[2] As is discussed in more detail subsequently, these 22 industries combined with the excluded non-competing sectors (e.g. crude and refined oil, natural gas, certain metals and minerals, and fishing and forestry products) accounted for the great bulk of the change in US net trade balance with the LDCs between 1963 and 1975, i.e. about 93 per cent of trade losses and 86 per cent of trade gains. The actual labour force employed in these 22 sectors represented 10 per cent of the total US labour force in 1975.

TABLE 5.3 US EMPLOYMENT EFFECTS RESULTING FROM CHANGES IN NET TRADE BALANCES WITH DEVELOPING WORLD BETWEEN 1963 AND 1975 FOR SAMPLE OF AFFECTED INDUSTRIES[a]

Sector	Change in US trade balance[b] 1963–75 $[(X_{j75} - M_{j75}) - (X_{j63} - M_{j63})]$	Change in direct and indirect output[b] ΔY_j	Net employment effects[b]
	In millions of dollars at 1972 prices		Number of jobs
4 Food and feed grains	1825	2093	67,308
26 Canned and frozen foods	− 292	− 280	− 6433
27 Grain mill products	176	280	3066
33 Miscellaneous food products	560	694	8410
39 Apparel	−1409	−1589	−78,945
52 Industrial inorganic & organic chemicals	411	816	14,231
53 Agricultural chemicals	280	450	8216
65 Footwear and other leather products	− 537	− 544	−32,821
71 Blast furnaces and basic steel products	530	1380	28,558
82 Other fabricated metal products	101	308	8631
83 Engines, turbines and generators	283	432	8571
84 Farm machinery	318	381	9470
85 Construction, mining and oil field machinery	490	563	13,867

No.				
86	Material handling equipment	385	426	12,024
87	Metal working machines	239	398	14,652
88	Special industrial machinery	622	692	20,676
89	General industrial machinery	165	392	12,060
92	Typewriters and other office equipment	464	472	15,447
93	Service industry machines	423	531	11,238
103	Motor vehicles	1490	2199	33,376
104	Aircraft	1488	1895	55,877
115	Musical instruments, toys, sporting goods	−183	−189	−8168
	Total employment gains			345,678
	Total employment losses			−126,367
	Net employment gains			219,311

a For criteria used in defining affected industries see text.

b See equations (1) and (2) in text. Note that the average employment-output ratios are not explicitly shown in the table.

c The change in the net balance between the two years will be positive if the size of the export surplus has increased, or, if an export surplus has been replaced by a previous import surplus, or, finally, if the size of the import surplus has been reduced and *vice versa*, for a negative net balance.

basis of the following equations:

$$\Delta E_j = E_j/Y_j \times \Delta Y_j, \quad \text{and} \tag{1}$$

$$\Delta Y_j = (I - A)^{-1} [(X_{j'75} - M_{j'75}) - (X_{j'63} - M_{j'63})] \tag{2}$$

where

ΔE_j = change in US employment in sector j due to trade with LDCs between 1963 and 1975;

ΔY_j = change in direct and indirect output in sector j resulting from changes in net trade balances with LDCs;

E_j/Y_j = average employment-output ratio for sector j, 1962–75;

$(I - A)^{-1}$ = Leontief-inverse for 1972 expressed in terms of 157 sectors;

$(X_{jt} - M_{jt})$ = net trade balance between the US and developing world in sector j and year t, t = 1963, 1975, respectively;

subscript j = 22 sectors listed in Table 5.3.

Table 5.3 summarises the estimated direct and indirect employment effects of the change in US–LDC trade between 1963 and 1975. Before analysing these results a few qualifications should be made about some implicit assumptions underlying the estimates based on equations (1) and (2). First, the 1972 input-output matrix is assumed to reflect the structure of the American economy throughout the period under consideration. Secondly, in computing employment losses or gross job displacement it is assumed that a one dollar net increase in LDC imports in sector j substitutes exactly for one dollar of domestic production in sector j.[1] The dollar-for-dollar assumption implies that for a given domestic income the total dollar expenditure on a particular category of goods (sector) remains constant even though some or all the goods in the category may change in price. Considering the fact that most sectors embrace a variety of different products and that even for generic goods (say shoes or automobiles) the imported variety may not be a perfect substitute for the domestic alternative, the assumption of a dollar-for-dollar substitution is likely to overstate the actual degree of substitution. Consequently, estimates of job losses resulting from increased imports from, or reduced exports to LDCs, based on this hypothesis as presented in Table 5.3, should be considered as upper bound figures.[2]

---

[1] Thus, for example, if US expenditure on imported footwear products rises by x dollars because of a fall in import price, then expenditure on domestic footwear would decline by x dollars.

[2] In the next section of this paper an alternative procedure for estimating employment effects is presented which attempts to measure the actual substitution among imports from developing and developed countries, respectively.

After having spelled out some of the assumptions underlying the estimates appearing in Table 5.3, we turn next to an examination of that table. The first observation is that between 1963 and 1975 the changing trade pattern between the US and the developing world — i.e. the incremental US—LDC trade — contributed to a *net* increase of about 220,000 jobs in the affected industries. Compared to the size of the US labour force (84.8 million in 1975) or even the increment to it between 1963 and 1975 (13.7 million) this net increase due to trade with LDCs is quite insignificant.[1] A more important fact which is revealed by Table 5.3 is that the employment gains were spread among 18 sectors while the employment losses were highly concentrated in only 4 industries. The sectors which appeared to have gained most employment-wise from increased trade with LDCs were food and feed grains (about 67,000 jobs), aircraft (56,000 jobs), motor vehicles (33,000 jobs), and blast furnaces and basic steel products (29,000 jobs). These sectors combined with the other gaining industries shown in Table 5.3 may have contributed about 346,000 new jobs during the period under consideration.

The sectors which lost jobs as a result of the changing US—LDC trade pattern were apparel (79,000 jobs), footwear and other leather products (33,000 jobs), musical instruments, etc. (8,000 jobs) and canned and frozen foods (6,000 jobs) for a combined total employment loss between 1963 and 1975 of about 126,000 jobs.

At this stage it should be recalled that only those sectors which underwent a change in net trade balance of more than 175 million dollars between the two benchmark years are included in the sample of industries appearing in Table 5.3. Another five sectors (wood products, plastic products, radio and TV receiving sets, watches and clocks, and jewellry and silverware)[2] displayed negative changes in their trade balances *vis-à-vis* LDCs ranging between 28 and 173 million dollars. The total employment losses attributable to these sectors were of the order of 14,000 jobs.

Thus, in conclusion, we come up with an estimate of about 140,000 jobs lost in the US over a 12-year period in sectors which underwent a worsening of their trade balances with the developing world. This estimate is somewhat lower than that obtained by Charles Frank of about 44,000 jobs a year displaced by rapid import growth in the US from 1964 to 1971.[3] More important than coming up with an exact estimate is the observation conveyed by our analysis of extreme sectoral concentration of job losses, with apparel accounting for about 56 per cent and footwear and leather products for about 24 per cent, respectively, of total employment losses. It is clear that a major change in the pattern of US imports from the developing world in recent

---

[1] In other words, increased trade between the US and the third world contributed about 1.6 per cent of the addition to the US labour force between 1963 and 1975.
[2] The corresponding sector numbers are 43, 63, 98, 113 and 114.
[3] See Charles R. Frank, Jr., *Foreign Trade and Domestic Aid* (Washington DC, Brookings Institution), pp. 36—7.

years has been the growth of clothing imports (which is included in the above apparel sector) from about 267 million dollars in 1967 to almost 3 billion dollars in 1976 and a concomitant displacement of DC sources by LDC producers.[1]

II ALTERNATIVE ESTIMATE OF EMPLOYMENT EFFECTS OF US–LDC TRADE: A STRUCTURAL DEMAND MODEL

The preceding discussion has been helpful in determining the scope of US trade with the third world, its changing character, and some estimate of the cumulative employment effects over the recent past. It is useful, at this point, to use the data to generate some more simple tests of the importance of this trade as it affects US employment. In this section we will describe the nature of the tests we prepared, summarising the results that we obtained, and make several conclusions based on those tests.

In a few words, the previous section made clear our belief that the scale of US–LDC trade is, for the moment at least, insignificant as it relates to US overall employment and that only adjustments in certain industries to changing conditions are of any concern. Employment losses in the recent past have been localised to a few industries and have been outweighed by gains which are spread over a large range of other industries.[2] In addition, it appears that the LDC trade profile is fairly distinct from US trade with the developed world.[3] Indeed, other studies have found that reduction in tariff barriers and restrictions in general, leading to greater trade with the world as a whole, may *reduce* the number of US jobs,[4] contrary to our findings that increased trade between the US and LDCs is beneficial to US employment on a net basis.

In this section a simple structural model is built to estimate the year-to-year changes in US employment occasioned by trade with the developing world over the sample period. The principal assumptions underlying this model are that (1) adjustments in the labour market take less than one year; and (2) output is determined by demand. These two behavioural assumptions are discussed next.

---

[1] The share of imports from LDCs out of total US imports of clothing rose from 41 per cent in 1967 to about 80 per cent in 1975–76. See Keesing, *op. cit.*, p. 62.

[2] For example, job losses in the electrical components industry have been balanced by gains in other sectors of the same industry. On balance, the industry had an export surplus with LDCs.

[3] This issue is discussed in Section III. See Table 5.8.

[4] The same is true of increased foreign investment which produces a different mix of US exports and imports with the world. See Frank, R. and R. Freeman, *The Distributional Consequences of Direct Foreign Investment* (Academic Press, 1978).

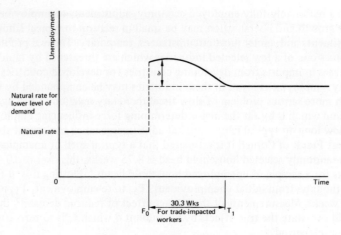

Fig. 5.1 Adjustment of employment to hypothetical reduction in demand

(1) *Adjustment lags*

Not least among the contributions of modern search theory is the conclusion that some level of unemployment is the necessary and natural outcome of the process of job search and matching labourers to positions. We accept this view of the world because it is clear that wage and price adjustments are not instantaneous and that capital and labour mobility are imperfect due to information constraints. It is consistent, then, to attribute any unemployment above this level to the same causes which create a pool of unfilled jobs and unemployed labourers in the first place — to wit, imperfectly mobile capital or labour and slow diffusion of wage and price signals. A second implication of the theory is that there are therefore two distinct components to be considered in explaining a given level of unemployment, the 'natural' rate and the cumulative effects of temporary adjustments around that rate.

For the moment we wish to focus on the longer term effects. To discuss these we will refer to Figure 5.1, where a hypothetical labour market is depicted. We accept both notions, that the impact effects of job losses are transitory, and that the numbers of jobs and employment in the long run are ultimately determined by the strength of demand.[1]

---

[1] Full employment can be thought of as the optimal link-up of men, machines, land and material. It is possible to trade in raw materials, invest across national boundaries and move labour. Of the four factors of production, land, labour, capital, and natural resources, only the first is not mobile.

In a reasonably fully employed economy, adjustments of employment to trade growth and liberalisation may be small in relation to typical labour adjustments and, under most circumstances, temporary. The real problem becomes one of a few selected industries which are threatened by rapid increases in imports from developing countries (or developed countries). Lastly, employment losses in these industries may be compounded by the much more serious problem of slow fiscal-monetary reaction to lost aggregate demand which is by far the major determining force influencing employment.

How long do typical labour market adjustments take? In a recent study by Robert Frank of Cornell it is estimated that a typical spell of unemployment for a randomly selected household head is 8.75 weeks, this rises to 10.48 weeks for a sample of unemployed household heads.[1] Plotting this in Figure 5.1, the time from initial unemployment, T_0, to re-employment, T_1, is roughly nine weeks. Measurements of the impact effect of reduced demand[2] therefore would overstate the true effects by an amount δ which falls to zero after the nine-week period.

Trade-affected workers seemed to fare slightly worse. Estimates of workers receiving trade adjustment assistance are that roughly 61 per cent of the males and 41 per cent of the females who found re-employment did so in 26 weeks. Another 21 per cent of males and 27 per cent of females were re-employed between the 27th and 52nd week.[3] The average for males was 30 to 40 weeks (depending whether one counts time out of the labour force and retraining time or not). Few studies have found evidence of longer waits than this. Consequently, the evidence seems to suggest that four quarters is sufficient for most of the short-term impact adjustments to have taken place. Even allowing for longer adjustment times for persons entering the unemployment pool from trade-impacted industries (a notion which the data seems to support), one year seems sufficient. For this reason we have used annual data in our simulations and anticipate that adjustments of employment to new demand levels will have occurred in that time.[4]

---

[1] Frank, R., *Econometrica*, Vol. 46, #2 (March 1978).

[2] For example, a shift in purchases of manufactured goods by less developed countries from the United States to Europe world represent a reduction in US aggregate demand.

[3] George R. Neumann, 'The Direct Labor Market Effects of the Trade Adjustment Assistance Program: The Evidence from the T. A. A. Survey: in *The Impact of International Trade and Investment on Employment*, A Conference on the Department of Labor Results, Wm. Dewall (ed.), 1976.

[4] The requirement for using annual data is therefore intended as an argument for using averaged data to smooth out short-term fluctuations which we are not interested in monitoring.

(2) Demand

A distinguishing feature of a study such as this one is that home-produced goods and foreign imports for most commodity classifications are imperfect substitutes. To measure the effects of trade on employment, one can either take the approach used by Leontief and ask what mix of capital and labour would be required to produce the home substitute for an imported commodity bundle, assuming perfect substitutability between imports and domestic goods as was done in Section I, or recognise that a reduction in imports will call forth a *different* mix of home goods in replacement for the foregone imports and calculate the employment needed to produce this new bundle of home goods.

In the latter case, one wishes to calculate, for example, how much US shoe production changes in response to a given reduction in imports. Because commodities are not perfect substitutes, however, replacement need not be one for one. Given that A_t is the economy input-output matrix at time t, a_t the labour-output vector,[1] $X_t - M_t$ net exports and D_t the domestic component of demand, one wishes to calculate the difference in

$$a_t(I - A_t)^{-1}(X_t - M_t + D_t) \tag{3}$$

between two periods. This is essentially the calculation of the first part of the paper – except that D_t is ignored – where estimates of a_t and A_t are obtained from published sources and were assumed to remain constant over the projection period.

An alternative procedure to estimate the effects of trade following the second approach is to impose a structure on the implied effects of trade on demand.[2] Writing domestic production (q_j) to consist of three components of demand; home use, non-LDC world demand, and LDC demand, the sum of the three components gives final output. LDC demand, in turn, is the aggregation of direct and indirect output requirements resulting from net US trade with LDCs ($X_{LDC} - M_{LDC}$) after substitution effects have been taken

---

[1] a_t here replaces the employment-output ratios (F_j/Y_j) used in the previous section (see equation 1). In section I average employment-output ratios prevailing over the period 1963–75 were used. As will be seen subsequently in the alternative procedure, a_t is estimated for each sector through regression methods.

[2] Such a procedure was used by Robert Baldwin and Wayne E. Lewis, 'U.S. Tariff Effects on Trade and Employment in Detailed SIC Industries' in *The Impact of International Trade and Investment on Employment*, A Conference on the Department of Labor Results, Wm. Dewald (ed.), 1976, to assess the impact effects of a 50 per cent tariff reduction. He assumed that the difference in question was of the form $a[1 - A]^{-1}[b_j][(X - M)]$ where $[b_j]$ is a diagonal matrix of substitution effects normally between zero and unity. He then used independent estimates of a, A, b_j to assess the impact of trade changes.

into account.[1] The foreign demand by developing countries is treated in an analogous way and home demand is treated as a function of domestic income. Adding these components together implies a relationship of the form,

$$q_j = a_{0j} + a_{1j}Y + a_{2j}\{(I - A)^{-1}(X_{DC} - M_{DC})\}_j$$
$$+ a_{3j}\{(I - A)^{-1}(X_{LDC} - M_{LDC})\}_j + \epsilon_j \qquad (4)$$

where the subscript refers to sector j, Y is domestic income unrelated to trade, $(I - A)^{-1}$ is the Leontief-inverse, and X − M is the vestor of US net trade balances. A 1972 input-output matrix furnished by the US Department of Labor, disaggregated into 157 sectors, was used for the estimate of A. In turn, a_{0j} through a_{3j} were estimated by regression methods over the period 1962–75.[2]

Strictly speaking, equation (4) above is correct over the sample period 1962–75 only if the coefficients of A do not change over time and other influences which determine demand for good j out of domestic income (secular trends for the use of certain types of goods and so forth) can be ignored.[3]

Marginal output employment ratios $(\Delta E_j/\Delta Y_j)$ were then applied to the difference in domestic production implied by a 10 per cent change in trade with less developed countries holding the level of non-LDC world demand, and domestic demand in equation (4), constant. (In most industries, fixed labour costs lead to marginal labour-output ratios which are below the average. In addition, average labour-output ratios have been falling over time.)

---

[1] That is, total effects on production from a change in LDC demand are $(I + [s_j])(I - a)^{-1}(X_{LDC} - M_{LDC})$ where $[s_j]$ is a diagonal matrix with entries s_j on the diagonal representing different substitutabilities. In the previous section it was assumed that s_j is zero − implying a dollar-for-dollar trade-off between imports and home goods, within sector j. Note that both b_j in the previous footnote and s_j measure the degree of substitutability between import and home goods.

[2] In other words, equation (4) was estimated for the 22(j) sectors, independently, on the basis of 14 annual observations covering the period 1962–75.

[3] In particular, we have not attempted to explain changes in relative prices or build an econometric model of the American economy. That would have required a massive research effort and moreover, would have included the idiosyncracies of the particular model employed. The procedure taken here, on the other hand, we feel is comparatively value-free in describing the order of magnitudes involved and their change over time. It is important, then, not to place too great a stress on the numerical values obtained for any specific industry. A more serious flaw in our data which is only partially rectified in our regressions, was the necessity of using the f.o.b. port of export trade values. Assuming tariff and transport costs were uniform over the period this would be corrected in the values of the estimated coefficients.

Two alternative equations were used to estimate the employment/output ratios, i.e.

$$E_j = b_{0j} + b_{1j}Y_j + b_{2j}T + \epsilon_j \tag{5a}$$

or

$$E_j/Y_j = c_{0j} + c_{1j}T + \epsilon_j \tag{5b}$$

where the time dummy (T = 1 in 1962, . . . , 14 in 1975) was omitted when it was insignificant.[1] Thus, in order to estimate the employment effects in sector j, of a hypothetical 10 per cent increase in the net US trade balance with the developing world (i.e. ΔE_j) the following equation,

$$\Delta E_j = b_{1j}a_{3j}\ [I - A]^{-1}(X_{LDC} - M_{LDC})_j \cdot 10^{-1} \tag{6}$$

was then calculated for the j industries (input-output sectors) described in the first section of the paper and summed over those industries.[2] The aggregate results which are presented below are discussed in terms of the effect that trade has had on US employment each year between 1962 and 1975, in contrast with the figures in the first part of the paper which cover cumulative changes.

Employment estimates derived from structural model

On the basis of the structural model described above, the effects of a hypothetical 10 per cent change in trade between the US and LDCs on US employment were estimated for each one of the 14 years in the sample period.[3] Table 5.4 presents the combined job gain and loss figures for the sample of 22 most affected industries. As was already mentioned in Section I, the criteria which were used in selecting these industries were that they produced competing products for which the US net trade balance (either positively or negatively) changed by at least 175 million dollars (at constant 1972 prices) over the period 1963–75.[4] These 22 industries, when added to the non-competing industries (crude petroleum and natural gas, refined

[1] b_2 and c_1 were uniformly negative, b_0, b_1, c_0, uniformly positive. Correction for auto-correlation was routinely made for comparison with the uncorrected equations.

[2] The employment/output coefficient b_{1j} in equation (6) was based on either its regression estimate as obtained from equation (5a), or, alternatively, from equation (5b), where $b_{ij} = c_{0j} + c_{1j}T$.

[3] That is, a year-by-year 10 per cent increase in all trade flows with LDC was considered. The increase in question is a per cent of each year's historical trade flows with accumulative effects from previous years.

[4] Radio and TV receiving sets which showed a net change of 173 million dollars and electrical transmission equipment which showed gains of 334 million dollars are treated elsewhere.

TABLE 5.4 ESTIMATES OF MARGINAL JOB GAINS AND LOSSES FROM A HYPOTHETICAL 10 PER CENT
INCREASE IN US TRADE WITH DEVELOPING COUNTRIES
(based on 22 affected industries) (thousands of jobs)

Year	Job gains[a] Lower bound (1)	Job gains[a] Upper bound (2)	Job losses[b] Lower bound (3)	Job losses[b] Upper bound (4)	Net gain (loss) Lower bound (1) – (4)	Net gain (loss) Upper bound (2) – (3)
1962	4.38	8.63	– 0.72	– 2.30	2.08	7.91
1963	4.29	8.42	– 0.76	– 2.34	1.95	7.66
1964	5.16	9.88	– 1.03	– 2.87	2.29	8.85
1965	5.19	9.52	– 1.24	– 2.73	2.46	8.28
1966	5.82	10.39	– 1.35	– 2.94	2.88	9.04
1967	5.63	10.39	– 1.79	– 3.24	2.39	8.60
1968	6.61	11.82	– 2.71	– 4.61	2.00	9.11
1969	5.88	10.81	– 3.43	– 4.86	1.02	7.38
1970	6.10	10.80	– 4.29	– 5.93	0.17	6.51
1971	6.18	10.45	– 4.01	– 5.49	0.69	6.44
1972	6.86	10.51	– 8.00	– 9.97	–3.11	3.51
1973	9.29	15.45	–10.04	–12.22	–2.93	5.41
1974	12.23	19.53	–10.85	–12.64	–0.41	8.68
1975	13.28	21.44	–11.98	–13.96	–0.68	9.46

[a] Gaining industries include numbers 4, 26, 27, 52, 53, 71, 82, 83, 84, 85, 86, 87, 88, 89, 92, 93, 103, 104.
[b] Loosing industries include numbers 26, 33, 39, 65, 115. For industry descriptions use Table 5.3

petroleum, certain metals, forestry and fishing products, etc.), accounted for the great bulk of the *change* in US net trade balances with LDCs over the period under consideration, i.e. approximately 93 per cent of trade losses and 86 per cent of the trade gains.[1] In terms of labour force, the sectors covered by Table 5.4 represent about 10 per cent of the US labour force in 1975. The estimates in Table 5.4 refer to a range of possibilities which depend upon (a) the particular equations used (for example, whether alternative specification (5a) or (5b) was used to estimate the employment-output ratios) and (b) the procedures which were used to obtain the coefficients, a_{3j}, b_{1j}, c_{0j}, and c_{ij} in equations (4), (5a) and (5b), respectively.[2] The values in Table 5.4 are arrived at by taking alternative values of individual coefficients yielding, respectively, lower and upper bound combinations for job gains and losses.

The primary implication of these estimates based on the structural model is that on balance the net effect of growing trade with the third world has been helpful to US employment with the possible exception of the years at the end of the period 1962–75, as can be seen from Figure 5.2. Whether one looks at the upper bound figures or lower bound figures, however, it is clear that the direction of job change has been somewhat negative since roughly 1966. Prior to that, the effect seems to have been fairly stable and probably positive.

A significant feature of the figures is that net employment effects of a hypothetical 10 per cent change in positive or negative trade balances in no year are larger than 9.46 thousands of jobs or lower than −3.11 thousand jobs. Thus, for the sample of selected industries which embraces the great bulk of US trade gains or losses with LDCs between 1963 and 1975, the net effect of trade on employment is likely to have been very small and positive.

Clearly, the concern about the effects of LDC trade on employment, therefore, cannot be justified by the absolute magnitudes (which are small) as over the direction of change, rate of increase, and the concentration of job losses in a few negatively affected industries. For example, historical imports from LDCs in constant 1972 dollars over the period 1963–75 grew at the average annual *rate* of just over 11 per cent. US gross national product by comparison, grew at the rate of about 4 per cent over the same period. These figures obscure the even faster growth rates of imports which occurred in the second half of the period. Hence, a hypothetical comparison would show much greater job effects in the later years were the *growth* of trade with LDCs to have been cut, say, to a 5½ per cent average growth rate, rather than the actual 11 per cent. Such an experiment after four years would require reducing the actual trade flows by roughly *20* per cent and after ten years, by

---

[1] Trade losses and gains in this context are defined, respectively, as the sum of the negative or positive changes in US trade balances with LDCs over the period 1963–75.

[2] For example, when the Durban–Watson statistics were inconclusive, the coefficients were re-estimated to correct for possible auto-correlation.

40 per cent. The figures in Table 5.4 would then have to be appropriately scaled up or down by a factor of two and four, respectively. Lastly, as a scan down the columns (1) and (4) will reveal, uncompensated trade effects on jobs have been growing over the period. Thus, in 1962, job gains were roughly 4–8,000, by 1975 they were 13–21,000, more than doubled. Job losses show even greater changes, from 1000 in 1962 to 12,000 thousand in 1975.

Another striking feature of Table 5.4 is that it shows that trade over this period can be divided into three periods. This is clearly revealed in Figure 5.2 which is based on Table 5.4. In the first period, roughly 1962 through 1966, employment effects seem to have been mildly positive and fairly stable. From 1966 on, however, these effects seem to have deteriorated as the composition of trade changed. This decline continued until 1972–73 when it reached its lowest point. From 1973 on, the trade pattern appears to have changed again and employment effects rose thereafter.

The explanation for the change after 1973 appears to be the great increase in US exports of machinery to LDCs after that period including automobiles, aircraft (non-military) and industrial and farm machinery. Trade figures representing this shift are presented in Table 5.5 below. As will be seen shortly, the magnitudes involved are quite large relative to total US–LDC trade. In the period 1973 through 1975, for example, in the industries covered in Table 5.5, net exports rose 79 per cent for a total of 3216 million dollars.

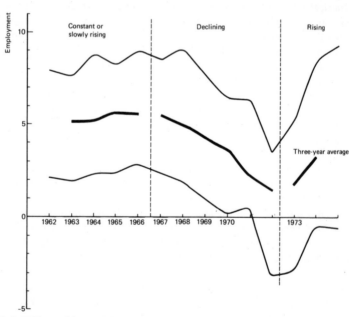

Fig. 5.2   Effect of hypothetical 10 per cent increase in US trade with
           developing countries on employment in selected sectors
           (thousands of jobs)

TABLE 5.5 NET TRADE WITH DEVELOPING COUNTRIES IN SELECTED MACHINERY SHOWING HIGH GROWTH RATES IN THE PERIOD 1970–75 (millions of 1972 dollars)

Year	(82) Fabricated metal products	(85) Construction, mining and oil-field machinery	(86) Material handling equipment	(87) Metal working machines	(88) Special industry machinery	(93) Service industry machines	(103) Motor vehicles	(104) Aircraft	Total	Growth over previous year (%)
1962	87	315	212	217	382	93	652	174	2132	
1966	125	300	195	217	372	184	919	349	2661	
1970	131	378	209	201	452	234	867	560	3032	3.3
1971	124	352	188	241	440	221	857	711	3134	3.4
1972	99	421	187	237	467	245	863	765	3284	4.8
1973	104	540	229	272	596	298	1042	977	4058	23.6
1974	138	734	345	316	749	418	1461	1426	5587	37.7
1975	193	772	587	441	989	530	2193	1569	7274	30.2

NOTES These sectors constitute 25.3 per cent of all US exports to LDCs in 1975; this is up from 23.0 per cent in 1970 and 21.6 per cent in 1973.

III FURTHER CHARACTERISTICS OF US–LDC TRADE, 1963–75

This section attempts to highlight some further characteristics of the US–LDC trade pattern with special reference to domestic employment effects.

Sectors displaying greatest positive or negative changes in US net trade balance with LDCs and changes in actual employment, 1963–75

To explain the consolidated findings of Section II, it is helpful to have at hand an indication of the disaggregated trade flows involved. We have already seen that the size of LDC trade relative to US GNP is quite small, but rising. The ratio of US imports from LDCs to US GNP rose from 1.06 per cent in 1962 to 2.55 per cent in 1975 and the corresponding export ratio went up from 1.24 per cent to 2.48 per cent over the same period. The relative growth of LDC imports is much less pronounced when oil is excluded, i.e. 0.79 per cent to 1.19 per cent between 1962 and 1975 (see Table 5.2).

Table 5.6 shows the sectors which underwent the largest absolute changes in net trade balances. Of those sectors where the US trade balance with LDCs worsened[1] between 1962 and 1975, $7005 millions of 1972 dollars or roughly 50 per cent was due to oil or oil-related products. From 1963 to 1969, US imports of crude petroleum and natural gas in real terms was nearly constant. From 1970 to 1975, even allowing for price changes, it increased over sevenfold in real terms. Of the remaining sectors, apparel and footwear showed the greatest losses.

An examination of Table 5.6 reveals that those industries which were most negatively affected from a net trade standpoint, and which, therefore, lost jobs because of it, were apparel, footwear and other leather products, canned and frozen goods, radio and TV receiving sets, and the non-competing sectors, crude and refined petroleum and metals. Sectors which gained jobs, on the other hand, include a wide range of industries: food and feed grains, grain mill products, industrial inorganic and organic chemicals, agricultural chemicals, blast furnaces and basic steel products, fabricated metal products, engines, turbines and generators, farm machinery, construction machinery (including oil field and mining), other industrial machinery, motor vehicles and aircraft.

It is interesting to note that the sample of 22 most affected sectors accounts for only 10.4 per cent of the US labour force and has been declining slightly over the period under consideration. Actual employment over the period 1963–75, in contrast with the hypothetical effects of greater trade between the US and LDCs previously estimated, fell from 1,987,000 in 1962 to 1,901,000 in 1975 for industries in our sample whose net trade balance

---

[1] A worsening in the US trade balance *vis-à-vis* developing countries, can take the form of a reduction in the export surplus, the appearance of an import surplus instead of a previous export surplus, or an increase in the import surplus.

A. Sectors in which US net trade balance changed by more than $300 million, 1963–75

Sector #		Amount
4[a]	Food and feed grains	1825
12	Crude petroleum and natural gas	-5679
33	Miscellaneous food products	560
39	Apparel	-1409
47	Paper products	1037
52	Industrial inorganic and organic chemicals	411
60	Petroleum refining and related products	-1326
65	Footwear and other leather products	-537
71	Blast furnaces and basic steel products	530
84	Farm machinery	318
85	Construction, mining and oilfield machinery	490
86	Material handling equipment	385
88	Special industrial machinery	622
92	Typewriters and other office equipment	464
93	Service industry machines	423
94	Electrical transmission equipment	334
103	Motor vehicles	1490
104	Aircraft	1488

B. Sectors in which US net trade balance changed by $200–300 million, 1963–75

Sector #		Amount
3	Cotton	261
6	Forestry and fishery products	276
26	Canned and frozen foods	-292
53	Agricultural chemicals	280
73	Primary Copper and copper products	205
83	Engines, Turbines and generators	283
87	Metal working machines	239

C. Sectors in which US net trade balance changed by $100–200 million, 1963–75

Sector #		Amount
8	Iron and ferroalloy ores mining	-164
24	Meat products	128
27	Grain mill products	176
29	Sugar	-160
43	Millwork, plywood and other wood products	-136
78	Fabricated structural metal	137
82	Other fabricated metal products	101
89	General industrial machinery	165
98	Radio and TV Receiving sets	-173
105	Ship and boat building and repair	108
109	Scientific and controlling equipment	130
112	Photographic equipment and supplies	117
115	Musical instruments, toys, sporting goods	-183

Circled sectors are the 22 affected sectors in our sample. See Table 5.3 and text for definition of criteria used in selecting these sectors.

[a] Circled sectors are the 22 affected sectors in our sample. See Table 5.3 and text for definition of criteria used in selecting these sectors.

worsened. On the other hand, actual employment in industries displaying improved trade balances in our sample, rose from 4,541,000 in 1962 to 4,701,000 in 1975. In addition, a crucial observation is that the employment losses were highly localised and concentrated essentially in four industries while employment gains were spread out more evenly over a large number of sectors, thus confirming the estimates derived in Section I.

It would thus appear that the losses, while smaller, are more visible than the gains. Over the period under consideration *actual* employment in the negatively affected industries in our sample above fell by 84,000 workers, while the positively affected sectors gained 160,000 workers. Therefore, it is reasonable to assume that the net increase of 76,000 actual employment growth during 1962–75, could be accounted for by the growth in US trade with the developing world.

Import growth sectors and concomitant export growth

Growth of imports into the US from developing countries over the period under consideration has been impressive, i.e. in excess of 11 per cent a year at constant prices. However, it is important to keep in mind that the base from which these imports start is very small – in many cases less than a million dollars in 1962 – and that the growth of exports to the less developed countries has been almost as large. Furthermore, at the level of disaggregation used, many sectors displayed considerable simultaneous import and export growth.

Table 5.7 is presented to show the extent of absolute trade changes as well as relative changes by sector. In the first part of this table, under A, sectors showing absolute increases in imports to the US of more than $100 million dollars (at constant 1972 prices) between 1963 and 1975 are listed. The extent of export increase in the same sectors is also shown in the right-hand column. If natural resource (essentially non-competing) trade is eliminated and those sectors which show a concomitant increase in exports to LDCs, are eliminated, then only eight sectors remain: canned and frozen foods, sugar, apparel, plywood and wood products, plastic products, footwear and leather, clocks and clock devices, and sporting goods and musical instruments. Of these, only apparel and footwear show substantial net changes.

The same story is repeated when relative changes are considered, as in part B of Table 5.7, which includes all sectors which displayed at least a 100 per cent increase in imports from LDCs to the US, over the period 1970 to 1975, when the bulk of the growth took place (trade figures were so low in the early part of the period, 1962–75, for many sectors that unrealistically large ratios would result if 1962 were chosen as a base year). Out of 28 industries which are in this category, less than half do not show commensurate growth of exports. Keeping in mind that initially many of these sectors displayed large US export surpluses, emphasising growth rates alone would clearly have been misleading.

Dissimilarities between the US–LDCs and US–DCs trade patterns

There are some interesting differences between the trade pattern of the US:
(a) *vis-à-vis* the developing world; and (b) *vis-à-vis* the developed world. More
specifically, for a number of sectors the net trade balance of the US with
LDCs is in the opposite direction than with respect to the developing countries
(DCs). Table 5.8 includes sectors for which the trade balance *vis-à-vis* LDCs
and DCs was of opposite sign for three or more years during the period 1962
to 1975. Sectors appearing in Table 5.8 include miscellaneous food products;
fabrics, yarn and thread mills; petroleum refining and related products; blast
furnaces and basic steel products; other fabricated metal products; engines,
turbines and generators; motor vehicles; and musical instruments and sporting
goods. The US exports to LDCs manufactured products while importing
fabrics and petroleum. In contrast, the US tends to display an import surplus
in manufactured products with DCs.

Trade adjustment assistance as it relates to LDCs

The policy importance of trade adjustments depends, of course, principally on
how easy it is to identify correctly industries which are harmed by trade to
the extent that they require aid. Labour unions have typically asserted that
job losses have been *greater* than the typically low estimates reached by
economists.[1]

Our data, as related to LDCs, suggest (a) that the overall employment
effects of US–LDC trade are small, (b) that the negatively affected industries
are more localised and visible, and (c) that the gaining industries are more
spread out and less visible. However, our study is not extensive enough as it
stands to more than suggest broad sectors which were affected and our chosen
emphasis on LDC trade further limits its applicability to all trade.

---

[1] We quote the President of the Amalgamated Clothing and Textile Workers
Union in a speech delivered to a US Department of Labor Conference,
2 December 1976.

> But there is no question that jobs have been lost — and that the number
> stretches into the hundreds of thousands, even millions — depending on
> when you want to start counting . . . Even if we cannot provide irrefutable
> macro data there are plenty of micro data . . . to the hundreds of thousands
> of individuals who have lost their jobs because of imports, to talk about
> the broad picture is most unpersuasive.

He quotes, sympathetically, a union member's letter to him,

> We at the H.A. Leinsheimer's Men's Clothing have been closed down because
> of imports. Is it fair for us to be out of jobs and isn't there a way to deal
> with this business through legislation?

TABLE 5.7 SECTORS DISPLAYING LARGEST ABSOLUTE AND

A. *Sectors showing import changes from LDCs of $100 million or more 1972 dollars, 1963–75*

Sector #		Amount	
		Import increase	Export increase
8	Iron and ferroalloy ores mining	164	0
12	Crude petroleum and natural gas	5703	24
(26)	Canned and frozen foods	314	22
29	Sugar	172	12
(39)	Apparel	1568	159
43	Millwork, plywood and other wood products	157	31
52[a]	Industrial inorganic and organic chemicals	448	859
60	Petroleum refining and related products	1301	– 25
63	Plastic products	174	76
(65)	Footwear and other leather products	556	19
71[a]	Blast furnaces and other basic steel products	109	639
91[a]	Computers and peripheral equipment	112	104
95[a]	Electrical industrial apparatus	182	259
98[b]	Radio and TV receiving sets	913	740
101[b]	Electronic components	644	637
113	Watches, clocks and clock operated devices	114	29
(115)	Musical instruments, sporting goods, toys	229	46

[a] Sectors in which export increase is *larger* than import increase.
[b] Sectors in which export increase is 80 per cent or more of import increase.

B. *Sectors showing greatest relative US import growth from LDCs between 1970 and 1975: (Ratio of 1975 import (export) value at constant 1972 prices, to 1970 import (export) value). Only sectors for which real imports doubled are included*

Sector #		Ratio of end of period values to base period values	
		R.G.†	R.G. of E.††
6	Forestry & fishery products	2.72	
12	Crude petroleum and natural gas	7.92	
30	Confectionery products	2.40	
31	Alcoholic beverages	3.10	(2.75)
37	Miscellaneous textile goods	2.91	
39	Apparel	2.54	
40	Miscellaneous fabricated textile products	2.04	(2.18)
46	Furniture and fixtures	2.04	
48	Paperboard	4.00	(2.08)
52	Industrial inorganic and organic chemicals	3.38	
53	Agricultural chemicals	2.17	(3.33)
61	Tyres and inner tubes	2.11	(2.33)
65	Footwear and other leather products	4.08	(2.59)
66	Glass	2.07	
82	Fabricated metal products	4.85	
88	Special industry machinery	3.50	(2.21)
91	Computers and peripheral equipment	14.25	
94	Electrical transmission equipment	3.47	(2.36)
95	Electrical industrial apparatus	2.89	(2.06)
96	Household appliances	9.86	(2.31)
97	Electric lighting and wiring	2.14	
98	Radio and TV receiving sets	3.96	(2.91)
101	Electronic components	4.70	(4.14)
102	Miscellaneous electrical products	3.00	
103	Motor vehicles	5.33	(2.58)
113	·Watches, clocks and clock operated devices	19.00	(5.17)
114	Jewellry and silverware	2.39	
157	Musical instruments and sporting goods	3.11	(2.10)

† R.G. = *Relative Growth*
†† R.G. of E. = *Relative growth of exports*

TABLE 5.8 NET TRADE PATTERN, 1962–75, IN MILLIONS OF CONSTANT 1972 DOLLARS, FOR SELECTED INDUSTRIAL COMMODITIES SHOWING OPPOSITE TRADE BALANCES BETWEEN US–LDC AND US–DEVELOPED COUNTRIES (DC) TRADE

Sector	Miscellaneous food products		Fabrics, yarn and thread mills		Apparel		Agricultural chemicals		Petroleum refining and basic steel products		Blast furnaces and basic steel products		Other fabricated metal products		Engines, turbines and generators		Motor vehicles	
	Trade balance		Trade balance		Trade balance		Trade balance		Trade balance		Trade balance		Trade balance		Trade balance		Trade balance	
Year	DC (1)	LDC (2)	DC (1)	LDC (2)	DC (1)	LDC (2)	DC (1)	LDC (2)	DC (1)	LDC (2)	DC (1)	LDC (2)	DC (1)	LDC (2)	DC (1)	LDC (2)	DC (1)	LDC (2)
1962	416	-1324	-168	-88	-258	-76	23	116	260	-551	-187	307	-45	97	165	144	265	652
1963	505	-1328	-169	-138	-276	-76	-20	110	311	-582	-310	348	-20	92	163	144	308	703
1964	618	-1522	-142	-115	-307	-107	39	160	300	-659	-233	430	27	94	112	168	233	837
1965	586	-1190	-233	-183	-336	-133	-42	86	279	-809	-1014	395	35	122	191	232	282	888
1966	472	-1269	-238	-239	-365	-148	10	134	257	-771	-1139	302	21	125	99	240	-221	919
1967	423	-1133	-163	-208	-343	-203	19	158	251	-759	-1105	297	-12	132	100	232	-527	867
1968	463	-1449	-259	-201	-420	-327	49	161	195	-839	-1949	320	-49	122	-19	265	-1507	883
1969	510	-1016	-251	-206	-487	-457	44	113	134	-878	-1133	440	-66	124	-39	257	-2108	877
1970	621	-1091	-270	-184	-544	-541	40	115	129	-1047	-905	513	-101	131	-107	240	-2953	867
1971	659	-1002	-340	-214	-783	-535	47	114	129	-1120	-2192	276	-122	124	-180	250	-4195	857
1972	614	-1097	-252	-276	-582	-1043	22	198	123	-1227	-2131	160	-212	99	-227	264	-4869	863
1973	949	-1052	-93	-225	-555	-1229	64	294	-332	-1594	-1726	475	-234	104	-205	331	-5002	1042
1974	900	-631	135	-197	-379	-1281	71	454	-512	-2963	-2597	802	-258	138	24	382	-5023	1461
1975	563	-768	176	-94	-344	-1485	88	390	-122	-1908	-2045	878	-264	193	143	427	-3296	2193

NOTE Positive figures denote an export surplus, negative figures an import surplus.

In Table 5.9 are listed the distribution of Trade Adjustment Assistance petitions by industry over the period October 1962 to May 1974 – roughly the same period covered by our study. As would be expected from our data, the industries receiving the most petitions (in terms of affected workers) are textiles, leather, certain miscellaneous manufacturing, and electrical equipment. Changing trade flows with LDCs however, cannot be held responsible for the bulk of these petitions as can be seen in the case of electrical equipment (Sectors 94–102). This classification covers a range of products from electrical transmission equipment, electrical industrial apparatus, household appliances, electric lighting and wiring, radio and TV receiving sets, telephone and telegraph apparatus, radio and communication equipment, electronic components, and miscellaneous electrical products. Of these, only radios and TVs (Sector 98) show an import surplus from LDCs.

While growth of imports from LDCs in these areas is quite spectacular (see Table 5.7.B), Table 5.7A shows that in *absolute* terms, only industries 95, 98 and 101 (industrial apparatus, radios and TVs, electronic components) showed import increases of 100 million or more in 1972 dollars. In each case there was a larger or nearly as large an export increase. For the electrical industry as a whole, there is an export surplus with LDCs. In fact, the export surplus increase in electrical transmission equipment between 1963 and 1975 of 334 million 1972 dollars alone is enough to more than outweigh the 173 million loss in radios and TVs. Taken as a whole, we believe it is fair to conclude that trade with developing nations has been beneficial to our employment in this industry and that losses have been balanced by gains elsewhere. Thus, in general, the petitions for trade adjustment assistance listed in Table 5.9 can only to a very limited extent, be attributed to a change in US–LDC trade. The bulk of them must be attributed to the worsening US–DC trade pattern. Perhaps only in leather products were some of the granted petitions occasioned by greater imports from LDCs. It is very significant, in this connection, that the sector which appeared to be most negatively affected in terms of employment as a result of a change in US–LDC trade (see Section I), namely apparel, was not granted any trade adjustment assistance during the period 1962–74.

IV SUMMARY AND CONCLUSIONS

The major conclusion which came out of this study is that the net overall effects on US employment, resulting from the changing nature of the pattern of trade between the US and the developing world over the period 1963–75, were insignificant compared to the size of the US labour force and its increase during this period. Furthermore, the net employment effects are much more likely to have been positive, on balance, rather than negative as the alternative procedures used in this study to estimate these effects revealed.

An equally important conclusion is that – notwithstanding the marginal nature of the *net* effects – the pattern and commodity composition of trade

TABLE 5.9 DISTRIBUTION OF TRADE ADJUSTMENT ASSISTANCE PETITIONS BY INDUSTRY, OCTOBER 1962–MAY 1974

Industry	Standard industrial classification	Certifications		Denials	
		Petitions	Workers	Petitions	Workers
Metal mining	10	0	0	1	650
Food and kindred products	20	0	0	1	163
Textiles	22	6	2900	18	10,876
Apparel	23	0	0	3	1126
Chemicals	28	0	0	2	1300
Rubber	30	6	4790	6	3073
Leather	31	37	11,173	67	13,617
Stone, clay, and glass	32	8	2320	8	1920
Primary metals	33	1	400	7	1982
Fabricated metals	34	3	450	1	200
Non-electrical machinery	35	2	676	6	3925
Electrical equipment	36	16	15,025	22	10,205
Transportation equipment	37	2	2150	3	700
Miscellaneous manufacturing	39	14	4785	4	5960
Totals		95	44,849	149	55,697

SOURCE Bureau of International Affairs, US Department of Labor as referenced by George R. Neumann, *op. cit.*

between the US and LDCs underwent substantial changes which, in turn, affected the level and composition of employment among a number of affected US sectors. The major change in the US–LDCs trade pattern at the macroeconomic level, described in Section I, was the rising relative importance of this trade as compared to US GNP. Both the rates of growth of US exports to and imports from the developing world during the period under consideration were considerably larger than the rate of growth of US GNP. Furthermore, the increasing dependence of the US on imports from LDCs is only partially attributable to the phenomenal rise in the value of oil imports. The income elasticity of demand for non-oil imports from LDCs in the US – expressed at current prices – was around 1.5 per cent over the whole period and considerably higher in the second half of this period, i.e. 1970–75. Clearly, this trend reflects the success which a limited number of newly industrialised developing countries have achieved in exporting manufactured commodities and penetrating the US market.

Estimates conducted in Section II to look at employment effects of trade on a year-by-year basis revealed several significant features of the changing trade pattern over time. In addition to confirming the generally beneficial effect on US employment that trade with LDCs has had, it pointed to a dramatic turn-around in the direction of the employment effect over time. From 1966 to 1973, the employment effects of trade were positive but falling through time, from 1973 on they have risen dramatically. It is likely that the concern generated by changing trade patterns in the last half of the 1960s and early part of the 1970s is misplaced in light of the turn-around taking place since 1973. Our data do not go past 1975 but it would be worth following this with subsequent data as they become available.

As discussed in Sections I and II, two alternative procedures were used to estimate the effects of US–LDC trade on US employment. The first step in deriving these estimates consisted of identifying a sample of affected industries. The criteria adopted in selecting these industries were that the latter produced competing goods for which the net trade balance with LDCs had improved or worsened by at least 175 million dollars between 1962 and 1975. These criteria yielded a set of 22 sectors out of 117 sectors producing tradeable goods in the 1972 input-output of the US economy, which provided the basis of the computations.

The first procedure attempted to estimate the cumulative employment effects for each of these 22 sectors resulting from the changes in the net balance of trade between the US and LDCs in the two benchmark years, 1963 and 1975. By pre-multiplying the sectoral changes in these net trade balances by the Leontief-inverse, the direct and indirect output effects were derived. In turn, the corresponding employment effects were obtained on the basis of average sectoral employment-output ratios. The main underlying assumption of this procedure was that any change in imports entails an equivalent change in home production within a sector. Home production is considered a perfect substitute for imports at the industry level. This procedure yielded estimates of total cumulative employment gains resulting from the changing pattern of trade between the US and LDCs of about 346,000 jobs, spread among 18 sectors. On the other hand, employment losses were estimated to have amounted to about 126,000 jobs, between 1963 and 1975, and were concentrated in only four sectors (apparel, footwear and other leather products, musical instruments and canned and frozen foods). Thus, the changing trade pattern between the US and the developing world is likely to have contributed to a net increase of roughly 220,000 jobs in 22 most affected industries.

The second procedure to estimate employment effects relied on a somewhat less naïve structural demand model which was estimated over the period 1962–75. A number of coefficients linking domestic production in the US to foreign demand in developing and developed countries, and home demand, respectively, were derived from regression equations – one for each of the 22 sectors. Likewise, employment-output ratios were obtained on the basis of two alternative equations, covering the period 1962–75. One of the implications of this procedure – in contrast with that previously described – is that the extent of substitutability between home products and imports within an industry is endogenously determined rather than assumed to be perfect.

This simple model was then used to estimate the effects on US employment of a hypothetical 10 per cent change in the prevailing US–LDC trade pattern for every year of the sample period. In this fashion, the annual changes in the commodity composition and bilaterial trade balances of US–LDC trade were captured. The results of this procedure confirmed the marginal and generally positive impact of trade on employment. It also highlighted a tendency for the changing composition of US–LDC trade to yield higher absolute job gains and losses over time and particularly since 1970. Again, the very high sectoral concentration of job losses in industries negatively affected by trade appears to be the real reason for public concern rather than the overall net employment effects which, if anything, tended to be positive.

The changing commodity composition of trade and magnitudes of trade balances between the US and developing world is further analysed in Section III. It is shown that the pattern of trade between the US and the developing world is quite dissimilar to that between the US and the developed world. In particular, net changes in trade balances *vis-à-vis* the two groups have tended to move in opposite directions in a number of sectors. Finally, it is shown that of the actual petitions for trade adjustment assistance during the period under consideration, only an insignificant part could be attributed to a worsening in US–LDC trade.

In the light of all the evidence we have examined we feel it extremely unwise for the United States to attempt to implement domestic incomes and employment policies based on trade-reducing measures and especially so as they relate to US–LDC trade. Protectionistic measures as they relate to US–LDC trade are more likely to reduce domestic employment than increase it.

Discussion of Paper by Professors Grinols and Thorbecke

Professor Giersch introducing the discussion said that Grinols and Thorbecke had submitted an interesting paper with definite empirical conclusions. Two alternative procedures led to the result that, as a whole, US trade with the developing world over the period 1963–75 had insignificant effects on employment in the US. The net effect was positive rather than negative. It had fallen until 1973; afterwards it had risen dramatically. There was a high concentration of job losses in some industries and this explained public concern. But the US would be ill-advised if it adopted trade-reducing measures *vis à vis* LDCs, as they were 'more likely to reduce domestic employment than increase it'. He liked the conclusions and their forward-looking implications, but had some doubts about the underlying calculations, their meaning, and their prognostic value.

Professor Giersch started from the pure logic of trade; it suggested the following propositions:

(1) Trade had a positive effect on welfare. It either raised incomes at given levels of employment or reduced inputs, including employment, at given levels of income. This held for both trading partners together, and for each of them if the trade balance was in equilibrium.

(2) The economising effect which trade had on the input of labour per unit of income could be overcompensated by an export surplus (trade *cum* resource transfer: investment abroad or foreign aid) which raised output and employment[1]). This was one possible situation in which trade had a positive employment effect.

(3) Over a period of time — with a given trade balance — trade could involve the use of more labour per unit of domestic absorption (have an employment-creating effect) if the volume of exports needed to buy the given volume of imports rose for the domestic economy. We normally called this a deterioration of the commodity terms of trade, including what mattered here: the single factoral terms of trade.

Grinols and Thorbecke were so happy in presenting a result that mitigated the present concern about unemployment that they lost sight of the question whether the employment-creating effect of the past was really due to (i) trade as such, (ii) a surplus on trade account (investment abroad), or (iii) a deterioration of the single factoral terms of trade. At a conference on trade and welfare participants would have emphasised the resource-saving or productivity effect of trade. His personal hunch was that the dramatic positive employment effect of US trade with LDCs after 1973 was mainly

---

[1] Under conditions of full employment equilibrium the positive employment effect of the resource transfer just compensated the negative employment effect of the domestic absorption that it displaced.

due to the sharp deterioration of the single factoral terms of trade caused by the oil price hike. Everyone in the West must work more if they wanted to have the same real income that they would have enjoyed at the lower oil price. If we had to pay a higher real price for oil we should expect the oil countries to absorb more of our domestic product. Table 5.1, especially column (4) (US Exports to LDCs), was compatible with this presumption. But the table, although fairly detailed in other respects, failed to make this point explicit; it lacked a column showing US-exports to OPEC countries in constant prices. Unless that were done somebody might conclude: How beneficial an even sharper increase in the price of imported oil would have been for employment in the US!

The authors, in estimating the employment effects on various sectors and industries over the period 1962 to 1975, used an input-output table of the US economy for 1972. Although less than ideal, this appeared to be the best possibility. But when they selected the sectors which they presumed to have been affected most strongly, they used as a criterion a change in the US net trade balance by an absolute amount ($175 million at 1972 prices) rather than a common percentage. This suppressed smaller sectors which might be quite dynamic – a less-important drawback in a purely historical exercise, but quite relevant for policy conclusions relating to the future.

The authors in their first calculation, which they called naïve, based their *ex post* estimates on the *average* rather than the incremental employment output ratios for the 22 sectors selected. This was likely to have led to too low results for the displacement effects. Simulations made at the Kiel Institute showed that the incremental employment output ratios for the adversely affected industries tended to be distinctly higher. As to the employment-creating effects on the export side, he presumed that there was an upward bias. The firms that provided the additional exports were likely to be less labour-intensive than the average.

Another source of error connected with the use of input-output tables for such calculations could be the assumption, often made only implicitly, that the import of a finished product displaced labour at all vertical stages of production down to the raw material level. Such displacement might be the case but it need not be. A shirt imported from Hong Kong could well be made of artificial fibres produced in the US; electronic equipment imported from Taiwan might well contain integrated circuits (ICs) from Texas Instruments. We could gain little information about this from published statistics, but businessmen continued to tell him that it often payed to shift only certain labour-intensive stages of production to LDCs. If this was true, negative employment effects or – to turn it around – the gains from trade in economising the scarce factor – might be greater than estimated on the basis of input-output tables. He would be most interested in the authors' judgement of this point.

Table 5.3 gave results for each of the 22 industries selected. They excluded, apart from the small sectors, all resource-based trade that was considered to be complementary rather than substitutive. The authors summarised the contents of Table 5.3 by saying that 'the incremental US–LDC trade contributed to a net increase of about 220,000 jobs'. He had difficulty in understanding the precise meaning and would, therefore, like to ask whether it was correct to say that the US economy would have had 220,000 jobs less in 1975 if trade with LDCs had been frozen with the 1963 level and pattern? What he was after was the nature of the implicit reference system. A comparison of colums (4) and (7) in Table 5.1, showed that exports were always higher and grew much faster (14 per cent) than imports (without oil). He gathered from this that the job gain estimated must be largely due to the sizeable increase of the export surplus in non-oil trade – explicit and implicit resource transfers.

The conclusion that 'the employment gains were spread among 18 sectors while the employment losses were highly concentrated in only 4 industries' was plausible and consistent with similar calculations for some European countries (UK, Belgium, France). However, these were the *net* employment effects for the individual industries. They would tell the whole story only if each industry consisted of just one firm or plant that could solve the adjustment problem internally without the hardships of interfirm-adjustment (via the labour market and the capital market), that entailed search unemployment.

It was a little surprising to read that 'trade flows with LDCs cannot be held responsible' for the 'Trade Adjustment Assistance Petitions' shown in Table 5.9 and to read that the bulk of these petitions 'must be attributed to the worsening US–LDC trade pattern', after having been introduced to the subject by the sentence: 'As would be expected from our data, the industries receiving the most petitions are textiles, leather, certain miscellaneous manufacturing, and electrical equipment'. Electrical equipment was referred to as an explanation for the apparent contradiction because of its large scope. We were told that in each subsector there was a larger, or nearly as large, an export increase, and that the increase in export surplus in electrical trans-mission equipment alone was more than enough to outweigh the loss in radios and TVs. However, it seemed to him that if transmission equipment and TVs were not being produced in the same plants and by the same people, a considerable adjustment problem must be hidden behind these figures which the authors balanced against each other. On the other hand, he shared the authors' surprise about the fact that trade adjustment assistance had not to be granted to the apparel industry, although this industry was most strongly affected by developments in US–LDC trade. To learn more about the adjustment problem one would have to adopt an approach that went down to the plant level; i.e. even further than Table 5.9.

On the basis of a structural model, this time with *incremental* output employment ratios calculated from time series, the authors simulated the yearly aggregate job gains and job losses for the 22 US industries selected that would have resulted from a 10 per cent change in trade with LDCs. The result was given in Table 5.4. If he understood the simulation and the Table correctly, the exercise was aimed at isolating the employment effects that were due to changes in the commodity composition of trade with LDCs (what might be called the pattern effect) from the unevenness in the growth of actual import and export volumes. The growth rates implied were 10 per cent for each year for each sector. This compared with the actual average of 11 per cent for all 22 sectors together that was found in reality. Whether the difference between the 11 per cent and the 10 per cent was significant for the result was a question which the authors did not deal with. Nor did they check the cumulative employment effects according to his method against the 220,000 jobs gained according to the naïve calculation. The difference was most significant even for the upper bound net gain.

If this interpretation of the simulation was correct, the text was obscure. It was not the actual job gains and job losses that the table showed, but only the effect that a smooth 10 per cent annual increase of trade in each sector would have had.

The pattern effect, as isolated by the authors, was labour saving from 1966 until 72/73. The reversal of the trend thereafter was attributed to the increasing importance of automobiles, aircraft and machinery in exports to LDCs. But were these products really more labour-intensive than those which they replaced in relative importance? As this was not immediately plausible, he wondered how much was due to the worsening of the single factoral terms of trade after the oil embargo. The use of constant 1972 dollars seemed to cloud the issue.

While the negatively affected industries in the sample lost 86,000 jobs in the period under consideration, the positively affected industries gained 160,000. According to the authors, the difference (a net increase of 74,000 jobs) could be accounted for by the growth of trade with LDCs, i.e. neither by trade with DCs nor by domestic absorption. Professor Giersch failed to see why. How did this compare with the 220,000 jobs gained according to the naïve calculation, with the 107,000 jobs gained according to the upper bound in the less naïve calculation or with the 11,000 according to the lower bound?

Table 5.8 showed sectors in which the US balance of trade with LDCs moved in opposite directions to the US balance of trade with DCs. While the US tended to have an import surplus in manufactured products in trade with DCs it paid for fabrics and petroleum from LDCs by exporting manufactures to them, e.g. blast furnaces, engines, turbines, generators and motor vehicles. These appeared to support his point that the employment-creating effect of economic relations between the USA and the LDCs — apart from a deterioration in the single factoral terms of trade — was largely due to the resource transfer rather than to trade as such.

Professor Giersch suggested that points for discussion were: How to cope with the adjustment problem if the LDCs wanted to achieve their goal of a 25 per cent share in world manufacturing production; and how to make use of the export surpluses of some developed countries for the development of LDCs.

Professor Grinols explained that the first (naïve) measure took actual trade and average employment/output ratios. The second model was different. It took a hypothetical 10 per cent increase in the level of the trade pattern in a given year and used marginal employment/output ratios. For the second situation to get back to the position in the first required an average rate of growth of the whole trade flow over the period. So they had shown that at the end of the period a 10 per cent change represented a much smaller trade effect than was implied by a change in the growth rate over the entire period which would telescope over time. If one replaced the marginal employment/output ratio by the larger average one, and there was substitution of home for overseas output on a one-for-one basis, then taking the cumulative trade figures at their historical levels should give the required answer.

Professor Hines wondered how trade between developed and underdeveloped countries could help both. The paper used an input-output table and he wanted to take an example. If trade were to lead to an increase in output and employment in underdeveloped countries, the increase in trade must assume bigger imports of raw materials. When an underdeveloped country expanded, the bigger employment content from these products seemed to arise in developed and not underdeveloped countries. So one found an increase in employment in the developed country, which was reversed when there was a depression in that country.

However, since this sector was an enclave in an underdeveloped country, it was not a base for development there. One therefore had a contraction in employment both in the developed and in the underdeveloped country. What, then, was the nature of the development of trade and employment in the two types of country which led to what the authors of the paper had observed? He suggested that attention should be given rather to encouraging development in underdeveloped countries that would generate enough income to support both domestic activity and imports.

Related to this was consideration of the pricing pattern linked to trade between developed and underdeveloped countries. If primary products did not generate enough income to lead to development in underdeveloped countries, and so to get imports from developed countries, than under-developed countries would remain peripheral. What one had was the result of fluctuations in demand inside underdeveloped countries. If so, who benefited? And was the employment-creating effect sustainable? Or did it fluctuate with demand by developed countries for primary products? It was important to look at the role of the underdeveloped countries as creators of autonomous demand both for themselves and for developed countries too.

Professor Maillet noted that the results of this study were analogous to the hypotheses put forward by Professor Giersch and to those of some other studies. These were concerned with the link between the development of trade between underdeveloped and developed countries and unemployment. If the results were favourable, this might be because the imports of underdeveloped countries could increase more than their exports, due to the financial aid (loans or grants) given to them by the developed countries.

He wondered whether the benefit was to employment in the developed or the underdeveloped countries? As for the practical character of the studies, they took technology as unchanged. Perhaps one of the reactions of economic agents was to develop technology to reduce imports. If so, this was defensive behaviour on the part of developed countries. If this were the case, the conclusions were not entirely valid and could not be extrapolated without great care. For elaborate forecasts, it would be necessary to imply substantial modifications in technological coefficients, taking into account the fact that the technology was not the same for imported and exported products. This kind of study was indispensable if we were to reach important economic and social conclusions.

Lord Kaldor suggested that there was nothing in the paper that was inconsistent with his own, since it dealt with a different kind of problem. Here one had a country, like Portugal, producing cheap shoes and textiles because it had learned the techniques of modern mass production. However the 'opening of trade' between Portugal and the UK did not mean free import of goods by the UK. There was continuing protection and, after 1945, when the new international trading system was being established, it was argued that underdeveloped countries should be free to protect themselves in a way that developed countries should not. If underdeveloped countries had to import freely from developed countries, they could never develop their own export industries. Their industries were protected, and the question was whether the (industrial) exports of underdeveloped countries were good or bad for the developed countries. The paper found that the supposed ill-effects in developed countries did not materialise and Lord Kaldor was not surprised. Under-developed countries were in a very different position from countries like Japan or Federal Germany. They were not saturated with imports, but in need of them. Hence their increased exports were matched by additional imports. Their imports enabled them to develop faster; their increased exports were not a source of deflation in the importing countries, because the propensity to invest in these countries was large.

If there were ill-effects on unemployment in the developed countries, this was because the production and exports of developing countries were in light labour-intensive industries. Their imports were of more complex capital goods and machinery which they could not manufacture themselves and in which the value of output per unit of labour input was relatively high. However, he was not sure whether there was much in this. The fact was that losses in the developed countries were concentrated in a few industries, while the benefits were widely spread. We should not restrict trade from underdeveloped countries simply for reasons of unemployment. Despite what people might think from his earlier remarks, he agreed in general with the dangers of indiscriminate protection. Those who spoke most loudly against protection were countries like Japan and Germany which wanted free access to large markets. So what he had said in his paper about the dangers of potential imbalances in trade applied to trade *between* developed countries.

One might go on to ask what would happen if the process of industrialisation of developing countries continued. By the end of the century, 25 per cent of manufacturing output of the world might well be produced in developing countries. This was not bad for the world because it meant greater output and greater two-way trade. The only worry for developed countries was if there were constraints on the use of raw materials and fuel. Then, if the continuing development of the richer countries required imports of primary products from less-developed countries (which was not always the case), the industrialisation of the developing countries would leave fewer resources for the developed countries, which could hold back the development of developed countries. There had been many references to oil but OPEC could do what it did only because there were very few sources of oil. Oil was a very important, indeed an indispensable, product. At present, there was no clear overall limit visible to raw material and energy supplies but perhaps their supply could not be expected to increase for ever.

Professor Modigliani pointed out that a lot of the discussion had supposed it was true that the development of trade led to an increase in the use of labour. He had always been brought up to think that international trade was intended to free labour to do other things so as to increase welfare.

Professor Grinols replied to the discussion. He suggested to Professor Modigliani that the situation was like a Robinson Crusoe facing diminishing returns. One might then ask if it was bad for him to go on picking more and more coconuts, and why he did it. The answer presumably was that he did it because he wanted more coconuts.

An export surplus and deteriorating terms of trade came to the same thing. A country had to send out more labour in the form of goods than in the past. If one regarded full employment as an objective in its own right this was desirable, although in theory one could always maintain full employment via the correct monetary policy.

He had been interested in studies which showed that the marginal employment/output ratio was greater than the average. His study had reached the reverse conclusion, and he and his colleague had tried to see whether the technology they were dealing with was not sufficiently sophisticated. Lord Kaldor suggested that a marginal employment/output ratio lower than the average ratio was exactly what one would expect if one abandoned classical economics.

Professor Grinols believed that the problem was one of adjustment. Few industries were affected by imports from less-developed countries: in the USA it was industries such as shoes and textiles. More microeconomic studies of adjustment were now needed and some were being conducted. His own study was static but had taken a great deal of effort. Professor Hines' problems were ones of how to study the effect of such trade on less-developed countries. If a country gave up the gains from trade, it needed something in return. Yet giving up trade with less-developed countries did not lead to compensating gains in employment.

Professor Modigliani wondered whether employment was good in itself, or a necessary evil. In Table 5.3 one got a gain of 220,000 jobs. Having selected certain industries, one got a bigger increase in the surplus than in the deficit. Given the sample of industries studied, he did not think it surprising that one found a gain in jobs. The question was how the different increases and decreases compared with the totals. The authors' particular sample might have concentrated more on one kind of situation than another.

Professor Grinols replied that the reason they had used a sample rather than the complete matrix was only lack of time. If one took the industries with trade losses, then the sample covered 93 per cent of the total losses.

PART THREE

Macroeconomic Analysis

6 Involuntary Unemployment*

A. G. Hines
BIRKBECK COLLEGE LONDON, UK

INTRODUCTION

The characterisation of involuntary unemployment is of importance both for economic theory and policy. It is important for theory in as much as it delineates that unemployment which is attributable to the malfunctioning of the economic system and not to the voluntary decisions of individual workers. It is due to a deficiency in aggregate demand whose primary cause is insufficient autonomous expenditure and it manifests itself in an unsatisfactory co-ordination of economic activity in production and exchange. It is important for policy since it circumscribes that unemployment for which demand management at the appropriate level of decision-making is the correct response. It is also important for measurement, for example, quantifying the magnitudes relevant to policy responses.

In this paper, we do three things: consider alternative characterisations and rationalisations of involuntary unemployment, set out two models which fit each of the two basic alternative characterisations, draw out the implications for Keynesian theory and demand management policy of the different methods by which profitability is altered in each model to induce the required response of output and employment, and discuss how the theory and policy are affected by the behaviour of prices and money wages.

I CONCEPTS OF INVOLUNTARY UNEMPLOYMENT

The point of departure for a consideration of involuntary unemployment must be Keynes' (1936) characterisations of it.[1] (a) First, there is the famous one.

> Men are involuntarily unemployed if, in the event of a small rise in the price of wage goods relative to the money wage, both the aggregate supply of labour willing to work for the current money-wage and the aggregate demand for it at that wage would be greater than the existing volume of employment.

---

* This paper is part of a wider enquiry into aggregate economic theory. I am indebted to my colleague John Muellbauer for valuable comments.
[1] Keynes, *General Theory*, pp. 15, 26, 16–17, 7.

(b) Moreover, and this is important for our subsequent discussion, he associates this with another which he regards as equivalent. There is involuntary unemployment, 'if aggregate employment is [not] inelastic in response to an increase in the effective demand for its output'[1] (c) A third is that there is involuntary unemployment when the real wage is not equal to the marginal disutility of labour, i.e. when the second classical postulate does not hold. (d) Finally, as Kahn (1976) has reminded us, Keynes had another.

> . . . the population generally is seldom doing as much work as it would like to do on the basis of the current wages . . . More labour would, as a rule, be forthcoming at the existing money-wage if it were demanded.

It should be clear that the first definition or characterisation is stronger than all the others. Thus, the conditions given in the first cannot be met if the second is not, i.e. if there is a full employment level of aggregate demand. Moreover, as we shall see, as is required by (c), in an equilibrium with deficient aggregate demand in which the conditions in (a) are met, 'the second classical postulate' does not hold, i.e. the marginal rate of substitution of income for leisure is not equal to the real wage. Kahn opts for (d). So also do Barro and Grossman (1976) and Malinvaud (1977), at least implicitly. Kahn thinks that the first definition is unnecessarily complicated for reasons which we summarise as follows. The introduction of the response of the labour supply to a fall in the real wage into the definition is unnecessary and in any case, the sign of this response is moot in principle. An inverse relationship between the demand for labour and the real wage does not hold empirically and as Keynes himself admitted, his theory could have been put over more simply without it and his practical conclusions would thereby have even greater force.

However, it is obvious that (a) implies (d). Moreover, while (d) is sufficient, it is not necessary for the existence of involuntary unemployment. To see this, consider the definition of the classical notion of voluntary unemployment which Keynes gives. '[V]oluntary unemployment [is] due to the refusal or inability of a unit of labour . . . to accept a reward corresponding to the value of the product attributable to its marginal productivity'.[2] It is clearly seen that this is the opposite of involuntary unemployment in senses (a)–(c), but not in the sense of (d) which is formally consistent with all unemployment being voluntary.

We will analyse models based on characterisations (a) and (d). We will also consider some implications of the relationship between voluntary and involuntary unemployment.

---

[1] Word in parenthesis added.
[2] *Loc. cit.*, p. 6.

II THE TRADITIONAL DISCUSSION OF INVOLUNTARY UNEMPLOYMENT

Most of the discussion of involuntary unemployment is concerned with the famous definition and stems from Keynes' explanation of why workers would not accept a reduction in the real wage rate brought about by a reduction in money wages but would accept if it were the result of an increase in the price level of wage goods. Attention focused upon the motives behind the behaviour of the individual or the representative worker which this implied.

In the interpretation given by the Walrasians, Keynes' theory was assumed to rest on the assumption of rigid money wages. The concept of involuntary unemployment was therefore taken to imply that workers suffered from money illusion. The individualistic interpretation having been accepted, the problem subsequently became one of accounting for this behaviour without the assumption of money illusion. Two explanations were offered, one based on search theory, the other on relativities.

(a) The one derives from the non-tatonnement, imperfect information and search class of models.[1] In an economy that does not operate to anounced wages and prices, more information about the value of his human wealth in the economy is conveyed to the ith worker employed in a particular firm by a change in a price index of a representative bundle of wage goods than by a change in his money wage in that firm. He will therefore more readily believe the message conveyed by the former and accept a reduction in real wages brought about by an increase in the price level. The message conveyed by the latter requires supplementation by additional information to be obtained through search before the worker will acquiesce in a reduction in real wages which arises from a cut in money wages in the firm in which he is currently employed.

This is not the place for a full discussion and critique of the theory of search unemployment.[2] For the present purpose, it is sufficient to make two observations.

The first is that the search theory is exclusively concerned with the behaviour of the individual worker and firm. An aggregate theory is not an integral part of it. Except in so far as probability distributions can be so regarded, it contains no well-defined aggregate demand or supply functions either at the level of particular sectors or at the level of the whole economy. It therefore possesses no proper notion of a market. For example, according to the theory, excess demand and excess supply as measured by unfilled vacancies and unemployment can co-exist in the same micro labour market and need not be the result of aggregation over markets. This is in contrast to both Walrasian and Keynesian theory in which there exist well-defined demand

---

[1] For a discussion along these lines see Alchian (1970).
[2] For an exposition see the essay in Phelps (1970). For a critique see Hines (1976).

and supply functions at the individual and sectoral levels in the former and at the individual and aggregate levels in the latter.

The second is that since search unemployment can occur at full employment — indeed, together with frictional unemployment it constitutes the only categories of unemployment admissable at full employment — it is clearly not involuntary. It is therefore clear that search theory cannot be used to illuminate the concept of involuntary unemployment even though it can offer an explanation of why an involuntarily employed worker may not offer to lower the money wage. Furthermore, involuntary or demand deficient unemployment may occur because of unintended consequences of the behaviour of the voluntarily unemployed workers. For if these workers reduce their current expenditure on goods and services while they are specialised in the activity of search, a cumulative contraction of aggregate expenditure can ensue which would result in involuntary unemployment.

We have observed that the search model does not contain within itself a theory of the aggregate economy. However, what has just been said above indicates that the Income Expenditure Theory or the Quantity Theory can be pressed into service. Based on the former, it could be argued that, to offset the undesirable and unintended aggregate consequence of search, the government should maintain aggregate demand at the full employment level by the use of whatever instrument is appropriate. Using the latter, it would be said that it is the duty of the government to maintain monetary stability in the face of such disturbances.

It should be noticed how this is reminiscent of the Keynes v classics debate. In the search model, the problem arises from the imperfect information which is available to workers and firms who are assumed to be dynamic monopolists/ monopsonists. The first best cure is the provision of better and cheaper information. But this may not be a feasible short-run policy. In the case of the classics, the voluntary unemployment is deemed to be the result of a conventional monopoly, namely a combination of workers who resist the theoretical first best policy of a cut in money wages. But the alternative Keynesian policy for achieving full employment is deemed to be more feasible on social grounds. Since these different theoretical approaches can be in agreement about policy, it appears possible to avoid questions such as the genesis of involuntary unemployment and the theoretical models and policy prescription to which they give rise. But this is not the case.

For if a Keynesian demand management policy is applied successfully we need to know why it works. More importantly, if such a policy is applied unsuccessfully, or is not applied because it is expected not to work, we need to know whether this is the result of a flaw in the Keynesian theory, or in the alternative (e.g. the search theory) which is supposed to explain the observed unemployment, or whether it is the result of a change in the environment or in the initial conditions which one or the other theory cannot comprehend because the change makes crucial assumptions on which they rest inapplicable. For instance, we shall show that policies designed to cure Keynesian unemployment are not appropriate to classical unemployment and vice versa. This must call into question the terms of the truce on which the Keynes v. classics debate was ended. Again, we shall show that if money wages behave in certain ways, traditional Keynesian demand management policies may be rendered inapplicable.

(b) The other explanation of why a cut in money wages is resisted is based on the hypothesis that the central consideration governing the behaviour of employed workers is wage relativities. A change in the price level of wage goods is accepted because it is universal and therefore leaves relativities unchanged. A reduction in the wage restricted to the ith category of worker in the jth firm/industry is not. It is therefore resisted either by the individual worker who quits and searches or by the organised resistance of all the workers in the firm/industry. In the latter circumstance, the workers are laid off by the employer. In either case, though more reasonably in the second, unemployment is said to be involuntary.

This explanation is unexceptional in itself. And, although it does not help to rationalise involuntary unemployment, it is less unhelpful than the search theory if only because it is more likely to invite attention to the macro circumstances of an economy in which a wage cut can be put forward as a theoretically correct response and to prompt a discussion of whether the objective of greater employment can be achieved by other means. However, like the search model, it focuses upon the response of employed workers to alternative methods of cutting real wages, regarding the reduction in it as the policy rather than the consequence of the demand management policies implemented to reduce unemployment.

I wish to argue for an alternative rationalisation of Keynes' first characterisation of involuntary unemployment. According to it, a state of widespread unemployment is observed. It is hypothesised that this is the result of deficient aggregate demand for goods and therefore is involuntary. Prices adjust within the unit period to make the aggregate demand for goods equal to the aggregate supply, i.e. the goods market clears and there is no corresponding excess supply. However, demand for goods is deficient relative to full employment productive potential. It is proposed that the autonomous demand for goods be increased. Assume that this is done. Then, if the unemployment were indeed involuntary, i.e. caused by a deficiency of aggregate demand, we should observe the following: an increase in the price level of wage goods at given money wages, hence a reduction in the real wage: increased actual profits and expected profitability at the as yet unchanged level of production: an increase in the demand for labour and a supply which is as least as great as the pre-existing level of employment: increased output and employment. On this view, the Keynes characterisation of involuntary unemployment is to be regarded as a test for the existence of deficient aggregate demand, and is inseparably and simultaneously linked both to the theory of effective demand and the determination of the level of employment and output and to the policy of demand management.

We elaborate upon this below.

III INVOLUNTARY UNEMPLOYMENT WHEN THE GOODS MARKET CLEARS

The context for this model and the one that follows may be said to be the 'reappraisal' view of the economy.

(a) It is a decentralised market economy which does not operate to announced and generally market clearing prices. It is an economy with uncertainty. It is therefore a sequential economy with active markets at all dates and one in which actual transactions in one market or decisions taken in the sphere of production determine optimal behaviour in other markets. It is a monetary economy in which money must intermediate between transactions in any pair of goods. Exchange is voluntary and when transactions are put through at non-market clearing prices, the short side realises its plans and the long side is rationed by some mechanism other than market prices. The last two assumptions concern all pairs of goods and all transactions and are therefore stronger than is necessary for our present purpose. It is necessary only that labour cannot be exchanged directly for goods and that the min condition of voluntary exchange and non-price rationing of the long side should apply to the labour market.

We consider a short period in which the relevant features of the past are embodied in the given stock of equipment, labour force, stock of money, transformation functions, state of long- and short-term expectations, a vector of prices, etc. The future is unknown and unknowable. Decisions have to be taken at the beginning of the period which will determine autonomous expenditure, demand and production and hence the degree of utilisation of the labour force, equipment, etc., during the current period.

We assume that the first market to open is the market in assets of differing degrees of liquidity (i.e. differing dates of maturity or conversion into means of payment at par). The following sequence of events takes place in this market. Based on uncertainty concerning the future yields of assets and set off against the stock of money, taking into account the transactions demand and precautionary demand (including the precautionary demand of workers based on income uncertainty), liquidity preference determines the money rate of interest. The rate of return on all other assets, including that on physical assets, is now adapted to be consistent with the money rate of interest. As of a given state of long-term expectations, the rate of return on physical assets, determines the level of investment. This level of investment, together with other expenditures not derived from current productive activity, e.g. the consumption of rentiers out of wealth, the consumption of workers out of initial money balances and government expenditure, constitutes the level of autonomous expenditure.

Given the level of autonomous expenditure and the vector of money prices and wages, the programmes of the agents, *viz* constrained optimisation, determine the functions appropriate to the behaviour of firms and workers in the labour and goods markets and the level of employment and output are thereby generated.[1,2]

We now make the assumption that the goods market always clears. This implies that when there are changes in the level of demand and hence in production, the price of output changes such that excess demand is always zero.[3]

The assumption of flexible prices of goods means that whenever demand changes, there is a change in actual profitability for some firms (at the very least retailers), which leads to a change in expected profitability thereby inducing the associated response in output and employment. And, when the goods market clears, but transactions take place in the labour market at a money wage and a price level associated with excess supply of labour, there is said to be involuntary unemployment.

We can describe the associated general equilibrium, or rather, the consistent solution to the system for the period, by making use of the aggregation device of the representative worker consumer and firm who have an intertemporal (two-period) planning horizon.[4]

(b) Given expectations concerning the variables which determine profits in period 2, the representative firm maximises profits in period 2 conditional upon its period 1 decisions. Its maximisation problem in period one can then be represented as follows: Maximise with respect to x_1, l_1, i_1

$$U_\pi = \pi_1 + \pi_2 \ (i_1, l_1, x_i, p_1, w_1, \Psi) \tag{1}$$

[1] To keep the unit period reasonably self-contained, it is assumed that the multiplier process works itself out within the unit period and hence before the asset market reopens. The implication is that short-term expectations are fulfilled so that firms judge the point of effective demand correctly.

[2] So called fix-price models, to be discussed below, focus almost exclusively on the role of alternative configurations of the wage price vector in the determination of the levels of output and employment in different regimes. See for example, Barro and Grossman (1976) and Malinvaud (1977). For an exposition, but explicitly in the context of an intertemporal model of the representative firm and household, see Muellbauer and Portes (1977).

[3] This is consistent with market-clearing prices changing with technical conditions of production as demand and production vary.

[4] It is sometimes more useful to work with a model in which each firm has the same profits functions and each consumer has the identical utility function. The aggregate functions, for example, the consumption function, are then derived by aggregation over the employed and unemployed. A treatment along these lines is provided by Malinvaud (1977). This is particularly helpful when, for example, rationing in the labour market consists of employment at fixed hours of work or unemployment. However, the model of the representative worker and firms are sufficient for the task in hand.

where

$$\pi_1 = p_1 x_1 - w_1 l_1$$

subject to

$$l_1 = l(y_1), l'(y_1) > 0, l''(y_1) < 0 \tag{2}$$

$$i_1 = h(i_0) + y_1 - x_1, \tag{3}$$

$$i_1 \geqslant 0, y_1 \geqslant 0, x_1 \geqslant 0.$$

$$h(i_0) \leqslant i_0$$

where π_1 and π_2 are profits in period 1 and 2 respectively, x is sales and y is production, l is labour employed, i is inventories and ψ represents all those factors which influence expectations of next period's profits which do not depend on the variables of the current period. It is assumed that expectations are held with complete certainty but an explicit probabilistic approach can be adopted.

Since the goods market is assumed to clear, so that the firm is not constrained in that market, it expresses its notional demand in the labour market. Similarly, since it is on the short side of the labour market, by hypothesis, $l^d(.) - l^s(.) < 0$ where $l^d(.)$ and $l^s(.)$ are notional demands and supplies, the firm expresses its notional supply in the goods market. Thus maximisation of (1) subject to (2) and (3) as of given states of (short-term) expectations yields effective demand and supply functions for the current period (i.e. period 1) which depend upon prices and initial conditions only:[1]

$$x^s = x^s (w, p, i_0, \psi) \tag{4}$$

$$l^d = l^d (w, p, i_0, \psi) \tag{5}$$

Correspondingly, given expectations concerning period 2, the representative household is assumed to maximise with respect to c_1, l_1 and m_1 the utility function in which period 2 decisions have been solved out,

$$U_H = U_H (c_1, T_1-1, T_2, m_1, \theta) \tag{6}$$

subject to

$$m_0 + w_1 l_1 = p_1 c_1 + m_1 \tag{7}$$

and to the additional restriction

$$l_1 = \bar{l} \tag{8}$$

c_1 is current consumption, m_0 and m_1 are initial and end-of-period money balances respectively, T is time endowment, and θ those aspects of expecta-

---

[1] Variables without a time subscript belong to the current period.

tions concerning period 2 which do not depend on the value of the variables in the current period. U is assumed to be increasing in all its arguments and

$$c_1 \geqslant 0, T_i > l_i \geqslant 0, \quad i = 1, 2.$$

This yields the effective demand function

$$c^d = c^{-d} (w, p, m_0, l, \theta) < c^d (w, p, m_0, \theta) \tag{9}$$

where the time endowments have been subsumed in the functional form. The consumption function is employment-constrained, since the worker faces a labour sales constraint. This is the Keynesian consumption function rationalised in terms of Clower's dual-decision hypothesis. Since the worker does not perceive a supply constraint in the market for wage goods, the notional supply function for labour

$$l^s = l^s (w, p, m_0, \theta) > \bar{l} \tag{10}$$

is the effective labour supply. However, it cannot be realised because demand for labour is insufficient. When there is no constraint on employment, the notional functions $l^s(.)$ and $c^d(.)$ are the joint outcomes of a single optimisation problem and depend only on prices, initial endowments and expectations. When there is a binding constraint on available employment, the link between the labour supply decision and the consumption demand decision is broken. It is readily seen that the 'second classical postulate' does not hold.

Applying min conditions,

$$c = \min (c^d, c^s) \tag{11}$$

$$l = \min (l^d, l^s)$$

and assuming that autonomous expenditure is always met, the equilibrium which is illustrated in Figure 6.1 is characterised by

$$x = c^{-d} (\underset{+}{w}, \underset{-}{p}, \underset{+}{m_0}, \underset{+}{l}, \theta) + z = x^s (\underset{-}{w}, \underset{+}{p}, \underset{+}{i_0}, \psi) \tag{12}$$

$$l = l^d (\underset{-}{w}, \underset{+}{p}, \underset{-}{i_0}, \psi) < l^s (\underset{+}{w}, \underset{-}{p}, \underset{-}{m_0}, \theta) \tag{13}$$

The solution exhibits unemployment and we wish to ascertain whether it is involuntary. To do so, we carry out a comparative static type exercise under the assumption of given long-term and short-term expectations. We increase autonomous expenditure remembering that the price of wage goods must rise to induce the increase in supply and to maintain the balance between supply and demand. The effect on output and employment is illustrated in Figure 6.2.

Taking derivatives, the effect of the increase in autonomous expenditure is as follows:

$$x_z = x_p^s p_z \tag{14}$$

$$l_z = l_p^d p_z \tag{15}$$

where $p_z = 1/(x_p^s - c_p^{-d} - c_l^{-d} l_p^d)$

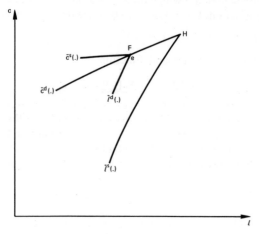

Fig. 6.1

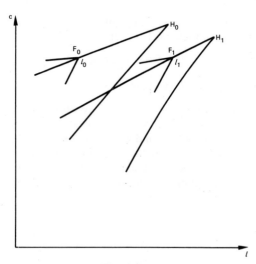

Fig. 6.2

We assume that the magnitude of own price effects exceeds that of indirect effects i.e.

$$| x_p^s - c_p^{-d} | > | c_l^{-d} l_p^d |$$

Thus

$$p_z > 0$$

Hence

$$x_z > 0, l_z > 0$$

Since, by hypothesis, the goods market clears, the increase in output is equal to both the increase in aggregate demand and in aggregate supply.

In the labour market, the increase in employment is equal to the increase in the demand for labour

$$l_z^d = l_z > 0$$

$$l_z^s = l_p^s p_z$$

The sign of the change in the labour supply of both employed and unemployed workers with respect to the increase in the price of wage goods is ambiguous. For those in employment before the expansion in aggregate demand, the real wage received is lower. Suppose we assume that the substitution effect is dominant. Then on this score, the labour supply is reduced. However, the price increase also reduces the purchasing power of initial money balances or wealth and, on this score, consumption is reduced and labour supply is increased. Hence, the supply of labour increases if the real balance effect outweighs the purchasing power of the wage effect when the latter is assumed to be zero or negative.[1] It does not appear unreasonable to suppose that the influence of this wealth effect exceeds any real wage effect even if the latter is negative. But even if this is not the case, so long as labour remains in excess supply after the system has adjusted to the disturbance, the labour supply must exceed the original level of employment.

It should also be observed that an increase in autonomous expenditure unaccompanied by a rise in the price of wage goods will not result in an expansion of output and employment. At the price level at which the market cleared, an increase in autonomous expenditure generates excess demand. The original market-clearing quantity now corresponds to the effective supply which, given the min condition, is also the equilibrium quantity. With excess demand for goods and excess supply of labour, the system moves into the regime of classical unemployment.

We may summarise the position reached as follows. An increase in

---

[1] In principle, these propositions also apply to unemployed workers who are also assumed to hold money balances and whose labour supply is also their notional supply.

exogenous expenditure raises the price of wage goods. The higher price induces the increased supply and maintains a cleared goods market. It is this which lowers the actual real wage (of workers in employment) at the current money wages. And the reduction in the real wage occurs prior to any increase in the demand for labour. Until employment and output rise there is no corresponding fall in the marginal product of labour. The changes in the demand for labour and consequently in employment are therefore not the cause of the reduction in the real wage. Moreover, since labour is in excess supply, additional workers can be taken on at the existing money wage. It should be stressed that this does not require the assumption of a rigid money wage. It only requires that transactions take place in the labour market at a wage above the market-clearing one. Indeed if it is assumed that money wages are falling in the face of excess supply and hence that there is downward pressure on prices from falling costs, the price of wage goods still rises relative to the money wage.

We see, then, that the model yields the test statements which establish the existence of involuntary or demand deficient unemployment in the given situation.

IV INVOLUNTARY UNEMPLOYMENT AND GENERALISED EXCESS SUPPLY

Another model is suggested by the alternative characterisation of involuntary unemployment given as (d) in section I above. It is assumed that, in addition to the excess supply of labour at the given money wage, there is also excess supply of goods at the price at which transactions take place. This is the case which is studied by Barro and Grossman and Malinvaud.

A dual-decision hypothesis can be seen to apply to the firm's behaviour in the labour market as well as to the behaviour of workers in the goods market. Solving the firm's optimisation problem on p.149 subject to the additional restriction

$$x = \bar{x} = \bar{c} + z < x^s(w, p, i_0, \psi) \tag{16}$$

we obtain

$$l = l^d = l^{-d}(w, p, i_0, x, \psi) < l^d(w, p, i_0, \psi) \tag{17}$$

Application of the min conditions now shows that in equilibrium at the given money price of labour and goods, output and employment are jointly determined by the effective demand for labour and for goods which are the quantity constrained functions

$$l = l^{-d}(w, p, i_0, x, \psi) < l^s(w, p, m_0, \theta) \tag{18}$$

$$x = c^{-d}(w, p, m_0, l, \theta) + z < x^s(w, p, i_0, \psi) \tag{19}$$

The test for the existence of involuntary unemployment is that at given wages, prices and expectations, an increase in autonomous expenditure should raise output and employment.

$$x_z = 1/(1 - c_l^{-d} l_x^{-d}) > 0 \tag{20}$$

$$l_z = l_x^{-d}/(1 - c_l^{-d} l_x^{-d}) > 0 \tag{21}$$

The equilibria are illustrated in Figure 6.3.

We see that the demand for labour and goods increases when autonomous expenditure is raised. The supplies of goods and labour are unaffected. But since both goods and labour are in excess supply, more are forthcoming at the ruling price/wage constellation. Therefore output and employment increase.

It should be observed that when the goods market clears, the multiplier involves terms in the supply of goods and in the difference between supply and demand with respect to price. In generalised excess supply, it involves terms in demand with respect to quantities only. In the former case the multiplier works through prices.

In the latter, it works through quantities. In generalised excess supply the price of wage goods is an exogenous variable. If it is increased simultaneously with exogenous expenditure, we have

$$dx = \frac{(c_p^{-d} + c_l^{-d} l_p^{-d}) \, dp + dz}{1 - c_l^{-d} l_x^{-d}} > 0 \tag{22}$$

$$dl = \frac{(l_p^{-d} + l_c^{-d} c_p^{-d}) \, dp + l_x^{-d} \, dz}{1 - c_l^{-d} l_x^{-d}} > 0 \tag{23}$$

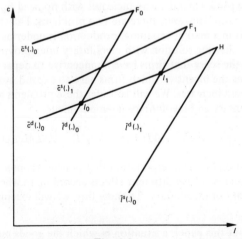

Fig. 6.3

we take $l_p^{-d} = 0$ so long as the representative firm is sales constrained.

We then see that although the multiplier does not operate through prices, it is modified by them and that in principle, the sign of the multiplier could be reversed since dx and dl are not signed unambiguously.

It should also be noticed that an increase in the price of wage goods on its own has a deflationary effect. Thus,

$$x_p = c_p^{-d} + c_l^{-d} l_p^{-d}/(1 - c_p^{-d} l_x^{-d}) < 0 \tag{24}$$

$$l_p = l_p^{-d} = l_p^{-d} + l_c^{-d} c_p^{-d}/(1 - l_x^{-d} c_l^{-d}) < 0 \tag{25}$$

The same conclusion follows in the Keynesian model which becomes equivalent to the model of generalised excess supply when the price level is not an endogenous variable and is at a level higher than that which clears the goods market.[1]

We may conclude from the foregoing that the alternative test for the existence of involuntary unemployment is therefore met. No reference need be made to the response of the demand for or the supply of labour to changes in the price-wage ratio as neither variable is required to change. The demand for labour and employment increases with the demand for goods. So long as labour remains in excess supply, the increase in employment is consistent with any direction of change in the real wage since the marginal product of labour exceeds the real wage. In this model, whatever influences the behaviour of the real wage is assumed to be independent of the change in the demand for goods and the subsequent changes in output and employment.

All this appears congenial. We have an operational concept of involuntary unemployment which is not in conflict with any empirical data concerning the behaviour of real wages in relation to output and employment. The test for the existence of involuntary unemployment is now that output and employment expand when demand increases with no need for an increase in the price wage ratio. However, there are two problems. They arise from the simple fact that in a market economy, production is undertaken for profit. The first is whether the solution with involuntary unemployment is an equilibrium in the sense that firms have no incentive to depart from it. The second concerns the incentive which firms have to expand output when aggregate demand increases. We will consider these problems after we have compared voluntary and involuntary unemployment.

V INVOLUNTARY AND VOLUNTARY UNEMPLOYMENT

It is an implication of our interpretation that policies proposed for the cure of unemployment will have different effects according to whether unemployment is voluntary or involuntary. To show this, we will examine the effects

---

[1] Throughout this paper, a situation in which the goods market clears but the labour market does not is said to be one of Keynesian unemployment.

of policies such as changes in money wages, prices and autonomous expenditure in the model in which the goods market clears, in the model of generalised excess supply and in the model of classical unemployment.

We consider first the effects of a cut in money wages. It is convenient to begin with the regime of generalised excess supply where we find

$$x_w = x_w^{-d} = c_w^{-d}/(1 - c_l^{-d} l_c^{-d}) > 0 \tag{26}$$

$$l_w = l_w^{-d} = l_c^{-d}/(1 - l_c^{-d} c_l^{-d}) > 0 \quad l_c^{-d} c_w^{-d}/(1 \tag{27}$$

We take $l_w^{-d} = 0$ for a sales-constrained firm.

$$l_w^s > 0$$

A reduction in the money wage rate reduces output, employment and the supply of labour.

In the Keynesian model, a reduction in the money wage at an unchanged price level of wage goods creates excess supply in a hitherto cleared goods market. With goods in excess supply, the effective demand for labour becomes the quantity-constrained demand

$$l^d = l^{-d}(.)$$

The system is pushed into the regime of generalised excess supply and the analysis of the effect of a wage cut in that regime applies.

In contrast, consider the regime of classical unemployment. It is characterised by a too high real wage

$$l^d(.) < l^s(.), \text{ and } x^s(.) < x^d(.)$$

Since firms are on the short side of both markets, the equilibrium is determined by their behaviour alone and is given by

$$x = x^s(w, p, i_0, \psi) < c^{-d}(w, p, m_0, l, \theta) + z \tag{28}$$

$$l = l^d(w, p, i_0, \psi) < l^{-s}(w, p, m_0, c, \theta) \tag{29}$$

In the discussion of this regime, it is usually assumed, explicitly or implicitly, that, although there is excess demand in the goods market, the prevailing price level of goods is nevertheless consistent with a full employment general equilibrium as of a given stock of money. The too high real wage and the consequent failure of both markets to clear is therefore attributed to the too high money wage. This must be the basis for the claim that, in classical unemployment, the observed unemployment is voluntary. To check this claim we study the effects of a reduction in the money wage rate, the proposed remedy for voluntary unemployment, as well as the effects of the proposed remedy for involuntary unemployment, with either a simultaneous increase in autonomous expenditure and the price of wage goods or an increase in autonomous expenditure at a given price of wage goods.

In the case of a reduction in money wages, we find:

$$x_w = x_w^s < 0 \tag{30}$$

$$l_w = l_w^d < 0$$

$$x_w^d = c_w^{-d} + c_l^{-d} l_w^d > 0 \tag{31}$$

$$l_w^s = l_w^{-s} + l_c^{-s} c_w^s = l_c^{-s} c_w^s < 0 \tag{32}$$

We therefore see that, given a reduction in the money wage, output and employment increase. The demand for wage goods by workers is likely to be reduced while the supply is increased. The excess demand for goods is therefore reduced. The demand for labour increases and the supply decreases. Hence the excess supply of labour is reduced. But given that after the change,

$$l^{-s}(.) \geqslant l^d(.),$$

both the aggregate demand for and supply of labour are greater than the original level of employment. We conclude that what we shall now call the test for the existence of voluntary unemployment is met. And, since unemployment is voluntary in classical unemployment, we see that the effect on output and employment of a reduction in money wages is the opposite of what it is in the Keynesian model or in generalised excess supply.

Now suppose that we were to apply the policy appropriate to involuntary unemployment in the Keynesian model to the case of classical unemployment, i.e. increase autonomous expenditure and the price level.

We then find

$$dx = x_p^s \, dp + dz > 0 \tag{33}$$

$$dl = l_p^d \, dp > 0 \tag{34}$$

$$dx^{-d} = (c_p^{-d} + c_l^{-d} l_p^d) \, dp + dz > 0 \tag{35}$$

$$dl^{-s} = l_c^{-s} c_p^s \, dp > 0 \tag{36}$$

We therefore see that although there are no multiplier effects, with the possible exception of the change in the labour supply the qualitative responses are similar to those obtained in Keynesian unemployment and in generalised excess supply. However, on closer inspection, we find that the similarity is due entirely to the effect of the increase in the price level. For, if autonomous expenditure alone changes, as is easily found from equations (28) and (29) there is no effect on the demand for and supply of goods or the demand for labour. However, since it is assumed that autonomous expenditure is always met, this implies the crowding out of the private consumption of workers by means other than the operations of the price mechanism. This is in marked contrast to our findings in Keynesian unemployment and in generalised excess supply. It is explained by the fact that at a given wage and price level, in classical unemployment, output and employment are determined by the behaviour of firms and the change in autonomous expenditure by itself does not provide any incentive for them to alter their behaviour.

The fact that an increase in the price level relative to the money wage increases output and employment appears to suggest that there are elements of unemployment present in classical unemployment that are not voluntary. However, we have seen that an increase in autonomous expenditure leaves output and employment unchanged which implies the absence of involuntary unemployment. We also assumed that in the initial situation, the price level of wage goods was in a 'correct' relationship to the money supply. It must therefore be the case that the increase in the price level is best interpreted as occurring in the economic environment described in search theory, in which voluntary unemployed and searching workers overestimate the real purchasing power of current wage offers and accept employment, thereby engaging in a less than optimal amount of search. The level of unemployment which is in fact voluntary is reduced because prices transmit wrong information to workers. In the conceptual framework to which search theory belongs, this conclusion depends on adaptive as distinct from rational expectations on the part of workers. We cannot go further into the matter here. Nevertheless, this explanation of why output and employment increase when prices rise in classical unemployment, clearly improves understanding of the basic theoretical positions of Keynesians and monetarists.

VI PROFITABILITY AND SUPPLY RESPONSE

(a) In the preceding sections, we have examined how output and employment respond to various disturbances according to the regime in which the economy finds itself and hence according to whether unemployment is voluntary or involuntary. However, we have not been sufficiently explicit about the incentives which are necessary to motivate the appropriate actions by firms and workers. Moreover, in part, we have been following the tradition of the fix price method in assuming that agents are price-takers as well as quantity-takers in the market in which they are on the long side. But the analysis is incomplete if we continue to treat agents as price-takers in a class of models which purports to deal with proper decentralised economies in which production and exchange are not to announced prices. Hence, if we are to consider the two questions posed at the end of section IV, namely, can a given solution state of these models persist, and what incentives agents have to alter their quantity responses given exogenous disturbances, we have to specify which agents set prices and how. For, given the level of autonomous expenditure, expectations etc., a satisfactory explanation of what determines the level at which output and employment are determined requires a theory of what determines the wage price vector. Correspondingly, given the wage price vector, expectations etc., a theory of what determines autonomous expenditure is required for a complete explanation of the level at which output and employment are determined.

We cannot enter into a full discussion of price and wage determination here. It will however be sufficient for our purpose if we assume that the representative worker and firm have power to alter money wages and prices and that this power is used, if it is used at all, before the beginning of period t based on the outcomes experienced during t − 1 and on expectations for t. For the most part, we will be concerned with the representative firm though the behaviour of workers will turn out to be crucial in the sequel.

(b) Let us now consider whether agents have any incentive to depart from any given solution in the regimes of Keynesian unemployment and generalised excess supply once it is established.

When output is limited by demand, i.e. when demand is not sufficient to guarantee full employment of labour and autonomous expenditure is constant, in the model in which prices clear the goods market within the unit period, the representative firm is under no pressure to alter its output or employment. It is already producing all that it notionally wishes to at the ruling price. In the model in which goods are in excess supply at the equilibrium corresponding to the given wage and price vector, the question is whether the firm has any incentive to lower price at the beginning of the following period. If it conjectures that there is a kink in the demand function which it perceives itself to face at the ruling price, there may be no such incentive.

In the labour market the question is why the firm does not consider it profitable to offer additional employment at the going level of prices and wages on the expectation that workers would purchase the additional output with the labour incomes generated thereby. Under Keynesian unemployment and in generalised excess supply, the individual firm does not have such an expectation because it correctly perceives that only a fraction of its outlay on wages will be spent on its own product. At the level of the whole economy, even if the behaviour of all firms were to be sufficiently co-ordinated so that they were aware of the relationships between aggregate demand and factor payments, if they all expanded employment and output simultaneously, the resulting expenditure on goods and services would be less than their outlay because the marginal propensity to consume is less than unity. Moreover, even if workers were to offer to reduce money wage rates, an offer which they are unlikely to make for both individualistic and collective reasons, this will not constitute an effective signal to firms to expand output and employment. Indeed, as we have already seen, when unemployment is involuntary, a reduction in money wage rates reduces employment and output. However, when unemployment is voluntary, faced with an offer to reduce money wages, firms would react by expanding employment and output because these are limited by the existing level of profitability at the given level of demand.

(c) This leads us into the question of the incentive which firms have to expand output and employment when there is a change in a relevant parameter. Let us consider the reaction of firms to an increase in exogenous expenditure in Keynesian unemployment and in generalised excess supply.

In the model in which price clears the goods market, the matter is straightforward. When autonomous demand increases, firms (including retailers, middlemen etc. as appropriate) increase prices. The rise in price relative to the wage increases the actual profits of those firms who are directly affected. It also increases expected profitability for those firms who now perceive an increased demand and hence a higher price for their products. An increase in aggregate supply is thereby induced. This conclusion holds irrespective of whether short-run returns are increasing, constant or diminishing.

In the model of generalised excess supply, in which wages and prices are given and firms are regarded as price-takers, the source of the incentive for the expansion of employment and output when autonomous demand increases is the excess of the marginal product of labour over the real wage.

However, both in the model in which prices clear the goods market and in the model of generalised excess supply, it can be seen that Keynesian-demand management may run into difficulties when it can no longer be assumed that money wages stay constant when aggregate demand is increased. In the model in which the goods market clears, prices rise when aggregate demand is increased. Wages may then be raised within the unit period in order to maintain the real wage rate, i.e. except on conditions to be agreed in advance, workers are no longer willing to accept the reduction in real wages which the successful application of demand-management policies require. In generalised excess supply, prices need not rise when aggregate demand is expanded. However, when there is an autonomous wage push, firms raise prices according to the mark-up rule in order to prevent an erosion in profit margins or in anticipation of such erosion. In either case, we must examine the effect on output and employment if prices and wages rise in the same proportion when autonomous demand is increased.

In the model in which the goods market clears, we have

$$x_z = \frac{x_w^s w + x_p^s p}{A + B + C} \tag{37}$$

$$l_z = \frac{l_w^d w + l_p^d p}{A + B + C} \tag{38}$$

where

$$A = (x_p^s - c_p^{-d})p$$
$$B = (x_w^s - c_w^{-d})w$$
$$C = c_l^{-d}(l_w^d w + l_p^d p) = 0$$

In generalised excess supply, we have

$$dx = \frac{dz + (c_w^{-d}w + c_p^{-d}p)\gamma + c_l^{-d}(l_p^{-d}p + l_w^{-d}w)\gamma}{1 - c_l^{-d}l_x^{-d}} \tag{39}$$

$$dl = \frac{l_x^{-d}dz + l_x^{-d}(c_p^{-d}p + c_w^{-d}w)\gamma + (l_p^{-d}p + l_w^{-d}w)\gamma}{1 - c_l^{-d}l_x^{-d}} \tag{40}$$

$$\gamma = \frac{dp}{p} = \frac{dw}{w}$$

In Keynesian unemployment, the multiplier works through the difference between the response of the demand and the supply of goods and the response of the demand for labour to the changes in wages and prices. Given that prices and money wages change in the same proportion, real wages are unchanged and hence the demand for labour and the supply of goods are unchanged. However, the demand for labour and hence employment would increase if firms demanded more inventories in anticipation of capital gains to be made if they expected the rate of inflation to persist. The supply of labour is reduced because of the real balance effect of higher prices. Similarly, workers' demand for goods is reduced or crowded out by the real balance effect of higher prices and is thereby made consistent with the unchanged supply and the higher level of autonomous expenditure which constitutes a prior claim on output.

In the case of generalised excess supply, the effect of the multiplier, which does not work through prices, is modified by the change in wages and prices. In principle, the change in output could be negative and the demand for labour may be increased because of firms' decisions or inventories in the light of their expectations.

We see then that in both cases, the change in employment and output cannot be signed unambiguously. Moreover, it may happen that production, inventories and demand cannot be brought into a consistent relationship within the confines of the models as they stand. In the Keynesian model this means that there might not be a market clearing level of γ. In the model of generalised excess supply, this means that the exogenous price and wage change and the changes in demand and output may not generate a consistent solution. All this is in the context of a closed economy. In the open economy, the discrepancy between demand and output could be met by running down foreign exchange reserves to pay for imports. This, then, is one way in which a connection between a budget deficit and the balance of payments can be established.

The amendments to the argument that are necessary when wages and prices do not increase in the same proportion are relatively straightforward.

(d) Thus far, our technological assumption has been that of short-run diminishing returns in production.

However, especially in manufacturing industry, production is usually subject to constant rather than diminishing returns in the short run. With firms having discretion over price, at given wage rates, the profitability of additional output depends on the technological conditions of production in relation to the pricing policy of firms.

It is often assumed that price is set on the basis of a mark-up on variable costs. It is also usual to assume that the technology exhibits constant returns in the short run. Ignoring the distinction between average variable costs and unit labour costs and that between output and sales and assuming a constant markup, β.

$$p = (1 + \beta) \, wl/x, \, 0 < \beta < 1 \tag{41}$$

where

$$x = al, \, a > 0 \tag{42}$$

whence

$$p = \gamma w, \, \gamma = (1 + \beta)/a \tag{43}$$

Prices are constant if productivity, the money wage and the mark-up are constant. There is therefore a constant addition to profits with each additional unit of output. Moreover, if there are significant overhead costs, total costs per unit of output decline with output. Therefore, profits per unit of output increase as output expands. However, increased profits cannot be made until output is actually expanded.[1] Thus, if an increase in demand is signalled, firms must perceive that it will be sustained if they are to undertake additional production.

Now, the original assumption of diminishing returns is common to both the fix price and the Keynesian model. Therefore, if we change the technological assumption in the one, we have to change it in the other. But the change in technological assumptions unifies both models since in the Keynesian model, an increase in autonomous expenditure does not have to be accompanied by an increase in the price of wage goods in order to be effective, and in the fix price model, the profitability of additional output does not require the marginal product of labour to be in excess of the real wage.[2] Under the changed technological assumption, we do not have rising supply price and we lose the concepts of market clearing and of excess demand. But the notion that output is limited by demand remains. The mark-up pricing hypothesis is also applicable. And independent price push is now possible in addition to wage push.

It should be clear that in comparison with the model in which firms set prices to clear the goods market or that in which the marginal product of

---

[1] It should be noted that the equations (41) and (42) together imply that $w/p < \alpha$ irrespective of how the real wage and employment move together over the cycle.

[2] From a longer term perspective, it could be that prices are increased with the trend in demand. However, it is not clear that this is applicable to a situation which is one of generalised excess supply.

labour exceeds the real wage, the route to the increased profitability which is required to induce firms in the capitalist economy to expand employment and production when autonomous demand increases is more tenuous and that given the validity of the mark-up pricing hypothesis, the central issue in the model of the closed economy is the determinant of the behaviour of money wage rates.

VII CONCLUSIONS

We have used the framework of the reappraisal of Keynesian economics to study the notion of involuntary unemployment. We have considered the four characterisations put forward by Keynes and shown that they reduce to a basic one, namely, that involuntary unemployment is that unemployment which can only be cured by an expansion of aggregate demand. However, in the model in which the goods market clears and the labour market does not, a rise in the price of wage goods relative to the money wage rate is required to induce the expansion in employment and output. We have argued that much of the discussion of involuntary unemployment in the literature is misdirected in as much as it focuses upon the microeconomics of labour markets — specifically, it focuses on explanations and evaluations of the behaviour of individual workers or groups of workers — rather than on the state of the macro economy. We have shown that the concept of involuntary unemployment must rest upon models of states of the economy which exhibit unemployment and which enable us to examine how, in each such state, output, employment and the demand or the supply of labour and goods respond to different policies designed to cope with the unemployment. We have shown that the model in which demand is deficient relative to productive potential and in which the goods market clears but the labour market does not is the basic model of Keynesian involuntary unemployment. The reason is that in it, an increase in autonomous expenditure associated with an increase in the price of wage goods at given money wages, and therefore associated with a rise in profits, is the only policy that can reduce such unemployment within the given institutional framework. Moreover, while a change in autonomous expenditure is the driving force, the mechanism of price and wage response modifies or may even reverse the sign of the response of the system to a change in autonomous expenditure. It should be stressed yet again that an exogenous money wage does not necessarily mean a rigid money wage.

By analysing the consequences of a change in autonomous demand and of a cut in money wages, we have established that classical unemployment is voluntary. Due allowance must be made for the possibility that voluntary unemployment may be influenced by misleading information conveyed to workers by prices and for the fact that an unintended consequence of the search which may be involved is a reduction in expenditure and the consequent generation of involuntary unemployment. Involuntarily unemployed workers may also search.

By analysing the effect on observed unemployment of those policies that are relevant, perhaps in the framework of an econometric representation of the economy in question, it should be possible to distinguish empirically between the different types of unemployment.

We have shown that involuntary unemployment also arises in fix price models, especially in the model of generalised excess supply. However, in this model, a reduction in real wages, hence a rise in profits, through a rise in the price of wage goods is not a necessary accompaniment of an expansion in demand and the associated increase in output. Increased profits are assured in as much as the marginal product of labour exceeds the real wage at the existing level of employment.

Constant real wages and a reduction in unemployment when demand is increased can also be obtained in the model of endogenous price of wage goods by changing its technological assumption to one of constant variable costs on equipment in place. We must also take cognisance of the fact that, in the decentralised economy, firms and workers do set prices and wages. Quantities and the appropriate set of prices are then jointly determined. As a first step, we assumed that firms follow a mark-up pricing rule. Trade unions set money wages and a theory of the rules by which they do so has to be added. We have not gone into this matter here. We have not provided a full and formal treatment of models in which prices and wages are set endogenously by firms and workers, and models in which there are short-run constant returns. However, what has been presented is sufficient both to merge the endogenous price and the fix price models and to show that demand management is at risk if prices and wages rise in response to each other even if they change in the same proportion, thereby keeping real wages constant. The situation is clearly exacerbated through the effect on profitability if, given productivity growth, money wages rise more than in proportion to prices or if, when costs increase, real wages cannot be reduced.

REFERENCES

Alchian, A. A. (1970), 'Information Costs, Pricing and Resource Unemployment' in E. S. Phelps (ed.) *Micro-economic Foundations of Employment and Inflation Theory* (Norton).

Barro, R. and H. Grossman (1976), *Money, Employment and Inflation* (Cambridge University Press).

Clower, R. (1965), 'The Keynesian Counter-revolution' in Hahn, F. and F. Brechling (eds.), *The Theory of Internal Rates* (Macmillan).

Keynes, J. M. (1936), *The General Theory of Employment, Interest and Money* (Macmillan).

Kahn, R. (1976), 'Unemployment as seen by the Keynesians' in G. D. N.

Worswick (ed.), *The Concept and Measurement of Involuntary Unemployment* (George Allen and Unwin).

Hines, A. G. (1976), 'The Micro-economic Foundations of Employment and Inflation Theory', in G. D. N. Worswick (ed.), *The Concept and Measurement of Involuntary Unemployment* (George Allen and Unwin).

Hines, A. G. (1971), *On the Reappraisal of Keynesian Economics* (Martin Robertson).

Malinvaud, E. (1977), *The Theory of Unemployment Reconsidered* (Blackwell).

Muellbauer, J. and Portes, R. (1977), 'Macroeconomic Models with Quantity Rationing', *Birkbeck College Discussion Paper, No. 54.*

Discussion of Professor Hines' Paper

Mr Honkapohja said that, since the original contributions in the 1960s from Patinkin, Clower and Leijonhufvud, there had been keen interest in so-called disequilibrium or fix-price theory. On the one hand, mathematical economists had studied some basic propositions in general multicommodity, multiagent models; other economists had provided simple macroeconomic models, more specifically directed towards policy questions. Professor Hines gave yet another exposition, utilising a macroeconomic framework, directed towards matters of policy. There were, however, several features of the paper which made it worthwhile, even if the results it derived were already familiar from earlier work.

Professor Hines tied his exposition closely to some older doctrinal issues: to the definition of involuntary unemployment, rigidity of money wages etc., and this was not often done in recent literature. Professor Hines began by quoting definitions of involuntary unemployment from Keynes's *General Theory*, and suggested that definition (d) could incorporate voluntary unemployment. Mr Honkapohja said he would probably contrast definitions (a) and (b), taken together with (c) and (d). Different issues were present:

(1) in (a) and (b), one considered the effect of a change in a parameter (the price of wage goods in (a) or effective demand in (b)) on unemployment, etc.

(2) in definitions (c) and (d), one simply asked whether there was excess supply of labour in a given situation, but said nothing about its cure or origin. Thus (c) would seem to be consistent with any type of unemployment, irrespective of its cause.

Later in the paper Professor Hines seemed to consider as involuntary unemployment that unemployment which was caused by deficient demand. The classical case, in which firms did not find it profitable to employ more labour when there was excess demand for goods was ruled out. It should be noted that this was in marked contrast to Professor Malinvaud, who, in his paper, called any rationing of workers' supply of labour involuntary unemployment.

In the second section of his paper, Professor Hines reviewed the traditional discussion of involuntary unemployment, in particular, search theory and wage relativities. Mr Honkapohja pointed out that aspects of search and of imperfect information were being used more and more in the research into disaggregated disequilibrium or fix-price models.

Turning to the more formal part of Professor Hines' paper, Mr Honkapohja noted that Professor Hines constructed a fairly standard simple macroeconomic disequilibrium model. The main features were: (i) a snapshot of the economy in a given period; (ii) asset markets operated first, and determined the level of investment and other components of autonomous demand by interest rates and returns on assets, (iii) given this, and wage and price optimisation by agents subject to certain constraints, one obtained behavioural functions which then determined unemployment and output.

Professor Hines considered two possible cases; in the first, the price of goods cleared the market for goods, and money wages were exogenous; in the second, both prices and money wages were exogenous. These cases were called 'Keynesian' and 'generalised excess supply' respectively. The formal model was reminiscent of the models of Barro—Grassman or Malinvaud. But Mr Honkapohja wanted to know why inventory behaviour was introduced into the model of the firm? It seemed to be totally unnecessary, since the paper considered only short-run questions. Not even comparative statics with respect to initial inventories was studied.

Mr Honkapohja also wanted to know why the effective/notional demand and supply functions of the household were written as separate arguments (p, w, m_0) when in view of the budget equation (f), only real wage and real balances mattered. There was some confusion later which seemed to be due to this formulation.

Assuming clearance of the goods market, Hines showed that the comparative statics of autonomous expenditure were as one would expect. There was some confusion, however, since the signs in (13) implied that $1^s_2 < 0$. This was generally not true, as indeed Professor Hines noted in the ensuing discussion. In fact, $\partial 1^s/\partial p < 0$ implied that the real wage effect dominated that of real balances. The comparative statics confirmed Keynes's first definition of involuntary unemployment L^d and 1^s were higher after the increase in autonomous expenditure.

Similarly in the case of excess supply in both markets, Keynes' test of involuntary unemployment was satisfied. However, part of the argument seemed to be misleading. Mr Honkapohja believed that the real wage had a definite relation with *ex post* employment

$$(\partial l/\partial (w/p) > 0).$$

In Section V the regime of classical unemployment was considered, and it was seen that autonomous expenditure had no effect on classical unemployment.

Finally, Professor Hines considered profitability signals which caused output expansion in Keynesian unemployment and generalised excess supply, as well as considering price-makers, mark-ups etc.

As a central subject for discussion, Mr Honkapohja wanted to consider how useful it was to say that unemployment was involuntary when it was due to a deficiency of aggregate demand for goods. Somehow the alternative formulation that one was off the supply curve seemed more straightforward. One could then enquire into reasons for it (whether classical or Keynesian) and policies to cure it.

As had been pointed out in the paper, one had to take into account the possible consequences of demand management on wages and prices. Thus, in definition (b), difficulties might appear if the behaviour of wages and prices was sufficiently adverse.

Mr Honkapohja felt that on the whole, he would opt for the fact that there was merely, 'unemployment'. He would then look into the general structure to find the causes of, and cures for, it. Alternatively, he would include the classical régime in 'involuntary unemployment'.

Professor Hines explained that the distinction he was trying to make between voluntary and involuntary unemployment was a simple one. The question was whether, if there was excess supply in the labour market, anything could be done by workers about the terms on which they offered their labour services, to ameliorate unemployment. Or did this require action from others? For example, unemployment might be voluntary because it was theoretically possible for all workers to reduce their money wage. With given prices, this could lead to a net increase in employment. With involuntary unemployment, the collectivity of labour, acting in the same way, could not increase employment but only reduce it. This was the fundamental distinction.

Professor dos Santos Ferreira agreed strongly with Professor Hines that Keynesian unemployment could best be viewed as a situation in which there was excess supply in the labour market, but the goods market cleared. However he did not think Professor Hines' characterisation of involuntary unemployment, as one which would be cured only by an expansion of aggregate demand, to be very fruitful or even faithful to the spirit of Keynes' work. To admit that Keynes attributed the existence of unemployment in his own time to a lack of effective demand for goods should not lead us to pretend that demand-deficient unemployment was the only kind of involuntary unemployment.

When Keynes referred to involuntary unemployment as a situation in which the real wage was above the marginal disutility of labour (characterisation (c)) or when he said that 'the population . . . is seldom doing as much work as it would like to do on the basis of the current wage' (characterisation (d)), he was just simply telling us that workers were off their supply curve, because of a lack of demand *for labour*. This excluded frictional unemployment, but was consistent with 'classical', no less than with Keynesian unemployment. In order to distinguish voluntary from involuntary unemployment, one must refer to the adjustment process. The former was the result of workers' resistance to *any* form of *real* wage adjustment, the other is the consequence of 'an unsatisfactory co-ordination of economic activity in production and exchange', as Professor Hines correctly stressed.

It left labour as a whole with no method whereby it could bring about a *real* wage adjustment, even if it accepted a cut in the *money* wage. So, one would expect Keynes to refer to the effect on employment (and the real wage) of a cut in the money wage as a positive test for whether unemployment was involuntary. But, assuming that money wages were sticky downwards, Keynes preferred a negative test: unemployment was involuntary when an increase in the price of wage goods, even without a compensatory rise in money wages, was not followed by a labour withdrawal (characterisation (c)). If prices were endogenous and cleared the goods market, and if we assumed diminishing returns in production and competitive markets, an increase in the price of wage goods would be the result of an increase in effective demand (characterisation (b)). However, since this increase in effective demand might be the consequence of a reduction in the money wage, through a real balance effect, demand-deficient unemployment might be in some degree voluntary.

On the other hand, in the fix-price model, an exogenous increase in prices would reduce 'classical' unemployment and meet the Keynesian test for involuntariness (characterisation (a)), as Professor Hines seemed to admit. Besides, the effect of a cut in money wages on 'classical' unemployment did not even seem to be quite unambiguous. In any case, if prices did not adjust to clear the goods market in spite of the existence of excess demand, we were confronted with an unsatisfactory co-ordination of economic activity. To say that unemployment was voluntary in such a situation appeared to represent a pre-Keynesian position, attributing responsibility for that unsatisfactory co-ordination exclusively to workers' behaviour. This was certainly the opposite of what Professor Hines wanted to show.

Professor Bergmann had a strong feeling of unreality, not in the theory but in its lack of contact with real issues in the USA today, or at least in the past few years. This scenario was consistently encountered. Problems were perceived, and there was a demand that the government should do something, but the argument then was that the sufferer was to blame for his suffering, so that nothing helpful could be done. This was followed by a scramble by the other side to negate what was being done. Professor Bergmann thought that something similar must have been happening at the time of the *General Theory*. In the economic crisis of the 1930s, some people were asking the government to do something, while others were claiming that the unemployed were responsible for their own problems. Keynes said this was not the case. Unemployment was not a result of workers' own behaviour if one looked at the problem in the right way.

In a sense, the opponents of such a view were trying to say that the person in trouble had caused his own problem, and used this attitude as the basis for deciding whether governments should act. This argument could be beside the point. For example, it might be possible for an unemployed man to present himself to the employer outside the usual conditions of work. If he did not, the argument was that it was his own fault that he was unemployed. But then one needed to call in sociologists and psychologists, and to realise that perhaps one could not hold people to this notion of accountability. Perhaps one could help people, even if in a sense they were responsible for their own problems.

Keynes might have been mistaken in trying to resolve the problem by saying that the situation was not the fault of the employee. Perhaps he should say that it was, though it was hard to see how this could help and might be simply self-defeating. Perhaps what one came to was not whose fault it was, but to whether government intervention was reasonable or not. Much of the discussion in the conference contributed little to this.

Professor Holt said the distinction between voluntary and involuntary unemployment might not be helpful. For example, one could say that the demand for money could be traced to the transactions, precautionary, and speculative motives. But it would then be hard to say what the motivation was for holding a particular dollar. The same was true for the unemployed worker. One could not look at a particular worker, and say whether he was voluntarily or involuntarily unemployed. Unemployment was a state through which labour flowed, and the amount of unemployment depended on various factors. At one point anyone could accept a job, if he would take a low enough wage or status. Looking at motivation was less helpful than looking at the process. Workers were like businessmen who, during a recession, were faced with high unemployment and low profits, and there was nothing they could do. If all were powerless, then only the government could do something. If it turned out that the government too was powerless because printing money led to inflation, then it was a very difficult situation indeed. The conclusion was that no-one could do anything about the problem.

He felt that trying to say how much unemployment was involuntary was not very helpful because all unemployment at the micro level was both voluntary and involuntary. What one needed to do was to examine the micro-level processes and analyse what was going on. One saw, for example, the need to improve information about the labour market; to get a better match between the man and the job; to provide better working conditions, etc. One then obtained good employee relations and low labour turnover, etc. These kinds of action altered the unemployment rate and affected inflation. Institutional factors like trade unions could lead to greater pressures toward inflation. Analysing the finer-grain processes was better than continuing to use the Keynesian aggregate analysis and policies exclusively. Professor Hines did well in tackling the question, but why did he tackle it?

Lord Kaldor thought the conference was making heavy weather of the issue. There was no difference between an excess supply of labour and an excess supply of goods. There was excess supply whenever the market was not cleared. There was involuntary unemployment when the market could not find employment for all workers at the given supply price. The Walrasian demand and supply schedules were schedules of *maximum* quantities. Given the wage rate, this meant that at a particular wage *up to* a given maximum, that a number of people, or any lesser number, were available to work. The difference between a maximum number and those actually working was the excess supply. If one had a downward-sloping demand curve for labour, one could say that there existed a simple 'equilibrium' or market-clearing price.

Some economists, for example Pigou in 1932, had thought that unemployment was 'voluntary'; there was an equilibrium wage, but if the trade unions asked for more than this, then the number unemployed would be limited by demand. The silliness of this supposition lay in assuming that because certain results flowed from a downward-sloping demand curve for cabbages, the same thing was equally true of the labour market. It was the source of the assumption of the falling marginal productivity of labour in the short run. We knew from empirical studies that the wage rate (in real terms) was positively correlated with employment and not negatively. The 'real' demand curve for labour for the economy as a whole was a rising rather than a falling one and this made nonsense of all theories that assumed that labour 'priced itself out of the market'. It could not do so; the world was not made that way.

Professor Parkin thought the distinction between voluntary and involuntary unemployment was both misleading and unnecessary. One could see that it was misleading if one looked at the summary definition in the paper. If there were one million unemployed, then one could take two actions. One could increase aggregate demand and wait for unemployment to fall to 500,000. One could then say, that there were 500,000 involuntarily unemployed. Second, one could hold aggregate demand constant and introduce a general payroll subsidy, matched by some fiscal manoeuvre. One could then assume that this would reduce unemployment, but a reduction would then not be a result of increased aggregate demand. One would therefore say that it could not be involuntary. So one had involuntary unemployment in the first case, and voluntary in the second. All definitions of involuntary unemployment were prone to this ambiguity. One defined unemployment in terms of an answer to a question. One then developed models to answer the question: what happens to unemployment if one then takes a given political action? One wanted non-zero effects, and he felt that the whole discussion was pointless.

Professor Henin argued that the discussion showed how difficult it was to distinguish between voluntary and involuntary unemployment. Professor Hines did this in terms of the elasticity of employment to changes in aggregate demand, but he was preoccupied with political questions. A discussion in terms of channels or periods would give a secondary distinction. If so, one would have the most direct definition, which was that one must see whether a worker was on his offer curve or not. Even in this sense, one could get back to what Professor Hines was saying if .the offer curve was controlled by trade unions. This was a more direct definition. If there was voluntary unemployment, workers could reduce the valuation of wages in terms of disutility, and so lower the supply curve of labour. This could be effective, if the processes of the market responded to a reduction in the wages demanded. This acceptance did not bear on wages but on the supply of labour.

Professor Henin asked about eventual relationships between these definitions of involuntary unemployment and the offer curves used in Professor Holt's paper. Professor Holt analysed one kind of equilibrium unemployment that was different from the Keynesian type. The two types of unemployment did co-exist in present economic conditions but they could not be seen theoretically as merely additive.

Professor Hines replied on technical points to Mr Honkapohja. Inventories were exogenous because he wanted to see the effect of events in the current period without any hangover. This had implications for the way in which problems were modelled. The property of homogeneity was not lost because one could divide one equation by another.

Professor Bergmann had raised the question of the individual unemployed. He was not happy with this kind of example and wanted to get away from it, because it was the collective behaviour of labour over wages that was important. He thought it was important to look at the situation studied by economists who considered a portfolio of jobs. As one scaled this up and down, on a first approximation the amount of unemployment occurring left the structure of jobs, of the unemployed (and the level of demand) unchanged. He would leave aside here what type of worker was most affected.

On whether the distinction between voluntary and involuntary unemployment was helpful, perhaps Lord Kaldor had put the issue most clearly. The question was what were the appropriate policies for dealing with unemployment. If Pigou was right, it was theoretically possible to have an economy where a reduction in wages increased employment. He would call this voluntary unemployment, as distinct from a situation where no set of actions by workers could change the situation, but a change in aggregate demand was necessary. To anticipate what would be said in Professor Malinvaud's paper, if one disaggregated the labour market, one would find some Keynesian and some classical unemployment. It followed that the policies pursued would determine, not only how the unemployment rate behaved, but what happened to inflation as well. If there were general involuntary unemployment, a change in employment resulting from an increase in aggregate demand would be inflationary. In another situation, one might say that one could cure unemployment, but at an unacceptable price in terms of inflation.

Professor Hines wanted to emphasise that voluntary unemployment was not a rare case, and not one which the labour market ever generally faced. One could say that classical unemployment could not be prevented, but that involuntary unemployment could, though to do so required political action from outside the market.

As for why discussion was necessary, he would like to make two points. When one went beyond Keynesian analysis, one had to study the response of wages and prices, and the autonomous behaviour of workers relative to demand management policies. If wages and prices increased together with aggregate demand, it then became a question of how far classical demand management policy was appropriate. In particular cases, one found that an increase in autonomous demand did not have the desired effect because of the response of wages and prices.

As for whether the distinction between voluntary and involuntary unemployment was useful, Professor Hines did not know whether he would reach the same conclusions as Professors Bergmann and Parkin. What he read now about the situation in the 1930s was exactly the same as for them. One had to deal with both economic and political factors. There were the same arguments and the same policy stances as in the 1930s. It was therefore important to try to categorise types of unemployment, and to find policies appropriate to dealing with each of them.

Sir Austin Robinson commented lightheartedly that forty-five years ago, when he and his friends had been looking at these issues in Cambridge, they had fallen into every trap imaginable in the very early days of macroeconomics. But they had tried to be clear what they were doing, whether they were talking about monetary or real wages, and above all, how far the supply and demand curves were or were not independent of each other. He thought that almost every fallacy of their discussions of forty-five years ago had been repeated during this session.

7 Macroeconomic Rationing of Employment

E. Malinvaud
IEA, PARIS

INTRODUCTION

J. M. Keynes started his *General Theory* with the obvious assertion that when involuntary unemployment exists, the labour supply is not met (which he calls the negation of the 'second postulate' of classical theory). During recent years it became common among some theorists to say that workers are then *rationed* in their labour supply.

Why this substitution of words? Because involuntary unemployment is seen as part of a more general phenomenon in which economic agents cannot fulfil all their plans and are thus rationed in various respects. In particular, we have been used to think that unemployment results from a too low demand for goods, i.e. from a situation in which firms are rationed in their supply of goods since they cannot produce and sell as much as would be most profitable for them at prevailing prices and wage rates. Discussing the foundations of such a conception, in order to reappraise its power and limitations, has led us to view it as deriving from a theory of general equilibrium with price rigidities and quantity rationing.[1]

This paper will consider some of the points raised by the application of the latter theory to problems of involuntary unemployment. To avoid misunderstandings, let it be said from the start that the paper will not consider whether, when unemployment prevails and is likely to be durable, one should organise the rationing of the labour supply (also called 'rationing of jobs') or leave it as it is. This is clearly a relevant and difficult question at present, but the essentially macroeconomic approach that will be followed here cannot be fully appropriate for its examination.

The present reconsideration of general theories aims at a better explanation of the impact of various policies, in particular of the macroeconomic policies used by western governments. But it is still at the stage of maturation, in which the exact significance of the new developments has not yet been brought out. We must know that this reconsideration may have important

[1] Such is the point I tried to make in part I of E. Malinvaud, *The Theory of Unemployment Reconsidered* (Basil Blackwell, Oxford, 1977).

consequences for our views on the respective effectiveness of various policies; but we must also be careful not to jump too quickly to conclusions. Indeed, various theoretical questions should still be answered and a number of appropriate econometric studies performed before we can feel confident of what we have recently learned.

Two of these theoretical questions will be considered here. Both of them proceed from the major claim of the new theories, namely the logical possibility of a second type of macroeconomic unemployment beyond the commonly considered Keynesian unemployment. This classical unemployment would appear in a situation where firms would not find it profitable to recruit the whole labour force even though they would be faced with an excess demand for their output.

The questions then are: can Keynesian and classical unemployments co-exist when a disaggregated representation of production is introduced? Is classical unemployment of secondary importance because an excess demand for goods always forces prices up and makes an increase of production profitable?

These questions will be considered in turn in the second and third parts of this paper. The first part will be devoted to a simple presentation of the new macroeconomic theory of involuntary unemployment, as it follows from the consideration of a general equilibrium with rationing. Technicalities will be deliberately avoided, so that the bare essentials of this theory appear.

I DEMAND, CAPACITY AND FULL EMPLOYMENT OUTPUT

Let us begin with the simplest expression of the prevailing conception on involuntary unemployment and the way to cure it.

The source of the trouble is considered to be an insufficient aggregate demand for goods. If this demand is denoted d, output y is limited to the amount d. Then, given labour productivity β, employment is limited to d/β. If the labour supply is L, involuntary unemployment is equal to $L - d/\beta$.

Now demand depends both on some autonomous instruments of economic policy (for instance government demand g) and on the level of output through the distribution of incomes. If we write d (y, g) to represent this relationship, output y is determined by the solution of the equation:

$$y = d (y, g) \tag{1}$$

A small change δg of the instrument generates an increase $\delta y = k d'_g \delta g$ of aggregate demand and output, k being the multiplier:

$$k = \frac{1}{1 - d'_y} \tag{2}$$

Unemployment is then reduced by $k d'_g \delta g/\beta$.

When this well-known theory is presented, it is common to stress not only that employment d/β is assumed to be smaller than the labour supply L, but also that output d is smaller than the productive capacity $\bar{y}$ of existing equipment. One easily introduces the new theory by relaxing these two hypotheses.

1. *Two types of involuntary unemployment*

Let us then say that output is bound to be the smallest of the three numbers d, $\bar{y}$ and β L: demand, capacity, and full employment output, as we shall say.

$$y = \text{Min}\left\{d, \bar{y}, \beta\, L\right\} \tag{3}$$

Then three cases must be distinguished, assuming for the time being the three numbers to be different:

(1) If d is the smallest of the three numbers, the prevailing Keynesian theory applies as indicated above. There is an excess supply of labour and potentially also an excess supply of goods because, by hypothesis or more exactly by the definition of what capacity $\bar{y}$ means, it is profitable for firms to produce at full capacity if there is a sufficient demand and they can recruit enough labour.

(2) If β L is the smallest, there is an excess demand for goods $(d > y)$ and also an excess demand for labour: firms would like to produce as much as the minimum of d and $\bar{y}$, but they do not find enough labour. This situation of generalised excess demand has been called for long 'demand inflation', or 'repressed inflation' when one wants to insist on the fact that prices and wages have not gone up enough to wipe out excess demands.

(3) If $\bar{y}$ is the smallest, there is again an excess demand for goods, but with an excess supply of labour. Involuntary unemployment exists and is equal to $L - \bar{y}/\beta$. Such an unemployment due to a lack of equipment might be called Marxian, because the excess labour supply might be explained by an insufficient past capital accumulation; but it is more commonly called classical: indeed what is involved is probably not an absolute physical lack of equipment, but rather a lack of profitable productive capacities (present prices and wages being considered, the existing equipment stock makes it most profitable to produce up to $\bar{y}$ and not beyond).

Between these three types of situations there are, of course, intermediate cases. Particular attention is given to the situation in which excess demand is exactly zero, both for goods and for labour. This requires:

$$d = \bar{y} = \beta\, L \tag{4}$$

and we may then speak of a 'Walrasian equilibrium'.

2. *Macroeconomic behaviour*

Even with such a fully aggregated model we must recognise that d, $\bar{y}$, β and L are not fixed numbers; they are functions of many variables. The theory of involuntary unemployment must consider in particular what may be these functions. Let us try to do it briefly here.

Aggregate demand depends, of course, on various instruments of economic policy. It may be enough for the present purpose to identify two of these instruments:[1] government demand g and the rate of taxation τ. It also depends on the purchasing power of income and wealth, which in turn depends on output y, the real wage w and the price level P. Hence, we may replace equation (1) by the following one:[2]

$$d = d (y, w, P, g, \tau) \tag{5}$$

d is of course increasing with y and g, decreasing with P and τ. We may also take it for granted that it is an increasing function of w because the marginal propensity to spend out of wages is larger than the marginal propensity to spend out of profits (for consumption and investment).

The labour supply depends of course on the real wage rate and on the purchasing power of non-labour incomes, which means here that it depends on w, P. and τ. Existing econometric studies show, if I am well informed,[3] that the labour supply is a slowly increasing function of w and a decreasing function of real non-labour incomes, i.e. an increasing function of P and τ. We may then write:

$$L = L (w, P, \tau) \tag{6}$$

It must also be recognised that the recorded labour force is a decreasing function of the unemployment rate u, which will play a role here:

$$u = 1 - \frac{y}{\beta L} \tag{7}$$

This should be made explicit if L were to be identified with the recorded labour force and u with recorded (involuntary ?) unemployment. It will be easier to avoid this complication here, remembering then that L and u are not directly interpretable as the corresponding notions that are found in official statistics.

---

[1] Monetary policy, which involves liquidity questions, is deliberately left aside here.

[2] Any precise representation of the distribution of transfer incomes is bound to be quite complex. It will not be attempted here, which means that this distribution is taken as being exogenous except for its dependence on τ and P.

[3] See for instance O. Ashenfelder and J. Heckman, 'The Estimation of Income and Substitution Effects in a Model of Family Labor Supply', *Econometrica* (January 1974); J. Smith, 'Family Labor Supply over the Life Cycle', *Occasional Papers of the NBER* (Spring 1977); D. Gayer, 'The Effects of Wages, Unearned Income and Taxes on the Supply of Labor', *International Economic Review* (February 1977).

As was mentioned above, capacity $\bar{y}$ is whatever output it is most profitable for firms to produce considering their existing equipment stock. This is somewhat flexible to the extent that (i) some old equipments may be operated or left idle, (ii) active equipments may be run more or less intensively, i.e. with the use of more or less labour. The exact value of capacity mainly depends on the real labour cost, which will be identified here with w. Hence, we shall write:

$$\bar{y} = \bar{y}(w) \tag{8}$$

this being a decreasing function of w.

Average labour productivity β is a complex function of many factors. It is fairly rigid in the short run but is then correlated with the level of output. We shall simply write here:

$$\beta = \beta(y) \tag{9}$$

β being understood to be an increasing function.

3. *Macroeconomic policies*

Equations (3) and (5) to (9) define a small macroeconomic model expressing a very simple version of the new theory of the short-term equilibrium with rationing. These six equations contain six variables that are taken as endogenous: y, d, $\bar{y}$, β, L, u. They also explicitly introduce four new variables, which are then considered as exogenous in the short run; not only do we find the traditional instruments of budgetary policy, g and τ, but also a simple representation of the price system by w and P. This stresses the fact that the new theory analyses the short-term adjustments as if they were made only on quantities and not at all on prices. This is, of course, an exaggeration, but an appropriate exaggeration because we now know that in the short run adjustments are indeed made much more through changes in quantities than through changes in prices.

Since the wage rate and the price level are somewhat independent of supplies and demands, they may be manipulated to some extent by economic policy. Hence w and P may be considered as providing of rough representation of the instruments of income and price policy.

It is not the place here to proceed to a full discussion of this small model, not even to exhibit explicitly under which conditions concerning the exogenous variables each one of the three types of istuation will occur. The methods for such a discussion have been explored elsewhere.[1] Attention will be limited here to considering how the unemployment rate u reacts to changes

---

[1] See for instance part III in *The Theory of Unemployment Reconsidered, op. cit.*, or G. Laroque, 'The Fixed Price Equilibria: Some Results in Local Comparative Statics', *Econometrica* (1978).

in two particularly interesting instruments of economic policy: government demand g and the real wage rate w.

A change δ *g of government demand has no effect* (*in the short run*) *on u if unemployment is classical.* Indeed, $y = \bar{y}$, u, β and L are then jointly determined by the four equations (6) to (9), in which g does not occur. Such a change then reacts only on aggregate demand, i.e. on the extent of rationing on the goods market.

If unemployment is Keynesian, the traditional multiplier applies. More precisely $\delta y = k$, δg, the multiplier being given by (2) and account being taken of the fact that $d'_g = 1$ if g is precisely government demand. The exact formula for δu is then found to be:

$$\delta u = -k \left[1 - \frac{y\beta'}{\beta} \right] . \frac{\delta g}{\beta L} \tag{10}$$

It is the product of three terms: the multiplier k, the size of the autonomous change relatively to full employment output $\delta g / \beta L$ and a middle term that differs from 1 by the elasticity of labour productivity with respect to output, an elasticity that is, of course, much smaller than 1. (In applications one should also take into account the elasticity of the recorded labour force with respect to unemployment.)

An increase δw *of the real wage rate pushes* u *up if unemployment is classical.* Indeed, $\delta y = \bar{y}'$. δw is negative. In order to approximate δu by an easily interpretable formula, let us assume d, $\bar{y}$ and βL are close to each other, so that the situation does not differ much from a Walrasian equilibrium. Then we can write:

$$\delta u = \left[\frac{wL'_w}{L} - \left(1 - \frac{y\beta'}{\beta} \right) \frac{w\bar{y}'}{\bar{y}} \right] . \frac{\delta w}{w} \tag{11}$$

the elasticity of the labour supply with respect to w is positive and the elasticity of capacity is negative.

But an increase δw *of the real wage rate pushes* u *down if unemployment is Keynesian* Indeed, $\delta y = kd'_w$. δw is positive and the same kind of approximation as above gives:

$$\delta u = \left[\frac{wL'_w}{L} - k \left(1 - \frac{y\beta'}{\beta} \right) \frac{wd'_w}{d} \right] . \frac{\delta w}{w}$$

Since the elasticity of the labour supply must be small, especially in the short run, the second term in the square bracket must dominate the first one.

Other applications of the model are of course feasible and interesting. But the two preceding ones are the most significant in exhibiting the sharp distinction between Keynesian and classical unemployments. The distinction is, however, too sharp as we realise as soon as we turn our attention to a less aggregated model.

II INTERSECTORAL DIFFERENCES, THE MULTIPLIER AND MOBILITY

In any real situation a careful study of unemployment requires consideration of what is happening in various regions and industries. Theory also must recognise that a great diversity exists at the micro level. But the way of modelling this diversity is far from obvious because it implies a representation of the whole productive system, which is not easily made simple.[1]

Here attention will be limited to a representation based on the following extreme assumption: production is made directly from labour in n distinct sectors, each one of them using its own equipment and confronting its own demand as well as its own labour supply; in other words the demands for the goods of the various sectors are not substitutable for one another (in the short run) and workers are not mobile from one sector to another (in the short run). Although actual unemployment has a definite relation with such a lack of substitutability and mobility, no real economy fits this extreme assumption, which can only claim to provide a rough approximation; the sectors should be viewed as being defined so as to make the approximation as good as possible. The type of goods produced, the professional qualification required from the labour and the location considered should all play a part in the definition of such sectors. A short-hand expression may be to say that a sector is a specific industry in a specific region.

1. *The statistical distribution of unemployment*

Let the productive capacity, the demand for goods and the labour supply in sector i be respectively $\bar{y}_i$, d_i and L_i. If productivity is β_i, output y_i is the minimum of the three numbers d_i, $\bar{y}_i$ and $\beta_i L_i$. Excess demand, excess capacity and unemployment in sector i are easily defined.

In order to study unemployment in the whole economy, so as to discuss how it can be cured by various policy measures, one should specify how d_i, $\bar{y}_i$, β_i and L_i depend on various explanatory factors. Since the purpose is here to consider macroeconomic policies one needs not precisely to identify those factors that play only on one or a few sectors. Hence, modelling may proceed along two successive steps:

(i) define the statistical distribution of the microvariables;
(ii) characterise how this distribution depends on a few macro-variables.

---

[1] A very interesting discussion on the role of disaggregation in models such as the one of the preceding section has been recently provided by J. Muellbauer ('Macrotheory vs. Macroeconometrics: the Treatment of Disequilibrium in Macromodels', Birkbeck College). Although his main aim is to clarify econometric applications, his paper bears definite similarities with what is presented in this section.

Proceeding to the first step, let us write:

$$\bar{y}_i - \beta_i L_i = e + sx_i \tag{13}$$

and consider the cumulative distribution function $F(x)$ of x_i over all n sectors ($i = 1, 2 \ldots n$). We do so because we want to keep F as a fixed function whatever the macroeconomic situation may be, whereas we want to be free to introduce variations in e and s. It will be convenient to speak of e as the average excess capacity (over full employment output) and of s as the dispersion of excess capacities; e may be positive, zero or negative, s is positive, the distribution F may be viewed as having a zero mean.

Similarly let us write:

$$d_i - \beta_i L_i = \epsilon + \sigma \xi_i \tag{14}$$

and consider the cumulative distribution function $\phi(\xi)$ of the ξ_i, which we assume to be distributed independently of the x_i. We may speak of ϵ as the average excess demand (over full employment output) and of σ as the dispersion of excess demands.

Knowing e, s, F, ϵ, σ, ϕ we can compute many interesting quantities, for instance:

P_K: the proportion of the n sectors in which production is limited by lack of demand $y_i = d_i$ (Keynesian situation);

P_C: the proportion of the sectors in which production is limited by lack of equipment $y_i = \bar{y}_i$ (classical situation);

u : the aggregate unemployment rate;

v : the ratio of vacancies to the labour force.

An appendix is devoted to derive exact formulae for such quantities as functions of e, s, ϵ and σ (the functions of course depend on F and Φ). The following results are obtained.

The proportion P_K (respectively P_C) is an increasing[1] function of e (resp. ϵ) and a decreasing function of ϵ (resp. e). The Keynesian situation becomes more frequent when excess capacity increases or excess demand decreases. The proportion P_K decreases with s (at least in a neighbourhood of a Walrasian equilibrium). It increases with σ if ϵ is larger than e and zero.

Assuming for simplicity the full employment output $\beta_i L_i$ to be the same quantity y^0/n in all sectors and productivity β_i to be distributed independently of x_i and ξ_i, the unemployment rate u is found to be a decreasing function of both e and ϵ; it even obeys the very simple equations:[2]

$$\frac{y^0}{n} \cdot \frac{\partial u}{\partial e} = -P_C \qquad \frac{y^0}{n} \cdot \frac{\partial u}{\partial \epsilon} = -P_K \tag{15}$$

[1] Here and later 'increasing' should be understood by the mathematician to mean 'non-decreasing' and 'decreasing' to mean 'non-increasing'.

[2] Rigorously speaking, these equations are true only at the limit when the number of sectors is infinitely large, F and Φ being then absolutely continuous.

If the average excess demand is reduced by 1 per cent of the average full employment output, the unemployment rate increases by 1 per cent multiplied by the proportion of sectors that are in a Keynesian situation. Remember again that this result should be corrected for the induced decrease of the recorded labour force.) The unemployment rate is also an increasing function of the dispersions of excess demands and excess capacities s and σ (at least in a neighbourhood of a Walrasian equilibrium).

Similar relations can be derived concerning the ratio v of vacancies to the labour force, namely:

$$\frac{y^0}{n} \cdot \frac{\partial v}{\partial e} = \text{Prob}\left\{ \beta L \leqslant \bar{y} \leqslant d \right\} \quad \frac{y^0}{n} \cdot \frac{\partial v}{\partial \epsilon} = \text{Prob}\left\{ \beta L \leqslant d \leqslant \bar{y} \right\}. \tag{16}$$

in which Prob R is meant as the proportion of sectors where relation R stands.

2. *Budgetary and income policies*

On such a multisector economy, one can discuss the impact of the macro-economic policies already considered in the first section: budgetary policy acting on government demand g or on the tax rate τ, price and income policy acting on the price level P or on the real wage rate w. In order to make such a discussion possible, one only needs to specify how e, ϵ, s and σ are related to g, τ, P and w.

Neither budgetary policy nor price and income policy seem, at first sight, to have any definite consequence on intersectoral dispersions. Indeed, in order to make the discussion easy, we shall take s and σ as being independent of g, τ, P and w. Moreover, the behaviour equations of part I will be taken as appropriate for tracing the consequences on the average excess capacity e and excess demand ϵ. But this will require for realism a fixed and common labour productivity:

$$\beta_i = \beta \tag{17}$$

Let us, indeed, pose the following equation for the labour supply, transposing equation (6) of part I:

$$L_i = \frac{1}{n} L(w, P, \tau) \tag{18}$$

Assuming such an equation is appropriate because, when macroeconomic policy acts on w, P and τ, it concerns all sectors simultaneously and indistinctly. Similarly the change of capacity in sector i will be assumed to depend on w and the change of the demand addressed to sector i to depend on w, P, g, τ, as well as on aggregate output through the distribution of incomes within the whole community.

But labour productivity in sector i can hardly be related to aggregate output y; if it were considered as variable, it ought rather to be related to y_i. Then in order to keep the equation $d_i = \beta_i L_i + \epsilon + \sigma \xi_i$, we ought to assume that the deviation $\beta_i L_i$ from its average value is added to $\sigma \xi_i$, making this term somehow dependent on y_i, hence indirectly on the aggregate exogenous variables. Even if the β_i were fixed but variable between sectors, a similar difficulty would occur when we would assume β_i to be independent of the deviation of d_i from its mean. Going into such complications would serve no good purpose here. This is why equation (17) is assumed.

This being made, a simple transposition of the behaviour equations of part I leads to:

$$ne = \bar{y}(w) - \beta L(w, P, \tau) \tag{19}$$

$$n\epsilon = d(y, w, P, g, \tau) - \beta L(w, P, \tau) \tag{20}$$

The model is now complete when account is taken of

$$y = \sum_{i=1}^{n} \text{Min} \left\{ d_i, \bar{y}_i, \beta L_i \right\} \tag{21}$$

Let us then consider an increase of government demand δg, all other exogenous variables remaining fixed. Output does not change in sectors that are in classical or inflationary situations, because neither capacity nor full employment output change in these sectors. For sectors in the Keynesian situation we can write: $\delta y_i = 1/n \,] d_y' \delta y + \delta g]$ (where account is taken of $d_g' = 1$).

Summing up, we find:

$$\delta y = P_K (d_y' \delta y + \delta g) \tag{22}$$

or

$$\delta y = k^* \cdot \delta g \tag{23}$$

with

$$k^* = \frac{P_K}{1 - P_K d_y'} \tag{24}$$

Moreover, it follows from (20) that $n\delta\epsilon = d_y' \cdot \delta y + \delta g = k^*/P_K \, \delta g$. Hence, according to (15) the unemployment ratio is reduced and obeys the simple formula:

$$\delta u = -k^* \cdot \frac{\delta g}{y^0} \tag{25}$$

which replaces (10) and is very similar to it.

In the multisector model the impact of the budgetary policy is still represented by a very simple multiplier rule. The only difference is that the multiplier k given by formula (2) is replaced by the multiplier $k^{\star}$ given by formula (24). One checks that the new multiplier $k^{\star}$ is equal to the old one k when all sectors are in a Keynesian situation. One also sees that it decreases to zero when the proportion of sectors in such a situation decreases.

By how much is the new multiplier smaller in the case of a concrete economy? The answer is not easily given. On the one hand numerical computation shows that the reduction may be quite significant (with $d_y' = 1/2$ $P_K = 2/3$ we find k = 2 and $k^{\star} = 1$). On the other hand estimation of P_K is difficult; we know that for instance in France the proportion of industrial firms who would have produced more if they had received a larger demand varied between 55 per cent and 88 per cent during the past twenty years;[1] but this is only for industry and our sectors must be viewed as larger than firms (although a single establishment of a much larger corporation does in some cases make the labour market of a town).

Even though we cannot give a precise answer to the question raised, we see that the revision is worth making in our theoretical thinking. It suggests a reason why the simple multiplier theory is never quite true.[2] It also helps us to realise why the sharp distinction that appears in the most aggregated model between Keynesian and classical unemployment should be replaced by the notion of a whole spectrum of situations from the purely Keynesian to the purely classical extremes. The proportions P_K and P_C, which then have a major significance, do not need to be observed directly, their impact may be estimated indirectly by using currently reported statistical quantities, as was shown by J. Muelbauer.[3]

The same notion of a continuous spectrum comes again to mind when one considers *the impact of an increase of the real wage rate*. Indeed, it is shown in the appendix that u then changes according to the formula:

$$\delta u = [\cdot \ \eta_L - (1 + d_y' k^{\star})(P_K \eta_d + P_C \eta_{\bar{p}} + P_I \eta_L)] \cdot \frac{\delta w}{w} \tag{26}$$

in which η_L, η_d and $\eta_{\bar{y}}$ designate the elasticities, with respect to the real wage rate, of the labour supply, the demand for goods and the productive capacity,

---

[1] During the same period the proportion of industrial firms that could not produce more by lack of equipment varied between 7 per cent and 31 per cent; the proportion of those that could not produce more by lack of labour varied between 3 per cent and 19 per cent. Lack of raw material is usually insignificant, but sometimes becomes a bounding constraint.

[2] It should be noted that, in actual econometric models which undoubtedly are of Keynesian inspiration, the multiplier is much smaller than in the simple theory. This is not only because of foreign trade and of the automatic fiscal stabilisers but also because of the varying extent of 'rationing on the goods markets' (accumulation or decumulation of involuntary inventories, of commands in order books, and so on).

[3] See reference on page 179.

whereas $P_I = 1 - P_K - P_C$ is the proportion of sectors experiencing repressed inflation.

This formula may be compared with equations (11) and (12), which, in the macroeconomic model, concerned respectively the classical ($P_C = 1$) and the Keynesian ($P_K = 1$) situations. When $\beta' = 0$, these equations appear as particular cases of (26).

We may easily derive from (26) *the condition for an increase in the real wage rate to lower the rate of unemployment.* We find the simple condition:

$$\frac{P_K}{P_C} > \frac{\eta_L - \eta_{\bar{y}}}{\eta_d - (1 - d'_y)\eta_L} \tag{27}$$

assuming the denominator to be positive, which we have already assumed in the macroeconomic model when commenting on equation (12). For instance, with $\eta_L = 0.1$, $\eta_y = -0.1$, $\eta_d = 0.25$ and $d'_y = 0.5$, the condition would simply be that P_K be at least as large as P_C; it would therefore practically always be met because the Keynesian situation is more frequent than the classical one, a proposition toward which we shall turn our attention in the third part.

3. *Mobility and structural changes*

Dealing with a multisector model permits not only a more realistic approach to the study of macroeconomic policies than by a simple macroeconomic model, but also a discussion of some of the 'structural' aspects of unemployment. In particular we may consider here briefly two propositions which have sometimes been taken as contradictory to one another.

(i) increasing the mobility of labour should reduce involuntary unemployment;

(ii) when an economy is experiencing a fast restructuration of its productive sector, one may observe simultaneously a high labour mobility and a high involuntary unemployment.

These two propositions actually refer to different aspects of labour mobility. The first one concerns exogenous measures intended to stimulate a more mobile behaviour of workers, the demands for goods and the productive capacities being given; mobility is stimulated by information on the labour market conditions in other areas and trades, or by special grants for reducing the costs of moves and professional changes.

The second proposition concerns the induced or forced mobility that workers have to accept, given their behaviour, when the demands for goods and the productive capacities undergo particularly fast transformations. But both propositions are related to the same property: *involuntary unemployment increases when the intersectoral dispersion of market conditions increases.*

Indeed, measures intended to stimulate a more mobile behaviour may be said to aim at reducing this intersectoral dispersion. Workers should move from sectors in which there is an excess supply of labour (Keynesian or classical unemployment) to sectors in which there is an excess demand for labour (inflation). Hence, $d_i - \beta_i L_i$ or $\bar{y} - \beta_i L_i$ will increase when at least one of them is negative and decrease when both are positive. Without going into mathematical technicalities, we understand that the impact of such a change is similar to the one following a decrease of s and σ in equations (13) and (14).

We should note here that intersectoral dispersion may also be reduced by measures that increase the 'mobility' of the demands for goods, i.e. the substitution of a new demand addressed to a sector experiencing an excess supply (Keynesian situation) as against an old demand addressed to a sector experiencing an excess demand (inflation or classical situation). Measures reducing barriers to competition on the goods markets may in principle have the same favourable effect on employment as measures increasing mobility on the labour market.

It is also natural to associate large values of s and σ in (13) and (14) to cases when the economy undergoes fast and therefore partly unexpected transformations. Indeed, the three intersectoral distributions concerning respectively the demand for goods d_i, the productive capacities $\bar{y}_i$ and the supply of labour L_i are unlikely to match each other well in such cases, because time is required for their reciprocal adjustments.

Conditions are spelled out in the appendix under which an increase of s (or σ) increases the unemployment rate u, the average excess capacity e and excess demand ϵ remaining fixed. Suffice it to say that they are quite general. One also finds, not surprisingly, that the sensitivity of u to s (respectively σ) is maximum when ϵ (resp. e) is very large and e (resp. ϵ) is equal to zero: the sensitivity of the unemployment rate to the dispersion of sectoral demands is the highest when capacities are nowhere bounding and when the average demand is equal to the average full employment output. The maximum sensitivity can even be given a simple, and intuitively appealing, expression: a 1 per cent change in $\sigma(\delta\sigma/\sigma = 0.01)$ induces a change in $u(\delta u)$ which is equal, in per cent, to the mean absolute deviation of $\sigma\xi_i$ divided by twice the labour productivity β.

This notion of a maximum sensitivity *a contrario* agrees with common sense: increasing labour mobility would serve no purpose in the fight against unemployment if, in all regions and all activities, there would exist some involuntary unemployment.

III LOOKING BEYOND THE SHORT RUN

The new theory of fixed-price equilibria, which aims to be more realistic for the study of short-term phenomena than was the old theory of equilibrium with fully flexible prices, imposes on economists the task describing the transition from one short-term equilibrium to another.

In particular, for the subject of this paper, the question must be faced whether classical unemployment has not a natural tendency to vanish quickly whereas Keynesian unemployment would be more stable. Indeed, the few figures quoted above about the rationing of French industrial firms suggest that producers lack demand much more often than equipment. This might be due to the dynamic working of the whole economy.

A simple argument supporting this view might run as follows. When classical unemployment prevails, firms are not able or willing to fully meet the demand for their output; buyers are competing one against another to be served first, which induces an increase of the price of output. Then production becomes more profitable. Capacity is extended either through investment or even by a more intensive use of existing equipments; employment is raised and unemployment reduced. The process goes on until full employment is reached or at least until capacity matches the demand for goods.

There are three quite valuable reasons for studying this process more closely. In the first place the preceding argument is not complete. As usual when questions of general equilibrium are involved, we must check that the conclusions are not reversed when account is taken of some effects that partial equilibrium analysis neglects.

In the second place the process may require enough time for classical unemployment to be more than of theoretical interest and to justify specific policy measures. Indeed, the building of new productive capacities cannot be taken as fast.

In the third place it is not unimportant to know whether classical unemployment ends up in full employment or in Keynesian unemployment. If the classical situation originated from a sudden exogenous drop of profitability it is not unimportant, for the framing of economic policy, to know whether it will be spontaneously and quickly restored or whether a stable Keynesian situation will soon appear in which capacities, even though not fully used, would still be insufficient to permit full employment ($d < \bar{y} < \beta L$).

This article cannot claim to propose a dynamic theory of involuntary unemployment, a theory that would represent the working of an economy operating through a sequence of fixed price equilibria.

Such a theory is needed and I should like to contribute to it elsewhere. But it is too complex and difficult to be presented in a few pages at this stage. Even brief remarks about it may, however, lead to some suggestive and hopefully valuable insights into what could be appropriate corrective economic policies.

(1) The dynamic theory that is looked for must exhibit two types of intertemporal links concerning on the one hand the revision of prices and remuneration rates, on the other hand the accumulation of capital in its dual form: investment and saving. A good deal of econometric research exists that provides the best basis for specifying these links. But abstract thinking may also help in leading to the specifications that are likely to be most appropriate.

In particular, consideration of a multimarket or multisector model, such as the one discussed in the second part, may be useful. Bent Hansen has very clearly shown this for the laws describing the revision of prices and remuneration rates.[1] The same is true for the behaviour equations concerning capital accumulation. With respect to investment, firms that are constrained by lack of demand behave differently from firms that are constrained by lack of equipment, even though the difference is not absolutely clearcut because of expectations: most firms feel that they may in the future experience lack of demand as well as lack of equipment.

It is too simple, but illuminating, to consider that the investment of firms is related negatively to their excess capacity in sectors that are in the Keynesian situation whereas it is related positively to profit margins in sectors that are in the classical situation. The respective roles of average excess capacity and average profit margin then depend on the frequencies P_K and P_C.

(2) Considering the simple argument aimed at showing that classical unemployment should soon vanish if it ever occurs, we are led to raise two questions that seem to be particularly relevant, beyond the one concerning the lag in the building of new capacities. Will not the rise of prices lead to a rise in wages, which will wipe out the increase in profit margins? Will not the rise of prices depress demand, hence profitability?

In these times of rapid inflation we know that changes in prices and changes in wages are intimately related. It would be quite inappropriate, when considering the impact of the first ones, to neglect the induced changes in wages, which counteract them to a large extent. But one must also recognise that they do not counteract them fully. Econometric studies on the short-term fluctuations of wages and prices show that a price rise has a durable depressing impact on the real wage rate, hence a positive impact on profit margins if it is due to buyers' competition in a sellers' market.[2]

The induced increase of nominal wages, however, makes the sensitivity of profit margins to excess demand for goods still less strong than it appears to be at first. One moreover knows, again from econometric studies, that this sensitivity is weak in manufacturing, not zero as proponents of the strict cost-plus theory claim, but small.

(3) Price rises have a depressing effect on aggregate demand for goods, because of real wealth effects and because the marginal propensity to spend is higher on real wages than on real profits. This is a reason for the reduction of the proportion of sectors that experience classical unemployment, since such unemployment is simultaneous with an excess demand for goods. This reason may be stronger and operate faster than the induced increase of productive capacities.

[1] Bent Hansen, 'Excess Demand, Unemployment, Vacancies, and Wages', *Quarterly Journal of Economics* (February 1970).

[2] Econometric studies also show that a rise of nominal wages does increase real wages because the induced rise of prices does not fully compensate it. These results contradict Keynes' doubts as to the possibility of exogenous actions on the real wage rate.

But putting this depressing effect in the forefront suggests that, when classical unemployment spontaneously tends to vanish, it ends up in Keynesian unemployment rather than in full employment. In other words, a situation in which lack of profitability has resulted in an insufficient building of new capacities may manifest itself after a while more by a lack of demand than by a lack of capacities.

IV SOME CONCLUSIONS

Looking at the rationing of employment that involuntary unemployment means, this paper has tried to show why some recent theoretical developments provide a new vision of the major and essential contribution of J. M. Keynes: analysis of involuntary unemployment should first concentrate on analysis of the aggregate demand for goods. These recent developments enrich our understandings of various aspects of the phenomenon; new considerations are brought in and naturally raise opposition because they are unfamiliar and probably not yet placed in the proper perspective.

Forty years ago many economists were finding it difficult to accept the Keynesian theory because they were slow to understand that stabilising factors, on which they relied for the restoration of full employment and whose existence was not disproved, could not act quickly enough. They were slow to understand that a theory of the short-term general equilibrium was needed and that Keynes had presented such a theory, an appropriate one moreover. Similarly today, it may very well be that the classical aspect of involuntary unemployment is not negligible but that we find it difficult to reconsider our earlier theories and to recognise how slow-acting are the stabilising factors that come into play when capacities are insufficient.[1]

APPENDIX

Let us consider

$$\bar{y}_i - \beta_i L_i = e + sx_i \tag{1}$$

$$d_i - \beta_i L_i = \epsilon + \sigma\xi_i \tag{2}$$

$$d_i - \bar{y}_i = \epsilon - e + \sigma\xi_i - sx_i \tag{3}$$

in which x_i and ξ_i are distributed independently from one another with respective cumulative distribution function $F(x)$ and $\Phi(\xi)$.

To avoid complications it will be assumed here that these two distributions

---

[1] This is the reflection I am tempted to make when considering the review article 'Malinvaud on Keynes', by R. F. Kahn, *Cambridge Journal of Economics* (December 1977).

are absolutely continuous with densities $f(x)$ and $\phi(\xi)$. Strictly speaking, such an hypothesis requires that we deal with probabilities rather than with frequencies in a finite population. But considering probabilities and expected values rather than frequencies and observed values implies no real loss of significance as long as the population size n is large.

1. *Probability of the Keynesian situation*

This may occur in two ways. It may be that:

$$d_i < \beta_i L_i < \bar{y}_i \tag{4}$$

or equivalently:

$$\epsilon + \sigma\xi_i < 0 < e + sx_i \tag{5}$$

(Since the distributions are absolutely continuous we need not consider cases in which equalities hold.)

The event defined by (5) has probability:

$$\Phi\left(-\frac{\epsilon}{\sigma}\right)\left[1 - F\left(-\frac{e}{s}\right)\right] \tag{6}$$

It may also be that

$$d_i < \bar{y}_i < \beta_i L_i \tag{7}$$

or equivalently:

$$\epsilon - e + \sigma\xi_i - sx_i < 0 \quad e + sx_i < 0 \tag{8}$$

This event has probability:

$$\int_{-\infty}^{-\frac{e}{s}} \Phi\left(\frac{e - \epsilon + sx}{\sigma}\right) f(x)\, dx \tag{9}$$

Thus P_K is the sum of (6) and (9):

$$P_K = \Phi\left(\frac{-\epsilon}{\sigma}\right)\left[1 - F\left(\frac{-e}{s}\right)\right] + \int_{-\infty}^{-\frac{e}{s}} \Phi\left(\frac{e - \epsilon + sx}{\sigma}\right) f(x)\, dx \tag{10}$$

From this formula we easily derive:

$$\frac{\partial P_K}{\partial e} = \frac{1}{\sigma}\int_{-\infty}^{-\frac{e}{s}} \varphi\left(\frac{e - \epsilon + sx}{\sigma}\right) f(x)\, dx \tag{11}$$

$$\frac{\partial P_K}{\partial \epsilon} = \frac{-1}{\sigma}\left\{\varphi\left(\frac{-\epsilon}{\sigma}\right)\left[1 - F\left(\frac{-e}{s}\right)\right] + \int_{-\infty}^{-\frac{e}{s}} \varphi\left(\frac{e - \epsilon + sx}{\sigma}\right) f(x)\, dx\right\} \tag{12}$$

The right-hand side in (11) is clearly non-negative since φ and f are non-negative. Similarly the multiplier of $-1/\sigma$ in (12) is non-negative because it would be the expected value of $\varphi(e - \epsilon + sx/\sigma)$ if x were distributed according to f(x) for $x < -e/s$ and with the probability $1 - F(-e/s)$ for $x = -e/s$. The probability P_K is increasing with e and decreasing with ϵ.

We also find:

$$\frac{\partial P_K}{\partial s} = \frac{1}{\sigma} \int_{-\infty}^{\frac{-e}{s}} x\varphi \left(\frac{e - \epsilon + sx}{\sigma}\right) f(x) \, dx \tag{13}$$

$$\frac{\partial P_K}{\partial \sigma} = \frac{1}{\sigma^2} \left\{ \epsilon\varphi \left(\frac{-\epsilon}{\sigma}\right) \left[1 - F \left(\frac{-e}{s}\right)\right] - \right.$$

$$\left. \int_{-\infty}^{\frac{-e}{s}} (e - \epsilon + sx) \, \varphi \left(\frac{e - \epsilon + sx}{\sigma}\right) f(x) \, dx \right\} \tag{14}$$

In order to discuss the signs of this derivative it is convenient to consider the case in which φ and f are symmetrical around zero. Then, if $e = \epsilon$, the sum in the right-hand side of (13) is negative because it is negative for $e > 0$, it is a decreasing function of e for $e < 0$ and it would be equal to zero for $e = -\infty$. *A fortiori* this sum is negative if $e > \epsilon$ because then extra weight is given to negative values of x. Hence, we conclude that P_K is a decreasing function of s, except perhaps if $\epsilon - e$ is positive and large enough.

The derivative (14) of P_K with respect to σ may also be written as:

$$\frac{\partial P_K}{\partial \sigma} = \frac{\epsilon}{\sigma^2} \varphi \left(\frac{-\epsilon}{\sigma}\right) \left[1 - F \left(\frac{-e}{s}\right)\right]$$

$$- \frac{1}{s} \int_{-\infty}^{\frac{-\epsilon}{\sigma}} \xi f \left(\frac{\epsilon - e + \sigma\xi}{s}\right) \varphi(\xi) \, d\xi \tag{15}$$

The first term has the sign of ϵ and the sum of the second term is negative, except perhaps if $e - \epsilon$ is positive and large enough. Hence P_K is an increasing function of σ in a neighbourhood of the Walrasian equilibrium ($e = \epsilon = 0$). It is also an increasing function if $\epsilon > 0$ and $\epsilon > e$.

These results concerning P_K may of course be directly transposed to P_C by interchanging e, s, F, f respectively with ϵ, σ, Φ, φ.

2. *The unemployment rate*

Total unemployment is the sum of unemployment in those sectors that are in the Keynesian situation with those that are in the classical situation. We shall write the unemployment rate u as:

$$u = u_K + u_C \tag{16}$$

To compute each one of these two terms we shall work out the formulae for the case in which:

$$\beta_i = \beta \quad L_i = \frac{L}{n} \tag{17}$$

But it is clear that the same formulae apply whenever (β_i, L_i) is distributed independently of (x_i, ξ_i).

Unemployment coming from sectors in the Keynesian situation, $u_K L$, is the division by β of the sum of the discrepancies $\beta_i L_i - d_i = -\epsilon - \sigma\xi_i$. We shall consider again the two cases (5) and (8). It will then be convenient to write:

$$\beta u_K L = n\gamma \text{ (5)} + n\gamma \text{ (8)} \tag{18}$$

It will also be convenient to introduce the new functions

$$G(x) = \int_{-\infty}^{x} zf(z)\, dz \quad \Psi(\xi) = \int_{-\infty}^{\xi} \zeta\varphi(\zeta)\, d\zeta \tag{19}$$

The expected contribution γ (5) of the discrepancies $-\epsilon - \sigma\xi_i$ when (5) holds is easily found:

$$\gamma \text{ (5)} = \left[-\epsilon\Phi\left(\frac{-\epsilon}{\sigma}\right) - \sigma\psi\left(\frac{-\epsilon}{\sigma}\right) \right] \left[1 - F\left(\frac{-e}{s}\right) \right] \tag{20}$$

which may also be written as

$$\gamma \text{ (5)} = \Omega\left(\frac{-\epsilon}{\sigma}\right) \left[1 - F\left(\frac{-e}{s}\right) \right] \tag{21}$$

with the definition:

$$\Omega(\xi) = -\epsilon\Phi(\xi) - \sigma\Psi(\xi) \tag{22}$$

Similarly the expected contribution γ (8) is:

$$\gamma(8) = \int_{-\infty}^{-\frac{e}{s}} \Omega\left(\frac{e - \epsilon + sx}{\sigma}\right) f(x)\, dx \tag{23}$$

It is not useful to write the long formula that would give u from (16), (18), (21), (23) and two other equations transposing (21) and (23). But we can consider the derivatives, writing y^0/n for $\beta L/n$:

$$\frac{y^0}{n} \cdot \frac{\partial^u K}{\partial e} = \frac{\partial}{\partial e} \left[\gamma(5) + \gamma(8)\right] \tag{24}$$

This is easily computed, when account is taken of

$$\frac{d\Omega}{d\xi} = -(\epsilon + \sigma\xi)\varphi(\xi) \tag{25}$$

One finds

$$\frac{y^0}{n} \cdot \frac{\partial^u K}{\partial e} = \frac{-1}{s\sigma} \int_{-\infty}^{0} t\varphi\left(\frac{t-\epsilon}{\sigma}\right) f\left(\frac{t-e}{s}\right) dt \tag{26}$$

Let us denote the right-hand member as T and note its symmetry. We can write:

$$\frac{y^0}{n} \cdot \frac{\partial u_K}{\partial e} = T = \frac{y^0}{n} \cdot \frac{\partial u_C}{\partial \epsilon} \tag{27}$$

Derivation of $\gamma(5) + \gamma(8)$ with respect to ϵ leads to:

$$\frac{y^0}{n} \cdot \frac{\partial u_K}{\partial \epsilon} = -\Phi\left(\frac{-\epsilon}{\sigma}\right)\left[1 - F\left(\frac{-e}{s}\right)\right] - \int_{-\infty}^{\frac{-e}{s}} \Phi\left(\frac{e-\epsilon+sx}{\sigma}\right) f(x)\, dx - T \tag{28}$$

Comparison with (10) and (27) leads to the simple formula:

$$\frac{y^0}{n} \cdot \frac{\partial u}{\partial \epsilon} = -P_K \tag{29}$$

An increase in the average excess demand which is equal to 1 per cent of full employment output decreases the unemployment rate by P_K per cent, as if it concerned only those sectors experiencing Keynesian unemployment. In other words the proof shows that only infinitely small effects follow from the fact that some sectors will shift from one situation to another.

Derivation of $\gamma(5) + \gamma(8)$ with respect to s similarly leads to:

$$\frac{y^0}{n} \cdot \frac{\partial u_K}{\partial s} = -\frac{eT + W}{s} \tag{30}$$

where by definition:

$$W = \frac{1}{s\sigma} \int_{-\infty}^{0} t^2 \varphi\left(\frac{t-\epsilon}{\sigma}\right) f\left(\frac{t-e}{s}\right) dt \tag{31}$$

Hence

$$\frac{y^0}{n} \cdot \frac{\partial u_G}{\partial \sigma} = -\frac{\epsilon T + W}{\sigma} \tag{32}$$

But this last expression appears, with an opposite sign, in the derivation of $\gamma(5) + \gamma(8)$ with respect to σ so that

$$\frac{y^0}{n} \cdot \frac{\partial u}{\partial \sigma} = -\Psi\left(\frac{-\epsilon}{\sigma}\right)\left[1 - F\left(\frac{-e}{s}\right)\right] - \int_{-\infty}^{\frac{-e}{s}} \Psi\left(\frac{e-\epsilon+sx}{\sigma}\right) f(x)\, dx \tag{33}$$

Now, equation (19) shows that $\Psi(\xi)$ is non-positive if the distribution Φ has a zero mean. But the right-hand side of (33) would be the expected value of $-\Psi(e - \epsilon + sx/\sigma)$ if x were distributed according to f(x) for $x < -e/s$ and with the probability $1 - F(-e/s)$ for $x = -e/s$. Hence u is a non-decreasing function of σ. Moreover, the derivative $\partial u/\partial\sigma$ would be maximum if a probability 1 were given to the maximum value of $-\Psi(\xi)$, which is achieved for $\xi = 0$ and is equal to half the mean absolute deviation of the ξ_i.

$$\frac{y^0}{n} \cdot \frac{\partial u}{\partial \sigma} \leqq -\Psi(0) \tag{34}$$

The maximum is achieved when $\epsilon = 0$ and $F(-e/s) = 0$.

3. *Impact of an increase of the real wage rate*

To avoid useless complications in notation let us write the equations (18) and (19) of the main text as:

$$ne = \bar{y}(w) - \beta L(w) \tag{35}$$

$$n\epsilon = d(y, w) - \beta L(w) \tag{36}$$

Let us also consider the equation:

$$y = (1 - u)\,\beta L(w) \tag{37}$$

We can write, using (29) and its transposed:

$$\beta L.\,\delta u = -P_C\,.\,n\delta e - P_K\,.\,n\delta\epsilon \tag{38}$$

Equations (35) to (37) imply:

$$n\delta e = (\bar{y}' - \beta L')\,\delta w \tag{39}$$

$$n\delta\epsilon = (d'_w - \beta L')\,\delta w + d'_y\delta y \tag{40}$$

$$n\delta\epsilon = \{\,d'_w - [1 - (1 - u)\,d'_y]\,\beta L'\}\,\delta w - \beta L d'_y \delta u \tag{41}$$

Hence

$$\beta L(1 - P'_K\,d'_y)\,\frac{\partial u}{\partial w} = [1 - (1 - u)\,d'_y P_K]\beta L' \tag{42}$$

$$- (P_K\,d'_w + P_C\bar{y}' + P_I\beta L')$$

Equation (25) of the main text directly follows because, at a Walrasian equilibrium $u = 0$, $\beta L = \bar{y} = d$, hence

$$\frac{wL'}{L} = \eta_L \quad \frac{wd'_w}{\beta L} = \eta_d \quad \frac{w\bar{y}'}{\beta L} = \eta_{\bar{y}} \tag{43}$$

Discussion of Professor Malinvaud's Paper

Lord Kaldor introduced the paper. He believed that it made an important contribution to the theory of involuntary unemployment. It was important for many reasons, only one of which was that unemployment was largely involuntary. After the discussion of Professor Hines' paper, he was glad to find that Professor Malinvaud thought the distinction between voluntary and involuntary unemployment important. There was a growing tendency to think that all unemployment was voluntary, and a consequence of the fact that labour had 'priced itself out of the market'. Professor Malinvaud described situations where there was involuntary unemployment, and his approach was a novel one with great potential. The paper displayed Professor Malinvaud's usual elegance, precision and economy of assumptions. Unlike most writers, Professor Malinvaud explicitly said that involuntary unemployment was either Keynesian, as a result of insufficient demand, or classical (or Marxian), due to an insufficiency of work places or equipment.

Lord Kaldor began by looking at Professor Malinvaud's examples. The economy was constrained by one of three factors, namely, demand (d), capacity ($\bar{y}$) or the effective labour force (βL). βL represented labour capacity, or output capacity seen from the labour side. This distinction was similar to the one Harrod made between the warranted and natural rates of growth. In Walrasian equilibrium the three variables were equal.

$$d = \bar{y} = \beta L.$$

There were various possibilities and here he would interpret what he thought Professor Malinvaud meant to convey. There were in fact two kinds of Keynesian situation and two kinds of classical situation. First, one had the normal Keynesian situation:

$$d < \beta L < \bar{y}$$

Demand was the effective constraint, but output capacity was greater than the labour force. The solution here was to remove the demand constraint on employment and thereby bring about a fuller use of capacity.

Second, one had the abnormal Keynesian situation of demand inflation, which was unlike that considered in the *General Theory* (though explicitly allowed for in exceptional cases). This might arise from excessive exports, excessive investment or excessive government expenditure. Here the labour force was *less* than demand. If one ignored guest workers, this had been the situation in the Federal German Republic at various points since 1950. This was a Keynesian situation of demand inflation or 'overfull employment'. There would be inflation unless one permitted the entry of foreign labour.

There were also two kinds of Marxian (or classical) unemployment. First, there was the normal Marxian situation of the reserve army. Here: $\beta L > \bar{y} \geqslant d$.

In other words, there was unemployment because demand was too small to employ the whole labour force. Excessive accumulation led to a Marxian crisis situation. This second Marxian situation can be characterised by

$$\bar{y} \geqslant d > \beta L.$$

In other words, output capacity, though not necessarily smaller (or greater) than demand, tended to exceed the available labour force, thereby bidding up wages.

Professor Malinvaud's conclusions were as follows. Short-run exogenous changes had an effect on quantities rather than prices, and therefore led to rationing of some kind. With involuntary unemployment, workers were rationed for jobs. With $\bar{y}$ greater than d, there was excess capacity so that sellers were rationed. If there was excess demand for goods as in the second Keynesian situation, or as in the second Marxian situation, then buyers were rationed.

Professor Malinvaud considered five endogenous variables. The labour force was to some extent a function of the real wage, with the first differential, w' positive; a higher real wage led to a bigger supply of labour. It was open to argument whether w' was large or small. The labour force might be highly responsive or it might not. $\bar{y}$, output capacity, was also a function of real wages but here $\bar{y}'$ was negative. An increase in real wages would lead to a reduction in capacity because less labour was now combined with each item of capital, i.e. there was a rise in the marginal costs curve. The magnitude of this effect depended on whether the short-run cost curve was of a reverse-L type, or a gently increasing function (as in Marshall) β (which stood for productivity) was a function of actual income, y, with β positive. Productivity was thus assumed to be positively correlated with income or employment. Unemployment was equal to $1 - y$ (actual output) divided by the labour potential, βL.

There were four exogenous variables. One of these was the wage rate, though Lord Kaldor found it hard to know what Professor Malinvaud meant by this. Normally real wages were an endogenous factor depending on productivity etc. He could see that the real wage could be exogenous if there were a real supply price of labour, with w' being very large' i.e. when the response of the labour supply to a change in real wages was large. However, he did not believe this to be a realistic assumption. From the real wage one could calculate residual consumption per worker.

Keynesian and classical unemployment had different responses. In the Keynesian situation an increase in real wages would reduce unemployment. In the classical situation, a rise in real wages, if anything, would increase it. If there were an increase in demand through government expenditure (g) or tax changes (t) these were treated as exogenous factors. There would be no effect on unemployment if unemployment was classical, because $\bar{y}$ governed employment and was not changed by changes in g or t.

Professor Malinvaud went on to break down his macroeconomic equations into microeconomic components. He obtained totals from what happened in individual sectors, whether industries or regions, using a broad disaggregation

into two or three sectors, or a very fine one. To do this Professor Malinvaud
adds a suffix i to variables, where i ranged from 1 to n. Lord Kaldor thought
that a dual designation was needed, with two kinds of suffix, i and j, where j
referred to the region and i to the industry.

There were two basic macroeconomic equations for overall unemployment.
First, $y_i - \beta L_i$ could be negative. These elements were shown as the sum of
two components: first, of e, which was the mean value of the difference for
all sectors, and second, of s, which was the deviation of a particular sector
from the mean. In any one sector, unemployment represented the difference
between average unemployment for the economy and that obtaining in the
sector. This dealt with chemical unemployment.

For Keynesian unemployment, when $d_i - \beta_i L_i$ was negative Professor
Malinvaud used Greek rather than Latin symbols so that one had ϵ for e, and
ξ for s.

Professor Malinvaud then showed how the deviations were important and
how a reduction in deviations of one kind (say, between ξ and ϵ) affected the
inequalities of the other kind (say, between s and e).

This kind of analysis showed the situation in the economy in terms of the
ratio between the proportion of sectors suffering from Keynesian unemployment P_K, and those suffering from classical unemployment P_C. Unemployment was unlikely to be totally Keynesian or totally classical.

Lord Kaldor was not quite clear what Professor Malinvaud meant by the
'economy', so he was not clear exactly what he meant by 'sectors' either.   .
One interpretation would be to treat as the 'economy' the whole world, which
was a non-trading region (since there was so far no trade with the moon or the
planets). Another approach would be thinking of countries like France or
Germany, or regions like the EEC, as a single 'economy'. There were all sorts
of possibilities. If one took the world as a whole, one could allow for very
different proportions between the sectors with Keynesian and classical
unemployment in different countries. If one was considering an individual
country, one would have to introduce export demand as a distinct element
in the model.

Professor Malinvaud had a demand function where demand was a function
of employment. In other words, this was a kind of consumption function.
However, he had no explicit investment function. One would introduce such
a relationship where investment was a function of a change in aggregate
demand rather than aggregate demand itself. Professor Malinvaud also had the
price level in money terms as exogenous, though variable. Lord Kaldor
wondered how both the real wage and the price level could be treated as
exogenous *if* β (output per head) was also given. There was also government
expenditure and taxation.

These were the elements, but one needed exports as well. Exports behaved
similarly to investment and one should treat them in the same way. One also
needed imports, and a marginal propensity to import which was normally
taken as a linear function of income. In other words $M = mY$. Once one had
gone this far, other conditions followed. If there were unemployment, one

needed to know the nature of the disequilibrium. The use of the word disequilibrium suggested something temporary with a movement towards its elimination, even if only a slow one. In practice, some unemployment would be eliminated, but perhaps not all. For example, one could allow for different kinds of competitive situation. Walrasian equilibrium assumed perfect competition. Then one could say the situation would tend towards equilibrium. However, if one had imperfect competition, the natural consequence of free entry would be that βL was less than $\bar{y}$. This was the situation we normally had in mind when we used the word 'oligopoly' in a broad sense, which usually involved the existence of excess capacity in 'equilibrium'. It paid firms to maintain reserve capacity for various reasons. Even in 'polypoly', as he had shown in a paper in 1935, and as R. G. Lipsey had shown in an article in the *Economic Journal* for September 1978, one had decreasing costs in equilibrium with free entry because each firm reduced its output with the arrival of every new competitor, and this process went on until it was brought to a halt owing to a rise in costs (a fall in β, which must always occur when output fell below some minimum level). This was the meaning of the assertion that competition tended to push firms towards their break-even point, and this implied the existence of excess capacity in equilibrium. There was therefore no natural trend towards the elimination of excess capacity and this resulted from the nature of competition.

There were some sectors where there was perfect competition, as with raw materials. Here the world had a central market which set the prices for both sellers and buyers over a wide area. (This was because in a highly organised central market, the margins absorbed by intermediaries [the 'traders'] were very small. It was therefore possible both for sellers to obtain a higher price and for buyers to pay a lower price than if they traded in local markets.) One could consequently extend the model to include natural resources as well as capital in $\bar{y}$. As Walras had shown, economic progress involved the continual substitution of capital for natural resources resulting from technical progress, thereby offsetting the short-run condition of diminishing returns due to the scarcity of land.

Professor Malinvaud took no account of the interdependence of demand between sectors. If one allowed $\bar{y}$ to represent the natural resource constraint in the primary sector, one could have classical unemployment there and Keynesian unemployment in the manufacturing sector. But the introduction of international trade had important implications. One could then have, not two but three kinds of unemployment. First, aggregate demand might be too small. Second, there might be a shortage of capacity. Third, there might be a balance of payments constraint. This introduced a situation which could not be cured by simple Keynesian techniques of stimulating demand. If one called the classical situation one of structural unemployment, then here one had a kind of quasi-structural unemployment. He would name this kind of unemployment after List (who first drew attention to it) and call it Listian unemployment. It was very different from either Marxian or Keynesian unemployment.

To complete the model, Lord Kaldor introduced a further equation. Here W represented world trade, either the sum of all imports or of all exports, as follows:

$$W = \sum_{1}^{\mu} M, j = 1 \ldots$$

Of course, each country would not necessarily be in balance of payments equilibrium. One therefore had $\overline{M}$ for actual or maximum feasible imports (as governed by the balance of payments) and M^* for optimal imports (corresponding to full employment). The difference between actual and optimal imports could be zero or negative. One then had a final equation:

$$\overline{M}j - M_j^* = \alpha + \beta z$$

where α and β stood respectively for the mean level of the shortfall of imports and of its dispersion. For any particular region the shortfall of $\overline{M}$ over M^* was the measure of Listian unemployment. This had difficult policy implications in that, if one assumed equilibrium in the balance of payments for each country, the shortfall of the countries with Listian unemployment depended on the sum of the $M^{*'}$ of the countries which had *no* Listian unemployment, since they imported all they wished to import. World employment could be raised by reducing the disparities between a region's share of world trade, Wj, and its imports at full employment, M_j^*

Professor Modigliani agreed with Lord Kaldor that Professor Malinvaud's paper was very pleasant reading because of its clarity, precision and stimulative capacity. Perhaps it was most useful in the way that it dealt so systematically with the subject. Because of shortage of time, he would concentrate on the shortcomings of the paper, though again emphasising how excellent he thought it was.

The main shortcoming, in his view, was an inadequate treatment of so-called classical unemployment and a resulting failure to appreciate its scope and seriousness. Malinvaud seemed to think that as long as demand was there, this type of unemployment would take care of itself in short order, because excess demand would cause the price of labour to increase relative to wages and other prices. This response, by increasing profit margins and total profits, would produce both the incentive to, and the means for, an expansion of capacity, thus leading to a gradual elimination of the unemployment. One might note in passing that under oligopolistic market structures of the type modelled by Sylos-Labini and Bain, capacity could be expanded while price was kept constant — in order not to attract new entrants — by straining existing plant, lengthening delivery times or even rationing.

But one must be aware of the fallacy of composition: what worked for a single market might not work for the entire economy. It was well known, for instance, that lack of demand was economy-wide, the process of correction was much more complex and uncertain since it must pass through an increase in real money supply.

Two cases of classical unemployment which were economy-wide and did not tend to be self-liquidating, were mentioned. One case occurred when powerful unions (or other forces) fixed the real wage which might be enforced through formal indexation, as in the case of Italy, or through informal indexation. If aggregate supply and, correspondingly, aggregate demand for labour, was a decreasing function of the real wage, a given real wage might be too high for full employment. This could happen because costs and/or the mark-up were an increasing function of output. The resulting unemployment would be of the classical variety because an increase in aggregate money demand would increase prices and wages but not employment (at least not permanently). In an open economy the same result would occur, even if the aggregate supply function were horizontal, so long as the aggregate demand, domestic and foreign, for the domestic output was a decreasing function of domestic prices relative to foreign prices. In this case the real wage and resulting real unit cost set a limit to the aggregate amount of employment that was consistent with current account balance. An expansion of nominal demand could expand employment only at the cost of an unsustainable deficit which must terminate through a curtailment of nominal demand or through devaluation and inflation. Aggregate demand policies could raise employment only in so far as wages lagged behind prices and then only through a process of maintained (and possibly accelerating) inflation. In addition, a significant rise in the real wage, not justified by technological progress, might make it hard to maintain aggregate demand and might pave the way for rising unemployment by sapping the incentive to invest and thus expand, or even maintain, the stock of capital.

It might be argued that one could accommodate a higher real wage without squeezing profits through higher capital intensity, resulting in greater labour productivity. But in this case there would tend to be insufficient national saving to provide the entire labour force with the capital needed. Classical unemployment would then take on the appearance of an aggregate lack of capital. This situation was similar to the second case of classical unemployment that had long been known to characterise some underdeveloped countries. Here one frequently found a dual economy. One sector had high capital intensity and relatively high wages; but lack of capital forced the rest of the population to be employed, or underemployed, in the traditional sector at low wages.

He had no doubt that these and related cases of classical unemployment could be worked into Professor Malinvaud's analysis by clarifying the distinctions between short- and long-run adjustments and between failures in individual markets and failures that were economy-wide in nature.

Professor Kolm wanted to comment on three important points in Professor Malinvaud's model. First, the use of the adjective 'Marxian' for the case where production was limited by capital deserved comment. It was not clear that this was Marx's model for normal periods, and it was certain that it was not his model for crises, where he considered that production was limited by effective demand. Professor Malinvaud attributed to Marx one case, limitation by capital. Lord Kaldor had commented that Marx considered two cases: limitation by capital and limitation by demand. In fact, all three cases were discussed by Marx, since he also considered the case where all the labour force was employed. There, Marx said, wages tended to rise and workers to reproduce *à la* Malthus. Second, with most profits being directly invested as retained earnings, and with financial constraints on firms, the propensity to spend out of profits (on capital and consumption goods) might be bigger than the propensity to spend out of wages. This was contrary to the traditional view. Third, the output elasticity of labour productivity might not be as small as was suggested. It was, for instance, 2/3 with an elasticity of output for employment of 3, a standard order of magnitude.

Professor Hines saw the paper as a continuation of Professor Malinvaud's earlier work. He would like to see clarification of the time frame within which Professor Malinvaud was working, and some indication of policy implications.

Professor Hines said that if one had n sectors — he would leave open how one defined them — the number with Keynesian or classical unemployment could vary. There were then two problems. First, there was no explanation of what caused a change in the economy from a proponderance of one type of régime to the other. In the short-run period of the model, was the percentage accounted for by each regime given or was there a theory to account for variation?

One policy implication seemed to be that, given the percentage of sectors operating under each régime, a different mix of policy might be necessary. Perhaps one had a trade-off in the sense that a policy curing Keynesian unemployment would not deal with classical unemployment and *vice versa.*

Sir Austin Robinson was glad Professor Modigliani had introduced the relationship between non-appropriate technology and unemployment. He wanted to ask a question. To an industrial economist like himself, the concept of capacity was a very difficult one. Few firms were perfectly balanced in the sense that one would reach the limit of the capacity of all processes at the same time. The question was therefore how one handled shortages and bottle-necks and the answer was that one brought in imports. A large part of imports in industrialised countries simply reflected shortage of capacity; and shortages were not always of equipment; they could be shortages of skilled labour. Sir Austin was not happy with the tendency ordinarily to treat labour as homogeneous. In most industries there were different levels of skill. For example, in the Cambridge University Press, with which he had been concerned, overall capacity had been much greater than capacity in terms of compositors. Similarly in the building industry one needed certain numbers of people with particular skills before one could take on a contract. A complete model therefore needed to bring in limits due to shortages of skill as well as of equipment. With equipment, the gestation period could vary from a few months to two or three years. With skills the period of training might be much longer. The solutions to shortages and bottlenecks could be very different, according to what caused the limits to capacity.

Professor Henin thought it interesting that Professor Malinvaud stressed problems arising from diversity of structure and of constraints in the economy, showing how the value of the multiplier changed according to the distribution of constraints among sectors. Professor Henin wondered whether the value of the multiplier was not even more directly affected by the distribution of unemployment among the population. For example, it was possible that the marginal propensity to consume of the unemployed was higher than for the rest of the population.

The idea of the balance of payments constraint was important, but he was not sure it could be treated by adding another constraint on the same level as the others. If one had an economic policy decision aimed at achieving external balance like a decrease in government expenditure, or the imposition of import controls, that would alter the configuration of the rationing process.

Professor Holt had noted the parallel between Professor Malinvaud's paper and work by Tobin on a model of unemployment which considered the impact on labour markets of random variation in supply and demand. 'Rationing' seemed to represent a loose end in the paper. Where there was rationing the price mechanism did *not* make the decision, but then who got the job? What took over from the price mechanism? He therefore saw a connection here with his own paper where 'availability' did the 'rationing'. Both he and Professor Malinvaud had started from the classical model. He had tried to use a search/turnover process to take the decisions. The ratio of vacancies to unemployment influenced both jobs and unemployment rates to achieve a balance. Professor Holt said he had found with an indeterminate equilibrium, with a lower wage rate, greater output occurred, and *vice versa*. This resulted from the technical production and labour participation processes.

Professor Timofeev noted that the conference had moved on to important papers of theory and policy which raised terminological issues. He agreed with those who thought that we should concentrate more on real problems, and the real content of the situation rather than concepts and would like to give examples of situations where economists from socialist and western countries had come into greater agreement because of contact with real problems. For example, an economist whom he knew, who worked for the United Nations, had published a book which used the terminology of Keynes, though not the Keynesian theoretical structure. When he looked at estimation of Keynesian concepts, Professor Timofeev was convinced that at the heart of the Keynesian system lay the recognition that free markets did not automatically bring total consumption and total output into harmony. It was therefore important that we should begin to discuss the difficult real-world process of adjustment. Professor Malinvaud thought there were two kinds of involuntary unemployment, one of which was Marxian, with labour capacity greater than output capacity. So, in his own way, Professor Malinvaud showed that capitalism led to the growth of the stock of capital equipment.

Professor Malinvaud claimed that the model gave the basis for practical policy decisions, but ignored important socio-economic relations. It was mainly concerned with the influence of the wage rate, prices, taxes etc. Professor Malinvaud should also look at broader factors. For example, he left aside the movement of labour, where there was currently great discussion.

Marxian economists disagreed with the idea that one could solve unemployment by providing more capital. Mundell had written suggesting that trade unions could achieve nothing. Professor Malinvaud dealt mainly with quantitative factors and not sufficiently with qualitative aspects of the human production factor, for example, training, development and housing conditions. All these affected the quality of the labour supply.

Professor Giersch underlined the fact that in Federal Germany in the 1950s there had been unemployment because of capital shortage. The situation was improved through capital accumulation. Fifteen years later, capital accumulation had overtaken the labour supply so that there was an overadjustment of real wages leading again to unemployment due to capital shortage. Similarly, the kinds of skill mentioned by Sir Austin Robinson were also short.

One of the reasons for unemployment in Western Europe was therefore the fundamental changes in the exchange rate between Europe and the USA, with Europe now an area with higher unit labour costs. This was certainly true of Belgium, Germany, the Netherlands and Switzerland, and probably of Italy. More investment was needed to create jobs, but this required expected profits to be high enough for those who were responsible for autonomous investment. The situation was aggravated because the European countries could no longer imitate the USA. The technological gap had disappeared and European countries had to take care of innovation for themselves and also to bear the costs of innovation. Perhaps the situation was like that in the 1930s where there had been stagnation with a shortage of technical innovation leading to a lack of investment.

On oligopoly, Professor Giersch said one could see firms which, when demand was high, forced customers to queue up for products. There was then a shortage of capacity (and thus of capital) in these firms. The shock of the recent recession had then led to timidity. Those firms had performed best during the recession that had built up customer queues during the previous prosperity. The fact was that managers in monopolistic and oligopolistic firms were not criticised for failing to maximise profits. Satisficing behaviour was quite acceptable. This became important in a period of structural change where the technological gap with the USA had been closed for much of industry and the capital accumulation process represented a bottleneck.

Professor Giersch referred to 'Listian' unemployment. In the 1950s the balance of payments had acted as a constraint on Germany after the Korean boom. At that time Professor Giersch had been working in the OEEC and found that this problem was a result of bottlenecks whose removal required importation. He had, therefore, written an article on the acceleration principle and propensity to import. This seemed to be relevant to the UK now, which ran into balance of payments difficulties whenever the level of demand was high. The problem was comparable to the problems of underdeveloped countries which suffered from structural unemployment of the Marxian kind. It linked up with what Lord Kaldor had said about income elasticities. The UK was perhaps in a position where it could not sustain change because the necessary alteration in relative prices would lead to a rise in profits that was politically unacceptable.

Professor Bergmann had been amused at the course of the discussion. Lavish praise for the paper had been combined with desire to challenge its central point, namely, the problem of differential sectoral demand, with some industries running out of capacity sooner than others. She wondered how real the problem was. It did not appear to have existed in the 1930s, though it did seem to have existed at times in the USA. For example, Charles Schultz had said that in the 1950s there was unemployment for this reason. A problem was that the generation of information led back to unemployment via restrictive measures. Perhaps there had been similar problems in the 1970s. She thought there was a potential problem, and we were likely to run into this. She believed that the way investors decided on investment led to the creation of excess capacity, with each industry behaving as seemed best in its own circumstances. There had been little study of this issue, and if Professor Malinvaud thought it was as important as he implied in his paper, it was necessary to make a detailed analysis, industry by industry.

Professor Bergmann wondered whether there was a gap between the social costs of seeking a job to the individual and the cost of excess capacity. And was there a problem for industry because of this? There had been no discussion of the issue because economists did not like this kind of variable. They were trained not to know how to deal with it. This seemed to raise a problem of how economists should be trained.

Professor Malinvaud began his reply to the discussion by saying that speakers had taken him well beyond what his own contribution would itself have justified. He would concentrate on two main issues. The first was the relation between models like his own or that of Professor Hines and evolution over time. The second was the use of sectoral analysis and what its notation could offer.

Professor Malinvaud said that agents reacted to changes in economic conditions more by adapting quantities than prices, or rather adapting quantities more quickly than prices. An analysis of this adjustments system had been a major contribution of thought and observation in the last decade. One had built a theory in which quantities adapted instantaneously but prices only after a time. This was an oversimplification but it was helpful as a first approximation. (Of course, when one had a financial sector, then for most types of security the rate of interest adjusted quickly.)

Were prices and real wages rigid in the short run? What Lord Kaldor and Professor Modigliani said surprised him because he had considered in his paper for this conference only the short run. In this context, which may be thought of as concerning studies for three to eighteen months at most, the course of the general price level and of the real wage rate were pretty much predetermined. He thought many difficulties in accepting the premises of the new theories revealed a lack of freedom in the modes of thinking and a too strict adherence to classical teaching.

The same comment applied to those who did not want to speak of prices and incomes policies, as if no exogenous action on prices and incomes was feasible. Certainly a prices and incomes policy was possible: one had seen this at work in the UK where it had reduced inflation from 17 per cent to 7 per cent per annum.

However, he accepted that his own paper was particularly inadequate from one point of view. It was necessary to go on working on the dynamics of the economic development processes, and in particular on the process leading from one short-run equilibrium to another. For example, Mr Honkapohja had in a research paper looked at some of these issues. Professor Malinvaud said he also had been working elsewhere on a dynamic process operating on the one hand through changes in prices and wages, on the other hand through capital accumulation, i.e. both investment and savings. This process neglected other changes such as changes in industrial structures or changes in socio-political factors. However, though he had restricted himself to the main economic factors, and felt that in many places the formulation was inadequate, he had realised that looking at such a process one had to face broader issues. In considering equilibrium over time, one needed to bring in all kinds of theoretical issues. In particular, one would have to look again at the theories of economic growth and of business cycles, and to reformulate them.

Professor Malinvaud said he thought it was important to try to give a model with a sectoral breakdown. By a sector he meant an industrial branch in a region, as Lord Kaldor had suggested. It was necessary to start with a model that was very simple compared with reality. The sector was characterised by having production capacity and labour availability, which he had also defined. But the demands addressed to the sectors which also differed, depended on the level of income in the whole economy. So what he had given was something of a caricature. However, he wanted to make this caricature as little deforming as possible in the simplification it made compared with reality. Professor Kolm was right when he said that one could decompose sectors and that the sectors might be very large or very small.

The division of the economy into sectors with classical and with Keynesian unemployment was not given. In part it would result from past macroeconomic development, which he had not introduced; but it also resulted, for example, from the distribution of incomes, the distribution of excess capacity, and so on. So, to Professor Henin he would say that this was a complex phenomenon and that a deeper study in any country would in fact show that each branch was in its own situation.

Professor Henin had also asked about the multiplier and disparities in behavioural relations. In particular he agreed with Professor Henin that the size of the multiplier would depend on the consumption functions of the unemployed and the employed. This was implicitly introduced in the aggregate demand function for goods and services.

8 Structure and Involuntary Unemployment*

Jean-Paul Fitoussi
UNIVERSITE LOUIS PASTEUR, STRASBOURG, FRANCE

and

Nicholas Georgescu-Roegen
UNIVERSITE LOUIS PASTEUR AND VANDERBILT UNIVERSITY, USA

> It is therefore misleading to reason on aggregative equilibrium as if it displayed the factors which initiate change and as if disturbance in the economic system as a whole could arise only from those aggregates.
>
> Joseph A. Schumpeter, *Business Cycles*

I INTRODUCTION: ARITHMOMORPHISM VERSUS DIALECTICS

Involuntary unemployment is a product of the industrial revolution. As a cyclical phenomenon, it existed until roughly the end of the Second World War. Some fluctuations still exist, but they are small and not as regular as during the earlier period dominated by business cycles. Moreover the problem appeared to have been solved by macroeconomic regulation of the Keynesian type. The unemployment which continued during the greater part of this period was considered as the 'full employment level of unemployment'. But the worsening of the phenomenon since the end of the sixties has shown that chronic unemployment remains the most relevant social problem. Hence, though the worsening of unemployment can be pin-pointed in time, its existence is a permanent characteristic of the industrial economic system.

But cyclical unemployment has recently become chronic unemployment.

* This is a revised version of the paper presented to the Conference. The authors wish to thank R. Dos Santos Ferreira for his comments and valuable suggestions concerning an earlier version, and to acknowledge the useful information provided by T. Aldrich Finegan.

The following tables – retracing the series of the low and the high rates of unemployment in the US since 1892[1] emphasise this conclusion.

Year	Low	High	Year	Low	High	Year	Low	High
1892	3.0		1918	1.4		1956	4.2	
1894		18.4	1921		11.7	1958		6.8
1902	3.7		1926	1.6		1960	5.5	
1904		5.4	1933		25.2	1961		6.7
1906	1.7		1944	1.2		1969	3.5	
1908		8.0	1949		5.9	1971		5.9
1913	4.3		1953	2.9		1973	4.9	
1915		8.5	1954		5.6	1975		8.5

	Before 1954	After 1954
Average low	2.5	4.5
Average high	11.9	6.7
Range	9.4	2.2
Average wave length	8.1	4.8

From this series, one can see the striking difference between the oscillation of unemployment before and after 1954, in two periods of industrial change. A fundamental question thus presents itself: what is the cause of this historical change?

The answer we propose in this paper is that both the emergence of unemployment, now and in the past, and its permanence in recent times are due to qualitative structural changes. For this reason we must point out from the outset that to deal with qualitative changes – whether in economics, biology, political sciences, or even astrophysics[2] – one must necessarily resort to the dialectical method. Furthermore, the nature of all actuality is dialectical, and this characteristic is especially pronounced in the case of

[1] The tables were calculated by continuing the series constructed by Lebergott (1964, pp. 512, 522).

[2] The most important notions forced upon us by a continuously changing actuality are dialectical: e.g. workable competition, tastes, long-run, short-run, democracy, good justice, valuable contributions, etc. Species, for example, is a dialectical concept precisely because the species, not the individual, is the vehicle of biological evolution. For the doubting arithmomorphic enthusiast, let us also mention 'a sufficient number of observations', a notion that cannot possibly be chased away from the foundations of probability (Georgescu-. Roegen, 1971).

unemployment.[1] This is why most economists who in the past have tackled the problem of unemployment in a serious way — from J. B. Say, T. R. Malthus, D. Ricardo and Karl Marx to J. A. Schumpeter, A. C. Pigou, G. Myrdall, A. H. Hansen and Lord Keynes — have done so primarily through dialectical reasoning. But in more recent times economists have turned to using purely arithmomorphic models instead — as is now the fashion in modern economics. Undoubtedly, such models play a very important role in all sciences. To use an arithmomorphic simile for verifying already developed dialectical reasoning is an absolutely necessary methodological step (Georgescu-Roegen, 1966, 1971). In economics this methodology was used by none other than the propounder of dialectical economics, Karl Marx, and over years has been used by many others, Lord Keynes in particular.[2] But it is an elementary truth, although we usually prefer to ignore it, that arithmomorphic models cannot incorporate the emergence of the novelty. If they could, nothing would prevent us from printing out the entire evolution of our whole planet until the end of eternity.

[1] The economic specialists who composed the USA President's Committee to Appraise Employment and Unemployment Statistics (1962) began their report by explicitly stating that 'there is no single definition of the labour force or of unemployment which is obviously *the* correct one'. In considering the question 'how shall we define the state of being unemployed?', they simply mentioned one case after another to prove that the concept slides into its opposite through an inextricable dialectical penumbra. To cite here only two illustrations: There is, first, the case of the unemployable (another dialectical quality). Second, there are individuals who *might* like to have a job but are not looking for one because they *believe* that they cannot find one. Are they 'unemployed'? And how can we discover who is such a 'discouraged worker'? (Finegan, 1978). Is, for example, a retired professor a discouraged worker because he believes that he could not find any job to his liking?

[2] It may not be superfluous to belabour the evidence. Keynes' *General Theory* contains only one diagram (p. 180), and an extremely elementary one at that. The famous work at the same time abounds in dialectical expressions. One can cite at will: approximate statistical comparisons of incommensurable collections based 'on some broad element of judgement rather than on strict calculations' (p. 39); expectations 'foreseen sufficiently far ahead' (p. 48); existing facts 'known more or less for certain' (p. 147); decisions 'taken as a result of animal spirits . . . , and not as the outcome of a weighted average of quantitative benefits multiplied by quantitative probabilities [but reflecting] the nerves and hysteria and even the digestions and reactions to the weather [of their authors]' (p. 161f). Also, outside some spotty simple algebraic expressions, only the first section of Chapter 20 contains an argument cast in mathematical form, which, symptomatically, Keynes considers superfluous (see also note 9, below). Patinkin (1976, p. 22f), who quotes Keynes' blunt denunciation of the 'symbolic pseudo-mathematical methods', is completely right in his verdict that Keynes' merits lie 'in his creative insights about fundamental problems', not 'in rigor and precision'.

Certainly, if we are interested only in anonymous actions that simply repeat themselves — to which Pareto wanted to confine the domain of economics — mathematical models can be very enlightening. This is no longer true if things do not keep repeating themselves. Pareto's analogy of the navigator who does not need to take account of geology is ill-conceived: a navigator would have to take account of geology if the shores of the oceans changed as often as economic life.

The prevailing unlimited confidence that economists have in arithmomorphic models is responsible for many fallacies and unwarranted claims that still make the rounds. Take the loud claims that disaggregated dynamic economic models are the best blueprints for a development planner. These models cannot explain even purely quantitative growth — as immediately becomes apparent if one tries to see what corresponds in actuality to the paper-and-pencil symbolism (Georgescu-Roegen, 1974).

II UNEMPLOYMENT AND DISEQUILIBRIUM THEORIES: EQUILIBRIUM VERSUS DISEQUILIBRIUM IN THE MARKET PROCESS

Especially in recent times, arithmomorphic models have been the choice of most writers on unemployment. Reference is made to the school of thought that has proposed to study disequilibrium instead of equilibrium. Some of the disequilibrium models have a definite value as similes of some dialectical reasoning — the best achievement in this respect being Keynes's famous model of his *General Theory*. But on occasion the analytical models of disequilibrium that are accompanied by claims of greater penetration involve shortcomings of various natures.[1]

Even those models that would hold water throughout offer only a description of how an economic system may live with market disequilibrium. To explain how this is possible, special rules are thought up so as to bring about the desired result. We will take a closer look at this kind of model in the Appendix to this paper by examining the Analytical Foundations of Disequilibrium Theories. But at this juncture three important shortcomings of the disequilibrium theories deserve unstinted emphasis.

First, the point of departure is a given constellation of prices that remains invariable throughout the period under consideration. 'In the beginning there were the prices', one might say, thinking of the familiar Biblical verse.

Second, no explanation whatsoever is offered of how these prices came

---

[1] See Appendix. Here, as elsewhere in the text, 'disequilibrium model' refers to the kind of model using the fix-price method. In fact such models, as Malinvaud rightly points out, are equilibrium models. They are based on the assumption that quantities react significantly faster than prices. Nevertheless we refer to them as disequilibrium models, because in some sense supply and demand differ in them.

about. As Schumpeter used to say in discussing the possibility of unstable equilibrium, perhaps an angel from the sky called them out.

Third, the disequilibrium theorists have been so concerned with explaining how an economic system can live with a given disequilibrium that they have ended up with a theory which implies that any given disequilibrium must continue forever.

This new development represents a complete *volte-face* from the explanation of the market process propounded by Léon Walras and, in an even more cogent way, by Alfred Marshall. To recall, they taught that, if no exogenous factors intervene to change the preference or the technical parameters, any disequilibrium between demand and supply will ultimately disappear. In a nutshell appropriate for the present discussion, the basic idea is as follows (cf. Patinkin, 1956, p. 37). The Monday markets open with some quantities offered for sale; the quantities have been determined by previous decisions (say, those made on the preceding Saturday). On these markets, some prices will be established by a partly random process that will also take into account the reasons that governed the previous decisions. There is no claim that these prices will clear all the markets. But Marshall's argument (in particular) does not stop with Monday's outcome. The economic process, indeed, continues on Tuesday, with new quantities and newly formed prices. Only by a miraculous coincidence will the Tuesday markets clear completely. But unless we deny to all consumers and producers the ability to learn from past experience, the new configuration of prices and quantities must normally be nearer the equilibrium than that of Monday. Such an adjustment, involving both prices and quantities, will day after day bring the system nearer and nearer its equilibrium defined on the basis of the prevailing economic behaviour. And even though the exact equilibrium may not be reached within a finite duration, the tendency of the system to move toward it is always at work. The only reason why this tendency may be disturbed is the emergence of some innovation in the broadest sense of the term.

In contrast with the neo-classical explanation of the market process, the disequilibrium approach deals only with what happens on Monday and stops there, as if there were no Tuesday, Wednesday, and so on. This, and not the fact that the disequilibrium approach focuses on another element of the market process, is the fundamental difference between the two schools of thought. In the disequilibrium theory, prices are unexplained parameters; they come from the past and completely dominate the market; quantities simply adapt to these fixed prices. Moreover, there is no tâtonnement at all; the adaptation is instantaneous (a one-day affair). This is the basis for the new school's explanation of the chronic unemployment of our own era.

The disequilibrium theory thus emerges as a theory of static disequilibrium, a disequilibrium that perpetuates itself because the Tuesday market is just a repetition of the Monday market. To be sure, some supporters of the disequilibrium theory mention that prices cannot remain constant as time goes by (e.g. Malinvaud, 1977). But if they mean that both prices and quantities adapt themselves even in the absence of any innovations, they must necessarily imply that the market configuration must tend toward equilibrium. Obviously, if this is the case, there can hardly be any claim of a true revolution with respect to the neo-classical teaching, nor even of a Keynesian counter-revolution.

Thus, by introducing the idea that, given time, prices also adjust so as to reduce any excess supply or excess demand, we parry the objection that disequilibrium theories are theories of static disequilibrium. But the price to be paid for this defence is the very relevance of those theories *vis-à-vis* the old equilibrium doctrine.

The proper approach, the most fruitful in economic theory thus far, emerges from Marshall's teachings. This is to start with a system in equilibrium, look for the causes that may throw it into disequilibrium, and study their possible effects. Once this is done, we must try to find out the reactions by which the system tends towards the new equilibrium. For to any disequilibrium there is always a corresponding conceptual equilibrium. Disequilibrium theories simply begin with a certain disequilibrium and end with it.

The only snag in Marshall's teachings on how the system moves toward equilibrium, first through short-run adaptations and later through long-run adaptations, lies in a misinterpretation of his methodology. Many economists came to believe that long-run adaptations to a given disequilibrium always operate and actually bring the system into equilibrium. However, Marshall never taught this inept interpretation of theoretical reasoning in economics; otherwise, he would not have insisted on the irreversibility of the long-run supply curve. Keynes's famous protest against the long-run equilibrium missed the core of the matter. The important thing for the economic process is not that 'in the long run we are all dead' – which is an undeniable fact. What is important is that the proper long-run adaptations (in the sense in which this term is used in economic theory) have little chance to begin working. Short though our lives may be in comparison with the time dimension of the economic process, one disequilibrium comes after another in such rapid sequence that we may seldom witness pure long-run forces at work. Before a new form enters the field, some innovation comes to introduce a new production function. This is particularly true of the modern industrial age – as we shall argue presently.

III UNEMPLOYMENT AND EVOLUTIONARY CHANGE

In a somewhat imprecise way the problem of unemployment may be represented by the following parable. At the great feast provided by nature and prepared by the community, some people are seated at the table and enjoy in varying degrees their meals. Others, however, can find no place at the table and must be content with the usually scanty leftovers. They cannot partake of the ordinary meal, they are told, because they have not contributed in any way to the preparation of the feast. To which they retort that they have tried very hard to do so by offering to work in the kitchen, but that there was no place for them there either. The problem now is to explain how such a situation may have come about.[1]

One possible answer is that there are not enough 'pots and pans' to permit the employment of all would-be workers. This case may be identified with 'overpopulation' in a special sense, namely when the marginal productivity of labour is zero. Obviously marginal pricing cannot work then; other rules for distribution must be adopted that conceal this kind of unemployment. The situation is characteristic of many agrarian economies, where through various institutional arrangements many people can earn a subsistence income greater than their individual contribution to the national product (Georgescu-Roegen, 1960). But the case deserves special attention because it reveals the influence that a continuously growing population, or even a sudden swelling of the labour force with women and youth, can have on industrial unemployment in western countries.

Whereas in the overpopulated agrarian countries the hidden unemployment can be imputed to the extremely low productive capacity per capita, the opposite condition was used by Karl Marx to explain the unavoidable increase in unemployment to such a level that it will ultimately bring about the downfall of capitalism. As he argued, capitalists contribute to a continuous structural change, because they invest a steadily increasing proportion of surplus value in constant capital, that is, in the physical capacity for production (Georgescu-Roegen, 1960a). Marx's implicit assumption was that under capitalism constant capital not only increases (a fact that by itself would rather increase employment), but also becomes continuously more efficient. Better machines replace men — an idea that goes back to Ricardo and to a large extent is perfectly valid.

We owe to Schumpeter, however, a far more refined and more penetrating structural analysis of unemployment under capitalism. As we remember, Schumpeter attributed the phenomenon of general disequilibrium — hence of unemployment — to a steady flow of novelties that arise from within the economic process itself (provided this process is not identified exclusively with what happens on the markets).

Schumpeter's point of departure was that the economic process feeds upon the product of the inventive idle curiosity that constitutes a main character-

---

[1] In what follows we shall ignore the suggestion that some individuals are not entitled to a seat because they have kept moving around the kitchen hoping all the time to find a 'better' job. It cannot be denied that some people remain unemployed because of their 'job-searching', but the phenomenon has only a marginal relevance.

istic of the human species: this is the source of the flow of the inventions of new things or of new ways of doing things. It is incontestable that such inventions have occurred continually but without any regularity, not even a stochastic one. Incontestable also is the fact that ever since the Industrial Revolution they have become far more frequent.

Naturally, not all technical inventions can find an immediate practical application; and those that do are not of equal importance. Schumpeter argued that as unused inventions accumulate over time, some entrepreneur will base his venture on one or another invention that seems to present a greater chance of economic success. Then many others will imitate the initiator(s). A movement of the economic system away from the previous situation will thus be produced by novelty or, as Schumpeter preferred to say, by innovation. Certainly, this movement implies a powerful disturbance, with workers being drawn from the older activities by an increase in new labour demand designed to provide future production. The disequilibrium that occurs during the first stage could be represented by the situation to which Malinvaud (1977) referred as 'repressed inflation'.

But entrepreneurs would not be entrepreneurs if they were not over-enthusiastic about their ventures. In the end, it will emerge in the new markets that the new captains have created a productive capacity too large for the final demand facing it. A large part of the capacity will become idle and unemployment will soar – a delayed result of the novelty that has been incorporated into the economic system.

Now, if this were all, we would expect the system ultimately to reach a new equilibrium. To be sure, that would take a rather long time, because decumulation is a far slower process than accumulation. A pair of shoes may be produced in a day, but we must walk miles on end to decumulate them in the proper sense of the term (Georgescu-Roegen, 1968; 1971; 1974). So, before long, new entrepreneurs embark upon another batch of innovations that have emerged from the continually produced inventions. The story (i.e. the cycle) thus repeats itself. (Needless to recall, Schumpeter did not include only technological novelties among innovations; for our own epoch we must take into consideration the novelties created by new fiscal rules, new economic developments, and new international contacts as well.)

Briefly, it is the steady emergence of novelties, bringing about structural changes, that prevents the economic system of modern times from reaching a Walrasian equilibrium. As a matter of fact, two of the greatest economists have explained the cause and the maintenance of economic disequilibrium by a structural analysis – Marx by referring to the structure of capital investment, and Schumpeter, to the structure altered by the perennial flow of innovations. However, the temper that now prevails in orthodox economics is to regard only work taking the form of mathematical models (the more mathematically complex, the better) as important. Even the structural studies of Marx and Schumpeter are belittled as 'vague and impressionistic', which is the verdict of Baumol (1970).[1,2]

In spite of this verdict, we propose to continue in the same furrow and argue with additional points that the permance of unemployment in this epoch is due to a continuous structural change brought about by novelties. This proposition means not that only one kind of unemployment — structural unemployment — is worth studying, but that at the source of any unemployment one finds structural change. Such an explanation is both particular and universal. Particular, because change always has an area of application. Universal, because evolution results from an ongoing process of change. 'Novelty' is, in effect, multidimensional; it can be expressed by innovation — a change of taste or of technique, the expansion of markets — or by institutional evolution — alteration of fiscal rules, unemployment compensation, the length of the work week. It can also be brought about by the transformation of a country's international relations and new economic developments. In short, it can manifest itself in many areas and cannot by its nature be constrained by a taxonomy. Hence the concept of 'innovation' that we shall consider must be understood in the broadest sense of the term. This sense, we should note, includes also any new measure instituted by the government with the intention of eliminating some undesirable aspect of the prevailing equilibrium, a phenomenon that has become quite frequent during the past forty years or so.

But although we have been inspired by Schumpeter's theory, our position differs from his. This does not mean that we find his theory inadequate. On the contrary, we believe that Schumpeter's theory of business cycles is one of the truly great economic contributions of all time, comparable only with those of Adam Smith, Ricardo and Marx. What we claim is that if Schumpeter arrived at the conclusion that the flow of novelties produces the cyclic fluctuation of unemployment, it was only because the economic reality which he had witnessed was such that the incorporation of novelties into the economic system was a bandwagon phenomenon. As John Theophilus Desaguiliers wrote in 1744, the inventors of the steam engine were not 'philosophers to understand the Reasons or mathematicians enough to calculate the Powers, and to proportion the Parts; [they] . . . luckily by

---

[1] Structural studies being thus *praeoccupatio non grata*, we economists have lost contact with actual phenomena in a dangerous measure. One salient case is the phenomenon of inflation, towards which the prevailing teachings based on a mechanistic description of aggregated coordinates are totally impotent. (For a structural analysis of inflation see Georgescu-Roegen, 1968 and Fitoussi, 1971.)

[2] A different verdict exists, however. A salient illustration is given by Francois Perroux, who insisted in his work on the necessity of a structural analysis of the economic process.

accident found what they sought for'. (Cited by Dickinson, 1963).[1]

This situation has completely changed since the Second World War. Enterprises no longer produce only products in the strict sense; they now produce inventions as well. Inventions no longer have to accumulate until some 'leaders' feel that it is about time to convert an invention into an innovation. The temper of the business world is nowadays geared to producing invention and using innovation as fast as it can get them. We live now by R & D, one of the greatest innovations, whose influence upon the structure of business activity has been recognised by many authors (including Schumpeter himself).

One consequence is that innovations come up now with such dazzling frequency that the economic system is constantly maintained in disequilibrium, with a persistent unemployment.[2] The main reason is familiar. Any successful innovation causes older activities to shrink or completely interrupt their production (since complete decumulation demands an utterly impractical long time under adverse circumstances). This creates what is known as structural unemployment, which in the usual literature is considered to have only marginal importance. We maintain, however, that in our own epoch, most unemployed workers represent structural unemployment. But it is not legitimate to think that macroeconomic disequilibrium and structural disequilibrium are mutually independent. The former can be – and *is*, according to Schumpeter – the consequence of a structural change. Conversely, the impact of macro-disequilibrium acts very selectively, in clearly circumscribed regions of a system of partial markets: decentralised economies are characterised by a system of markets that are not perfectly co-ordinated. Hence the distinction between structural and deficient demand unemployment is not always relevant. Moreover, there are also several aggravating factors that characterise the new structure of the world's economic system.

First, because modern technology requires increasing specialisation, it becomes increasingly difficult for many unemployed people to find new jobs. The just-adopted innovation generally requires new skills, which is responsible for the fact that jobs are begging although chronic unemployment may be high.[3] Unemployment thus lasts longer.

Second, enterprises no longer tend to gather together in a few centres. We do not find only Manchesters or Pittsburghs any more. Unemployed people from one location may find it difficult to know about vacancies in other locations, and even if they know, they may not always find the change of place a convenient solution. Structural unemployment thus meets with still another friction.

---

[1] We may also mention that the inventor of another important energy convertor, the electrical dynamo, was a workman, without any R & D facility.

[2] On the frequency of innovation, see Lebergott (1964).

[3] A survey by *Business Week* revealed that shortages of highly skilled workers are becoming increasingly common (*Business Week*, 5 June 1978).

Third, it is in the nature of the process itself to generate excess capacity (in the physical sense). The plasticity of the structure of demand comes up against the relative rigidity of the structure of production. Hence investors are likely to overreact to any increase in demand regardless of its structural origin. This means not that adaptations in capacity are systematically oversized with regard to the supplementary demand which generates them — the converse may be true — but that the duration of the supplementary demand is generally difficult to evaluate. Nor does this mean that the entrepreneurs are always wrong in their expectations of effective demand. But two factors aggravate the difficulty of forecasting. The first is obviously obsolescence, a phenomenon which has some connection with novelty. The second is competition. Competition is not a state but a process. As a process it often has the effect when the market shrinks of developing excess capacity (Gaffard, 1979). The time horizon of the investment coincides only by chance with that of demand. This problem certainly has some relevance when the optimal scale of new investment is high. Thus, when the automobile industry in the United States was faced in the late 1950s with a sudden increase in demand caused by peoples' sudden desire (a novelty, to be sure), to have a second car in the family, its managers reacted by building a capacity to satisfy that additional demand within a few years. After the temporary excess demand was satisfied, the industry ended up with too large a capacity, for they now must satisfy only the replacement demand and whatever increase may be attributed to the population growth. The result is that, because of technological and financial advantages, the industry now works near capacity during only part of the year.[1] If decumulation were a simple affair, this disequilibrium would vanish quickly.[2]

The tendency of the managers to overinvest may also result in building more than one plant. After the air clears, the superfluous plants have to be closed because of well-known laws of returns to scale of operations.[3]

Fourth, it is by now a well-known fact that one fateful novelty of post-Second World War has been the development of many underdeveloped

---

[1] For the reasons why a firm may choose between two alternatives — to work with a given capacity and vary the working time, or to keep this time constant and vary the capacity used — see Georgescu-Roegen (1971a).

[2] Incidentally, graduate schools in the United States adopted exactly the same policy as the automobile industry when the universities were confronted (around 1960) with the sudden increase in the number of applicants for admission to college. As a result, the greatest difficulties of many graduate schools stem from their present excess capacity (Georgescu-Roegen, 1975).

[3] If one were willing to pay more attention to facts than to mathematico-imaginative endeavours, one could see from the press wires that this case is sufficiently frequent. For example, Bulova Watch, which maintained three plants (two in the United States and one in Switzerland), recently closed its New York plant in order to maintain the operation of the Swiss plant at a profitable level (*The New York Times News Service*).

countries and the spectacular development of others, such as Japan. In most cases, the newly created industries adopted the latest techniques and were far more efficient than the old physical plants in the western world, which, without any possibility of being decumulated, eventually had to close down.[1] The situation in the electronic, apparel and shoes industries is common knowledge.[2] World employment suffered a structural displacement because a great amount of hidden unemployment from formerly non-industrial economies was attracted into new industrial activities operating at a lower real wage-rate, in efficiency terms, than those prevailing in the old advanced economies.

IV STRUCTURAL DISEQUILIBRIUM AND ASYMMETRICAL ADAPTATIONS

We have mentioned so far only what we believe to be the main categories of structural change in the super-industrial era. Even a more extensive study probably could not exhaust all causes. For, as Schumpeter (1939, p. 11) observed, 'it is obvious that the external factors of economic change are so numerous and important, that if we beheld a complete list of them we might be set wondering whether there is anything left in business fluctuations to be accounted for in other ways'. But, also with him, we believe that innovations are the main causes of disequilibrium, whether on the labour market or on other markets. Great novelties have emerged in the economic world since Schumpeter's time, and they are responsible for the change in the western world from wide fluctuations in unemployment to persistent unemployment.

Thus, in a mobile, perpetually changing economy, consumer habits and the industrial pattern alter continuously. Change may be external to the partial system on which one is reasoning, but it is inherent in economic evolution itself: e.g. change of tastes and behaviour, new technologies and new products, and changes in social conventions. These continual structural shocks require that microdecisions be adapted constantly and assure the permanence of market disequilibrium. Certain factors provide the basis for the permanent existence of market disequilibria. They explain why prices and quantities do not have and cannot have an infinite speed of reaction. This is precisely why the adaptive process of the various economic agents becomes lasting and produces redistributive effects (we shall call the dispersion of partial disequilibria around their macroeconomic average 'structural

---

[1] What to do with obsolete plants is a far more important economic problem than it appears from this angle. Take an absolute economic planner. What ought he to do if one day he finds on his desk a blueprint that renders obsolete, say, all existing steel plants, which still have a useful life of some thirty or forty years?

[2] To cite an example for this phenomenon, too: some 700 workers lost their jobs when one Genesco plant in Huntsville, Alabama, closed because of 'outdated facilities and competition from imports' (UPI wire).

disequilibrium'). The first of these factors is the high level of uncertainty in the present world, in which something novel is likely to occur almost every day. The second is the great difficulty, almost impossibility, of knowing what is actually happening in a world which, because of structural novelties, has reached a crushing complexity, and which, in addition, often changes before information reaches the inquiring individual.[1] The third is the friction exercised on the adaptations by several institutional rules which have come into being on the basis of the idea that some price rigidities would help prevent disequilibria associated with novelties.

But if the adaptations of the economic agents were symmetric, structural disequilibrium would not have macroeconomic effects. Now, asymmetry characterises nearly all movements in the economic space, and yet is usually eluded in theoretical representations or reduced to the status of an epiphenomenon. It is, however, the manifestation of a constraint essential for the understanding of economic and social phenomena, i.e. irreversibility. The manifestations of asymmetry are numerous — precisely because they represent the local application of a more general principle — and reflect objective or subjective constraints, but none of them is irrational (Fitoussi, 1979). Asymmetry is in particular the medium through which structural disequilibrium produces its consequences in terms of unemployment and inflation.

The first asymmetry we shall speak of has been evoked in the preceding section. It concerns the pair accumulation-decumulation. For a basic asymmetry governs the domain of material production: while a stock of natural resources can be decumulated as fast as one wishes, this is not true of the stock of industrial equipment. Each kind of equipment has its specific decumulation time. These specific times retard structural changes. It follows that the differential evolution of various sectors, induced by structural disequilibrium, will clash with a countervailing trend; the result of this clash will probably be a worsening of unemployment, since it is reflected in a loss of capital, i.e. abrupt disinvestment. Thus, the delay imposed by decumulation on structural changes is generated by the relative inertia of industrial structures. If one adds to the problem of the physical stability of industrial structures that of the tendency toward stability of organisations, this delay becomes multidimensional. The plasticity of structures thus comes up against an objective obstacle — the internal decumulation delay — and an institutional obstacle. For the structural pattern of an economy itself produces the institutions responsible for maintaining it, i.e. stabilisation policy, development of the public sector, concerted practices and coalitions, pressure groups, etc.

[1] We do not deal with the issue of information because some substantial work has already done (e.g. Phelps *et al.*) so that the imperfection of information provides a theoretical basis for the imperfect flexibility of prices is demonstrated e.g. by Gordon and Hynes (1970).

But asymmetry not only affects the pair accumulation-decumulation, but by way of corollary is reflected in the behaviour of the managers of existing plant. In spite of the fact that for the reasons shown in this paper we maintain that price rigidity is not the cause of persistent unemployment, we do not intend to deny that in the western world some prices are sticky. There are, above all, the institutions that in western countries regulate salaries and wages. Nor do we intend to deny that price rigidity increases the friction of adaptations, that is, it aggravates the duration of the unemployment generated by innovations. A series of substantial papers have concentrated on the relation between price rigidity – especially, of wage-rate rigidity – and unemployment.[1] Some of them are based on a fully choice-theory approach. There is no longer any need, therefore, to invoke the hypothesis of an institutionally determined wage, or monetary illusion, to justify imperfect regulation by the price system.

Hence, the second application of the general asymmetry principle concerns the domain of prices and quantities. Pure adjustment by prices and pure adjustment by quantities delimit a spectrum within which all combinations are possible. In this continuum we hypothesise that the adaptations gravitate closer to prices with regard to upward adjustments, closer to quantities with regard to downward adjustments. These two types of adjustment are in any event simultaneous, since the asymmetry of price movements has for corollary an asymmetry in the opposite direction of movements of quantities. This result may be derived in a number of ways. For example, Galli (1978) argued, on the basis of the existence of production adjustment costs, that the movement of prices relative to that of quantities is greater in the case of an increase in demand than in the case of a decrease. Dieffenbach (1977) derived the same result in combining the Marshallian dynamic with the voluntary exchange hypothesis. The argument implies that one assumes that the elasticity of supply is much greater than the elasticity of demand.

We incline towards another explanation, which is that the asymmetry reflects rather the behaviour of economic agents under the conditions of continuous uncertainty that now prevail in western countries. Between the two possible modes of adaptation to an increased demand – increased prices or increased quantities – a manager will naturally reject that which represents a course difficult to reverse – which is to increase the present capacity or, if

---

[1] Two kinds of approach provide a theoretical basis for this rigidity. The first starts from the Keynesian hypothesis that wage-earners resist a fall in their relative wages and introduce into the utility functions the set of relative wages (e.g. Trevithick, 1976; Annable, 1977). The hypothesis has also been amended to take into account 'the real wage rate resistance' (Hicks, 1974). The second (Azariadis, 1975; Bally, 1974; Gordon 1976) base the relative rigidity of wages on the existence of implicit contracts between employers and employees whereby real wages remain stable in the presence of stochastic fluctuations of demand. But this second approach concludes that unemployment is always voluntary.

this is not fully used, to hire more workers on the basis of the typical conditions of the labour contracts (Fitoussi, 1971, 1974).

That such an asymmetrical behaviour towards the structural changes generated by a novelty necessarily leads to an increase in unemployment is a point which has some roots in Keynes' *General Theory*. But the point may be presented in a framework that is both more general and more precise. We start with the reasonable assumption that for small displacements supply varies proportionally to excess demand. The asymmetry of the managerial behaviour is then translated by the formula

$$\Delta S_i = s_{i, t+1} - s_{i, t} = \lambda_i X_{i, t} \quad i \in [n], \tag{1}$$

where s_i is the supply of commodity G_i, X_i is the excess demand and

$$\lambda_i = k_i + h_i \Delta_i, \quad k_i, h_i > 0, \text{ with} \tag{2}$$

$$\Delta_i = 1 \text{ if } X_i < 0, \Delta_i = 0 \text{ if } X_i > 0. \tag{3}$$

These conditions imply that when price changes, entrepreneurs will not fully adapt to their short-run supply curve, SS^1, because they are not certain about the durability of the change. Instead, they follow a course of adaptation under uncertainty, Ea' if prices increase, and Ea if they decrease. It follows that there is a kink at point E (Figure 8.1).

Hence if p_i is the price of G_i and if we put $Y_i = p_i X_i$ and introduce the notation $F^* = -F$ whenever $F < 0$, then

$$S = \Sigma p_i \Delta s_i = \sum_{1}^{n} k_i Y_i - \Sigma h_j Y_j^*, \tag{4}$$

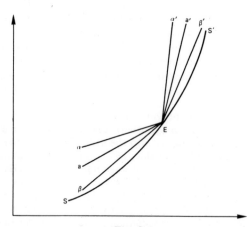

Fig. 8.1

where the last sum extends only over the negative excess demands. This relation shows that the aggregate supply is subject to an influence that can be decomposed into two main components: one related to the aggregate excess demand and one related to the aggregate negative excess demand (Fitoussi, 1971). The implications of this result are highly relevant. Let k and h be the arithmetic means of $[k_i]$ and $[h_j]$, respectively, and let

$$k_i = k + a_i, h_j = h + b_j \tag{5}$$

Relation (4) may be written

$$S = k \sum_1^n Y_i - h\Sigma Y_j^* + \sum_1^n a_i Y_i - \Sigma b_j Y_j^*. \tag{6}$$

Further

$$T = \sum_1^n a_i Y_i - \Sigma b_j Y_j^* = \Sigma a_p Y_p - \Sigma a_q^* Y_q - \Sigma (a_r + b_r) Y_r^* + \Sigma (a_s + b_s)^* Y_s^* \tag{7}$$

and if $a = \text{Max } [a_i]$, $b = \text{Max } [b_j]$, the last relation becomes

$$T = \alpha[a\Sigma Y_p + (a + b)\Sigma Y_s^*] - \beta[a\Sigma Y_q + (a + b)\Sigma Y_r^*], \tag{7a}$$

for some values $\alpha, \beta > 0, \alpha + \beta = 1$,

Now, if a and b are of the second order of importance with respect to k and h — which is a reasonable supposition — the last two terms of relation (6) may be neglected. Hence

$$S \simeq k \sum_1^n Y_i - h\Sigma Y_j^*, \tag{7b}$$

which proves that, if the aggregate excess demand is null, supply decreases approximately in proportion to the aggregate negative excess demand. Relation (7) always leads to (7b) if — as portrayed in Figure 8.1 — the cone $\alpha'E\beta'$ representing all possible Ea′ lines has no common element with $\alpha E\beta$, the cone containing all possible Ea lines.

More generally, relation (7b) signifies that the variations of production undergo a twofold effect: a macroeffect operating in the usual direction, and a structural effect — the effect of the dispersion of microeconomic disequilibria — which generates a slowing down of the growth of output. In any case, an aggravation of the structural disequilibrium is likely to be followed by a decrease of the rate of growth (if the economy has been growing aggregatively). The same relation also proves that an explanation which pays attention only to aggregate equilibrium cannot bring to light important phenomena due to structural changes, i.e. to structural disequilibria.[1]

If we consider this result together with the asymmetrical reaction of wages and prices, the result is that any aggravation of the structural disequilibrium causes an increase both in the level of unemployment and in the inflation rate. We have in this an explanation for the curious and troublesome situation of inflation accompanied by an intolerable level of unemployment (Fitoussi, 1971).[2]

V SUMMARY AND CONCLUSIONS

In this paper we defend the thesis that the cause of economic disequilibria, and hence of the phenomenon of unemployment, is the novelties that punctuate the evolution of the economic process. This is Schumpeter's theory of economic development. But we amended his theory by arguing that in the period following the Second World War some fateful novelties have changed the picture to which he referred. These are, particularly, the momentous innovations of R & D, and the communication established between the labour markets of western nations and those of the developing countries. Novelties that impose structural changes are produced from within the economic process itself. A steady flow of inventions is now produced by R & D and immediately converted into actual innovations. There is no time, therefore, for adaptations to soften the disequilibrium caused by one novelty before the next novelty comes on the scene. Hence the resilient persistence of disequilibrium, and implicitly, of unemployment. The second fateful innovation falls in line with Schumpeter's theory. We need only add that since development of the formerly undeveloped nations is a continuous process, its repercussions on the labour markets of the western nations are also a persistent phenomenon.

Our analysis therefore establishes unemployment as a structural phenomenon. The principle of the explanation is as follows: if it is true that any evolution of effective demand is accompanied or produced by a modification of its structure, transfers between markets and between sectors will characterise economic evolution. There is thus constant pressure towards the modification of production structures which generates the simultaneity

---

[1] Needless to add, in the case of complete Walrasian equilibrium all $X_i = 0$; hence (1) becomes idle. But that formula is not intended for analysing Walrasian equilibrium.

[2] The argument has also been developed by Archibald (1970) and Tobin (1972), but the main objective was to explain the price co-ordinate and the equilibrium component of unemployment. For Archibald, e.g., the problem was to explain short-run movements around the Phillips curve. Our model, however, explains why one may have a simultaneous aggravation of inflation and unemployment.

of the isolated processes of accumulation and decumulation. It is then easy to understand that structural disequilibrium – i.e. the differential evolution of the structures of demand and production – produces unemployment because of the impossible mobility of installed capital and the asymmetry of movements in prices and quantities. Because structural disequilibrium and macroeconomic disequilibrium are linked, the structural/conjunctural dichotomy loses its relevance.

In the main text as well as in the Appendix we take a position against those disequilibrium theories that explain the existence of unemployment today by the fact that there was unemployment the day before and that base their analytical models on the assumption of price rigidity. However, there can be no valid explanation of one phenomenon if we just begin and end with that phenomenon or if we explain its existence today by its existence yesterday. For, as Schumpeter was often heard to protest against the purely monetarist theories of business cycles (which, to recall, argue that one prosperity grows out of the previous depression), such theories boil down to the notion that the cause of business cycles was the overproduction of apples in the Garden of Eden.

To explain a phenomenon, we must reduce it to a proximate cause, to something more general and also more elemental. This does not mean that all phenomena can be so reduced. Many are brute fact. Indeed, a theory is intellectually satisfying only when it rests entirely on brute facts. The inquisitive activity of the human mind, which is responsible for the inventions of all sorts which influence the economic process, is not a brute fact, but can be regarded as a valid proximate cause of innovations.

The great physiologist, Claude Bernard, set up a very interesting rule for deciding whether an explanation or a statement suggesting a relation between two phenomena is sound. The rule is that each valid explanation requires not only some proof but also a counterproof. Following this stringent rule, we would like to mention the counterproof of our thesis. Before the Industrial Revolution paved the way for the capitalist system, in no part of the world did unemployment of the sort prevalent under that system exist. And it did not exist simply because inventions occurred extremely rarely, and even when they occurred they did not always attract the interest of producers. Those societies were served by a practically invariable technology. Basically, they were in a non-evolutionary state.[1] That is why they had no involuntary unemployment.

---

[1] During the Middle Ages, for example, the overwhelming majority of people spent their budgets in a practically invariant pattern. That explains why economists then were unable to arrive at the notions of demand and supply schedules (Georgescu-Roegen, 1967).

REFERENCES

(These references relate to both text and Appendix)

Annable, J. E. Jr. (1977), 'A Theory of Downward-Rigid Wages and Cyclical Unemployment', *Economic Inquiry* (July).

Archibald, C. C. (1970), 'The Structure of Excess Demand for Labour', in *Microeconomic Foundations of Employment and Inflation Theory* (Norton).

Arrow, Kenneth J. and Gerard Debreu (1954), 'Existence of Equilibrium for a Competitive Economy', *Econometrica*, **22** (3) (July), 265–90.

Azariadis, C. (1975), 'Implicit Contracts and Underemployment Equilibria', *Journal of Political Economy* (October).

Bally, N. (1974), 'Wages and Employment under Uncertain Demand', *Review of Economic Studies* (January).

Barro, Robert J. and Herschel I. Grossman, (1971), 'A General Disequilibrium Model of Income and Employment', *American Economic Review*, **61**, 82–93.

——— (1976), *Money, Employment and Inflation* (Cambridge University Press).

Baumol, W. J. (1970), *Economic Dynamics*, 3rd ed (Macmillan).

Benassy, Jean-Pascal (1974, 1977, 1978), 'A Neokeynesian Model of Price and Quantity Determination in Disequilibrium' in *Equilibrium and Disequilibrium in Economic Theory*, G. Schwödlauer (ed.) (D. Reidel Publishing Company, 1977, ed. 1978), pp. 511–44.

Bushaw, D. W. and R. W. Clower, (1957), *Introduction to Mathematical Economics* (Richard D. Irwin).

Clower, R. W. (1965), 'The Keynesian Counter-Revolution: A Theoretical Appraisal', in F. H. Hahn and F. P. R. Brechling (eds.), *The Theory of Interest Rates* (Macmillan) pp. 103–25.

Dickson, H. W. (1963), *A Short History of the Steam Engine* (Frank Cass).

Dieffenbach, B. C. (1977), 'Aggregate Effective Demand and Supply Curves', *Economic Inquiry*, (April).

Finegan, T. Aldrich (1978), 'The Measurement, Behaviour and Classification of Discouraged Workers', paper prepared for the National Commission of Employment and Unemployment Statistics.

Fitoussi, J. P. (1971, 1973), *Inflation, équilibre et chômage* (Editions Cujas, 1973).

——— (1974), 'De l'inflation d'équilibre à la stagflation: théorie et vérification empirique', *Economie Appliquee*, no. 1.

——— (1979), 'Emploi, structure et régulation', *Revue Economique*, no. 1

Gaffard, J. L. (1979), *Efficacité de l'investissement, croissance et fluctuations* (Editions Cujas).

Galli, G. (1978), 'Asymmetry and Ratchet Effects of Aggregate Demand on Industrial Prices', Massachussetts Institute of Technology, mimeo.

Georgescu-Roegen, N. (1951), 'Relaxation Phenomena in Linear Dynamic Models', reprinted in NG-R, 1966.

——— (1952), 'A Diagrammatic Analysis of Complementarity', reprinted in NG-R, 1976.

—— (1955), 'Limitationality, Limitativeness, and Economic Equilibrium', reprinted in NG-R, 1966.

—— (1960), 'Economic Theory and Agrarian Economies', reprinted in NG-R, 1966, 1976.

—— (1960a), 'Mathematical Proofs of the Breakdown of Capitalism', reprinted in NG-R, 1966.

—— (1965), 'Process in Farming v. Process in Manufacturing: A Problem of Balanced Development', reprinted in NG-R, 1976

—— (1966), *Analytical Economics: Issues and Problems* (Harvard University Press).

—— (1967), 'Utility', *International Encyclopedia of the Social Sciences*, Vol. 16.

—— (1968), 'Structural Inflation-Lock and Balanced Growth', reprinted in NG-R, 1976.

—— (1969), 'The Economics of Production', Richart T. Ely Lecture, reprinted in NG-R, 1976.

—— (1971), *The Entropy Law and the Economic Process* Harvard University Press).

—— (1971a), 'Process Analysis and the Neoclassical Theory of Production', reprinted in NG-R, 1976.

—— (1974), 'Dynamic Models and Economic Growth', reprinted in NG-R, 1976.

—— (1975), 'Economics and Educational Development', *Journal of Educational Finance*, 1–15.

—— (1976), *Energy and Economic Myths* (Pergamon Press)

Gordon, D. F. and A. Hynes (1970), 'On the Theory of Price Dynamics', in Phelps *et al.*, *Microeconomic Foundations of Employment and Inflation Theory* (Norton).

Gordon, D. F. (1976), 'A Neo-Classical Theory of Keynesian Unemployment', in *The Phillips Curve and the Labor Market*, K. Brunner and A. H. Meltzer (eds.), Supplementary series to the *Journal of Monetary Economics*.

Hicks, J. H. (1939), *Value and Capital* (Clarendon Press).

—— (1974), *The Crisis in Keynesian Economics* (Basil Blackwell).

Hildebrandt, Kurt and Werner Hildebrandt, (1977), 'Sur la contribution de Malinvaud au renouvellement de la théorie du chômage', CNRS, Séminaire d'économétrie de M. Edmond Malinvaud, 7 March 1977, miméo.

—— (1978), 'On Keynesian Equilibria with Unemployment and Quantity Rationing', *Journal of Economic Theory*, 18, 255–77.

Keynes, John M. (1936), *The General Theory of Employment, Interest and Money* (Macmillan).

Korliras, P. G. (1978), 'Non-tâtonnement and Disequilibrium Adjustments in Macroeconomic Models', in Schwödiauer (ed.), 463–95.

Lebergott, S. (1964), *Manpower in Economic Growth* (McGraw-Hill).

Leijonhufvud, A. (1968), *On Keynesian Economics and the Economics of Keynes* (Oxford University Press).

Malinvaud, E. (1977), *The Theory of Unemployment Reconsidered* (Blackwell).

Measuring Employment and Unemployment, President's Committee to Appriase Employment and Unemployment Statistics, Washington, DC, 1962.

Negishi, Tagashi (1972), *General Equilibrium Theory and International Trade* (Elsevier).
—— (1978), 'Existence of an Unemployment Equilibrium', in Schwödiauer, *op. cit.*, 457–510.
Patinkin, Don (1956), *Money, Interest, and Prices* (Row Peterson).
—— (1976), *Keynes' Monetary Thought: A Study of its Development* (Duke University Press).
Phelps, E. S. *et al.* (1970), *Microeconomic Foundations of Employment and Inflation Theory* (Norton)
Roos, Charles F. (1935), 'Economic Theory of the Shorter Work Week', *Econometrica*, 3, 21–39.
Schumpeter, J. A. (1939), *Business Cycles* (McGraw-Hill).
Schwödiauer, Gerhard (ed.) (1978), *Equilibrium and Disequilibrium in Econometric Theory* (Reidel).
Solow, Robert M. (1957), 'Technical Change and the Aggregate Production Function', *Review of Economics and Statistics*, 39, 312–20.
Tobin, J. (1972). 'Inflation and Unemployment', *American Economic Review*.
Trevithick, J. A. (1976), 'Money Wages Inflexibility and the Keynesian Labor Supply Function', *Economic Journal* (June).
Walras, L. (1926, 1954), *Elements of Pure Economics*, W. Jaffe tr. (Irwin).

Appendix: An Examination of the Analytical Foundation of Disequilibrium Theories

Jean-Paul Fitoussi and Nicholas Georgescu-Roegen

1. The necessity of analytical similies and the usefulness of specific models

As we noted in the main part of the paper, the use of an arithmomorphic simile to verify an *already developed* dialectical reasoning is a necessary step in economic methodology. Some problems, however, are so complicated that they can be represented to some degree of satisfaction only by a highly complex system of the same general nature as Walras' or Pareto's. The inherent mathematical difficulties of such general systems make it extremely difficult to arrive at logically firm answers to the most relevant questions. To verify the claims associated with a general model — or, in its absence, to verify the correctness of the initial dialectical reasoning — only one means seems available: to replace the general simile by a simple, yet completely specific model. Such a step is just as fruitful methodologically as its predecessor — that of using an analytical simile to verify a dialectical reasoning. One of the most important applications of this methodological procedure is Malinvaud's recent monograph on the disequilibrium theories of unemployment (1977).

The problem to which Malinvaud addressed himself is of primary importance for both theory and policy. The old Keynesian idea that some aggregate disequilibrium is responsible for unemployment took a specific form with the work of Patinkin (1956) and subsequently and in broader perspective with that of Clower (1965). Recently, several authors, beginning with Barro and Grossman (1971) have cast this idea into some simplified but unspecified models. Slightly different though these models are, they all tend to explain how a complex system may live with any disequilibrium. Instead of ultimately disappearing if exogenous factors do not intervene — as Walras and, in a more cogent way, Marshall taught — disequilibria may be perpetuated indefinitely. That is why — the new school asserts — chronic unemployment as we have it today exists. The new theory being, in its strictest formulation, a theory of static disequilibrium, it cannot possibly offer any physiological analysis of the market. Its characteristic model offers only a mechanico-descriptive view of that process (Georgescu-Roegen, 1966).

2. Disequilibrium theories: general observations

The main analytical claims of the disequilibrium theories — claims that, in addition to their simplicity, account in large part for the growing popularity of those theories — are two (Malinvaud, 1977, pp. 12f, 78):

P_1. To absolutely every constellation of money-prices $(p_1, p_2, \ldots, p_j)$, there corresponds *one and only one* specific type of disequilibrium. In other words, the type of disequilibrium, DIS, is a point function of the price constellation:

$$DIS = DIS (p_1, p_2, \ldots, p_j).$$ (1)

P_2. For each type of disequilibrium, there exist some rationing procedures that allow the disequilibrium to persist at the given price constellation.

In this paper we propose to show that within the usual framework of disequilibrium theory there are some disturbing exceptions to these claims. However, contrary to what Hildebrandt and Hildebrandt (1977–78) have recently maintained, there is no ambiguity involved in the determination of the disequilibrium patterns, provided the *purely analytical* solutions that have no economic relevance are set aside (as they should be in any model of actuality). But as we shall show, for substantially frequent constellations, the analytical models of economic disequilibrium break down completely. Still more important, rules for rationing if there is shortage may fail to achieve their aim (Section 13).

In view of the fact that, as far as the cause and nature of unemployment are concerned, swords have been crossed over Walrasian versus non-Walrasian economics, we thought it instructive to examine the Walrasian explanation of equilibrium from the same viewpoint adopted by the disequilibrium analysis (Section 9). We have recalled an older result that refutes the current belief in the general existence of a Walrasian equilibrium and hence in the notion that the Walrasian system is applicable to any economic condition. That counter-example reflects the case of 'overpopulation'. This time, we have added still another counter-example, which reflects 'overcapitalisation' and is equally pertinent to chronic unemployment (Section 12).

A special feature of this paper is the fact that we have taken into account the essential difference between labour time and labour power. The distinction — introduced and used only by Karl Marx — is important in many problems, for example, in that of the utilisation of existing physical plants. But for any analysis of employment its importance is paramount. Yet the authors of unemployment models have followed the practice used in the standard theory and have clung to an analytical representation of the production process, that ignores the distinction. We thought the occasion very opportune for exposing this old, deep-rooted fallacy (Section 5), the verdict being that not only the analytical models of unemployment but also the production theory limited to the behaviour of a single firm have still, so it seems, a long and thorny way to go.

Since Malinvaud's re-examination embodies the main ideas developed by the previous contributors, it appeared natural to refer the following analysis to the framework made numerically explicit in his essay.

3. A review of analytical assumptions

The logical way to begin the proposed re-examination of the disequilibrium models is by listing the general assumptions made, explicitly or implicitly, by practically all writers on disequilibrium. For even if one shares the philosophy widely popular among large circles of economists which is that we should not quarrel about axioms, one should none the less be aware of as many as possible that are involved in an argument.

A. *The period for which the market process is described is so short that (i) the size of the population remains constant and so does the size of the labour force, which consists of N individuals; (ii) the tastes of the population are invariable; and (iii) there exists a constant number, P, of production units operating with unchanging technical recipes and constant material scaffolds.*

B. *During the same period only one trading act takes place in each market.* This means that during that period workers are hired only once and they also buy their good only once. The closest correspondence to such a duration in actuality is obviously the day. We may therefore refer hereafter to this period as 'the day.'[1]

C. *The price constellation is an economic element that cannot be affected by the behaviour of the economic agents – consumers, producers, government. Consumers seek to maximise their ophelimities and firms seek to maximise their profits by adjusting the quantities they but or sell to the given price constellation. The government simply spends some given funds at the given prices.* There also are some special assumptions that are usually adopted in order to simplify the demand and supply schedules. Some of these assumptions are made for the sole purpose of obtaining structures amenable to simple algebraic manipulations. Malinvaud was right in adopting this procedure. For as long as one's approach is confined to a mechanical description of a given process, a specific algebraic model is an excellent didactic tool.

D. *In addition to money there are only two commodities: a homogeneous labour and a general consumer good, hereafter called 'commodity'.* The fact that capital is not recognised as a commodity does not mean that capital equipment *per se* does not exist. In a completely integrated process, capital equipment may be maintained constant within each production unit as a part of its normal activity. A capital market, therefore, is not necessary. However, the situation is different for natural resources. Even in a completely integrated process there must exist some material input flows. It is true that during one

---

[1] Barro and Grossman (1971, p. 84) propose the label 'week'. But this term may be misleading, since it does not convey the strong restriction assumed by the models.

'day' there cannot be any appreciable increase in the scarcity of natural resources. Also, royalties are manmade; nature does not have check-out counters. Yet in an actual market economy royalties are part of cost, side by side with wages. But the authors of the models under discussion have followed the traditional practice of standard economics, which is to ignore this issue. [1] The curious outcome is that, although their authors do not seem aware of the fact, these models represent a pure labour theory of value in a sense not intended perhaps even by Marx.

E. *All individuals and all firms are identical.* In other words, all individuals have the same ophelimity function and all firms operate according to the same technical recipe and possess the same type of physical facilities.

4. A critique of structures: the ophelimity function

The most debatable of all these assumptions is certainly that concerning the price-quantity relationships (assumption C). However, the same assumption raises a different kind of issue, which concerns the analytical structure of both the ophelimity function and the production function.

These two concepts have acquired their present currency only by a repetitive, almost automatic, use. As a result, the issue of whether they are valid analytical representations of the corresponding phenomena has received little attention, and some correlated aspects of those concepts have even received none. As far as analytical representation is concerned, we are to a large extent justified in assuming simple structures — linear, quadratic, etc. — in our specific illustrative models. But it would be a fatal mistake to leave out, whether by neglect or for reasons of simplification, any essential feature of reality.

Let us deal first with the ophelimity function. Unless we assume that the world ends at the end of the day, this function must depend on money. The justification is simple. Not only boiled, baked, fried, etc. potatoes but also raw potatoes must be included in the ophelimity function for they *can be converted into the former at some specific rates.* That is, raw potatoes have an 'indirect' utility. Similarly, money has an indirect utility because it can be converted into direct utilities at some specific, albeit somewhat uncertain, rates in the future (Hicks, 1939, p. 33). Obviously, this is true for money as well as for raw potatoes only as long as there will be a tomorrow, however uncertain that tomorrow may be.

That is not all. Once we introduce money as a store of value into the ophelimity function, the thorny issue of whether the arguments of that function should be stocks or flows comes up in full force. Indeed, the ophelimity pertaining to a day — which is assumed not to be the last one —

[1] This is usually done by simple silence. Malinvaud (1977, p. 33) seems to be an exception, as he justifies the omission by explaining that a three-commodity model cannot have room for natural resources as well.

must be a function of *all flows consumed during that day as well as of all stocks existing at the end of the day*. 'Consumed' is used here in the strictest sense. Accordingly, one cannot consume money. One can only exchange it against goods, which may be consumed or held as stocks. The important point that not all flows come from or go into a stock is established in economics by leisure.

The ophelimity function must therefore have the form

$$U = U(x, l; s, m), \tag{2}$$

where x is the flow of the commodity consumed during the day; s is the corresponding stock at the end of the day; $l = B - L$ is leisure (with L being the work time performed and B the biosociological maximum of working hours that can be performed during the day); and m is the amount of money at the end of the day.[1] The price of the commodity and the wage rate being p and w respectively, the budget of the individual is

$$I = ps_0 + wB + m_0 = p(x + s) + wl + m, \tag{3}$$

where the subscript zero indicates *stocks* at the beginning of the day.[2] Hence, its optimal distribution is determined by the additional, but not too familiar equation

$$\frac{U_x}{p} = \frac{U_l}{w} = \frac{U_s}{p} = U_m. \tag{4}$$

This argument shows that by using for the ophelimity function the simple formula

$$U = 2 \log x + \log (B-L) + \log m, \tag{5}$$

one implicitly assumes that the individual has no initial stock of the commodity and consumes all that he buys during the same day.[3] Explicitly

F. *Households do not stock the commodity.* If we also assume (which by now seems quite natural) that 'in the morning' the identical individuals have

[1] Most authors make the ophelimity function depend on 'real money', i.e. on m deflated by the price of a physical unit of the commodity. However, if one takes this price as money unit – as Barro and Grossman (1971, p. 84) do – then the deflation of m is only a necessary transformation, not a structural aspect of the ophelimity function. See also the following footnote.

[2] To our knowledge, only Bushaw and Clower (1957) have considered a utility function that depends on both flows and stocks. But they assumed that both consumption and trading go on continuously, an assumption that compelled them to introduce an additional relation between flows and stocks different from the natural one, which is so clearly shown by a discrete framework (such as that assumed here).

[3] With this form of the ophelimity function – used by, among others, Malinvaud (1977, p. 41) and Benassy (1978, p. 522) – it is immaterial whether we make it depend on m or on m/p, as long as p is assumed constant.

the same amount of liquid money m_0, the supply of working hours, the demand for the commodity, and the final money balance are

$$L = (3Bw - m_0)/4w, x = (Bw + m_0)/2p, m = (Bw + m_0)/4. \qquad (6)$$

These formulae, however, are valid on the assumption that there are no constraints to the individual's reaching the maximum of this ophelimity and that

$$m_0 < 3wB. \qquad (7)$$

If $m_0 \geqslant 3wB$, the individual is too rich to want to work, in which case the solution of (4) is a corner solution:

$$L' = 0, x' = 2m_0/3p, m' = m_0/3, \qquad (8)$$

with $x' \geqslant x$ and $m' \geqslant m$.

5. A critique of the standard production function: funds, flows and working hours

The form of the production function used by the models under discussion raises far more complicated issues. In fact, that form involves perhaps the greatest fallacy of standard economic theory. To recall, in 1894 Philip Wicksteed introduced the concept of production function by simply stating that the equation

$$q = F(x, y, z, \dots) \qquad (9)$$

represents the relationship between the product and the factors of production — with the current vapid terminology, between output and inputs. During the almost hundred years elapsed since, economists have made no attempt to see whether Wicksteed's simple formula represents a production process adequately. To recall only the salient points of a previous analysis of this issue, Wicksteed's formula, now the standard one, omits two cardinal aspects of the production process.[1]

The first omission concerns the *essential* difference between fund and flow factors, that is, between the agents of the process (labour power, capital equipment and Ricardian land) and the materials transformed by them.

---

[1] Georgescu-Roegen (1976, chs. 2, 4, 5). Endeavours have been made to specify at least the dimensionality of the symbols in (9), some writers arguing that the symbols must represent quantities, others, that the symbols must represent flow rates with respect to time. The two views still circulate as two completely equivalent descriptions of one and the same phenomenon. Yet they would be equivalent only if all production processes were indifferent to size — an idea that cannot possible be accepted.

Because of this distinction, the analytical representation of any such process requires at least two relationships:

$$q = \Psi(H, K, T), \tag{10}$$

$$q = \Psi(x, y, z, \ldots, v), \tag{11}$$

where H, K, T represents (generically) the amounts of labour power, capital and Ricardian land, and $q; x, y, z, \ldots$; and v represent the flow rates of the product, of the ordinary inputs, and of waste.

The second element omitted by the standard theory is the duration of the process, specifically, the number of hours, $t \leqslant 1$, the process is in operation every day (the day being taken as the unit of time). It is important to note that this duration should not be confused with the working hours of one shift; t may cover several shifts and also include overtime. Since the *daily* production is $Q = tq$, (10) and (11) become

$$Q = t\Psi(H, K, T), \tag{12}$$

$$Q = \Psi(tx, ty, \ldots, tv). \tag{13}$$

This representation brings to light several important problems. One is the idleness of capital in development planning; another concerns the structure of the cost of production. But the new representation reveals the elementary fact that, if $t < 1$, the daily output can be increased without necessarily increasing the agents, not even the labour power.

Instead of using (12) and (13), the usual models of market disequilibrium are based on some highly simplified form of the standard production function

$$Q = F(Z), \tag{14}$$

where $Z = tH$ is *the amount of labour services*. There seems to be no exception to this practice.[1] Take the particular form used by Malinvaud (1977, pp. 51, 63), which with our notations is

$$Q = (\sqrt{1 + 2aZ} - 1)/a. \tag{15}$$

If the representation of a reproducible production process by (14) is to comply with the truth that *doubling the working time of any given set of factors doubles the output*, F must reduce to $Q = AtH$, where A is a constant determined by the existing material funds. However, in the analytical models

---

[1] See Patinkin (1956, p. 128); Barro and Grossman (1971, p. 85; 1976, p. 11); Korliras (1978, p. 480); Benassy (1978, p. 522); and Negishi (1978, p. 504), although this author simply speaks of 'labour'. Some authors – e.g., Negishi (1972) – do not even allow us to know whether they have in mind labour power, H, or labour services, since their argument is carried out in abstract symbols of 'labour inputs'.

of disequilibrium the usual assumption is that decreasing marginal returns prevail for all scales;[1] hence for any Z

$$F''(Z) < 0. \tag{16}$$

Occasionally, one hears the argument that if the output were not a function of labour services we could not account for the fact that managers may substitute between working hours and labour power. But the idea is a superficial interpretation of facts (as we shall see presently in some detail), and is related with the practice of using 'employment' to mean labour services. A salient illustration is offered by Keynes himself: in one place he defines 'the quantity of employment' as the ratio between the total wage bill and the wage rate of 'ordinary labour' (1936, p. 41). The dimension of the co-ordinate thus defined is that of labour *services*, man-hours, not of labour *power*, which is measured in men.[2]

6. Further remarks about the production function

For any given production unit — with K^0 and T^0 given — the *scale* of operation is determined only by the size of the labour force employed, H. The daily output is then proportional to the operating day of the production unit,

$$Q = t\Psi(H, K^0, T^0) = tf(H) \tag{17}$$

From all we know, the curve represented by this function of H is S-shaped. For t = 1 (a full working day) the curve is represented by $OQ^iQ^mQ^*$ in Figure 8.A1.[3] There is an inflexion point H^i such that $f''(H^i) = 0$ and

$$f''(H) > 0 \text{ for } 0 < H < H^i, f''(H) < 0 \text{ for } H^i < H < H^*, \tag{18}$$

where H* corresponds to the maximum scale of operations

$$Q^* = f(H^*), \tag{19}$$

with

$$f'(H) = 0, \text{ for } H \geqslant H^*. \tag{20}$$

---

[1] This practice is, again, general: Barro and Grossman (1971, p. 85; 1976, p. 11); Korliras (1978, p. 480), Negishi (1978, p. 504); Benassy (1978, p. 522). Malinvaud's formula obviously satisfies (16).

[2] A most curious fact, which apparently has not aroused attention: the basis of Keynes reasoning on this matter is purely dialectical, essentially identical to that by which Karl Marx argues that any concrete labour represents some general, abstract labour.

[3] There is no danger in using from now on the same letter to denote both the amount of a co-ordinate and the corresponding point in a diagram, and the diction will be greatly simplified thereby.

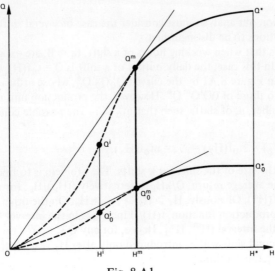

Fig. 8.A1

There is also an optimum scale of operation H^m for which $f(H)/H$ is a maximum. For analytical convenience, we shall also assume (as is ordinarily done) that the third derivative $f'''(H)$ exists.

As an instructive illustration, we shall occasionally use

$$f(H) = -H^3 + 6H^2 + 3a (a + 4)H, 0 \leqslant a, \tag{21}$$

which yields

$$H^i = 2, H^m = 3, H^* = 4 + a. \tag{22}$$

Before proceeding to examine the problems raised by the shape of $f(H)$, let us point out still another incongruity of the standard literature, where the production function is frequently represented by

$$Q = F(Z, K), \tag{23}$$

even in works dealing with crucial problems (e.g. Patinkin, 1956, p. 128; Solow, 1957, p. 313; Barro and Grossman, 1976, pp. 105 and 107). The incongruity becomes obvious if we note that Q and Z, in contrast with K, involve the time dimension. In fact, whenever labour cost is equated with the product of the wage rate by the amount of 'employment', alternatively, by 'labour', there is a confusion between the amount of a fund factor and the amount of its services.

7. *The case of several labour shifts*

In continuation our analysis must consider the case of several shifts. There are two situations to be distinguished.

The first is that when working hours of a shift, $t_0 \leqslant B$, are exogenously determined. In this case, the daily output of a shift is $Q = t_0 f(H)$, and is represented in Figure 8.A1 by the curve $0Q_0^i Q_0^m Q_0^*$, whose ordinates are in the ratio t_0 to those of $0Q^i Q^m Q^*$. However, the production unit may work with any number, n, of shifts, such that $nt_0 < 1$. The possible combinations are

$$Q = t_0 f(H_1) = 2t_0 f(H_2) = \ldots = nt_0 f(H_n), \tag{24}$$

where H_k is the size of the shift for k shifts. The problem is to find which k maximises the average return, Q/kH_k, alternatively $f(H_k)/H_k$, for a given Q, $0 < Q < nt_0 f(H^*)$. Obviously, $H_1 > H_2 > \ldots > H_n$. On the other hand, for an S-shaped production function, $f(H)/H$ increases in the interval $[0, H^m)$ and decreases in the interval $(H^m, H^*]$. Hence, for any $Q < t_0 Q^m$, the solution is $k = 1$. The second shift will be introduced only after H_1 reaches the level H' determined by the condition

$$f(H') = 2f(H'/2). \tag{25}$$

This equation admits a solution $H' < H$ if and only if

$$2F^*(H/2) > Q^*. \tag{26}$$

Alternatively, if the *second* solution ^1H of

$$Q/H = Q^*/H^*, \tag{27}$$

which always exists, satisfies the condition,

$$^1H < H^*/2. \tag{28}$$

Otherwise, the second shift will be introduced only after H_1 reaches the maximum level, H^*.[1]

To clarify this point, let us now take the working hours of a shift as the unit of time and denote by δ the new measure of the day. Let us also assume that (21) represents the daily output of a shift. The solution of (25) is $H' = 4$. Hence, for $0 < Q < Q' = 12a^2 + 48a + 32$, one shift provides the optimum solution, a result that is represented only by the section $0Q'$ of the production curve $0Q^*$ (Figure 8.A2). A change occurs at $Q = Q'$, when a second shift may be introduced. The third shift will be introduced only after the size of the

---

[1] It may be well to remember that not all scales of a production function are necessarily used in business practice. Thus, even if (26) is not satisfied, the production unit will pass from one shift to two shifts without first using H^*.

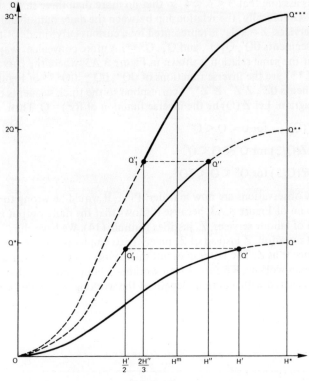

Fig. 8.A2

shift in the two-shift solution reaches the level H'' determined by

$$f(H'') = (3/2)f(2H''/3), \tag{29}$$

which expresses the same condition as (25). Similarly, the solution (29) exists if and only if the second solution ^2H of

$$f(H)/H = Q^*/H^* \tag{30}$$

satisfies

$$^2H < 2H^*/3 \tag{31}$$

In the case of our numerical illustration, we have $H'' = 18/5$ with $Q'' = 2F(H'') = 21.6a^2 + 86.4a + 62.2$. After Q exceeds Q'' the optimum operation requires three shifts.

We may continue in the same way for another and another shift. However, for the object lesson of our illustration it is not necessary to go further. We may thus assume that $3 < \delta < 4$, so that no more than three shifts should be possible. Graphically, the relationship between the daily output and the labour services, $\mathbb{Z} = kH_k$, is represented by a curious curve made of the three broken segments $0Q'$, $Q_1'Q''$, and Q_1'', Q^{***}. A more convenient way to represent the same relation is shown in Figure 8.A3, where the curves $0\mathbb{Z}^*$, $0\mathbb{Z}^{**}$, $0\mathbb{Z}^{***}$ are the inverse functions of $0Q^*$, $0Q^{**}$, $0Q^{***}$ of Figure 8.A2. The segments $0\mathbb{Z}'$, $\mathbb{Z}'\mathbb{Z}''$, $\mathbb{Z}''\mathbb{Z}^{***}$ correspond to the thick segments of the other diagram. Let $\mathbb{Z}(Q)$ be the inverse function of $f(\mathbb{Z}) = Q$. Then,

$$\mathbb{Z} = \mathbb{Z}(Q) \qquad \text{for } 0 < Q < Q' \tag{32}$$

$$\mathbb{Z} = 2\mathbb{Z}(Q/2) \text{ for } Q' < Q < Q''$$

$$\mathbb{Z} = 3\mathbb{Z}(Q/3) \text{ for } Q'' < Q < 3Q^*.$$

A few observations are now in order. First, it would be wrong to think that the diagram of Figure 8.A3, because it shows that the daily output is a function of labour services, $\mathbb{Z}$, justifies formula (14). We have chosen a different notation, $\mathbb{Z}$ instead of Z, precisely to emphasise that $\mathbb{Z}$ is not the same concept as Z. The latter does not distinguish between 8 men working 1 hour, 1 man working 8 hours, 4 men working 2 hours, etc. In other words, Z is not associated with a definite length of the working day whereas $\mathbb{Z}$ is. If,

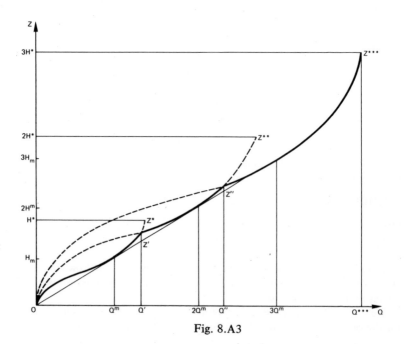

Fig. 8.A3

for example, $Z' < Z < Z''$, the working day is twice the working time of one shift.

Second, as one should have expected, the optimum average return is the same for any number of shifts. In actuality, however, there is a new complication. A regimen of several shifts involves some additional costs. Hence, when the diagram of Figure 8.A3 is used to represent the total cost, some discontinuous jumps must separate the three segments at the points corresponding to Q' and Q''. The optimum average return is therefore not the same for all shift regimens.

We may now consider the case in which the working hours of a shift may vary freely up to a maximum, t_0. A given output Q, $Q < Q_0^* = t_0 Q^*$, of a single shift may be obtained in an infinite number of ways by variation of the working hours and the labour power employed. The optimal combination is that which will minimise the variable cost. But since in the case under consideration labour is the only *variable* factor, for the optimal solution we have to minimise only the input of labour services, tH, *without any regard for the level of the wage rate.*[1]

For the labour services, we have

$$s = th(Q/t), \tag{33}$$

where h is the inverse of f. The minimum of s involves the sign of

$$ds/dt = h(Q/t) - h'(Q/t)Q/t. \tag{34}$$

On any interval of free variation of the argument Q/t, this familiar expression changes its sign from negative to positive for $Q/t = Q^m$, provided this value is compatible with the constraints of the problem. But $Q/Q^* \leqslant t \leqslant t_0$, hence that solution is acceptable if and only if $Q < t_0 Q^m = Q_0^m$. In this case, the optimal solution consists of the optimal scale, H^m, used during

$$t = Q/Q^m. \tag{34}$$

If $Q > Q_0^m$, ds/dt is negative over the entire interval of variation of t; hence the minimum of s corresponds to using $H = h(Q)$ for the maximum number of working hours, t_0.

The optimal solution as Q varies from 0 to Q_0^* is represented by the kinked line $H^m Q_0^m Q_0^*$ (Figure 8.A1), again a quite unorthodox result.[2]

However, since the unit may now choose the working hours of a shift, it does not necessarily have to move into decreasing returns even if $Q > Q_0^m$. If

---

[1] The variable cost of any given output must always be minimum. In the case of more than two variable factors the condition leads to the scale line whose equation involves the price ratios of all these factors. Naturally, in that case the optimum solution depends on prices (Georgescu-Roegen, 1976, ch. 2).

[2] Obviously, if $Q > Q_0^*$, no solution exists with a single shift. And if $Q > Q^*$, an additional plant is needed.

$Q \leqslant Q^m$, the unit may use enough optimal shifts, H^m, of $t \leqslant t_0$, so that the daily output be Q. Only if $Q^m < Q \leqslant Q^*$ must the unit operate in the region of decreasing returns. The final result is that, if the working hours of a shift are not pre-determined, the relation between the daily output and the labour services (properly determined) is represented by $H^m Q^m Q^*$ (Figure 8.A1). By inversion, we obtain a representation analagous to that of Figure 8.A3, which is

$$Z = (H^m/Q^m)Q, \text{ for } 0 \leqslant Q \leqslant Q^m, \tag{36}$$

$$Z = h(Q), \qquad \text{for } Q^m \leqslant Q \leqslant Q^*.$$

Here again we must note that Z is not just a number of man-hours. For the first interval, the size of the labour power employed is given, H^m; for the second interval, the working day is given, $t = 1$. An even more important observation is that for the first interval the number of shifts is indeterminate; hence we cannot say how many members of the community are actually employed. Even if $Q < t_0 Q^m$, the unit may employ any number of shifts. The upshot is that even though relation (36) is much simpler than that obtained for the condition in any general model assumed in the preceding section, its use in a general model may lead to greater analytical complexities. The point is that although the wage bill is the same regardless of how many shifts are used to produce $0 < Q^m$, the income distribution and hence the demand for the commodity and the supply of labour do vary with the number of shifts.

8. The optimal scale of production

In the preceding sections we have considered the purely technical problem of a production unit called to produce a given daily output with the least cost. One point for the thesis developed in those sections deserves emphasis at this juncture. The optimal solution does not consist in minimising the 'labour input', tH, as such, in which case it would be possible to substitute t for H and *vice versa*. Even when the labour regimen allows the production unit to choose its operating hours freely, for every Q there is only one optimal t (determined by the optimal H). This should also be true when the production unit comes to adjusting its market behaviour optimally.

Turning now to consider this problem, we shall adopt the simplifying assumption — implicit in all standard models, whether of equilibrium or disequilibrium — that only one shift can be used. The question now is what t, $t \leqslant B$, maximises the unit's profit.

For our purpose it is now useful to consider the total cost function

$$T(Q) = T_F + twH = T_F + twh(Q/t), \tag{37}$$

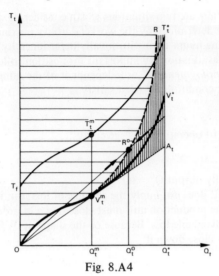

Fig. 8.A4

where T_F is the fixed cost and w is the wage rate.[1] If w is assumed constant, $T(Q)$ is represented by $T_F T_t^*$, and the variable cost, $T_V = twh(Q/t)$, by $0V_t^*$ (Figure 8.A4).[2]

If p is the price of the commodity, the profit is

$$\Pi = t[pf(H) - wH] - T_F. \tag{38}$$

Since Π is a linear function of t and the coefficient of t is always positive (in acceptable conditions), it follows that for whatever H, Π is an increasing function of t. Profit is then maximised when t has the greatest possible value. The conclusion is that the value of t that maximises profit is t = B, provided the production unit can choose it so.[3]

---

[1] We must not gloss over the fact that the fixed cost represents the earnings of the services of the material agents. Interest is counted even in communist economic systems. The disequilibrium models usually ignore this co-ordinate; e.g. Benassy (1978); Barro and Grossman (1971). In their 1976 volume, Barro and Grossman include the capital fund in the production function, but use a different formula from (37). The omission not only vindicates the point made earlier – that such models reflect a pure labour theory of value – but also does away with the condition in which firms must close down (thus contributing to involuntary unemployment) for the reason that receipts are smaller than the fixed cost.

[2] The inverted S-shape of $0V_t^*$ follows from (18), and from (20) it follows that the marginal cost for Q_t^* is infinite.

[3] The point recalls Karl Marx's objection against the argument of Nassau Senior that profit is earned in the last hour of the working day. Formula (38), however, vindicates Senior.

Analytically, there are two situations worth considering. In the first, the working hours are determined by the workers' utility maximisation; in the second, the working hours are institutionally determined by law.[1] But whatever the actual situation, an important proposition follows from (38):

The optimal employment, H^0, is independent of the number of *working hours, t*. The only condition H^0 must satisfy is

$$pf'(H^0) = w.[2] \tag{39}$$

The optimal *scale* of operations, Q^0, given by

$$wh'(Q^0) = p, \tag{40}$$

determines the daily output $Q_t^0 = tQ^0$.

Maximum profit does not imply the absence of loss, but if the loss is greater than T_F the production unit must close down in order not to lose more than the unavoidable loss. Because of the shape of $0V_t^*$, it is obvious that the unit must close down if

$$p < V_t^m/Q_t^m. \tag{41}$$

Hence, the *analytical* solutions of (39) and (40)[3] are valid if and only if

$$H^0 \geqslant H^m, Q^0 \geqslant Q^m. \tag{42}$$

The case that distinguishes the disequilibrium models is that in which the production unit is rationed. This means that it can sell at most a given $\bar{Q}_t$, such that $\bar{Q}_t < Q_t^0$. For a general picture, let $V_t^m R$ be the locus of the point (Q_t^0, pQ_t^0) representing the receipts for the optimal output as p varies. From (40) it follows that the equation of $V_t^m R$ is

$$R_t(Q_t) = wQ_t h'(Q_t/t), \tag{43}$$

and we shall write $\bar{R}_t = R_t(\bar{Q}_t)$. If $(\bar{Q}, p\bar{Q})$ is in the domain shaded vertically in Figure 8.A4 – $RV_t^m A_t$ with $V_t^m R$ excluded – the unit can increase its profits by producing less, namely, Q_t^0. This is no longer possible if that point is in the closed domain $T_t 0 V_t^m R$, shaded horizontally. To produce less than $\bar{Q}_t$ would decrease the profit available at that output. Finally, if $(\bar{Q}, p\bar{Q})$ is in the domain below $0V_t^m$ and $V_t^m A_t$, the firm must close down.

---

[1] Malinvaud (1977) is apparently the only author to consider in detail both these situations.

[2] Let us not fail to note that there is only a formal similarity between this relation and the ultra familiar one of the standard theory. The latter, when it is not written in an incongruous form, is $pF'(Z) = w$. Cf. Malinvaud (1977, p. 52).

[3] By *analytical* solutions we mean those solutions that may satisfy an equation without complying with the restrictions of the model involved.

The optimal output of the unit is

$$Q_t = \bar{Q}_t, \text{ if } pQ_t \geqslant \max[\bar{V}_t, \bar{R}_t], \tag{44}$$

$$Q_t = Q_t^0, \text{ if } \bar{Q}_t > Q_t^m \text{ and } \bar{V}_t \leqslant p\bar{Q}_t \leqslant \bar{R}_t, \tag{45}$$

$$Q_t = 0, \quad \text{if } (\bar{Q}_t < Q_t^m \text{ and } p\bar{Q}_t < \bar{V}_t) \text{ or } (\bar{Q}_t \geqslant Q_t^m \text{ and } pQ_t^m < V_t^m). \tag{46}$$

For the particular production function (21), we have:

$$Q_t^m = (9a^2 + 36a + 27)t, \quad V_t^m = 3wt. \tag{47}$$

9. A map of Walrasian disequilibria

A few object lessons can be derived by applying the preceding results first to the Walrasian equilibrium. To this purpose, we shall use the simple diagram devised by Edgeworth and subsequently adopted by Hicks for the analysis of multimarket equilibrium.[1] For the system that involves only labour and a general commodity, we may consider the value of the wage rate, $w = \alpha(p)$, that would clear the labour market when the participants act on the knowledge that the commodity price is some given p. As we shall see presently, the function $w = \alpha(p)$ is always linear. Hence, if S_L and D_L are the Walrasian supply of and demand for labour, respectively, the locus of the pairs for which the excess supply of labour $\Sigma_L = S_L - D_L$ is null, is represented by the straight line 0b (Figure 8.A5). This line divides the plane into two domains; above 0b, $\Sigma_L > 0$; below 0b, $\Sigma_L < 0$.

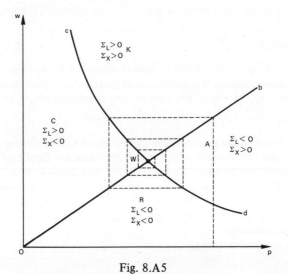

Fig. 8.A5

[1] Cf. Georgescu-Roegen (1976, p. 365). Some diagrams used by Malinvaud (1977, Sec. III) and Benassy (1978) are Edgeworth's diagrams.

Similarly, we can define a function $p = \beta(w)$, along which the excess supply of the commodity, $\Sigma_X = S_X - D_X$, is null. The curve cd, represented by this function, also divides the plane into two domains; $p > \beta(w)$ where $\Sigma_X > 0$, and $p < \beta(w)$ where $\Sigma_X < 0$.

A priori, we may expect that the plane (p, w) should thus be divided into four distinct domains (as shown in Figure 8.A5), each one associated with a particular type of initial disequilibrium:

- (K) Keynesian: $\Sigma_L > 0, \Sigma_X > 0$
- (C) Classical: $\Sigma_L > 0, \Sigma_X < 0$
- (R) Repressed inflation: $\Sigma_L < 0, \Sigma_X < 0$
- (A) Anticlassical: $\Sigma_L < 0, \Sigma_X > 0$

The terminology is that used by Malinvaud (1977, pp. 30f) with the exception of the last (A), which he discards from the outset as 'uninteresting' (which is not true in general).

The idea of Edgeworth and Hicks is that one can explain the movement of prices toward their Walrasian equilibrium by an algorithm based on Figure 8.A5 instead of by the more controversial *tâtonnement*. Successive adjustments may proceed from one market to another in a cobweb fashion, as shown by the interrupted lines. The algorithm will bring the price constellation nearer and nearer the Walrasian equilibrium, W, represented by the intersection of the two lines, $\Sigma_L = 0$ and $\Sigma_X = 0$, (provided that they intersect and also have a 'nice' shape).

Since all P production units are assumed to be identical, the total daily output is

$$Q = tP\Psi(H/P, K^0, T^0), \tag{48}$$

where H is now the total *number of men* employed. P being constant in the case under consideration, it is harmless but greatly convenient to write this relation in the same form as that used in the preceding sections, i.e. as

$$Q = tf(H). \tag{49}$$

We now come to the crucial consequence of our new analytical representation of a production process, which is that *the Walrasian supply of labour power is completely inelastic*. Certainly, every man wants to be employed for his desired supply of labour time. It is only *this last supply that varies with the price constellation*. Moreover, as we have seen, the demand for labour power also is independent of the supply of working hours. There are two important conclusions.

First, in all circumstances,

$$Q = Lf(H), \tag{50}$$

where L represents the working hours, the individual worker is willing to supply in each particular situation.

Second,

$$\Sigma_L = N - D_L, \tag{51}$$

where D_L is given by (39), i.e. by

$$w = pf'(D_L), \tag{52}$$

provided receipts cover at least the variable cost. This last condition is $f(D_L)/D_L > f'(D_L)$, from which it follows that

$$D_L \geqslant H^m, \tag{53}$$

and hence

$$w \leqslant pf(H^m)/H^m = pf'(H^m). \tag{54}$$

The boundary of this *closed* domain is a straight line denoted by 0i in Figure 8.A6 as well as in our subsequent graphs.

Alternatively, (p, w) may belong to the complement of (54), which is the domain *above* 0i. Then, all firms must close down: $D_L = 0$, which implies $S_X = 0$. Relation (51) becomes $\Sigma_L = N > 0$ (a discontinuity that will prove to be quite relevant for the disequilibrium analysis, Section 10 below). Since in the domain above 0i, also $\Sigma_X < 0$, the initial pattern is classical in all cases.

For the subsequent analysis, the domain of (54) need only be considered. There are three distinct patterns that require separate handling.

(A): $H^m \leqslant N < H^*$. This is the 'normal' case on which standard models, whether of equilibrium or disequilibrium, are based.

Because of (52), $\Sigma_L = N - D_L = 0$ is equivalent to the linear relation

$$w = pf'(N), \tag{55}$$

represented in our graphs by 0b. From (54), it now follows that the slope of 0b is never greater than that of 0i (Figure 8.A6a).

Let L now be the *unrestricted* supply of labour time of the individual and x the *unrestricted* demand of the individual. The Walrasian total supply of the commodity is $S_X = Lf(D_L)$ and the unrestricted total demand $D_X = Nx + G/p$, where G is a fixed amount of money that represents the demand of the 'government' and must be spent entirely at any price p whatsoever. Hence, the commodity market clears if and only if

$$\Sigma_X = Lf(D_L) - Nx - G/p = 0. \tag{56}$$

If the ophelimity function has the form (5), this relation becomes[1]

$$3pEf(D_L) = 2w(NE + 2A), \tag{57}$$

[1] Especially when specific numerical structures are used, one should ascertain the dimensional homogeneity of all relations. In the case of the formulae derived from (21) one should take into account the fact that all the numerical coefficients in that expression have the dimension commodity/ (time) (labour power)^i i = 3, 2, 1, respectively.

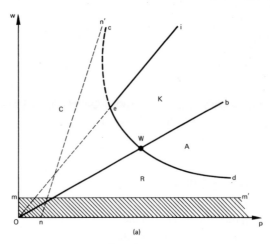

Fig. 8.A6a

where

$$E = 3Bw - m_0, \quad A = 2Nm_0 + 3G. \tag{58}$$

Within the non-negative orthant of the plane (p, w), (57) is represented by the curve cd. If

$$\Lambda(k) = 3f(D_L) - 2Nk > 0, \tag{59}$$

the intersection of cd with the line $w = kp$ corresponds to a unique $E > 0$. Indeed, Λ is a decreasing function of k for any k such that $f''(D_L) < 0$, as proved by the sign of

$$\Lambda'(k) = 3f(D_L)/f''(D_L) - 2N. \tag{60}$$

Therefore, cd intersects 0i at a point, e. It also has two asymptotes. One asymptote is mm', which is represented by $E = 0$; it delimits the domain of unavailable price constellations (7). The second asymptote, nn', is

$$w = kp - 4Ak^2/9Bf(D_L) \tag{61}$$

where k is given by $\Lambda(k) = 0$. Its slope is therefore greater than that of 0i.

Only the branch of cd below the point e is relevant for the economic model. To the east of the kinked line ied, $\Sigma_X > 0$; to the west of it, $\Sigma_X < 0$. The plane (p, w) is divided into the relevant domains K, C, A, R, as shown by the thick lines in Figure 8.A6a.

The Walrasian equilibrium constellation, $W(p_W, w_W)$, exists and is unique. By putting $D_L = N$ in (57) and noting that $w_W = p_W f'(N)$, we obtain

$$[3f(N) - 2Nf'(N)] E_W = 4Af'(N).$$

However, one curious feature must be remarked. The line ei is only one part of the boundary between the domains K and C; it is not part of the locus $\Sigma_X^0 = 0$. For values of w above e, *there is no value of p that clears the commodity market*. The cobweb approach to equilibrium cannot therefore work unless the initial price constellation does not differ too much from that of the Walrasian equilibrium. This analytical result is sufficiently surprising if viewed only from the general analysis of Walrasian equilibrium. But apart from this, it deserves attention because it represents a catastrophe situation stronger than that of the usual models of catastrophe.

(B): $N > H^*$. Since $f'(N) = 0$, the system may be rightly characterised as 'overpopulation'. It obviously cannot operate according to the principle of marginal pricing of Walrasian economics. We have here a striking counter-example to the position that Walrasian economics can work in all circumstances and that at least one Walrasian equilibrium always exists, a position which has acquired the status of incontestability through the famous theorem elegantly proved by Arrow and Debreu (1954). What is more, the relevance of this case is not purely academic only. Overpopulation in the above sense has been a far more dominant situation in history than that in which marginal productivity of labour is positive.

If there is overpopulation there is involuntary unemployment in an entirely different sense from the current use of the term. Employment is H^*, with, paradoxical though it may seem, a maximum working time (which now may be split between several individuals who thus share the 'unwanted leisure'). The resulting output satisfies first the demand of the 'government', D_G, representing some percentage, ρ, of the total output. The rest is shared among all consumers in the same ration, r:

$$Bf(H^*) (1 - \rho) = Nr. \tag{63}$$

Most of the distribution is achieved by transfers in nature outside any price system and according to a rationing rule analogous to that suggested recently by Malinvaud for the classical unemployment (Section 13 below).[1]

(C): $N < H^m$. In this case, the labour market can never clear. If $w > pf(H^m)/H^m$, we conclude as before that $D_L = 0$ and $\Sigma_L = N > 0$. And if $w \leqslant pf(H^m)/H^m$, then $D_L \geqslant H^m$; hence $\Sigma_L < 0$. If $D_L = 0$, then $\Sigma_X < 0$; and if $D_L \geqslant H^m$, the commodity market again clears only if (56) is satisfied.

The pattern is described by Figure 8.A6b, again by the thick, solid lines. No price constellation corresponds to the Keynesian case. What is more, *there is no Walrasian equilibrium*, for nowhere can we have $\Sigma_L = 0$. This is still another counter-example to smooth-sailing Walrasian economics. The situation may be described as 'underpopulation' or, perhaps more tellingly, as 'overcapitalisation'.

---

[1] The foregoing points form the substance of a 1960 essay reprinted in Georgescu-Roegen (1976, ch. 6).

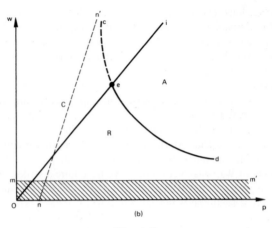

Fig. A6b

10. Preliminary considerations of disequilibrium theory

The idea that an economic system can live with disequilibria of some sort or other necessarily implies that the demand of some buyers or the supply of some sellers normally have to remain unsatisfied. This raises the thorny problem of determining which particular individual or which particular production unit will remain unsatisfied and to what extent.

The answers hinge on a series of factors, most of which are imponderable: the economic acumen of the individual (as a consumer, a worker, or a manager), his location, his eagerness to strike a contract, the chance of his finding a favourable partner, the amount of 'money' he possesses, etc. No analytical formula could possibly embrace all these variables for a positive answer in each case.

For purely analytical purposes, however, the issue can be circumvented by some expedient assumptions. The assumption that all people and all firms are identical (assumption E) comes easily to mind. But because of the Principle of Insufficient Reason, all buyers (or all sellers) should then come out of the market equally unsatisfied. Unemployment would then pertain to working hours instead of individuals. It would be a continuous attribute instead of a discontinuous one as is the case in actual conditions, in which an individual is either fully employed *for the day* or is not employed at all.

It is thus assumed, first, that in a market oversupplied with workers who seek employment a worker is satisfied either completely or not at all (e.g. Malinvaud, 1977). Because of the complete identity of the workers, who is employed and who is not must be decided by pure hazard – a curious assumption as far as the actual world is concerned. A second assumption is anti-symmetrical to the preceding one. On the commodity market, the unemployed individuals are always completely satisfied, whereas those who are employed may have to be rationed, in which case they share the balance of the effective supply equally.[1] In contrast with the rules for individuals, firms always share equally the demand for the commodity, and, hence, the supply of labour.[2]

We should also recall the novel idea of disequilibrium theory, namely, that prices are not affected by the behaviour of the economic agents – the production units and the households. These agents adapt only the quantities transacted at the given price constellation. The adaptation is based on what once was regarded as a tautology, namely, that the quantities bought must be equal to the quantities sold. But there also is an additional, not always explicit, idea, which is that the commodity market, not the labour market is the wheel of the adjustment.

Three basic ideas will aid the organisation of the otherwise entangled picture of disequilibrium theory.

(I): *First*, if (p, w) is the given price constellation, no unit can work with H workers unless

$$w \leqslant pf(H)/H, \tag{64}$$

and none could work at all outside the domain of (54).

(II): *Second*, the characteristic assumption of disequilibrium approach is that the excess supply of the commodity, $\Sigma(H)$, cannot be positive at the disequilibrium employment $H = N_1$. The excess supply is

$$\Sigma(H) = Lf(H) - H(x - x') - Y_m, \tag{65}$$

where x' denotes the demand of the unemployed worker and Y_m stands for the minimum necessary output, $Nx' + G/p$. We may also put

$$\Sigma_X^0 = \Sigma(N) = Lf(N) - G/p. \tag{66}$$

(III): *Third*, as we have seen in Section 9, if a production unit cannot employ D_L workers because $N < D_L$, in order to maximise its profit it must seek to employ as many workers as the preceding conditions would allow. This means that $\Sigma(N_1) = 0$. Hence,

$$D_L > N \Rightarrow N_1 \leqslant N. \tag{67a}$$

If $D_L \leqslant N$, $\Sigma(N_1)$ may be negative. And, as we shall see by an additional

---

[1] We may note in passing that this rule contradicts the common fact that individuals with higher incomes are ordinarily more efficient buyers than the others.

[2] Malinvaud (1977, pp. 50f) seems to be the only author who considers the case of non-identical firms. But, in the end, he adopts an aggregate production function which does not specify the share of each individual firm.

argument later on, the rule is

$$D_L \leqslant N \Rightarrow N_1 \leqslant D_L. \tag{67b}$$

Naturally, even in this set up, some sort of *tâtonnement* is indispensable for arriving at the disequilibrium scale that satisfies both (II) and (III). Yet disequilibrium theories disregard this necessity completely, and *pour cause*: since there is only one market during the day, one would have to fall back on contracting and recontracting (which would upset the whole apple cart).

11. The map of static disequilibria: first part

For a qualitative analysis that may pinpoint the details of the various situations, we shall again assume that the ophelimity function has the form (5).

The problem of which type of disequilibrium corresponds to a given price constellation hinges on the relative position of two curves in the plane (H, Q). The first is the straight line AB, representing the effective demand for the commodity,

$$Q_1 = H(x - x') + Y_m, \tag{68}$$

for the employment level H.[1] The second is 0Q*, representing the output of the commodity,

$$Q_2 = Lf(H), \tag{69}$$

for the same employment (see Figure 8.A10, below). In order to avoid the division of many of the subsequent analytical findings into cumbersome subcases, we shall include in the function (69) the extension $Q = Q^*$ for $H > H^*$.

Because $\Sigma(0) < 0$ and $\Sigma(H) < 0$ for any value of H greater than some ^0H (which may be zero), the equation $\Sigma(H) = 0$ has an even number of roots in the interval $(0, {}^0H]$. As we shall prove presently (although it is intuitively obvious from Figure 8.A10), this number may only be 0 or 2 (including the case of a double root).

Let us put

$$\phi(N; E, H) = 2w(HE + 2A)/3Ef(H). \tag{70}$$

---

[1] It may be natural to think that $x' < x$, which entails that the slope of AB is positive. However, whether that is so or not depends on the sign of the coefficient of dl in the relation $(U_{xx}U_m^2 - 2U_{xm}U_xU_m + U_{mm}U_x^2[w(U_{xm} - U_{mm}) + U_{ml} - U_{xl}]\,dl$, which cannot be ascertained in general. In the case of 'independence', however, that coefficient is always positive; hence, with increased leisure (decreased income from work), the demand for the commodity decreases, and $x' < x$. Curiously, however, in our case the specific formula of x' coincides with that established in (8) for an individual too rich to work!

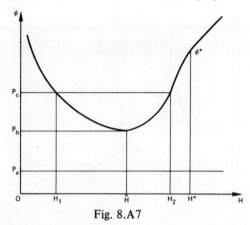

Fig. 8.A7

This sign of $\Sigma(H)$ is the same as that of $p - \phi$. For any given E, the shape of ϕ, regarded as a function of H, is that shown in Figure 8.A7. Namely, for $H = 0$, $\phi = \infty$, and for $H \geqslant H^*$, $\phi = 2w(HE + 2A)/3Ef(H^*)$. The function $\phi(H)$ also has one and only one minimum, corresponding to H determined by the equation:

$$\varphi(H) = f'(H)/[f(H) - Hf'(H)] = E/2A. \tag{71}$$

Let us note, first, that, because of the general S-shape of $(f(H), \varphi(H) \geqslant 0$ if and only if $H \geqslant H^m$. Moreover, $\varphi(H^m) = \infty$ and $\varphi(H) = 0$ for any $H \geqslant H^*$. Finally,

$$\varphi'(H) = ff''(f - Hf')^2 < 0 \tag{72}$$

for $H^m < H < H^*$. It follows that for any given E, there is a unique $\check{H}$,

$$H^m \leqslant \check{H} = \check{H}(E/2A) \leqslant H^*, \tag{73}$$

for which ϕ is a minimum.[1] Conversely, to any given H not smaller than H^m, there corresponds one and only one value of E such that $H = \check{H} (E/2A)$.

Let us now put

$$p = \check{p}(E) = \phi(N; E, \check{H}). \tag{74}$$

In the plane (p, w), this function is represented by $\mathcal{H}$(Figures 8.A8 and 8.A9). It is immediately clear that $\check{p}(0) = \infty$ and $\check{p}(\infty) = \infty$. Therefore $E = 0$ is an asymptote of $\mathcal{H}$. There also is another asymptote, zz', given by

$$w = 3pf(H^m)/2H^m - 2A/3BH^m; \tag{75}$$

its slope is greater than 0i.

---

[1] The concavity of ϕ does not necessarily remain always positive. ϕ'' might be zero for some H, $\check{H} < H < H^*$. But this does not affect the current argument.

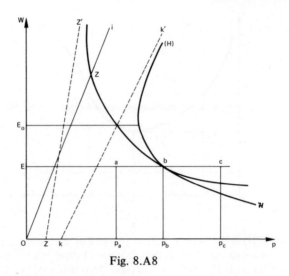

Fig. 8.A8

The sign of $d\check{p}/dE$ is the same as that of

$$\Delta(E) = \check{H} - 2Am_0/E^2 . \tag{76}$$

Since $\Delta(0) = -\infty$ and $\Delta(\infty) = H^m$, $\Delta(E) = 0$ has an uneven number of roots. For the particular form (21), (71) becomes

$$EH^2(H - 3) = 3A(a + H)(4 + a - H) \tag{77}$$

by substituting $H = 2Am_0/E^2$, it is immediately seen that $\Delta(E) = 0$ has only one solution. It is analytically convenient to assume that the function $f(H)$ is such that (76) has only one root, in which case $\mathcal{H}$ has the shape shown in Figure 8.A8. Perhaps this is true for all 'regular' production functions. However, for the strict argument, $\mathcal{H}$ has a somewhat equivalent property: a line $p = \lambda w$ that intersects $\mathcal{H}$ does not intersect it again. Let us assume that $p = \lambda w$ intersects $\mathcal{H}$, which means that

$$3\lambda/2 = (\check{H}E + 2A)/Ef(\check{H}) \tag{78}$$

has a solution $E > 0$. The derivative of the right-hand side with respect to E is simply $-2A/E^2 f(\check{H}) < 0$. Hence, (78) cannot have a second solution. In particular, $0i$ intersects $\mathcal{H}$ once, at Z. Since (71) and (74) yield

$$f(\check{H}) = 2w/3p \tag{79}$$

the value of $\check{H}_z$ corresponding to Z, is given by $f'(H_z) = 2wf'(H^m)/p$.

There exists a still more important property of $\mathcal{H}$. In the plane (p, w),

$$p = 2w(HE + 2A)/3Ef(H) \tag{80}$$

represents a one-parameter family of curves, the parameter being H. This

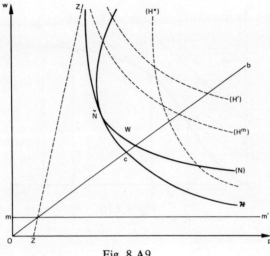

Fig. 8.A9

family constitutes the basis of disequilibrium analysis. Analytically, we shall allow H to vary freely from 0 to ∞.

Each curve (80), denoted thereafter by (H), has two asymptotes: $E = 0$ and

$$w = 3pf(H)/2H - 2A/3BH, \qquad (81)$$

denoted by kk'. (The slope of kk' is never greater than that of zz'.) The right-hand function of (80) has a unique minimum corresponding to

$$E_m(H) = \sqrt{2Am_0/H} \qquad (82)$$

Moreover, (H) is convex toward the west, since $d^2p/dw^2 > 0$ (Figure 8.A8).

Next, we should ascertain whether the family of curves (80) has an envelope. If it exists, the envelope is determined by eliminating the parameter H from (80) and the derivative of that equation with respect to H. This derivative yields

$$3pf'(H) = 2w. \qquad (83)$$

By substituting this value of H for Ȟ in (80) we obtain the envelope of that family. But (83) is the same equation as (79); hence the function determined by it and (80) is Ȟ(E/2A). Therefore, the envelope of the family (80) is ℋ.

However, ℋ is tangent not to all curves (H), but only to those for which $H \geqslant H^m$. The reason is that (71) has no positive solution otherwise. If the last condition is satisfied, (H) is tangent to ℋ at one and only one point (Figures 8.A8 and 8.A9). Indeed, if the same (H) were tangent in more than one point, it would mean that to the same Ȟ there would correspond more than one value of E – which would contradict (79). This last condition implies that if E (of the tangent point) increases from 0 to +∞, the parameter corresponding

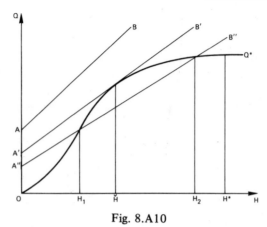

Fig. 8.A10

to the tangent curve decreases from H^* to H^m. The point of tangency of
(H^*) is at $p = \infty$, and that of (H^m) at $w = \infty$ (as shown in Figure 8.A9). If
$H' < H^m$, (H') does not intersect (H^m) and belongs entirely to the open
domain east of (H^m).

The curve $\mathcal{H}$ divides the plane into two domains with crucial properties for
disequilibrium mapping. If a price constellation (p_a, w) is represented by a
point a belonging to the domain west of $\mathcal{H}$ (Figure 8.A8), then, as seen from
Figure 8.A7, $p_A < \check{p}(E)$, and, hence $\Sigma(H) < 0$ for any H. AB does not
intersect $0Q^*$ (Figure 8.A10).

If $b(p_b, w)$ is on $\mathcal{H}$ then $p_b = \check{p}(E)$, and $\Sigma(H) < 0$ except that $\Sigma(\check{H}) = 0$.
$A'B'$ is tangent to $0Q^*$ at $\check{H}$ (Figure 8.A10). Through b passes *only one* curve
of the family (80). This curve, which corresponds to the parameter H, is
tangent to $\mathcal{H}$.

Finally, let us consider a point belonging to the east of $\mathcal{H}$, say, $c(p_c, w)$.
From Figure 8.A7 it follows directly that in this case, the condition $p_c = \check{p}(H)$
is always satisfied for two and only two values of H, $H = H_1$ and $H = H_2$,
$H_1 < \check{H} < H_2$. $A''B''$ intersects $0Q^*$twice, at point corresponding to H_1 and
H_2 (Figure 8.A10).[1]

Therefore, through any point belonging to the domain east of $\mathcal{H}$ pass two
curves of the family (80), (H_1) and (H_2), as shown in Figure 8.A9. The dual
proposition, however, is not true: two curves do not always intersect each
other, not even at infinity. If they intersect, the value of E^0 pertaining to

---

[1] For Figure 8.A10, we should note that if w remains constant, Lf(H) does
not shift if p varies. As p increases, AB shifts lower and its slope decreases.
Needless to add, H_2 may be greater than H^*, but that is only an analytical
solution.

intersection must be non-negative and satisfy the equation

$$E^0 [H_2 f(H_1) - H_1 f(H_2)] = 2A[f(H_2) - f(H_1)],$$ (84)

where (here and hereafter) notations are such that $H_1 < H_2$. If $f(H_2)/H_2 > f(H_1)/H_1$, the solution of (84) is positive; the two curves intersect and intersect only once. In the contrary case, $E^0 < 0$ and the curves do not intersect.

There are four distinct and exhaustive cases.

1: $H^* < H_1$. From (84) it follows that $E^0 = 0$, hence, $p = \infty$. The two curves meet at infinity.

2: $H^m < H_1 < H^*$. In this case, $0 < E^0 < \infty$. The two curves intersect at a finite distance.

3: $H_2 < H^m$. The two curves never intersect, since $E^0 < 0$.

4: $H_1 < H^m < H_2$: There are two subcases. First, the equation $f(H_2')/H_2' = f(H_2)/H_2$ has a non-trivial solution (which is unique if it exists). Second, this solution does not exist; we then put $H_2' = 0$. The two curves intersect at a finite distance if $H_1 > H_2'$, and at infinity if $H_1 = H_2' > 0$. If $0 < H_1 \leqslant H_2'$, the two curves never intersect.

We shall also need to know the relative position of a pair of curves (H). The sign of $p(H_1) - p(H_2)$ is the same as that of

$$-E[H_2 f(H_1) - H_1 f(H_2)] + 2A[f(H_2) - f(H_1)].$$ (85)

If the curves intersect, this sign is positive for $E < E^0$, and negative for $E > E^0$. Hence, (H_1) intersects (H_2) from above and from the west. We must note that if $H^* < H_1$, (H_1) and (H_2) intersect at $E^0 = 0$, hence (H_2) is to the east of (H_1). If the curves do not intersect at all, then (85) is positive, which means that (H_1) is to the east of (H_2).

Another crucial element of the problem is the sign of

$$\Sigma_X^D = Lf(D_L) - D_L(x - x') - Y_m.$$ (86)

The associate curve, D, represented by

$$D(p, w) = E[3f(D_L) - 2D_L f'(D_L)] - 4Af'(D_L) = 0,$$ (87)

is asymptotic to $E = 0$, since $f'(D_L) = 0$ implies $p = \infty$. For relevant situations, $H^m \leqslant D_L < H^*$, in which case the coefficient of E is always positive. Therefore, any line $w = \lambda p$, $\lambda \leqslant f(H^m)/H^m$ intersects D at a finite distance. In particular, D intersects $0i$ at a point c' for which $E = 4A/H^m$ (Figure 8.A11).

12. *The map of disequilibria: second part*

As in Section 10, we shall being with the normal case of disequilibrium models.

A: $H^m \leqslant N < H^*$. We shall represent the family of curves (79) in Figure

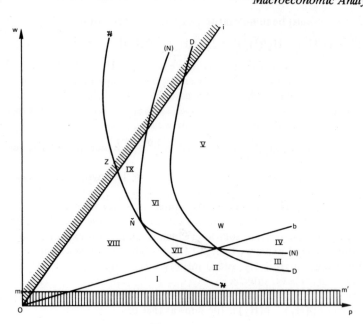

Fig. 8.A11

8.A11 without any regard for the relevance of the points (p, w). Before proceeding to its analysis, several points need to be established.

First, let us recall that E_w, corresponding to the Walrasian equilibrium prices, satisfies (62) and that $\check{E}$, corresponding to the tangency point of (N) and $\mathcal{H}$, satisfies (71), in which N has been substituted for H. From the two equations it follows that $\check{E} < E_w$, which means that $\mathcal{H}$ intersects 0b below W, at c.

Second, let $H_1 < H_2$ be the two intersections of Q_1 and Q_2 — i.e. of (68) and (69) — when they exist. From

$$3pEf(H_1) = 2w(H_1 E + 2A), \quad 3pEf(H_2) = 2w(H_2 E + 2A), \tag{88}$$

it follows, by subtraction and the mean theorem, that

$$3p[f(H_2) - f(H_1 0]/(N_1 - N_2) = 3pf'(\theta) = 2w, \tag{89}$$

for some unique θ such that $H_1 < \theta < H_2$. And since $pf'(D_L) = w$, we obtain the important result that[1]

$$D_L < \theta < H_2. \tag{90}$$

---

[1] Relation (90) is the crux of the fact that the relation between price constellations and disequilibrium types is never ambiguous.

Third, D belongs to the domain east of $\mathcal{H}$. Indeed the two curves could not intersect, because there is no point $\check{H}$ such that $\check{H} = D_L$. The slope of AB is $E/6p$ and that of the tangent to $0Q^*$ at H is $Ef'(H)/4w$. If these slopes were equal,

$$f'(H) = 2w/3p; \tag{91}$$

hence, $\check{H} \neq D_L$.

Fourth, from (62) and (87) it follows that D passes through W (an expected result), where it intersects (N) from above and from the west. For the Walrasian equilibrium prices, (p_0, w_0), the straight line AB intersects $0Q^*$ at the point corresponding to $N = D_L$ and at a second point, N_2, which by (90) is such that $N_2 > N = D_L$. Let now $0 < w/p - w_W/p_W < \epsilon$, where ϵ is sufficiently small. To w/p, there corresponds $D'_L = N - \Delta N$. Because of the continuity of $f'(H)$, from (89) it follows that the corresponding line AB that passes through the point corresponding to D'_L intersects $0Q^*$ the second time in N'_2 such that $N < N'_2 < N_2$. D passes, therefore, through the intersection of $(N - \Delta N)$ and (N'_2). From what we know about the relative positions of the curves (H) with respect to $\mathcal{H}$, that intersection is above (N).

However, D cannot intersect (N) at a *relevant* point different from W, for that would mean that $D_L = N$ for two different ratios w/p (which is impossible).

Fifth, we will find that in some cases $H_1 < D_L < H_2 < N$. This situation raises a crucial question. Since both H_1 and H_2 are possible *analytical* disequilibrium solutions, is the solution indeterminate? The answer is that the *economically relevant* solution is completely determinate, with employment at H_1.

Let Π_1 and Π_2 be the profits corresponding to H_1 and H_2, respectively. From

$$\Pi_2 = pLf(H_2) - wLH_2, \Pi_1 = pLf(H_1) - wLH_1, \tag{92}$$

it follows that

$$(\Pi_2 - \Pi_1)/L = p[f(H_2) - f(H_1)] - w[H_2 - H_1]$$
$$= [pf'(\theta) - w][H_2 - H_1].$$

From (90), it follows that $\Pi_1 > \Pi_2$. Hence, in order to maximise profit under constraint, the production units must necessarily employ H_1.

Bearing in mind the findings of the preceding section concerning the relative positions of any pair of curves (H_1) and (H_2), as well as that of any (H), $\mathcal{H}$ and D, we arrive at the following description of each of the domains into which, (N), $\mathcal{H}$, D, and 0b may divide the constellations (p, w), as shown in Figure 8.A11.[1] There may be either eight or nine domains according to

[1] The constraint represented by (64) will be taken into account later.

whether N is greater or smaller than H_Z, that is, according to whether the point of tangency of (N) and $\mathcal{H}$ is higher or lower than Z.

I. $Q_1 = Q_2$ has no solution. Moreover $D_L > N$, as is always the case below 0b. According to rule III of Section 10, the production units should choose the scale that is nearest to D_L. Hence, the disequilibrium solution is full employment with a uniform rationing of the commodity for all.[1] The case is known as repressed inflation (on the thought that rationing may be eliminated by increasing the production capacity of the physical plants).

II. $N < H_1 < H_2$ and $D_L > N$. Since $\Sigma(D_L) < 0$, the order is $N < D_L < H_1$. The pattern is again repressed inflation.

III. This case differs from II in that $\Sigma(D_L) > 0$; hence, $N < H_1 < D_L < H_2$, which also represents repressed inflation.[2]

IV. In this sector, just as in all sectors above (N), $H_1 < N < H_2$. Since here $N < D_L$, the producers would like to hire all workers (in order to obtain the maximum possible profit). However, at full employment production exceeds demand, because $\Sigma(N) > 0$. According to the characteristic tenet of disequilibrium theory, this contradiction can be eliminated if and only if the producers hire H_1 workers, in which case production (not to be confused with supply) is equal to the demand under constraint.[3] The unemployment is caused by a lack of demand at full employment. The pattern is that of Keynesian disequilibrium.

V. The only difference between this sector and IV is that now $D_L < N$. Now $\Sigma(D_L) > 0$, hence, $H_1 < D_L < H_2$. The producers cannot therefore sell all their optimal supply, $Lf(D_L)$. The solution is again represented by H_1, i.e. by a Keynesian disequilibrium.

VI. Since this sector is below (N), we have, as in some previous cases, $N < N_1 < N_2$, with $D_L < N$, and $\Sigma(D_L) < 0$. In this case, the producers can choose to work with their optimal scale. There is unemployment, $N - D_L$, with production falling short of demand. Consumers have to be rationed. The situation is known as classical disequilibrium.

VII and VIII. In both these sectors, $D_L < N$, and also $D_L < H_1$, since $\Sigma(D_L) < 0$. The pattern is again classical.

IX. This domain exists only if $N < \check{H}_z$. It differs from VI only in that $N < H_1 < H_2$. But since still $D_L < N$, the pattern is again classical.

---

[1] On this point, more in Section 13.

[2] It is clear that in this case, as in some others, the *disequilibrium* solution is the same in all three domains, I, II and III. Only the initial patterns may differ in II. However, there is no ambiguity in either classification. We want to overemphasise this point because during the meeting we stated that repressed inflation may overlap with Keynesian unemployment. *The statement was wrong.* Our error was caused by not realising that not all *analytical* solutions of $Q_1 = Q_2$ are economically *relevant* and that the classification of the disequilibrium does not always coincide with that of the initial conditions (Section 9).

[3] On this point, more in Section 13.

It may be well to note that cd, defined by (56), cuts D from above. This observation allows us to see that classical disequilibria develop from initial conditions that are classical disequilibria (Figure 8.A6a). However, some classical initial conditions may lead to Keynesian disequilibria. Initial Keynesian disequilibria always lead to Keynesian unemployment. But Keynesian patterns may also develop from some anti-classical initial conditions. These last conditions may end up as repressed inflation disequilibria, but not all initial repressed inflation situations change their pattern. Knowing these changes should help economic policy (if it is based on disequilibrium theory), because any economic policy must act on the initial causes, not on their outcomes.

To determine the loci of constant unemployment we must eliminate those elements of our map that, for one reason or other, have no relevance to this problem. To begin with we must eliminate the curves (H) for any $H > N$. These curves are tangent to $\mathcal{H}$ below $\check{N}$. But even the remaining curves must be amputated, as it were. The branch above their point of tangency $\check{H}$ must be eliminated. The reason is that through each point of such a branch there passes another curve, (H), that corresponds to a lower value of H. As we have seen, if $H_1 < H_2$, disequilibrium cannot be at H_2. The relevant loci of Keynesian unemployment, for $H^m < H_1 < N$, are the lower branches of the curves (H_1). For the curve (H^m), however, whose point of tangency with $\mathcal{H}$ is at $E = \infty$, there is no branch to be eliminated. The same applies to the curves (H) such that $H < H^m$. These, as we have seen, do not intersect each other, but follow in successive order above (H^m).

But there is still more. No production unit can employ H workers if the price constellation is such that

$$wH > pf(H). \tag{94}$$

This means that the branch of (H) above the intersection, j_H, of (H) with the straight line $0b_H$ represented by $wH = pf(H)$, must also be eliminated if j_H happens to be on the branch of (H) that has not been already eliminated by the previous operation (Figure 8.A12). For j_H we have

$$E(j_H) = 4A/H. \tag{95}$$

From this relation and from the result, mentioned earlier, that D intersects $0i$ at a point for which $E = 4A/H_m$, it follows that (H^m) and D intersect on $0i$ at $j_H m$.

The locus, j, of j_H is obtained by substituting H from relation (95) into (79), which yields

$$pEf(4A/E) = 4wA. \tag{96}$$

For the shape of this curve, we must note that, because of the continuity properties assumed about $f'''(H)$,

$$3Bwf'(0) = 3Bp[f'(o)]^2 + 2Af''(0) \tag{97}$$

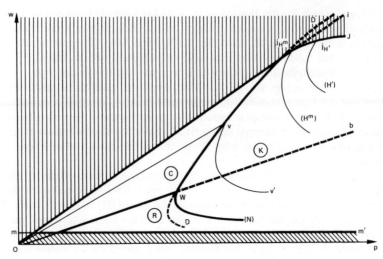

Fig. 8.A12

is an asymptote of J, provided $f'(0) \neq 0$. If $f'(0) = 0$, the upper branch of J
has a parabolic shape. $E = 0$ also is an asymptote of J, but the lower branch of
J presents no relevant interest. In fact, only the branch above $j_H m$ is
economically relevant. Indeed J is tangent to Oi at $j_H m$. Any straight
line $w = kp$, $f'(0) < k < f'(H^m)$, intersects J in two points, as is proved
by the shape of the curve representing $f(H)/H$. Only if $k = f'(H^m)$ do these
two points coincide, namely, with $j_H m$. But D is intersected only at one point
by any straight line $w = f'(H)p$, $H^m < H < N$. Hence, the constellations that
are not eliminated by (94) are represented by the lower branches of the
curves (H), for which $H < H^m$.

On the basis of the foregoing observations, the relevant map of static
disequilibria for the case under consideration, (A), is represented in Figure
8.A12. The shaded areas represent price constellations for which the system
cannot possibly work. The relevant domain, delimited by Oi, D, and Ob,
corresponds to classical unemployment. The domain delimited by D, J, and
(N) corresponds to Keynesian unemployment. Finally, the domain delimited
by mm′, Ob, and (N) corresponds to repressed inflation.[1]

But the most salient result (about which more later) is this. The locus of a
given employment level N_1 such that $H^m \leqslant N_1 \leqslant N$, is a kinked line Ovv′
(the segment below mm′ being, of course, excluded). On Ov, the equation of
which is $w = f'(N_1)p$, the pattern is classical. At v the pattern becomes

---

[1] The patterns corresponding to points on any one of the boundaries are
not ambiguous, although they may reflect mixed features, as this is most
obvious in the case of D.

Keynesian and the locus is vv', the relevant branch of (N_1). For $N_1' < H^m$ the locus is only the branch of (N_1') below $j_{N_1'}$, and the pattern is Keynesian throughout.

B: $N < H^m$. Since no price constellation can now satisfy both $w = f'(N)p$ and $wN \leqslant pf(N)$, the analytical 0b lies above 0i. *There is, therefore, no Walrasian equilibrium.* Price constellations above the line $wN = pf(N)$, represented by 0b' (Figure 8.A13a), are unavailing. The domain between the branch of (N) below j_N and J corresponds to the Keynesian pattern. The branch of the curve (N_1), $N_1 < N$, is the locus of Keynesian employment N_1. The domain between 0_{j_N}, (N), and mm' corresponds, as before, to repressed inflation.

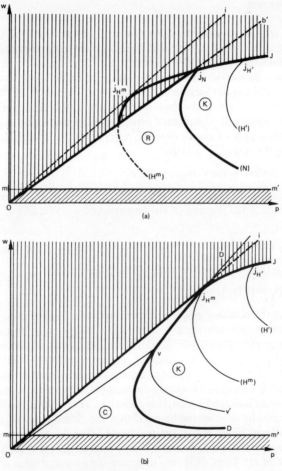

Figs. 8.A13a–A13b

Because not all plants can be manned at their optimal capacity, H^m, the situation just considered reflects a deficit of population. There is thus underpopulation or, equivalently, overcapitalisation. In this case, the most we can hope to achieve is full employment, not Walrasian equilibrium.

C: $H > H^*$. In this case again no Walrasian equilibrium exists. The corresponding map is represented by Figure 8.A13b. There are only two patterns: Keynesian above D, and classical below D. The employment isoquants for $N_1 \geq H^m$ have the same kinked shape, Ovv', as in Figure 8.A12. And for $N_1' < H^m$, they again are the branches of (N_1') below J.

13. Rationing rules

As we have seen, in various situations of disequilibrium there is a need for some rationing in order to assure that the economic disequilibrium can exist in all situations, as the new theory wants it. One such specific rule for rationing the consumers in the case of classical unemployment has been suggested by Malinvaud (Section 10). Let r, $r = x - u$, $u > 0$, be the rationed amount of the commodity the employed worker is allowed to purchase. Knowing (by some still unexplained procedure) this restriction, such a worker will adjust his supply of labour time, L', accordingly. If the ophelimity function has the form (5), we have

$$L' = L - pu/2w = (Bw - m_0 + pr)/2w. \tag{98}$$

The production must now satisfy the constraint demand of the employed workers as well as the demand of the unemployed workers and of the government:

$$3pr[f(D_L) - 2D_L f'(D_L)] = 2(A - 2D_L m_0)f'(D_L) - 3(Bw - m_0). \tag{99}$$

The rub is that this equation may fail to determine r, if

$$f(D_L)/2D_L = f'(D_L). \tag{100}$$

Indeed, as the ordinary graph of the average and marginal productivity of labour would immediately show, this equation always has at least one solution, $D_L > H^m$. That is not all: (100) is a differential equation, whose integral is $f(H) = \alpha\sqrt{H}$. For this function, (99) is completely indeterminate, a snag that cannot be set aside as long as the production function satisfies the standard assumption (16). However, the snag persists in a somewhat smaller form even for an S-shaped production function. True, such a production function cannot be represented by $\alpha\sqrt{H}$ over the closed interval $[H^m, H^*]$, which is pertinent to the model defined by (A). Yet the production function can be represented by $\alpha\sqrt{H}$ over any closed interval $[H', H'']$ such that $H^m < H'$, $H'' < H^*$. Then, (99) fails to determine r for any value of D_L belonging to that interval. The point is highly important, because it proves that rationing rules for classical unemployment may break down for other ophelimity functions as well.

For the case of repressed inflation, the same rule leads to

$$\Sigma_X^0 = Lf(N) - Nx-G/p = u\,[pf(N)\text{-}2Nw]\,/2w. \tag{101}$$

Because for repressed inflation $\Sigma_X^0 > 0$, u cannot be positive unless $pf(N) > 2wN$, which means that the receipts of the firms must be greater than twice the wage bill. If prices do not allow this to happen, the rule, simple and transparent though it appears *prima facie*, becomes inoperative. Other rationing rules may have the same fate.

Disequilibrium theory counts on possible rationing only for the commodity and labour power, but not for labour time (probably because the latter co-ordinate is absent from the standard framework). However, Keynesian unemployment (which, according to the same theory, is the more relevant in actuality), could be eliminated by rationing labour time.

The idea is not far-fetched. To recall, in 1933 the United States Congress passed a law reducing the work week to thirty hours for the sole purpose of reducing the massive unemployment of that time. (The law was never put into effect.) Charles Roos (1933), who immediately set out to analyse the implications of such a measure, also remarked that 'Theorists have generally very glibly referred to the supply of labor without specifying the length of the work week, whereas obviously, if all workers were employed on a forty-hour average work week, some would be unemployed if the work week could be suddenly increased to fifty hours'. In retrospect, one can only wonder why economic theorists still continue to ignore the labour time in the analysis of production and unemployment.

If L^0 is the exogenously determined labour time, the corresponding demand for the commodity of an employed worker is

$$x^0 = 2(wL^0 + m_0)/3p. \tag{102}$$

The proper L^0 for the elimination of Keynesian unemployment is given by

$$L^0\,[3pf(N) - 2wN] = A. \tag{103}$$

This equation always has a solution, L^0, for any relevant price constellation.

In the case of a classical pattern, however, rationing the number of working hours would make matters worse since it would diminish an already insufficient production. Classical unemployment, so it seems, is a harder nut to crack.

14. Concluding remarks

Two additional observations should be made in closing. The first concerns a specific feature of the ordinary disequilibrium model. Any model must, of course, be consistent within itself. But a model intended to represent a process that presumably goes on without any distinction between one day and the next must also be consistent as an *algorithm*. This means that its final outcome must satisfy the same assumptions as those imposed on the initial conditions. For example, a model requiring that all initial co-ordinates be positive must ensure that all final co-ordinates also be positive. The model cannot represent what happens on Tuesday if the conditions inherited from Monday do not belong to the same axiomatic set as those of Monday morning.[1]

Malinvaud's assumption about the initial conditions (which is representative of the usual disequilibrium models) is a case in point. All individuals start with the same amount of money, m_0; the government has a fund G. The business sector has no initial money balance. By the end of the day, that sector is in possession of the profit

$$\Pi = pLf(N_1) - wLN_1 = G + 2(N - N_1)m_0/3 + N_1(3m_0 - Bw)/4, \quad (104)$$

which is always non-negative if $E \leqslant 4A/N_1$ (as we have seen). This profit consists of the government expenditure G, the expenditure by the unemployed, in all $2(N - N_1)m_0/3$, and the net change in the balances of the employed, $N_1 \Delta m = N_1(3m_0 - Bw)/4$.

The process by which disequilibrium is reached thus fundamentally changes the distribution of money between the various participants. For the model to represent the next-day process as well, some additional rules must be introduced for re-establishing the initial distribution. Naturally, one would think of taxing away the whole profit, which would restore the initial position of the business sector, and using the proceeds for doing the same for individuals and the government itself. Alternatively, one may propose distributing Π among the households 'according to a predetermined distribution pattern' (Barro and Grossman, 1971, p. 84). Unfortunately, things are not so easy even for the very simple model under consideration. That recipe obviously fails if Π = 0. In this case, the employed absorb all the money in the community. The only way to restore the initial distribution is for the government to tax away the entire savings of the employed and use the proceeds for subsidising the unemployed by a negative tax and endowing itself again with G. But even if Π > 0, the distribution of profit among the investors (assumed to include the government) would not do as a general rule. Δm may still be negative, since $N_1 E < 2A$ requires only

$$3N_1 \Delta m + 2m_0(N - N_1) + 3G > 0. \quad (105)$$

The intervention of the government is then necessary for siphoning the savings of the employed either for subsidising the unemployed, or financing itself, or doing both. The simplest rule is therefore for the government to tax all savings and profits and to practise negative tax (which might include the employed as well).

The idea of a business sector that operates constantly without profit after

---

[1] We should note that the Walrasian model is consistent in this sense.

taxes and a government that may have to practise negative taxation is so remote from the prevailing system that our model is utterly inadequate to serve as a guide for policy.

The second observation is a reminder: no process of a dialectical nature can be adequately represented by an arithmomorphic blueprint. Only mechanical processes ('mechanical' being understood in its extensive sense used in epistemology) can be so represented. For dialectical processes we can, at most, resort to an analytical simile (Georgescu-Roegen, 1966; 1971). Being the product of a heroic mental jump between the two irreducible modes of cognition, a simile can nonetheless be useful in some particular way. Ordinarily, it can make us aware of some unsuspected difficulties or of latent errors in some of our conventional notions. That is, if a simile cannot tell us what to do, it may tell us what not to do or not to believe.

Take the current notion that to reduce unemployment one should either increase the wage rate or decrease prices (which is tantamount to increasing the purchasing power of wages). From Figure 8.A12 it is immediately obvious that in the case of classical unemployment the contrary is true: one must either increase prices or decrease wages (up to a certain level).[1] The same map shows that, contrary to Malinvaud's assertion (1977, p. 66), even in the case of a Keynesian disequilibrium increasing wages may increase unemployment, if the disequilibrium corresponds to a point on (H) above the turning point, which corresponds to (81).

To justify the map of Figure 8.A12, let us first note that from (81) and (95) it follows that

$$E_m(H) < E_j(H). \tag{106}$$

Hence for $H < H^m$, H is always backward-bending below J. (See also Figure 8.A13). For $H^m \leqslant H \leqslant N$, let a_H be the intersection of (H) and the straight line $w = f'(H)p$. For a_H we have

$$E_a(H) = 4Af'(H)/[3f(H) - 2Hf'(H)]. \tag{107}$$

For the equality $E_m(H) = E_a(H)$ to be satisfied over some non-zero interval, f must be a solution of the differential equation

$$[3f - 2Hf'(H)]\sqrt{2AM_0} = 4Af'(H)\sqrt{H}. \tag{108}$$

This yields

$$f = c(2A + \sqrt{2AM_0H})^3. \tag{109}$$

For this function, which can be valid only for a true subinterval of $[H^m, H^*]$, the turning point of (H) is on D. Functions therefore exist for which the turning points may be on either side of D.

An example of a function with a continuous derivative that fits the map of

---

[1] That this also is a simple consequence of (52) is a familiar point.

Figure 8.A12 is

$$f(H) = 3\sqrt{3}H^2/16 \qquad\qquad \text{for } 0 \leqslant H \leqslant 4/3,$$
$$f(H) = \sqrt{H-1} \qquad\qquad\quad \text{for } 4/3 \leqslant H \leqslant 10, \qquad\qquad (110)$$
$$F(H) = (-3H^2 + 62H - 311)/3 \quad \text{for } 10 \leqslant H \leqslant 11/3,$$

for which $H^i = 4/3$, $H^m = 2$, $H^* = 11/3$. N may have any value such that $H^m < N < 10$.

The extremely simple formula (7), assumed for utility, is responsible for the fact that in the model under consideration, a decrease in prices always reduces Keynesian unemployment. But if the ophelimity function is assumed to have only the generally accepted properties, no definite sign can be attributed to $\delta N_1/\delta P$ on the basis of relation (65) which defines Keynesian disequilibrium. The conclusion that the disequilibrium theory offers us no guide on how to remedy Keynesian unemployment is not without value. On the contrary, it is worth remembering.

Discussion of the paper by Professors Fitoussi and Georgescu-Roegen

Professor Modigliani began by saying that this paper had a broad sweep, considering philosophical issues, and with Schumpeter very much in evidence. A major purpose was to explain why there had been such a sharp change in the pattern of unemployment before and after the Second World War. It was certainly true that since 1945 there had been less cyclic variation in unemployment but it was not clear to him whether the authors were saying that the average level had been higher or lower in the second period. Nevertheless, they wanted a model to explain what had happened. They began by rejecting disequilibrium theories like those of Professor Malinvaud. They castigated him for understandable reasons, criticising him for talking of disequilibrium without looking for a mechanism to put it right. Malinvaud assumed a given level of prices which was there for ever. If there was disequilibrium at these prices there was no reason why disequilibrium should ever end. Malinvaud did not search for an equilibrating process like that of Marshall's long run. Of course, there was no such thing as long-run equilibrium in the sense of a state reached but only a direction in which the system moved.

The authors explored unemployment along Schumpeterian lines as a reaction to the innovation process. Innovation disturbed equilibrium. The economic system then sought to re-establish it, so that there was a continuous move towards re-establishment of equilibrium. As we all knew, Schumpeter believed that innovation went in waves, though Professor Modigliani had always found it hard to see why. According to the authors, Schumpeter seemed to be correct until the Second World War, with unemployment a cyclical phenomenon. Since the Second World War however, there had been the Schumpeterian innovation to transform all Schumpeterian innovations. This was R & D expenditure which made innovation an induced process. Innovation still disturbed the system and led to unemployment and its reabsorption, but the flow was now steadier. Unemployment was not cyclical but permanent. The authors gave a number of factors which they thought caused unemployment today to represent a steady state situation. They thought there was persistent excess capacity with geographical dispersion. However, they gave no hard evidence on the existence of excess capacity. The authors further mentioned two reasons for the way unemployment responded. First, there was wage and price rigidity. Prices did change, but slowly, so that the adjustment process was also slow. Second, there was a supposed asymmetry in the response of modern managers to changes in demand. They responded to increased demand by increasing output less than they reduced it when demand fell. He was not quite clear whether the authors were talking about the speed or the extent of this response because the paper seemed contradictory. The reason why the modern manager behaved this way was that he was risk-averse. The paper went through various transformations to show that dispersion of demand led to unemployment. What he was not clear about was whether if there was zero excess demand output would be stable or whether it would then fall. The appendix to the paper was devoted to a formal and severe criticism of Professor Malinvaud and pointed to some shortcomings which led to some questionable results.

Professor Modigliani said he had two main criticisms of the paper. First, there was the asymmetric response he had already noted to increases and decreases in demand. In the paper, output responded less to increases than to decreases but he imagined that one could credibly support the reverse case. One could say that it was easy to increase output with existing capacity; only when new capacity was needed was there risk. When demand increased, business did not want their competitors to get a big share of the increase, hence they would respond fully. On the other hand, one could argue that workers disliked falling output because it led to unemployment, so that business would try not to fire workers but to reduce prices, accumulate inventories etc. In general, he was wary of asymmetries, including the one in the paper. He acknowledged, however, that American experience might be different from that in Europe. In Europe, employers seemed to be reluctant to hire workers because it was difficult to fire them later. One implication was that if demand increased this might not lead to a rise in output, or at least in employment. But then a fall in demand might also not lead to a fall in employment. In any event, this mechanism was not mentioned in the paper.

Second, in his view, the bearing of this source of unemployment was not too serious. The main thesis was that unemployment resulted from innovation. He was sympathetic to this view, but one ought to distinguish between whether unemployment had changed in nature, and whether or not it had increased on the average. He himself had reservations about a presumed increase in average unemployment after the Second World War, at least up to the seventies. There had certainly been smaller and fewer cycles since the Second World War, but he thought that was due to the application of Keynesian economics. The reason we had no more 1929s was that economists were smarter. Why was this not a possible explanation? Of course, since 1970, as a result of stagflation economists had become increasingly doubtful about their ability to manage exogenous inflation or to end the momentum of inflation, but he thought we had learned a great deal about the management of aggregate demand.

As for the average level of unemployment, the authors seemed to recognise only one source, that resulting from the loss of jobs through the disequilibrium generated and maintained by the process of innovation. This view of unemployment was consistent with models like that of Holt which showed that a steady flow of job losers could give rise to a stable pool of unemployed even though the losers would eventually find new jobs, because of the time required to find a job. But the authors neglected the many other sources of flow into the pool of unemployed — people fired because of shifts in private and public demand between products and regions, or because of fluctuations in aggregate demand, job quitters, new entrants and re-entry into the labour force.

All of these flows were important if one wanted to understand why there was an equilibrium rate of unemployment (the so-called full-employment unemployment) and why that rate was, say, around 5 per cent in the USA, but much lower in the Scandinavian countries or in the Federal Republic of Germany. For very open economies, and in the presence of multinational corporations, this diversity could not be so readily explained by the innovation model. The higher level for the USA seemed rather to be explained by the much larger flows of labour relative to the labour force, and perhaps longer job-search time, arising from such factors as the size of the country, the heterogeneity of the population and the greater freedom of firing which in turn generated a larger flow of job openings and greater readiness to quit. A small homogeneous country with appreciable restrictions on firing would be characterised by smaller flows.

In Professor Modigliani's view, the rise in the average rate of unemployment in the last few years must be seen as the intended result of aggregate demand management policies designed to bring inflation under control.

In conclusion, it seemed to him that the paper brought attention to an important phenomenon. There was a combination of the fact that dynamic innovation in society was good, but perhaps while it was good the conclusion was that one should not allow it to move too quickly because that led to unemployment. Nevertheless, he thought the authors took too partial a view, and in a broader perspective what they had to say could be more valuable.

Professor Georgescu-Roegen could not see how Professor Modigliani had reached the conclusion that he wanted 'to give hell' to Professor Malinvaud. He had taken the Malinvaud model as the basis for his criticism because that model was the most specific and precise of the set of such models, and was also the latest presentation of disequilibrium theory. All that he had done was to deal with the problems raised by the theory just as any scholar would.

Professor Georgescu-Roegen was prepared to accept most of what Professor Modigliani had said in addition. The paper he had presented together with Professor Fitoussi had not attempted to 'finish' dealing with the problem of unemployment. The authors simply wanted to point to what they believed to be its true cause. An analogy might be supplied by a river which sometimes flooded. One obviously needed more bridges, dams, etc. but this did not mean that the flooding was caused by the bridges and dams. The paper sought to show how the late capitalist society paid for its extravagant growth, often by developing a wrong technology. In the USA people spoke of 'another Edsel', because the Edsel was a car which had been carefully researched and advertised, but which in the end proved to be a total failure. Other worrying developments had been due to Madison Avenue advertising technology. Salesmen kept coming along and saying, 'What we sold you last year was rotten; now try this *new* gadget'. Why did we have to worry about Keynesian teaching if there were no innovations? And Walras and Marshall were perfectly right in saying that, with no disturbances, the economic system would move towards an equilibrium. Professor Georgescu's criticism of disequilibrium theory concerned the point that, given prices and real wages, this led to a static (determined) disequilibrium. He did not think that represented the factual truth.

Mr Kaser wanted to take up Professor Modigliani's introductory observation that the appendix to the paper was substantially focused on Professor Malinvaud's recent work, including his paper for this conference. The authors used three models, listed in the appendix. These were the Keynesian, classical, and repressed inflation models. These had been considered in the discussion of Professor Malinvaud's paper, and indeed had also been explored in some respects by Professor Hines.

Mr Kaser wanted to deal with the statement in the appendix that 'individuals seek to maximise their utility and firms seek to maximise their profits'. He suggested that in the real world individuals, in their role as trade unionists, were in fact willing to share work, and that multiplant businesses were prepared to share profits. Any of either that were not inclined to share in such a way could be compelled to do so by even the most libertarian governments through the conventional taxation system. Of course, in appealing to the real world an economist was often only urging his hearers to accept his own model, but he would like to quote a few empirical cases which, perhaps surprisingly, no-one had yet mentioned in the conference.

Two of Professor Malinvaud's macroeconomic models of involuntary unemployment required the profitable employment of capacity $\bar{y}$ in all its sectoral uses, namely, the Keynesian and classical situations. The early discussion had not considered the repressed inflation model whose conditions ruled, as Lord Kaldor had earlier noted, in the West immediately after the Second World War. Mr Kaser wanted to add that the model was relevant to eastern Europe today where sectoral production was clearly determined by the availability of employment, and not by profitability. Examples could be found in the coal mines of Wales in 1947 and today in Poland, but it was part of Mr Kaser's argument that it was not only in the repressed inflation model that the profit margin constraint could be relaxed. The instrument was the transfer of income, particularly between enterprises and through the aegis of the government. The role of government was also relevant to the distribution of personal income, which Professor Malinvaud assumed stable. Intersectoral financial transfer reduced Professor Malinvaud's equilibrating function for labour mobility. Shop stewards notoriously preferred labour mobility, though they could occasionally be overruled by their trade unions or government. Professor Timofeev had implicitly invoked the role of social transfers in his criticism of the authors' approach, and this could similarly modify the starting assumption of Professor Hines's paper, namely 'the simple fact that in a market economy production is undertaken for profit'.

One could rather say that in some western European countries there was pressure for production to be undertaken for employment reasons. Individual instances readily came to mind in the UK and in France (Lip). Japanese corporations were well known for their policy of employment maintenance. All such cases suggested a voluntary reduction of wage rates, or sometimes of hours worked. However, Mr Kaser's principal contention was that enterprises might well be motivated to produce up to or even beyond the break-even point provided that subsidies were paid if profits became negative. To avoid inflation, such subsidies must be financed from current profits or household income. But there were two vehicles for such transfers. First, households could be taxed. Second, multiplant firms could indulge in cross-subsidisation or be taxed. Marris's theory of managerial capitalism supported the idea of employment maintenance by pointing to various motivations. The important one here was the desire of these managers of a large firm to maintain its turnover to resist takeover by another. Professor Giersch had similarly mentioned the satisficing principle.

Professor Modigliani had already noted that transfers that were capital-deepening would be frustrated, either because savings were too small, or because an open economy could not maintain a low enough interest rate. Mr Kaser's own proposition should be followed through, partly by taking account of different propensities to consume between households and enterprises, as mentioned by Professor Kolm, or through raising the multiplier by distributing expenditure for the employed to the unemployed, as had been mentioned by Professor Henin.

Sir Austin Robinson said that, when confronted by a mathematical model, he always asked himself whether that model was covering all the relevant and important issues. He had no doubt that structural employment was important, but wondered whether the authors were looking at what mattered most. Unemployment in the 1970s was perhaps more largely a consequence of the growth of the economies of Japan, Hong Kong, Singapore and other developing countries. Again, he thought of the oil crisis, of Britain's entry into the EEC and of the problem within the EEC of finding where the member countries' comparative advantages lay. There were also changes in income distribution, in tastes and in technology. These helped to cause structural unemployment.

What was it that limited the capacity of a country to adapt to the new situation? He thought there had been far too little work by economists on the practicable rate of adjustment by an economy with only price incentives. In wartime there could be rapid change because of controls. There was nothing of this in the paper. Perhaps one needed more work on these practical problems of how fast an economy could adjust. He thought that prices could handle such changes satisfactorily if they were no greater than, say, 2½ per cent of change per annum. In Europe today he was not surprised that there was structural unemployment. Countries could not adjust as rapidly as was needed at the moment.

Professor Malinvaud limited his discussion to four types of consideration.

First, concerning the scientific approach to the study of unemployment, he would easily accept the role of dialectics, especially in order to impose a complete grasp on the phenomenon. But then modelling had still a complementary role to play for the consolidation of dialectical discoveries and for the study of their consequences.

There was also agreement on the fact that explanations of unemployment should bring in time in an essential way (the unemployment of the 1970s could not be fully understood without reference to the events of the 1960s). Irreversibility and asymmetry were then important, as always when time was involved. Static models were not necessarily useless, but they were certainly partial.

Second, since unemployment was a disequilibrium phenomenon, rapid innovations could in some circumstances make unemployment worse. He was *a priori* ready to give credit to the main argument of the paper, namely that the present unemployment was structural and caused by technological innovations.

However, as a dialectician, he would find it hard to accept this as the whole explanation. He thought the authors were too pessimistic about our ability to absorb unemployment. He could point to periods in history when innovation was high and unemployment low, and did not think one could fully explain recent unemployment in these terms.

Third, Professor Malinvaud thought there was also agreement on the role of uncertainty in the behaviour of the firm. This might explain the increase in unemployment first in 1971 and then in 1973. He was quite happy to accept what the authors said about asymmetry, but was perplexed at the claim that a fundamental reason for present unemployment was the 'growth mania' of the new managerial class. One could not argue simultaneously that managers were too much growth-oriented and that, because of uncertainties, they did not build the productive capacity that was needed.

Fourth, as for the Appendix, Professor Malinvaud was ready to accept most of it and to recognise that the theory of general equilibrium under fixed prices and quantity rationing raised still more problems than he had dealt with in his own writings. In particular he agreed that a precise analysis of unemployment ought not to deal only with the labour input but to distinguish between number of employees and hours of work.

He did, however, have considerable difficulty with the last sentence of the Appendix. 'Models that aim only at simply describing possible disequilibriums, even when they are not affected by short-comings of the kind pointed to in this Appendix, cannot shed much light on the cause of unemployment and on its impact on the adaptation of markets.' He thought the Appendix showed how difficult it was to create such models. But since unemployment was a disequilibrium, there was no alternative when one wanted to supplement dialectics by more analytical reasoning.

Professor Bergmann wanted to look at a narrow point, namely the contribution of the increase in frictional unemployment to current unemployment problems. She agreed that attention to job turnover and to the role of search in the labour market process was valuable, but this theoretical emphasis had led to airy statements on its large importance. In an extreme case, one could say that all unemployment resulted from turnover, so it was necessary to do some measurement. Her own work had measured the extent of frictional employment and the extent to which an increase in turnover had led to increase in unemployment with demand constant. Figure 12.2 in her own paper showed that white males had a 2½ per cent probability per month of being hired. 1 per cent of the 6½ per cent unemployment rate could be attributed to frictional unemployment. We could take it that frictional unemployment showed up in vacancies. If frictional unemployment resulted from search, then only an ability to find a job vacancy was confirmed.

If innovation led to unemployment, we could talk of demand shortage. So if one really were interested in frictional unemployment, one was interested in the match between job creation and job destruction. If when anyone left a job it was immediately refilled, there was no frictional unemployment. However, we had not even begun to explain the increase in unemployment which had occurred.

Professor Henin turned to the main theme of the paper, which was that a major cause of unemployment was change. Maybe most economists wanted to say rather that the main cause was uncertainty about the way in which change occurred in the economy. But Professor Henin thought that a more essential and more operative answer was to note that such a change occurred in a decentralised economy, where, unlike the models by Walras and Pareto, there was no perfect mechanism for the *a priori* co-ordination of plans. This was the very message of disequilibrium theory. There might be a wide variety of models saying that. But the important point was that – to be relevant – they had to speak about an economy with imperfect co-ordination.

Professor dos Santos Ferreira referred to the appendix to the paper. He did not share the authors' interpretation of the general equilibrium model with quantity rationing, but wanted to stress that the distinction which they introduced between the amount of employed manpower and the length of the working day seemed to him a potentially important innovation. However, he did not think that this distinction was introduced in the most fruitful way, nor that it considerably modified the working of the Malinvaud model. The authors considered exclusively the influence of consumer behaviour and institutional factors on the length of the working day. In fact, working time was the result of (constrained) optimisation by the firm, taking account of the increase in the average hourly wage rate resulting from overtime. It would be interesting to consider the effects upon the different equilibrium regimes of the variability of working time as a consequence of firms' rather than of workers' behaviour.

Professor Frey referred to structural change on the side of labour supply. There was a big change in work force participation, and participants knew that he looked for a change in participation by the aged in future.

He wondered whether it would be better to renounce bad technological progress or to find better technological progress than in the last decade. He referred to a 1965 report on technology in the USA which had pointed to a drastic reduction in hours of work per week.

Dr Gordon was surprised to read in the paper that most unemployment was frictional unemployment caused by frequent structural change resulting from innovation. That, to her, was structural unemployment. To her, an increase in frictional unemployment resulted from the fact that people left jobs or were fired, even though there was no change in output. This might be very difficult in practice to distinguish from cyclical unemployment.

Professor Modigliani had said that he did not see why innovation should come in waves. What Schumpeter had actually said was that innovations were implemented in waves. This was important here because there was no reason why that was less true now than it used to be. It was true that there was now more research and development, but there was still the same phenomenon of the wave-like implementation of innovation.

Professor Hines agreed that one should discuss the different shocks to which an economy was subject, and that the method of adaptation to these was unimportant. The framework which he and Professor Malinvaud both used could be made to encompass them.

The appendix to this paper looked at the disequilibrium method which could be used where prices did not adjust. Most economists now seemed to agree that a quantity response was perhaps the most immediate reaction to a shock. There was not a Walrasian market-clearing vector of prices, but some prices adjusted faster than others. For example, as in the paper, capital markets cleared more quickly. Adjustment might be more rapid for product markets as compared with labour markets, though these did adjust and it was recognised that quantity adjustment might operate rather than price adjustment. If there was no adjustment of prices in the goods market, one could have an increase in imports. Whether foreign exchange was then available had implications for the adjustment of goods prices.

One also had to look at the implications for profit. The authors did say that, in a market economy, one must start from some rate of profit. Whether this would lead to growing unemployment would depend on wages, prices and the rate of interest. If one by-passed this system, what was the alternative mechanism? Perhaps one could not talk in terms of the general level of profitability and of cross-subsidisation. One would then have to find a new way of generating a level of activity. However, it was necessary to develop our models for doing that.

Professor Holt did not think one could link frictional unemployment to the number of unemployed. The idea was not sound. There were severe difficulties in identifying voluntary and involuntary unemployment. It was necessary to study the costs and benefits of unemployment, and these concepts were then not very useful, even though Professor Bergmann's measure was a very ingenious one.

Lord Kaldor said the issues raised in the Georgescu-Roegen–Fittousi paper had been discussed as far back as the 1920s at the Kiel Institute. The unemployment then being experienced in Germany was put down to technical change. He agreed with Professor Malinvaud that there was no evidence that technical change was now so much faster than a few years ago or that that particular feature explained the radical difference in the rate of unemployment and the gravity of the situation in western countries today. In the 1960s, OECD countries took it as a matter of course that aggregate output would grow by 5 per cent per annum and argued that stability was unimportant. Some countries grew more rapidly than others. In the UK with much unemployment in the previous decades and a good deal of emigration, there had been twenty years during which unemployment had been less than 2 per cent.

All that had now changed, and he thought it was important to ask why the capitalist world had grown so quickly for so long. There had been harmonious development. Even though there were intersectoral pressures, all went well, and consumption and production moved in step. There was no rapid increase in prices, but no collapse either. He thought the latter had been prevented by the readiness of governments to build up stocks, while technical progress in land-saving inventions had helped the output of raw materials and fuel to increase rapidly. This harmony had now vanished, and things had gone haywire. However, he did not think one should conclude that we were entering on a new age where we could not sustain the working population in employment. In ten years' time, he suspected that we should find that many of the fears in this discussion were premature.

Professor Fitoussi replied to the discussion. The paper intended to say that unemployment was affected not only by variations in aggregate demand, but also and sometimes more importantly by the way in which they took place. A general reduction of income, for example, had discriminatory effects. The first impact would be on some markets rather than others. Therefore macroeconomic reasoning should not be abandoned. But one had also to look at structural effects. In some situations the structural effect was far more important than the global effect.

He agreed with Professor Henin that we need a theory of imperfect co-ordination of markets, but he disagreed on the fact that the theory of general equilibrium with rationing provided such a framework. This theory worked in terms of co-ordination through quantities rather than prices, so one had trial and error models with full co-ordination through quantities.

A productive way of working on a theory of imperfect co-ordination was to look at the asymmetries which characterised the economy. There was general agreement among the economists about the existence of such an asymmetry in variations of prices. Thus price movements had an upward bias. But this was only part of the story. As a corollary there was an asymmetry in quantity variations; *an inverse asymmetry*. So quantity movements had a *downward* bias. Macroeconomic equilibrium was by nature stochastic, since such an equilibrium was the resultant of a plurality of disequilibria. It was the null average of a series of excess demands of contrary sign. A structural disequilibrium was therefore associated with macroeconomic equilibrium. One had partial markets in imbalance, with structural disequilibrium leading to positive effects on prices and negative effects on quantities. Hence to the Phillips curve, which was an inverse conjunctural relation, we had to add a direct structural relation between inflation and unemployment. The important point was to understand that the two relations were complementary.

To Sir Austin Robinson, Professor Fitoussi replied that the factors the former emphasised produced a structural imbalance. He himself had not only been concerned with innovation in the technical sense. 'Novelty' was multidimensional. It could be expressed by innovation – a change of taste, technique, the expansion of markets – or by institutional evolution – alteration of tax rules, unemployment compensation, the length of the working day. It could be brought about by the transformation of a country's international relations, as in the case of economic developments affecting bargaining power. In short, it could be manifested in many areas, and could, by its nature, be constrained by a taxonomy. So the shocks of innovation led to some unemployment through the worsening of structural disequilibrium. For Professor Robinson this meant that this effect was most important for structural unemployment, but it also had an impact on aggregate demand and production. One of the models in the paper showed that structural disequilibrium led to a fall in the production or in its rate of growth.

To Professor Malinvaud, Professor Fitoussi pointed out that the paper did not argue that dialectical reasoning was the only possibility. However, one needed to combine it with analytical reasoning, otherwise one would not see the mistakes in the dialectical process. This was an essential basis for the progress of economic science.

At the conference, the distinction had been discussed between frictional unemployment, structural unemployment, and unemployment resulting from deficient demand. He did not believe that one could distinguish in this way between structural and involuntary unemployment. He thought that structural change led to unemployment and that, for most economists, involuntary unemployment was the most significant and relevant type. Changes in real demand and in structures led to involuntary unemployment. So even if we had a situation where excess demand was zero, we might have unemployment. He had tried to show that even if there was good macroeconomic demand management, this would not solve all the problems of involuntary unemployment.

Professor Georgescu-Roegen also replied to the discussion. He pointed to the extensive recent literature on modern innovations. This phenomenon was well-known and had been recognised by many writers, for example, Galbraith. There had been studies of the rhythm of innovations over the past 150 years. However he thought there was a difference of several orders of magnitude between different decades. After 1945, innovation had become much more frequent, especially in electronics and chemicals. It was not possible to deny that this increase had led to more frequent exogenous shocks to the economic system. Since prices (in this case) adapted more rapidly than quantities, any innovation led to difficulties. He did not want to get into the semantics of the various types of unemployment, but simply wanted to show that innovation necessarily led to 'frictional' unemployment.

Professor Fitoussi and he had referred to the difference between dialectical and analytical models, and to the legitimate importance of the former. Professor Malinvaud's contribution had been concerned with specific functions rather than with a general model. In doing what he had done, Professor Georgescu-Roegen had only pointed to some of the inconsistencies of that specific presentation. If one represented prices and wages in a plane, one had an area of Keynesian unemployment, another for classical unemployment, and other kinds. The unsatisfactory point of this theory was that it led to different types of equilibrium in some cases, depending on the position of prices. There was therefore ambiguity. By modelling unemployment situations, one could solve such an analysis mathematically to show what actually was happening. For Keynesian equilibrium, one had one description of the situation, just as one might identify a square among all quadrilaterals. But the system did not explain the actual reason for unemployment. It did not address itself to the real-world problems.

Professor Bergmann mentioned the lengthening of the period of unemployment. This was a point made in general. In a more precise analysis, it bore on the impact of innovations.

Professor Holt had said it was not clear that all problems were looked at from one point of view. He thought that opinion was justified. Causes were hopelessly multiple.

On the criticism of the paper by Professor Robinson, Professor Georgescu-Roegen said it would be foolhardy to try in a relatively short paper to set out the policy measures required to solve the complex problem of unemployment. He and his colleague had not tried to do this, but to show how continuous shocks, caused by innovations of all sorts, were responsible for chronic unemployment.

9 Unemployment and Inflation: Facts, Theories, Puzzles and Policies

Michael Parkin
UNIVERSITY OF WESTERN ONTARIO, LONDON, ONTARIO, CANADA

INTRODUCTION

This paper has four objectives. First it seeks to review the facts about unemployment and inflation with an emphasis on putting recent experience into a longer-term perspective. Additionally, a review of the facts, although in themselves well-known, provides an accessible statement of those features of the world which, as a minimum condition, any acceptable theory must be able to explain. The second objective of the paper is to review the alternative explanations for the facts about the relationship between unemployment and inflation and to evaluate critically those alternatives partly in the light of their ability to explain the observed behaviour of unemployment and inflation and also, and very importantly, in the light of their consistency with other well-known facts about human behaviour which are embodied in all acceptable economic theories. The third objective is to identify and highlight puzzles and paradoxes present in the existing state of knowledge. Hopefully this will serve to put into sharp focus the ongoing research task in this area. Finally the paper analyses, in the light of the existing state of knowledge, the key alternative policy recommendations for dealing with the twin problems of unemployment and inflation.

The paper is divided into four main sections which deal with each of these matters in turn. The bulk of the paper however is concerned with the second item raised above. But first the facts will be reviewed.

I THE FACTS

The recorded facts about unemployment and inflation cover a large number of countries and a relatively long time span. Ideally all the relevant time-series and cross-section data should be reviewed in order to establish the full range of unemployment and inflation behaviour experienced. However, problems concerning the cross-country comparability make any cross-section work in this area hazardous and require painstakingly detailed qualifications to allow for differences in measurement across countries. Further, space limitations preclude such a comprehensive account. Recognising its limited scope, it has been decided to focus on the unemployment and inflation experience of one country, the United States, and for the time period running from 1914 to 1978. The facts about unemployment and inflation in the US for this time period are set out in Figures 9.1 to 9.7 and are summarised in Figure 9.8.[1]

It is immediately apparent that there is no strong simple bivariate relationship between unemployment and inflation taking the period from 1914 to 1978 as a whole. However, there are some strong simple relationships within certain subperiods. From 1914 to 1921, for example, there appears to be a well-defined steeply sloped inverse relation between the two variables which would give a zero inflation rate of something like 8 per cent of unemployment and would give a 4 per cent reduction in inflation for each 1 per cent point rise in unemployment. The subperiod from 1921 to 1929 continues to display a strong negative relationship but one which has shifted. Inflation now would be zero at approximately 3½ per cent unemployment and the relationship is much flatter than before with a 1 per cent rise in unemployment now being associated with a 2 per cent fall in inflation. The fifteen years between 1929 and 1944 are characterised more by a giant anti-clockwise loop than by a simple bivariate relationship. If one attempted to fit a single line through that period it would be extremely flat with a 1 per cent point change in unemployment being associated with less than 1 per cent point change in inflation and with a zero inflation rate of unemployment of somewhere in excess of 10 per cent.

After the Second World War, ignoring the last years of the war, there appears to be an almost vertical relation between inflation and unemployment, inflation falling from 13 per cent in 1947 to virtually zero in 1949–50, with unemployment increasing from a little under 4 per cent to a little over 5 per cent. By comparison with the interwar years, the early postwar years are extremely placid: 1950–54 is characterised by a strong counter-clockwise loop pattern which, in the subperiod 1954 to 1959, is exactly reversed with a strong clockwise loop. There is no clear slope to the relation between inflation and unemployment through this period. In the five years from 1959 to 1964, there is hardly any variability in the rate of inflation, it remaining virtually constant at 1 per cent and unemployment itself only moves through the range 5.2 to 6.7 per cent and is mainly held steady at around 5½ per cent. Thus, for this subperiod, there is simply too little independent variability in either of the two variables to see any clearcut relationship. Of the postwar years, it is the period from 1965 to 1969, taken together with the set of points for the period from 1959 to 1964, which traces out a clear inverse relation between the two variables. Since 1969 the unemployment–inflation relation seems to have developed a positive slope and is characterised by two clockwise spirals around this positive slope.

---

[1] The data are listed in Appendix 1.

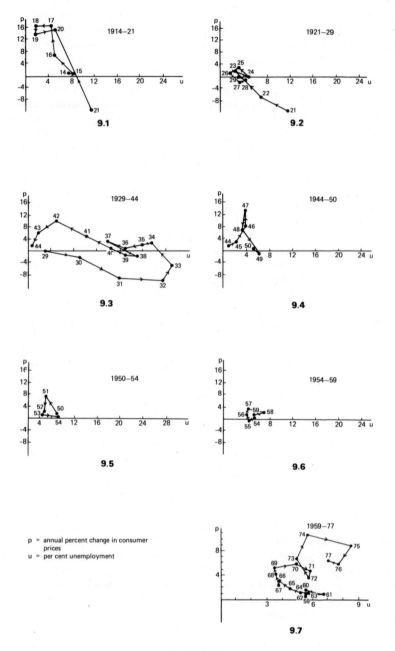

p = annual percent change in consumer
    prices
u = per cent unemployment

Figs. 9.1–9.7

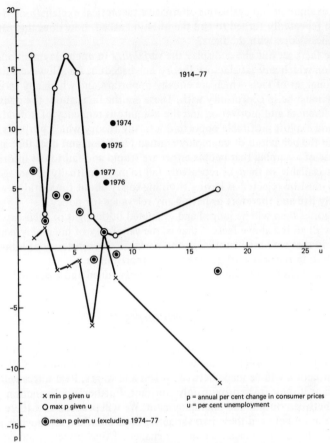

Fig. 9.8

The summary Figure 9.8 gives a vivid picture of the range of variability of inflation at each rate of unemployment (grouped in per cent point ranges) over this sample period. It also however shows vividly one further matter of great importance, namely, the fact that the inflation–unemployment experience since 1974 is wholly outside the range of prior experience within this sample.

The question of central policy relevance concerns explaining why we are now experiencing a new extreme of unemployment and inflation and the more important question of what can be done to return to a more agreeable state of affairs. However, we cannot answer questions like these until we have a satisfactory explanation for *all* the facts. That is, the turbulent 20s and 30s as well as the more placid 50s and early 60s. This will be kept centrally in mind when examining and evaluating alternative theoretical explanations. The facts will be repeatedly turned to and the question asked: how does this particular hypothesis cope with the facts?

The facts set out above display the *variability* in unemployment and inflation which any satisfactory theory must account for. However, there is an additional set of facts which are equally important and which any satisfactory theory must be in conformity with. These are the facts about the *constancy* of preferences and motivation and the ubiquitous tendency of individuals to seek and exploit profitable opportunities. Any theory which purports to explain the behaviour of unemployment and inflation and does that at the expense of assuming that people either are stupid and fail to use information that is available to them or repeatedly fail to make mutually advantageous trades must be rejected as having anything to say about the world in which we actually live and therefore as having any relevance for policy.

Theories then will be judged and evaluated in the light of their capacity to cope with all the above facts — that is, the variability of unemployment and inflation that we have historically observed and the constancy of human behaviour in the search of gainful trade opportunities.

The key alternative theories will now be examined and evaluated.

II THEORIES

In reviewing the alternative theories of unemployment and inflation a slight oversimplification will be made in the interests of streamlining the discussion. No distinction will be made between prices and wages. Real wages will be treated as if they are approximately constant. Further, no distinction will be made between output and unemployment. We will proceed as if there were a rigid relation between these two variables. Thus inflation, although it will generally be taken to mean the rate of change of final prices, could equally be meant to imply the rate of change of money wages. (These two variables would of course have a different mean reflecting productivity growth.)

Also, there are slight differences in timing of changes in wage and price movements on the one hand and output and employment movements on the other. However the detailed quarter-by-quarter timing is not going to be of central concern.

Theories about the relationship between unemployment and inflation date back at least to the time of David Hume (1741), who clearly believed that a change in the quantity of money gave rise first to a change in the level of output and employment and then subsequently to a change in wages and prices. The relationship between these two variables was first explored empirically by Irving Fisher (1926) and subsequently by A. J. Brown (1955) and Phillips (1958) whose name the supposed inverse relation between the two variables bears. Following Phillips' work, empirical evaluations of the Phillips curve (not all of them sympathetic to the approach) have mushroomed and have been surveyed by Laidler and Parkin (1975). There has also been an outpouring of theoretical work seeking to explain the facts, surveyed again by Laidler and Parkin (1975) and also by Robert J. Gordon (1977) and Anthony Santomero and John Seater (1977). This survey seeks to complement and update these earlier surveys. However, it is useful to begin the review with the earliest postwar attempt to provide a theory of the 'Phillips curve' by Richard Lipsey (1960). Even though this contribution clearly predates modern theoretical constructions, it nevertheless provides a useful basis for sharpening up the questions which have been the central concern in more recent theoretical developments.

(1) Lipsey's theory of the Phillips curve

Lipsey's theory of the Phillips curve consists of two *ad hoc* behavioural propositions and one identity. The first behavioural proposition is that prices rise in proportion to proportionate excess demand. That is,

$$\Delta p = \alpha x \tag{1}$$

where p is the log of the price level, x is proportionate excess demand. An identity defines excess demand in terms of vacancies and unemployment as

$$x = v - u \tag{2}$$

where v is the vacancy rate and u the unemployment rate (both as proportions of the labour force). A second behavioural relation explains changes in unemployment as depending positively on quits which take place at a constant rate β and negatively on hirings which are proportional to unemployment (the number of people looking for jobs) and the vacancies (the number of jobs available), i.e.

$$\Delta u = \beta - \gamma uv \tag{3}$$

Using the third equation to eliminate vacancies from the second and then eliminating excess demand from the first, gives Lipsey's theory of the Phillips curve as

$$\Delta p = \frac{\alpha \beta u^{-1}}{\gamma} - \alpha u - \frac{\alpha}{\gamma} \frac{\Delta u}{u} \tag{4}$$

Thus these assumptions yield the prediction that there will be an inverse relation between inflation and unemployment when unemployment is steady (when $\Delta u = 0$) and that, as unemployment changes, so the rate of inflation will be higher (lower) the faster unemployment is falling (rising). There will be a unique unemployment rate at which the rate of inflation is zero and that is given by

$$u^* = \sqrt{\beta/\gamma} \tag{5}$$

This zero-inflation unemployment rate depends positively on the quit rate (β) and negatively on the hiring rate parameter (γ).[1]

How does Lipsey's model square with the facts? Its prediction of a generally negative correlation between inflation and unemployment seems to be broadly in line with the long-run average facts. Its prediction of anti-clockwise loops in inflation-unemployment space appears to be consistent with the evidence for the period from 1929 to 1944 and from 1950 to 1954 but inconsistent with the evidence for any other subperiod. Further, although it is superficially consistent with the 1929 to 1944 experience, the sheer size of the loop and the large movement in inflation with virtually zero movement in the unemployment rate between 1932 and 1934 as well as between 1942 and 1944 constitute a considerable problem as does the departure from the pure counter-clockwise loop as the US economy went into the 1938 recession. Further, in terms of this theory, the shifts in the zero-inflation unemployment rate as well as in the slope of the relationship between the two variables can only be 'explained' by arbitrary shifts either in the reaction of prices to excess demand (α), the quit rate (β) or the hiring propensity (γ). There are enough parameters to be able to cope with the facts but, to explain the facts in terms of arbitrary changes in parameters seems hardly satisfactory.

There is a more important set of criticisms of the Lipsey hypothesis, however, arising from a consideration of individual economic behaviour. First, exactly whose behaviour is equation (1) supposed to describe? Is it the behaviour of suppliers or demanders or some kind of reduced-form representation of what 'the market' does with no individual behaviour being described by the equation? This question needs an answer for two reasons; first, if α is a variable, it is necessary to establish the factors upon which its value depends so that variations in it may be predicted and incorporated into a fuller theoretical analysis: further, it is necessary to verify that no other variables belong in the equation and that the rate of price change responds to excess demand and only to excess demand (or vice versa, i.e. that excess demand responds only to price change and to no other variables). Second, and of crucial importance, the Lipsey theory provides no explicit guidance as to what it is that determines the quantity of unemployment (or employment). The proposition usually employed in economic analysis, that demand equals supply, provides a ready method for determining the quantity. However in that case there would be no excess demand and therefore no price change

---

[1] This representation of Lipsey's model is based on that contained in footnote 32 of Lipsey (1960). Everything that is presented here is to be found in that footnote although Lipsey himself did not draw out the full implications of his model, in particular its predictions of a counter-clockwise loop. Instead, Lipsey went on to develop an elaborate theory of the loops based on the aggregation of micro Phillips curves and the hypothesis that the degree of dispersion across individual labour markets was systematically related to the business cycle. Subsequent empirical work has shown that explanation for the loops to be non-viable. (See, in particular, Archibald, 1969.)

according to equation (1). The alternative of allowing demand and supply to be unequal raises two problems. First, how is the quantity determined and second, how do economic agents behave in a situation in which they cannot behave according to the equations that describe their normal demand and supply behaviour? Lipsey's own (implicit) 'explanation' is hardly satisfactory. It virtually overthrows the whole of the conventional supply and demand apparatus and makes mechanical assumptions about flow excess demand behaviour which have no choice or price theoretic content. Indeed, the question posed concerning the first equation has equal force concerning the third. Whose behaviour is described by the proposition that unemployment changes negatively with both the unemployment and vacancy rate? Are the decisions being made on the demand side or the supply side or in some weighted average way on both?

It is these questions arising from the lack of a satisfactory choice and price theoretic basis for the Phillips curve that gave rise to the vast amount of theoretical work that has been undertaken in recent years. There has not, however, been a single theoretical development which has found universal acceptability. Instead, there have been two broad developments, one which may be characterised as the disequilibrium approach and the alternative equilibrium approach. The equilibrium approach itself has had two major branches, one which characterises aggregate behaviour as the outcome of a continuous auction in all markets (including labour) and one which places primary emphasis on the implicit contractual nature of transactions in the face of costly information and uncertainty. These modern developments are now reviewed in turn.

(2) Disequilibrium models

(a) Phelps' price-setting story. Within the spirit of the disequilibrium models, Edmund Phelps (1967) offered a 'story' which sought to rationalise, although with an important modification having far-reaching implications, the basic price adjustment equation, equation (1), above. For Phelps, equation (1) describes the behaviour of firms. (His analysis in Phelps (1967) is conducted in terms of wage setting and labour markets but in Phelps and Winter (1970) the analysis is applied to commodity markets.) Firms set prices and their objective is the maximisation of present value. Put at its simplest, in order to achieve their objective, firms change their prices by the amount which on the average they expect other firms to change their plus (or minus) an amount to allow for any reduction (or increase) in their market share which they seek to achieve. Aggregating over all firms produces an equation similar to (1) but with the important addition of the expected rate of inflation. That is,

$$\Delta p = \Delta p^e + \alpha x \tag{6}$$

where Δp^e is the expected rate of inflation. Equation (6) above represents a considerable improvement over equation (1) for, by starting with a consideration of individual price setters' behaviour, rather than an *ad hoc* price adjustment rule, it avoids the now widely acknowledged error of explicitly building money illusion into the price adjustment process. Inflation is no longer necessarily zero when excess demand is zero so that any rate of inflation (so long as it is fully expected) can be associated with equilibrium.

Phelps develops a generalisation of Lipsey's third equation to yield the prediction that inflation will deviate from its expected rate by an amount that is greater the smaller the unemployment rate and the faster unemployment is falling, i.e.

$$\Delta p - \Delta p^e = f(u, \Delta u) \tag{7}$$
$$(-), (-)$$

In order to give empirical content to Phelps' theory, an hypothesis about the formation of expectations is required. Phelps provided this in the form of the familiar Cagan (1956) adaptive expectations formulation. That is

$$\Delta p^e - \Delta p^e_{-1} = \lambda(\Delta p_{-1} - \Delta p^e_{-1}) \tag{8}$$

The key predictions of the pair of hypotheses embodied in (7) and (8) for the behaviour of inflation and unemployment are first that there will be a unique unemployment rate u^* at which any fully expected rate of inflation is possible. At unemployment rates below u^* the actual inflation rate will exceed the expected rate and thereby, via proposition (8), cause expected inflation to rise and, as a result, cause the actual inflation rate to rise. Conversely, at unemployment rates above u^*, actual inflation will be below expected inflation thereby reducing both expected and actual inflation. If there is a cycle in aggregate demand, this cycle will, via the expectations mechanism, generate *clockwise* loops in inflation—unemployment space. Over the long run there will be no systematic tendency for inflation to be correlated with unemployment. It will never be possible to observe a short-run inverse relation (short-run Phillips curve) since any change in unemployment which would lead to a movement along a short-run Phillips curve would, at the same time, change the actual rate of inflation and therefore the expected rate of inflation thereby shifting the short-run curve. Thus, all movements in inflation—unemployment space would represent a mixture of shifts of and movements along short-run Phillips curves.

In terms of its capacity to fit the broad stylised facts of Section I, this modification of Lipsey's hypothesis hardly fares any better. As already noted, from 1914 to 1929 there are virtually no discernible loops of any kind despite sizeable movements of both variables. From 1929 to 1944 the loops go in the opposite direction to those predicted by this adaptive expectations augmented Phillips curve. It is the period 1954 to 1959 and again from 1959 to 1964 that this hypothesis works at its best. However, it cannot cope with the later years unless we invoke some arbitrary parameter shifts which have moved the natural unemployment rate.

Furthermore, the problems posed above concerning Lipsey's model remain.

The essential contribution of Phelps' analysis is to remove money illusion from an otherwise largely *ad hoc* price adjustment equation. Also the explicit analysis of the determination of quantities in the face of unequal demand and supply and a choice theoretic analysis of the interaction of price and quantity determination is absent.[1]

This last problem however has been addressed by the mainstream branch of disequilibrium theorists. It is to a review of that work that attention is now turned.

(b)   Clower–Barro–Grossman–Malinvaud disequilibrium quantity deter-mination. The pioneering work on quantity determination when supply and demand are unequal was done by Robert Clower (1965) and has been most thoroughly developed by Robert Barro and Herschel Grossman (1971, 1976) and recently taken up by Edmond Malinvaud (1977). The basis of all these models is that for some reason that is not specified in the analysis, money prices (and wages) are given and are not necessarily equal to their market-clearing values. In such an event, notional demands and supplies being unequal, plans which are the outcome of a utility or profit-maximising calculus within the framework of the market-clearing paradigm cannot be implemented. When agents attempt to implement their plans they are frustrated. In effect, this imposes an additional set of tighter constraints upon individual maximising behaviour and changes the form of excess demand functions to include quantity as well as price variables. (in terms of Keynesian analysis, the attrac-tion of this approach is that it rationalises the role of income as an argument in the consumption function and the change in income (the acceleration principle) as an argument in the investment function.) Of course, in the face of a difference between *aggregate* supply and *aggregate* demand, there is an infinity of ways in which that aggregate may be allocated to individuals. The existing stock of disequilibrium models makes the simplest and crudest *ad hoc* assumptions about this allocation process. Typically, each individual agent bears a fixed share of the total discrepancy between demand and supply. Agents are not allowed to use economic resources to shift the burden of the disequilibrium away from themselves and on to others by any device (and of course by the initial assumption of the model, least of all by changing the price offer at which they are willing to trade).

These models do provide an account of how quantities could be determined in the face of a discrepancy between demand and supply. Further, they provide an account of the movements of output and employment in response to an aggregative shock which are broadly in line with the stylised facts presented in the first section of this paper.

However these models pay a high price for their success. First they assume an *ad hoc* price adjustment process which is not allowed to interact in any

---

[1] Though Phelps and Winter (1970) do deal with this problem at the level of the individual firm.

explicit way with the maximising decisions of individual agents. Prices are parametric for all decisions. Second, they assume an entirely arbitrary rationing procedure with no economic analysis of why the 'disequilibrium' falls on the particular individuals that it does. These two problems can be seen as really being one: put more simply, these models fail to explain why rational economic agents refuse to engage in mutually advantageous trades. This major shortcoming must cast serious doubt on the usefulness of disequilibrium models at least as currently specified.

Whilst, from the middle 1960s to around 1970, this approach to modelling the aggregate economy looked extremely promising, that promise now seems to have largely faded. Whilst it is too early to reject the approach out of hand and whilst it still has many adherents and indeed continues to attract imaginative scholarly contributions, it is hard to see how the approach can satisfactorily meet the objections stated above without in effect taking on board the major insights and analytical apparatus of the alternative equilibrium models.

(3) Equilibrium models

(a) Continuous spot auctions. Equilibrium models of economic fluctuations have a long tradition going back at least to Irving Fisher (1911) and form the basis of Milton Friedman's (1968) work in this area. The modern treatment of equilibrium models, foreshadowed in Lucas and Rapping (1969) and Mortensen (1969), have been given their clearest statement in Lucas (1973) and have featured in much recent work especially by Thomas Sargent (1973) and Robert Barro (1977).[1]

The essence of the approach is that observed price level (or inflation rate) and unemployment rate are determined by the intersection of aggregate demand and aggregate supply schedules. The expectations augmented Phillips curve, equation (7) above, explicitly becomes an aggregate supply function. It determines the quantity of output supplied (or labour demanded, or unemployment that will be chosen) as a function of the actual price (or wage) level relative to the expected level. Economic agents are assumed to be rational in the sense that they respond only to *relative* prices but they are placed in a setting in which they cannot distinguish relative price movements from movements in the general price level. As a consequence, a change in a 'local' money price will convey some information with which to make an exact inference about movements in the latter variable. Therefore, a rise in a particular price (or wage) will be interpreted in part as a rise in the relative price of the commodity (or labour service) in a particular local market. Viewed in this way, the 'Phillips curve' needs to be read the opposite way around from that of Lipsey and Phelps. It is the equation that tells us how much

[1] The most rigorous general equilibrium development of the approach is to be found in Lucas (1973).

unemployment will be generated for a given discrepancy of the actual from the expected price level. Furthermore, the underlying Lipsey and Phelps story which puts the change in the unemployment rate in the relationship will no longer apply. However, costs of adjustment on the supply side can be invoked in order to rationalise a distributed lag of past unemployment rates in the relationship. The supply story explicitly embodies the natural rate hypothesis implying that purely nominal disturbances which are fully anticipated have no real effects. Thus the aggregate supply function of Lucas may be written as

$$-\phi(u_t - u^*) = \Delta p_t - \Delta p_t^e + \epsilon_t \tag{9}$$

where ϵ_t can be thought of as incorporating any lagged values of unemployment as well as embodying a purely random disturbance.

Now that there is an explicit story underlying this aggregate supply relation, it is possible to say more than was hitherto possible concerning the parameter ϕ. Lucas shows that the value of this parameter will depend on the ratio of the total variance of price to the variance of relative price. In an environment in which the variance of relative prices is small, a change in a particular price will be read as indicating a change in the absolute price level and evoke a small quantitative (and therefore unemployment) response, whereas in an environment in which there is a large variance of relative prices, a change in a relative price will convey little information about the absolute price level and will be read as a change in relative prices thereby invoking a large quantitative (and unemployment) response.

The demand side of the equilibrium model is a conventional IS-LM aggregate demand function which, expressed in its unemployment form, may be written as

$$u_t = \psi_0 - \psi(m_t - p_t) + \eta_t \tag{10}$$

where m is the log of the nominal money supply and the parameter ψ_0 embodies all other sources of shift in the aggregate demand function. Where the supply locus, equation (9), and the demand locus, equation (10), intersect determines the unemployment rate u_t and the price level p_t (and of course equivalently the inflation rate Δp_t) given m_t, ϵ_t, η_t and p_t^e.

In order to maintain consistency, rational economic agents not only respond to relative prices, but also form their expectations in the most efficient way possible. Specifically, in order to form expectations they presume that all other agents are as rational as they are and that the price level will in fact be determined by equations (9) and (10). Formally their expectations are formed by taking the mathematical expectation of the price level conditional on all the information (I) available to them at that time. That is

$$P_t^e = E_t(P_t \mid I_t) \tag{11}$$

Treating the money stock as having an expected value at t of $\widehat{m}_t$, the solution to the above model for deviations of the price level from its expected level, the unemployment rate and the expected price level is as follows

$$P_t - P_t^e = \frac{\phi\psi}{1 + \phi\psi}(m_t - \widehat{m}_t) - \frac{(\phi\eta_t + \epsilon_t)}{1 + \phi\psi} \tag{12}$$

$$u_t = u^* - \frac{\psi}{1 + \phi\psi}(m_t - \widehat{m}_t) + \frac{(\eta_t - \psi\phi\epsilon_t)}{1 + \psi\phi} \tag{13}$$

$$p_t^e = m_t^e - \frac{\psi_0}{\psi} + \frac{1}{\psi}u^* \tag{14}$$

Thus the price level will deviate from its expected level in proportion to deviations of the actual money stock from its expected level as well as by a random component reflecting the disturbances η and ϵ. Similarly, unemployment will deviate from the natural rate in inverse relation to unanticipated money stock and as a result of the distrubances η and ϵ. Finally, the expected price level depends solely on the expected money stock as well the aggregate demand function parameters and the natural unemployment rate.

It should be noted that, although the money stock has been treated here as the only aggregate demand-influencing variable the value of which is random, other variables entering through the parameter ψ_0 could also take on the same characteristic.

To give this model full empirical content it is necessary of course to specify a procedure for generating the expected value of the money stock. This is typically done by using a mixture of a reaction function analysis together with whatever order of ARIMA process is required to reduce the forecasting errors of the money stock to a white noise process. This is the formulation which was employed by Barro (1977a).

The main predictions of this model evident from the above equations are easy to summarise. First the model predicts that unemployment will on the average equal the natural rate and that it will be independent of the rate of inflation. Second, there is no general presumption for any particular slope to the relation between inflation and unemployment since in general, the expected rate of inflation will not be constant and will depend on the expected change in the money stock. This means that changes in the actual rate of inflation will depend on both the expected and unexpected components of changes in the money stock whereas changes in unemployment rate will depend only on unexpected changes in the money stock. Third, if the expected money stock (or expected change in the money stock) is constant, there will be an inverse relation between inflation and unemployment. Fourth, the slope of that relation will not necessarily be constant but will depend on the relative variances of the general price level and relative prices. If relative prices are tightly distributed, then a small change in relative prices will be read as indicating a change in the general price level and will not evoke a large quantitative response implying a steep short-run Phillips curve. If that variance is large the Phillips curve will be flatter.

A recent study by Robert Barro (1977a) has addressed this question in terms of an explicit econometric model. Modifying equation (9) to incorporate a distributed lag in the unemployment rate as well as to incorporate a shift arising from a change in conscription regulations, Barro finds that this model explains well the actual movements in unemployment in the United States throughout the entire sample period studied and does extremely well in the postwar years. There is one important exception in the middle 1930s. The model cannot readily account for the persistence of unemployment in the middle 1930s (1934/35/36). Barro does not unfortunately in that paper analyse the implications of the model for price movements.

A more impressionistic evaluation of the model can be performed by returning to the charts in Part I and asking how it copes with the pattern of unemployment and inflation displayed there. For the period from 1914 to 1931, there appears to be a well-defined inverse relation between inflation and unemployment but one, the slope of which is becoming flatter. This would seem to suggest that the expected rate of money supply growth through that period was constant, implying a constant expected rate of inflation so that actual changes in the money stock relative to that expected money stock growth rate were giving rise to the tracing out of a short-run Phillips curve. The flattening of the curve through the period would arise if the variance on relative prices was increasing relative to the variance of the absolute price level. A key test of the model would involve establishing whether or not that was in fact so. Casual evidence would suggest it possible since this was a period of great turbulence in the world economy. However, casual impressions are no substitute for hard empirical evidence. That the expected money stock growth rate might have been relatively stable through this period is at least in line with the facts about the then-operating monetary system based on a gold standard mechanism which provided an anchor for the money supply growth rate.

In 1934 the US dollar was devalued against gold. This may be presumed to have substantially increased the expected rate of growth of the money stock and expected rate of inflation in the ensuing few years as a reaction to the increased dollar value of gold reserves inside the Federal Reserve system. Thus, the sharp rise in the inflation rate in 1934, while unemployment was almost 25 per cent of the labour force, would, according to this model, have to be attributed to a rise in the expected rate of inflation from this revaluation of gold. As this process was going on, an unexpected change in reserve requirements led to a sharp unexpected contraction of the money stock in 1937–38 thereby generating the contraction of 1938. The strong recovery from that recession is seen as being associated with an initially unexpected increase in monetary growth which, by 1943–44, was followed by substantial reduction in inflationary expectations as a result of wartime monetary stringency and controls.

The early postwar years are extremely easy to explain in the equilibrium rational expectations model. This is the period through which Barro's model tracks extremely closely. The relatively stable inflationary expectations (and money supply growth rate expectations) through the early postwar years and right up to the end of the 1960s are to be seen largely as arising from the nature of the international monetary system based on fixed exchange rates and a fixed dollar price of gold. This provided a solid anchor for the monetary system and for long-term money supply growth rate expectations and, with actual money supply growth rates in the 50s and 60s staying in the 2 to 7 per cent range and for the most part at the lower end of that range, fairly stable money supply growth rate and inflationary expectations were generated. With the abandonment of the gold exchange standard in 1972, money supply growth expectations no longer had a firm anchor and, in the current environment, such expectations have to be formed on the basis of an evaluation of an ill-understood political process. Recent monetary policies have given no indication that money supply growth rates are going to be contained at low inflationary levels and therefore inflation expectations in the 7 to 10 per cent range seem to have become firmly established.

The above account of the history of unemployment and inflation in the US from 1914 to 1977 told through the eyes of the equilibrium rational expectations model is of course nothing more than a story. However, it is a consistent story and one which represents a considerable improvement upon the alternatives reviewed above. There are, however, problems for this approach. A minor problem concerns the lack of an explicit modelling of the variability of the natural rate of unemployment. The formal analyses treat the natural rate as a constant whilst in empirical work it becomes necessary to allow for shifts in the natural rate such as, for example, Barro's adjustment based on changes in draft regulations. However, this is not a problem in principle at all. The natural rate of unemployment can readily be viewed as being determined by real factors including unemployment insurance, taxes and minimum wage laws, without changing the essence of the approach.

A major problem for the approach, however, lies in the fact that, as an empirical matter, those variations in unemployment induced by unexpected inflation (i.e. unexpected money supply growth) should be serially uncorrelated whilst any systematic serially correlated unemployment has to be 'explained' as the result of supply side adjustment lags due to some type of transactions or adjustment costs. Hall (1975) has calculated that for the postwar US only 1.7 per cent of the variance of unemployment can be attributed to unexpected inflation whilst 98.3 per cent of that variance must be attributed to variations in the natural rate of unemployment and therefore is left without any explicit explanation in the analysis. Lucas' own formulation of the aggregate supply function, being very closely related to his own earlier work with Leonard Rapping (Lucas and Rapping, 1969) can rationalise a distributed lag in the unemployment rate as part of the aggregate supply response. However, in order to hold the economy in the depths of a recession of 1932/33/34 for so long it seems essential to invoke the proposition that money supply growth was unexpectedly low in each of those years whilst the expected money supply growth rate increased.

Robert Hall (1975) has provided an ingenious alternative explanation for the persistence of unemployment to that based on adjustment costs but one which is (despite Hall's statement to the contrary), entirely within the spirit of the equilibrium auction model analysis though supplemented with an explicit search theory. Drawing on the insights of John R. Harris and Michael P. Todaro (1970), Hall develops a two-sector analysis in which there is a rigid wage sector (the government sector) and a flexible wage sector (the rest of the economy). In the face of a reduction in aggregate demand, the wage level in the rigid wage sector refuses to respond and, as a result, although the wage in the non-rigid sector falls, the widened gap between the rigid and non-rigid sector increases the payoff to job search. As a result, workers remain unemployed for longer in the hope of finding a more highly paid rigid wage sector job. Whilst the basic analysis is correct and does indeed generate the prediction of persistence of unemployment, it is difficult to believe that any sizeable fraction of the (almost) 25 per cent of the labour force that was unemployed in 1932/33/34 was searching for a government sector job. Equally implausible is the proposition that this has applied to the American (or any other) economy during the years since 1974.

A further problem with this class of models is the assumption that markets clear in the sense that an auction market clears every period. Of course this issue could be fudged by defining the period to be long enough such that market clearing on the average over the period made sense. However, as a matter of description, many markets for commodities and most markets for labour do not appear to resemble spot auctions. Rather they appear to involve the trading parties entering into either explicit or implicit contracts with each other embodying rules for the conduct of each party contingent on the realisation of specific unforecastable or too expensive to forecast events.

It is to the class of models which pay explicit attention to this feature of the world which attention is now turned.

(b) Implicit (and explicit) contracts. The basic idea underlying the contract approach to the modelling of employment, output and inflation fluctuations is that in a situation of uncertainty, agents can gain by trading with each other not only factors of production and goods but also by trading risk. That is, they can enter into an implicit (or often explicit) contract for a prespecified period which sets out rules for the determination of prices and quantities and also rules for the date at which the contract will be renegotiated contingent upon future random events in such a way that any risk associated with their trading activities are shared in an efficient manner. A central problem in developing a theory of contracts is that of focusing on a relevant small number of dimensions to the contract. The minimum dimensions which an economic analysis needs to take account of are first of all the contract's price rule, second a quantity rule and third, what might be called a renegotiate rule. Each rule may be fixed or may be specified as a function of variables whose realisations will be drawings from stochastic distributions. How the price and quantity variables respond to various shocks will clearly depend upon the

details of the contracts. Whether these details will turn out to be of critical importance for predicting unemployment and inflation movements is not yet clear for, as we have already seen, a continuous auction model at least is able to tell a story which is broadly consistent with the facts. However, many insights are available from the contracts approach. There are three main strands in the development of this approach which will be considered separately.

(i) Azariadis–Bailey–Gordon: efficient risk sharing. Three related papers by Costas Azariadis (1976), Martin Neil Bailey (1974) and Donald F. Gordon (1976), develop a basic theorem on one of the minimum conditions of an efficient contract which is of central importance in understanding some aspects of labour markets. The analyses presented by these three authors differ in detail but are identical in essentials. Only labour market contracts are analysed although, as Grossman (1978a) has shown, they readily extend to commodity markets. Firms are assumed to be risk-neutral and households risk-averse. There is therefore a potential gain from trading risk, firms being able to buy labour and simultaneously sell insurance against income fluctuations resulting in a lower net labour cost than would arise if households had to absorb all the uncertainty about real incomes themselves. The specific theorem proved is that for any given employment level there always exists a fixed wage which gives the households the same level of utility as a random wage would but which is associated with a higher expected profit for the firm. Thus this analysis predicts that real wages will be sticky, a prediction which seems to be entirely in line with the stylised facts.

However, there is a major problem in that this analysis has nothing to say about the determination of *money* wages and, therefore, the absolute price level. The entire analysis is conducted in real terms and the prediction is that *real* wages will be sticky. More strongly, the analysis seems to imply (although I have not seen an explicit examination of this question) that all labour contracts will be fully indexed so that any price level uncertainty is completely removed from the contract. Such contracts would imply considerable flexibility in absolute wages and prices (but of course rigidity in the real wage).

The problem of demand-induced unemployment seems to be one of money wage and not real wage rigidity. It is a reluctance of the money wage and price level to fall in the face of a fall in the money stock (or other determinant of aggregate demand) rather than a real wage rigidity which is at the centre of the problem.

Thus, although providing an underpinning for rigidity of real wages, this efficient risk-sharing analysis does not seem to provide a convincing account of why we observe nominal wage and price rigidities in the face of nominal shocks.

(ii) Optimal price setting models. An alternative group of models developed by Barro (1972), Bruno (1977), and Mussa (1977) go to the opposite extreme

of those just considered and assume (though do not explain why) that prices are fixed in money units. There are setup costs to price adjustment so that continuous price change as implied by an auction model is always inefficient. Instead of continuous price adjustment, prices are set and held for a period and then changed in a step jump. The frequency of the changes and the size of the step are chosen by firms so as to maximise expected profit. This is done by balancing the cost of having a price away from the instantaneous profit-maximising price against the cost of changing the price. The quantity rule employed in these models is that the price setter will always satisfy demand so long as the quantity demanded can be supplied at a marginal cost less than or equal to the price that has been set. However, if the quantity demanded exceeds that quantity then the firm will ration and supply the quantity which maximises its instantaneous profit.

Barro's model examines only situations in which the expected trend rate of inflation is zero and shows that as an approximation an equation like (1) above can be derived as an average over firms and over a finite time interval. The parameter α which relates price change to excess demand depends positively on the variance of demand or more simply on the degree of uncertainty about the firm's demand curve.

Bruno and Mussa focus on the effects of a change in the anticipated trend rate of inflation on the frequency and step size and show that prices are adjusted both more frequently and with a bigger step as the expected trend rate of inflation increases.

These analyses provide an alternative rationale for the short-run Phillips curve based on price-setting (and wage-setting) firms who implicitly contract with households to supply goods (or demand labour) at a preannounced *money* price and to satisfy the household's demands (or supplies of labour) so long as the marginal cost of production does not exceed the price (or the marginal product of labour does not fall short of the wage) but in that latter event to ration the household until the next price review period.

It may appear that these models provide a choice theoretic rationalisation for rationing and therefore rehabilitate the 'disequilibrium' models. However, it is a long step from asserting that an individual firm will ration to the prediction that rationing will be prevalent and present in the aggregate. If firms are setting their prices in the manner described by Barro, Bruno and Mussa, there will presumably at any point in time be a distribution of prices as different firms will change their prices on different dates. Therefore some firms will be rationing at a time when others are not. It is therefore not possible to make general predictions about aggregative rationing without a careful analysis of the distribution of prices and of demands.

There is no problem in these models concerning the stickiness of money wages and money prices. Both are sticky because it is costly to adjust them. However, simply invoking adjustment costs without some convincing story as to why firms set their prices in money units in the first place rather than, for example, contingent upon the value of some general price index, does not seem to be very illuminating. Furthermore it is hard to see why price adjustment costs *per se* would be large enough to give rise to the degree of sluggishness in money wage and price adjustments that seems to be present in the world.

(iii) Indexing of contracts. The question as to why firms enter into contracts denominated in money units rather than indexed contracts is analysed by Jo Anna Gray (1976, 1978) and Stanley Fischer (1977a). Their analyses relate explicitly to labour markets. The basic framework, set out most simply in Gray (1976), is one in which both real (or more accurately supply) and nominal (or more accurately demand) shocks hit the economy and in which contracts are characterised by four parameters. First, an initial money wage is set. Second, a coefficient of responsiveness of the money wage to the general price level (a degree of indexing) is specified and, third, a contract length is set.[1] Fourth, the contract specifies a rule for the determination of the quantity of employment. This feature of a contract was not brought out explicitly in the work of Gray and Fischer but is dealt with in some detail by Barro (1977). The basic objective is to minimise the variance of output and employment from the levels that would obtain if there was a continuous auction taking place. The continuous auction does not take place (implicitly) because it would be too costly to organise. Trading under contracts characterised by the set of parameters set out above implicitly constitutes the least-cost way of organising trades. Given the assumed optimality criterion it is shown that in general it will not be optimal fully to index contracts. The optimal degree of indexing will in fact depend upon the ratio of the variance of nominal disturbances to the variance of total disturbances (real and nominal). Only if the only source of uncertainty is nominal will it be optimal fully to index. If nominal disturbances are seen as unimportant and real disturbances dominate then it will be efficient not to index at all. This result is derived even in the absence of indexing costs. If there are costs of indexing in the form of monitoring the index and adjusting wage schedules, then indexing will not take place unless nominal disturbances are greater than some critical value. Optimal contract length is also shown to be a decreasing function of the amount of uncertainty.

These analyses are potentially of great importance for they suggest a nontrivial reason why indexing may not be prevalent and why contracts may be fixed in money units. However, they are not without their problems. First, the objective of minimising the variance of real output and employment relative to the values which would prevail under a continuous auction is not obviously the relevant criterion for optimal choices by firms and households.

---

[1] Gray (1976) and Fischer (1977a) deal only with the first two aspects of an indexed contract, whilst Gray (1978) deals with the question of optimal contract length.

It would be more convincing if these analyses could be couched in terms of expected profit-maximising firms and expected utility maximising households than in terms of a rather arbitrary minimisation of employment and output variance relative to its auction value. Further, the quantity (employment) determination rule in these analyses is one which always places the firm on its demand curve. Households are assumed to be willing to work even though the marginal disutility of work exceeds the real wage and also willing to accept a situation in which the reverse inequality holds. This implies that households and firms entering into contracts of this type do so knowing that circumstances will arise in which they will have blocked trades which are mutually advantageous. It is not clear why such contracts should ever be written. However, as Fischer (1977b) has argued, such contracts do seem to be a feature of the actual world. It remains a mystery however as to why.

The contracting literature which has just been reviewed clearly provides some insights into the question of why nominal prices might be sticky. It also provides a potential reason why unemployment might be more persistent than would be implied by a continuous auction model even where expectations are formed using all the available information. An examination of a model embodying these features has been examined by Stanley Fischer (1977c).

The key difference between the equilibrium auction models and the contract models is in their underlying 'story' about the aggregate supply side. For the auction model, costly adjustment of factor inputs puts autoregressiveness into the aggregate supply response which supplements a non-autoregressive response to unanticipated price changes. For the contract model, costly contract negotiation and price setting makes the current departure of aggregate supply from its full employment level depend not only on current period unanticipated inflation but also on unanticipated inflations which occurred earlier in the term of any existing contracts. Either way there is an autoregressive component to the aggregate supply (and unemployment) response and it is hard to see how a discriminating test between the two approaches involving aggregative data will be devised. The facts which the auction hypothesis can explain, can be explained by contracts and *vice versa*. The puzzles for the auction approach are equally puzzling for the contract view of the world.

But let us now turn to a more systematic consideration of the major puzzles in this area.

III PUZZLES

Throughout the preceding section an attempt has been made to present the alternative theoretical approaches designed to explain unemployment and inflation and to check those theories both against the facts about those two variables as well as for their conformity with rational profit and utility

maximising behaviour. Many puzzles and problems have been thrown up
en route. This section seeks to highlight the major puzzles and to suggest
possible fruitful lines of research which they indicate.

The major puzzles of course are questions concerning the explanation for
particularly awkward episodes. The episode of the immediate past and present
is of course one of key importance. Why has the inflation and unemployment
record of the last four years been so far out of line with our earlier experience?
The other major awkward episode was the period following the movement into
the Great Depression. The fact of the Great Depression and its depth are not
mysterious. However, the persistence of a high rate of unemployment through
the middle 1930s with a sharp increase in the inflation rate constitutes a major
puzzle. A puzzle of these two episodes is really the same puzzle and one to
which the same answer must be sought.

As the previous section indicates, we do not have an overabundance of
satisfactory theories. The only analysis which is capable of telling a story which
approximates to the facts is that embodying rational expectations and
including, on the supply side, sluggish adjustment of employment either for
reasons based on the contract story or for reasons arising from costs of
adjustment embedded into a Lucas-type aggregate supply curve. Neither of
the available rationalisations for slow adjustments of nominal wages and prices
and consequently persistence of unemployment seems readily to cope quantitatively with the persistence of the Great Depression and are even hard to
square with the persistence of modern recessions such as the most recent one.
A key problem then is to find a convincing rationalisation for the persistence
of unemployment in excess of the natural rate. Just what are the significant
costs of adjustment which give rise to such slow nominal price and wage
changes and thereby generate persistent depressions of employment? I suspect
that the answer to this question is not going to be found solely or even mainly
as a result of further theoretical innovation. On the contrary, I suspect that
careful and perhaps even tedious empirical work is required. We need to know
precisely what kinds of contracts explicitly and implicitly, but more
important implicitly, characterise labour markets. Are there important
differences in the implicit contracts in different types of markets and, if there
are, is it the case that unemployment typically arises in markets characterised
by a specific kind of contract? If so, why is it in the interests of both parties to
enter into such contracts? By focusing on the distribution of contract types
and the resultant distribution of employment and unemployment variability,
we should be able to shed more light on the question of whether or not the
characteristics of contracts have a crucial role to play in an analysis of the
persistence of output and employment movements.

To check out the Lucas story further requires a careful empirical evaluation
of costs of adjustment on the demand for factors — especially labour. Again
cross-section evidence would seem to be of critical importance here. Are there
some sectors where the cost of adjustment of labour input is particularly great
and others where it is relatively low? We should observe that unemployment

persists longest in those sectors of the economy where adjustment costs are greatest. Is this the case? Further, can the adjustment costs that can be objectively measured quantitatively account for the degree of observed persistence in unemployment?

However, I suspect that the critical problem in explaining persistence is not going to reside in identifying precisely what the important costs of contracting and factor input adjustment are but rather in establishing precisely how agents use information in order to form their expectations of the general price level (and inflation rate). Whilst the insights of rational expectations embodied in the equilibrium and contract models have revolutionised our perceptions, our current method for empirically implementing the hypothesis of rational expectations is surely too naïve and must itself be one of the major reasons why we can explain so little in terms of unexpected price changes and have to rely so much on *ad hoc* adjustment or contracting costs. Whilst it is a defensible scientific strategy to postulate unobservable *constants* such as preference functions, the use of unobservable *variables* such as the expected inflation rate or expected money supply growth rate makes convincing hypothesis testing and rejection virtually impossible. Whilst the basic message of rational expectations, that agents make efficient use of all relevant information, is surely correct, precisely what the relevant information is and precisely what efficient use means when information is costly to acquire is by no means transparent. Assuming that agents know the true model (whilst the economics profession remains ignorant) seems to be going too far. The very fact that we are puzzled by the persistence of the Great Depression and the persistence of above natural unemployment in various phases of the postwar business cycle should at least create some doubt that the average economic agent can, on the basis of an expectation of the money stock, form an expectation held with much confidence concerning the immediate future price level. Clearly what we need as a first step in the process of figuring out how expectations are formed is a set of measurements of expectations themselves. I do not see how we can duck this and at the same time retain a method of analysis in which expectations play a central role. It is probably going to be impossible to construct objective measures of expectations for any period, let alone periods long past. However, for the recent past and future there is no reason why measures of expectation should not be constructed, based on explicit surveys. The survey technique, when applied to attempting to explain why people behaved in certain ways, for example, investment intention surveys, is rightly rejected. However, where the central matter of concern is to know what a person believes (right or wrong) then a survey approach would seem less objectionable (although of course not foolproof). The qualitative surveys of expectations about economic variables which are routinely conducted in most major countries could provide a basis for such independent expectations measurements and one method for converting such qualitative data into a quantitative series has been suggested by John Carlson and Michael Parkin (1975). With such independent observations of inflationary

expectations it becomes possible to check out independently the properties
of the aggregate supply function as well as the process whereby expectations
are formed. For periods long past where direct measurement of this kind is
impossible, a careful reconstruction of precisely what information was
available at each relevant stage in history together with a careful documentation of what was then known (or believed) about the working of the economy
might make possible the construction of a widely acceptable measure of
expectations. However, such will always have an element of subjectivity in it.
One matter of critical importance in conditioning expectations of money
supply growth which was used in the story concerning the equilibrium models
explanation of the interwar years as well as recent experience above, is the
nature of the monetary system (national and international) within which
monetary policy is operating. The role of a fixed value for some basic
commodity such as gold and the role of the exchange rate regime (and regimes
in other countries) in influencing money supply growth expectations clearly
needs to be explored. I suspect that when we have done a better job on
measuring or developing acceptable proxies for expected money supply growth
we shall find that there were indeed prolonged periods in which positive or
negative prediction errors prevailed. It will be rather like looking at a time-
series of coin tosses and noting ten heads in a row despite the fact that each
toss had an unbiased equal chance of being either heads or tails.

Although the models discussed in the previous section (with the exception
of the Lipsey analysis) were all in the 'natural rate' tradition and implicitly
assumed a fixed natural rate of unemployment, there is of course no reason to
suppose that the natural rate is in fact a constant. Analyses of the determination of the natural rate and the effects of taxes and unemployment insurance
arrangements upon the rate are undoubtedly going to have an important part
to play in explaining some of the movements of unemployment, and it is clear
that in recent years the natural rate has increased. To some extent an
analysis of what determines the natural rate is separable from the problems that
are being discussed in this paper. However, there are some questions concerning
the variability of inflation and the level of inflation and the natural rate of
unemployment which have not been resolved and which are implicit in some
of the above models. The price-setting stories of Bruno and Mussa, for
example, suggest that as the expected trend rate of inflation increases, prices
will be adjusted both more frequently and in bigger steps. This implies that
there will be an increase in the variance of relative prices across individual
firms. In that event, along the lines of the analysis of Mortensen or Hall
(referred to in the preceding section), the payoff to search activity will
increase. This could therefore give rise to a positive relation between
unemployment and the anticipated rate of inflation. An explicit working out
of these conjectures might provide a theoretical rationalisation for the
apparent tendency for the relationship between unemployment and inflation
to have become positive in recent years. Again, however, there would be a
need for careful empirical work to check out whether the variance of relative
prices is in any way correlated with the trend rate of inflation.

In sum, the major puzzles which confront us in this area are empirical and concern the explanation of the more extreme periods of unemployment or inflation (or both). It is these extreme observations rather than 'normal' periods which provide the main testing ground for alternative theories and, whilst no doubt some theoretical innovations are going to be necessary, we are not going to resolve the puzzles by *a priori* reasoning. A careful formulation testing and rejection of hypotheses, implying the careful measurement of all the relevant variables, is the only basis on which we shall make further progress.

IV POLICIES

The policy questions concerning unemployment and inflation fall in two areas: (i) activism vs. passivism in monetary policy and (ii) the use of incomes policies as an adjunct to an active monetary policy for containing inflation. Specifically in the current context the question may be posed as: should aggregate demand be given an upward kick by (temporarily) increasing the money supply growth rate or should money supply growth be stabilised (and possibly gradually reduced) and secondly, should some kind of price and wage policy be implemented?

In the current state of knowledge it is hard to see how activism in demand management can be defended. It is true that it is possible to construct an internally consistent theoretical model based either on contracts or on inertia in a Lucas-type aggregate supply function with rational expectations in which a rise in the money stock relative to the expected money stock will increase employment (reduce unemployment) and without much of a rise in the inflation rate. However, we do not know how to raise the actual money supply growth rate relative to the expected money supply growth rate. The process whereby monetary policy expectations are formed is ill-understood. Furthermore, active variations in money supply growth make it more difficult for agents in the future to form expectations which will not turn out to be falsified. All the existing models point to the need for a greater degree of predictability (and steadiness) in the growth rate of the money supply. This would stabilise inflationary expectations and lead to lower forecasting errors and therefore lower departures of unemployment from its natural rate.

If there is one single active intervention needed it is clearly to change the institutional arrangements for controlling the money supply so that a lower and more steady growth rate can be delivered in the future. The details of such a change are beyond the scope of this paper but would presumably involve changes both in the technique of monetary control (moving away from interest rate targets to monetary base targets) and changing the degree of dependence of monetary policy on short-run political considerations.

A further problem pointing strongly against activism is the imprecise knowledge we have at any time (and especially at the present time) concerning the value of the natural unemployment rate. We do not know the extent to which current unemployment is induced by unanticipated inflation and the extent to which it represents 'natural' i.e. *real* forces. Any monetary policy strategy which targets the money stock on to an unknown natural unemployment rate is almost certain to lead to long-term inflationary problems and large gyrations in money supply growth rates.

As regards the effects of incomes policies, our theoretical knowledge of their effects both on aggregate and allocative behaviour is virtually non-existent. However, a great deal of empirical work has been done attempting to measure the effects of policies of the type employed in the past and with the broad verdict that they help a little in reducing the inflation rate below what it otherwise would have been, but not much. A full catalogue of their allocative and distributive consequences is not available to us. The broad verdict of the profession seems to be that incomes policies of types hitherto practised are of zero or perhaps even negative value. However, advocates of incomes policies are the ultimate messengers of hope and always seeking to suggest new versions of their product which will overcome the problems with the old variety. A current fad is for a tax-based incomes policy, a policy which would vary the tax rate applicable to corporate profits in direct relation to the scale of wage and price change on the corporation's labour inputs and outputs. Whilst there does not appear to be a rigorous theoretical analysis of the effects of such a policy in the literature, it is easy to see how one could analyse the effects of such a policy in the context of the models presented in Section II above. In the context of a price- (or wage-) setting model of the Barro–Bruno–Musa variety, it is clear that such a tax-based incomes policy would in effect raise the cost of price (and wage) adjustment. The predictions of these models is that in that event prices and wages would be adjusted less frequently and involve on the average more temporary rationing by firms as they approach the price review date. However, there would be no change in the relation between the expected rate of inflation and actual inflation rate. The key prediction therefore from this class of model would be for a flattening of the Phillips curve and for the curve to pivot on the natural unemployment rate. Thus, whether such a policy raised or lowered the inflation rate would depend on whether the economy was above or below the natural unemployment rate. At the natural rate the policy would have no effect on the inflation rate but would of course have detrimental allocative effects. Below the natural rate, inflation would be lower than otherwise and above the natural rate, higher than otherwise. In terms of the Lucas aggregate supply model, the tax would have similar effects via its operation on the effective private marginal costs of producers. A careful working out of the propositions just stated in the context of these models would be a valuable contribution to the literature. It is hardly needed, however, to buttress the already overwhelming administrative arguments against this particular form of incomes policy.

The preceding discussion of policy towards unemployment and inflation has been entirely prescriptive and normative. That is the way we normally discuss these matters. However, we are now becoming increasingly aware that policy is made by politicians who are themselves ordinary economic agents seeking to maximise their own utility subject to budget constraints and additional constraints imposed upon them by constitutions and costly-to-change institutions. If the existing theories of the determination of inflation and unemployment which explain these problems as the consequences of unexpected policies are broadly correct, then a rigorous positive analysis of the behaviour of policy-makers themselves is going to be essential both to the complete understanding of why inflation and unemployment fluctuate in the way that they do and to achieving a more satisfactory macroeconomic performance.

BIBLIOGRAPHY

Archibald, G. C. (1969), 'The Phillips Curve and the Distribution of Unemployment', *American Economic Review*, Papers and Proceedings, 59 (2), 124–34.

Azariadis, C. (1975), 'Implicit Contracts and Underemployment Equilibria', *Journal of Political Economy*, 83, no. 6 (December), 1183–202.

Bailey, M. N. (1974), 'Wages and Employment under Uncertain Demand', *Review of Economic Studies*, 41 (January).

Barro, R. J. (1972), 'A Theory of Monopolistic Price Adjustment', *Review of Economic Studies*, 39, 17–28.

—— (1977a), 'Unanticipated Money Growth and Unemployment in the United States', *American Economic Review*, 67, no. 2 (March), 101–15.

—— (1977b), 'Long-Term Contracting, Sticky Prices and Monetary Policy', *Journal of Monetary Economics*, 3, no. 3 (July), 305–16.

—— (1978), 'Thoughts on Keynesian Economics', University of Rochester Discussion Paper, August.

—— and H. I. Grossman (1971), 'A General Disequilibrium Model of Income and Employment', *American Economic Review*, 61 (1), 82–93.

—— (1976), *Money, Employment and Inflation* (New York, Cambridge University Press).

Brown, A. J. (1955), *The Great Inflation: 1939–1951* (London, Oxford University Press).

Bruno, M. (1977), 'Price and Output Adjustment: Microfoundations of Macro Theory', Harvard Institute of Economic Research Discussion Paper No. 534, February.

Cagan, P. (1956), 'The Monetary Dynamics of Hyperinflation', in M. Friedman (ed.), *Studies in the Quantity Theory of Money* (Chicago, Ill., University of Chicago Press).

Carlson, J. A. and J. M. Parkin (1975), 'Inflation Expectations', *Economica* (NS), 42 (166), 123–38.

Clower, R. W. (1965), 'The Keynesian Counterrevolution: A Theoretical Appraisal', in F. H. Hahn and F. Brechling (eds.), *The Theory of Interest Rates* (London, Macmillan).

Fischer, S. (1977a), 'Wage Indexation and Macroeconomic Stability', *Journal of Monetary Economics* Supplement (Carnegie-Rochester Conference Series, vol. 5), 107–47.
—— (1977b), 'Long-Term Contracting, Sticky Prices and Monetary Policy: A Comment', *Journal of Monetary Economics*, 3, no. 3 (July), 317–24.
—— (1977c), 'Long-Term Contracts, Rational Expectations and the Optimal Money Supply Rule', *Journal of Political Economy*, 5, no. 5, 191–206.
Fisher, I. (1911), *The Purchasing Power of Money* (New York, Macmillan). (Latest edition, New York, A. M. Kelley, 1963.)
—— (1926), 'A Statistical Relation Between Unemployment and Price Changes', *International Labour Review* (reprinted as 'I Discovered the Phillips Curve', *Journal of Political Economy*, 81 (2), pt. 1, March/April (1973)), 496–502.
Friedman, M. (1968), 'The Role of Monetary Policy', *American Economic Review*, 58, no. 1, 1–17.
Gordon, D. F. (1977), 'A Neoclassical Theory of Keynesian Unemployment', *Journal of Economic Inquiry*, 431–59.
Gordon, R. J. (1977), 'Recent Developments in the Theory of Inflation and Unemployment', *Journal of Monetary Economics*, 2, no. 2 (April), 185–220.
Gray, Jo Anna (1976), 'Wage Indexation: A Macroeconomic Approach', *Journal of Monetary Economics*, 2, no. 2, 221–35.
—— (1978), 'On indexation and Contract Length', *Journal of Political Economy*, 86, no. 1 (February), 1–18.
Grossman, H. I. (1978a), 'Employment Fluctuations and the Mitigation of Risk', Brown University Discussion Paper, May.
—— (1978b), 'Why Does Aggregate Employment Fluctuate?', Brown University Discussion Paper 6/78 processed.
Hall, R. E. (1975), 'The Rigidity of Wages and the Persistence of Unemployment', *Brookings Papers on Economic Activity*, 2:1975, 301–35.
Harris, J. R. and M. P. Todaro (1970), 'Migration, Unemployment and Development: A Two-Sector Analysis', *American Economic Review*, 60 (March), 126–43.
Hume, D. (1741), 'Of Money', in *Essays* (Oxford University Press).
Laidler, D. and M. Parkin (1975), 'Inflation: A Survey', *Economic Journal* (December), 741–809.
Lipsey, R. G. (1960), 'The Relationship Between Unemployment and the Rate of Change of Money Wage Rates in the UK, 1862–1957: A Further Analysis', *Economica* (NS), 27 (105), 1–31.
Lucas, R. E., Jr. (1972), 'Expectations and the Neutrality of Money', *Journal of Economic Theory*, no. 4 (April), 103–24.
—— (1973), 'Some International Evidence on Output, Inflation Trade offs', *American Economic Review*, 63, no. 3, 326–34.
—— and L. A. Rapping (1969), 'Real Wages, Employment and the Price Level', *Journal of Political Economy* 77 (September), 721–54.
Malinvaud, E. (1977), *The Theory of Unemployment Reconsidered* (Oxford, Basil Blackwell).
Mortensen, D. T. (1970), 'A Theory of Wage and Employment Dynamics', in E. S. Phelps *et al.* (1970).

Mussa, M. (1977), 'The Welfare Cost of Inflation and the Role of Money as the Unit of Account', *Journal of Money, Credit and Banking*, IX, no. 2 (May), 276–86.

Phelps, E. S. (1967), 'Money Wage Dynamics and Labor Market Equilibrium', *Journal of Political Economy*, 76 (4), pt. 2, 678–711 (Amended reprint in E. S. Phelps *et al.* (1970).)

—— *et al.* (1970), *The Microeconomic Foundations of Employment and Inflation Theory* (New York, Norton).

—— and S. E. Winter, Jr. (1970), 'Optimal Price Policy Under Atomistic Competition', in Phelps *et al.* (1970), 309–37.

Phillips, A. W. (1958), 'The Relationship Between Unemployment and the Rate of Change of Money Wage Rates in the UK, 1861–1957', *Economica* (NS), 25 (100), 283–99.

Santomero, A. M. and J. J. Seater (1977), 'The Inflation-Unemployment Trade-Off: A Critique of the Literature', Philadelphia Federal Reserve Research Papers, no. 21, Department of Research, Federal Reserve Bank of Philadelphia.

Sargent, T. J. (1973), 'Rational Expectations, the Real Rate of Interest and the Natural Rate of Unemployment', *Brookings Papers on Economic Activity* 2:1973, 429–72.

Appendix 1

DATA FOR THE UNITED STATES

Year	Rate of inflation % p.a.	% Unemployment
1977	6.5	7.0
6	5.8	7.9
5	9.2	7.7
4	10.9	8.5
3	6.3	5.6
2	3.3	4.9
1	4.3	5.6
1970	5.9	4.9
1969	5.4	3.5
8	4.2	3.6
7	2.6	3.8
6	3.1	3.8
5	1.7	4.5
4	1.2	5.2
3	1.2	5.7
2	1.1	5.5
1	1.1	6.7
1960	1.5	5.5
1959	0.9	5.5
8	2.7	6.8
7	3.6	4.3
6	1.4	4.1
5	−0.2	4.4
4	0.4	5.5
3	0.8	2.9
2	2.2	3.0
1	7.6	3.3
1950	1.0	5.3
1949	−1.0	5.9
8	7.4	3.8
7	13.4	3.9
6	8.2	3.9
1945	2.3	1.9

Year	Rate of inflation % p.a.	% Unemployment
4	1.7	1.2
3	6.0	1.9
2	10.1	4.7
1	4.9	9.9
1940	1.0	14.6
1939	−1.4	17.2
8	−1.9	19.0
7	3.6	14.3
6	1.0	16.9
5	2.5	20.1
4	3.3	21.7
3	−5.3	24.9
2	−10.8	23.6
1	−9.2	15.9
1930	−2.6	8.7
1929	0	3.2
8	−1.4	4.2
7	−1.9	3.3
6	0.9	1.8
5	2.5	3.2
4	0.2	5.0
3	1.8	2.4
2	−6.6	6.7
1	−11.3	11.7
1920	14.7	5.2
1919	13.8	1.4
8	16.1	1.4
7	16.1	4.6
6	7.3	5.1
5	1.0	8.5
1914	1.3	7.9

Sources (1) *Consumer Price Index (Annual Rate of Change)*
1913–70: *Historical Statistics of the United States Colonial Times to 1970*, Part I, Bicentennial Edition (US Bureau of the Census, Washington, DC, 1975), p. 210.
1971–77: *Monthly Review* (US Department of Labor, Bureau of Statistics, June 1978), p. 87.
(2) *Per cent Unemployed (per cent of the Civilian Labour Force)*
1913–70: *Historical Statistics of the United States Colonial Times to 1970*, Part I, Bicentennial Edition (US Bureau of the Census, Washington, DC, 1975), p. 135.
1971–76: *Statistical Abstract of the United States: 1977* (US Bureau of the Census, Washington, DC, 1977), p. 395.
1977: *Monthly Labour Review* (US Department of Labor, Bureau of Statistics, June 1978), p. 70.

UNEMPLOYMENT AND INFLATION IN THE UNITED STATES 1914–77

Unemployment range	Mean unemployment	Frequency (no. of years)	Minimum inflation	Maximum inflation	Mean inflation
< 2%	1.6	6	0.9	16.1	6.8
> 2% but < 3%	2.5	2	1.8	2.9	2.3
> 3% but < 4%	3.5	12	−1.9	13.4	4.5
> 4% but < 5%	4.5	9	−1.4	16.1	4.4
> 5% but < 6%	5.4	13	−1.0	14.7	3.0
> 6% but < 7%	6.7	3	−6.6	2.7	−1.0
> 7% but < 8%	7.6	4	1.3	9.2 (1.3)[a]	5.5 (1.3)[a]
> 8% but < 9%	8.6	3	−2.6	10.9 (1.0)[a]	2.9 (−0.8)[a]
> 9%	17.5	12	−11.3	4.9	−2.0

[a] ( ) excluding 1974–77

Discussion of Professor Parkin's Paper

Professor Kolm introduced the paper. He considered that Professor Parkin's well-ordered, sympathetic and critical survey of the relations between inflation and unemployment, and especially of the theories about it, was an extremely useful contribution on a topic of paramount importance. It was thus especially important to be aware of some serious involuntary limitations of this study which were, however, more due to the literature under review than to the reviewer.

First, the survey was restricted to the Anglo-Saxon literature. This was a severe limitation, since the most important ideas in this field, as in other in economics, originated in other languages before they were rediscovered in English. He would note several examples.

Second, in his review of the facts about the inflation—unemployment relation in the USA, Professor Parkin should have shown on the same diagram their trends since 1953 — the 'post—Korean' period. He would then have put in evidence the regularity of the 'upward clockwise inflation-unemployment spiral', the observation and the theory of which had made it possible to forecast the 1974—75 crisis five years in advance.[1] This paper had forecast for 1974—75 a crisis which would be 'the deepest since the Great one'. The crisis would be caused by especially strong and simultaneous stabilisation policies in 1973—74, the aim of which would be to fight increased inflation. This inflation would result from the 1972 reflations, which were designed to fight the 1971 recession, itself introduced by the deflationary 1969 anti-inflation policies. The depth of the 1974—75 depression would result from the strength of the deflationary measures, themselves a result of the high inflation rate. The average inflation rate increased in each cycle because political pressures forced governments to reflate before inflation could be brought back to its earlier low level. The theory of the international synchronisation of the cycle — partial since 1966, perfect since 1971 — of its importance in the crisis and inflation, and of its economic causes, was added later. We could now add that, in essence, these developments would have occurred even without the oil price increases. These added relatively little to world inflation at that time, and their deflationary effects were purposely uncompensated by some governments in order to fight inflation.

Third, Professor Kolm said that his own paper, just mentioned, explained in particular the upward shifts in short-run Phillips curves, which Professor Parkin found inexplicable. They were loops rather than curves, and there had been public reflation at a still high inflation rate because of the political costs — to politicians — of the slump. More generally, Professor Parkin seemed unaware that capitalism in the second half of the twentieth century was a

---

[1] Kolm, 'L'avenir du capitalisme americain' (Cepremap, 1969), and *Revue d'Economie Politique* (January 1971).

different animal from what it was before, because of systematic and large macroeconomic policy-making and global demand management.

The relationships between the macroeconomic situation and dynamics, macroeconomic policies, and the political process, were thus essential. They were barely mentioned by Professor Parkin at the end of his paper, in spite of recent American contributions — Nordhaus's 'political cycle' of 1975 in particular — and of studies of the relations between the macroeconomic situation and elections (especially in France and the USA).

Fourth, since governments manipulated macroeconomic policy to try to put the economy in a favourable state about election time, the direction of the loops in an inflation—unemployment diagram was an essential question for these policies and thus for the performance and evolution of the system. Professor Parkin rightly mentioned the spontaneous counter-clockwise loops of the Lipsey model, and the clockwise tendency introduced into Phelps's model by expectations if unemployment fluctuated. This could happen under the effects of macroeconomic policies. However, Phelps's model could also generate counter-clockwise loops, because the presence of Δu in the function f created what might be called a Lipsey effect. The model thus could explain all the historical facts on an *a priori* basis.

Fifth, after these government policies, the second most important cause of unemployment and inflation in the various countries was international economic relations. This was proved by all theoretical and empirical knowledge. This question was by-passed by Professor Parkin. He was aware of its existence, but the only fact he mentioned in this field was that American inflation in the 1960s was low because of the international monetary system. But inflation had been much more rapid in other countries during this period; France, for instance. Professor Parkin argued that the fixed-rate gold-exchange standard provided an 'anchor' for the 'system' and for 'money growth expectations'; but American inflation was lower than that abroad, and, on the world scale, this regime provided the opposite: there was no constraint on the dollar outflow. Of course, the inflation of the 1970s and the transformation of the international monetary system were closely related, but this happened through other links, and went both ways in dynamic feedbacks. Persistently high unemployment and low growth in the USA up to the mid-1960s explained low inflation in this period.

Sixth, in considering the history of the 'Phillips curve', the contributions by François Simiand in the 1920s and by Tinbergen and Pollak in 1939 were omitted from Professor Parkin's review. The first works on the microeconomic foundations of the inflation—employment relationship were also ignored; for example, S. Kolm, 'La theorie de la relation inflation—chômage', *Revue économique*, March—April 1970). Several big empirical models, which contained relevant information about the relationship between inflation and employment, were not even mentioned.

Seventh, expectations of inflation were probably the most important question in Professor Parkin's analysis. Rightly so . . . but they were also its weakest point. The paper centred around an American fantasy called 'rational expectations'. Professor Parkin thought it to be 'the only acceptable theory'. He rightly criticised some of its aspects or applications, such as the idea that the public knew the correct model of the economy. (This would at least exclude most professional economists from the set of 'rational economic agents'.) But Professor Parkin endorsed other ideas, some of which were just absurd. One was that 'the average economic agent' forecast the rate of inflation by the intermediary of a forecast of the rate of monetary expansion. The public knew practically none of the facts or beliefs which would be necessary for that: statistical definition, figures, theory, facts and effects of monetary policy, and the rest.

Professor Parkin presented one particularly amusing application of the idea: the 1934 devaluation of the dollar, he argued, created inflation in the USA. This would surprise no-one: an increase in foreign prices and net demand and a foreign surplus had produced an inflow of reserve money. However, the reason given was that the increase in the dollar value of gold reserves induced the public to forecast an increase in the quantity of money and thus in the inflation rate, hence this increase. In fact, the 'rational expectations' theories presented here were far-fetched, and merely a device to have the rate of inflation depend exclusively upon the increase in money supply. More generally, these theories failed to consider properly the effects on expectations of the costs and constraints of knowing and computing, of memorising and remembering, of gathering, storing, processing and applying information. These costs and constraints were different for the various agents and for the economist. Contrary to Professor Parkin's optimistic view, people were stupid, overselves included; but we could be intelligent enough to know why. We should finally note that actual agents' expectations were not point estimates.

The most important factor in expectations of inflation was the *extrapolation of the recent derivatives* of the price level: the price level itself (derivative of degree zero), the rate of inflation (logarithmic derivative), the absolute or relative increase in the rate of inflation, etc. In the period 1966−74, people in France successively extrapolated derivatives of increasing degree, up to the fifth derivative of the price level. (See S. Kolm, *Le Monde*, 15 and 19 March, 1974.) In English, the general principle of this idea was first mentioned by John Fleming in *Inflation* (London 1976).

Eighth, Professor Parkin rightly emphasised the question of the dispersion of rates of inflation and of relative prices. But his comments missed some essential points. Both *ex ante* uncertainties and *ex post* dispersions across dates and commodities were of importance, both for global inflation rates and for relative prices, and for prices of commodities defined both by their nature and by the seller or buyer. A central point in Professor Parkin's presentation was the relative importance of the time dispersions of the rate of inflation and of relative prices. However, this factor was likely to have little importance in an individual country, since the two dispersions varied together, and with the average rate of inflation. In fact, the socio-psychological effects of the uncertainty of relative prices (incomes included) and of returns on a assets were the essential social cost of inflation.

Changes in the variability of relative prices with the rate of inflation were well established since Jean Gabillard's book *La fin de l'inflation*, 1952 (In English, see Parks, 'Inflation and relative price variability', *Journal of Political Economy*, February 1978). It was explained by the fact that the various prices had different periodicities of adjustment. These periods tended to become shorter when inflation was more rapid, and this had the opposite effect. But one could show that the first effect remained more important.

Professor Parkin's authors applied this cause of dispersion to firms' prices for the same commodity. But this was just the case where to do so was least valid since quite often a number of phenomena induced these firms to change their prices at the same dates: the use of standard calendar dates (daily, weekly, monthly, quarterly, yearly), oligopolistic agreements, collective bargaining, 'price leader' firms, etc.

Moreover, what validity was there in the story of an agent witnessing an increase in a price and attributing it either to a change in relative prices or to the inflation rate, or, presumably, to some mixture of both? Agents witnessed many prices, and from this they made the distinction and knew what was happening.

Ninth, to explain variations in employment, too much was expected from the effect of unemployment compensation, taxes and minimum wage laws on the so-called 'natural rate' of unemployment. For instance, they could not help in explaining the drastic increase in unemployment of 1974.

Tenth, on macroeconomic policies, Professor Parkin's only recommendation was 'passivism', i.e. constant growth rate of the money supply. This old discussion was thus not dead. The only scientific attempt to justify 'passivism' was Milton Friedman's paper, first published in *Economie Appliquée* in 1951, and later as 'The effects of a full-employment policy on economic stability'. This model had been shown to be an extremely specific and unrealistic one, built specifically to yield this result. Macroeconomic policy affected only the scale of the deviation of global income from its average. The part of global demand influenced by macroeconomic policy was assumed to be always uncorrelated with fluctuations in the remainder, etc. (See S. Kolm, 'Inflation et relation inflation-chômage induits par les incertitudes de la politique économique', *Revue d'Economie Politique*, May 1975). To advocate 'passivism' was to recommend governments and central banks not to use the information they had, i.e. to recommend them to be what was called 'irrational' in the discussion of 'rational expectations'. The political and sociological context of macroeconomic policy must also be recalled here.

Eleventh, discussing the anti-inflation tax, Professor Parkin asserted that there were 'overwhelming administrative arguments against' this. However, such a tax had now existed in France for five years.

Finally, the paper contained several imprecise or unexplained assertions: prices and price variations were not distinguished clearly enough in various places; an observed change in a nominal price was called a change in a relative price; a monetary policy aiming at an unknown 'natural' rate of unemployment was not inflationary if it believed in and aimed at one which was above the actual one; rationing by all firms was not necessary for the existence of global rationing; the problem of demand-induced unemployment was not only one of money wage and price rigidity (through Pigou, liquidity, or other nominal, effects); it was also one of real wage rigidity (through firms' employment and production decision).

In conclusion, Professor Kolm wanted to say that the importance and comprehension of these questions were, in his view, a definite proof of the stimulus and important issues raised by Parkin's paper.

Professor Södersten wanted to make a simple point about the effects of the oil crisis. The essence of this was that it represented a drastic redistribution of income to the OPEC countries. Receipts from sales of oil increased from $30 billion per annum to S120 billion over a very short period. Moreover, the marginal propensity to save within OPEC was high. Savings therefore increased very dramatically, and from a world point of view, there was a disequilibrium between savings and investment. The developed countries, from whom most of the increased oil revenues came, had very conservative governments, so that restrictive policies were introduced. There was a redistribution of income and assets, and therefore a transfer problem. Between the mid-1970s and 1980s something like $300 billion had to be dealt with, and the only countries that could swallow sums on that scale were the members of the OECD. At bottom, the crisis of the 1970s was therefore a crisis of deficiency of demand on an international scale leading to cumulative effects, including classic unemployment.

Investment in Sweden had fallen dramatically, so that it might be difficult to employ the labour force fully in the future. One might then have Keynesian and classic unemployment together at a time when the world was still confronted with this basic transfer problem between OPEC and the rest of the world. Professor Södersten did not think the politicians of the West were up to solving the problem. There had been a moment when the USA could have chosen to show statesmanship under President Ford, but it has merely threatened the Arabs in an attempt to keep prices down. Professor Södersten in this case thought we should employ economic theory as an Occam's Razor, using simple explanations first. On the world level this was a straightforward Keynesian problem.

Dr Kaufman asked Professor Parkin if he sincerely believed the stories implicit in the Lucas—Phelps models whereby firms (workers) perceived changes in their nominal prices (wages) and altered their production (job attachment) to the extent that such changes represented changes in relative prices (real wages) rather than inflation. Rather than acting in this way, firms seemed to base their production decisions on changes in sales, and he suspected workers reacted primarily to job opportunities.

In the contract theory models espoused by Bailey and Azariadis workers were assumed to be more risk-averse than firms. Real wages were fixed, and firms responded to fluctuations in aggregate demand by laying off workers. The workers allegedly viewed these layoffs as preferable to a situation in which real wages were flexible. While the authors' assumption about relative risk aversion seemed plausible, workers should be concerned about fixing their real *income* rather than their real *wage*. Layoffs might have the same effect on real incomes as did flexible wages, and hence might not be preferable.

Dr Kaufman applauded Professor Parkin's honesty in three areas. Parkin admitted that current rational expectations models were of limited value for policy purposes, that rational expectations theorists needed to incorporate the fact that information in the labour market might be costly and difficult to acquire, and that the events of the Great Depression had yet to be adequately explained by either monetarists or non-monetarists.

He noted that the US unemployment rate fell from 14.6 per cent in 1940 to 1.2 per cent in 1944. In discussing this decline Professor Parkin mentioned only unexpected money growth coupled with a reduction in expected inflation following the imposition of wage and price controls. He asked Professor Parkin what fraction of this decline in unemployment he would attribute to these phenomena.

Dr Kaufman mentioned the probability that the natural rate of unemployment itself was determined by the level of aggregate demand to the extent that conditions prevailing when unemployment was held below the current natural rate (albeit temporarily) might create incentives for investment in human and physical capital which would in turn *reduce* the natural rate of unemployment. To this extent expansionary monetary and fiscal policies might have enduring effects even within the natural rate framework. Finally, even if we accepted the extreme assumption that altering the current unemployment rate was a zero sum game, incorporation of a positive rate of time preference implied that the Federal Reserve System should fool people now and pay for this later. Thus, Professor Parkin's prescription of a constant growth rate of money did not follow from the discussion presented in the text.

Professor Eastman noted that, thus far, the conference had discussed unemployment resulting from inadequate real demand. The problem was that if we took measures to increase demand we did not know how to ensure that we got an impact on unemployment rather than prices. Professor Parkin gave data showing that the relationships between inflation and unemployment were irregular. We all wanted to know more about the costs of inflation which Professor Kolm had discussed, but there must be benefits from inflation as well, or there would be less of it. It seemed that, perhaps after a lag, the victims defended themselves, but the root cause of inflation must be that some benefited from it. If one went back into history, one saw that the increase in the money supply in the USA had begun because the USA did not want to be taxed in order to fight the war in Vietnam. That increase in the money supply had spread elsewhere. There were big lags before the public appreciated what would happen, both in the USA and in other countries. However, the learning process now seemed to be complete. Public opinion was at last sensitive to changes in the money supply, most of which were fiscal in origin. To reverse the inflationary process would therefore take time.

Taking up what Professor Eastman had said, *Lord Kaldor* pointed out that historically great inflations ended suddenly and not gradually, though it was often not clear why.

Professor Eastman therefore explained that what he claimed to be inconsistent was the relationship between unemployment and inflation.

Professor Henin thought the paper important because it gave a competent and honest statement of the monetarist view. It showed that there was now a debate between those with disequilibrium theories who wanted government intervention and those who took a view which, in name of equilibrium theories, expressed ultra-liberal ideas. Professor Parkin claimed that the intellectual difficulty of the idea of disequilibrium concerned expectations. But, on an equilibrium view, to talk of continuing unemployment was to talk about recurrent failures of expectations.

More generally, perfect expectations did not preserve us from cumulative disequilibria, as had been shown ten years previously in the context of multisector, multicapital-goods models by F. Hahn and others.

Professor Henin said that Professor Parkin's honest survey let us see clearly the weakness of the 'equilibrium' or 'liberal' view. It was not acceptable to explain persistent unemployment by a systematic autocorrelation of errors, and to discuss rigidity of supply was to use a very *ad hoc* argument in this nearly perfect world. The more recent story of contracts might be more firmly grounded but, in any case, consistent explanation of a lack of adjustment in the short run reintroduced rationing as an unavoidable consequence. This had two very destructive implications for the liberal or equilibrium view, the first implication theoretical and the second concerned with economic policy.

At the theoretical level, if one recognised the existence of rationing, then one had to consider those disequilibrium models that were concerned with the spillover effects of such rationing. An equilibrium approach was no longer the relevant theory. At the economic policy level, if price fixing by economic agents led to rationing, then external diseconomics would be generated. There would be a difference between private and social adjustment costs and for an optimal solution to be reached state must intervene. Then Liberalism was no longer relevant policy.

Of course, intervention would be selective, coping with the microeconomic costs of adjustment and internalising the external diseconomics of the social costs of inflation.

Professor Henin thought that the concept of rational expectations was too important to be left to monetarists. However, the idea that economic agents were gathering information according to some structure was very sound and might be the only way to understand changes in expectations.

Professor Holt was worried that Professor Parkin argued that the policy

questions concerning unemployment and inflation fell only into the areas of
(i) activism versus pacificism in monetary policy and (ii) the use of incomes
policies as an adjunct to active monetary policy. He did not think the policy
alternatives so limited. One could make use of manpower programmes;
Professor Rehn's marginal wage subsidy; a reduction in government legislation
on minimum wages, etc. Professor Parkin was sceptical about active demand
management, but Professor Holt thought we should try harder. Take the OPEC
shock as an example. It had increased both unemployment and inflation.
Estimates were being made for the USA that the cumulative lost production
was of the order of $500 billion, and unemployment rates were greater than
at any time since the 1930s. For some minority groups, the unemployment
rate was 45 per cent. It was not an adequate answer just to say that we were
ignorant and therefore we could do nothing. Professor Parkin also said that a
tax-based income policy was a new fad. But perhaps it would push the Phillips
curve downwards — there might be a significant effect on expectations.

On rational expectations, he was astounded at the gap between glib
assumptions about what information firms had and used, and what they
actually did. There was much use of crude rules of thumb, and many
businesses seemed to react only when serious crises forced them to do so. We
needed a model but he was not sure that rational expectations was the best
available.

To Professor Kolm, he would say that he wondered whether inflation
caused the dispersion of prices, rather than *vice versa*.

Professor Georgescu-Roegen thought there were more important factors
than the level of the rate of inflation. We used generally Western ideas in
writing about inflation. In Latin America and South East Asia it had a different
mechanism, as, for example, in Brazil, where rates of inflation were very high.
The reasons for resorting to inflation were different institutional frameworks.
We therefore needed to look at the structure of inflation rather than at its rate.

Professor Modigliani disagreed profoundly with the paper. Professor Parkin
posed many issues but the real one was what price in unemployment we would
pay in order to reduce inflation. Professor Modigliani did not think it was true
that we tolerated inflation because we gained from it. Those whom one would
think would gain from it most, like businessmen, were all against it. We
tolerated inflation because we did not want unemployment. If inflation was
as costly as some participants had suggested, one needed to have an inflation
target path in order to bring its rate down ultimately to low levels. He was
prepared to accept the conservative view that we needed more slack in the
economy until inflation abated, but there was a case for a gradual reduction
in the rate. When he said this, he assumed that the short-run Phillips curve had
some curvature — a positive second derivative. In the absence of curvature,
gradualism would no doubt lose most of its merit.

Professor Modigliani was sorry that Professor Parkin was so attracted by
the rational expectation theory in the macroeconomic context. He would
yield to no-one in admiration of the idea of rational expectation, particularly

since it had been thought of by one of his students, Muth, but he thought that the correct idea would be non-irrational expectations. However, he accepted that this was a grey area. While he believed that hypothesis was relevant with respect to certain individual markets, its relevance at the macroeconomic level was an entirely different matter. For one thing, it was inconsistent with the classic tâtonnment process in which economic agents respond to their experience of excess demand or supply. In any event, economic policy makers would not lose all power as soon as one allowed for long-run contracts. Professor Parkin should look at Phelps's paper, which showed, in the context of multiperiod contracts, what was the rational expectation path which, if universally believed, would lead to zero inflation without departing from full employment. It involved the solution of high-order difference equations. So, to entertain rational expectations economic agents would also be required to have super-mathematical ability.

Professor Modigliani noted that it was when a problem seemed unbeatable that it disappeared. How could this problem of inflation go away? He thought that a run of good luck in terms of exogenous shocks and avoidance of unfavourable policy-induced shocks would help enormously.

Professor Hines explained that he owed Professor Parkin replies to some of his previous writings, and that these would come. He agreed with Professor Modigliani that one should not necessarily accept the notion that agents in the economy took good decisions. There was nothing in the propositions that there were no adequate expectations or that rational learning processes did not exist which committed anyone to anything in the paper. So, for example, if in an organised labour market trade unions set prices, why could they not learn to change their behaviour? Perhaps incomes policies were not always faulty but a part of the educational process.

Lord Kaldor pointed out that Milton Friedman, in a letter to *The Times*, had gone a long way in conceding that money was not the only thing that mattered, but that the oil price was also important, as well as the exchange rate and import prices. He held firm only on the role of trade unions, insisting that wage increases could not generate inflation. Once that last bastion fell, the whole disagreement between monetarists and others would become a semantic issue. He wondered how far Professor Parkin would go along with this. However, in his more recent Nobel lecture, Friedman had given up everything except an empirical generalisation showing an inverted Phillips curve – i.e. that unemployment and inflation were positively, not negatively, related. This deprived the 'Phillips curve' of all its previous significance.

Professor Parkin made some clarifications. Professor Kolm had referred to his 'almost perfect' paper, but Professor Parkin did not want to claim that the world would be totally perfect if there were no government policy and the money supply were kept constant. This was not his view at all.

He wanted, however, to begin with rational expectations. Central to the way he had described these in his paper was the current class of rational expectations models, all based on Muth's original analysis. The idea was applied in a very naïve way. One began by supposing that everyone knew, and could solve, the true model, and so could predict the true rate of inflation. Often people were concerned only with the money supply, but fiscal policy could come in too. This model was naïve but it was a benchmark from which one could move on. What was needed now was a start to serious work on the measurement of expectations. If one could not measure a phenomenon, one could not hypothesise about it. If one did measure it, then one might get time-series which would allow the analysis of important problems. His own work for the UK had been done at a time when the rational expectations theory was not well-known and he had not taken account of it. He had tested an alternative hypothesis, namely, that we learned by adopting a level of time derivative that was roughly constant. When the rate of inflation was low, namely, less than 2 per cent, nothing seemed to determine expectations. There was simply a certain amount of noise in the system. At a moderate rate of inflation, expectations became adaptive; at a very high rate of inflation, what happened was not easily explicable. After the pound had been devalued in 1967, a survey found an increase in inflationary expectations, for obvious reasons.

More work was needed on how expectations responded to monetary and fiscal policy. The ideas about expectations in the *General Theory* gave a good description of how expectations responded to policy, suggesting a weak effect of policy on expectations.

Professor Georgescu-Roegen commented that by 'expectation' Professor Parkin referred to what was expected and not to the corresponding state of mind, which involved probabilities. He thought that to recognise the difference between the two concepts, that would settle the difference between Professors Parkin and Modigliani.

Professor Parkin replied to the discussion. The Keynesian hypothesis was effectively saying that if there was no new information there was no basis for changing expectations. Professor Parkin was not himself asserting a rationalist view. He agreed with Professor Henin that one could not ignore the basic approach of assuming that economic agents were doing their best in the face of costly information.

He now wanted to turn to the supply side. In his paper he had suggested that rationing models, while emphasising the supply-side response, had not yet gone far enough. When they did so, as Professor Malinvaud wanted, it would be difficult to distinguish them from other approaches. A lot depended on which way round one viewed the Phillips curve. One approach was to see prices as indicating quantities. Lucas, for example, said that there was a response only to relative prices, which he then aggregated to show that aggregate excess supply would respond positively to the unexpected component in inflation. This did not, however, explain the stylised facts on unemployment and inflation. What North American conservatives did was to introduce distributed lag adjustments. Many thought they represented the costs of changing the response of the labour force to taxation, etc. However, the story needed to be about the world we lived in, and to fit the stylised facts which it was initially intended to explain. Professor Parkin thought it realistic to take the view that firms announced prices and then saw what quantities were demanded at those prices. This enabled them to decide whether to change the prices. He preferred this story, but in terms of periods for which prices were set. It seemed to be necessary to consider the costs of having prices at non-optimal levels for certain periods of time. In terms of quantitative factors, it was not clear why labour contracts should be for periods of, say, three years, or which firms should set prices for, say, six to twelve months. There were therefore two alternatives, and one did not seem too plausible.

On policy matters, he thought the conference was in agreement on everything except on what would have been the appropriate response to the shock of the oil price increase. Perhaps there was virtual agreement on other issues, where differences that remained were perhaps only about the size of the second decimal place. However, he did not think it had been wise to increase the rate of growth of the money supply in the USA in 1971 to 12 per cent for M_2 and 19 per cent for M_1 and then bring it down so quickly. That action had been inappropriate. Nor was the present rate of fluctuation in the money supply desirable. There were two issues. First, could one control money supply? Second, had one the political will to do so? He had no doubt that we could control the money supply in the technical sense but had doubts about the political will.

On the response to the oil price increase, he was agnostic. He would not have accommodated it by increasing the money supply, but he did not think one could say that an accommodatory monetary policy would have led to less unemployment. There would have been a major problem whatever was done. Perhaps one would have had a little less unemployment if one had allowed rather more inflation, but increasing the money supply to accommodate the shock must have made it harder for agents to predict what would happen to prices, and so made it harder to maintain full employment. He was not sure one could by monetary accommodation avoid the consequences for employment of a real shock of that magnitude.

Professor Parkin did not think he had been indulgent to his friends and harsh to his enemies. He had simply put over the view that the Chicago School had important things to say. He also thought there was a great deal of ignorance that needed clearing up. In fact, he thought Professor Kolm's scenario was like his own. The apparent exception lay in Professor Kolm's view on the role of expectations in the build-up period. He thought we could treat France over the next twelve to eighteen months as an interesting test of whether expectations were adapting or whether the amount of monetary growth was affecting the level of inflation. If the rational expectations view was correct, we should not expect a permanent increase in the French inflation rate, but a fall in unemployment. Of course, in France the money supply figures were published only with a nine to twelve months' lag and this was good for the monetary authorities.

To Dr Kaufman he wanted to say that he did not feel able to explain what had happened in 1941–44. He did, however, agree with Professor Georgescu-Roegen. This was why he emphasised the importance of contracts. For example, Brazil had wound down inflation by using their contracts.

As for Friedman's views, he thought it important to say that, on the whole, Friedman dealt with a closed economy. So what he said did not carry over to the world economy, with exchange rates, capital markets, and balance of payments imbalances.

10 Recent and Prospective Trends of the Demand for Labour in the Federal Republic of Germany: An ex-post Analysis and some Simulation Results with a Macro- and Linked-Industry Model

Christoph Koellreuter
PROGNOS, EUROPEAN CENTRE FOR APPLIED ECONOMIC
RESEARCH, BASEL, SWITZERLAND

I INTRODUCTION

In this paper I shall try to analyse recent and future trends of the demand for labour and its determinants in the FRG at the national level as well as in selected industries.

First this is done for a typical pre-recession time period in the early seventies (1970–73) and then for a time span of eight quarters (1976: 1 to 1977:4) after the 1974–75 recession. The main purpose of this ex-post analysis is to find answers to what factors have caused the changes in the post-recession short- to medium-term trends of two to four years in the demand for labour in the FRG as a whole and in German key industries. The time horizon of this discussion is clearly short- to medium-term. It is not the ambition of this paper to find out what is the new long-term trend in the demand for labour for the next ten to fifteen years ahead.

The investigation has been done using the analytical framework offered by an econometric macro and industry model elaborated at PROGNOS Ltd and the Institute for Applied Economic Research of the University of Basle.[1]

Because the way in which the trends in the demand for labour are interpreted depends heavily on the econometric equations and models used for the

[1] For the macro model see Ditzler, Koellreuter and Kugler (1978); The industry model is described in Koellreuter (1978); see references at end of chapter.

analysis, the main features of these models will first be reviewed in the second and third sections of this paper. This discussion will be followed by the ex-post analysis of recent trends in the demand for labour before and after the 1974–75 recession mentioned above.

Finally an estimate of the growth of the demand for labour in the FRG during the period 1978–80 will be presented. This 'control forecast' has been calculated with the models mentioned.

A series of scenarios based on assumptions which depart from the set of exogenous variables underlying the control solution will form the last section of this paper.

It will be the main objective of this final part to show whether specific policies – such as are recommended in certain quarters – can lead to an improvement in the short- to medium-term employment prospects in the FRG as a whole and its key industries. Several questions – suggesting the formulation of alternative scenarios – will be asked:

(1) Can a policy of wage restraint restore full employment (as recommended by the German Economic Council)?[1]

(2) Is a Swiss-style monetary policy the clue to more growth and employment, counting on a possible causal chain of zero inflation – improvement of international competitiveness – more growth and employment?

(3) Or would the familiar Keynesian reflationary measures do the job?

A scenario with a higher increase of raw material prices than assumed in the control forecast, and an examination of the effects of industry-specific wage increases on employment in that industry, follow the more policy oriented scenarios.

II THE MODELS USED FOR ANALYSIS AND SIMULATION: THE QUARTERLY MACRO-MODEL FRG IV

The quarterly macro model FRG IV contains 32 behavioural equations and 13 identities.

The consumption function has been modelled along Duesenberry–Davis lines[2] although with an important modification. Following an idea of the McCracken report (OECD, 1977, p. 42) a sort of a discomfort index has been considered as an additional variable explaining the average propensity to consume. According to our estimation seems to be the inflation rate which exerts an important negative influence on private consumption. The implied

---

[1] See 'Sachverständigenrat zur Begutachtung der gesamtwirtschaftlichen Entwicklung', *Jahresgutachten 1977/78*, p. 11 and especially p. 138

[2] Cf. Duesenberry (1949, p. 90) and Davis (1952).

short-run propensity to consume with 0.35 to 0.4 is rather high compared with e.g. American standards.[1]

Adaptive inflationary expectations work just the other way round in the case of the modified neo-classical Jorgenson type investment functions[2] (business fixed investment) where they enter the user cost of capital variable with a negative sign.

When entrepreneurs expect lower product prices in the future, capital costs incurred in the present are more burdensome and have therefore an increased negative impact on investment.

The relatively high price-elasticity of German exports – more than one – is another important feature of the macro-model. The demand for German exports is no longer price inelastic, as it used to be until the 1974/75 recession.[3]

This important new structural feature of the German economy shows the new situation confronting the German export industry. This set-up is characterised by a strongly revalued Deutschmark and a new international division of labour which brings those branches of German industry producing relatively standard products (e.g. the branches producing chemicals and iron and steel) under heavy price pressure.

The demand-for-labour function is modelled as a manhours' equation and follows a neo-classical approach. Output, capacity utilisation, relative factor prices and disembodied technical progress are the determinants of the demand for labour in the macro-model. The employment-wage elasticity at -0.2 and the employment-output elasticity at 0.75 are very close to the median estimates quoted by Hamermesh (1976, pp. 514, 518) from a series of US studies on the demand for labour. Similar coefficients have been estimated for the Netherlands (Driehus, 1972, p. 37) and the FRG (Franz, 1977, p. 15). A disembodied technical progress parameter in the range of 3 per cent p.a. seems to be a result which is not unexpected for this type of labour demand function.[4] As will be seen in later sections of this paper, the choice of the neo-classical approach gives relative factor prices and the phenomenon of factor substitution an important part to play in the determination of labour demand, such as may be difficult to accept for someone who perhaps prefers more realistic labour demand models. On the other hand the wage capital-cost ratio has increased rather markedly in the periods under consideration in this

---

[1] Cf. Evans (1969, p. 68).

[2] For the estimation of the first Jorgenson investment function (Jorgenson 1963, 1965) for the FRG see Koenig (1976).

[3] Cf. the export equation in the quarterly model FRG II (Koellreuter and Kugler, 1976). The export demand is still price-inelastic in the case of Switzerland (data coverage 1965:1 – 1974:4) as can be seen from some still unpublished work at the Institute of Applied Economic Research of the University of Basle.

[4] See Driehus (1977, p. 16).

paper, and the same holds true for all scenarios covering future periods to be presented below. Substitution of capital for labour is a one-way street. Empirically observed, as well as all likely possible future, developments of the wage/capital-cost ratio will only accelerate or decelerate this process.

In this sense the influence of relative factor prices on employment at a macro level is very similar to the influence of real wage cost on employment in a clay-clay vintage model.[1]

It has not been possible to get statistically significant and economically reasonable results for the user-cost-of-capital variable in the relative factor price term, when inflationary expectations are included, as in the case of the investment functions of the model. It seems that adaptive inflationary expectations are important with respect to capital-widening but not with respect to capital-deepening decisions.

Actual hourly wage rates are modelled according to a modified version of the productivity theory as proposed by Kuh (1967). The Phillips approach (1958) could not be identified in a statistically acceptable way.

A second wage equation, where actual hourly wage rates are primarily explained by contractual hourly wage rates, can be used for wage policy simulations.

The labout supply is determined inside the model. In this context the 'discouraged workers' hypothesis could be confirmed.

The equations for gross and net profits and other non-wage income, as well as for net wages, are relatively simple. Together with an equation for indirect taxes minus subsidies they imply a rudimentary government/social security submodel. The relatively low elasticity of net wages with respect to gross wages of 0.67 (before 1975 but 1 or 0.81) gives evidence of the relatively strong progression of the German wage-tax system. Several simulations with the model showed that, out of an increase of the gross wage sum of 1 billion DM, about 600 millions DM are taken away by the government and the social security system.

This points crucially to the negative impact of the German tax and social security system on the size of the multipliers one may expect in the case of possible expansionary measures. The price equations reflect mainly the cost-push approach. Demand-pull elements are also of some importance.[2]

In the monetary sector of the model, the short-term interest rate is primarily explained as a function of the real value of money (M1) and real GNP. The long-term interest rate results from a distributed lag of the short-term interest rate.

The US dollar exchange rate of the DM is determined in the model by the inflation rate differential between the US and the FRG. The elasticity of the exchange rate with respect to the relative price variable amounts to -2.6

---

[1] Cf. Den Hartog and Tjan (1976, p. 52).
[2] Both hypotheses are also compatible with neo-classical assumptions. See Eckstein and Fromm (1968, p. 1162).

in the second quarter. This points to strongly extrapolative elements in the formation of expectations (the 'overshooting' phenomenon). The corresponding long-run elasticity is not significantly different from one – thus well in line with the purchasing power parity theory. Trade balance effects are taken into account with the ratio of German industrial production to the US industrial production. The interest rate differential (or the relative money supplies in the forecast version of the model) is the third variable determining the behaviour of the exchange rate.[1]

The exchange rate equation is the corner stone of the monetary sector but perhaps also of the whole macro-model. Exchange rate movements – which can be induced by variations of the money supply – are of crucial importance for the internal price level (via import prices) and *vice versa*. But they are equally important for the real elements in the model via the high export price-elasticity.

We shall see later that our macro-model, which incorporates distinct features of today's world of flexible exchange rates, may show that certain propositions in which economists used to believe, or still believe, can only be true under the conditions of a system of fixed exchange rates.[2]

III THE MODELS USED FOR ANALYSIS AND SIMULATION: THE QUARTERLY MODEL FRG-INDUSTRY III

As an extension of the macro-model FRG IV, the quarterly model FRG-INDUSTRY III has been constructed by the author to provide an instrument for the analysis, forecast and simulation of the demand for labour and its determinants in selected industries of the FRG.

The normal approach to constructing an industry model consists in the conversion of final expenditure categories – determined in a macro-model – into gross outputs by industrial sectors by making use of the inverse Leontief matrix of technical coefficients for a base year. The problem of changing coefficients is generally solved by estimating adjustment equations for the deviations between actual gross output and the hypothetical values one gets by multiplying the base year Leontief inverse with the final demand vector.[3]

Instead of concentrating our efforts on estimating good adjustment equations for the deviations mentioned above, we have preferred to consider the factors responsible for the changing coefficient problem as being technical

---

[1] For the exchange rate equation with monthly data see also Bernholz and Kugler (1978).

[2] One example is provided by our scenario 'Wage Restraint'. Because the exchange rate tends to 'overshoot' movements of internal prices, a policy of general wage restraint does not continue to pay off in all cases in an open economy; the contrary is true. See section VI of this paper.

[3] Cf. Preston (1975, p. 615) and Schluter (1974, pp. 100–2).

progress, changing relative prices, factor substitution, and a changing product mix within and between sectors, in a rather more explicit way.

In place of deriving gross output by industry directly from final demand components by means of the input-output technique, it is the absorption of a certain product group (ABS_i) which is first explained. In a second step exports (EX_i) and imports (IM_i) of goods belonging to this product group are modelled. Gross output (GPX_i) of an industry is then defined by the following equation:

$$GPX_i = ABS_i + EX_i - IM_i$$

The not uncommon hypothesis is made that absorption, including imports as well as exports, depends on an adequately defined activity ('income') variable and on the relevant relative prices.

The activity variable in the absorption equations consists in a weighted index of production and final demand indices of domestic sectors consuming output of the product group under consideration. The weights are taken from the 1972 input-output matrix and the import matrix at current prices, as provided by the Deutscher Institut für Wirtschaftsforschung (1975).

In the case of the import equations it is the absorption which functions as the relevant income variable. The activity index for the exports of German industries reflects a weighted index of industrial production of the USA, the United Kingdom, France, Italy and Japan, weighted by the shares of each of these countries in German exports. Because one of the constraints under which the industry model has to operate consists in having only a small number of exogenous variables, it was not possible to find a more appropriate approach for modelling exports by industry.[1]

For the sake of simplicity it has been assumed that the relationship between gross output and output originating (value added) is constant over time.

Even if the main interest did not lie in shedding some light on the determinants of the demand for labour in particular industries it would be necessary to estimate employment and wage equations in order to reach one decisive factor influencing product and export prices by industry, that is unit labour cost. Prices (relative prices) are very important in our industry model. This is especially true for the exports and imports by industry.

The price equations (producer, export and import prices) are explained more or less as in the macro-model. Unit material costs enter the functions as additional right-hand variables.

Wages by industry are largely determined by the economy-wide wage trend. Industry prices and productivity modify the national wage trend in specific industries.

Employment functions by industry are similar to that in the macro-model:

---

[1] The FRG-INDUSTRY-model III will also be used for forecasting and simulation purposes in a quarterly to semi-annual rhythm at PROGNOS Ltd; the available budget does not allow over-expensive forecasting rounds.

output, relative factor prices[1] and disembodied technical progress are the explanatory factors. Because it is employment which has been estimated and not manhours,[2] the maximum employment–output lag is much longer (on the average: 4 quarters) than in the macro-model.

Further research is necessary to show whether the empirical results for the technical-progress parameters, as well as the relative factor-price terms, can be accepted or may have to be modified: in two industries the relative factor-price term has not been statistically significant and the lag distribution of this variable is comparatively short in other industries.

These perhaps not wholly convincing results are the logical result of the 'estimation philosophy' applied to constructing this model as well as the macro-model.

Economic theory is readily accepted as a source of hypotheses about the economic behaviour that need to be modelled – especially so far as the set of explanatory factors and the sign of their influence is concerned. But economic theory is usually of relatively little value in providing *a priori* insights into the maximum lengths and the shapes of lag distributions. The decision on the choice of the appropriate lag structure is therefore made on statistical grounds. This has been dome by first estimating the lag distributions in all equations without any *a priori* restrictions.[3] This relatively free and pragmatic approach also implies that factors which should actually be included according to the theoretical model are left out when it has not been possible to get statistically significant coefficients.

During the estimation process it became more and more clear that most equations showed systematic deviations between observed and estimated values of the dependent variable after 1975: 1. This was always indicated by a relatively low Durbin Watson figure. The presumption that structural shifts in the coefficients have taken place proved to be right in a number of cases (especially in the import equations). The corresponding tests have been made by estimating coefficients of structural dummy variables which have been introduced into all equations for all right-hand variables. These structural dummy variables have the value of the corresponding right hand variable after 1975: 1, and zero otherwise. If these coefficients proved to be statistically significant they have been included in the final version of the equation.[4]

---

[1] Because price indices for investment by industry do not exist in the FRG the user-cost-of-capital variable (equipment investment, without inflationary expectations) of the macro-model had to be used.

[2] Data for manhours are only available for workers but not for all employees.

[3] It is natural that data limitations force the investigator to set an *a priori* limit to the maximum lag to be tested. It is not denied that this has been a problem when estimating this model because the author could only be supplied in due time with data for the period 1969:1 to 1977:4.

[4] Due to the limited time available these tests only could be undertaken for the single time span 1975:1 to 1977:4. The tests were not made in the case of the price equations.

A summary of the estimation results for the equations of the FRG-INDUSTRY model III are given in Tables 10.1 to 10.4.

The industry model covers six selected industries (iron and steel, chemicals, non-electrical machinery, road vehicles, electrical machinery and textiles).[1] Manufacturing as a whole has also been modelled.

The production of six further industries (building trade suppliers, non-ferrous metals, other metal products, plastics, food and beverages and construction industry) is also included in the model. Production of these industries is explained comparatively simply by a demand indicator for the output of these industries. The results are not presented here.

IV THE DEMAND FOR LABOUR AND ITS DETERMINANTS IN THE FRG IN TOTAL AND IN SELECTED INDUSTRIES 1970–74 AND 1976–78

In this section recent employment trends and their determinants will be discussed within the framework of the two econometric models described in the last two sections.

The time horizon of the analysis is short- to medium-term. The models used would not allow a long-term perspective. But neither is it our purpose to discuss purely cyclical, quarter to quarter, movements.

Because the first few quarters after the recession trough of 1975 had a predominantly cyclical character (see Figure 10.1), an attempt to identify the new medium-term trend of the late seventies cannot start before the first, or even the second, quarter of 1976. Thus we do not possess data for more than eight quarters after the 1974–75 recession (1976:1 – to 1977:4) which may provide evidence about the characteristics of the new trend.

The old trend of the early seventies with which we would wish to contrast the new trend of 1976:1 to 1977:4 is best measured from the peak quarter before the 1971 recession to the peak quarter before the 1974/75 recession in terms of the production of each industry. Despite all efforts to find adequate time segments for the calculation of the old and new trend rates[2] there still remains an element of arbitrariness which affects the results of our analysis. In Figure 10.1 and 10.2, as well as in Table 10.5, the old and new trend rates of output and employment in selected industries, in total manufacturing and in the whole national economy (only Table 10.5) are given.

While the 1976/77 trend of growth of output of total manufacturing (3.4 per cent) and of the whole German economy (3.5 per cent) still amounts to about two-thirds to three-quarters of the 1970/73 trend rate, the fall in the output trend rate has been most dramatic in the chemical industry (6.6 per cent 1971–73 to 0.8 per cent 1976–77). The output trend rates in iron and

---

[1] These six industries cover 67 per cent of manufacturing exports and 54 per cent of all manufacturing employment (1976).

[2] The trend rates in this paper are in all cases calculated as compound growth rates on an annual basis; the selected periods are shown in Figures 10.2 and Table 10.5.

steel, in non-electrical machinery and in textiles, all of which were already below average in the period 1970/73 decreased further. The decrease in the above average trend rate of electrical machinery has been only slight. This does not continue to hold true for the year 1977, when output growth from quarter to quarter in this industry was near zero. The great exception is the road vehicle industry, where the trend rate in output growth increased in the 1976/77 period compared with the 1970/73 period.

The decline of output trends is reflected in a similar fall of employment trends.[1] Whereas in the pre-recession period chemicals, road vehicles and electrical machinery still showed positive employment trend rates, nearly all the industries under consideration (and including total manufacturing and the national economy as a whole) have shown negative employment growth in the period 1976:1 to 1977:4. The single exception is the road vehicle industry. Before we discuss further what has caused the decline in the short- to medium-term employment trends it is necessary to indicate how this will be attempted.

All the equations covering the direct as well as the indirect determinants of employment that are of interest for the purposes of this analysis have been estimated in logarithms. This enables us to express the growth rate of the dependent variable as the weighted sum of the growth rates of the right-hand variables where the weights are given by the estimated long-run partial impact elasticities. The employment equations can then be written as follows:[2]

$$g_N = a_1 g_x + a_2 g_{W/UCC} + T$$

g_N	= output growth rate
$g_{W/UCC}$	= growth rate of relative factor prices
W	= wage rate
UCC	= user-cost-of-capital
a_1	= employment-output elasticity
a_2	= employment-wage elasticity (or more precise: elasticity of employment with respect to the wage-capital-cost-ratio)
$a_1 g_x$	= output effect on employment
$a_2 g_{W/UCC}$	= impact of changes of relative factor prices on employment
T	= impact of disembodied technical progress

[1] Employment trends are always measured for a time span which starts and ends four quarters later than the output trend and the other factors determining employment taken in account in our investigation. This was found to be necessary because our estimation results point at an average maximum lag of adjustment of employment to output of about four quarters.

[2] This way of writing the equation implies the neglect of the so-called joint effect.

TABLE 10.1 FRG-INDUSTRY MODEL III. ESTIMATES OF THE 'INCOME'- AND PRICE-ELASTICITIES OF THE ABSORPTION, THE EXPORTS AND IMPORTS OF SELECTED MANUFACTURED GOODS IN THE FEDERAL REPUBLIC OF GERMANY (Data Coverage: 1970:2–1977:4)

	'Income' – elasticities[a]						Price – elasticities[b]						$\bar{R}^2$	DW
	before 1975:1			after 1975:1			before 1975:1			after 1975:1				
	1 Quarter	4 Quarters	'Long Run'	1 Quarter	4 Quarters	'Long Run'	1 Quarter	4 Quarters	'Long Run'	1 Quarter	4 Quarters	'Long Run'		
Absorption														
Iron and steel	1.41	1.41	1.41	1.38 / 1.36 (after 1976:1)	1.38 / 1.36 (after 1976:1)	1.38 / 1.36	0.44	−1.15	−1.15	0.44	−1.15	−1.15	0.85	1.6
Chemicals	1.66	1.66	1.66	1.65	1.65	1.65	–	–	–	–	–	–	0.94	1.7
Non-electrical machinery	0.65	0.65	0.65	0.64	0.64	0.64	−1.0	−1.6	−1.6	−1.0	−1.6	−1.6	0.94	1.9
Road vehicles	1.38	1.38	1.38	1.38	1.38	1.38	–	–	–	–	–	–	0.79	1.4
Electrical machinery	1.97	1.97	1.97	1.97	1.97	1.97	−0.82	–	–	−0.82	–	–	0.84	1.3
Textiles	0.37	0.37	0.37	0.37	0.37	0.37	−0.29	–	–	−0.23	–	–	0.73	1.9
Manufactured goods	1.01	1.01	1.01	1.01	1.01	1.01	–	–	–	–	–	–	0.97	1.9
Exports														
Iron and steel	1.11	1.11	1.11	1.11	1.11	1.11	0.24	1.49	1.49	0.24	1.49	1.49	0.89	1.3
Chemicals	1.81	1.81	1.81	1.81	1.81	1.81	–	−0.62	−0.62	–	−1.29	−1.29	0.98	1.3
Non-electrical machinery	1.53	1.75	2.38	3.05	1.60 (after 1977:1)	1.60	−0.41	−1.20	−1.20	−0.41	−1.20	−1.20	0.97	2.2
Road vehicles	3.06	1.58	1.58	3.07	1.62	1.62	–	0.76	−0.76	–	−0.76	−0.76	0.93	2.2
Electrical machinery	1.76	2.37	2.37	1.76	2.37	2.37	−0.97	−2.00	2.00	0.97	−2.00	−2.00	0.91	2.3
Textiles	2.20	2.20	2.20	2.20	2.20	2.20	−0.78	−1.56	−1.56	−0.78	−1.56	−1.56	0.96	1.1
Manufactured goods	0.97	1.85	1.85	0.98	1.88	1.88	−0.22	−0.40	−0.40	−0.94	−1.69	−1.69	0.99	2.3

	1.17	2.08	2.08	1.18	2.1	2.1	-0.20	-0.46	-0.46	-1.02	-1.28	-1.28	0.99	1.5
Total German exports of goods	1.17	2.08	2.08	1.18	2.1	2.1	-0.20	-0.46	-0.46	-1.02	-1.28	-1.28	0.99	1.5
Imports														
Iron and steel	–	–	–	–	–	–	-1.35	-1.78	-1.78	0.63	-1.78	-1.78	0.71	1.2
Chemicals	1.28	1.28	1.28	1.33	1.33	1.33	-0.43	-0.43	-0.43	-3.95	-3.95	-3.95	0.97	1.8
Non-electrical machinery	0.63	0.63	0.63	0.63	0.63	0.63	–	–	–	–	-1.2	-1.2	0.88	1.4
Road vehicles	0.84	1.39	0.78	0.78	1.46	1.46	-2.16	-2.16	-2.16	-2.16	-2.16	-2.16	0.96	1.7
Electrical machinery	0.68	1.18	1.18	0.76	1.25	1.25	–	-1.52	-1.52	–	-2.85	-2.85	0.98	2.4
Textiles	2.57	2.57	2.57	2.68	2.68	2.68	–	-3.19	-3.19	–	-1.09	-1.09	0.92	1.7
Manufactured goods	1.44	1.44	1.44	1.47	1.47	1.47	-0.62	-0.62	-0.62	-0.62	-0.62	-0.62	0.87	1.8

	2.43	2.15	2.15	2.43	2.15	2.15	0.19	0.19	0.19	0.19	0.19	0.19	0.99	1.9
Total German imports of goods	2.43	2.15	2.15	2.43	2.15	2.15	0.19	0.19	0.19	0.19	0.19	0.19	0.99	1.9

[a] The following variables have been used as proxies for 'income':

Absorption: Indicator of domestic demand for the goods produced by the industry under consideration = weighted activity index of domestic sectors (industries and final demand sectors) consuming these goods.

Imports: Absorption of the goods under consideration

Exports: Weighted index of industrial production of the USA, the UK, France, Italy, and Japan: Weights: Shares of these countries in German exports.

[b] The following variables function as relative prices:

Absorption: Ratio of the price index of absorption of the goods under consideration to the price index of total absorption in the economy;

Imports: Ratio of import prices to absorption price index of the goods under consideration

Exports: Ratio of export prices of the German industry under consideration to export prices of foreign competitors.

For any details, also for tables 10.2, 10.3 and 10.4: see Keollreuter, C., BRD-INDUSTRIEMODELL III, Diskussionspaper Nr. 20 der Basler sozialökonomischen Institute.

TABLE 10.2 FRG-INDUSTRY MODEL III: ESTIMATES OF THE EMPLOYMENT-OUTPUT AND THE EMPLOYMENT WAGE ELASTICITIES FOR SELECTED MANUFACTURING INDUSTRIES IN THE FEDERAL REPUBLIC OF GERMANY (Data Coverage: 1971:1–1977:4)

| | Employment-Output elasticity | | | | | | Employment-Wage elasticity[a] | | | | | | Disembodied Technical Progress[b] | | | |
| | before 1975:1 | | | after 1975:1 | | | before 1975:1 | | | after 1975:1 | | | before 1975:1 | after 1975:1 | $\bar{R}^2$ | DW |
	1 Quarter	4 Quarters	'Long-Run'	1 Quarter	4 Quarters	'Long-Run'	1 Quarter	4 Quarters	'Long-Run'	1 Quarter	4 Quarters	'Long-Run'				
Employment																
Iron and steel	–	0.10	0.10	–	0.10	0.10	–	–0.25	–0.25	–	–0.25	–0.25	–	–0.15	0.67	1.2
Chemicals	–	0.16	0.20	–	0.16	0.20	–0.03	–0.14	–0.14	–0.03	–0.14	–0.14	–	0.11	0.93	1.9
Non-electrical machinery	0.14	0.58	0.68	0.14	0.58	0.68	–	–	–	–	–	–	1.46	1.52	0.99	1.3
Road vehicles	–	0.68	0.89	–	0.68	0.89	–	–0.04	–0.34	–	–0.04	–0.34	–	after 1974:i –0.11	0.94	1.0
Electrical machinery	0.32	0.62	0.62	0.32	0.62	0.62	–0.20	–0.20	–0.20	–0.20	–0.20	–0.20	2.67	2.67	0.99	2.0
Textiles	0.19	0.51	0.51	0.07	0.21	0.40	–	–	–	–	–0.04	–0.09	6.75	3.00	0.99	1.4
Manufacturing	0.24	0.55	0.64	0.24	0.55	0.64	–	–	–	–	–	–	3.58	3.58	0.99	0.9
As comparison (from the quarterly macro-model FRG IV)																
Employment (manhours)	0.75	0.75	0.75	0.75	0.75	0.75	–	–0.05	–0.20	–	–0.05	–0.20	3.1	3.0	0.99	1.6

[a] Elasticity of employment with respect to relative factor prices (Ratio of gross wage rate to user cost of capital).
[b] Trend rate in per cent p.a.

TABLE 10.3 FRG-INDUSTRY MODEL III: ESTIMATES OF THE REACTION ELASTICITIES IN THE EQUATIONS DETERMINING THE GROSS WAGE RATE FOR SELECTED INDUSTRIES IN THE FEDERAL REPUBLIC OF GERMANY. (Data Coverage: 1970:1–1977:4)

	Elasticity of the industry gross wage rate with respect to the national gross wage rate			Elasticity of the industry gross wage rate with respect to the labour productivity of the industry			Elasticity of the industry gross wage rate with respect to the producer price index of the industry			$\bar{R}^2$	DW
	1 Quarter	*4 Quarters*	*'Long-Run'*	*1 Quarter*	*4 Quarters*	*'Long-Run'*	*1 Quarter*	*4 Quarters*	*'Long-Run'*		
Gross wage rate (gross wage sum per employed)											
Iron and steel	–	0.70	0.70	–	0.23	0.23	0.20	0.18	0.18	0.99	2.2
Chemicals	–	0.75	0.75	0.13	0.13	0.13	–	0.25	0.25	0.99	2.0
Non-electrical machinery	–	0.83	0.83	0.32	0.74	0.74	0.48	–	–	0.99	2.0
Road vehicles	–	0.55	0.55	0.38	0.38	0.38	0.54	0.54	0.54	0.99	2.0
Electrical machinery	–	0.81	0.81	0.19	0.19	0.19	–	0.29	0.29	0.99	2.0
Textiles	–	0.86	0.86	–	–	–	0.13	0.13	0.13	0.99	1.8
Manufacturing	–	0.71	0.71	0.24	0.24	0.24	0.27	0.27	0.27	0.99	2.0

TABLE 10.4 FRG-INDUSTRY MODEL III: ESTIMATES OF REACTION ELASTICITIES IN THE PRICE EQUATIONS FOR SELECTED INDUSTRIES IN THE FEDERAL REPUBLIC OF GERMANY (Data Coverage: 1970:2–1977:4)

	Elasticity of industry prices with respect to the unit labour cost of the industry			Elasticity of industry prices with respect to the unit material cost of the industry			Elasticity of industry prices with respect to the degree of capacity utilisation of the industry			Elasticity of industry prices with respect to other factors[k]			$\bar{R}^2$	DW
	1 Quarter	4 Quarters	'Long-Run	1 Quarter	4 Quarters	'Long-Run'	1 Quarter	4 Quarters	'Long-Run	1 Quarter	4 Quarters	'Long-Run		
Producer prices														
Iron and steel	—	—	—	0.51	0.51	0.51	—	0.15	0.15	0.54	0.31	0.31[a]	0.98	1.7
Chemicals	0.11	0.11	0.15	0.50	0.68	0.68	0.08	—	—	—	0.05	0.05[b]	0.99	0.9
Non-electrical machinery	0.32	0.48	0.48	—	0.28	0.62							0.99	0.9
Road vehicles	0.17	0.42	0.42	—	0.24	0.55	0.06	0.12	0.12	0.67	0.67	0.67[c]	0.99	1.8
Electrical machinery	0.03	0.37	0.37	0.32	0.51	0.51	0.20	0.21	0.21				0.98	1.8
Textiles	0.26	0.33	0.33					0.15	0.15				0.99	0.6
Manufacturing	0.16	0.43	0.43	0.68	0.68	0.68	0.30	0.30	0.30				0.99	1.6
Export prices														
Iron and steel	—	—	—	0.73	—	—	0.71	0.71	0.71	1.02	1.12	1.12[d]	0.99	2.0
Chemicals	—	—	—	0.71	1.06	1.06	0.32	0.32	0.32	0.01	−0.03	—[e]	0.99	0.99
Non-electrical machinery	0.12	0.47	0.47	—	0.27	0.72	—	0.26	0.26				0.99	1.2
Road vehicles	0.16	0.16	0.16	0.12	0.47	1.00	0.06	0.06	0.06				0.99	1.6
Electrical machinery	0.40	0.45	0.45	—	0.44	0.67	0.30	0.30	0.30				0.99	1.8
Textiles	0.12	0.12	0.12	0.26	0.26	0.26				0.35	0.35	0.35[f]	0.99	1.5
Manufacturing	—	0.26	0.26	0.91	0.91	0.91	0.08	0.20	0.20	0.06	0.06	0.06[g]	0.99	1.2

CONTINUATION TABLE 10.4 FRG-INDUSTRY MODEL III: ESTIMATES OF REACTION ELASTICITIES IN THE PRICE EQUATIONS FOR SELECTED INDUSTRIES IN THE FEDERAL REPUBLIC OF GERMANY (Data Coverage: 1970:2–1977:4)

	Elasticity of import prices with respect to the raw material price index (HWWA) on DM-Basis			Elasticity of import prices with respect to the export prices of foreign suppliers on DM-Basis			Elasticity of import prices with respect to the prices of domestic competitors (producer prices)			Time trend rate in % p.a.	$\bar{R}^2$	DW
	1 Quarter	4 Quarters	'Long-Run'	1 Quarter	4 Quarters	'Long-Run'	1 Quarter	4 Quarters	'Long-Run'			
Import prices												
Iron and steel	0.19	0.42	0.42	0.23	0.65	0.65					0.98	1.9
Chemicals	0.54	0.54	0.54	0.14	0.47	0.47					0.98	1.3
Non-electrical machinery	-0.7	-0.14	-0.14[h]	0.34	0.79	0.79				-3.5	0.99	1.2
Road vehicles				0.05	0.41	0.44	0.28	0.34	0.34		0.99	1.5
Electrical machinery	–			0.01			–	0.20	0.37		0.98	1.5
Textiles	0.19	0.19	0.19	0.62	0.62	0.62[i]	0.02	0.31	0.31[j]	+2.8	0.98	0.5
Manufactured goods	0.28	0.28	0.28								0.99	0.6

[a] Prices of imports of steel products.
[b] Raw material prices on DM-basis.
[c] Prices of imports of textile products and raw material prices on DM-basis.
[d] Prices of imports of steel products.
[e] Export prices of foreign competitors.
[f] Producer prices of the textile industry.
[g] Export prices of foreign competitors.
[h] Oil price effect.
[i] Weighted index of prices of imported goods under consideration in this model.
[j] Degree of capacity utilisation in the textile industry.
[k] Import prices, raw material prices, export prices of foreign suppliers (competitors) etc.

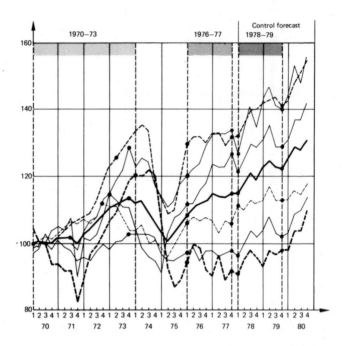

Fig. 10.1 Recent and prospective trends in manufacturing and selected
manufacturing industries in the FRG. Indices of industrial production
1970 = 100

(S) = Iron and steel
(C) = Chemicals
(N) = Non-electrical machinery
(V) = Road vehicles
(E) = Electrical machinery
(T) = Textiles
(M) = Manufacturing

E	7.2	C	0.8	C	3.5
C	6.6	E	6.2	E	5.4
M	5.0	V	6.0	V	3.4
S	2.6	M	3.4	M	3.6
V	4.5	T	0.0	T	0.4
T	3.1	N	0.5	N	3.2
N	0.8	S	−1.3	S	4.4

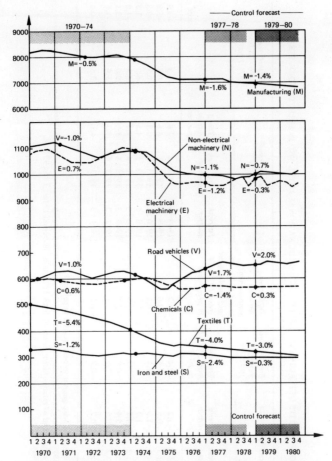

Fig. 10.2 Recent and prospective trends in the demand for labour in manufacturing and selected manufacturing industries in the FRG. Employment in 1000 persons

The output effect can be split up into the absorption, import and export effects by making use of the definition equation for production:

$$X = ABS + EX - IM$$

X	= output
ABS	= absorption
EX	= exports
IM	= imports

TABLE 10.5 THE DEMAND FOR LABOUR AND ITS DETERMINANTS IN THE FRG ON THE NATIONAL LEVEL AND IN SELECTED INDUSTRIES 1970–74 AND 1976–78

	Employment trend[a] 1970–74			Employment trend[a] 1977–78	Difference between employment trend 1977–78 and employment trend 1970–74 in percentage points	Output trend[a] 1970–74			Output[a] trend 1976–77 from 1976:1 to 1974:4	
	1st peak quarter	2nd peak quarter	Trend rate in per cent	Trend rate from 1977:1 to 1978:4[b]		1st peak quarter	2nd peak quarter	Trend rate in per cent		xxx
Iron and steel	1970 : 1	1974 : 2	−1.2	−2.4	−1.2	1969 : 4	1974 : 1	2.6	−1.3	−3.9
Chemicals	1971 : 2	1973 : 3	0.6	−1.4	−2.0	1969 : 4	1973 : 1	6.6	0.8	−5.8
Non-electrical machinery	1971 : 2	1974 : 4	−1.0	−1.1	−0.1	1970 : 2	1973 : 4	0.8	0.5	−0.3
Road vehicles	1970 : 2	1974 : 2	1.0	1.7	0.7	1970 : 1	1973 : 1	4.5	6.0	1.5
Electrical machinery	1971 : 2	1974 : 2	0.7	−1.2	−1.9	1970 : 3	1973 : 4	7.2	6.2	−1.0
Textiles	1970 : 1	1974 : 1	−5.4	−4.0	1.4	1969 : 3	1972 : 4	3.1	0.0	−3.1
Manufacturing	1972 : 2	1974 : 2	−0.5	−1.6	−1.1	1971 : 3	1973 : 4	5.0	3.4	−1.6
National economy	1972 : 2	1974 : 3	−0.7	−0.9	−0.2	1971 : 3	1973 : 4	4.1	3.5	−0.6

[a] Annualised seasonally adjusted trend rates from indicated peak quarter to peak quarter in per cent.
[b] Employment figures for the period 1978 : 1 to 1978 : 4 have been forecast on the basis of the corresponding employment equations (see Ditzler, Koellreuter and Kugler (1978, pp. 29–33)), assuming the same trend of output and of relative factor prices through 1978 as in the period 1976 : 1 to 1977 : 4.
xxx = Difference 76/77 to 70/74 in percentage points.

TABLE 10.5 (continued) CONTRIBUTIONS OF THE DETERMINANTS FOR THE DEMAND OF LABOUR TO THE EMPLOYMENT TRENDS IN THE PERIODS 1970–74 AND 1976–78. IN PERCENTAGE POINTS OF THE EMPLOYMENT TREND[c]

Upper panel

	Output effect 70–74	Output effect 76–77	Output effect xxx	Impact of disembodied technical progress 70–74	Impact of disembodied technical progress 76–77	Impact of disembodied technical progress xxx	Impact of changes of relative factor prices 70–74	Impact of changes of relative factor prices 75–77	Impact of changes of relative factor prices xxx	Output effect: Absorption effect 70–74	Output effect: Absorption effect 76–77	Output effect: Absorption effect xxx	Output effect: Import effect 70–74	Output effect: Import effect 76–77	Output effect: Import effect xxx
Iron and steel	0.3	-0.1	-0.4	—	0.1	0.1	-1.5	-2.4	-0.9	0.1	-0.2	-0.3	0.1	0.0	-0.1
Chemicals	1.3	0.2	-1.1	—	-0.1	-0.1	-0.7	-1.5	-0.8	1.0	0.1	-0.9	-0.4	-0.4	0.0
Non-electrical machinery	0.5	0.4	-0.1	-1.5	-1.5	0.0	—	—	—	-1.0	0.7	1.7	0.0	-0.7	-0.7
Road vehicles	4.0	5.4	1.4	—	0.1	0.1	-3.0	-3.8	-0.8	3.2	4.5	1.3	-2.4	-2.1	0.3
Electrical machinery	4.3	3.7	-0.6	-2.7	-2.7	0.0	-0.9	-2.2	-1.3	3.9	4.0	0.1	-1.1	-1.2	-0.1
Textiles	1.5	0.0	-1.5	-6.8	-3.0	3.8	-0.1	-1.0	-0.9	2.8	0.3	-2.5	-1.9	-0.7	1.2
Manufacturing	3.0	2.0	-1.0	-3.5	-3.6	-0.1	—	—	—	2.2	1.8	-0.4	-0.1	-0.6	-0.5
National economy	3.1	2.6	-0.5	-3.1	-3.0	0.1	-0.7	-1.0	-0.3	2.3	2.6	0.3	-0.8	-1.1	-0.3

Lower panel

	Output effect: Effect of production for domestic market 70–74	76–77	xxx	Output effect: Export effect 70–74	76–77	xxx	Import effect: Absorption effect 70–74	76–77	xxx	Import effect: Price effect 70–74	76–77	xxx	Export effect: Absorption effect 70–74	76–77	xxx	Export effect: Price effect 70–74	76–77	xxx
Iron and steel	0.2	-0.2	-0.4	0.1	0.1	0.0	—	—	—	—	—	—	0.1	0.1	0.0	0.0	0.0	0.0
Chemicals	0.6	-0.3	-0.9	0.7	0.5	-0.2	-0.3	0.0	0.3	-0.1	-0.4	-0.3	0.7	0.5	-0.2	0.0	0.0	0.0
Non-electrical machinery	-1.0	0.0	1.0	1.5	0.4	-1.1	0.0	-0.2	-0.2	0.0	-0.5	-0.5	2.9	2.0	-0.9	-1.4	-1.6	-0.2
Road vehicles	0.8	2.4	1.6	3.2	3.0	-0.2	-1.6	-1.4	0.2	-0.8	-0.7	0.1	3.2	3.5	+0.3	0.0	-0.5	-0.5
Electrical machinery	2.8	2.8	0.0	1.5	0.9	-0.6	-0.8	-0.9	-0.1	-0.3	-0.3	0.0	2.0	1.1	-0.9	-0.5	-0.2	0.3
Textiles	0.9	-0.4	-1.3	0.6	0.4	-0.2	-1.6	-0.7	0.9	-0.3	0.0	0.3	0.8	0.6	-0.2	-0.2	-0.2	0.0
Manufacturing	2.1	1.2	-0.9	0.9	0.8	-0.1	-0.2	-0.4	-0.2	0.1	-0.2	-0.3	1.0	1.1	0.1	-0.1	-0.3	-0.2
National economy	1.5	1.5	0.0	1.6	1.1	-0.5	-0.8	-1.1	-0.3	—	—	—	2.5	1.6	-0.9	-0.9	-0.5	0.4

xxx = Difference 76–77 to 70–74 in percentage points

[c] The effect of a determining factor on the employment trend corresponds to the product of the annualised seasonally adjusted trend rate of the determining factor (for the same time span as for the output trend) times the estimated partial elasticity of this factor (and the pre-recession share exports, imports and absorption to gross production in the case of the export, import and absorption effect): for an exact explanation see the text.

TABLE 10.5a CONTRIBUTIONS OF CHANGES IN THE ABSORPTION, IMPORT AND EXPORT EFFECT TO THE CHANGE IN THE OUTPUT EFFECT ON EMPLOYMENT FROM 1970–73 PERIOD TO THE 1967–77 PERIOD

Contributions of changes in determining factors in per cent of the changes of the output effect

	Changes in output effect in percentage points	Absorption effect	Import effect		Export effect		Sum of the contributions
			Absorption effect	Price effect	Absorption effect	Price effect	
Iron and steel	−0.4	75	\{ 25		–	–	100
Chemicals	−1.1	82	−27	27	18	–	100
Non-electrical machinery	−0.1	−1700	200	500	900	200	100
Road vehicles	1.4	93	14	7	21	−35	100
Electrical machinery	−0.6	−17	17	–	150	−50	100
Textiles	−1.5	−67	−60	−20	13	–	100
Manufacturing	−1.0	40	20	30	−10	20	100
National economy	−0.5	−60	60	–	180	−80	100

The subeffects on employment are then defined as follows:

$$a_1 \frac{ABS}{X} g_{ABS} = \text{absorption effect}$$

$$g_{ABS} = \text{growth rate of absorption}$$

$$a_1 \frac{IM}{X} g_{IM} = \text{import effect}$$

$$g_{IM} = \text{import growth rate}$$

$$a_1 \frac{EX}{X} g_{EX} = \text{export effect}$$

$$g_{EX} = \text{export growth rate}$$

$$a_1 \left(\frac{ABS}{X} g_{ABS} - \frac{IM}{X} g_{IM} \right) = \text{effect of production for domestic market}$$

The import and export effects on employment are further subdivided into an absorption and a price effect:

$$b_1 a_1 \frac{IM}{X} g_{ABS} = \text{import absorption effect}$$

$$b_2 a_1 \frac{IM}{X} g_{PIM} = \text{import price effect}$$

$$b_3 a_1 \frac{EX}{X} g_{FD} = \text{effect of foreign demand}$$

$$b_4 a_1 \frac{EX}{X} g_{PEX} = \text{export price effect}$$

$$b_1 = \text{absorption-elasticity of imports}$$

$$b_2 = \text{price-elasticity of imports}$$

$$b_3 = \text{elasticity of exports with respect to foreign demand}$$

$$b_4 = \text{price-elasticity of exports}$$

$$g_{ABS} = \text{growth rate of absorption}$$

$$g_{PIM} = \text{growth rate of relative import prices}$$

$$g_{FD} = \text{growth rate of foreign demand}$$

$$g_{PEX} = \text{growth rate of relative export prices}$$

It is not only the lower output growth rate which has caused the lower employment trend. In the light of our neo-classical employment equations it is also the acceleration in the operation of the wage-capital-cost ratio which contributed to this process. As can be seen in Table 10.5 the decline in the employment trends between the two periods under consideration would not have taken place at all in the case of the whole economy, or only to the extent of 20 per cent (textiles), 25 per cent (iron and steel), 30 per cent (electrical machinery) and 60 per cent (chemicals) in the case of these specific industries. It has to be emphasised that this view is based on strictly partial equilibrium evidence. The same holds true when we state that in most of the industries under consideration employment would not have shrunk in the post recession period if the wage-capital-cost-ratio had not increased any further in the period 1976/77 (e.g. in iron and steel where the impact of the change in relative factor prices on employment amounts to −2.4 percentage points, which is equal to the negative employment trend rate during the same period).

It needs to be said that at least one-third of the increased impact on employment of changes of relative factor prices cannot be explained by nominal wage increases but is due to the fall in the user-cost-of-capital (mainly caused by a reduction in the long-term interest rate). A sizeable change in the impact of disembodied technical progress between the two periods under consideration occurred only in textiles where the technical progress parameter fell nearly to 50 per cent of its pre-recession value.

The long-term employment-output elasticity is of major importance in regard to the impact of changing output trends on changes of employment trends. With an employment output elasticity of 0.1 it is in the steel industry that employment is likely to be hurt least by declining output trends. Iron and steel is followed by chemicals, with an elasticity of 0.2, whereas textiles, electrical and non-electrical machinery form the medium range of elasticity values of 0.5 to 0.7. In the road vehicle industry employment is most sensitive to output variations (an employment-output elasticity of 0.9). The importance of the employment-output elasticity has to be kept in mind when we now start to discuss how the absorption, import and export trends determine the output-effect on employment in the way described above.

It is not necessary to analyse the pre-recession trend rates or the pre-recession output-effect on employment. The investigation will be limited to a discussion of what factors contributed to the *change* in the output-effect in the period 1967/77 as compared with the time period 1970/73.

On the one hand this type of analysis has the advantage of giving emphasis to *changes* in trends — the real question of interest in this context. On the other hand it may have the disadvantage of giving a negative effect in cases of a positive but decreasing trend rate and a positive effect in cases of a decreasing negative trend rate. This is troublesome, especially in all those cases where the different factors contributing to the net change in the output effect on employment have opposing signs and are relatively large compared with the net change in the output-effect. Despite these shortcomings it is hoped that Table 10.5a gives some clues to what factors are mainly responsible for the change in the output-effect on employment as between the two periods 1970–73 and 1976–77.

As far as the whole German economy is concerned, it is the decreased trend rate in foreign demand for German goods (from 2.5 to 1.6 percentage points of the employment trend) which contributed 180 per cent to the increase in the negative employment trend rate, from –0.7 per cent (1972–73) to –0.9 per cent (1977–78). The negative change in the import effect takes the second place, while the change in the absorption effect and in the export price effect have been working in the opposite direction, mitigating the negative impact of the first two factors. One of the reasons[1] for the difference in the contributions of the various different factors to the change in the output-effect on employment in respect of the economy as a whole and in respect of the manufacturing sector – to be discussed below – must have been the very different development of the service sector of the German economy – characterised by a rising trend rate with respect to its domestic market and a declining trend rate with respect to foreign markets.

For manufacturing it is not primarily the changes in the export-effect but in the domestic absorption-effect which caused as much as 40 per cent of the decrease in the output-effect on employment of one percentage point. A further 50 per cent of the change of the output-effect comes from imports. Thus almost the whole negative change in the output-effect stems from a decreased contribution of the production for the domestic market.

The situation in specific industries is again different from manufacturing as a whole. The negative impact of the change in the domestic absorption is of greater importance in iron and steel and chemicals. These two basic industries have been badly hurt by the low growth rate of the German economy. This effect is so overwhelming that the import and export effects play a less marked role on the decrease of the output-effect on employment in these industries.

Textiles fall to a certain extent into the same category. But it is interesting to note that the period 1976–77 in comparison with the period 1970–74 has been characterised by a decline of the negative import-effect on employment in the textile industry.

The negative movement of the output-effect on employment in electrical and non-electrical machinery stems primarily from deteriorating export trends. A positive change in the domestic-absorption-effect has mitigated this negative contribution to the change in the output effect in each of these industries. This phenomenon reflects the improved 1976–77 investment trends compared with the early seventies. The only industry for which a positive change in the output-effect on employment can be found is the road vehicle industry. It is primarily the change in the domestic-absorption-effect which is sustaining the positive change in the output-effect on employment.

[1] In addition to any reasons relating to the way in which our analysis has been conducted.

Our findings do not lead to any unique explanation of the decline in the output-effect on employment. The negative changes in the output effect on employment during the past-recession period from 1976:1 to 1977:4 as compared with the pre-recession period in the early seventies have to be explained by domestic as well foreign developments. Changes in absorption-effects at home and abroad seem to play a major role, but the importance of the change in relative import- and export-prices on the change in the output-effect on employment when comparing the two periods cannot be denied.

V DEMAND FOR LABOUR IN THE FRG 1978–80: ESTIMATED CHANGES IN TOTAL AND IN SELECTED INDUSTRIES

Whereas in the last section certain equations from the econometric models FRG IV and FRG-INDUSTRY III have been used to provide partial impact elasticities in order to get some idea as to the quantitative contributions of the different determinants of the demand for labour to the changes in the employment trends, in this section the macro and the combined industry model will be used for forecasting purposes.

We shall try to present a view of the probable development of the demand for labour in the FRG the period 1978–80. We must stress that we mean by 'probable development' not simply the development that seems most likely in the eyes of the author. On the contrary, the control forecast which will be presented in this section must be regarded as a fairly optimistic view of the period 1978–80, taking into account the information available in August 1978. The main purpose of this forecast lies in securing a benchmark solution for the models concerned which is not completely unrealistic for purpose of the simulations that will follow in section VI, where we shall study the consequences of making variations of certain assumptions underlying the control forecast for the demand for labour. The role which has to be played by the control forecast justifies a few remarks about the set of values for the exogenous variables for which the models have been solved for purposes of the forecasting period of 1978:1 to 1980:4.

After the minor 1977 recession in France, Italy and the UK (so far as industrial production is concerned) it is assumed that the recent recovery in industrial production in these countries continues during the next few quarters. On the other hand it is assumed that the quarter-to-quarter growth rates of industrial production in the US will continue to fall from mid-1978 to the second half of 1979. The effects of this development on the quarter-to-quarter growth in the large European countries will be felt at latest in the first half of 1979. 1980 being an election year in the US as well as in the FRG will have its positive effect on quarter-to-quarter growth not only in these countries but also in France, Italy, the UK and Japan.

The implications of this international scenario for the period 1978–80 for the year-to-year growth rates of industrial production can be found in Table 10.6; graphic illustration is given in Figure 10.3. The control forecast assumptions regarding export prices and US dollar exchange rates of Germany's major trading partners as they affect our models are also presented in Table 10.6. They reflect very much a status quo view of the development. The exchange rate assumptions are based on the purchasing power parity approach and allow for some overshooting in both directions.

The modest expansionary measures decided by the German government last year are taken into account to a slightly optimistic extent. The German promises made at the recent Bonn summit are not included in the calculations. German monetary policy is assumed to be more restrictive on a quarter-to-quarter basis. It is thought that the exchange-rate-induced monetary expansion in the first quarter 1978 will be offset and that a slight adaptation of the monetary targets to the lower inflation rate will occur in the future.

The results for the main endogenous variables of the models FRG IV and the linked model FRG-INDUSTRY III[1] are also given in Table 10.6. A further revaluation of the DM and a decrease in the German inflation rate, with GNP growth rates ranging from 2.5 per cent to 3.7 per cent p.a. and with slightly improving employment prospects[2] are the main results.

In the second part of this section we shall discuss the demand for labour and its determinants, as projected within our control forecast. The somewhat optimistic assumption with respect to the exogeneous variables, in combination with the way our models behave, indicate an improvement of the employment trends during the period 1979–80 compared with the 1977–78 period. This is the case for the whole economy and for total manufacturing, as well as for all the industries under consideration; this can be seen in Table 10.7. Positive changes in the output-effect and a positive impact of changes of relative factor prices contribute to these results in nearly all industries.

A more modest increase in contractual hourly wages (around 5 per cent p.a. for 1978–80) and an end to the fall of the user-cost-of-capital (mainly caused by a relatively stable long-term interest rate which in turn is the result of the adaptation of monetary policy to slower real growth and a lower inflation rate) leads to a reduction in the positive trend rate of the wage-capital-cost ratio. Of the improvement in employment trends (1979–80 in comparison to 1978–79), 40 per cent (for the whole economy) and more than 100 per cent (for road vehicles, electrical machinery), can be explained by the positive impact of changes in the relative factor prices. That the change in the output-effect on employment is negative for the whole economy (1978–79 in comparison to 1976–77) but positive for total manufacturing can be explained by the slow growth of real government expenditures through

---

[1] The solution has been elaborated by making use of a limited number of added factors.

[2] The macroeconomic employment outlook would become negative if the technical progress parameter had not been reduced by one percentage point in accordance with our estimate of the further development of the potential output in Germany.

1979 compared with the period 1976–77 and the better export prospects (which are much more important for manufacturing than for the economy as a whole) during period of the forecast.

As can be seen in Table 10.7a, it is again the change in the domestic

TABLE 10.6 THE DEMAND FOR LABOUR IN THE FRG: 1978–80. A PROBABLE DEVELOPMENT ON THE NATIONAL LEVEL AND IN SELECTED INDUSTRIES

Control forecast elaborated with the quarterly models FRG IV and FRG-INDUSTRY III for the period 1978:1–1980:4. Percentage changes from previous year

		Forecast		
	1977	1978	1979	1980
Exogenous variables				
Industrial production				
United States	5.6	4.8	3.8	5.5
United Kingdom	1.2	3.2	3.7	3.0
France	1.6	3.3	4.6	3.7
Italy	0.9	1.9	3.7	3.0
Japan	3.9	4.9	5.2	6.0
Export prices				
United States	4.4	6.1	5.0	5.5
United Kingdom	18.2	10.1	10.8	10.1
France	10.0	8.7	9.8	11.0
Italy	20.4	11.9	13.0	14.0
Japan	3.6	1.1	0.0	0.0
US dollar exchange rates per unit of national currency				
United Kingdom	−3.4	5.0	−3.9	−4.0
France	−2.9	1.9	−9.6	−6.0
Italy	−5.9	−1.7	−10.3	−10.0
Japan	10.7	18.0	4.3	4.0
Combined index of industrial production of the United States, United Kingdom, France, Italy and Japan (Weights: shares of these countries in German exports)	2.4	3.4	4.1	4.0
Combined index of export prices of the United States, United Kingdom, France, Italy, and Japan on US dollar basis (Weights: shares of these countries in German exports)	8.9	10.4	2.1	4.4
HWWA index of raw material prices on US dollar basis	10.2	0.8	3.2	6.2
USA: Money supply (M1)	7.4	5.3	6.4	6.5
Wholesale prices	6.4	6.8	6.8	6.8
FRG: Resident population	−0.2	−0.3	−0.3	−0.3
Resident population of German nationality, 15–64 age group	0.5	0.6	0.6	0.5
Employees of foreign nationality	−2.9	−3.9	−3.9	−1.7
Money supply (M1)	8.7	9.9	5.8	6.1
Government consumption at current prices	5.0	7.6	6.1	7.6
Public investment at current prices	1.1	11.9	4.5	7.9
Net transfers (Government/social security to households) at current prices	8.3	7.3	5.0	5.5
Wages: Contractual hourly rates	6.9	5.3	4.9	5.1
Stockbuilding (actual rate, 1970 prices, billion DM)	6.9	4.0	1.7	4.7

TABLE 10.6 (*continued*)

		Forecast			
		1977	*1978*	*1979*	*1980*
Selected endogenous variables (adjusted for unequal numbers of working days in the year)					
Gross national product (1970 prices)		2.8	2.6	2.5	3.7
Private consumption (1970 prices)		3.1	3.0	4.1	2.9
Gross fixed capital formation (1970 prices)		3.2	3.0	2.9	2.6
Exports (1970 prices)		4.7	4.5	5.4	7.4
Imports (1970 prices)		5.5	4.8	7.2	5.8
Dependent employment		0.1	−0.2	0.2	0.4
Prices: GNP		3.7	3.9	2.5	2.6
Private consumption		3.9	2.3	1.9	1.7
Equipment investment		3.2	1.1	0.2	0.7
Long-term interest rate (yield of government bonds) per cent per annum (annual average of end of quarter figures)		6.1	5.4	5.5	5.5
US dollar exchange rate					
US cents per DM (annual average of monthly averages)		43.2	48.0	50.3	52.9
percentage change from previous year		8.7	11.2	4.7	5.2
Manufacturing	production	3.3	3.3	4.1	3.9
	employment	0.3	−2.1	−0.1	−1.4
Iron and steel	production	−4.7	3.6	1.3	7.8
	employment	−2.9	−1.6	−0.3	−0.3
Chemicals	production	0.4	3.7	4.3	4.8
	employment	1.5	−1.5	0.6	0.2
Non-electrical machinery	production	0.1	3.4	3.6	4.7
	employment	−0.7	−0.8	1.9	−0.1
Road vehicles	production	8.4	1.5	3.9	4.2
	employment	6.1	−0.0	0.8	0.4
Electrical machinery	production	7.5	0.9	5.9	5.5
	employment	−0.6	1.3	−0.1	−0.8
Textiles	production	−1.5	5.3	2.1	1.6
	employment	−3.0	−3.5	−1.6	−2.8

absorption effect which is important for the now positive change in the output-effect on employment in iron and steel and chemicals. The change in the output-effect on employment is negative for road vehicles and electrical machinery. In road vehicles it is mainly the change in the foreign demand effect; and in electrical machinery the change in the domestic absorption effect that is responsible for this development. Non-electrical machinery receives positive contributions to its positive change in the output-effect from all subeffects. The recent acceleration in the revaluation of the DM is felt: the change in relative export prices has a negative influence on the change in the output-effect in chemicals, road vehicles, electrical machinery, textiles and manufacturing as a whole.

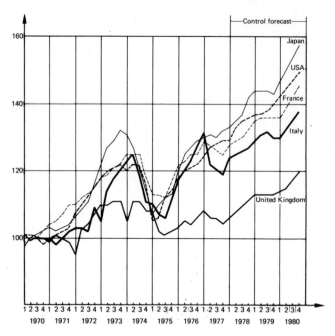

Fig. 10.3 Industrial production of the USA, the UK, France, Italy and Japan
1970 = 100

VI THE DEMAND FOR LABOUR IN THE FRG 1978–80 UNDER ALTERNATIVE ASSUMPTIONS

As already mentioned in the introduction, it will be the main purpose of this last section of my paper to investigate the effects of specific policies through which various groups believe that they could improve the employment situation. This analysis will be made by the means of simulations with our econometric models.

The simulation results for the following scenarios will be presented:

(1) *Scenario 'Wage Restraint'*

The models have been solved for the same set of assumptions as they have been made for the control forecast with the exception of a lower increase of contractual hourly wage rates (3.5 per cent p.a. instead of 5.0 per cent p.a.).

TABLE 10.7 THE DEMAND FOR LABOUR AND ITS DETERMINANTS IN THE FRG ON THE NATIONAL LEVEL AND IN SELECTED INDUSTRIES 1978–80
(Control Forecast) AND 1976–78 AS COMPARISON

| | Employment trend[a] | | | Output trend[a] | | | Contributions of the determinants of the demand of labour to the employment trends in the periods 1976–78 and 1978–80 in percentage of the employment trends[d] | | | | | | | | |
| | | | | | | | Output effect | | | Impact of disembodied technical progress | | | Impact of changes of relative factor prices | | |
	1977:1 to 1978:4[b]	1979:1 to 1980:4[c]	x	1976:1 to 1977:4	1978:1 to 1979:4	xxx	76–77	78–79	xxx	76–77	78–79	xxx	76–77	78–79	xxx
Iron and steel	-2.4	-0.3	2.1	-1.3	4.4	5.7	-0.1	0.4	0.5	0.1	0.1	—	-2.4	-0.9	1.5
Chemicals	-1.4	0.3	1.7	0.8	3.5	2.7	0.2	0.7	0.5	-0.1	-0.1	—	-1.5	-0.3	1.2
Non-electrical machinery	-1.1	0.7	1.8	0.5	3.2	2.7	0.4	2.2	1.8	-1.5	-1.5	—	—	—	—
Road vehicles	1.7	2.0	0.3	6.0	3.4	-2.6	5.4	3.1	-2.3	0.1	0.1	—	-3.8	-1.2	2.6
Electrical machinery	-1.2	-0.3	0.9	6.2	5.4	-0.8	3.7	3.2	-0.5	-2.7	-2.7	—	-2.2	-0.8	1.4
Textiles	-4.0	-3.0	1.0	0.0	0.4	0.4	0.0	0.2	0.2	-3.0	-3.0	—	-1.0	-0.2	0.8
Manufacturing	-1.6	-1.4	0.2	3.4	3.6	0.2	2.0	2.2	0.2	-3.6	-3.6	—	—	—	—
National economy	-0.9	-0.4	0.5	3.5	2.4	-1.1	2.6	1.8	-0.8	-3.0	-2.0	1.0	-1.0	-0.8	0.2

a Annualised seasonally adjusted trend rates from indicated first quarter to final quarter in per cent.

b The employment forecast for the period 1978:1–1978:4 has been calculated on the basis of the corresponding employment equation assuming the same trend of output and relative factor prices through 1978 as in the period 1976–77.

c The employment forecast for the period 1980:1–1980:4 is not the model forecast but has been calculated according to the corresponding employment equation assuming the same trend of output and relative factor prices through 1980 as in the period 1978–79.

d The effect of a determining factor on the employment trend corresponds to the product of the annualised seasonally adjusted trend rate of the determining factor (for the same time span as for the output trend) times the estimated partial elasticity of this factor (and the pre-recession share exports, imports, and absorption to gross production in the case of the export, import, and absorption effect); for an exact explanation see section IV.

x Difference 79–80 to 77–78 in percentage points
x

xxx Difference 78–79 to 76–77 in percentage points

TABLE 10.7 (continued) CONTRIBUTIONS OF THE DETERMINANTS OF THE DEMAND FOR LABOUR TO THE EMPLOYMENT TRENDS IN THE PERIODS 1976–78 AND 1978–80 IN PERCENTAGE POINTS OF THE EMPLOYMENT TRENDS^d

	Absorption effect			Import effect			Effect of production for domestic market			Export effect		
	76–77	78–79	xxx	76–78	78–79	xxx	76–77	78–79	xxx	76–77	78–79	xxx
Iron and steel	-0.2	0.2	0.4	0.0	-0.1	-0.1	-0.2	0.1	0.3	0.1	0.3	0.2
Chemicals	0.1	0.9	0.8	-0.4	-0.4	0.0	-0.3	0.5	0.8	0.5	0.2	-0.3
Non-electrical machinery	0.7	1.0	0.3	-0.7	-0.2	0.5	0.0	0.8	0.8	0.4	1.4	1.0
Road vehicles	4.5	3.4	-1.1	-2.1	-0.9	1.2	2.4	2.5	0.1	3.0	0.6	-2.4
Electrical machinery	4.0	3.0	-1.0	-1.2	-0.8	0.4	2.8	2.2	-0.6	0.9	1.0	0.1
Textiles	0.3	0.1	-0.2	-0.7	-0.2	0.5	-0.4	-0.1	0.3	0.4	0.3	-0.1
Manufacturing	1.8	2.2	0.4	-0.6	-0.9	-0.3	1.2	1.3	0.1	0.8	0.9	0.1
National economy	2.6	2.0	-0.6	-1.1	-1.3	-0.2	1.5	0.7	-0.8	1.1	1.1	0.0

	Import effect						Export effect					
	Absorption effect			Price effect			Absorption effect			Price effect		
	76–77	78–79	xxx	76–77	78–79	xxx	76–77	78–79	xxx	76–77	78–79	xxx
Iron and steel	—	—	—	—	—	—	0.1	0.2	0.1	0.0	0.1	0.1
Chemicals	0.0	-0.3	-0.3	-0.4	-0.1	0.3	0.5	0.3	-0.2	0.0	-0.1	-0.1
Non-electrical machinery	-0.2	-0.1	0.1	-0.5	-0.1	0.4	2.0	2.6	0.6	-1.6	-1.2	0.4
Road vehicles	-1.4	-0.8	0.6	-0.7	-0.1	0.6	3.5	1.4	-2.1	-0.5	-0.8	-0.3
Electrical machinery	-0.9	-0.6	0.3	-0.3	-0.2	0.1	1.1	1.4	0.3	-0.2	-0.4	-0.2
Textiles	-0.7	-0.2	0.5	0.0	0.0	0.0	0.6	0.6	0.0	-0.2	-0.3	-0.1
Manufacturing	-0.4	-0.8	-0.4	-0.2	-0.1	0.1	1.1	1.3	0.2	-0.3	-0.4	-0.1
National economy	—	—	—	—	—	—	1.6	1.4	-0.2	-0.5	-0.3	0.2

TABLE 10.7a CONTRIBUTIONS OF CHANGES IN THE ABSORPTION, IMPORT AND EXPORT EFFECT TO THE CHANGE IN THE OUTPUT EFFECT ON EMPLOYMENT FROM THE 1976–77 PERIOD TO THE 1978–79 PERIOD (Control Forecast)

	Changes in output effect in percentage points	Contributions of changes in determining factors in per cent of the changes of the output effect					
		Absorption effect	Import effect		Export effect		Sum of the contribution
			Absorption effect	Price effect	Absorption effect	Price effect	
Iron and steel	0.5	80	–20 (brace)		20	20	100
Chemicals	0.5	160	–180	180	–40	–20	100
Non-electrical machinery	1.8	17	6	22	33	22	100
Road vehicles	–2.3	48	–26	–26	91	13	100
Electrical machinery	–0.5	200	–60	–20	–60	40	100
Textiles	0.2	–100	250	50	50	–50	100
Manufacturing	0.2	200	–200	50	100	50	100
National economy	–0.8	75	25 (brace)		25 (brace)		100

(2) *Scenario 'Tighter Money'*
This scenario is characterised by a lower growth rate of the money supply (M1); 1977—78: 6.0 per cent (control: 9.9 per cent); 1978—79: 5.2 per cent (control 5.8 per cent); 1979—80: 4.7 per cent (control: 6.1 per cent)

(3) *Scenario 'German Reflation'*
The consequences of a stylised German reflation package as promised at the Bonn summit are investigated. For the sake of simplicity only a simulation for higher growth rates of nominal government consumption than assumed in the control forecast is undertaken: 1977—78: 10.1 per cent (control: 7.6 per cent), 1978—79: 8.3 per cent (control: 6.1 per cent), 1980—79: 7.3 per cent (control: 7.6 per cent).

These more policy-oriented scenarios are finally supplemented by scenarios with other deviations from the control forecast:

(4) *Scenario 'Higher Raw Material Prices'*
A further model run assumes higher increases of raw material prices from the first quarter 1979 onwards than in the control forecast. The probable effect of this development on economic trends in other industrial countries as a factor leading to reduction in production and higher inflation rates is also taken into account.

(5) *Scenario 'Industry Specific Wage Hike'*
The last scenario actually consists of seven different model runs, in which gross wages per employee in a single industry have been assumed to increase by a rate which is two percentage points higher per annum than in the control forecast.

The GNP developments resulting from the assumption of the different scenarios are presented in Figure 10.4.

(1) Scenario 'Wage Restraint'

One of the most actively discussed topics in the FRG, touching theoretical as well as economic policy issues, has been the policy recommendation put forward by the German Economic Council[1] that a policy of wage restraint would lead to more growth and employment. The results of our model run as represented in Table 10.8 point to a more or less neutral result when judged by yearly GNP growth rates.

The effect of a policy of wage restraint on real private consumption is positive, as can be explained by the following factors: the fact that the

---

[1] See 'Sachverständigenrat zur Begutachtung der gesamtwirtschaftlichen Entwicklung', *Jahresgutachten 1977/78*, p. ii and especially p. 138.

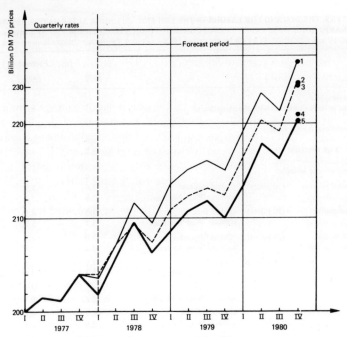

Fig. 10.4 Quarterly model FRG IV: Forecast of real gross national product
of the FRG 1978:1–1978 under alternative assumptions

Scenarios: 1 'German Reflation'
2 'Control Forecast'
3 'Wage Restraint'
4 'High Raw Material Prices'
5 'Tighter Money'

government/social security system takes about 60 per cent out of any increase
in the gross wage sum also works the other way round in the case of a
decrease in this aggregate (scenario 'Wage Restraint' compared to the control
solution): the wage component of disposable income will not be hurt to the
same extent as the gross wage sum.

The lower increases of wages lead to lower unit labour cost, and via the
price equations to a lower inflation rate. The real purchasing power of the
public net transfers to private households, fixed in nominal terms, will
increase. Together with the increase in other real non-wage income, and with
an increased average propensity to consume (consumers react positively to a
lower inflation rate according to our consumption function), the effect of a
policy of wage restraint on real private consumption will be positive.

It has to be mentioned that the way the German tax and social security

TABLE 10.8 THE DEMAND FOR LABOUR IN THE FRG 1978–80 UNDER ALTERNATIVE ASSUMPTIONS
SCENARIO *'WAGE RESTRAINT'* VERSUS CONTROL FORECAST. (Elaborated with the quarterly models
FRG IV and FRG-INDUSTRY III for the period 1978:1–1980:4. Percentage changes from previous year)

			Forecast		
			1978	1979	1980
Exogenous variables are the same in both scenarios with the exception of					
Wages: contractual hourly rates					
Control forecast			5.3	4.9	5.1
Scenario 'Wage Restraint'			3.7	3.4	3.6
Selected endogenous variables					
Gross national product	(70 prices)	control forecase	2.6	2.5	3.7
		scenario 'Wage Restraint'	2.8	2.5	3.5
Private consumption	(70 prices)	control forecast	3.0	4.1	2.9
		scenario 'Wage Restraint'	3.2	5.0	3.3
Gross fixed capital Formation	(70 prices)	control forecast	3.0	2.9	2.6
		scenario 'Wage Restraint'	3.3	2.6	2.5
Exports	(70 prices)	control forecast	4.5	5.4	7.4
		scenario 'Wage Restraint'	4.3	4.8	6.2
Imports	(70 prices)	control forecast	4.8	7.2	5.8
		scenario 'Wage Restraint'	5.2	8.7	6.6
Dependent employment		control forecast	−0.2	0.2	0.4
		scenario 'Wage Restraint'	0.0	0.4	−0.1
Prices: GNP		control forecast	3.9	2.5	2.6
		scenario 'Wage Restraint'	3.3	1.6	1.4
Private consumption		control forecast	2.3	1.9	1.7
		scenario 'Wage Restraint'	1.9	1.1	0.5
Equipment investment		control forecast	1.1	0.2	0.7
		scenario 'Wage Restraint'	0.9	−1.1	0.4
Long-term interest rate (yield of government bonds) per cent per annum (annual average of end of quarter figures)		control forecast	5.4	5.5	5.5
		scenario 'Wage Restraint'	5.3	5.2	4.8
US dollar exchange rate US cents per DM (annual average of monthly averages)		control forecast	48.0	50.3	52.9
		scenario 'Wage Restraint'	48.4	51.6	55.6
percentage change from previous year		control forecast	11.2	4.7	5.2
		scenario 'Wage Restraint'	12.1	6.5	7.8

system operates, and that net transfers to households are fixed in nominal
terms, is crucial to this result. The same holds true for the assumption that
government consumption and public investment are fixed not in real but in
nominal terms. In this case the government sector will give a real stimulus to
the economy thanks to a lower inflation rate. If these assumptions were

altered the model could easily generate a negative impact on real private consumption from a policy of wage restraint.

The impact of a policy of wage restraint is negative on business fixed investment. After one year, that is also the case for fixed investment as a whole. This is mainly due to the negative effect of lowered inflationary expectations on investment.

Exports are affected negatively by the additonal revaluation of the DM to offset the decrease in the inflation rate. Relative factor prices increase because the user-cost-of-capital adapts rapidly to the lower inflation rate (this is true for the long-term interest rate as well as the price index of equipment investment): the decrease in the growth of the user-cost-of-capital exceeds the decrease in the wage rate. Employment therefore is affected negatively by a policy of wage restraint in our neo-classical context![1]

Whereas the scenario 'Wage Restraint', under the given assumption, generates an overall outcome with respect to economy-wide growth which corresponds almost completely to the control forecast, it has definite structural effects: the shares of real private and public consumption in GNP increase whereas the investment and export shares decrease. This structural aspect of a policy of wage restraint is important for the impact on output and employment in the manufacturing sector of the economy, because quite a few manufacturing industries depend more on exports and investment than do other sectors of the economy. The change in the output-effect on employment of a policy of wage restraint is negative when compared to the control forecast in the cases of non-electrical and electrical machinery and road vehicles, as can be seen in Table 10.9. The change in the output-effect is zero for the more consumption-oriented industries, such as chemicals, textiles and for manu-facturing as a whole.

Because the additional effect of changes in relative factor prices is negative in all industries – wherever it has been identified – the employment trends deteriorate in all industries (except in manufacturing as a whole where employment trends are not affected). The deterioration in the output-effects on employment is in nearly all cases due to the adverse development in relative export and import prices, which in turn is the result of the additional exchange rate revaluation exceeding the reduction of the increase of internal prices. The change of the effect of domestic absorption on the output-effect-on-employment is positive in all industries, with the exception of non-electrical machinery and iron and steel which are affected by the negative investment trends.

The combination of a flexible exchange rate, tending to overshoot internal price movements at least temporarily, with a high and short-lagged price-elasticity of export demand and with investment also determinated by

[1] The last scenario 'Industry Specific Wage Hike' will show that the usual result still holds on a micro level.

TABLE 10.9 THE DEMAND FOR LABOUR AND ITS DETERMINANTS 1978–80 IN THE FRG UNDER ALTERNATIVE ASSUMPTIONS SCENARIO 'WAGE RESTRAINT' VERSUS CONTROL FORECAST

	Employment trend[a,b] 1979:1–1980:4			Output trend[a] 1978:1–1979:4			Contributions of the determinants of the demand for labour to employment trends in percentage points of the employment trends[c] Output effect			Impact of disembodied technical progress			Impact of changes of relative factor prices		
	(1)	(2)	(3)	(1)	(2)	(3)	(1)	(2)	(3)	(1)	(2)	(3)	(1)	(2)	(3)
Iron and steel	-0.3	-0.9	-0.6	4.4	4.3	-0.1	0.4	0.4	0.0	0.1	0.1	0.0	-0.9	-1.4	-0.5
Chemicals	0.3	0.2	-0.1	3.5	3.5	0.0	0.7	0.7	0.0	-0.1	-0.1	0.0	-0.3	-0.4	-0.1
Non-electrical machinery	0.7	-0.2	-0.9	3.2	1.9	-1.3	2.2	1.3	-0.9	-1.5	-1.5	0.0	-1.2	-1.3	-0.1
Road vehicles	2.0	1.5	-0.5	3.4	3.0	-0.4	3.1.	2.7	-0.4	0.1	0.1	0.0	-0.8	-0.9	-0.1
Electrical machinery	-0.3	-0.5	-0.2	5.4	5.2	-0.2	3.2	3.1	-0.1	-2.7	-2.7	0.0	-0.2	-0.4	-0.2
Textiles	-3.0	-3.2	-0.2	0.4	0.4	0.0	0.2	0.2	0.0	-3.0	-3.0	0.0			
Manufacturing	-1.4	-1.4	0.0	3.6	3.6	0.0	2.2	2.2	0.0	-3.6	-3.6	0.0			
National economy	-0.4	-0.8	-0.4	2.4	2.4	0.0	1.8	1.8	0.0	-2.0	-2.0	0.0	-0.8	-1.2	-0.4

(1) Control forecast
(2) Scenario 'Wage Restraint'
(3) Difference between scenario 'Wage Restraint' and control forecast in percentage points

[a] Annualised seasonally adjusted trend rates from indicated first quarter to final quarter in per cent.
[b] The employment forecast for the period 1980:1–1980:4 is not the model forecast but has been calculated according to the corresponding employment equation assuming the same trend of output and relative factor prices through 1980 as in the period 1978–79.
[c] The effect of a determining factor on the employment trend corresponds to the product of the annualised seasonally adjusted trend rate of the determining factor (for the same time span as for the output trend) times the estimated partial elasticity of this factor (and the pre-recession share exports, imports, and absorption to gross production in the case of the export, import, and absorption effect); for an exact explanation see section IV.

CONTINUATION TABLE 10.9 CONTRIBUTIONS OF THE DETERMINANTS OF THE DEMAND FOR LABOUR TO THE EMPLOYMENT TRENDS IN PERCENTAGE POINTS OF THE EMPLOYMENT TRENDS[c]

	Absorption effect			Import effect			Effect of production for domestic market			Export effect		
	(1)	(2)	(3)	(1)	(2)	(3)	(1)	(2)	(3)	(1)	(2)	(3)
Iron and steel	0.2	0.1	−0.1	−0.1	−0.1	0.0	0.1	0.0	−0.1	0.3	0.4	0.1
Chemicals	0.9	1.0	0.1	−0.4	−0.5	−0.1	0.5	0.5	0.0	0.2	0.2	0.0
Non-electrical machinery	1.0	0.2	−0.8	−0.2	−0.1	0.1	0.8	0.1	−0.7	1.4	1.2	−0.2
Road vehicles	3.4	3.8	0.4	−0.9	−1.3	−0.4	2.5	2.5	0.0	0.6	0.2	−0.4
Electrical machinery	3.0	3.3	0.3	−0.8	−0.9	−0.1	2.2	2.4	0.2	1.0	0.7	−0.3
Textiles	0.1	0.2	0.1	−0.2	−0.3	−0.1	−0.1	−0.1	0.0	0.3	0.3	0.0
Manufacturing	2.1	2.4	0.3	−0.9	−1.0	−0.1	1.2	1.4	0.2	0.9	0.8	−0.1
National economy	2.0	2.3	0.3	−1.3	−1.6	−0.3	0.7	0.7	0.0	1.1	1.0	−0.1

	Import effect						Export effect					
	Absorption effect			Price effect			Absorption effect			Price effect		
	(1)	(2)	(3)	(1)	(2)	(3)	(1)	(2)	(3)	(1)	(2)	(3)
Iron and steel	–	–	–	–	–	–	0.2	0.2	0.0	0.1	0.2	0.1
Chemicals	−0.3	−0.3	0.0	−0.1	−0.2	−0.1	0.4	0.4	0.0	−0.1	−0.2	−0.1
Non-electrical machinery	−0.1	0.0	0.1	−0.1	−0.1	0.0	2.6	2.6	0.0	−1.2	−1.4	−0.2
Road vehicles	−0.8	−1.1	−0.3	−0.1	−0.2	−0.1	1.4	1.4	0.0	−0.8	−1.6	−0.8
Electrical machinery	−0.6	−0.6	0.0	−0.2	−0.3	−0.1	1.4	1.4	0.0	−0.4	−0.7	−0.3
Textiles	−0.2	−0.2	0.0	0.0	−0.1	−0.1	0.6	0.6	0.0	−0.3	−0.3	0.0
Manufacturing	−0.8	−0.8	0.0	−0.1	−0.2	−0.1	1.3	1.3	0.0	−0.4	−0.5	−0.1
National economy	–	–	–	–	–	–	1.4	1.4	0.0	−0.3	−0.4	−0.1

(1) Control forecast
(2) Scenario 'Wage Restraint'
(3) Difference between scenario 'Wage Restraint' and control forecast in percentage points.

inflationary expectations, leads to these unusual results that are not found
with a very open economy with a system of fixed exchange rates.

(2) Scenario 'Tighter Money'

In some quarters it is believed that the relatively tight monetary policy
(combined with a voluntary policy of wage restraint) in Switzerland, which
has led to the extremely low Swiss inflation rate, is the clue to the astonishing
best-recession export performance of the Swiss economy, and the basis of the
internationally above average growth rate of real GNP in Switzerland in 1977.

In a scenario 'Tighter Money' the models have been solved for lower growth
rates of the money supply M1 in order to evaluate whether a Swiss-style
monetary policy would generate the results certain people are hoping for.
The results are presented in Tables 10.10 and 10.11. The most astonishing
result consists in the positive impact of the restrictive monetary policy on
employment. In this scenario the user-cost-of-capital increases as compared
to the control forecast as a result of the tighter money supply. The wage-
capital-cost-ratio increases less markedly in the scenario 'Tighter Money' than
in the control forecast, and this has, as we know, a positive effect on
employment in our neo-classical context.

The increased user-cost-of-capital affects investment negatively. The
restrictive monetary policy leads to a higher revaluation rate of the DM, which
in turn hurts exports. These two effects are sufficient to reduce the growth
rate of output or the whole economy. The lower output and the higher
employment trend generate a lower increase of labour productivity and, for a
given wage trend, a higher increase in unit labour cost and therefore more
inflation. This has a negative impact on real private consumption (via a lower
increase in real disposable income and a lower average propensity to consume).
The effects on industrial output trends are clearcut: the deviation of the
output-effect-on-employment from the control forecast is always negative —
mainly as a result of a negative change in the absorption and export price
effects.

Despite the negative impact of the change in the output-effect, the
employment trends improve in all those industries where the relative-factor-
price term affects employment. This is mainly due to the already mentioned
increase in the user-cost-of-capital.

(3) Scenario 'German Reflation'

Familiar Keynesian policies of reflating demand through increases in government expenditures work very well in the context of the models FRG IV and
FRG-INDUSTRY-III, despite the heavy neo-classical overtones in some sectors
of the models, as can be seen from the results represented in Tables 10.12 and
10.13. The resulting higher inflation rate helps investment (by increasing
inflationary expectations which lower the user-cost-of-capital) and exports

TABLE 10.10 THE DEMAND FOR LABOUR IN THE FRG 1978–80 UNDER ALTERNATIVE ASSUMPTIONS SCENARIO *'TIGHTER MONEY'* VERSUS CONTROL FORECAST. (Elaborated with the quarterly models FRG IV and FRG-INDUSTRY III for the period 1978:1–1980:4. Percentage changes from previous year)

			Forecast		
			1978	1979	1980
Exogenous variables					
are the same in both scenarios with the exception of the					
Money supply (M1)					
Control forecast			9.9	5.8	6.1
Scenario 'Tighter Money'			6.0	5.2	4.7
Selected endogenous variables					
Gross national product	(70 prices)	control forecast	2.6	2.5	3.7
		scenario 'Tighter Money'	2.1	2.2	3.2
Private consumption	(70 prices)	control forecast	3.0	4.1	2.9
		scenario 'Tighter Money'	2.7	4.0	2.4
Gross fixed capital formation	(70 prices)	control forecast	3.0	2.9	2.6
		scenario 'Tighter Money'	2.0	1.7	1.6
Exports	(70 prices)	control forecast	4.5	5.4	7.4
		scenario 'Tighter Money'	3.2	4.8	6.3
Imports	(70 prices)	control forecast	4.8	7.2	5.8
		scenario 'Tighter Money'	4.0	6.7	4.7
Dependent employment		control forecast	−0.2	0.2	0.4
		scenario 'Tighter Money'	−0.6	0.8	0.6
Prices: GNP		control forecast	3.9	2.5	2.6
		scenario 'Tighter Money'	3.9	2.7	3.0
Private consumption		control forecast	2.9	1.9	1.7
		scenario 'Tighter Money'	2.9	2.1	2.0
Equipment investment		control forecast	1.1	0.2	0.7
		scenario 'Tighter Money'	0.8	−0.2	1.0
Long-term interest rate (yield of government bonds) per cent per annum (annual average of end of quarter figures).		control forecast	5.4	5.5	5.5
		scenario 'Tighter Money'	6.1	6.5	7.0
US dollar exchange rate					
US cents per DM (annual average of monthly averages)		control forecast	48.0	50.3	52.9
		scenario 'Tighter Money'	48.9	51.3	54.5
Percentage change from previous year		control forecast	11.2	4.7	5.2
		scenario 'Tighter Money'	13.2	4.9	6.3

(via a lower revaluation rate of the DM). These effects are additional to the traditional Keynesian effects of an increase in government expenditures on consumption and investment.[1]

Because the user-cost-of-capital (apart from inflationary expectations) increases more than the wage rates, the impact on employment of the change

[1] The multiplier implied in our model FRG IV amounts to 1.30 in 1978 and to 1.75 in 1979 and 1980 (measured in 1970 prices).

TABLE 10.11 THE DEMAND FOR LABOUR AND ITS DETERMINANTS 1978–80 IN THE FRG UNDER ALTERNATIVE ASSUMPTIONS SCENARIO 'TIGHTER MONEY' VERSUS CONTROL FORECAST

| | Employment trend[a,b] 1979:1–1980:4 | | | Output trend[a] 1978:1–1979:4 | | | Contributions of the determinants of the demand for labour to the employment trends in percentage points of the employment trends[c] | | | | | | | | |
| | | | | | | | Output effect | | | Impact of disembodied technical progress | | | Impact of changes in relative factor prices | | |
	(1)	(2)	(3)	(1)	(2)	(3)	(1)	(2)	(3)	(1)	(2)	(3)	(1)	(2)	(3)
Iron and steel	-0.3	0.2	0.5	4.4	4.1	-0.3	0.4	0.4	0.0	0.1	0.1	0.0	-0.9	-0.3	0.6
Chemicals	0.3	0.5	0.2	3.5	3.3	-0.2	0.7	0.7	0.0	-0.1	-0.1	0.0	-0.3	-0.1	0.2
Non-electrical machinery	0.7	0.4	-0.3	3.2	2.8	-0.4	2.2	1.9	-0.3	-1.5	-1.5	0.0	-1.2	-0.5	0.7
Road vehicles	2.0	2.3	0.3	3.4	3.0	-0.4	3.1	2.7	-0.4	0.1	0.1	0.0	-0.8	-0.5	0.3
Electrical machinery	-0.3	-0.2	0.1	5.4	5.0	-0.4	3.2	3.0	-0.2	-2.7	-2.7	0.0	-0.2	-0.1	0.1
Textiles	-3.0	-3.0	0.0	0.4	0.2	-0.2	0.2	0.1	-0.1	-3.0	-3.0	0.0			
Manufacturing	-1.4	-1.6	-0.2	3.6	3.4	-0.2	2.2	2.0	-0.2	-3.6	-3.6	0.0			
National economy	-0.4	-0.3	0.1	2.4	2.3	-0.1	1.8	1.7	-0.1	-2.0	-2.0	0.0	-0.8	-0.6	0.2

(1) Control forecast
(2) Scenario 'Tighter Money'
(3) Difference between scenario 'Tighter Money' and control forecast in percentage points

a Annualised seasonally adjusted trend rates from indicated first quarter to final quarter in per cent.
b The employment forecast for the period 1980:1–1980:4 is not the model forecast but has been calculated according to the corresponding employment equation assuming the same trend of output and relative factor prices through 1980 as in the period 1978–79.
c The effect of a determining factor on the employment trend corresponds to the product of the annualised seasonally adjusted trend rate of the determining factor (for the same time span as for the output trend) times the estimated partial elasticity of this factor (and the pre-recession share exports, imports, and absorption to gross production in the case of the export, import, and absorption effect); for an exact explanation see section IV.

CONTINUATION TABLE 10.11 CONTRIBUTION OF THE DETERMINANTS OF THE DEMAND FOR LABOUR TO THE EMPLOYMENT TRENDS IN PERCENTAGE POINTS OF THE EMPLOYMENT TRENDS[c]

	Absorption effect			Import effect			Effect of production for domestic market			Export effect		
	(1)	(2)	(3)	(1)	(2)	(3)	(1)	(2)	(3)	(1)	(2)	(3)
Iron and steel	0.2	0.1	-0.1	-0.1	-0.1	0.0	0.1	0.0	-0.1	0.3	0.4	0.1
Chemicals	0.9	0.8	-0.1	-0.4	-0.3	0.1	0.5	0.5	0.0	0.2	0.2	0.0
Non-electrical machinery	1.0	0.8	-0.2	-0.2	-0.1	0.1	0.8	0.7	-0.1	1.4	1.2	-0.2
Road vehicles	3.4	3.4	0.0	-0.9	-0.9	0.0	2.5	2.5	0.0	0.6	0.2	-0.4
Electrical machinery	3.0	2.6	-0.4	-0.8	-0.5	0.3	2.2	2.1	-0.1	1.0	0.9	-0.1
Textiles	0.1	-0.4	-0.5	-0.2	0.3	0.5	-0.1	-0.1	0.0	0.3	0.2	-0.1
Manufacturing	2.1	1.7	-0.4	-0.9	-0.5	0.4	1.2	1.2	0.0	0.9	0.7	-0.2
National economy	2.0	1.7	-0.4	-1.3	-1.0	0.3	0.7	0.7	0.0	1.1	1.0	-0.1

	Import effect						Export effect					
	Absorption effect			Price effect			Absorption effect			Price effect		
	(1)	(2)	(3)	(1)	(2)	(3)	(1)	(2)	(3)	(1)	(2)	(3)
Iron and steel	-	-	-	-0.1	-0.1	0.0	0.2	0.2	0.0	0.1	0.2	0.1
Chemicals	-0.3	-0.2	0.1	-0.1	-0.1	0.0	0.4	0.4	0.0	-0.1	-0.2	-0.1
Non-electrical machinery	-0.1	-0.0	0.1	-0.1	-0.1	0.0	2.6	2.6	0.0	-1.2	-1.4	-0.2
Road vehicles	-0.8	-0.8	0.0	-0.1	-0.1	0.0	1.4	1.4	0.0	-0.8	-1.6	-0.8
Electrical machinery	-0.6	-0.3	0.3	-0.2	-0.2	0.0	1.4	1.4	0.0	-0.4	-0.5	-0.1
Textiles	-0.2	0.3	0.5	0.0	0.0	0.0	0.6	0.6	0.0	-0.3	-0.4	-0.1
Manufacturing	-0.8	-0.5	0.3	-0.1	0.0	0.1	1.3	1.3	0.0	-0.4	-0.6	-0.2
National economy	-	-	-	-	-	-	1.4	1.4	0.0	-0.3	-0.4	-0.1

(1) Control forecast
(2) Scenario 'Tighter Money'
(3) Difference between scenario 'Tighter Money' and control forecast in percentage points

TABLE 10.12 THE DEMAND FOR LABOUR IN THE FRG 1978–80 UNDER ALTERNATIVE ASSUMPTIONS SCENARIO *'GERMAN REFLATION'* VERSUS CONTROL FORECAST. (Elaborated with the quarterly models FRG IV and FRG-INDUSTRY III for the period 1978:1–1980:4. Percentage changes from previous year.)

			Forecast		
			1978	*1979*	*1980*
Exogenous variables					
are the same in both scenarios with the exception of					
Government consumption at current prices					
Control forecast			7.6	6.1	7.6
Scenario 'German Reflation'			10.1	8.3	7.3
Selected endogenous variables					
Gross national product	(70 prices)	control forecast	2.6	2.5	3.7
		scenario 'German Reflation'	3.1	3.3	3.6
Private consumption	(70 prices)	control forecast	3.0	4.1	2.9
		scenario 'German Reflation'	3.2	5.0	3.1
Gross fixed capital	(70 prices)	control forecast	3.0	2.9	2.6
formation		scenario 'German Reflation'	3.7	3.1	1.4
Exports	(70 prices)	control forecast	4.5	5.4	7.4
		scenario 'German Reflation'	4.5	6.6	8.2
Imports	(70 prices)	control forecast	4.8	7.2	5.8
		scenario 'German Reflation'	5.3	8.9	6.1
Dependent employment		control forecast	−0.2	0.2	0.4
		scenario 'German Reflation'	0.0	1.6	1.1
Prices: GNP		control forecast	3.9	2.5	2.6
		scenario 'German Reflation'	4.0	2.9	2.9
Private consumption		control forecast	2.3	1.9	1.7
		scenario 'German Reflation'	2.4	2.2	2.1
Equipment investment		control forecast	1.1	0.2	0.7
		scenario 'German Reflation'	1.2	0.5	1.1
Long-term interest rate (yield		control forecast	5.4	5.5	5.5
of government bonds) per cent		scenario 'German Reflation'	5.5	6.0	6.2
per annum (annual average of					
end of quarter figures)					
US dollar exchange rate					
US cents per DM (annual		control forecast	48.0	50.3	52.9
average of monthly averages)		scenario 'German Reflation'	48.0	49.4	51.3
Percentage change from		control forecast	11.2	4.7	5.2
previous year		scenario 'German Reflation'	11.1	3.0	3.7

in relative factor prices is positive for the economy as a whole as well as for all industries where this factor is significant.

The change in the output-effect-on-employment is positive in all industries. The absorption as well as the export and the import price effect, contribute to this result.

TABLE 10.13 THE DEMAND FOR LABOUR AND ITS DETERMINANTS 1978–80 IN THE FRG UNDER ALTERNATIVE ASSUMPTIONS SCENARIO 'GERMAN REFLATION' VERSUS CONTROL FORECAST

	Employment trend[a,b] 1979:1–1980:4			Output trend[a] 1978:1–1980:4			Output effect			Impact of disembodied technical progress			Impact of changes in relative factor prices		
	(1)	(2)	(3)	(1)	(2)	(3)	(1)	(2)	(3)	(1)	(2)	(3)	(1)	(2)	(3)
Iron and steel	−0.3	0.3	0.6	4.4	6.6	2.2	0.4	0.7	0.3	0.1	0.1	0.0	−0.9	−0.6	0.3
Chemicals	0.3	0.9	0.6	3.5	5.3	1.8	0.7	1.1	0.4	−0.1	−0.1	0.0	−0.3	−0.1	0.2
Non-electrical machinery	0.7	1.7	1.0	3.2	4.6	1.4	2.2	3.2	1.0	−1.5	−1.5	0.0	−1.2	−0.6	0.6
Road vehicles	2.0	4.4	2.4	3.4	5.4	2.0	3.1	4.9	1.8	0.1	0.1	0.0	−0.8	−0.5	0.3
Electrical machinery	−0.3	0.9	1.2	5.4	6.8	1.4	3.2	4.1	0.9	−2.7	−2.7	0.0	−0.2	−0.1	0.1
Textiles	−3.0	−2.8	0.2	0.4	0.7	0.3	0.2	0.3	0.1	−3.0	−3.0	0.0			
Manufacturing	−1.4	−0.8	0.6	3.6	4.6	1.0	2.2	2.8	0.6	−3.6	−3.6	0.0			
National economy	−0.4	0.2	0.6	2.4	3.1	0.7	1.8	2.3	0.5	−2.0	−2.0	0.0	−0.8	−0.6	0.2

(1) Control forecast
(2) Scenario 'German Reflation'
(3) Difference between scenario 'German Reflation' and control forecast in percentage points.

[a] Annualised seasonally adjusted trend rates from indicated first quarter to final quarter in per cent.
[b] The employment forecast for the period 1980:1–1980:4 is not the model forecast but has been calculated according to the corresponding employment equation assuming the same trend of output and relative factor prices through 1980 as in the period 1978/79.
[c] The effect of a determining factor on the employment trend corresponds to the product of the annualised seasonally adjusted trend rate of the determining factor (for the same time span as for the output trend) times the estimated partial elasticity of this factor (and the pre-recession share exports, imports, and absorption to gross production in the case of the export, import, and absorption effect); for an exact explanation see section IV.

CONTINUATION TABLE 10.13 CONTRIBUTIONS OF THE DETERMINANTS OF THE DEMAND FOR LABOUR TO THE EMPLOYMENT TRENDS IN PERCENTAGE POINTS OF THE EMPLOYMENT TRENDS[c]

	Absorption effect			Import effect			Effect of production for domestic market			Export effect		
	(1)	(2)	(3)	(1)	(2)	(3)	(1)	(2)	(3)	(1)	(2)	(3)
Iron and steel	0.2	0.5	0.3	-0.1	-0.1	0.0	0.1	0.4	0.3	0.3	0.3	0.0
Chemicals	0.9	1.3	0.4	-0.4	-0.5	-0.1	0.5	0.8	0.3	0.2	0.3	0.1
Non-electrical machinery	1.0	1.8	0.8	-0.2	0.2	0.0	0.8	1.6	0.8	1.4	1.6	0.2
Road vehicles	3.4	5.4	2.0	-0.9	-1.5	-0.6	2.5	3.9	1.4	0.6	0.8	0.2
Electrical machinery	3.0	3.9	0.9	-0.8	-0.9	-0.1	2.2	3.0	0.8	1.0	1.1	0.1
Textiles	0.1	0.2	0.1	-0.2	-0.4	-0.2	-0.1	-0.2	-0.1	0.3	0.5	0.2
Manufacturing	2.1	2.7	0.6	-0.9	-1.1	-0.2	1.2	1.6	0.4	0.9	1.2	0.3
National economy	2.0	2.6	0.6	-1.3	-1.7	-0.4	0.7	0.9	0.2	1.1	1.4	0.3

	Import effect						Export effect					
	Absorption effect			Price effect			Absorption effect			Price effect		
	(1)	(2)	(3)	(1)	(2)	(3)	(1)	(2)	(3)	(1)	(2)	(3)
Iron and steel	-0.3	-	-	-	-	-	0.2	0.2	0.0	0.1	0.1	0.0
Chemicals	-0.1	-0.4	-0.1	-0.1	-0.1	0.0	0.4	0.4	0.0	-0.1	-0.1	0.0
Non-electrical machinery	-0.1	-0.2	-0.1	-0.1	0.0	0.1	2.6	2.6	0.0	-1.2	-1.0	-0.2
Road vehicles	-0.8	-1.5	-0.7	-0.1	0.0	0.1	1.4	1.4	0.0	-0.8	-0.6	0.2
Electrical machinery	-0.6	-0.8	-0.2	-0.2	-0.1	0.1	1.4	1.4	0.0	-0.4	-0.3	0.1
Textiles	-0.2	-0.4	-0.2	0.0	0.0	0.0	0.6	0.6	0.0	-0.3	-0.1	0.2
Manufacturing	-0.8	-1.1	-0.9	-0.1	0.0	0.1	1.3	1.3	0.0	-0.4	-0.1	0.3
National economy	-	-	-	-	-	-	1.4	1.4	0.0	-0.3	0.0	0.3

(1) Control forecast
(2) Scenario 'German Reflation'

(4) Scenario 'Higher Raw Material Prices'

In this scenario it is assumed that raw material prices (presumably led by an oil price hike) will increase at a higher rate from the first quarter 1979 onwards than in the control forecast. The negative impact of this possible event on production and inflation in the US, the UK, France, Italy and Japan is taken into account, as can be seen in Table 10.14. The precise numerical deviations of the scenario 'Higher Raw Material Prices' from the control forecast are given in the same table, as well as the results for the main endogenous variables.

It is the over-shooting exchange rate that is over-compensating the cost-push effect coming from higher raw material prices. Astonishingly, as a result the German inflation rate is lower in this scenario than in the control forecast. The effect of this on investment and exports is negative, as we have already learned from the discussion of other scenarios. The overall growth which emerges in this scenario is so much lower than in the control forecast that the positive effect of a lower inflation rate on consumption is exceeded by the negative effect of decreased real income.

Slower growth also induces a fall in the long-term interest rate (for a given growth path of money supply) and hence in the user-cost-of-capital (apart from inflationary expectations). As a consequence relative factor-prices (the assumptions with respect to the trend of contractual hourly wage rates are not changed) increase. This in turn leads to a negative effect of this factor on employment, as can be seen in Table 10.15, both for the whole economy and for all industries in which relative factor prices play a role.

The change in the output-effect-on-employment is negative in all cases. The change is mainly caused by a decrease in the absorption effect at home and abroad,[1] as well as by a negative change in the export price effect (the revaluation effect).

(5) Scenario 'Industry Specific Wage Hike'

In seven different model runs it has been investigated how an industry-specific wage-hike affects employment in that industry. In each model run it has been assumed that gross wages per employee in the industry under consideration increase by a rate which is two percentage points higher p.a. than in the control forecast. At the same time wage development in the macro model has been exogenised as well. It has then been assumed that wages will also increase

---

[1] It is assumed that real foreign demand does not decrease for iron and steel, chemicals and electrical machinery. In all three cases the assumption is made that the implied oil price hike will have positive effects which compensate the negative ones, as happened in 1974. In the case of electrical machinery it is thought that a further and greater increase of the oil price will positively affect the nuclear power business.

TABLE 10.14 THE DEMAND FOR LABOUR IN THE FRG 1978–80 UNDER ALTERNATIVE ASSUMPTIONS SCENARIO *'HIGHER RAW MATERIAL PRICES'* VERSUS CONTROL FORECAST. (Elaborated with the quarterly models FRG IV and FRG-INDUSTRY III for the period 1978:1–1980:4. Percentage changes from previous year)

		Forecast		
		1978	*1979*	*1980*
Exogenous variables				
are the same in both scenarios with the exception of the				
combined index of industrial production[a] of the US, the UK, France, Italy and Japan	control forecast	3.4	4.1	4.0
	scenario 'Higher Raw Material Prices'	3.4	3.1	4.0
combined index of export[a] prices of the US, the UK, France, Italy, and Japan on US dollar basis	control forecast	10.4	2.1	4.4
	scenario 'Higher Raw Material Prices'	10.4	4.2	4.4
HWWA index of raw material prices on US dollar basis	control forecast	0.8	3.2	6.2
	scenario 'Higher Raw Material Prices'	0.8	9.4	6.2
Selected endogenous variables				
Gross national product (70 prices)	control forecast	2.6	2.5	3.7
	scenario 'Higher Raw Material Prices'	2.6	1.4	3.1
Private consumptions (70 prices)	control forecast	3.0	4.1	2.9
	scenario 'Higher Raw Material Prices'	3.0	3.6	2.1
Gross fixed capital formation (70 prices)	control forecast	3.0	2.9	2.6
	scenario 'Higher Raw Material Prices'	3.0	1.9	3.0
Exports (70 prices)	control forecast	4.5	5.4	7.4
	scenario 'Higher Raw Material Prices'	4.5	2.4	5.1
Imports (70 prices)	control forecast	4.8	7.2	5.8
	scenario 'Higher Raw Material Prices'	4.8	6.3	3.9
Dependent employment	control forecast	−0.2	0.2	0.4
	scenario 'Higher Raw Material Prices'	−0.2	−0.6	−1.0
Prices: GNP	control forecast	3.9	2.5	2.6
	scenario 'Higher Raw Material prices'	3.9	2.2	2.2
Private consumption	control forecast	2.3	1.9	1.7
	scenario 'Higher Raw Material Prices'	2.3	1.8	1.3
Equipment investment	control forecast	1.1	0.2	0.7
	scenario 'Higher Raw Material Prices'	1.1	0.1	0.3
Long-term interest rate (yield of government bonds) per cent per annum (annual average of end of quarter figures)	control forecast	5.4	5.5	5.5
	scenario 'Higher Raw Material Prices'	5.4	5.2	4.9
US dollar exchange rate				
US cents per DM (annual average of monthly averages)	control forecast	48.0	50.3	52.9
	scenario 'Higher Raw Material Prices'	48.0	51.9	55.9
Percentage change from previous year	control forecast	11.2	4.7	5.2
	scenario 'Higher Raw Material Prices'	11.2	8.1	7.7

[a] These indices remain at control forecast rates for iron and steel, chemicals and electrical machinery; see text for explanation.

TABLE 10.15 THE DEMAND FOR LABOUR AND ITS DETERMINANTS 1978–80 IN THE FRG UNDER ALTERNATIVE ASSUMPTIONS SCENARIO 'HIGHER RAW MATERIAL PRICES' VERSUS CONTROL FORECAST

	Employment trend[a,b] 1979:1–1980:4			Output trend[c] 1978:1–1980:4			Contributions of the determinants of the demand for labour to the employment trends[c]								
							Output effect			Impact of disembodied technical progress			Impact of changes of relative prices		
	(1)	(2)	(3)	(1)	(2)	(3)	(1)	(2)	(3)	(1)	(2)	(3)	(1)	(2)	(3)
Iron and steel	−0.3	−0.6	−0.3	4.4	3.4	−1.0	0.4	0.3	−0.1	0.1	0.1	0.0	−0.9	−1.1	−0.1
Chemicals	0.3	0.0	−0.3	3.5	2.7	−0.8	0.7	0.5	−0.2	−0.1	−0.1	0.0	−0.3	−0.4	−0.1
Non-electrical machinery	0.7	−0.9	−1.6	3.2	0.9	−2.3	2.2	0.6	−1.6	−1.5	−1.5	0.0	−1.2	−1.3	−0.1
Road vehicles	2.0	−0.6	−2.6	3.4	0.7	−2.7	3.1	0.6	−2.5	0.1	0.1	0.0	−0.8	−1.0	−0.2
Electrical machinery	−0.3	−1.1	−0.8	5.4	4.3	−1.1	3.2	2.6	−0.6	−2.7	−2.7	0.0	−0.2	−0.4	−0.2
Textiles	−3.0	−3.8	−0.8	0.4	−0.7	−1.1	0.2	−0.4	−0.6	−3.0	−3.0	0.0			
Manufacturing	−1.4	−2.3	−0.9	3.6	2.2	−1.4	2.2	1.3	−0.9	−3.6	−3.6	0.0			
National economy	−0.4	−1.5	−1.1	2.4	1.7	−0.7	1.8	1.3	−0.5	−2.0	−2.0	0.0	−0.8	−1.4	−0.6

(1) Control forecast
(2) Scenario 'Higher Raw Material Prices'
(3) Difference between scenario 'Higher Raw Material Prices' and control forecast in percentage points.

[a] Annualised seasonally adjusted trend rates from indicated first quarter in per cent.
[b] The employment forecast for the period 1980:1–1980:4 is not the model forecast but has been calculated according to the corresponding employment equation assuming the same trend of output and relative factor prices through 1980 as in the period 1978/79.
[c] The effect of a determining factor on the employment trend corresponds to the product of the annualised seasonally adjusted trend rate of the determining factor (for the same time span as for the output trend) times the estimated partial elasticity of this factor (and the pre-recession share exports, imports, and absorption to gross production in the case of the export, import, and absorption effect); for an exact explanation see section IV.

CONTINUATION TABLE 10.15   CONTRIBUTIONS OF THE DETERMINANTS OF THE DEMAND FOR LABOUR TO THE EMPLOYMENT TRENDS IN PERCENTAGE POINTS OF THE EMPLOYMENT TRENDSᶜ

	Absorption effect			Import effect			Effect of production for domestic market			Export effect		
	(1)	(2)	(3)	(1)	(2)	(3)	(1)	(2)	(3)	(1)	(2)	(3)
Iron and steel	0.2	0.0	-0.2	-0.1	-0.1	0.0	0.1	-0.1	-0.2	0.3	0.5	0.2
Chemicals	0.9	0.6	-0.3	-0.4	-0.3	0.1	0.5	0.3	-0.2	0.2	0.2	0.0
Non-electrical machinery	1.0	0.1	-0.9	-0.2	-0.1	0.1	0.8	0.0	-0.8	1.4	0.6	-0.8
Road vehicles	3.4	1.3	-2.1	-0.9	-0.4	0.5	2.5	0.9	-1.6	0.6	-0.3	-0.9
Electrical machinery	3.0	2.4	-0.6	-0.8	-0.5	0.3	2.2	1.9	-0.3	1.0	0.7	-0.3
Textiles	0.1	-0.2	-0.3	-0.2	-0.3	-0.1	-0.1	-0.5	-0.4	0.3	0.1	-0.2
Manufacturing	2.1	1.3	-0.8	-0.9	-0.6	0.3	1.2	0.7	-0.5	0.9	0.6	-0.3
National economy	2.0	1.7	-0.3	-1.3	-1.2	0.1	0.7	0.5	-0.2	1.1	0.8	-0.3

	Import effect						Export effect					
	Absorption effect			Price effect			Absorption effect			Price effect		
	(1)	(2)	(3)	(1)	(2)	(3)	(1)	(2)	(3)	(1)	(2)	(3)
Iron and steel	—	—	—	—	—	—	0.2	0.2	0.0	0.1	0.2	0.1
Chemicals	-0.3	-0.2	0.1	-0.1	-0.1	0.0	0.4	0.4	0.0	-0.1	-0.2	-0.1
Non-electrical machinery	-0.1	0.0	0.1	-0.1	-0.1	0.0	2.6	2.2	-0.4	-1.2	-1.6	-0.4
Road vehicles	-0.8	-0.1	0.7	-0.1	-0.3	-0.2	1.4	0.8	-0.6	-0.8	-1.1	-0.3
Electrical machinery	-0.6	-0.3	0.3	-0.2	-0.2	0.0	1.4	1.4	0.0	-0.4	-0.7	-0.3
Textiles	-0.2	-0.3	-0.1	0.0	0.0	0.0	0.6	0.5	-0.1	-0.3	-0.4	-0.1
Manufacturing	-0.8	-0.3	0.5	-0.1	0.0	0.1	1.3	1.1	-0.2	-0.4	-0.5	-0.1
National economy	—	—	—	—	—	—	1.4	1.2	-0.2	-0.3	-0.4	0.1

(1) Control forecast
(2) Scenario 'Higher Raw Material Prices'

TABLE 10.16 THE DEMAND FOR LABOUR AND ITS DETERMINANTS 1978–80 IN THE FRG UNDER ALTERNATIVE ASSUMPTIONS SCENARIO 'INDUSTRY SPECIFIC WAGE HIKE' VERSUS CONTROL FORECAST

| | Employment trend [a,b] 1979:1–1980:4 | | | Output trend [a] 1978:1–1980:4 | | | Contributions of the determinants of the demand of labour to the employment trends in percentage points of the employment trends [c] | | | | | | | | |
| | | | | | | | Output effect | | | Impact of disembodied technical progress | | | Impact of changes of relative factor prices | | |
	(1)	(2)	(3)	(1)	(2)	(3)	(1)	(2)	(3)	(1)	(2)	(3)	(1)	(2)	(3)
Iron and steel	-0.3	-0.9	-0.6	4.4	4.4	0.0	0.4	0.4	0.0	0.1	0.1	0.0	-0.9	-1.5	-0.6
Chemicals	0.3	-0.1	-0.4	3.5	3.4	-0.1	0.7	0.7	0.0	-0.1	-0.1	0.0	-0.3	-0.7	-0.4
Non-electrical machinery	0.7	-0.4	-1.1	3.2	1.5	-1.7	2.2	2.1	-1.1	-1.5	-1.5	0.0	-1.2	-1.9	-0.7
Road vehicles	2.0	0.7	-1.3	3.4	2.8	-0.6	3.1	2.5	-0.6	0.1	0.1	0.0	-0.8	-1.4	-0.6
Electrical machinery	-0.3	-1.2	-0.9	5.4	4.8	-0.6	3.2	2.9	-0.3	-2.7	-2.7	0.0	-0.2	-0.6	-0.4
Textiles	-3.0	-3.6	-0.6	0.4	0.0	-0.4	0.2	0.0	-0.2	-3.0	-3.0	0.0			
Manufacturing	-1.4	-1.6	-0.2	3.6	3.4	-0.2	2.2	2.0	-0.2	-2.0	-2.0	0.0			

(1) Control forecast
(2) Scenario 'Industry Specific Wage Hike'
(3) Difference between scenario 'Industry Specific Wage Hike' and control forecast in percentage points.

[a] Annualised seasonally adjusted trend rates from indicated first quarter to final quarter in percent.
[b] The employment forecast for the period 1980:1–1980:4 is not the model forecast but has been calculated according to the corresponding employment equation assuming the same trend of output and relative factor prices through 1980 as in the period 1978/79.
[c] The effect of a determining factor on the employment trend corresponds to the product of the annualised seasonally adjusted trend rate of the determining factor (for the same time span as for the output trend) times the estimated partial elasticity of this factor (and the pre-recession share exports, imports, and absorption to gross production in the case of the export, import, and absorption effect); for an exact explanation see section IV.

CONTINUATION TABLE 10.16 CONTRIBUTION OF THE DETERMINANTS OF THE DEMAND FOR LABOUR TO THE EMPLOYMENT TRENDS IN PERCENTAGE OF THE EMPLOYMENT TRENDS[c]

	Absorption effect			Import effect			Effect of production for domestic market			Export effect		
	(1)	(2)	(3)	(1)	(2)	(3)	(1)	(2)	(3)	(1)	(2)	(3)
Iron and steel	0.2	0.2	0.0	-0.1	-0.1	0.0	0.1	0.1	0.0	0.3	0.3	0.0
Chemicals	0.9	0.9	0.0	-0.4	-0.4	0.0	0.5	0.5	0.0	0.2	0.2	0.0
Non-electrical machinery	1.0	0.0	-1.0	-0.2	0.0	0.0	0.8	-0.2	-1.0	1.4	1.3	-0.1
Road vehicles	3.4	2.9	-0.5	-0.9	-0.9	0.0	2.5	2.0	-0.5	0.6	0.5	-0.1
Electrical machinery	3.0	3.0	0.0	-0.8	-0.8	0.0	2.2	2.2	0.0	1.0	1.7	-0.3
Textiles	0.1	0.0	-0.1	-0.2	-0.3	-0.1	-0.1	-0.3	-0.2	0.3	0.3	0.0
Manufacturing	2.1	2.1	0.0	-0.9	-0.9	0.0	1.2	1.2	0.0	0.9	0.8	-0.1

	Import effect						Export effect					
	Absorption effect			Price effect			Absorption effect			Price effect		
	(1)	(2)	(3)	(1)	(2)	(3)	(1)	(2)	(3)	(1)	(2)	(3)
Iron and steel	—	—	—	—	—	—	0.2	0.2	0.0	0.1	0.1	0.0
Chemicals	-0.3	-0.3	0.0	-0.1	-0.0	0.0	0.4	0.4	0.0	-0.1	-0.1	0.0
Non-electrical machinery	-0.1	0.0	0.1	-0.1	-0.2	-0.1	2.6	2.6	0.0	-1.2	-1.3	-0.1
Road vehicles	-0.8	-0.7	0.1	-0.1	-0.2	-0.1	1.4	1.4	0.0	-0.8	-0.9	-0.1
Electrical machinery	-0.6	-0.6	0.0	-0.2	-0.2	0.0	1.4	1.4	0.0	-0.4	-0.7	-0.3
Textiles	-0.2	-0.3	-0.1	0.0	0.0	0.0	0.6	0.6	0.0	-0.3	-0.3	0.0
Manufacturing	-0.8	-0.8	0.0	-0.1	-0.1	0.0	1.3	1.3	0.0	-0.4	-0.5	-0.1

(1) Control forecast
(2) Scenario 'Industry Specific Wage Hike'
(3) Difference between scenario 'Industry Specific Wage Hike' and control forecast in percentage points.

at a higher rate on the macro level. The increases in the growth rate of the national wage rate were calculated in accordance to the share of the gross total of wages of the industry under consideration in the gross total of national wages. This was made in order to allow for repercussions of industry-specific wage hikes which only could be calculated in the macro-model.

Such repercussions can only play a role in manufacturing as a whole, where the total of wages is large enough really to affect such macroeconomic aggregates as real disposable income and other decisive variables. As can be seen in Table 10.16, the impact of an industry-specific wage hike on the change of relative factor prices is clearly negative, and affects employment trends negatively in all industries where this effect has been identified. In iron and steel and chemicals it is only the substitution-effect which matters, because wage cost does not influence prices and therefore output in these industries (at least according to our equations). In all other industries the industry-specific wage hike leads to an increase of producer and export prices. This development exerts an additional negative influence on the absorption, export and import effect on employment. Because all three work intensively in the case of non-electrical machinery, the negative change in the output-effect-on-employment is largest in this industry. The negative wage-employment realtionship which we were forced to question on a macro level (see scenario 'Wage Restraint') still holds on the micro level, even in cases where the relative-factor-price term could not be identified in the employment equation (non-electrical machinery and manufacturing as a whole).

REFERENCES

Bernholz, P. and Kugler, P. (1978), 'An Empirical Model of the Short Run Fluctuations of Exchange Rates: The Case of the Deutschmark (DM) and the Swiss Franc (SFR), will be published in *Kredit und Kapital.*
Deutsches Institut für Wirtschaftsforschung (DIW) (1975), 'Input-Output-Rechnung für die Bundesrepublik Deutschland 1972', Heft 38, Berlin.
Davis, T. F. (1952), 'The Consumption Function as a Tool for Prediction', *Review of Economics and Statistics*, 34, 270–80.
Ditzler, C., Koellreuter, C. and Kugler, P. (1978), 'Quartalsmodell BRD IV – Oekonometrisches Modell für die Bundesrepublik Deutschland.' Discussion paper No. 20 of the two Economic Institutes of the University of Basle.
Den Hartog, H. and Tjan, H. S. (1976), 'Investment, Wages, Prices and Demand for Labour (a Clay-Clay Vintage Model for the Netherlands)', *Economist*, 124, pp. 32–82.
Driehus, W. (1972), *Fluctuations and Growth in a Near Full Employment Economy* (Rotterdam).
Driehus, W. (1977), 'Capital Labour Substitution, Technology and Employment', paper presented at OECD Experts' Meeting on Structural Determinants of Employment and Unemployment.
Duesenberry, J. S. (1943), *Income, Saving and the Theory of Consumer Behaviour* (Cambridge, Mass.).

Eckstein, O. and Fromm, G. (1967), 'The Price Equation', *American Economic Review*, 58, 1159–83.

Evans, M. K. (1969), *Macroeconomic Activity; Theory, Forecasting and Control; an Econometric Approach* (New York).

Franz, W. (1977), 'International Factor Mobility and the Labour Market: A Macroeconometric Analysis of the German Labour Market', *Empirical Economics*, 2, 11–30.

Hamermesh, D. S. (1976), 'Econometric Studies of Labour Demand and their Application to Policy Analysis', *The Journal of Human Resources*, 11, 507–25.

Jorgenson, D. W. (1963), 'Capital Theory and Investment Behaviour', *American Economic Review*, 52, 247–60.

Jorgenson, D. W. (1965), 'Anticipations and Investment Behaviour', in J. S. Duesenberry *et al.* (eds.), *The Brookings Quarterly Model of the United States* (Chicago and Amsterdam), pp. 35–94.

Koellreuter, C. and Kugler, P. (1976), 'Quartalsmodell BRD II', Discussion paper No. 11 of the two Economic Institutes of the University of Basle.

Koellreuter, C. (1978), 'BRD-Industriemodell III-oekonometrisches Branchen-konjunkturmodell fur die Bundesrepublik Deutschland auf Quartalsbasis', Discussion paper No. 20 of the two Economic Institutes of the University of Basle.

Koenig, H. (1976), 'Neoklassische Investitionstheorie und 'Investitionsverhalten in der BRD', *Jahrbucher für Nationalokonomie und Statistik*, 190, pp. 316–48.

Kuh, E. (1967), 'A Productivity Theory of the Wage Level; 'An Alternative to the Phillips Curve', *Review of Economic Studies*, 36, 333–61.

McCracken, P. *et al.* (1977), *Towards Full Employment and Price Stability* (Paris, OECD).

Phillips, A. W. (1958), 'The Relation between Unemployment and the Rate of Change of Money Wage Rates in the United Kingdom, 1861–1957', *Economica*, 283–99.

Preston, R. S. (1975), 'The Input-output Sector of the Wharton Annual and Industry Forecasting Model, in Fromm, G. and Klein, L. R. (eds.), *The Brookings Model: Perspective and Recent Developments* (Amsterdam, Oxford and New York), pp. 605–26.

Sachverständigenrat zur Begutachtung der gesamtwirtschaftlichen Entwicklung (German Economic Council) Jahresgutachten 1977–78.

Schluter, G. (1974), 'Combining Input-Output and Regression Analysis in Projection Models: An Application to Agriculture', *Agricultural Economics Research*, 26, 95–105.

LIST OF DISCUSSION PAPERS PREPARED HITHERTO

1. Gottfried Bombach, Nationale und europäische Probleme der Vermogens-poltik — Rückblick und Ausblick.
2. Peter Bernholz and Malte Faber, Interest Rate, Growth Rate, Rounda-boutness and Impatience — A Comment.
3. Peter Stolz, Marktmechanismus und behördliche Massnahmen in der Basler Getreide- und Brotversorgung des 18. Jahrhunderts.

4. Niklaus Blattner, Intraindustrieller Aussenhandel – Empirische Beobachtungen und theoretische Interpretationen.
5. Rene L. Frey, Das interregionale Wohlstandsgefälle als Problem des schweizerischen Föderalismus.
6. Niklaus Blattner, Die Arbeitsplatzsteuer – Ein Instrument zur Beeinflussung des Verhältnisses von Wohn- und Arbeitsplätzen im Kanton Basel-Stadt?
7. Niklaus Blattner, Die Hypothese von der Relevanz der organisatorischen Struktur in der Theorie der Firma.
8. Gottfried Bombach, Wettbewerbstheorie und Wettbewerbspolitik: Rückblick und Ausblick. Einleitung der Generaldiskussion beim wirtschaftswissenschaftlichen Seminar in Ottobeuren 1975.
9. Felix Wehrle, Einkommensverteilung in der Volksrepublik China.
10. Peter Stolz, Einige Indikatoren und Indizien zum Wachstum und zur Entwicklung der vorindustriellen Wirtschaft Basels.
11. Christoph Koellreuter und Peter Kugler, Quartalsmodell BRD II – Oekonometrisches Makromodell für die Bundesrepublik Deutschland.
12. Rene L. Frey, Das Recht auf Arbeit als gesamtwirtschaftliches Problem.
13. Peter Bernholz, On the Stability of Logrolling Outcomes in Stochastic Games.
14. A. Rutz and R. Zehnder, Eine Spektraltechnische Schätzung zum Kursverlauf der Schweizer Aktien.
15. H.-J. Buettler, J. F. Gorgerat, H. Schiltknecht und, K. Schiltknecht, Ein Multiplikatormodell zur Steuerung der Geldmenge.
16. C. Koellreuter und P. Kugler, Quarterly Model France I, A Short-Term Econometric Model of the French Economy.
17. P. Kugler, Some Remarks on a Modification of Tow Stage Least Squares (TSLS) for Undersized Samples.
18. Manfred Gaertner, A Political Economic Model of Wage Inflation.
19. Christoph Ditzler, Christoph Koellreuter und Peter Kugler, Quartalsmodell BRD IV- Oekonometrisches Modell für die Bundesrepublik Deutschland.
20. Christoph Koellreuter, BRD-Industriemodell III – ökonometrisches Branchenkonjunkturmodell für die Bundesrepublik Deutschland auf Quartalsbasis.
21. Christoph Koellreuter, Recent and Prospective Trends of the Demand for Labour in the FRG, An *ex-Post* Analysis and Some Simulation Results with a Macro and Linked Industry Model.

Discussion of Dr Koellreuter's Paper

Professor van de Klundert said this paper was based on simulation runs with two quarterly econometric models of Germany (FRG). A macro-model was linked with an industry model in order to present additional information for six selected industries. He thought Dr Keollreuter deserved much credit for the amount of preparation he had done and for the originality of his contribution to econometric model-building.

The main purpose of the paper was twofold. First, by running *ex-post* simulations before and after the 1974—5 recession, an impression was given of old and new trend rates (annual growth rates) of output and employment. Factors determining employment were used to impute differences in the growth rates of employment in the periods 1970—73 and 1976—77.

Second, by presenting policy and uncertainty scenarios, we learned what might happen if certain exogenous variables deviated from their values in the central projection, or in the control solution, for the period 1978—80.

Professor van de Klundert wanted to concentrate on macroeconomic results, given the time constraint. The macroeconomic model might be considered as more or less complete from a theoretical point of view. It contained demand equations, a description of the labour market, price relations, relations to determine the interest rate as well as the exchange rate of the Deutschmark against the US dollar and, last but not least, production potential as an endogenous variable. Although a discussion of the equations one by one might be interesting, he thought this was not the right place to do so. But an exception should be made for the relation explaining the demand for labour.

The demand for labour (manhours) was based on neo-classical theory. Accordingly, output, capacity utilisation, relative factor prices and disembodied technical progress were the determining factors. The specification of the equation could be found in Discussion paper no. 19 of the two Economics Institutes of the University of Basle (written in German). Professor van de Klundert wanted to thank Dr Koellreuter for supplying the information contained in this paper and the subsequent one on the industry model.

The modelling of the demand for labour raised the following points: First, the estimation of the equation in logarithmic form implied that the demand for labour could be derived from a Cobb—Douglas production function. The regression coefficients then appeared as expressions in terms of the elasticities of production. Now there was a production function in the model. In order to calculate production potential, a Cobb—Douglas function for the German economy was actually estimated. Applying the production elasticities found, it might be concluded that the regression coefficients of the labour demand equation were not equal to their theoretical values. This might, or might not, be a serious point. The question was: Should there be the same theoretical consistency with regard to production and the demand for factors at the macro level as was required at the micro level?

Second, in his paper, Dr Koellreuter observed that his approach was very similar to the 'clay-clay' vintage model applied to the Dutch economy by H. den Hartog and H. S. Tjan. This was true in the sense that both studies were applications of neo-classical production theory. However, there was an important difference in the specification of the substitution effect. In the 'clay-clay' vintage model, substitution depended on real wage cost, whereas in the paper by Dr Koellreuter the ratio between the wage level and the user cost of capital was central. It should be stressed that this difference in specification was not a necessary consequence of the choice made with regard to the production function. J. M. Malcomson, S. Nickel and others had shown that capital cost could play a role in a 'clay-clay' vintage model.

On the other hand, it was well known that a relation between labour input and real wage cost could be derived from a conventional production function. Different hypotheses could be tested, but Professor van de Klundert had no great confidence in the discriminative power of empirical data, at least on this subject. That left room for personal judgement. He felt rather uneasy about this. He thought substitution processes played a role in reality, but the ultimate quantitative effect of a nominal wage impulse on employment might differ substantially according to whether or not capital costs appeared in the equation modelling the demand for labour.

Third, said Professor van de Klundert, the macro-model of Dr Koellreuter and his associates related to gross national product and total dependent employment. The production activities of the government and the private sector were therefore added. It might be preferable to deal with employment in the government sector separately. The laws determining production and factor demand in the private business sector were not well suited to explain government behaviour in the same field.

Fourth, continued Professor van de Klundert, Dr Koellreuter pointed out that in his paper structural shifts were systematically taken into account. Dummy variables, with zero values before 1975 and the values of the relevant explanatory factors afterwards, were introduced in a number of equations. This raised a serious question. Was the available information at present sufficient to establish such a once-for-all change in behaviour and technology? If not, predictions based on the old structure might be as good as forecasts including the dummies. Inspection showed that structural changes in the equation representing the demand for labour were very small. But this was no great comfort as we were dealing with interdependent equations. Attention should be paid to the estimated production function, which was used to determine the degree of capacity utilisation in the economy. There was a substantial shift in 1974(1). The rate of disembodied technical progress of 3 per cent was reduced to 0.3 per cent p.a. For the production elasticities, highly implausible results emerged. Professor van de Klundert would hesitate to base projections on these outcomes of the estimation procedure. What may have happened during the 1974–75 recession was a loss of capacity in excess of normal proportions due to rationalisation and bankruptcies. Because the rate of depreciation was fixed in the model, such a possibility was *ipso facto* excluded.

Turning to the *ex-post* simulations, the purpose was to obtain an impression of the quantitative importance of the different explanatory variables in the demand for labour before and after the 1974–75 recession. In addition, the growth rate of output was split into its components by applying appropriate weights. Further, import and export growth rates were decomposed into price- and volume-induced effects. The intention was to determine which factors were mainly responsible for the slower growth rate of employment after the recession. The reported results for the whole economy were not entirely clear. According to the table, the difference between employment trends before and after the recession amounted to −0.2. In contrast with this the output effect, the impact of disembodied technical progress and the impact of changes in relative factor prices added up to a difference between reference periods of −0.7.

Two possible explanations emerged. In the macro-model the degree of capacity utilisation appeared as a fourth factor in the equation for labour demand. The difference between the two figures could be ascribed to this. If so, the degree of capacity utilisation must have had a positive effect, which was very unlikely. The second possible explanation was that output and employment trends related to different subperiods, as indicated in a footnote. In the macro-model this must lead to inconsistent results, because there was no time lag between employment and output in this case.

When these difficulties were resolved, there remained the question of the usefulness of the approach chosen by Dr Koellreuter. Differences in the demand for labour in the subperiods could not be fully explained by different outcomes for other endogenous variables. Ultimately, everything had to be traced back to the development of the exogenous variables and structural shifts in the regression coefficients. It would pay to isolate both sets of causal factors by means of simulation experiments for the second period. This would give a better impression of what happened during and after the recession of 1974–75.

The policy and uncertainty scenarios presented in the paper showed how the model worked. The results were sometimes rather unexpected. For instance, a policy of wage restraint led to lower levels of employment, despite the neo-classical flavour of the model. The reason was that the decrease in the user cost of capital exceeded the decline in the growth rate of nominal wages. Consequently, entrepreneurs were induced to substitute capital for labour. The spectacular development of the user cost of capital was the combined effect of a lower long-term interest rate and a cheapening in the price of equipment. Inflationary expectations were not taken into account, so that there was not the offsetting effect of a lower inflation rate on the cost of capital that one would expect. The lower inflation rate was reinforced by an extra appreciation of the Deutschmark. The appreciation of the national currency was so strong that it exceeded the ultimate internal price effect of a lower nominal wage level — what Dr Koellreuter called 'overshooting'. As a consequence, exports were lower and imports higher in the case of wage restraint than with the control forecast. Professor van de Klundert found it hard to believe that would really happen. The balance of payments would show a lower surplus on current account (because the Marshall–Lerner condition was fulfilled) as well as on capital account (because of the lower interest rate), whereas the exchange rate of the Deutschmark against the dollar would be substantially higher.

These results depended crucially on the estimated equation for the exchange rate, which was rather weak from a statistical point of view compared with the other equations (a small number of observations and lower t-values for certain coefficients). Moreover, the equation explained only the dollar exchange rate of the Deutschmark. The dollar exchange rates of other currencies were exogenous variables. In the policy simulations the values of these rates were the same as in the control forecast. The extra appreciation of the Deutschmark in case of wage restraint therefore implied an equal increase compared with all other relevant foreign currencies. Although a general appreciation of the Deutschmark was to be expected, he did not think that the regression equation for the dollar exchange rate generated the correct result for the overall appreciation. Professor van de Klundert stressed that he did not deny the possibility of extra appreciation in case of wage restraint. What worried him was the overshooting phenomenon, leading to implausible results.

In his paper on the model Dr Koellreuter pointed out that 'wrong' expectations were responsible for this. But whose expectations were meant? Were they always wrong, or was some form of adaptation possible in case of disappointment? On a more technical level, the question arose whether the model led to stable solutions.

Returning to the main issue, Professor van de Klundert thought it would be interesting to know the employment effect of wage restraint in case of a fixed exchange rate. This could be achieved by treating the exchange rate for the time being as an exogenous variable. If the result was worthwhile in terms of an increase in employment, a policy of wage restraint could be combined with a demand pull. As appeared from the scenario 'German Reflation', demand pull led to a depreciation of the Deutschmark. So, the second instrument of a demand pull could be used to stabilise the exchange rate in the case of a negative wage push. He wondered what the result of such an experiment would be.

The scenario 'Tighter Money' also led to some astonishing outcomes. For instance, it appeared that a restrictive monetary policy had a positive impact on employment. The user cost of capital was higher compared with the control forecast, and this led to substitution in favour of labour. There was no need to discuss the results of this scenario and the subsequent ones extensively, because what Professor van de Klundert had said about the principal relations of the model applied to other cases as well.

In conclusion, Professor van de Klundert said that even though he had made some criticisms of Dr Koellreuter's paper, he found his work very stimulating. It showed that simulation experiments based on econometric models were indispensable if we wanted to understand reality.

Dr Koellreuter agreed that on the manhours equation theoretical consistency had not been shown, but he was trying to forecast so that this was not his first priority. In an earlier version of the model he did have consistency; but including capital costs — as specified in the model — changed the value of the technical progress parameter drastically. The negative effect of the time trend on manhours had been taken over to a large extent by the relative factor-price term.

In a neo-classical context, capital costs should be included in the factor price term because decisions on the optimal factor mix were generally based on *relative* factor prices. Hamermesh in a paper in the *Journal of Human Resources*, (Autumn 76) had shown that wage/employment elasticities were significantly overestimated if capital costs were excluded.

It should be remembered that the ultimate effects of wage variations on employment could be determined only in a macroeconometric model. Studying the labour demand equation exclusively amounted to pure *partial* equilibrium analysis, with all its limitations. Without the inclusion of structural shifts in the parameters in certain equations, the regression results would have been bad. In practical projections with the model, the coefficients of the dummy variables for structural shift had been corrected to take account of the sort of criticism put forward by Professor van de Klundert.

The model had been used to discuss whether a once-for-all loss in capacity had taken place during the 1974—75 recession in Federal Germany by including a 0/1-dummy variable in the production function. This had been estimated for calculating potential output but the result had not been significant.

As for the *ex-post* analysis of the demand for labour and its determinants, the results reported for employment trends for the whole economy had to be corrected. A mistake had been made by not using the same time period for output and for manhours in the macro function. Qualitatively, the results still held but the actual numbers needed correction.

Professor Giersch thought there was confusion in the debate about wage restraints in the Federal Republic. There had been suggestions for relating the wage increase for 1978 to the increase in productivity. One would then expect inflation rates in Germany to drop to zero which could lead to an overshooting of the foreign exchange rate. He had suggested at the time that the pre-announced growth of money supply should be increased and that the central bank should intervene in the foreign exchange market. The central bank took the point and the increase in the money supply had been greater than originally announced.

One should take the money supply into account in models like Koellreuter's because it had important effects in a system of floating exchange rates. Different inflation rates in different countries were raising the demand for inflation proof assets. This leads to an explosion of some currency areas — those of the Swiss franc and the Deutschmark – while others – the dollar area – were imploding. The idea initially was that the size of a currency area was determined by geography, but this was no longer true.

Adaptive inflationary expectations in the inflation equation made the scenario one of increasing employment. Professor Giersch doubted the applicability of this to Germany. The short- to medium-term analysis covered only the upswing and he wondered what would happen when inflationary expectations were renewed. The German government was working through tax changes because government expenditure –like autonomous investment – was partially held back by pressure from environmentalists and by other legal constraints. Restrictions – like preventing the dismissal of labour – had raised the shadow price of labour above the actual one. Firms would be more cautious in taking labour on because they could not easily dismiss it when demand turned down.

Professor Henin suggested that the unexpected results in models came especially from over-adaptation. He wondered whether Dr Koellreuter had tested the model by longer simulation runs or by analytical methods. Did it work well over longer periods? Simulation often provided an extra method for validating a macroeconomic model where the general use of information in estimation made this necessary. He wondered whether the model was robust enough to changes in expectation because this was important for its qualitative results.

On the substitution of capital for labour. Professor Henin wanted to remark, on a technical plane, that, like Jorgenson in his well-known studies, Dr Koellreuter did not use a consistent neo-classical formulation. However, he knew well that in building a macro-model it was not always possible to keep all the restrictions suggested by pure theory. He wondered whether in forecasting one could use more of an equilibrium model. If not, perhaps bad specification was leading to error in estimating the relative strength of demand and relative-cost effects. If empirical estimation was wrong on that point, it was hard to see how the model could work well in explaining dynamic substitutions between factors.

Professor Odaka explained that in Japan one factor leading to unemployment was the same as in Germany, namely, the fall in the capacity of manufacturing industry to absorb more labour. In Japan this had been compensated by an increase in service activities. What had happened in West Germany?

The distributive system in Japan was protected from exchange rate appreciation. For example, the dollar was currently worth about 190 yen. Yet an air ticket was based on a rate of about 290 yen to the dollar. With books, the exchange rate was about 320. This sort of institutional barrier reduced competition for the Japanese service sector and could therefore lead to an increase in employment. This might not be the case in Germany, where there was competition with service industries in neighbouring countries.

Lord Kaldor threw in the suggestion that the reason why Japanese service industry was expanding employment as quickly as it was lay in the fact that wages in small-scale service industries were more under the influence of the balance between demand and supply. In Federal Germany wages resulted from collective agreements and it was less easy to separate wages in service industries from those elsewhere in the economy.

In the UK, one found that the fall in manufacturing employment was attentuated by the increase in service employment because there had been an increase in the gap between manufacturing and service wages. Since the service industry was a polypoly, with falling demand curves, a reduction in service wages led to lower break-even points for service businesses. Therefore, if the labour market became easier, there was an increase in the number of selling outlets and an increase in employment. There was a very large turnover of businesses in the service sector, but, with lower wages, more small businesses survived.

Professor Giersch agreed that in the Federal Republic banking, insurance and similar service activities were well regulated. They were not entrepreneurial but cartelised under the auspices of the government.

Professor Bergmann returned to the fact that in Koellreuter's model easy money was bad for employment. In the short run, conventional wisdom suggested the opposite, through the effect on investment. Substitution between capital and labour was a long-run factor. She would have greater confidence in the model if the lag structure brought this out. Of course, continuing easy money would have less effect on investment if investment opportunities dried up over time. She did not have complete confidence in the model, but thought it meritorious to have included money.

Professor Holt thought it curious that there was no Phillips curve in the model. Why was the Kuh approach used? And what was the difference between that and what the Phillips assumption gave? Professor Holt wondered whether there were other econometric models of the Federal Republic of Germany and why the Swiss should be building a model of Germany.

Professor Hines thought that much turned in the model on the user cost of capital. Why, if incomes policy was a substitute for monetary policy, did a fall in the cost of capital lead to an increase in unemployment, but a restrictive monetary policy increase the user cost of capital? He thought that symmetry should mean that incomes policy reduced the cost of labour and increased the cost of capital. Easy money should therefore go in the same direction.

Dr Koellreuter said that there had been little time to test the stability of the model. Actual runs of the model did not cover more than 12 quarters. For this period, the model proved to be stable. The exchange rate equation did not behave well for the forecasting period, so that another exchange rate equation, including relative money supplies instead of interest rate differentials, had been used.

The pure Jorgenson approach to the investment function had given bad results but the performance of the equation could be improved with adaptive inflationary expectations. One then got a positive effect of inflation on investment both in the short and the medium run. It had to be assumed that the effects of inflation on investment over a period of three to ten years might be quite different from its results in the short run.

Some participants had been worried about the results which the model gave with a tighter money supply. The reason for the results was that the simulation model took as exogenous factors that really were not. If wages could be allowed to adapt to the higher inflation rate in the scenario under consideration, relative factor prices would probably remain constant. The negative output effect on employment then would dominate and a restrictive monetary policy would have the usual negative impact on employment.

The reason why a Swiss group had built a model of the German economy was first, that the Federal Republic was Switzerland's main trading partner. It was significant that the first model of the FGR had been constructed in the Netherlands for the same reason. Second, PROGNOS AG – a consulting company in Basel, Switzerland, for whom Dr Koellreuter worked – had 80 per cent of its customers in the FGR.

Dr Koellreuter explained that it had been impossible to test the Phillips curve at the level of the industry, because of constraints of time and data. At the level of the economy, the Phillips approach did not work well for statistical reasons, and the Kuh model worked better. He agreed that one would like to have an exchange rate equation with better statistical properties but this was not possible because of limitations in data. There was no other way to catch the important effect which a fall in the inflation rate – due to a policy of wage restraint – would have on the exchange rate. Because an 'overshooting' exchange rate was very likely, international competitiveness might paradoxically be hurt by a policy of wage restraint in a world of flexible exchange rates.

For the outcome of a policy of wage restraint, government behaviour was very important. Wage restraint led, via a lowering of the inflation rate, to a redistribution of net real income towards non-wage earners compared with a model with no wage restraint. The positive net effect on real disposable income was due to the high marginal rate of taxation on wages in the FDR. From an increase of 1 billion Deutschmarks in the gross wage, social security contributions and wage taxes would take 600 million Deutschmarks. A corresponding change in marginal tax rates in favour of wage earners would naturally alter the results: a policy of wage restraint could then have a negative impact on the development of real disposable income. If government expenditure and transfers were fixed in real and not in nominal terms, the positive effect of a policy of wage restraint on real government expenditure and therefore on real GNP would not be observed in the way it had been in the model.

PART FOUR

The Labour Market

11 Wages and Job Availability in Segmented Labour Markets

BUREAU OF BUSINESS RESEARCH,
UNIVERSITY OF TEXAS AT AUSTIN, USA

I INTRODUCTION

Ever since the institutional labour economists rejected classical economic theory over six decades ago, there has been a deeply troubling schism in the foundations of our discipline that still has not been satisfactorily resolved. As a result, our ability to forecast inflation and unemployment suffers, and our policy analyses of structural and demand issues are often not very enlightening.

Research stimulated by the Phillips relation has helped to unify the conceptual worlds of labour economists, microeconomists, and macro-economists, but we can hardly claim to have achieved the creative synthesis that is so badly needed. On the one hand we had neo-classical price theory and on the other a great deal of institutional knowledge about how labour markets actually work. In recent years the microdynamics of the labour market has been modelled and search theory has been linked to the Phillips relation.[1] Many researchers, a sampling of whom are included among the references (pp. 406–8 below), have been working to improve our foundation of analytic knowledge but the links between wage and employment dynamics remain weak.

Clearly new ideas were needed, and one came from the development

---

[1] For examples see Phelps, (ed.) (1970) and work at the Urban Institute where the author, working with a research team composed of C. Duncan MacRae, William J. Scanlon, Stewart O. Schweitzer, Ralph E. Smith, Richard S. Toikka, and Jean E. Vanski, has studied many aspects of labour market dynamics relating to allocation by job availability, especially the transition probabilities between employment, unemployment and out-of-the-labour-force. This work culminated in a 180-equation model of the US labour market called RAAST (Race Age Sex Search Turnover) that predicts the dynamic behaviour of 16 demographic groups. Unfortunately lack of monthly wage data in the Current Population Survey prevented the joint analysis of wage effects. Some of the issues in modelling wage and availability together were discussed in Holt (1977).

economists, Todaro and Harris, who noted that, even though high industrial wages were paid in the cities of developing countries, the in migration from the traditional economy of the rural areas was inhibited by high urban unemployment rates.[1] Robert E. Hall [1970] studied data on US cities to determine whether the same phenomenon occurred in a developed economy. He found the same high positive correlation between wage and unemployment rates. He explained how high-wage cities would attract the unemployed who would leave low-wage cities, causing low unemployment. He also suggested reasons, such as reduced turnover and training, why employers could pay higher wage rates where unemployment was high. These relations make it possible for otherwise identical cities to reach different labour market equilibria. These researchers did not conclude that a basic revision of neo-classical labour market theory would be required. In another effort to

---

[1] See Michael Todaro (1969) and John Harris and Michael Todaro (1970).

Professor Parker commented on the parallel between this paper and the work on industrialising economies by Todaro and Harris. Since their seminal work was an important stimulus to both Robert Hall's and my work, it may be useful to point out some of their similarities and differences.

All these papers have the same general thrust in using two allocators in motivating labour participation, one being wages and the other the probability of finding a job. However, instead of viewing them in terms of two distinct behavioural motivations for migration, Todaro and Harris combine them multiplicatively into the single concept of expected income. While this helps to salvage the appearances of the classical model, they find that the policy implications are drastically different. Both wage subsidies to the industrial sector, and restraint on rural to urban migration would be required to achieve efficiency.

Todaro analyses migration flows to obtain an equilibrium unemployment rate that depends on the urban-to-rural wage differential and the rate of industrial expansion. There is a marked parallel to the turnover analysis of pages 395—6

The Harris—Todaro paper incorporates much of the classical competitive marginal-productivity model in a dual agricultural-industrial economy, but the effect of unemployment on migration is introduced through the expected income concept. In setting real wages by a politically motivated minimum wage they find, 'There will be a unique equilibrium associated with each possible value of the minimum wage, the locus of these equilibria is plotted . . . ' (p. 130). If the minimum wage had not been given by their institutional assumption (with virtually no theoretical or empirical support by the way), their equilibria would have been indeterminant. They *assume* that the labour surplus pushes the industrial wage down to the minimum wage, but they do not explore the process. In their static equilibrium, migration ceases when the combination of industrial wage and chance of finding a job is a stand-off compared with the agricultural wage. In this situation the industrial labour force accepts the expected income, and there would appear to be no

examine the dual effects of jobs and wages, Toikka [1976] analysed these impacts on labour participation.

In a recent paper the author [1978] attempted to meld classical price theory with search-turnover theory by introducing the ratio of vacancies to unemployment as a new allocating variable called 'job availability' to compliment wages. This paper started out to test that theoretical framework empirically, but instead it develops the theory more fully. Space does not allow inclusion of the empirical results which will be described briefly at the end, and reported in the later paper.

Because we seek to synthesise price and availability theory in a way that produces important *non*-classical results in terms of the equilibria to be expected, we start by briefly reviewing well-known market theory. The collective bargaining issue will not be considered.

---

disequilibrium that would strongly motivate behaviour which would put downward pressure on wages. Hence there would be no downward pressure in their model to force wages down to the political minimum. The equilibrium then is indeterminant because many combinations of wage and unemployment will yield the same expected income.

In summary they say, 'The essence of the argument is that in many developing nations the existence of an institutionally determined minimum wage at levels substantially higher than that which the free market would allow can, and usually does, lead to an equilibrium with considerable urban unemployment' (p. 129). They observe unemployment but their model explains it only by a minimum wage. However, they show no evidence in developing countries of the general existence of minimum wages. Even though their model is novel, rigorously formulated, and strongly supported empirically, they reach the traditional neo-classical conclusion that perverse governmental wage intervention is responsible for unemployment. They have not considered that industrial employers may well find a high wage–high unemployment urban economy to be strongly in their interests in terms of profits.

I applaud Harris and Todaro for their pioneering work. They have clearly seen the likely deviation from social optimum that occurs in their model, but they have not recognised the fundamentally important implications of introducing a second allocator in the analysis of the labour market.

It is significant to broaden the interpretation of their developmental analysis and apply it to transitions across market segments that are separated by barriers based on training, experience, discrimination or intercity distance, as well as to barriers between the rural and urban economies.

Harris and Todaro cite empirical support for the influence of both wages and unemployment on migration in Kenya and in the US during the depression of the thirties. Subsequent research on many developing countries has yielded substantial additional supporting evidence. See Henry Rempel 'Rural-Urban Migration and Urban Unemployment in Kenya', unpublished working paper, International Institute for Applied Systems Analysis, Schloss Laxenburg, Austria, August 1978.

II APPLYING NEO-CLASSICAL PRICE THEORY TO LABOUR MARKETS

Traditional price analysis postulates a demand curve $Q_d(P)$, supply curve $Q_s(P)$, and a price-adjustment mechanism in which the rate of change of price is a function of excess demand,

$$\frac{\Delta P}{P} = f[Q_d(P) - Q_s(P)]. \tag{1}$$

The market is in equilibrium when the condition, $0 = f(0)$, is satisfied.

Actually it is not necessary to specify the full adjustment relation (1) and equate it to zero to establish the unique equilibrium. Presumably any excess of *either* demand or of supply indicates the existence of disappointed individuals who will take actions that affect the generally known market price and move it toward its equilibrium level. Thus, the market equilibrium occurs at the unique price which clears the market.

This framework has been adapted to the labour market by introducing unemployment and vacancies attributable to lack of information at the micro level and other frictions which prevent *both* demand and supply from ever fully clearing. Continual turnover requires time-consuming job search and recruiting so that residual vacancies and unemployment *always are* present.

Let $J(W/P)$ and $L(W/P)$ be the demand for labour, and the supply of labour, respectively, as functions of real wages (W/P); see Figure 11.1. Vacancies V are unfilled jobs and unemployment U is composed of members of the labour force L who are not employed E.

$$V = J - E \tag{2}$$

$$U = L - E. \tag{3}$$

These residual variables fill the gaps between demand and supply on one hand and employment on the other. The ever-present 'disappointed'

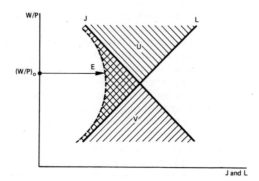

Fig. 11.1

employers and workers are stimulated by their situations to engage in specific recruitment, search, waiting and other behaviours that have impacts on individual wage offers, acceptances and other market transactions.

Turnover in the labour market continually generates new vacancies and unemployed workers. These stocks grow until enough mutually satisfactory job—worker matches occur that new hires offset the inflows of vacancies and unemployment, and a stock-flow equilibrium is reached. However, many equilibria can occur — with vacancies high and unemployment low, or *vice versa*, as shown by the curve in Figure 11.2. This stable relation between vacancies and unemployment derives from an equilibrium of the flows into and out of employment and the levels of vacancies, unemployment, and employment. Because of its importance in understanding labour markets, it will be rigorously derived in the next section.

We have described five labour market equations in six unknowns which yield the locus of employment levels shown by the dotted curve in Figure 11.1. For each wage level, J and L are determined. How many of these are matched in *employment* depends on how many vacancies and unemployed workers are generated by the turnover process and how fast the hiring process operates. These are reflected in the V-U relation.

The concept of market clearing ceases to be sufficient to determine an equilibrium because *both* residual variables, vacancies and unemployment, *always* exist applying opposite pressures on market transactions.

A wage-adjustment relation must be added to translate these pressures into wage changes,

$$\frac{\Delta(W)}{P} = f_V(V/U), \tag{4}$$

and equated to zero before a unique equilibrium real wage $(W/P)_0$ is

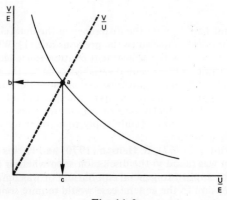

Fig. 11.2

obtained.[1] However, there is no basis for assuming the $\Delta(W)/P = 0$ when $(V/U) = 1$. Hence the market equilibrium is *not* likely to occur at the wage level corresponding to the intersection of the demand and supply curves. The unique equilibrium real wage $(W/P)_0$ is shown in Figure 11.1.

The Beveridge assumption that labour markets are in equilibrium when vacancies equal unemployment is simply not supported empirically. Unemployment usually far exceeds vacancies even in an inflationary labour market.

By combining the V/U curve of Figure 11.2 with the wage-adjustment relation of (4) vacancies are eliminated, and a Phillips relation is obtained:

$$\frac{\Delta W}{W} = F_U(U) + \frac{\Delta P}{P} \tag{5}$$

This is the essential theoretical foundation[2] for most of the empirical work on the Phillips curve.

The theory which has been sketched, as well as that which follows, can be applied to either a national macro market or to a compartmentalised labour market which does not interact with others.[3] It can also be extended to apply to segmented labour markets with interactions between the segments.

III ALLOCATION BY BOTH WAGES AND AVAILABILITY

The familiar results above are reviewed here to clarify and differentiate the introduction of 'job availability', the ratio of vacancies to unemployment, as a second allocating variable in the labour market. Like wages, availability is generated in the market process and is not simply an inherent quality characteristic of labour which accounts for a wage differential. 'Job availability' measured by the ratio of vacancies to unemployment reflects the availability of unfilled jobs relative to the unemployed workers who are available to fill them. It is a measure of *relative* job—worker availability in the market and is

---

[1] It is important here to note the difference in the determination of the equilibria of this model compared to the previous one (1). While market clearing sufficed there, now the adjustment relation is needed to determine the unique equilibrium. When residual variables occur as the result of imperfect knowledge, the search processes (that cause the adjustments which balance the market) affect not only its dynamic speed of adjustment but also its equilibrium level. The effectiveness of search processes affects system efficiency. These conclusions certainly apply to markets for other complex commodities such as housing.

[2] See R. A. Gordon (1967), B. Hansen (1970) and Phelps (1970).

[3] The question was raised in the discussion as to whether the analysis of this paper could be applied to general equilibrium or was limited to partial analysis. The extension to the general case would require some further development, but the results should carry over.

a sensitive index of the prevailing balance between employer recruitment and worker job search.[1]

Labour supplied and employment demanded are both affected by the V/U ratio in the market. When the employment demanded and supplied is regulated only by wages, there is a unique market-clearing wage as we have seen above. However, when they are regulated by *both* wages and availability, then there is a whole locus of wage-availability combinations that satisfy the demand, supply, and flow conditions which are necessary for equilibrium. Pressures to make wage adjustments are generated by deviations from the equilibrium locus.

To put the issue in its boldest form, if increased job availability *encourages* the labour participation of workers and *discourages* employers from creating jobs (because workers are hard to find) — just as occurs under traditional theory with wage increases — then a balance between the demand and supply of labour *could* always be achieved by changing availability without ever requiring a wage adjustment.

We do not suggest that availability does the whole job of regulating labour markets, but only that it does part of the job along with wage. When both allocators are operating, a relationship exists between them, but there is indeterminancy about where the market system will settle. There are *multiple* equilibria that may be equally stable. This is in sharp contrast to the above neo-classical theory in which there tends to be a unique equilibrium value for real wages.

The basic concept of allocation by both wage and availability has been presented earlier in sketchy form.[2] The purpose of this section is to develop the concept more formally in a theory of segmented labour markets and to relate it to neo-classical price theory.[3]

---

[1] In using this measure we, of course, recognise that some jobs are filled by people who were out-of-the-labour-force rather than unemployed, but in equilibrium a roughly equal number of people drop out of the labour force. We also recognise that other jobs are filled by people already employed. Such job changing simply fills one vacancy by producing another.

[2] See R. E. Hall (1970) and the discussion by Holt, and Holt (1978).

[3] The E_d and E_s functions, (6) and (9), which were designed to maintain as far as possible the parallel with the classical demand and supply analysis proved difficult to understand. At the conference Professor Henin correctly interpreted the E_d and E_s curves as reflecting employer and worker behaviour constrained by the micro search-turnover processes of the labour market which involve both vacancies and unemployment. Thus each of these curves does not reflect pure employer behaviour or worker behaviour, but already incorporates some of their interactions.

Professors Henin and Kolm also were bothered by having two distinct concepts of demand J and E_d, and two of supply L and E_s. This formulation was difficult to sort out.

continued on next page.

Demand for Labour

The demand for workers E_d is assumed to depend on the real wage W/P, the aggregate demand[1] for real goods and services D, and the vacancy to employment ratio which reflects the difficulty of recruitment in the labour market. The demand for employment is

$$E_d = E_d(W/P, V/E, D) \tag{6}$$

There was also some difficulty in keeping track of the number of equations and the number-endogenous variables which is necessary for demonstrating that we are one equation short and hence have an indeterminant equilibrium. The analysis seems clearer when presented in the more basic form below which does not strain to preserve the parallels with traditional supply and demand.

The system of equations which determines the static equilibrium can be summarised as follows:

$J = J(W/P, V/E)D$	(A)	$S = S(V, U)E$	(10)
$L = L(W/P, U/E)N$	(7)	$V = J - E$	(2)
$H - S = GE$	(12)	$U = L - E$	(3)
$H = H(V, U)$	(11)		

These numbered equations are basically those presented and discussed in the body of the paper except for equation (A) which was implicit in the E_d function (6).

The J function (A) is simply the aggregate of the J functions of individual employers which indicate the number of people that each would try to employ for given market conditions, i.e. real wage and the general ability to keep jobs filled as reflected in the market V/E ratio. The L function (7) similarly is the aggregate of worker labour force participation functions for given market conditions: real wages and ability to keep employed as reflected in the market's U/E ratio. How many of the jobs J and members of the labour force L will be engaged in employment matches E when the hire and turnover flows are in equilibrium depends on the speed of the search-turnover processes which are reflected in the other equations. Specifically (12) shows the excess of hires over separations which would be sufficient for employment growth at the constant rate G (which implicitly applies to aggregate real demand D, population N and capital as well). Hires and separations in turn depend in (11) and (10) upon the level of vacancies, unemployment and employment in the market. But they relate through (2) and (3) back to J and L, the basic decisions made by employers and workers.

These seven equations relate eight endogenous variables (J, L, W, V, U, H, S, E) and three exogenous variables, price level P, real demand D and population N which are determined outside the labour market system. On this basis the equilibrium of the labour market system is seen as indeterminant.

The resulting implicit equilibrium function relating real wage W/P, job availability V/U and exogenous demand (D/N) fully satisfies: employer

where its partial derivatives with respect to the three arguments are respectively: negative, positive and negative. This is a traditional aggregate demand function except that it adds an index of labour market tightness. Increasing V/E reduces employment demanded just as higher real wages would.

This labour-demand curve follows from aggregating the labour demand of profit maximising employers whose production operations are adversely

---

decisions on job J, worker decisions on labour market participation L and the stock-flow relations of the search-turnover process. Since employer and worker decisions already have taken full account of both real wages and the relative availability of vacancies and unemployed workers in the market, these decision-makers have no incentive to participate in additional adjustment processes that would move the market away from the above equilibrium relation. The adjustments of wages and prices (17), and of vacancies and unemployment (18) (quantity adjustments) are triggered by *deviations* of the labour market state from the equilibrium relation. The adjustment relations will not favour one equilibrium position over another – except through the influence of historically-given initial conditions. Further development of the adjustment relations will, of course, involve expectations. In the equilibrium analysis the expectations are assumed to be fulfilled.

Since equation (A) depends directly on an inverted production function,

$$D = \left(\frac{V/E + 1}{J(W/P, \, V/E)} \right) E$$

which reflects labour quality, recruiting costs, capital and monopoly power, we can *not* add a production function to obtain the equation needed for a unique equilibrium.

Recognising that prices are likely to be based on the mark-up of wages would add another equation, but also would transfer P to the list of endogenous variables, so the indeterminacy would remain.

The Harris–Todaro analysis which spells out marginal conditions, assumes competition, etc. encounters the same indeterminacy (see footnote 2 above).

The conclusion to be drawn from the analysis is that:

(1) The labour market equilibrium is genuinely indeterminant. Its current equilibrium is determined by the particular initial conditions which reflect previous history. Sufficiently strong shocks can move the market to a new position on the equilibrium locus.

or alternatively

(2) An unknown relation operates to establish the real wage, the vacancy-unemployment ratio, or some function of the two.

---

[1] The trend in labour productivity is involved and could be made explicit. In a dynamic theory, the demand for labour would relate to production decisions and be influenced by inventory levels and the backlog of orders as well as the demand for final goods.

affected by the tightness of the labour market.[1] The higher the ratio of vacancies to employment the higher are real recruiting costs, recruitment delays, labour turnover (because quits rise more than layoffs decline), and training costs. In addition labour productivity declines because: workers are more secure from the threat of layoffs; opportunities for working long hours by holding second jobs are greater; less skilled and motivated workers are attracted to participate in paid employment by the relative abundance of jobs; and fewer unemployed workers are in the market from which to recruit candidates whose qualifications match job requirements.

Although the demand for labour (6) reflects the employer's decision on the size of work force which is in his economic interest to employ, it is important to recognise that employers do not *control* employment. Rather that is the result of joint decisions by employers and workers to offer and accept employment. When an employer wants to increase his work force, he creates new vacancies, increases recruiting effort and its duration in filling them, and increases the wages offered or, what is the same thing in terms of labour costs, lowers hiring standards. The success of these measures, of course, depends on the availability of vacancies in the market with which the individual employer is competing so he must balance their costs against the benefits obtained from increasing his work force.

In deriving (6) the V/E term reflects both market aggregates and individual employer decisions. In the first instance V/E reflects the assumed condition of the labour market faced by individual employers. Then each employer makes his decision on both E_i and V_i which serves as an index of recruiting efforts. Adding these up for all employers yields an aggregate V/E ratio which may not be consistent with the initial assumption of market conditions. If not, a revised assumption about V/E is indicated, until the micro behaviour of employers is consistent with the aggregate condition of the labour market.

Note that the inclusion of the V/E ratio in the demand function has the effect of introducing supply conditions into the employer's decision process, since a high V/E ratio is accompanied by a low U/E ratio. The clean separation of supply and demand issues which characterises the neo-classical theory becomes somewhat smudged by the presence of market frictions. The employer's decision in weighing increased wage offers against recruiting effort already constitutes an adjustment to the supply side of the labour market which he faces. The employer must balance the supply elasticity to wage increases against the availability conditions prevailing.

Supply of Labour

The number of workers in the labour force available for work depends on real

---

[1] The sharp temporary rise in labour productivity which results from utilising slack labour when production increases with a virtually fixed work force is an important *dynamic* effect which does not affect the *static* demand for labour.

wages, the unemployment rate U/L, and Population N:

$$L = L_s(W/P, U/L)N \tag{7}$$

The effect of real wages in motivating paid employment in preference to leisure or household production is well known. The time spent unemployed, i.e. searching, waiting and not earning, obviously is a deterrent to participation in the labour market, and empirical studies clearly show that participation is inhibited by high unemployment rates. Actually individuals are continually entering and withdrawing from the labour force as part of the turnover process. If the probability per period of time of leaving the labour force is higher for unemployed workers than for employed workers, as it assuredly is, that alone is enough to ensure that labour participation declines with rising unemployment.[1]

Job availability regulates worker behaviour. When more jobs become available, unemployment is reduced and this induces more labour participation without necessarily requiring any change in wages. The increased labour force fills some of the new jobs, but not enough completely to prevent the fall in unemployment or there would be no job availability stimulus to increased participation. The strong tendency for participation changes to offset changes in unemployment has often been noted, but we want to stress that this is an important feature of the economic allocation process in labour markets.

In order to make the supply function of labour comparable to demand we need to express it in terms of employment rather than labour force by subtracting unemployment. Substituting (7) and using the U/E ratio rather than the unemployment rate we obtain:

$$E = L - U = \frac{L_s\left(W/P, \dfrac{1}{1 + E/U}\right)N}{1 + U/E} \tag{8}$$

This defines an employment supply function:

$$E_s = E_s(W/P, U/E, N) \tag{9}$$

where the partial derivatives of E_s with respect to (W/P), (U/E), and (N) are positive, negative and positive respectively.

The Vacancy—Unemployment Relation

If demand is partially regulated by vacancies and supply by unemployment, it is necessary to determine exactly how vacancies and unemployment relate to each other. A strong inverse relation between V and U has long been known, but adequate theory to explain it has received relatively little attention.[2]

---

[1] See R. E. Smith (1973).
[2] See C. C. Holt and M. H. David (1966), J. I. Foster (1974), Holt, MacRae and Schweitzer (1970), MacRae and Schweitzer (1970) and Holt, MacRae, Schweitzer and Smith (1971).

Research at The Urban Institute explains the V-U relation in terms of the separation flow of workers from employment, the hire relation which replaces them, and the growth rate of unemployment.

The flow of workers per month who leave employment S is influenced by the level of employment, the demographic composition of employment (since turnover rates are much higher for youth, women and minorities), and the tightness of the labour market (since quits rise more than layoffs decline when vacancies are high relative to unemployment).

The separation function is:

$$S = s(V/U)^q E \qquad (10)$$

where s is the weighted average of employment separation rates for the different demographic groups and $0 < q$ reflects the dominance of quits over layoffs as V/U rises.

The flow of new workers who are placed in jobs H increases with the number of workers searching and the number of vacancies to be filled. However, diminishing returns are experienced for both since increasing either alone has less and less effect. The following hire function has considerable theoretical and empirical support:

$$H = hV^v U^{(1-v)} \qquad (11)$$

For employment to grow, hires must exceed separations:

$$\frac{H - S}{E} = \frac{\Delta E}{E} = G \qquad (12)$$

where G is the growth rate of employment. Substituting (10) and (11) in (12) and making a simplifying approximation [which follows from $(s \gg G)$ and $(q \ll 1)$] yields:

$$(V/E)^{(v-q)}(U/E)^{1-(v-q)} = \left(\frac{s+G}{h}\right). \qquad (13)$$

This gives rigorous support and explanation for the inverse relation between vacancies and unemployment shown in Figure 11.2, but note that it is expressed naturally in terms of the vacancy and unemployment ratios, V/E and U/E.[1] If we specify a vacancy to unemployment ratio (V/U) as shown by the dotted line in Figure 11.2, its intersection with the V-U curve at point 'a' uniquely determines a value for V/E at point 'b' and a value for U/E at point 'c'.

In the above derivation of the V-U relation the level of real wages has not been taken into account although one might argue that high real wages would

---

[1] Although G varies with population growth and cyclical conditions, the employment growth rate is so small relative to the turnover rate that its fluctuations can be neglected.

be a stimulus to a fast-hire process and would inhibit separations. Although the data fits the above relation very well, wage effects might be explored.

The V-U relation will be affected by changes in the demographic composition of the work force or its growth rate.

Market Equilibrium

The V-U relation (13) enables us to express both the employment demand function (6) and the employment supply function (9) in terms of the (V/U) ratio which we have called 'job availability':

$$E_d = E'_d(W/P, V/U, D) \tag{14}$$

and

$$E_s = E'_s(W/P, V/U, N) \tag{15}$$

Equating employment demanded to employment supplied yields the equilibrium function:

$$E'_s(W/P, V/U, N) - E'_d(W/P, V/U, D) = 0 \tag{16}$$

whose partial derivatives with respect to (W/P) and (V/U) are positive so we see that for *given* aggregate demand level D and population N there is a locus of points relating real wages and job availability that is negatively sloped as shown in Figure 11.3. Since for *every* point on the line corresponding to a particular demand level: (i) the market clears in the sense that employment demanded equals employment supplied; (ii) the demand function which depends on both real wages and job availability is satisfied exactly; (iii) the supply function similarly is satisfied exactly; and (iv) the stock-flow relations

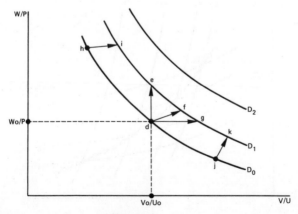

Fig. 11.3

of the turnover process are satisfied, the line constitutes a locus of equilibrium points. Population N is assumed to be given.

Once the labour market system settles to any of the equilibrium points (with demand D and prices P given) there is no motivation for either employers or workers to take actions which would change it. This is extremely important because it contrasts sharply with the neo-classical case of Figure 11.1 in which there was a unique wage equilibrium. When the supply, demand and V-U relations take full account of vacancies and unemployment, the system's equilibria characteristics are determined without specifying the adjustment processes. Those will be considered later.

We interpret the multiple equilibria (for a given level of aggregate demand) which occur when both real wages and job availability affect the behaviour of employers and workers as indicating that both are as satisfied with a relatively high wage, high unemployment situation as with a low wage, low unemployment one — at least as far as labour market adjustments are concerned.

Because of the significance of finding multiple equilibria and the plausibility of the underlying behavioural relations, a graphical derivation of the equilibrium line may be useful. Hold aggregate demand constant at D_0 and draw the iso-employment lines of the demand surface from (14) as dotted lines in Figure 11.4. At lower real wages and in slacker labour markets employers hire more workers. Draw the iso-employment lines of the supply surface from (15) as solid lines. Figure 11.4 shows greater worker employment at higher wages and tighter markets, but the full employment ceiling is evident as greater and greater wage and job availability increments are needed to induce more employment.

Where corresponding iso-employment lines intersect, employment supplied equals that demanded. The locus of these intersections is the curved line of

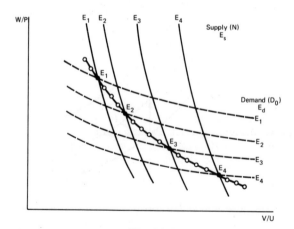

Fig. 11.4

circles that constitutes the multiple equilibrium points of the market. Although all of the small circles represent equilibrium points, their employment levels differ.[1] When real wages are high, unemployment is high and employment is low. When real wages are low the employment level is high.

When aggregate demand increases, the demand surface shifts right and upward and the new equilibrium locus moves similarly. See Figure 11.3 for D_1 and D_2.

Implications of Multiple Equilibria

In the classical model of (1) supply and demand responses to price and market clearing told the whole story in determining a unique equilibrium. In the neo-classical labour market model of Figure 11.1, imperfect information at the micro level caused vacancies and unemployment to occur. However, by limiting their effects to influencing wage changes, a simple unique equilibrium again occurred. However, when we recognised that supply and demand respond not only to wage but also are *directly* influenced by the presence of unemployed workers and unfilled jobs, we find that the equilibrium is indeterminant, that there is a trade-off between the wage and the job availability allocators and that there are multiple equilibria that are equally stable.[2]

Where such powerful economic allocators lead to indeterminant results, we should expect that other more subtle influences will play important roles in influencing which of the possible equilibria actually prevail. Discrimination based on race, sex and age, union bargaining, government regulations such as the minimum wage, historical and traditional wage differentials relating to region, occupation and industry all can have magnified effects on wage and unemployment patterns, when they do not run counter to the strong wage-equilibrating forces postulated by classical theory.

The point just made about relative prices and unemployment may also apply to the aggregate economy. There may be a trade-off between the usual levels of real wages and of unemployment.

---

[1] Figure 11.4, in showing the supply isoquants steeper than demand isoquants, assumes that workers are relatively more responsive to job availability than to real wages and employers are relatively more responsive to real wages. This realistic assumption leads to higher employment at lower wages and in tighter markets. Reversing the assumption leads to the opposite result, i.e. lower employment at lower wages. However, the negative slope of the employment locus is not affected. The author is indebted to Allan King for this observation.

[2] While the occurrence of indeterminant equilibria is perhaps surprising there seems nothing here that is inherently in contradiction with rational behaviour by either employers or workers. Steigler and others previously have incorporated optimal search in neo-classical models.

Wage and Availability Adjustment Processes

The labour market system cannot be expected to remain on the equilibrium locus unless adjustment processes operate to restore equilibrium once it is disturbed. Consider an equilibrium at point 'd' in Figure 11.3 when demand suddenly increases from D_0 to D_1. If all the adjustment were made in real wages, a new equilibrium could be established at point 'e'. On the other hand if job availability made the whole adjustment, a new equilibrium could be established at point 'g'. A combination of both adjustments might achieve equilibrium at point 'f'. With two allocating variables, two adjustment mechanisms can operate and we need to explore the nature of each.

The amount of the disequilibrium in such a market is appropriately measured by 'demand gap', the difference between the demand which 'corresponds' to the initial (disequilibrium) state and the new equilibrium state. Any point on the D_0 line would require similar adjustments to get a new equilibrium on the D_1 line. Given the demand gap $(D_1 - D_0)$ measure of disequilibrium, what will be the character of the two adjustment responses,

$$\Delta(W/P) = A_W(D_1 - D_0), \tag{17}$$

and

$$\Delta(V/U) = A_V(D_1 - D_0)? \tag{18}$$

At point 'd' wages are insufficient to attract the increased labour supply which is needed at the increased level of demand and for which the employers are willing to pay at the wage rate of point 'e' in order to obtain maximum profits. Clearly a profit motivation exists for making the wage adjustment in the right direction (the derivative of A_W is positive and the same for A_V), but the empirical evidence indicates that this adjustment is very slow, lasting longer than a year.

Increased demand applies a direct stimulus to the employer to increase vacancies and recruiting effort without necessarily changing wages. As a consequence unemployment is reduced. The increased revenue makes funds readily available for covering the increased costs of a larger work force.

While wage adjustments certainly occur, especially through changing hiring standards, the availability adjustment is likely to be more direct, effective and fast. The availability adjustment is particularly forceful when revenues fall and employers are under pressure to lower costs in order to protect profits and sometimes even firm survival. The alternative of lowering wages and waiting for workers to quit hardly seems responsive to the situation especially since the workers would tend to reduce the labour force by dropping out of unemployment but not necessarily leaving jobs. Experiments with the Urban Institute's RAAST model of the labour market indicates that much of the availability adjustment process occurs in a quarter and most is complete in a half-year.[1]

The relatively *fast* response of availability may explain why wages decrease so little when demand falls. For example, with demand at level D_1 in Figure 11.3 and the market at point 'g', assume that demand dropped to D_0. A very fast drop in job availability to point 'd' would leave virtually no downward pressure on wages. Some workers responding to reduced vacancies would have dropped out of the labour force. Those remaining in the labour force are willing to work at the old wage level and put up with the higher level of unemployment. Although employers face lowered demand and would like to lower wages, they now face a lower vacancy-to-unemployment ratio and have a better choice of workers and easier recruiting from the increased unemployment so they are willing to stay with the old wage. Availability allocation may largely account for the long-standing puzzle of sticky wages which respond little to even high levels of unemployment.

We have examined several adjustment relations that were functions of: excess demand (1); the vacancy to unemployment ratio (4); unemployment (5); and now with availability allocation, demand gap (17) and (18).

Solving (16) for demand and using a linear approximation to the logarithms of real wage and availability in the resulting function yields:

$$D = f_D(\ln W/P + k \ln V/U) \tag{19}$$

where the derivative of $f_D(\ )$ is positive. Substituting the co-ordinates of point 'd' in (19) to obtain D_0 and substituting in (17) yields

$$\Delta(W/P) = A_W [D_1 - f_D(\ln W_0/P + k \ln V_0/U_0)] \tag{20}$$

which can be rewritten to obtain a feedback wage adjustment relation:

$$\Delta(W/P) = A'_W [f_D^{-1}(D_1) - \ln W_0/P - k \ln V_0/U_0]. \tag{21}$$

Here we see that the adjustment is triggered by a function of demand D which determines the new equilibrium, and two negative feedback terms which reflect the current state of the system in moving toward that equilibrium.

---

[1] See Smith (1977).

Actually relations (10), (11) and (12) indicate in oversimplified form the dynamic stock-flow relations that are involved in the availability adjustment relation (18). They also supply first approximations to the probabilities for placing unemployed workers, separating workers and filling vacancies. The corresponding approximate probability distributions for vacancy durations and job tenures also are obtained.

For an analysis of the employment adjustment process which incorporates wages, vacancies and other variables see Holt and Lee (1977) and more fully Lee (1969). For a study of the vacancy response of firms see Holt, Toikka and Scanlon (1977).

It is interesting in (21) to see wages *increased* by: low current wages, which is expected, and by low current V/U (high current U) which is unexpected. This is explained by the fact that low wages and high unemployment inhibit labour participation and stimulate employers to increase production. Either raising wages or increasing job availability (lowering unemployment) will move the market toward equilibrium. The same derivation also applies to the availability adjustment of (18).

The wage adjustment relation (21) can be rewritten to indicate how a demand relation interacting with wage level and job availability can determine wage inflation:

$$\frac{\Delta W}{W} = A_W''\,[f_D^{-1}(D) - \ln W/P - k\,\ln V/U] + \frac{\Delta P}{P}. \tag{22}$$

Although this relation was derived in the context of the market moving toward an equilibrium determined by fixed demand D, the demand gap could be maintained by continuing changes in demand. However, the analysis of this paper, with the exception of the adjustment mechanisms, has not considered dynamic issues.

It has long been recognised that the Phillips curve relates endogenous variables but does not show how the inflation rate is regulated by exogenous demand. Equation (22) makes exogenous demand explicit.

Phillips Relations

The availability of two adjustments responding to the same disequilibrium in (17) and (18) and the fact that the availability response is much faster than the wage response suggests another way of formulating the wage adjustment process.

By observing the availability response we can infer the demand gap, and substitute it into the wage adjustment relation. Thus the wage adjustment is obtained as a function of the availability adjustment:

$$\Delta(W/P) = A_W\,[A_V^{-1}\,[\Delta(V/U)]]. \tag{23}$$

The availability allocation theory as used in (23) offers a basic interpretation of and rationale for stable Phillips functions relating endogenous labour-market variables.

Rewriting (23) in a plausible functional form which introduces a distributed lag to indicate that the wage response lags the quantity response and allows less than full response to price changes yields:

$$\frac{\Delta W}{W} = m_1\left(\frac{\Delta V}{V} - \frac{\Delta U}{U}\right) + m_2\left(\frac{\Delta P}{P}\right) + m_3\left(\frac{\Delta W}{W}\right)_{-1} \tag{24}$$

It is interesting that this Phillips relation responds to *changes* in unemployment rather than its level. This suggests a 'speed limit' policy in regulating aggregate demand which sometimes has been advanced by Art Okun. This Phillips relation would produce clockwise loops which often have been observed.

The last two terms will be highly correlated, so it will be difficult to obtain a good statistical estimate of their regression coefficients. Survey estimates of the price expectation term should be tested as a possible means of explaining rapid upward shifts of such Phillips relations.

Phillips relations usually stress unemployment and do not include vacancies. Using (13) we can write (24) in terms of changes in unemployment, employment, turnover rates and employment growth rate:

$$\frac{\Delta W}{W} = -n_1 \frac{\Delta U}{U} + n_2 \frac{\Delta E}{E} + n_3 \Delta \ln\left(\frac{s+G}{h}\right) + n_4 \frac{\Delta P}{P} + n_5 \left(\frac{\Delta W}{W}\right)_{-1} \quad (25)$$

Rapid increases in employment, even when no changes occur in unemployment because participation increases, have been thought to stimulate inflationary wage pressures. This Phillips relation displays that characteristic.

The bulge of young people in the labour market as a result of the post-war baby boom and the increasing inclination of women to seek paid employment contribute to high growth G and high separation rates s, both of which raise the non-inflationary unemployment rate.

A more conventional Phillips relation can be obtained by assuming that the price level is closely related to the recent wage level

$$\frac{P}{W_{-1}} = \frac{1}{S} \quad (26)$$

but subject to certain dynamic variations as the share of income going to labour, S, varies in response to events which create temporary opportunities to shift income shares such as war threats, OPEC, etc. Taking logs of (26) and substituting in (24) yields:

$$\Delta\left(\frac{\Delta W}{W}\right) = m_1 \Delta\ln(V/U) - m_2 \Delta\ln S + (m_2 + m_3 - 1)\left(\frac{\Delta W}{W}\right)_{-1} \quad (27)$$

and on integration,

$$\frac{\Delta W}{W} = m_0 + m_1 \ln V/U - m_2 \ln S + (m_2 + m_3 - 1)\left(\frac{\Delta W}{W}\right)_{-1} \quad (28)$$

This Phillips relation relates the wage inflation rate to job availability V/U, but contains an income share term which could be somewhat erratic. The price expectation term no longer appears explicitly.

The wage adjustment may respond to the demand gap at a *speed* depending on job availability. Quitting jobs to obtain higher wages may be an important aspect of the inflation process, and quits are known to respond both to

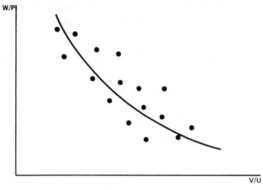

Fig. 11.5

vacancies and wages.[1] Perhaps (17) should be replaced with:

$$\Delta(W/P) = B_W(V/U)\ C_W(D_1 - D_0) \tag{29}$$

which would help to explain why wages are sticky downward in a slack market but respond rather quickly in a tight market. Support for such a relation can be found in optimal job search theory. This change in the adjustment process could be reflected in Figure 11.3 by the movements from h to i and from j to k.

Segmented Markets

To this point we have considered a single labour market of comparable, but not identical jobs and workers. If there were multiple but similar markets but without interactions, we would expect to find them scattered along the equilibrium locus as indicated in Figure 11.5.

Disturbances impacting on particular markets would tend to move them away from the equilibrium locus, but availability and wage adjustments would tend to decrease the deviations from equilibrium. The contention of this paper is that there may be little or no pressure to move wages in segmented markets toward a common level.

Should limited interactions occur between these segmented markets by movements of either workers or employers, then the pressures toward the equilibrium locus would be increased. This model of wages and unemployment rates in interacting labour markets might apply to different cities, regions, occupations or even possibly countries. Of course, special and persisting characteristics of the jobs or of workers would sustain differences in wages and unemployment that would not be eliminated by the adjustment processes.

[1] See J. P. Matilla (1974).

IV SUMMARY IMPLICATIONS OF THE WAGE-AVAILABILITY THEORY

We have developed the static theory of equilibria and adjustments toward them which follow from introducing the ratio of vacancies to unemployment as a second allocator in the labour market. The implications have been explored both for macro Phillips relations and for segmented submarkets. The following implications which follow from the theory need to be tested empirically:

(1) Labour markets have multiple stable equilibria which can occur with either high wages and unemployment, or low wages and unemployment.
(2) A labour market out of equilibrium could be brought into adjustment by *either* of two distinct processes, one affecting wages and the other job availability.
(3) In general both adjustments occur, but availability changes occur much faster and carry most of the load in cyclical adjustments. This may explain why wage inflation declines so little when demand declines, and hence why the Phillips curve is so flat at high unemployment rates.
(4) A wage adjustment relation is derived in terms of exogenous demand and negative feedback from wages and availability.
(5) A rationale for the Phillips relation is presented in terms of a linkage between wage adjustments and vacancy and unemployment adjustments.
(6) New dynamic variables, changes in vacancies, and changes in employment, are proposed for Phillips relations.
(7) Changes in the demographic composition of employment shift the Phillips relation because of differences in turnover rates.

V SUPPORTING EVIDENCE

Robert Hall's study [1970] discussed earlier indicated that the average weeks of unemployment per worker for twelve US cities maintained almost the same rank ordering over a four-year period indicating the absence of strong forces tending to equalise unemployment rates. This result persisted even after he had statistically standardised for age, marital status, family size, income and wages. With the same standardisation (except for wages) and holding sex and race constant he found for all four groups that average weeks of unemployment in the cities correlated positively with their hourly wages. Although the number of cities was small, the survey data for a sample of households was very rich.

The author, using a sample of forty US cities and two different measures of job availability, showed a uniform negative correlation between wages and job availability in three years (all different from Hall's). When an estimate was made of the wage and availability adjustment relations corresponding to (21)

by examining year-to-year changes of the cities, the expected signs were
obtained for the former but not for the latter. This result is consistent with
the faster response of job availability that is expected.

When city population, which studies have often linked to city wage levels,
was introduced along with job availability, the latter variable showed a
stronger relation with wages.

When a large cyclical decline occurred in *demand* between 1973 (with an
unemployment rate of 4.9 per cent) and 1975 (with an unemployment rate
of 8.5 per cent), very large reductions occurred in the job availabilities in the
cities and small changes occurred in their wage rates. Even though demand
had sharply decreased and hence the equilibrium locus had shifted sharply
to the left, its negative slope (in log terms) changed little.

The types of Phillips curves which are derived from the wage-availability
theory appear generally consistent with those which have found support
empirically.

VI CONCLUSION

Over all, the empirical support for the importance of availability as an
allocator in the labour market seems sufficient to merit substantially more
extensive testing of the wage-availability theory.

It is premature to try to draw policy implications from the theory, but it
is clear that its new insights may substantially change the interpretation of
labour market data. For example, the use of regional unemployment rates in
the allocation manpower programme funds, etc. would need to be reviewed.

Imperfect knowledge and structural frictions are by no means specific to
labour markets. Hence there may well be parallels to this theory development
in product markets where order backlogs, lead time, inventories and stock-outs
may well prove to be relevant availability variables which interact with price
allocation. This may explain why industrial product prices too are sticky and
often adjust more slowly than economists using classical price theory would
expect.

The neglect of institutional dynamics in this paper should not be
intepreted as suggesting that they are unimportant, but rather that we need
first to understand the market setting within which unions and firms operate.

REFERENCES

J. L. Foster, 'The Relationship between Unemployment and Vacancies in
    Great Britain (1958–72): Some Further Evidence', in *Inflation and Labour
    Markets*, D. Laidler and D. L. Purdy (eds.) (Manchester University Press,
    1974), pp. 164–96.
R. A. Gordon, *The Goal of Full Employment* (New York: Wiley, 1967).

R. E. Hall, 'Why Is Unemployment So High at Full Employment?', *Brookings Papers on Economic Activity*, 2 (1970), pp. 369–410.

B. Hansen, 'Excess Demand, Unemployment, Vacancies, and Wages', *Quarterly Journal of Economics* (February 1970), 84, 1–23.

John R. Harris and Michael Todaro, 'Migration, Unemployment and Development: A Two Sector Analysis', *American Economic Review* (March 1970), pp. 126–42.

C. C. Holt, 'Labour Market Structure: Implications for Micro Policy', *American Economic Review* (May 1978), 68, No. 2, 342–7.

———, 'Modeling a Segmented Labor Market', in Phyllis Wallace (ed.), *Women, Minorities, and Employment Discrimination* (Lexington Books, 1977).

———, R. S. Toikka and W. J. Scanlon, 'Extensions of a Structural Model of the Demographic Labor Market', in Ronald G. Ehrenberg (ed.), *Research In Labor Economics*, Vol. 1 (Johnson Associates, 1977).

———, R. E. Smith and J. E. Vanski, 'Recession and Employment of Demographic Groups', *Brookings Papers on Economic Activity* (1974), 3, p. 737–60.

———, C. Duncan MacRae, Stuart O. Schweitzer and Ralph E. Smith, 'Manpower Proposals for Phase III', *Brookings Papers on Economic Activity*, 3 (1971), pp. 703–22.

———, C. Duncan MacRae, Stuart O. Schweitzer and Ralph E. Smith, *The Unemployment-Inflation Dilemma: A Manpower Solution* (The Urban Institute, Washington, DC 1971).

———, 'Job Search, Phillips' Wage Relation, and Union Influence: Theory and Evidence', in E. S. Phelps *et al., Microeconomic Foundations of Employment and Inflation Theory* (New York: W. W. Norton, 1970).

——— and M. H. David, 'The Concept of Job Vacancies in a Dynamic Theory of the Labor Market', in *The Measurement and Interpretation of Job Vacancies*, National Bureau of Economic Research (New York: Columbia University Press, 1966).

———, C. D. MacRae and S. O. Schweitzer, 'Job Search, Labor Turnover, and the Phillips Curve: An International Comparison', in American Statistical Association, *Proceedings of the Business and Economics Section* (Washing (Washington, DC, 1970).

——— and Kry Sik Lee, 'Dynamic Economic Structure and the Econometrics of Linear Decision Analysis', *Stability and Inflation, Essays in Honor of A. W. H. Phillips* (Wiley, 1977).

L. Jacobsson and A. Lindbeck, 'Labor Market Conditions, Wages and Inflation – Swedish Experiences 1955–67', *Swedish Journal of Economics* (June 1969), 71, 64–103.

E. Kalachek and J. Knowles, *Higher Unemployment Rates 1957–60: Structural Transformation or Inadequate Demand.* Subcommittee on Economic Statistics of the Joint Economic Committee, 87th Cong., 1st sess., Washington, DC, 1961.

J. S. Lee, *Employment Decisions of Manufacturing Forms in Response to Demand Fluctuations: An Econometric Study*, unpublished Ph.D. dissertation, University of Wisconsin library (1969).

C. D. MacRae and S. O. Schweitzer, 'Help-Wanted Advertising, Aggregate Unemployment, and Structural Change', in G. G. Somers (ed.), *Proceedings of the Twenty-Third Annual Winter Meeting* (Madison: Industrial Relations Research Association, Dec. 1970), pp. 87–96.

Edmond Malinvaud, *The Theory of Unemployment Reconsidered* (Wiley, New York, 1977).

R. Meidner, 'Active Manpower Policy and the Inflation Unemployment Dilemma', *The Swedish Journal of Economics* (Sept. 1969), 71, 161–83.

J. P. Matilla, 'Job Quitting and Frictional Unemployment', *American Economic Review* (March 1974), 64, 235–39.

George L. Perry, 'Unemployment Flows in the U.S. Labor Market', *Brookings Papers on Economic Activity*, 2 (1972), pp. 245–92.

E. S. Phelps (ed.), *Microeconomic Foundations of Employment and Inflation Theory* (New York: W. W. Norton, 1970).

R. E. Smith, 'The Discouraged Worker in a Full Employment Economy', *Proceedings of the American Statistical Association*, Business and Economic Section (1973), pp. 210–25.

R. E. Smith, 'A Simulation Model of the Demographic Composition of Employment, Unemployment, and Labor Force Participation: Status Report', in Ronald G. Ehrenberg (ed.), *Research in Labor Economics*, Vol. 1 (Johnson Associates, 1977).

Charles L. Schultze, 'Has the Phillips Curve Shifted? Some Additional Evidence', *Brookings Papers on Economic Activity*, 2 (1971), pp. 452–67.

Michael P. Todaro, 'A Model of Labor Migration and Urban Unemployment in Less Developed Countries', *American Economic Review* (March 1969), pp. 138–48.

R. W. Toikka, 'A Markovian Model of Labor Market Decision', *American Economic Review* (December 1976), 66, p. 821–34.

Discussion of Professor Holt's Paper

Professor Henin introduced the paper. He said this was an important and original contribution to the representation of the labour market. It was also a complex paper. The point of departure was that Holt, after his contribution to the microdynamic theory of employment, was well placed to fill the gap between the theory of search or of turnover, etc. and the traditional theory of market equilibrium.

The paper tried to construct an equilibrium model in line with search theory. The principle on which it intended to reconstruct the labour market model was the use of two regulating variables. One was as in the traditional model; the real wage (W/P): the other, job availability was the relationship V/U, or the number of vacancies compared with unemployment. The fact that these were two allocating variables meant that there was a degree of freedom. There were a series of couples between W/P and V/U which were possible. We were faced with multiple equilibrium expressed in the form of a locus with a negative correlation between the two regulating variables which the traditional theory saw in the form of a downward sloping demand curve. This was the essential principle.

The initial presentation in the paper was clear and precise. It was essential to introduce availability, and especially V, as the difference between the number of jobs and the total number employed. Unemployment was the difference between the total labour force and the number employed. Figure 11.1 contrasted the traditional theory with that of Professor Holt. The idea was that because of frictions in the process of search the balance was not to be found at the intersection of the demand and supply curves, but on the left side of it. The situation shown by horizontal lines like that at E in Figure 11.1 led to the dotted line in Figure 11.2 which gave the total situation on a single curve. Of course, one did not necessarily have V = U which would be equivalent to the neo-classical equilibrium.

From them on, Holt took up his model as the central part of his contribution. A broadening of the earlier analysis going into the two allocative variables plus the idea of multiple equilibrium, formed the core of what he had to say. Professor Henin said he had felt in some difficulty over the concepts of supply and demand which Holt used. Compared with the definition of demand on pages 393–4, he was somewhat embarrassed by the concept of the supply of labour which he found difficult to interpret in behavioural terms. After discussion with Holt, he had obtained what he thought was the most faithful interpretation. Perhaps Professor Holt would not share this.

Following Professor Henin's own interpretation, one had to distinguish two concepts of supply and demand. First we had traditional or neo-classical supply and demand curves, which led to the J and L variables in Holt's paper; then we had supply and demand curves conditioned by market constraints. The idea was that, on an imperfect market, economic agents signalled demand

or supply shorter than their neo-classical plans. This distinction between
neo-classical and conditional functional functions was to be compared with the
famous Clower's distinction between notional and effective demands, but it
was very different. Effective demand differed from notional owing to
constraints on other markets. Conditioned demands here are related on
constraints on the same market. They expressed behavioural inhibition of
agents confronted to an imperfect market and led to some 'internalization' of
disequilibria.

In Holt's paper the conditioned demand curve followed from equation (6)
as a function of D and V/E. The conditioned supply curve followed from
equation (7) as a function of N and V/L. Both expressed stock values, so their
intersection gave the stock equilibrium on the labour market. But this stock
equilibrium was very indeterminate in so far as we did not get a definite
relationship between U and V. Such a relationship followed from conditions
for flow equilibrium. Flow equilibrium was reached for a given rate of growth
G of actual employment and gave a relationship between separation S and
recruitment H, both depending on V and U. Then flow equilibrium gave the
relationship between V and U which was needed for the determination of the
stock equilibrium. In terms of graphical analysis, it allowed us to know which
conditioned supply curve to connect with one given conditioned demand
curve. M. Henin proposed Figure 11.D1 as a complement to Professor Holt's
Figure 11.1.

The locus of Holt's equilibrium was given by the intersection of the
conditioned demand and supply curves, related by flow equilibrium conditions.
If demand D or labour force N were allowed to change, the equilibrium locus
was given as in Figure 11.4 in Professor Holt's paper.

The next interesting feature of the paper was when Professor Holt moved
on to the study of the dynamic adjustment process involving both real wage
rate and job availability. He used a symmetrical formulation, but Professor
Henin was not sure that this was possible. He thought one could not write
one independent adjustment equation for V/U (like (18)) because the adjust-

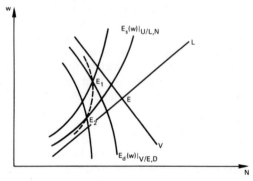

Fig. 11.D1

ment of job availability was implicitly given by the hiring and separation process, and then employment adjustment. In further discussion of adjustment in relation to the Phillips curve, Professor Holt said that segmentation was a major factor but the paper was too condensed really to cope with this issue.

Professor Henin wanted to say how interesting he found the new concept of supply and demand appearing in the paper, but he had to point out where some difficulties lay.

First, one had to distinguish between voluntary quits and laid off. Then, it was unsatisfactory to take G as an exogenous variable: if G was not given, every solution was indeterminate. One important question is whether unemployment could be called unvoluntary in such a model, where at equilibrium demand was equal to supply. Of course it was different from Keynesian unemployment, but the model did not support the liberal's view of equilibrium employment as in some sense optimal.

Professor Henin found himself wondering how far conditioned demand and supply curves could be derived from adjustment cost considerations. In that case, such functions would be unstable over time. Here one was confronted with the very limit of the methodology adopted by Professor Holt in his paper: to give a static image of a dynamic world. Able as was the photographer — and we had to admire his skill — there was some risk that the photography was slightly blurred.

Professor Holt accepted Professor Henin's interpretations and hoped that his introduction to the discussion had clarified the paper. The key point was that having learned the neo-classical model which was so simple, elegant and rigorous, it was hard to see the world in a new way. But the study of labour markets with segmentation showed that one had a situation that was very different from the standard, single-product neo-classical world. He had tried in his paper to treat complex markets simply. He had found basic concepts that looked sensible and had empirical support, yet when one put them into the model they led to conclusions that implied multiple equilibria and indeterminate solutions. This could be important both for the analysis of data and for policy.

Professor Holt then turned to Figures 11.D2 and 11.D3 which summarised the indeterminacy analysis. For simplicity of exposition, wages were held constant and the equilibrating adjustment was made in terms of job availability.

One might think of this in terms of different cities. Some cities would have high wage rates with slack labour markets and high unemployment. Others would have tight labour markets and relatively large numbers of jobs, but low wages. The migrant between cities would have to decide whether he would prefer a high wage with a high chance of unemployment, or a low wage with low unemployment. There was strong evidence, if one looked at less-developed countries, that *both* the unemployment rate and the wage rate influenced migration to cities.

In neo-classical trade theory, it was predicted that differences in wage rates

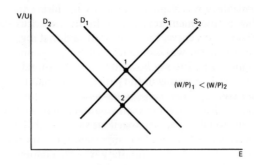

Fig. 11.D2

between cities would become equalised. Or, if there were more unemployment in one city than another, one again found gradual equalising adjustments. One expected wage rates to adjust labour supply to demand, but if people also responded to labour market conditions, which influenced how fast workers found jobs, one had the possibility of multiple equilibria. One could not then say that cities with different unemployment or wage rates were out of equilibrium. One would need to determine whether cities were off the equilibrium locus. Professor Holt feared that in the past we might have been misinterpreting stable differentials as disequilibria.

Figure 11.D2 showed demand curve D_1 and supply curve S_1, both regulated by job availability V/U and both conditional on real wages which were given and constant at level $(W/P)_1$. Equilibrium availability and employment were shown at point 1 (One should note here the parallel with Professor Malinvaud's analysis).

At a higher given real wage $(W/P)_2$, fewer workers were demanded (D_2) but the supply was greater (S_2). The result was a new equilibrium, at point 2. These two equilibrium points, when plotted in Figure 11.D3, fell on the locus of equilibrium points which related real wages and availability. Thus, when there were two allocators, there were many points of equilibrium.

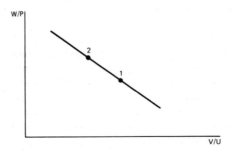

Fig. 11.D3

An exactly parallel exposition could have been made by holding availability constant and letting real wages regulate the market. As the paper showed, both of these modes of adjustment operated to bring about equilibrium, but the speed of wage adjustment was usually slower.

Professor Malinvaud fully understood that Professor Holt was dealing with fundamental questions, but questions that were difficult and intriguing. The message of the paper was that, considering how the labour market worked and given aggregate demand, there was not a single equilibrium but a full spectrum of equilibria corresponding to different degrees of pressure of the demand for labour and correlatively to different real wage rates. In one sense, those who had been recently thinking about the foundations of Keynesian theory would accept the importance of the level of the wage rate. (If the goods market was always cleared, there was a direct relationship between unemployment and the wage rate.) But Professor Holt brought in a new idea, namely that the dynamic adjustment of wage rates might lead to any limit within a full spectrum of limit equilibria. Professor Holt therefore made us go on to look at the process of adjustment of real wages.

Given aggregate demand and the labour force, the process in Professor Holt's model worked on two variables: the real wage rate W/P and the pressure of labour demand V/U. What was special was that the adjustments of the two variables depended on precisely the same function, namely the gap between the demand and the supply of work. A mathematician would call such a process 'singular'. Indeed, if adjustments of W/P and V/U were distinct functions of W/P and V/U, then one would expect to find a single limit equilibrium. What was the justification for saying that both variables reacted to exactly the same pressure of demand and to nothing else?

Whatever the answer to this fundamental question, Professor Malinvaud suggested that the formulation of the dynamic process, notably for V/U, had to rely on microeconomic formulations like those Professor Holt had used in earlier papers.

Professor Bergmann was not happy with Professor Holt's response to Professor Henin. In Figure 11.4, at E_1 there was one possible ratio V/U. This value of V/U came from equations (1) to (9). However, equations (10) and (11) were in themselves sufficient to give values for both V and U that were not consistent with the values at E_1. If so, there might be only one point where the value of V/U obtained. She would be surprised if the number of equilibrium positions was infinite.

Professor Holt, replying to Professor Bergmann, said she was implying that there was the same number of equations as unknowns. If she counted carefully, he could assure her she would find one equation short. Because the demand function had two allocating variables, it was actually a demand surface. There was also a supply surface and, of course, if two planes intersected they did so along a line, and not at a point. If one had an equilibrium line for a given aggregate demand, all points along it represented points of stable equilibrium. Then if aggregate demand changed, the new equilibrium point would fall on the new equilibrium line. But the adjustment process depended on the starting point, that was, say, the relative importance of wage and availability adjustments depended on the initial wage and the availability of labour. The adjustment of availability was a stock/flow process.

Professor Kolm said that, as always, Charles Holt presented a very interesting paper. He confessed, however, that he was under the impression that the model did not stand naturally on its feet from the start. This led to several original results, including that of 'multiple equilibria'. Specifically, Professor Holt introduced behavioural variables without introducing the corresponding behaviour. These were the 'availability' variables, unemployment U and vacancies V. Professor Holt saw the point well in his literary presentation but did not translate it into his formal model. He wrote, 'availability is generated in the market', the employer 'creates new vacancies' and 'makes his decision on both E_i and V_i' (the firm's hiring and vacancies). But this remark, and the corresponding one for labour supply, was not effectively formalised. Professor Holt's agents decided on only one independent variable instead of two (hiring and vacancies, or demanding and taking a job). Thus U and V appeared *de facto* as parameters in the model's equations, hence the 'multiple equilibria' result. In addition, there was a problem in the transformation of the variables U and V into V/U; but Professor Holt could have made both E_s and E_d depend directly upon both U and V, and thus, by simplification, upon V/U.

Professor Kolm thought the best way of commenting on the paper was to give what he thought should be the model. As in Professor Holt's paper, labour was assumed to be homogeneous. A firm i had three variables: total supply of jobs S^i, number of workers hired E_s^i, and the number of vacancies V^i. It chose their levels, but this gave only two independent choice (behavioural) variables because of the definitional identity $S^i \equiv E_s^i + V^i$. This choice depended upon the market parameters: demand for the firm's product d^i which one might write as a function of aggregate demand $d^i(D)$; real wage rate W/P; total unemployment U, which expressed how easy it was to find workers for hire; and total vacancies V, which expressed how tight was hiring competition from other firms (this was $V - V^i$, but V^i/V could be assumed to be small). We now had $V = \Sigma V^i$, $E_s = \Sigma E_s^i$.

Similarly, a worker j had three variables: his decision to seek a job: $D^j = 0$ if he did not and $D^j = 1$ if he did; his decision to take a job: $E_d^j = 0$ if he did not and $E_d^j = 1$ if he did; and his decision to be a jobless job-seeker: $U^j = 1$ if he was and $U^j = 0$ if he was not. But $D^j \equiv E_d^j + U^j$ by definition, so that there were only two independent choice (behavioural) variables. They depended upon the market parameters: real wage rate W/P; number of vacancies V, which expressed how easy it was to find a job; and total unemployment U, which expressed how tight was competition for jobs from fellow workers (U was assumed not to be a very small number). We now had $U = \Sigma U^j$, $E_d = \Sigma E_d^j$ (N would be introduced through the number of these j).

This gave three equations:

$$\Sigma E_s^i (W/P, U, V, D) = \Sigma E_d^j (W/P, U, V)$$

$$V = \Sigma V^i (W/P, U, V, D)$$

$$U = \Sigma U^i (W/P, U, V).$$

They usually determined the values of the three variables W/P, U, V, as a function of global demand D. There was generally no continuum of 'multiple equilibria'. Employment E was the common value of ΣE_s^i and ΣD_d^j for these values of these variables.

We could now continue by introducing dynamics, the evolution of V^i, U^j, E, etc. in time. Or perhaps we could be more specific about wage decisions and adjustments, and so on.

Professor Parkin said this was a clever and challenging paper, especially for those unhappy about working with market equilibria. He found it useful to link this to the analysis of segmented labour markets in less-developed countries. The demand for labour depended on the real wage and supply depended on the probability of being hired. If one equated supply and demand to find where there was equilibrium, then one obtained a locus like that relating V/U to the real wage in Professor Holt's model. In a less-developed country one had a subsistence wage in one sector which bolted down the system. Another model used the wage rate in a government sector. However, such solutions were not convincing and he would not want to hide behind a dynamic adjustment process.

What factor was at work in the real world? When the labour market tightened, this was either not productive or created disutilities. If one supposed that workers got utility from their real wage, or if the utility function had two arguments, the level of employment and the amount of labour input, one could then solve this to express unemployment as a function of the real wage or of V/U. If the relevant indifference curve coincided with Professor Holt's locue, one would get equilibrium. Otherwise there would be a problem because the real wage/labour market was not optimal. This was a line one could take. One could have a story deriving from utility maximisation in this situation which was either more explicit or showed that people cared where they were.

Professor van de Klundert said that, referring to equation (6), on the demand for labour, Professor Holt said that the trend in labour productivity could be made explicit. What did he mean? On a more fundamental point, Professor van de Klundert agreed with the general emphasis on quantitative adjustment rather than price adjustment in the labour market. However, he was not quite sure whether a symmetrical treatment of the adjustment process was right. There was asymmetry in the sense that there was more likely to be a quantitative adjustment if there was an excess supply of labour. If so, he wondered whether one could then deal with this by a non-linear Phillips relationship.

Professor Modigliani said he had high admiration for Professor Holt's work, but would criticise this paper, where he thought that perhaps Professor Holt's ideas had carried him away. He understood the motivation behind the paper because he had seen Holt's work on differences in wage rates and employment rates between cities. He thought this was important work. It solved questions like: why did General Motors pay more than the corner shop? At the cross-section level this was important, but he was worried when one took the analysis to the macroeconomic level. Moreover, when Professor Holt said that any level of aggregate demand was consistent with macroeconomic equilibria, he did not like this at all. Professor Holt was saying that forgetting the vacancy rate meant there was equilibrium at any level of demand because a falling demand allowed firms to increase prices and so reduce the real wage. Professor Modigliani was not sure whether Professor Holt really meant this but it was an important issue. It was also reflected in the way Professor Holt treated the Phillips curve. This used to be seen as the relationship of unemployment to the rate of charge of the price level and not the level of real wages. It showed why nominal money prices changed and not real wages.

At the end of the paper Professor Holt seemed to confuse real and nominal wages. Professor Modigliani believed that (in a closed economy) the labour market set nominal wages and that firms set real wages by their pricing policies. This brought him to the question of whether he believed in multiple equilibrium. His main reservation was that he saw the relationship between the vacancy rate and the real wage in a different setting.

First, one would expect the vacancy rate for a firm to be an increasing function of overall vacancies and a declining function of its relative wage. Next, one could conceive of the firm as having an optimal or target level of vacancies, depending on its product demand and labour supply conditions, and on the cost of delayed and lost sales. If one accepted this paradigm, then an increase in aggregate demand and hence in vacancies would lead firms to increase nominal wages in an attempt to raise relative wages and reduce vacancies. While this formulation leads to a relation between the rate of change of wages and the vacancy rate, one can readily arrive at a traditional Phillips curve by using the Beveridge relation to express vacancies in terms of unemployment. This paper represented an interesting attempt to deal with an important problem but he felt there were some large holes in it, and was in any case not sure that much could be learned about this problem at the aggregate level.

Professor Georgescu-Roegen said that early in his paper Professor Holt suggested that unemployment exceeded vacancies. Later he said that as the number of vacancies increased, unemployment declined. Did he have a case in mind where the two curves crossed, or was there an upper limit for the first and a lower limit for the latter?

Professor Rehn noted that Professor Holt dealt with situations where there were different levels of real wages. One could have the same level of real wage in a more regimented economy. Then different cities would have different levels of productivity, in which case the relationship between the real wage and productivity would differ, so one could have different levels of relationship between U and V.

Where Professor Holt suggested that one should not help monopolistic elements in the labour force to become unemployed, he would say that one should introduce regional development policies; then one would standardise the real wage over the whole country. He wondered whether this idea was consistent with Professor Holt's thinking.

Professor Grinols said that the essence of Professor Holt's methodology was to add a new variable to each side of the market. One therefore needed two variables to adjust, and the question was whether the wage or unemployment adjustment was larger relative to the other. However, when one talked of costs of adjustment, he thought an important question to ask was; what was it that the firm was optimising which led to such a description of adjustment?

Professor Holt responded to the discussion. He was working at the frontiers of economic analysis, and would treat the proposed theory with scepticism until empirical work had supported it. For example, he would accept, at least temporarily, Professor Modigliani's suggestion that the theory might have stronger relevance at the cross-section, microeconomic level than at the macroeconomic level. However, many areas were yet to be adequately explored. For example, perhaps the Phillips curve resulted from the fact that there were two adjustment processes. Perhaps both wage changes and availability changes were responses to a common cause, i.e. both reflected responses to labour market disequilibrium.

Professor Holt had wanted to test the theory but had then found that more theory was needed first. However, empirical studies which were available seemed to give the theory support.

On whether one could bring out a unique world from all of this, one answer would be that the initial conditions in the world were unique. But it did not necessarily follow that the adjustment processes would give a unique later history. He thought one would get a more satisfactory answer if one looked closely at the demand for labour and found how to make the firm's behaviour consistent with that of an external market.

Discrimination between those in the labour market on grounds of age, sex, etc. had its role. If one had a strong equilibrating mechanism and indeterminacy, then second-order effects (like discrimination) could have larger impacts than one might expect. He hoped it would be possible to make progress by sorting out how the two allocating mechanisms were operating.

Professor Kolm's comments were interesting, and on the surface convincing. However, while the employer decision on jobs S^i and the worker decision on labour force participation D^j were independent, the employer's employment decision E_s^i and the worker's employment decision E_d^j were *not* different variables whose sums could be equated. Indeed, the employment relation existed only when a single *joint* decision E^{ij} was made of an offer by employer j *and* its acceptance by worker i. $E^{ij}(W/P, U, V, D)$ was 1 if worker j was employed in firm i under the existing market conditions, otherwise 0. Hence, Kolm's employment equation would be replaced with $E = \Sigma_i \Sigma_j E^{ij}$ (W/P, U, V, D). The effect was to introduce E as an additional variable. More explicitly, if Kolm wanted to interpret E^{ij}_s as a job offer and E^j_d as the conditional decision that the offer would be accepted, those decisions could be independent. Then the relevant aggregated equations would be:

$$E = \sum_i \sum_j E^{ij}_s(W/P, U, V, D) \cdot E^j_d(W/P, U, V)$$

$$V = \sum_i S^i(W/P, U, V, D) - E$$

$$U = \sum_j D^j(W/P, U, V) - E$$

We again had four variables in three equations. Serge Kolm was quite right in stressing behaviour, but unfortunately, his correction was in error.

Professor Parkin had mentioned work on underdeveloped countries like that of Harris and Todaro. He himself would simply note that, when faced with a problem like this, the automatic response of an economist was to rescue the traditional theory. In this case, Professor Parkin would take the real wage and multiply it by one minus the unemployment rate. That gave the expected wage and left one with no concern. Professor Holt thought Harris and Todaro's work had profound theoretical implications. All of us were keen to preserve any existing paradigms and perhaps were too ready to reject new ones. Professor Parkin had behaved typically in suggesting that V/U was not really important. Nevertheless, this was an extremely wasteful process. In the US economy in recent years a huge job-search industry had grown up, so he would not take a polar position on this. A large amount of search activity was very wasteful. Testing out empirically what happened would have important results.

Professor Holt told Professor van de Klundert that equation (6) had no time trend for labour productivity, so he had not tried to introduce labour productivity as one would do in a full theory. If one were considering other types of market, this kind of analysis could have important implications. He was there thinking of very complicated markets like those for housing or consumer durables where one could show that availability was a major factor.

Professor Holt emphasised that he did not put great stress on the idea of indeterminacy itself. He was simply reacting to the classical theory which said that there was only one wage for a given type of labour. If there was variability in such wages, one needed to look for an explanation. Using two allocating variables led to a more complicated world.

Asymmetry in the adjustment mechanism might be important. In a tight labour market, the speed of adjustment might be different, for example, in labour turnover and in inflation rate charges. He did not want to suggest that GNP could be indeterminate, but perhaps a firm like General Motors was faced with a range of equally good wage policies. It could offer a high wage and do little recruiting, etc.

To Dr Grinols, Professor Holt explained that the empirical data made it clear that if there were a change in aggregate demand, the movement in the labour market would be almost all horizontal. In a tight market one would get a stronger inflationary response. Turnover models gave a first approximation to the adjustment process. The distinction between 'quits' and 'lay-offs' was important in the model. For example, one could see what happened when 'quits' were rising faster than 'lay-offs'.

To Professor Rehn, he would say that the model worked at the industry level rather than that of the economy. If there were no strong equilibrating efforts, collective bargaining would have bigger effects than usual.

Professor Holt concluded that there must be a notion of market segmentation, and one needed a unified theory that cut across this. His model might show why wages were sticky. It might be that availability rather than the real wage adjusted with changes in aggregate demand. The labour market might therefore work best if aggregate demand were stable.

12 Discrimination and Unemployment*

Barbara R. Bergmann
UNIVERSITY OF MARYLAND, USA

INTRODUCTION

As compared to white males, blacks and women in the United States tend to have a high incidence of unemployment, tend to earn lower wages when employed, and tend to be distributed across the range of occupations in a different way. The same is true for women and identifiably lower-class persons in most other countries.[1] With respect to any particular group in any particular country, there is likely to be disagreement as to the source or sources of these three problems. Some observers believe that the problems of these groups stem in the main from characteristics of their members, which cause them to shy away from certain jobs, to have or appear to employers to have lower productivity in certain jobs, and to have a high rate of separation from jobs. Other observers emphasise discrimination – the tradition-bound attitudes of employers which result in witholding access to certain jobs from group members who potentially might have normal productivity in those jobs.[2]

A considerable body of research supports the proposition that discrimination

* The author would like to thank Ralph Smith and Jean Vanski for making corrected estimates of labour force gross flows available to her.

Support was provided by the Computer Science Center of the University of Maryland and some of the materials incorporated in this work were developed with the financial support of the National Science Foundation Grant 77-14693. However, any opinions, findings, conclusions or recommendations expressed herein are those of the author and do not necessarily reflect the views of the Foundation.

[1] Women have higher unemployment rates than men in all OECD countries except the United Kingdom, Ireland, Canada, Finland and Japan. See Organisation for Economic Co-operation and Development, *Labour Force Statistics, 1964–1975* (Paris, 1977).

[2] For a discussion of the sources of black-white labour market differences see Stanley Masters, *Black-White Income Differentiations* (New York, Academic Press, 1975). For male-female differences see Ronald Oaxaca, 'Sex Discrimination in Wages' in O. Ashenfelter and A. Rees (eds.), *Discrimination in Labor Markets* (Princeton University Press, Princeton, 1973).

against women and blacks exists and is an important labour market phenomenon in the United States.[1] In this paper I shall discuss a number of theories of the workings of discrimination and their application to the problem of unemployment. Then with the help of a micro-simulated computer model of labour market processes which embodies some of these theoretical insights, I shall explore the effect of employment discrimination on the unemployment rate of discriminated-against groups and on economywide unemployment rate rates, and discuss the policy implications of these results.

I THEORIES OF DISCRIMINATION

One of the most influential of recent thinkers on the mechanisms and results of discrimination has been Gary Becker.[2] Becker's analysis can be summarised by saying that he characterises employers as being willing to hire any qualified person (regardless of race or sex) for any job, subject to a candidate's willingness to accept the offered wage. However, says Becker, employers will offer lower wages to candidates whose characteristics are such as to occasion psychic pain to the employer if he were to hire and thus associate with them. The Becker approach to discrimination can be thought of as a variant of the neo-classical theory of 'compensating wage differences'. The employer is paid a premium (by the worker) for putting up with the annoyance of associating on the job with a person of the wrong race or sex.

Becker's model of the process of discrimination is not particularly apt for exploring the unemployment problems (if any) occasioned by discrimination, because it is based on the neo-classical assumption that the labour market is continually cleared through a process of wage bidding by the unemployed, so that nobody, of whatever race or sex, could ever be unemployed because of a deficiency in demand for their labour. While Becker recognises that persons of certain race or sex have impaired employability because of employers' 'taste' for not associating with them, the wage differential applied to them after the bidding is over turns out to be just sufficient to make up for their impairment.

To economists interested in understanding the sources of the considerable unemployment problems of blacks and women, and at least exploring the possibility that discrimination might play a role, a description of labour market processes different from Becker's is therefore required. One result has been the development of a 'queue' theory of differential unemployment rates.[3]

---

[1] One set of estimates of the importance of discrimination in race/sex wage differentials is given by Alan S. Blinder, 'Wage Discrimination Reduced Form and Structural Estimates', *Journal of Human Resources*, 8 (Autumn 1973).

[2] Gary Becker, *The Economics of Discrimination* (University of Chicago Press, Chicago, 1957).

[3] See Lester C. Thurow, *Poverty and Discrimination* (Brookings Institution, Washington, DC, 1969).

In its crudest version, an unemployed worker would be hired for the next vacancy when he or she reached the head of an imaginary queue. Newly unemployed workers of the race/sex groups most acceptable to employers can break into the queue rather than joining on at the end, so that they reach the head more rapidly. In a more sophisticated version of the queue theory, each unemployed worker has a number of sweepstake tickets giving a chance at the next vacancy to be filled, with workers from the more desired race-sex groups holding more tickets per person, and thus having a higher probability of success. However, any unemployed person will eventually get a winning ticket and get a job.

The queue theory, unlike Becker's theory, does predict different unemployment rates for different groups, although it ignores wage issues. However, it tends, as we shall see, to give results which run counter to common experience.

Consider a labour market with N distinguishable groups, which is in a steady state, i.e. total employment and unemployment and group employment and unemployment are unchanging. Each unemployed member of group i has t_i sweepstake tickets, for which the prize is being taken on for the next vacancy. Further assume that members of group i leave employment at a rate of s_i. Because of the assumption of a steady state, persons in each group entering employment in each time period must equal the number leaving employment, so that for group i, the number flowing into employment is

$$\left(\frac{t_i U_i}{\Sigma t_i U_i}\right)(\Sigma s_i E_i) = s_i E_i, \quad i = 1, N \tag{1}$$

where U_i and E_i are respectively numbers unemployed and employed in group i.[1] The expression in the first bracket on the left represents the proportion of all the sweepstake tickets held by members of group i, while the expression in the second bracket on the left is the total number of 'winning' tickets per time period. Making the substitutions

$$LF_i - U_i = E_i, \quad i = 1, N$$

and

$$u_i = \frac{U_i}{LF_i}, \qquad i = 1, N$$

and dividing any of the equations (1) by any of the others gives

$$\frac{t_i}{t_j} = \frac{s_i}{s_j} \frac{u_j}{u_i} \frac{(1 - u_i)}{(1 - u_j)}, \quad i = 1, N; j = 1, N \tag{2}$$

---

[1] For a somewhat similar analysis with, however, rather different conclusions, see Stephen T. Marston, 'Employment Instability and High Unemployment Rates', *Brookings Papers in Economic Activity* (1976:1).

TABLE 12.1 ESTIMATED RATES OF US LABOUR FORCE FLOW, 1976
(PER CENT PER MONTH)

	Employment to unemployment (1)	Employment to not in labour force (2)	Total flow from employment (3)=(1)+(2)	Unemployment to not in labour force (4)
White males	1.6	1.9	3.5	11.7
White females	1.3	5.3	6.6	18.4
Black males	2.6	2.6	5.2	17.1
Black females	1.2	4.6	5.8	31.0

SOURCE US Labor Department unpublished gross flow data adjusted by
Ralph Smith and Jean Vanski.

Thus, if we believe in the queue theory, and know the group rates of
separation, we can deduce the degree of disadvantage of unemployed workers
of various groups in the job sweepstake. (We may call the quantity to the
right in (2) the 'advantage ratio' of the two groups.)

We do have available usable information on separation rates for the race/
sex groups in the US. A household is maintained in the Census Bureau sample
of the labour market survey for four successive months, and the reply of
each person who has been in the sample for at least two months can be
compared with his or her reply in the previous month. The result is a tabulation
of 'gross flows' from one of the three possible states (employed, unemployed,
not in the labour force) into one of the three states in the subsequent month.
In Table 12.1, data are presented on three of the gross flows, based on the raw
data as corrected by Ralph Smith and Jean Vanski.[1] The first two columns give
monthly rates of exit from the state of employment. The large absolute size
of these numbers is quite striking, particularly when it is considered that
persons who leave employment and re-enter it between the days of the
monthly survey are not included.

If we use the numbers in Table 12.1 to compute the advantage ratios
implied by the queue theory, as we have done in Table 12.2, we get a not
unreasonable answer for blacks, but a totally unreasonable answer for white
women. The rate of unemployment for white women is so low, considering
their rate of separation, that a belief in the queue theory involves believing
that employers have a considerable preference for white women over white
men in every job. Since this is patently untrue, further theoretical development
is obviously called for.

One obvious element of unreality in the queue theory and in Becker's
discrimination theory is their neglect of the phenomenon of occupational

[1] See Ralph E. Smith and Jean E. Vanski, 'Gross Change Data: The
Neglected Data Base' (Urban Institute, Washington, 1978).

TABLE 12.2 UNEMPLOYMENT RATES AND DEDUCED 'ADVANTAGE
RATIOS' UNDER A QUEUEING HYPOTHESIS, 1976

	Unemployment rate	*Advantage ratio* (t_1/t_i) *1976*
White males	6.4	1.00
White females	7.9	1.51
Black males	12.7	.70
Black females	13.6	.72

segregation, which is a prominent feature of labour markets everywhere, from
the most primitive economies to the most highly complex, whether capitalist
or collectivist. In the US, each race/sex group is grossly underrepresented in
certain occupations. In the United States 73 per cent of the managers and
administrators and 87 per cent of craft workers are white males, who are
53 per cent of the labour force, while only 21 per cent of the clerical workers
are not female.[1] The Soviet Union has integrated many of the occupations
which are all-male in the US, yet 98 per cent of orderlies, nurses and nurse-
maids, 95 per cent of garment workers, 95 per cent of public dining workers,
90 per cent of letter carriers and 85 per cent of economists are women;
91 per cent of enterprise directors and 95 per cent of automotive transport
and urban electrical transport workers are men.[2] That at least some of these
assignments of occupation to one sex or another do not derive from physio-
logically based differences in the sexes in tastes or productivity is suggested
by the fact that an occupation may be assigned to one sex in one country and
the other sex in another.

Some social scientists do hold firmly to the view that the occupational
segregation observed in the US derives in large part from racial differences in
human capital and from sex differences in commitment to the labour market
rather than discrimination by employers. The participants in these controversies
have based their positions on analyses of survey data sets which provide
information on individuals' wage income and on the individuals' characteristics
such as education and experience, but provide no information on the practices
of employers.[3] A new body of evidence is making itself felt in this controversy,

[1] U.S. Bureau of Labor Statistics, *Employment and Earnings.*
[2] Soviet data are from the chapters by Michael P. Sacks and Norton T.
Dodge in Dorothy Atkinson, Alexander Dallin and Gail Warshofsky Lapidos,
(eds.), *Women in Russia* (Stanford University Press, Stanford, 1977).
[3] See Jacob Mincer and Solomon Polachek, 'Family Investments in Human
Capital: The Earnings of Women', *Journal of Political Economy*, 82 (March/
April 1974). See also their note and that of Sandell and Shapiro in *Journal of
Human Resources* 13 (Winter 1978).

deriving from the records of lawsuits brought by women and blacks under Title VII of the Civil Rights Act, which prohibits employment discrimination on account of race or sex. These records are full of accounts of employer and union practices which have the effect of denying entry to certain kinds of jobs to women and black people.[1] Those practices designed to deny access to blacks have usually been less explicitly invidious than those designed to deny access to women, because differentiation of treatment by race has been more widely believed to be unjust than has differentiation of treatment by sex. Until recently the latter has seemed, even to most women, to be the natural order of things.

Once we accept that occupational segregation which is enforced or allowed to persist by employers[2] is a major element in discrimination, then a model which incorporates labour market segregation by race and sex becomes appropriate to an analysis of issues relating to unemployment. Admitting the element of occupational segregation brings up a number of questions which need to be attended to for a full understanding to be reached. One such question relates to the mechanism whereby a newly created job cluster is initially assigned to one race/sex group or another.[3] Another question relates to the conditions under which violations by individuals of the race/sex assignment of a job cluster occur.[4] Still another question is the mechanism by which reassignments of job clusters from one race/sex group to another occur, presumably motivated by employer problems with wages and recruitment.

The model to be described in the next section puts aside such questions, and assumes that in the short or medium run the job 'territory' assigned to each race/sex group is fixed. The model highlights the issue of supply-demand

---

[1] The record of the case of the American Telephone and Telegraph Company is an excellent example. AT & T used entirely different recruiting materials for men and women, and gave them different tests. See the chapter by Judith Long Laws in Phyllis A. Wallace (ed.), *Equal Opportunity and the AT&T Case* (MIT Press, Cambridge and London, 1976).

[2] When an employer does assign a person of an 'inappropriate' race or sex to a particular job, that person is not unfrequently subjected to physical and psychological harassment by other workers, who take the assignment as an assault on their status and self-image. This behaviour, which disrupts the work effort, tends to discourage both the victim and the employer from persisting. However, since employers have the power to discipline those carrying on the harassment, and most frequently fail to do so, it is perhaps not unreasonable to place the responsibility for the failure of integration on them in such cases.

[3] This issue has been treated by sociologists who have suggested that there is a tendency to assign a job cluster to women if the duties and status can be thought of as similar to women's duties and status in the family. See Valerie Oppenheimer, *The Female Labor Force in the United States* (University of California Press, Berkeley, 1970).

[4] See Rosabeth Moss Kantor, *Men and Women of the Corporation* (Basic Books, New York, 1977).

imbalances within market segments as a factor in explaining different unemployment rates of the race/sex group. These supply-demand imbalances may also be implicated in wage differentials, and we discuss this matter briefly below.

II A SIMULATION MODEL OF A SEGMENTED LABOUR MARKET

In this section we describe a model of the labour market which incorporates the element of occupational segregation by race and sex and also the elements of supply-demand imbalances. It also allows us to take account of differentials in the extent of movements out of jobs and out of the labour force displayed by the various race/sex groups, as documented in Table 12.1, above.[1]

Rather than present this model as a collection of equations, I have set it up as a computer micro-simulation, which allows a realistic portrayal of labour market dynamics.[2] In a micro-simulation model we follow fictional individuals through time, as they go in and out of the labour force and as they go in and out of employment. A worker's race/sex indentification and history influence his or her chances and behaviour, and the computer retains a memory of relevant portions of that history which allows us to model these effects. The behaviour of employers may similarly be modelled. Our interest centres, of course, not in what happens to particular fictional individuals, but on the unemployment rates by race/sex groups which sum up the experience of the individuals in the labour market.

The framework of our micro-simulation consists of parallel representations — one of the supply side of the labour market (workers and potential workers), and the other of the demand side of the market (job slots, some of which are occupied and some of which are vacant but which employers would like to fill). In Figure 12.1, the top row of circles represents persons; the number under each circle represents the ID number of the person, and the number in the circle gives the person's labour force status. To the left of the single vertical line are persons who are employed, and the number within each circle contains the ID number of the job slot that person is occupying. Circles between the vertical single line and the vertical double lines represent persons who are unemployed; this is indicated by a zero in their circle. Persons to the right of the double line are not currently in the labour market, and this is

[1] See also Claire Vickery, 'The Impact of Turnover on Group Unemployment Rates', *Review of Economics and Statistics*, 59, No. 4 (November 1977).

[2] For a fuller description of the model's mechanics see Barbara R. Bergmann, 'Empirical Work on the Labor Market: Is There any Alternative to Regression Running?', (*Proceedings of the 27th Annual Meeting of the Industrial Relations Research Association*, 1975).

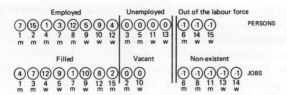

Fig. 12.1

indicated by −1 in their circle. Job slots are treated entirely analogously: some jobs are occupied (marked by the ID of the occupying person); others are vacant but looking for workers (marked 0), others are presently non-existent or 'not in the labour market' (marked −1).[1]

To represent occupational segregation (in this diagram only segregation by sex is represented), each person and each job has an 'm' or a 'w' below its ID number. Only a man is considered for jobs marked 'm' and women do not even apply for them. Nor do men apply for or get considered for jobs marked 'w'. In the rules of the model reported in this paper, we have maintained rigid segregation, but this set-up could easily be altered to allow persons from both groups to vie (perhaps with differing chances of success) for some of the job vacancies, if empirical estimates of the extent of the phenomenon could be developed.

In this model the number of jobs is not directly affected by any behaviour of the workers or jobseekers.[2] In particular, they cannot (or do not) cause an increase in the number of jobs by offering to work for lower wages. In this context, it makes sense to raise 'Keynesian' questions concerning demand shortages. We may characterise the supply-demand balance in the labour market overall or for any segment by defining[3]

demand deficiency rate =

$$\frac{(\text{employed} + \text{unemployed}) - (\text{filled jobs} + \text{vacancies})}{\text{employed} + \text{unemployed}} \times 100$$

[1] In the computer, a circle represents a memory space, the number in the circle represents the numerical value stored in that memory space, and the number below the circle is part of its 'address' in the computer memory.

[2] For a labour market simulation in which applicants' wage requirements do affect the number of jobs see Donald Nichols, 'The Equilibrium Level of Unemployment: A Simulation', in *Journal of Economic Theory*.

[3] This would make the Beveridge definition of full employment (vacancies equals unemployment) consistent with a demand deficiency rate of zero.

Using this definition, Figure 12.1 (which is intended to be merely illustrative) shows a 14.3 per cent and a 20.0 per cent demand deficiency rate for men and women respectively, and 16.7 per cent rate for the labour market overall. The corresponding unemployment rates are 28.6 per cent, 40.0 per cent and 33.3 per cent. The unemployment rate differs from the demand deficiency rate by the vacancy rate defined as vacancies/employed + unemployed. It is the characteristics of the dynamic simulation process which determine vacancy rate associated with given values of the demand deficiency and separation rates, and thus the unemployment rate.

The simulation runs by going through a three-step process for each working day:

Step 1. The hiring process occurs. Those involved are employers with job vacancies, all unemployed workers, and those employed workers who have on this or previous days made the decision to change jobs. For each job vacancy, 'interviews' are held. Workers of the appropriate race/sex groups are chosen at random to come to an interview. The probability that a worker would be willing to accept a job offer is taken to be an increasing function of the amount of time he or she has been searching.[1] The probability that an employer is willing to offer a job slot to a worker is taken to be an increasing function of the time the job has been vacant and of the worker's 'employ-ability grade'.[2] Random numbers are drawn to determine whether the job offer is made, and whether it is accepted. If the accession occurs, appropriate changes are made in the worker's status variable and in the job's status. The number of interviews allowed for each vacant job slot is a fraction of the number of searching workers. If, after the maximum number of interviews has occurred, a job is still unfilled, it remains vacant and is involved in the search process the following day.

Step 2. Separations from employment occur. For each race/sex group employed workers are chosen at random to leave their jobs, in accordance with the frequencies of columns 1 and 2 of Table 12.1. Each such event creates a vacancy which will be filled on some subsequent day.

Step 3. Some unemployed persons leave the labour force. Unemployed workers of each race/sex are chosen at random in accordance with the frequencies in column 4 of Table 12.1. Each of those who leave in this step is replaced by a new entrant. The net effect is to replace someone who has been

---

[1] Probability of a worker's acceptance $= 1 - A(1)^D$, where $A(1)$ is a parameter and D is the number of days the worker has been searching.

[2] Probability of employer's making an offer =

$$1 - A(2)^{D + A(3) \text{ (worker's employability grade)}}$$

where $A(2)$ and $A(3)$ are parameters, and D is the number of days the job has been vacant. Employability grades were assigned to have the same variance as the distribution of average durations reported by age and sex in the fall of 1972.

searching for a job for some time by someone who has just started his search, and is therefore less likely to accept a job offer in the next few days. A low rate of job acceptance leads to a high vacancy rate and a higher rate of unemployment for a given demand deficiency rate.

The model was run with differing sets of parameter values to produce simulated values for average unemployment rates and unemployment durations (without regard to race/sex) for the period 1969–73 which were then compared with US data. That set of parameter values which minimised the sum of squares of errors of simulation was chosen. For that period monthly vacancy data were available and were used to deduce the overall demand deficiency rate on a monthly basis.[1]

Using these parameter values, under the assumption that they hold within each race/sex segment of the labour market, and assuming perfect segmentation by race/sex groups, the model was run numerous times, each run simulating the period of a year. In each run a different value for the demand deficiency rates in the segments was assumed. The results are given in Figure 12.2, which shows the locus of simulated unemployment rates for each race/sex group when different values of the demand deficiency rates are assumed.

The difference between the unemployment rate of a group and the demand deficiency rate it experiences (measured in Figure 12.2 from the 45° line) can be taken to be equal to 'frictional unemployment' for that group, which is equal to the number of vacancies for that group. For each group, frictional unemployment increases in absolute amount as the demand deficiency rate decreases (moves to the right in Figure 12.2). The reason for this lies in the assumption (due to Holt[2]) embodied in the simulation that the likelihood of a worker accepting a particular job varies positively with the time he or she has been unemployed. At high demand deficiency rates, there are many unemployed workers who have already had long spells of unemployment, and who will accept the first job offered. Thus the probability that a particular job will continue vacant is reduced in such circumstances.

I have marked in Figure 12.2 the position for the year 1976 of each race/ sex group implied by its unemployment rate, assuming perfect segmentation, and assuming that the simulation set-up and parameters reflect a reasonable approximation to the behaviour of workers and employers. These results would indicate that about half of the difference in unemployment rates between white women and white men in 1976 was due to the difference in

[1] The parameter values used were $A(1) = A(2) = 0.95$, $A(3) = 0.31$. Parameter $A(4)$, which was the maximum proportion of all searching workers who may be interviewed for a vacancy in a single day was set at 0.09. With these parameters, an R^2 of 0.928 for simulated versus actual unemployment rates, and of 0.588 for simulated versus actual durations was achieved. For details, see Bergmann, *op. cit.*

[2] Charles C. Holt, 'Job Search, Phillips' Wage Relation and Union Influence: Theory and Evidence' in E. S. Phelps *et al.*, *Microeconomic Foundations of Employment and Inflation Theory*, (W. W. Norton & Co., New York, 1970).

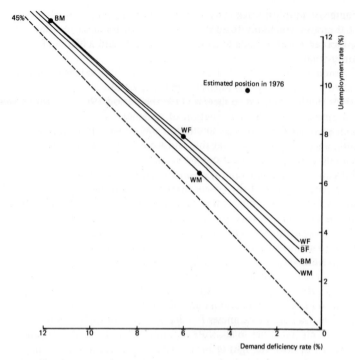

Fig. 12.2   Estimated relation between unemployment rates and demand
            deficiency rates, by race/sex group on the assumption of perfect
            segmentation

demand deficiency rates for the two groups, with the rest being due to the
higher rate of separation from employment of white women. For blacks of
both sexes a very high proportion of the excess in their unemployment rates
over the white male rate would appear, on these assumptions, to be due to a
shortage of jobs in the segment of the labour market to which they are
confined.

The ranking of race/sex groups with respect to deduced demand deficiency
rate does not match the ranking of groups by average wage. The median
income of full-time year-round workers in 1975 was $13,459 for white men,
$9848 for black men, $7737 for white women and $7392 for black women.
The advantage of black men over white women in terms of wage rates is even
more pronounced after correction for differences in education.[1] What this
means is that either a theory of wage differentials which relies exclusively on

[1]   See Blinder, *op. cit.*

the degree of supply-demand imbalance cannot be empirically supported, or that the model which produced the estimates of supply-demand imbalance is lacking in certain essential elements of the true situation. Both of these are probably true.

III SOME CONCLUSIONS

If we accept as a fact that there is considerable (if not absolute) segmentation of the labour market with respect to race and sex, and that the degree of supply-demand imbalance varies from one segment to the other, then breaking down discriminatory barriers to movement into certain occupations is an obvious way to move toward more equality in unemployment rates among race/sex groups. If present differences in separation rates were to persist, full equalisation of unemployment rates would not be possible, but the differences could be far less pronounced than they now are. It should be noted that for substantial equalisation of group unemployment rates we do not need to assume that more than a small proportion of women and blacks would be competent and willing to do some of the jobs that are now done by white men.

It is frequently asserted, even by representatives of blacks and women, that progress towards the breakdown of occupational segregation cannot be expected under current conditions of slack in the labour market because 'the jobs just aren't there'. The sizeable flows out of employment by white males documented in the gross flow data for 1976 imply that large numbers of new hires in jobs in the 'white male territory' occur even in years of high unemployment rates. While a plentiful supply of white males may well reduce the motivation of employers to try to place workers of other groups in jobs previously reserved for white males, employers are not failing to do so for lack of job openings. Nor should it be imagined that huge differences in required skills within the territories are the inhibiting factor in many cases. In the US, blacks are well represented in intracity trucking but grossly under-represented in intercity trucking; women frequently drive school buses but rarely drive public transit vehicles, and virtually no restaurant food is cooked by women.

While a move towards equalisation of group unemployment rates would be desirable for ethical and prudential reasons, the Keynesian assumptions we have made here preclude our making any claim that such a move would have the direct effect of reducing average unemployment rates. The best that might be said is that a reduction in the dispersion of supply-demand imbalances among occupations might be expected to relieve the inflation pressure associated with any average unemployment rate. This in turn might generate a policy response which would be more stimulative than it might otherwise be.

Discussion of Professor Bergmann's Paper

M. Salais introduced the paper. He said that differential unemployment rates, resulting from discrimination by employers against certain categories of labour, were nowadays very common. There seemed, indeed, to be a danger that at a time of high and rising unemployment, discrimination might increase to the point where certain categories of labour were excluded from employment altogether, or at least from good jobs. In her very interesting paper, Professor Bergmann tried to evaluate the intensity of job discrimination, by sex and race, in the USA. She suggested that higher unemployment rates among women and blacks were principally due to a shortage of jobs offered to them by employers, because this deficiency did not appear to be imputable to inadequate skills of the workers concerned or to excessive wage demands on their part.

M. Salais raised a number of points for discussion, in the order in which they occurred in the paper:

(1) How were we to define and measure discrimination, and what were its relations with labour market segmentation?
(2) The place of Mrs Bergmann's model in current flow-stock models of the labour market.
(3) Assumptions regarding the hiring process.
(4) A few remarks on frictional unemployment.

(1) *Discrimination and segmentation*

In what circumstances was it right to assume that employers discriminated against certain workers in filling job vacancies? In trying to answer this question we had to follow a number of rules. We had to consider similar jobs within a given class of work. Equally, the workers' productivity and the level of their education training and skills, must be similar. Differential unemployment rates must persist regardless of the phase of the business cycle and of the overall level of unemployment. In these circumstances, discrimination must be suspected if unemployment rates were regularly higher among certain workers. Even then, we must try to identify their cause. For example there were: (a) the behaviour of individuals, their mobility, their refusal of certain jobs or the intensity of their job-seeking. We must bear in mind that these factors were not independent of the level of job vacancies; e.g. an unemployed worker might be discouraged from further search by his failure to find a job. (b) the behaviour of employers in offering jobs and hiring workers in so far as employers' choice of personnel might be governed by criteria other than, or additional to, those imposed by rational economic calculation. The chief of these was expected productivity in relation to wage cost. Only such behaviour could be regarded as discriminatory. These other criteria might be: sex, race, age, a more or less explicit assessment that the worker would fit into the enterprise, and so on.

In this sense, discrimination seemed to M. Salais a more limited phenomenon than that connected with segmentation, although it certainly formed part of it. The analysis of segmentation, at least in terms of the far-reaching implications of segmentation theory, required consideration of the following factors:

(i) the structure of jobs, especially with respect to workers' qualifications, channels of mobility and the internal market organisation of enterprises;
(ii) the distribution of employed workers by training, skills and chance of upgrading or access to other jobs;
(iii) the connection between the structure of jobs and that of the employed work force, together with the mechanism of this connection.

This meant that we had to take account of sociological, institutional, and even historical factors. Be that as it may, Professor Bergmann looked for evidence of discrimination in the functioning of the labour market, with the help of a simulation model previously estimated on past data.

(2) *The place of the model among current flow-stock models*

M. Salais felt it would be useful to recall a few general features of flow-stock models, since this might lead us to a better understanding of Mrs Bergmann's simulation model. He was indebted to Professor Holt[1] for the main points he wished to make, and indeed for the notation, which was as follows:

U = stock of unemployed

V = stock of job vacancies

F = flow of hires

P_{oa} = offer-acceptance probability

T_s = mean search time

L = size of labour force

E = number of employed workers

$u = \dfrac{U}{L}$ = unemployment rate

[1] Especially, among his numerous interesting contributions, his paper on 'The Phillips Curve and Inflation and Unemployment' in E. S. Phelps *et al.*, *Micro-economic Foundations of Employment and Inflation Theory* (New York, 1970)

$$v = \frac{V}{E} = \text{vacancy rate}$$

$$f = \frac{F}{E} = \text{turnover rate}$$

T_u = unemployment duration

$$D = u - \frac{E}{L} v = \text{demand deficiency rate}$$

Given that, at least in the simplest case, the number of possible interviews per time unit was UV/T_s, the flow of hires per time unit was

$$F = \frac{UV}{T_s} P_{oa} \tag{1}$$

and therefore

$$u = \frac{1}{L} \cdot \frac{f}{v} \cdot \frac{T_s}{P_{oa}} \tag{2}$$

At two different moments of time, or as between two segments of the labour market, the difference in unemployment rates depended upon:

- (i) the size of the labour force, a larger labour force giving rise to returns to scale, all other things being equal:
- (ii) the turnover rate f. This was on the assumption of a steady state, the rate of job entry by hiring equalling the rate of job exit by resignation, dismissal, movement to non-employment, etc. All other things being equal, a higher turnover rate implied a higher unemployment rate;
- (iii) the vacancy rate v, a higher vacancy rate implying a lower unemployment rate;
- (iv) the mean search time T_s, that was, the average time needed for any worker to find a vacancy and obtain an interview. This was an indicator of the intensity of the search and of the degree of information on the part both of workers and employers;
- (v) the probability P_{oa} of a job being offered by an employer and accepted by an unemployed person.

This was a complex collection of determinants, interacting and acting simultaneously. The simulation model constructed by Professor Bergmann was obtained by (a) controlling the influence of E, f and v in the estimation, by fitting them to observed values for the period 1969–73; and (b) formulating certain hypotheses regarding the rules governing behaviour in the hiring process (T_s, P_{oa}). Professor Bergmann then looked, by means of simulation of the past, for those parameter values which yielded the closest approximation to the unemployment rates, and the average periods of unemployment, observed in the past.

It could easily be seen from equation (2) that the demand deficiency rate D could be rewritten in the form:

$$D = u - \frac{u_0^2}{u} \tag{3}$$

where $u_0 = \sqrt{(E/L^2)} \, f \, (T_s/P_{oa})$ was 'frictional' unemployment corresponding to D = 0. There one had a labour market where there was equilibrium between demand and supply. This 'frictional' unemployment depended only upon the turnover rate and hiring behaviour. He would presently have a little more to say about this concept of frictional unemployment.

It followed that u could be expressed as an increasing function of D, asymptotic to the second bisector in a design (u, D).

Using the model to simulate situations corresponding to various values of D, Professor Bergmann could draw the curves implied by (3) for different race/sex segments of the labour market. These curves were reproduced in her paper, and we could note that at any given moment the difference in the unemployment rates of two market segments was made up of two component deviations. One was due to the rates of frictional unemployment at a given D, and the other to differences in demand deficiency rates.

The second deviation was generally the larger, and this entitled us to conclude that discrimination derived largely from a deficiency of job offers to members of the group being discriminated against.

The same procedure could be followed, symmetrically, for average unemployment duration. In a steady state, this could be written:

$$T_u = \frac{U}{F} = \frac{1}{E} \cdot \frac{1}{v} \cdot \frac{T_s}{P_{oa}} \tag{4}$$

In the light of (4), deviations in unemployment durations appeared to be more direct indicators of the deficiency of job offers.

Similarly, the analysis of discrimination in terms of the advantage ratios of the queueing theory in Professor Bergmann's paper was actually very close to an analysis in terms of unemployment duration. Indeed, the advantage ratios were exactly inverse to the ratio between the unemployment durations of the groups considered, provided we took what M. Salais saw as the very necessary precaution of taking into account the balance of the flows between employment and non-employment. This was because only a surplus of exits over entries could be considered as leading to vacancies for the unemployed. Otherwise, we were bound to overestimate the employability of the unemployed by omitting the competition they encountered from direct entrants from non-employment. Table 12.1 showed no data by which the correction could be made, but if it were made, the resulting distribution of sex/race advantage ratios would probably be much closer to those in the Bergmann model.

(3) *Assumptions regarding the hiring process*

This was the crucial point of the simulation. Three probabilities might usefully be discussed:

   (i) the probability, P_1, of getting an interview in any unit of time; this was assumed to be constant;

  (ii) the probability, P_2, of an employer offering a job to a job-seeker; this was assumed to be an increasing function of the time the job had been vacant, and also of the worker's 'employability grade';

 (iii) the probability, P_3, of a job-seeker accepting this offer; this was assumed to be an increasing function of the time the worker had been looking for a job.

Obviously, P_1 had to do with T_s, and P_2 and P_3 with P_{oa}.

M. Salais now had a question. Empirical studies showed that the probability of finding a job diminished with the length of time a worker had already been unemployed. This appeared quite clearly in French data, as he had had occasion to note when examining figures from the French labour force survey. He wondered whether this was equally true of data from other countries? Certainly, it seemed reasonable to think that after a long search a worker would lower his sights and might be willing to accept less pay or a lower grade job. Such an attitude would increase his chances if it brought him closer to what the market had to offer. But other, stronger elements worked in the opposite direction:

  (i) there was a personal element, in that discouragement after a long search caused the worker to look less actively for a job. This would mean that P_1, the probability of being offered a job, was a decreasing function of search time;

 (ii) elements inherent in the hiring process:

    (a) there was the employer's unwillingness to take on someone who had been unemployed for a long time and, for this reason, was assumed *a priori* to be not very good. The duration of unemployment might be an additional reason for discrimination;

    (b) job offers might be made more quickly, within a given category of workers, to the individuals best suited to the employer's specifications. In the hiring process, job-seekers would be, as it were, creamed off, so that the first to be hired would be those best suited to the employer's requirements, especially those linked with qualitative discrimination. The others would find it much more difficult to obtain a job offer.

Professor Holt pointed out that Professor Bergmann's model could be used to look at the 'sorting process'. Published statistics were not for homogeneous groups. Some people found jobs quickly, others did not. So the mix in the unemployment 'stock' was hard to track and her simulation model could do so.

Professor Holt wanted to comment about the advantage ratio in equation (2). Professor Bergmann saw the worker as having 'tickets' for getting a job and looked at the probability of this happening. In the equation she compared the probabilities of the ith and the jth groups getting jobs and this led to a complicated expression. One could get the probability directly by taking, say, the number of unemployed in a group multiplied by the probability of getting a job derived from the flow of unemployed into employment. This must equal the rate of turnover multiplied by the employment stock. So one could obtain the probability of receiving a working 'ticket'. This was equal to the turnover flow divided by the number of unemployed.

M. Salais wondered whether these elements were correctly represented in the simulation. If due account were taken of the negative influence of search time on the probabilities P_1, P_2, P_3, might we not get a better adjustment, especially with respect to mean unemployment durations?

Similar observations could be made about the influence of the time a job had been vacant. Surely, if that time had been long, the employer might in turn be expected to feel discouraged, and this might lead him to reorganise the assignments of workers within the enterprise and/or to alter his demand for labour on the outside market. Other things being equal, workers could surely be expected to accept the best job offers first, leaving the remaining vacancies very hard to fill.

Finally, it seemed reasonable to assume that an increase in the number of unemployed workers would diminish the chance of each of them to obtain an interview.

In the light of all this, he would stress the need for direct surveys and empirical studies of employers' job-offer behaviour and hiring practices, of choice criteria and of methods of selecting workers.

(4) 'Frictional' unemployment

M. Salais was tempted to add to Professor Bergmann's conclusions, and this was why he put the word 'frictional' in quotation marks. Certain aspects of turnover, and of entry and exit behaviour in employment, had to do with discrimination. For example, dismissal practices were selective, in that certain categories – the least skilled, the young, women, the last to have been taken on – were the first to be made redundant. The same was probably true for assignments to unstable jobs.

It followed that changes in frictional unemployment might well also reflect discriminatory practices. They did not look large so far for the four groups mentioned, but might be larger for more disaggregated groups, especially

groups disaggregated by age. The whole question of workers' differential
vulnerability to unemployment might usefully be reconsidered from this
point of view.

Finally, the concept of frictional unemployment might conceal elements
of structural unemployment, such as higher turnover due to rapid changes in
employment structure by branches, regions or skills. They might lead to a
consequent increase in unemployment. M. Salais said that he had found all
these elements important in explaining the growth of unemployment in
France, even before the 1973–74 recession.

In conclusion, he wanted to say how useful simulation models were, even
though they might be unwieldy. They made it possible to do without the
simplifying hypotheses that must be made in dealing with a steady state,
independent of time. They also made it possible – or should do so – to test
the effects of certain structural transformations, e.g. slower growth of
employment, or of certain structural employment policies, e.g. how to break
down job barriers resulting from discrimination.

Professor Bergmann wanted to add a point on the fact that there was a
lower probability that employers would offer a job the longer anyone had
been unemployed. Her model had been fitted to US time series both for
unemployment and its duration. There was no series for completed spells of
unemployment but only for the time the person had been so far unemployed.
The average of completed unemployment durations might be shorter than the
average for incomplete ones if a number of people remained unemployed for
very long periods. The parameters of the model had been fitted in order to
track durations. So it had to allow some employees to have a lower probability
of employment for certain reasons. There were other stigmas as well as colour
and sex: for example, the fact that one had been employed in agriculture. She
thought further data were needed to reach correct conclusions.

Professor Henin pointed out that Professor Bergmann claimed that the
model perhaps raised Keynesian questions. It was surely desirable to distinguish
between voluntary leavers and those who were dismissed and he thought it
was a disadvantage of the model that it did not make this distinction.

On the notion of the rate of demand deficiency, he did not think Professor
Bergmann's method was completely justified. It could be seen as using excess
demand as the control variable. One needed such a variable but he wondered
whether the definition in the paper was the best one.

Professor Bergmann therefore took this as an exogenous variable. She
estimated the volume of demand for employment because she did not know
how many 'discouraged workers' there were. She assumed that jobs were more
likely to be filled by an employer the longer a candidate had been unemployed.
It might be wiser to use the rate of deficiency of demand adjusted for the
discouraged unemployed, which might be a better control variable.

In Table 12.2, where Professor Bergmann obtained an advantage ratio, she
found that white females, despite a higher unemployment rate, had an

advantage rate of 1.51, greater than that for men. This seemed to counter the argument on sex discrimination. However, in Table 12.1 the total flow of women from unemployment was higher, indicating a relatively high turnover. Women had more frequent job changes and went through the labour market more often. This was why unemployment for women was higher than for men.

Further analysis of this showed that women had a weak attachment to the labour market. Professional or single women, or heads of households, had lower turnover rates, similar to those of men. So perhaps there was a high overall unemployment rate for women because they were in a segment of the market where there were few attractive jobs and hence they were not well attached. A breaking of barriers in the labour market to give greater opportunity to women might lead to a fall in the turnover rate.

Dr Kaufman wanted to add that statistics showed that lay-offs had recently been very important. A job was often 'reserved' for a worker. How would the modelling of this affect Professor Bergmann's results?

Professor Parkin pointed out that there was a well-known alternative story for the USA. Broadly this was that Professor Bergmann's story was correct but that wages could not adjust because of minimum wage laws. As a result blacks and women were seen as low in productivity and therefore most likely to be unemployed. He wondered whether the evidence could or could not reject this. And was it implicit in what Professor Bergmann was doing in her analysis?

Professor Bergmann commented on the possibility that discrimination affected turnover. The evidence was strong and the story was told in the literature about dual labour markets where it was emphasised that the kind of job for the disadvantaged was that where long experience was not rewarded and where there was sometimes a very personal element of supervision in the job. The worker would leave, but with a high rate of turnover would get another job quickly. So discrimination was connected with turnover.

On distinguishing between voluntary leavers and those who were dismissed, one could reserve a different part of the computer's memory and make such analyses. She had done it in some of her models with the idea that those who were free to leave did so without a spell of unemployment. Turnover indicated the number of quitters, so that a group with more turnover would see fewer unemployed.

Professor Bergmann said she had a larger model covering the generation of the demand for labour which did distinguish the two groups. If behaviour was different, that too could be included.

Dr Kaufman's paper suggested that both the worker and the job disappeared from the search process but that tended to lengthen the duration of unemployment.

To Professor Henin she would say that the rate of demand deficiency which related to the labour force and so to 'job slots' was endogenous. She had assumed it away by supposing that the labour force was of constant size. As far as possible, the definition of the labour force should include those who would like to be back in it. This was a defect of many analyses.

On flow analysis and simulation, she pointed out that queueing theory assumed no segmentation. Simulation assumed complete segmentation. The reality was between the two. Simulation could deal with this, but would require data on the degree of segmentation. Here she was assuming no segmentation so that her model was not complete. Professor Bergmann said she welcomed the reminder that women found jobs because other women left the labour market. This was true of labour market segmentation. Women leaving jobs meant other women finding jobs. With segmentation of the labour market one had the warning that all acts of separation led to extra unemployment. The individual who became unemployed would almost at once be replaced. The extent of separation hinged on the length of time the worker was unemployed and the process for filling vacancies. Vacancy data had been discontinued in USA because the figures were so small. But this was an interesting question. The amount of unemployment due to friction was perhaps a very small part of the total, even with high, and perhaps overstated, turnover rates.

Mr Kaser wanted to raise a small point. Early in the paper it was pointed out that 85 per cent of economists in the USSR were women. He thought it likely, and Professor Khachaturov agreed, that many of these were in economic sections of factories, in planning, accounting etc. In the USA, where there were many women among professional economists, the percentage was nowhere near 85 per cent.

Professor Södersten reported a Swedish study which suggested that unemployment duration was longer in Sweden, even though unemployment rates were low. Also, when unemployment rose in 1969–72 during the recession, turnover was little affected but duration was roughly doubled. Women over 45 had the highest unemployment rates of all. This seemed contrary to the American findings. So Swedish economists had invented the 'captive worker' effect. It had been concluded that Swedish workers dared not leave their jobs for fear of unemployment. Perhaps if one were in a more homogeneous labour market than Sweden, things would turn out differently. He wondered how far turnover in the USA was linked to tightness in the labour market.

Professor Modigliani thought the relationship between the voluntary quitters and being fired was interesting, not least because it had implications for the shape of the Phillips curve. The implication was that the turnover rate did not change much during the cycle. One could call this Holt's Law because, as a first approximation, it said that turnover was independent of aggregate activity and unemployment. If, with a tighter labour market, fewer were fired but more quitted, turnover would be unchanged.

Professor Modigliani thought this was not true, and that one would find for the USA as he had found for Italy in a forthcoming paper, that on the whole the turnover rate did increase as unemployment fell and vacancies increased because quitters rose faster than the decline of those who were fired. He wondered whether Professor Bergmann had evidence that most who quitted had jobs already lined up. If not, there was the implication that the Beveridge curve relating unemployment to vacancies (and hence also the Phillips curve) might not be monotonically decreasing. Indeed, an increase in jobs and vacancies beyond some point might increase quits, and hence turnover, to the point of producing a rise rather than a fall in unemployment.

Sir Austin Robinson wondered whether Professor Bergmann used only national figures. One might get useful results from regional analysis, for example, comparing the East coast and the West coast of the USA. In the UK, he would be frightened of conclusions from national figures because there were regional differences in the labour mix. Structural unemployment was unevenly distributed and he wondered what the comparable position in the USA would be.

Professor Malinvaud explained that, as an econometrician, when he used simulation models he thought the results often were very dependent on the estimation of the parameters. He would then want to know how far the results were sensitive to the parameters and how these were precisely estimated. The paper was rather brief on this, simply saying that different values of parameters had been used.

Professor Holt said it was a unique characteristic of the model that it looked at industries. Since the model was a somewhat 'realistic' micro-economic model, it could be used to draw on diverse bodies of data and to fit them together. He wondered why Professor Bergmann had used optimal parameters only to get a model which dealt with *aggregate* data, particularly since this was a model with firms as well as industries. Did she plan to introduce the dynamics of vacancies and wages in the inflationary process? Such a model would be valuable.

M. Salais said that in France there had been studies of the evolution of unemployment. One obtained a result similar to that discussed by Professor Modigliani, i.e. an increase of involuntary unemployment.

Turnover also grew over a long period, of ten or fifteen years. This was hard to explain but he thought that the recent growth in unemployment had had little effect on turnover, though the duration of unemployment had increased.

On queueing theory, he would say that Table 12.2 was interesting. The average unemployment rates were higher for women than for men, but it was not the same for advantage ratios. He thought that it would be necessary to modify the computation of advantage ratios by taking into account all the flows between employment, unemployment and those not in labour force and by considering as new vacant jobs for unemployed only the balance between flows 'employment' to 'not being in labour force' and the reverse flows (direct entries from those not in labour force).

Professor Bergmann replied to Professor Parkin that it was correct that one could use her model to explain demand deficiency, and she had not in the paper looked at why it existed. Perhaps the problem could be alleviated by a reduction in wage rates, but her own view was that this was a social matter.

Some occupations were reserved for certain groups, and it was even harder to manipulate job assignments in terms of race and sex than to reduce wage rates.

To Professor Modigliani she said there was evidence that most quitters had jobs ready for them. As for the USSR, and Mr Kaser, she had suspected as much!

On durations, some use had been made of these as indicators of the bad situation faced by some groups. She took the view that we were losing resources here, and low duration of unemployment was often made up by higher frequency.

To Sir Austin Robinson she said that she had not done regional studies. Regional data for the USA were very bad and one needed a great deal of information for her kind of model to work realistically.

Professor Bergman agreed with Professor Malinvaud that she needed help from econometricians. The simulation model had advantages in realism and helped policy-makers and she did not like simply adding terms to equations. She tried to use what econometricians had to say, but they had told her what the characteristics of parameters should be rather than how to estimate them. She had had to 'hunt and pick' at the computer terminal. What was needed now was to find a methodology that was reproducible. She also needed a reduction of discretion so that she could not be accused of putting in parameters to prove her point. However, search techniques for parameters were not easy because similar techniques depended on the evaluation of analytic functions. The alternative was to run through the simulation a thousand times.

Professor Holt doubted whether macroeconomic data would help here. He knew of none that would help. Money to do such surveys would be valuable because one could then find out how those looking for jobs, and those seeking to employ the unemployed, actually behaved. This would be 'purer' and more 'scientific'. As for the sensitivity of the parameters, a change affected the unemployment rate little, but the distribution of durations very much. As a result, much of the search must be for parameters giving a good fit for the distribution of durations.

13 New Attitudes to Work

B Södersten
UNIVERSITY OF LUND, SWEDEN

INTRODUCTION

Economists have always had an ambiguous attitude toward work. The mainstream of economic theory has viewed work as sacrifice. Man worked in order to produce so that he could consume. According to neo-classical theory, a person or a household exchanged work for income, and leisure could be substituted for income. This assumed motivation for work gave rise to the well-known problem of the shape of the supply curve for labour.

Another quite different view of work has been present among economists ever since the origin of the discipline, even among those working in the classical and neo-classical tradition. Often this view has taken the form of 'asides', of an argument that has been presented in more essayistic or philosophical form, for instance by Knight (Knight, 1936, pp. 62 et seq). This view may be roughly summed up by the statement that man does not work in order to consume, but that work is an end in itself and that man consumes so that he may have a reason to produce.

The labour market has undergone important changes in most western countries since the Second World War. One of these has been the influx of women into the labour market and the sharp increase in the rate of labour force participation on the part of women that has occurred in the last two decades. It is argued here that the increase in the female rate of labour force participation may partly be explained in purely economic terms, but that new or changing attitudes should also be taken into account in order to obtain a more comprehensive explanation of this new phenomenon. Another different aspect of labour market behaviour concerns the new emphasis on the quality of working life, and the struggle for influence and self-determination on the part of the employees, that have been observed in recent years. Again it seems that new attitudes toward work are emerging which may have important implications for future forms of economic organisation.

The present paper consists of two parts. The first part analyses, in sections I to III, the growing preference for work outside the home, within the market economy, that women have manifested in the last decade or so. It is argued here that this phenomenon can partially be explained by the modern theory of the household, but that new attitudes toward work also account for a substantial part of this change. When discussing the increase in the female rate of labour force participation that has occurred, one should also take into account other repercussions of a general equilibrium nature, such as its effects on nativity. In this first part of the paper a specific aspect of discrimination connected with female labour force attachment is also dealt with. The second part of the paper discusses, in section IV to the end, changing attitudes toward work and their effects on forms of economic organisation.

In several countries a process of change toward an increased influence on the part of the employees is under way. The form in which economic life is organised will influence attitudes towards work, and changing attitudes will themselves be an important factor influencing subsequent forms of economic organisation.

I NEW ATTITUDES TOWARDS WORK AND LABOUR FORCE PARTICIPATION

One of the outstanding features of economic development in most western countries over the last two decades has been the increase in female labour force participation. Sweden is certainly a case in point here, but the same general phenomenon seems to apply to most western countries. Table 13.1 provides figures on labour force participation in Sweden since 1920.

TABLE 13.1 LABOUR FORCE PARTICIPATION RATE (NUMBER OF PROFESSIONALLY EMPLOYED AS A PERCENTAGE OF TOTAL (MALE OR FEMALE) POPULATION OVER 15 YEARS OF AGE)

Year	Men	Women
1920	90.2	27.1
1930	88.7	30.7
1940	87.5	29.3
1950	85.8	29.5
1960	79.9	32.0
1965	76.0	35.0
1970	73.2	38.0
1975	76.2	50.2

SOURCE Silenstam, P., Arbetskraftsutbudets utveckling i Sverige 1870–1965; C. Jonung, Kvinnorna i Svensk ekonomi; Arbetsmarknadsstatistisk arsbok 1974 o 1976

The rate of labour force participation among men has fallen somewhat, and currently measures roughly 75 per cent. The increase in the participation rate of the female labour force has, on the contrary, been very substantial. It has increased as a proportion of total female population in the relevant age groups by over 50 per cent in a matter of 15 years, from 32 per cent in 1960 to 50 per cent in 1975.

The increase in the rate of labour force participation on the part of women during the 60s and 70s is historically unique. The pattern varies somewhat among western countries, but the basic trend seems to be the same. This increase is all the more striking as the rate of female labour force participation had only shown a slight increase during the forty years from the end of the First World War to the end of the 1950s. The increased willingness among women to work outside the home is an important economic phenomenon that needs to be explained. It seems that changing attitudes toward work must be invoked as an important part of the explanation of this dramatic increase in the willingness on the part of women to work in the market economy witnessed during the last two decades. Traditional labour market analysis can hardly provide a satisfactory explanation for the increase in the female labour force participation. The post-war era has witnessed a rapid increase in real incomes. Cross-sectional empirical studies show that labour force participation rates of married women decline with increased incomes of husbands. If anything, this would seem to point to an increase in the demand for leisure as real incomes rise. Substitution effects, in the form of an increase in the relative price of household services (for instance), may be at work that may counteract the effects of an increase in real incomes. Still, it is hard to find any implications of traditional neo-classical theory that would lead us to expect the rapid and sustained increase in female labour force participation that we have witnessed during the last twenty years.

A better explanation may be constructed with the help of the modern theoretical developments within the framework of neo-classical theory that have facetiously been referred to as 'the new home economics' (Nerlove 1974). According to this new (Chicago-inspired) theory it is not the individual but the household that is the decision-making unit. What distinguishes the new theory from the traditional is that time enters into the model in an explicit and critical fashion (Becker, 1965). The technology of the household production function is described by a function in which time and commodities bought in the market appear as inputs. These inputs are then used within the household to produce 'utility' or the goods and services which lead to satisfaction.

This theory has several interesting implications which may help to explain developments in the labour market over the last two decades. As economic development advances the value of time increases. This increase in value is also caused by the fact that the amount of time available to a household cannot be increased, while material inputs can. Another factor making for an increase in the value per unit of human time is the investment in human capital, which has taken place over the last decades.

The new home economics seems to take it for granted that the man (or men) in the household will specialise in market-related activities. This can partly be attributed to biological factors and partly to the fact that the male usually has the higher income-earning capacity in the household. This can then explain why men exhibit higher rates of labour force participation than women.

The increase in the value of time may help to clarify why female labour force participation rates are increasing. With increased education and with higher real incomes the relative cost of time-consuming activities goes up. The incomes foregone by not engaging in market-related activities increase. Hence the household will substitute time-consuming household activities with goods bought in the market. This will lead to an increase in the rates of labour force participation on the part of women. This line of reasoning possesses a certain plausibility. It is, however, doubtful whether it can sufficiently explain more than a few aspects of the new labour market behaviour that we have observed in western countries during the last two decades.

For example, one of the reasons why people form households is that it is an accepted and convenient form for procreation and for raising children. It is true that the new home economics has something to say about the cost of raising children; we will shortly return to that topic in connection with a discussion of the falling rate of nativity that is concomitant with the rise in the female rate of labour force participation. But there are not only costs involved in having children; there are also benefits to be derived by the parents from having children. Here it seems that the modern theory of marriage and household behaviour (Becker, 1973, 1974) is very inadequate. In these matters it appears that attitudes come into play and that some down-to-earth reasoning about changing attitudes may provide as much illumination as the new home economics.

None the less there are also factors which should counterbalance the increase in the value of time that has led women to become more prone to work in the market place and less prone to work at home at time-consuming activities. One such 'distortion' is taxes. Taxes have increased sharply in all western countries during the post-war period. In Sweden, for instance, the portion of the GNP that goes to taxes, has increased from 20 per cent in 1950 to 50 per cent in 1975. There is a certain amount of variation according to size and kind of income that a household may have, but the taxable part of practically all incomes from work has grown dramatically during the last two decades.

A growing tax burden on households lowers the relative value of time spent in market-related activities as compared with domestic activities, since the latter are not subjected to taxation. This factor should therefore have a negative influence on the female labour force participation rate, since an increase in taxes should lead to a substitution of market-related activities by domestic, non-taxed activities.

Even though the modern theory that we have called the new home economics may successfully explain part of the increase in the female rate of labour force participation, it is doubtful whether it can offer more than a partial explanation. One reason is that the factors embodied in the theory should reasonably have been at work for a rather long period of time, while the increase in the female rate of labour force participation is a fairly recent phenomenon. It seems that other factors also have to be taken into account. Changing attitudes toward work are certainly one of these.

Men customarily specialise in market-related activities. This means that work outside the home will play a central role in their lives. Women, however, can also claim that work outside the home embraces a value of its own. Considerations of equality, independence and security can influence their decision to work outside the home.

Women become more equal to men if they, like men, can specialise in market-related activities. An independent source of income will probably increase the feeling of independence. Employment outside the home will allow for greater security: we may cite the case of the female professor who argued that tenure was more important for her security than marriage.

Preferences and attitudes are elusive concepts. Economic factors such as an increase in human capital formation and a rise in the value of time should lead to an increase in the female rate of labour force participation, even though other factors like higher taxation should have a countervailing effect. Still, new attitudes towards work, based on considerations like those described above, should also have exerted influence on participation rates. Basic factors such as general equilibrium considerations and processes of a cumulative nature will also have a strong bearing on women's labour market activity. It may not, in fact, be possible to distinguish between economic factors and changing attitudes.

Parents may harbour the attitude or preference that their daughter should marry and raise a family. Nevertheless they often want to give her a good education. The human capital, thus embodied in her, increases the value of her time. She may decide to substitute market-related activities for domestic activities. This will in turn influence her attitudes. She may avoid having children or limit the size of her family so as to increase her attachment to the labour force.

This may be viewed as an example of how economic factors will influence a woman's attitudes, and how changing attitudes in turn will affect her economic behaviour. Had the parents not invested in their daughter's education, her future attitudes would have been more in line with their own preferences, Furthermore, man is a social animal. Changing attitudes on the part of some persons will influence others. If some women in a neighbourhood begin working outside home, they may influence others. Social contacts for those women who specialise in domestic activities may be fewer, and their situation therefore less satisfactory. There may also be demonstration effects; women who work outside the home may exhibit an independence that will tempt other women in the neighbourhood to seek work outside home themselves.

In brief: changing economic conditions (increased formation of human

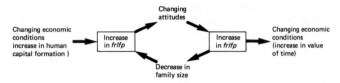

Fig. 13.1

capital, for instance,) may cause an increase in *frlfp* (female rate of labour force participation) which in turn gives rise to changing attitudes (increased evaluation of independence) which cause an increase in *frlfp*, leading to a decrease in family size with a subsequent increase in *frlfp* and so on.

The argument given above may be summarised with the help of Figure 13.1. A cumulative process, where economic conditions and changing attitudes interdependently strengthen and reinforce each other, may therefore be the most fruitful hypothesis for explaining the change in labour market behaviour that has been an important characteristic of the western economies in recent decades.

I shall now elaborate on the discussion of changing attitudes by considering two subtopics which are related to the increase in the female rate of labour force participation. The first concerns the fall in nativity that has characterised western economies in recent decades. The second has to do with the question of discrimination and labour force attachment.

II FEMALE LABOUR FORCE PARTICIPATION AND NATIVITY

The increase in the female labour force participation rate is interesting *per se*, but it also contains important implications in a general equilibrium setting. The most important of these concerns nativity. The increase in the female rate of participation in the labour force has been associated with a fall in nativity. The trend is clearly documented in the case of Sweden, as is shown in Table 13.2, and seems to hold true for most western countries.

The fall in nativity can partly be explained by the modern theory of marriage. There is, on the one hand, a positive correlation between family size and income. Most men are, for reasons that we need not consider here, completely specialised in market-related activities. An increase in male wage rates would therefore have a positive effect on family size and nativity due to income effects. An increase in the female wage rate will, however, have an opposite effect. An increase in female earnings will bring about a substitution effect, away from time-consuming activities like raising children and over to activities that require a larger number of inputs that can be bought in the market. It seems that the substitution effect caused by increased female wages has been the dominant factor determining the development of nativity.

According to the theory of marriage, education should not influence family

TABLE 13.2 NATIVITY

	Live births per 1000 of mean population	Net reproduction rates
1965	15.88	1.147
1966	15.80	1.121
1967	15.42	1.082
1968	14.29	0.992
1969	13.51	0.919
1970	13.70	0.924
1971	14.14	0.939
1972	13.82	0.916
1973	13.47	0.898
1974	13.46	0.899
1975	12.65	0.851
1976	11.96	0.806

SOURCE Statistisk årsbok 1977, p. 77.

size and nativity other than in an ambiguous fashion. Formation of male human capital should primarily have an income effect and lead to increased nativity. An increase in female human capital formation should have the opposite effect. It will increase the value of the time women dispose of and also increase the value of earnings foregone due to time-consuming domestic activities such as raising children. We would therefore expect higher levels of education among women to lead to the fall in nativity which actually has occurred during the last two decades. As the relative value of female time increases it will become relatively more and more costly to have children.

An important corollary of the line of argument pursued above concerns income distribution. The modern household will become increasingly dependent on two incomes, i.e. on the fact that both husband and wife work outside the home. The difference in pecuniary income between those households on the one hand in which the woman works in the market place and those on the other hand in which she engages in domestic activities will therefore increase with time. The opportunity cost in the form of earnings foregone will increase and the relative cost of raising children will increase with economic development and increasing female wages.

Again it is important, however, to view our problem in a cumulative perspective, and take general equilibrium considerations into account. An increase in female wages alone can hardly explain the fall in nativity which has been experienced during the recent decades. New attitudes are also at play. As women come to value market-related activities and independence more highly, their willingness to bear and care for children decreases. This, in turn, increases the demand for outside help in caring for children. The need for day-care facilities expands drastically. Such services are, however, very costly and the supply of them is highly restricted in most countries. The inter-relationships between family size, nativity and female labour force participation are important. A decrease in the size of families may be suggested as one of the explanations for the increase in the rate of female labour force participation. At the same time it is clear that a greater attachment to the labour force on the part of women will imply a negative influence on family size. It has been found that married women with a high degree of education participate more in the labour force and work longer hours than do married women with less education (Leibowitz, 1972). Some of the aspects of discrimination and attachment to the labour force are discussed below. It will be natural for a woman with a strong interest in work, career and independence to limit the size of her family so that she will not have to withdraw for too long or too frequently from the labour force. Changing attitudes toward work on the part of women which move in the direction of an increased preference for market-related activities will therefore have important repercussions on the rate of nativity and form part of the explanation for the fall in nativity that has occurred in western countries in recent years.

III PART-TIME WORK, LABOUR-FORCE ATTACHMENT AND DISCRIMINATION

We commented in the introduction that throughout the history of doctrine at least two diverging views on the nature of work have existed among economists. A partial explanation may be approached by first grouping work into two broad categories: one where work primarily consists of routine tasks, where no advancement is possible once the basic tasks have been mastered; one where the career ladder is an essential element and where continuous advancement is an integral part of the work history.

Needless to say, a division of work into two such broad categories is a gross oversimplification. Such a division, however, can be useful as a basis for clarifying some important points regarding new attitudes toward work.

The struggle for equality for women has opened the question of discrimin-ation. Different groups of women have varying attitudes toward work, just as they do in their views on discrimination. Differing views are logically related to which of the two broad groups mentioned above a given woman can be placed in. It is natural that women who aspire towards a career, often in competition with men, have a more militant view than their sisters who hold jobs where concern with a career is less critical. It should be observed that a 'natural' division of labour plays an important role in determining a person's attitudes towards work and views on discrimination.

It is well known that the division of labour with respect to sex is skewed in western countries, and that most women are clustered around a few occupations, such as services, retail trade, teaching and health care. Within these occupations they are concentrated in the lower levels of responsibility and pay. The majority of women who work are relegated to routine tasks of the kind in which possibilities for promotion are slim. These women may be strongly tied to the labour force, but a temporary leave of absence from the labour market will not negatively affect the future demand for their services or their career status in any major way. Women in this category are generally not discriminated against as individuals.

The women who strive for a career are in a very different position. For them a continuous attachment to the labour force is often absolutely essential. Any absence will have a very detrimental effect on their career possibilities. Hence the opportunity cost for bearing and raising children will be especially high in this group.

The distinction made above illuminates two interesting consequences. One concerns part-time work; the other a pertinent point regarding discrimination and social justice. Part-time work has increased sharply during the 1970s in several western countries. Sweden is a good case in point here. Views on part-time work are divided; some view it as a second-best solution, instead of unemployment; others as a good solution to the need for coping with family demands on the one hand, and the need for increased income and work experience on the other.

Just how large a proportion of part-time work is involuntary is difficult to say. In Sweden roughly 25 per cent of the labour force is occupied in part-time work. Of these, 7 per cent claimed that they would have liked to work more, had employment opportunities been available.

Part-time work or a reduced work week have become a pertinent topic of discussion in the 1970s. The motives behind the demands for shorter working hours are very different in different countries.

In Sweden, for instance, vociferous groups have argued in favour of a six-hour working day and a thirty-hour work week. In this field it has especially been groups of women, both women's sections within the established political parties and feminist groups, that have raised the demand for a six-hour working day. Their motives have primarily been egalitarian and family-oriented. They argue that if *all* employees work only six hours a day, both men and women will have time and energy left over to take part in political and social life outside the family. Thus, these demands for a six-hour working day have nothing to do with labour market conditions *per se*.

In some other western European countries the motives behind the demand for a shorter work week have been different and completely consequent on labour market conditions. The 1970s have witnessed an increase in the rate of unemployment both in Western Europe and in the United States. As employment opportunities have become more scarce and unemployment has taken on a chronic character, spreading employment by shortening the work week has become an interesting alternative in the political debate. So far, it has primarily been government representatives who have been promoting this argument, while representatives of the labour unions have taken a more hesitant attitude toward these proposals. If the unemployment rate is to remain as high in coming years as it has been in recent years, one may expect, however, that the demands for a shorter work week in order to solve the unemployment problem will become more insistent.

Attitudes towards discrimination will also critically depend on the nature of work. The majority of women, who are engaged in the type of work in which considerations of a career do not exist or are of secondary importance, are hardly being discriminated against in any meaningful sense of the word. It is especially the women in occupations in which a career ladder is fundamental who may rightfully claim that they are often the subjects of discrimination. The problems associated with discrimination become especially pertinent in connection with on-the-job training.

Women commonly have a large amount of general training behind them. In order to advance in their chosen professions, however, they also need specific on-the-job training. This type of training is typically provided by the firm. If the firm seeks to maximise its return on training costs, and if it is a risk averter, it may try to avoid taking women into its training programmes. This depends on a fact, well-known to it from experience, that women have a greater tendency than men to interrupt their working career and to drop out, at least temporarily, from the labour force. If this is the case, then women may, more often than men, turn out to be poor risks or 'lemons' (cf. Akerlof, 1966). It is then rational on the part of the individual firm to try to avoid recruiting women to its internal training programmes.

A specific woman may know, however, that her labour market performance will not be an 'average' one, and that she will not be a 'lemon'. She may have decided once and for all to stay in the labour force and to pursue her career. If this is the case, she may rightfully claim that she is discriminated against if she is not admitted to a training programme due to the bias of the recruitment process. Hence a case of social injustice may be in evidence. The situation described above gives rise to what we may call 'the dilemma of the ill-treated women'. The market economy cannot solve this problem on its own. If we introduce a broader view of social fairness into our consideration, we may regard the situation described above as a special case of market failure where an atomistic market economy fails to provide a solution that is both efficient and just (cf. Svensson, 1977, for a discussion of the concept of social fairness). In order to solve this dilemma some specific social action is called for. The logical solution would be to obtain a measure of the extra cost which the firm must incur in refraining from the application of discriminatory recruitment practices in its internal training programmes. Society should then pay a subsidy to the firm corresponding to the cost of opening its training programmes equally to both men and women.

So far, we have tried to demonstrate some effects of the new attitudes towards work which have emerged within the existing forms of economic organisation. Changing attitudes towards work do, however, also influence the demands for new forms of economic organisation. We will now continue with a brief discussion of some of the interconnections between work forms and new attitudes toward work.

IV ATTITUDES TOWARDS WORK AND FORMS OF ECONOMIC ORGANISATION

The neo-classical theory of the firm stresses the importance of responsibility and control on the part of business leaders and entrepreneurs (Knight, 1921, pp. 271 *et seq*). In its modern version this theory focuses on the concepts of metering and monitoring (Alchian and Demsetz, 1972).

This type of theory is rooted in a strongly hierarchical view of the employees of the firm. Alchian and Demsetz, for instance, take the superiority of team work as a point of departure. A firm is necessarily organised as a team. The method of organising production gives rise to the problem of 'metering'. The production function of the firm cannot be separated into different functions dependent on a single input factor (Alchian and Demsetz, 1972, p. 779); if Q is the amount produced, and X_1 and X_2 are the input factors, then $\delta^2 Q/\delta X_2 \neq 0$. Since distinct production functions for different inputs cannot be established, it is difficult to measure directly the productivity of each input. This is one factor which gives rise to the problem of metering. Furthermore, the net product of the team needs to be distributed among the members of the team. Thus metering concerns two fundamental aspects of team production as organised by the classical capitalist firm, or privately-owned corporation. The first aspect is the measurement of marginal productivity (meter = measure) and the second the distribution of factor incomes (meter = apportion). The other key concept in the modern version of the neo-classical is 'monitoring'. The team members, that is the employees, will, if left on their own, have a strong inclination to avoid work, according to Alchian and Demsetz. Therefore it is important that they be supervised. This is the monitor's duty.

The monitor alone concludes contracts with all suppliers of input factors. He observes the behaviour of input factors and can alter the composition of the team. Furthermore he has the right to the firm's surplus or residual.

But who supervises the monitor? Profits. The monitor needs no other supervisor since he receives the residual as payment for his services. The neo-classic tradition presents a mechanistic perspective on labour as a factor of production. Labour is hardly ever viewed as a true partner in production. Workers are treated as quite soul-less input factors, equivalent to capital. The theoretical attitudes of neo-classical economists such as Alchian and Demsetz have their more applied counterparts in what is commonly called 'scientific management'.

The pioneer in scientific management was F. W. Taylor who began to improve managerial methods at the end of the nineteenth century (Copley, 1923). Taylor and his colleagues were mainly interested in relatively routine work tasks; they noticed that workers' movements reminded one of a machine, and they arranged the actions efficiently to call for the least possible use of human energy. Taylor and his followers became experts at 'time and motion'; their work gave birth to the MTM method. To increase the workers' motivation they used piece-rate incentives.

The attitude towards work, and the view of employees that is implicit in neo-classical theory and in its practical applications, among which scientific management is one, are rigid and hardly very imaginative. The employers (the monitors) behave as simple profit maximisers, and the employees are only interested in material incentives. This view of work has also been criticised as being dehumanising.

By regarding the monitor's duties as one of the firm's most important functions, scientific management reveals its kinship with neo-classic tradition. The more effectively one can control and supervise the employees, the more effectively will the firm be managed, and the greater will be the surplus. Both lines of thought also view employees in a one-dimensional perspective, in which pecuniary rewards are the standard means of improving worker productivity.

Neo-classical theory on economic organisation and scientific management has been criticised from various angles. Writers of a marxist leaning have been very critical of neo-classical theory which has been attacked for being apologetic and for having a dehumanising attitude toward work. Scientific management has been characterised as a tool of manipulation on the part of management to deprive work of its meaning, and as an instrument for controlling the employees in order to increase profit (Braverman, 1974). It has even been argued that the whole system of distribution of labour that modern industry uses is an artifice basically employed to manipulate workers (Braverman, 1974).

Scientific management can be viewed as representing one extreme attitude towards work. It has undoubtedly exerted an important influence on the organisation of modern industry. But the strict supervision and the hierarchical organisation that is implicit in scientific management have also been challenged.

Attitudes toward work are, as has already been said, not primarily an object of study for economists. Other disciplines within the social sciences have also shown an interest in this field. Within social psychology and sociology there is another different tradition, whose approach and results differ markedly from those of scientific management. In brief, this tradition argues that participation produces better results than control. Two lines can be distinguished in this tradition: one is more economic, the other psychological. The writings of the American psychologist Abraham Maslow provide part of the philosophical or normative foundation for this school (see, for example, Maslow, 1970). According to Maslow, the satisfaction of human needs constitutes a hierarchy. Physiological needs are the strongest. When these are satisfied, other needs, like the demand for security, feelings of group acceptance, and appreciation (both self-esteem and appreciation by others), come into play. The highest need in Maslow's hierarchy is self-actualisation.

To satisfy this want, the individual must be given an outlet for his desires and an ability to influence his surroundings. More simply, he must be able to influence his work and his life. Participation in decision-making is, from this standpoint, superior to economic organisation based on hierarchy and strict control.

The nature of this subject makes it difficult to produce hard data and crystal-clear results regarding the economic effects of increased participation. A classic investigation in this field is the so-called Hawthorne study (Homans, 1950; Tannenbaum, 1966). These analyses began as a study of the effects of lighting on worker productivity at Western Electric's Hawthorne plant. They showed the difficult of confirming with any certainty simple connections between factors like productivity and variations in lighting. On the other hand, they demonstrated the existence of a clear and strong relationship between the workers' job satisfaction and their productivity. The attention which the workers received, the less restrictive supervision, and the increased opportunities to control their own work situations produced a feeling of increased well-being and thereby improved productivity. Productivity rose primarily because management became interested in the workers; when the employees were treated like individuals and allowed to participate in decisions about their work milieu and the production arrangements, their motivation and productivity also rose. Numerous studies have since confirmed these results, although isolated contradictory findings also exist.

Job satisfaction and workers' feelings of alienation have received much attention in the past decade. One well-known study of these problems is Blauner's (Blauner, 1964). According to Blauner, the workers' feelings of well-being or estrangement at their jobs depend to a significant extent upon their relation to their technical surroundings: can they manipulate and control the technical equipment themselves, or are they placed in a machine-oriented production system where jobs are defined to correspond with the machines, and only minimal opportunities remain for individual adjustment and control of the work-rhythm. Blauner distinguishes three important aspects of freedom at work: first, the ability to influence the immediate working conditions, including the production tempo and opportunity to move around freely at the workplace; second, the chance to visualise the whole work process and see a particular job as a part of a larger unit (otherwise, specialisation deprives the individual of the feeling that his contribution is meaningful); and third, the possibility for social integration with the firm, with feelings of estrangement and antipathy replaced by a sense of fairness and belonging.

The scientific discussion of alienation and participation has produced no clear conclusions. It appears, however, from the majority of the investigations of it that the employees' ability to influence decisions has positive effects on production, and that participation leads to increased well-being.

This approach, and the results that it has produced, can be viewed as the analytical underpinnings for another interesting new attitude toward work. Here, it may be argued that the individual seeks to fulfil his aspirations through collectivity. Employees in a number of countries have expressed dissatisfaction with the form of economic organisation that the traditional monitor-guided firm represents. Demands have been made for a more direct say in the guidance of the firm.

It may, of course, be somewhat arbitrary to call this search for influence over working conditions a 'new' attitude toward work. Still, demands of this kind seem to be gaining ground in many western countries and influence both the total supply of work and the choice of work and place of occupation. Needless to say, in times of low activity levels they will be less pronounced than in times of full employment. The trend seems, however, to be present, and to make its presence felt in good times as well as in times of less prosperity.

This new attitude towards work has several ramifications. One is that the approach through scientific management has proved less promising than its originators originally thought. Attempts at reorganising work around auto-mation and machine-oriented standardisation through the introduction of assembly line principles, for example, have revealed significant weaknesses.

Employees have often protested against extreme 'routinisation' and super-vision. At times, protests have found expression through wild-cat strikes, quality control problems, sabotage, and the like. More often, though, workers are believed to have 'voted with their feet' by avoiding strictly routinised tasks or by remaining only a short time at such work stations. Consequently, some firms have been forced to bear unexpected costs for absenteeism and high employee turnover and to settle for productivity levels below the technically feasible potential.

Employees have instead called for an increased influence over working conditions, for co-direction or *mitbestimmung*. At the firm level, empl yees have made demands both for a share of the control over working conditions and for some rights of decision *vis-à-vis* hiring practices. Again, Sweden may be used as a case in point.

In Sweden in recent years a great emphasis has been placed on working conditions. No worker is to be obliged to work under conditions which are dangerous or unhealthy. At every place of work the workers have their own 'ombudsman' who has the right to stop the work if he finds working conditions risky or unsatisfactory. He can then call in a representative for the state agency concerned with safety regulations and working conditions, who in turn can order the firm to make the necessary improvements for work to continue again.

The changes concerning the rules for lay-offs and termination of employ-ment are also important. According to the new legislation which has recently been passed by the Swedish Parliament, employment is, in principle, lifelong. Unless a formal contract has been agreed on to the contrary, no worker can be laid off if the firm has employment to offer. This means, in effect, that a worker who has been employed by a firm for a certain time cannot be fired unless the firm goes bankrupt or business conditions worsen to such an extent that a large portion of the working force must be laid off.

If, for instance, due to a recession, some workers must be laid off, the principle of 'last-in-first-out' should be applied. The seniority principle is further strengthened by the fact that every year worked after reaching the age of 45 is multiplied by two. When the business upturn comes, the firm must offer employment to the workers with seniority; here the principle of 'last-out-first-in' must apply. This legislation obviously aims at protecting the older – and often less competitive – workers, who are easily at a disadvantage in a capitalist setting.

Economists have judged the new legislation favourably or unfavourably depending on their political points of view. Those with neo-classical leanings and a more conservative frame of mind have criticised it for impairing the adaptability and the smooth functioning of the Swedish economy. Those who view the strivings toward industrial democracy more favourably argue that it is only natural to regard the labour force as a continuing entity in the firm, and that short-run fluctuations should be taken care of by adjusting other variables, such as incomes and prices, and not the amount of labour used in the firm.

The 'new' attitudes toward work which we have discussed above challenge the organisation of work as it is conceived in the classical capitalist firm, where a monitor organises work along hierarchical lines.

Neo-classical economic theory is a very supple instrument. It remains to be seen whether the privately owned firm, as described by neo-classical theory, is equally flexible and will manage to accommodate to the new attitudes towards work and the attendant demands for influence on the part of the employees, as well as their desire for meaningful work.

It may be added that the concept of the privately owned monitor-ruled firm has been challenged also on other grounds in the Scandinavian countries. In Denmark and Sweden proposals for 'fund socialism' have been launched by the trade unions and the social-democratic parties (Södersten, 1977). By having shares of profits go to a wage-earners' fund on the one hand, and, on the other, by letting a share of wages be used for purposes of capital formation, employees will obtain control of part of the share capital of the firms. This is another example of the dissatisfaction with the concept of the traditional capitalist firm being exhibited by employees.

It remains to be seen how the organisation of work will be affected in the future by these new attitudes toward work. Perhaps the classical monitor-guided firm will survive. New forms of economic organisation may also be tried, however. A logical development in some western countries may be that some kind of labour-managed market economy will emerge. In such a setting, employees will control the capital in the economy and run their own firms according to the rules of a market economy (cf. Vanek, 1970 and Meade, 1972). Thus the employees would then be able to organise work according to principles which are different from those applied in a monitor-guided firm (Steinherr, 1975).

V SOME CONCLUSIONS

In the developed western countries, work cannot be regarded as simply a way of earning a living. The supply of work and of work effort should not be viewed in purely pecuniary terms. Work is an important element of many people's lives, in the sense that it is a critical factor for satisfaction and self-actualisation.

In part this may be explained in purely economic terms. An increase in human capital formation and in female wages has made time more valuable. This has led to market-related activities increasingly being substituted for more time-intensive non-market activities. But to obtain a fuller explanation of the new trend in labour-market behaviour it seems necessary also to invoke changing attitudes or changing preferences. Work outside the home affords independence and a feeling of self-actualisation. Cumulative processes are also at work and, in the setting of general equilibrium, economic factors and changing attitudes reinforce each other. New attitudes also have important implications for the values attached to traditional family life and child-raising. Family size and nativity rates are falling, as witnessed in several countries, as domestic activities are being substituted by market-related activities.

An important new group that has appeared in the labour market is the group of women who are taking up occupations where a career ladder forms an important element. Here on-the-job training is often essential for advancement. Women in such occupations may often claim rightly that they are met by discrimination, since they are not being admitted to internal training programmes on equal terms with men. If social justice is to be achieved, this should be rectified. The efficient way of doing this is by paying a subsidy to firms so that the internal rate of return on training members of different sexes will be equalised.

Another interesting aspect of attitudes toward work concerns work satisfaction and forms of economic organisation. Dissatisfaction with working conditions in the traditional monitor-guided firm seems to be prevalent in several countries. This leads to a challenge of traditional heirarchical ways of organising work. Demands have been raised for increased participation on the part of employees. Again, this development may be described as a tendency to put more emphasis on the non-pecuniary rewards of work, combined with an increased interest in the quality of work. Working conditions are being scrutinised more closely, and demands for a satisfactory working environment have become more insistent. It remains to be seen whether these new attitudes can be reconciled with the dominant forms of economic organisation now existing in most western countries, or whether instead the evolution will head in the direction of some form of labour-managed system.

REFERENCES

Akerlof, G. (1970), 'The market for 'Lemons': Quality Uncertainty and the Market Mechanism', *Quarterly Journal of Economics*, 84.

Alchian, A. A. and Demsetz, H. (1972), 'Production, Information Costs and Economic Organisation', *American Economic Review*, 62, no. 1.

Becker, G. (1965), 'A Theory of the Allocation of Time', *Economic Journal*, 75.

Becker, G. (1973), 'A Theory of Marriage: Part I', *Journal of Political Economy*, 81.

Becker, G. (1974), 'A Theory of Marriage: Part II', *Journal of Political Economy*, 82.

Blauner, R. (1964), *Alienation and Freedom* (Chicago).

Braverman, H. (1974), *Labor and Monopoly Capital* (New York).

Copley, F. B. (1923), *Frederick W. Taylor* (New York).

Homans, G. C. (1950), *The Human Group* (New York).

Knight, F. H. (1921), *Risk, Uncertainty and Profit* (Boston).

Knight F. H. (1936), *The Ethics of Competition* (London).

Leibowitz, A. (1972), *Women's Allocation of Time to Market and Non-Market Activities* (New York).

Maslow, A. (1970), *Motivation and Personality*, 2nd edn (New York).

Meade, J. (1972), 'The Theory of the Labor-Managed firms and of Profit-Sharing', *Economic Journal*, 82.

Nerlove, M. (1974), 'Household and Economy: Toward a New Theory of Population and Economic Growth', *Journal of Political Economy*, 82.

Södersten, B. (1977), 'Industrial Democracy: Present and Future', *Scandinavian Review*, no. 2.

Steinherr, A. (1975), 'On the Efficiency of Profit-Sharing and Labor-Participation', mimeo.

Svensson, L. (1977), *Social Justice and Fair Distributions* (Lund).

Tannenbaum, A. S. (1966), *Social Physchology of Work Organisation* (Belmont).

Vanek, J. (1970), *The General Theory of Labor-Managed Market Economies* (Ithaca N.Y.).

Discussion of Professor Södersten's Paper

Dr Margaret Gordon introduced the paper. Unfortunately she had not received a copy until she arrived at the conference, so she had no elegantly prepared set of comments, and would speak from notes. She was pleased to find that the first half of the paper was concerned with the labour force participation of women — a subject on which she had herself done some writing.

She said she would first summarise the paper, and reserve her own comments until the end. The two parts of the paper — on the increasing labour force participation of women, and on changing attitudes towards work — were linked, because changing attitudes were emphasised in both parts.

The author began by contrasting the classical economists' view of work with a more modern attitude, which was held by some economists, but which also reflected the writings of sociologists and psychologists.

In the view of classical economics, work was a sacrifice or disutility. Man worked in order to consume, and traded-off increasing income from work against leisure — hence the shape of the labour supply curve. In the more modern view, work itself was a source of satisfaction.

In the first part, the author maintained that the increase in the labour force participation of women could not be explained very satisfactorily in classical terms. The acceleration of the increase in the 1960s and 1970s occurred in a period of rapidly-rising real income, when the classical interpretation would have predicted a withdrawal of women from the labour force. Moreover, not only the classical theory, but also cross-sectional survey data, showed that labour force participation rates of women were inversely related to the husband's income.

The Becker school of Chicago economists provided a more satisfactory interpretation. They treated the household as the decision-making unit, and regarded both time and market-produced goods as inputs to the household. As income from market activities rose, the value of time rose, and market-produced goods came to be preferred over time-consuming household activities. In addition, the value of women's time increased as educational levels rose. Both of these trends tended to induce wives to enter the labour market.

Nevertheless, since these tendencies had been going on over a long period, it was difficult to explain the recent acceleration of the rise in the labour force participation of women (in Sweden) without bringing in changing attitudes. Surely the desire of women for greater freedom, independence, and security of income had played a role.

The increase in the labour force participation of women had had several important repercussions. One of these had been the decline in the birth rate, which needed no elaboration, since a working wife would prefer to have fewer children. Another repercussion had been the accusation of discrimination against women.

In the author's view there were, broadly, two kinds of jobs that women obtained. In one type of job, chiefly in the trade and service industries, jobs were of a low-level type and offered few promotional opportunities. In these jobs, there was no discrimination against individual women. There were, however, other jobs that offered opportunities for career progression, and in these there was discrimination against women. Although an educational background was needed, one could not advance in these jobs without on-the-job training. It was rational for the employer to discriminate against women in providing it because of the high probability that they would withdraw from the labour force for child-bearing and rearing. In other words, women were poor risks, or 'lemons' in Akerlof's terms.

The answer to this problem was a social policy in which on-the-job training was subsidised by public funds on a differential basis, with higher subsidies for women. Dr Gordon said this had not been tried in the USA, but there were anti-discrimination and affirmative action policies, which had been at least partially successful.

The second part of the paper was concerned with the conflict between the neo-classical view that management must control the use of productive resources (monitoring and metering in Alchian's terms with profits as the governing force) and the increasing desire of workers to find job satisfaction, to be involved in controlling work and to have a part in the decision-making process.

Thus in several European countries was found the movement towards *Mitbestimmungsrecht*. This movement had not proceeded very far in the USA, because trade union leaders, Dr Gordon believed, feared that it would reduce the possibility of retaining independence at the bargaining table. But in a number of countries, including the USA, there was evidence of a revolt against routine, assembly-line types of work, through absenteeism, wild-cat strikes, and the like.

The author also referred to related developments, such as the *ombudsman* programme in Sweden and legal measures providing job security for long-service workers in Sweden and in several other European countries. Whether these interrelated developments involved a serious long-run threat to managerial control of the process of production Professor Södersten was not yet very clear.

Dr Gordon said she did not disagree seriously with the author's views, but would suggest certain amplifications and modifications.

In interpreting the increased labour force participation of women, she would emphasise the need to consider developments on the demand, as well as on the supply side, of the labour market.

Changes on the demand side were at least partially manifested in changes in occupational structure. At the beginning of the present century the vast majority of women workers in the USA were employed in agriculture, domestic service, or in semi-skilled factory jobs, especially in the textile and apparel industries. For the most part, the jobs were low-paid and demeaning. It was small wonder that a working-class man felt pride if his wife did not have to work, and that middle- and upper-income husbands considered it a disgrace for a wife to work.

Over the decades, the structure of demand for women had changed quite dramatically. The rise in labour force participation of women in the USA changed very gradually until the Second World War, but after that increased at an accelerated rate. There was not the sudden increase in the USA in the 1960s shown by the Swedish data.

Especially after the Second World War, there had been a pronounced increase in clerical, trade and service jobs for women, in professional jobs and (in the 1970s) in managerial jobs (this last development clearly influenced by affirmative action policies). It was true, as Professor Bergmann would emphasise, that occupational segregation was a pervasive phenomenon, but, on the whole, women's jobs were not as demeaning or low-level as they had been at the beginning of the century. Furthermore, as evidence of the influence of demand factors, there was a tendency for the labour force participation rate of women to rise particularly sharply in years when total employment rose rapidly. And, as a number of studies had shown, in recession the 'discouraged worker' effect outweighed the 'additional worker' effect, so that the number of women and other secondary workers withdrawing from the labour force tended to exceed the number entering it.

Dr Gordon's most serious quarrel with the Becker school related to its explanation of the positive correlation between the labour force participation of women and their educational attainment — a relationship that was quite pronounced in the USA. Dr Gordon sometimes thought that only women should write about the labour market behaviour of women. The Becker school explained this relationship on the ground that the value of an educated woman's time in the labour market exceeded the value of her time spent in the household by a larger margin than in the case of less-educated women. In her opinion, this involved an overly exclusive emphasis on pecuniary aspects of the matter. An educated woman gained a sense of achievement from her work, developed her potential capabilities, usually worked in a more pleasant environment than did a less-educated woman, and found more stimulating associations in her work.

Finally, Dr Gordon commented on the relevance of the paper to a conference on unemployment. There was a clear, if somewhat speculative, relationship. The changes in attitudes described by Professor Södersten had largely developed in a period of full employment, when the risk of prolonged joblessness was minimal, and when workers could make demands for greater job satisfaction in an atmosphere largely devoid of the fear of losing their jobs. The decade of the 1960s was also a period when educated youth rebelled against materialism and yet assumed that a good job would be available on their completion of education.

Dr Gordon asked whether a prolonged period of higher unemployment would lead to a reversal of these trends. In one respect there had been a reversal. College youth in the USA, and to some extent elsewhere, she believed, displayed much more concern about job prospects, studied harder, and preferred fields of study that were occupationally oriented.

In other aspects, changes in attitudes were not so clear. The protection of job security in Western Europe tended to prevent reversals of attitudes among adults, while at the same time enhancing youth unemployment, which had been the subject of her own recent research. Prolonged unemployment might well discourage a continued increase in the labour force participation of women. It could, indeed, lead to policies resembling those of the 1930s, in which married women were barred from various types of job.

The prospects were not very clear. In the very long run, however, she believed that the trends described in Professor Södersten's paper would be the prevailing trends of the future.

Professor Södersten said this was a very fair and clear analysis of the paper. So far as unemployment was concerned, some thought there were too many women in the labour market. There was also a problem in Sweden because of uneven development, related to the cost of strikes. In a short paper, he could not deal with all issues, but he hoped that what he had said was relevant.

Professor Hines made two observations on the proposition that unemployment of women and blacks would increase if wages were reduced. He agreed with earlier suggestions that variations in the employment of women and blacks were better explained by variations in economic activity. He saw these two groups as constituting a reserve of labour, as in less-developed countries. They moved in and out of the labour market as the demand for labour changed. In underdeveloped countries, these movements were to and from the subsistence sector, and in developed countries, into and out of unemployment. The number of women available did not fall, but even if it did, it was not clear that that would increase the employment possibilities open to them.

There was also the more speculative notion of the disutility of work, which related to workers and not to capitalists. Nor did he think it applied to the self-employed or artisan in the same way. Perhaps, as industrial democracy developed, and as we moved to more worker control, the idea of workers yielding only disutility would go. Perhaps Dr Gordon was talking in terms of professional women. It was not so much here that the shadow price of labour was higher, but that paid employment was more attractive. It was not perhaps a matter of women comparing unskilled work in the home with a job in the factory.

Professor Kolm saw the paper as touching on deep problems, and was glad it had been included in the conference agenda. One point posed was the nature of the relationship between work and leisure. He thought it possible that we should see the notion of work giving way to the general idea of activity. There might be less work in the future, but it might be more like that of the artist. It was essential for economists to study these issues, but they should do so with the help of sociologists, philosophers and psychologists.

One advantage was for the person who undertook the activity; the other for those who could exchange with him. A simple view would be that women were liberated in leaving home for the labour market. But children were once sent out in the same way.

One must remember that the firm was a collective organisation. Its 'political' organisation could be that of a monarchy, as now, or a democracy. On such organisation, he thought that Marx and Walras made the same distinction between labour and labour power. When sold, it was disposable and represented labour power. An important issue was control over labour when sold.

Recent contributions on the economics of the family were clearly interesting, but inadequate. The family was too often seen as the decision unit, and he thought this idea should be abandoned. If there were several individuals involved in such a decision, one could have intransitivity in utility functions. One must see that the family was the main factor in individual preference. One therefore needed a theory of individual socialisation, and to see all its effects, including changes in individual preferences.

On the law of work and unemployment, most western countries after 1945 had a law of employment. This was usually looked at in macroeconomic terms. One needed to realise that this was part of the social contract but that there were also more microeconomic weapons. This led to a discussion of employment like that taking place in Sweden, and of the possibility of restrictions on the rights of the employer.

As for democracy in work, the paper discussed developments in Sweden, but this assumed only a certain level of participation and in some enterprises workers could have the power of decision within ten to fifteen years. This would be a big social change. Professor Kolm thought this was an essential field of study for economists, but with an extension of their point of view. It was also a major field for social improvement.

Professor Kolm wondered what was the link to the current crisis. There were suggestions that the change in values began before 1970, and that this movement must now be dampened, together with the changes in values it caused. He thought, on the contrary, that to the extent that there was a crisis, one could find no link with what went on in eastern countries, or with what had happened to workers in the nineteenth century. There were many reasons why one was now asking deeper questions on the notion and the nature of both work and leisure.

Professor Frey wanted to bring Professor Södersten away from the field of female employment to that of the old. It was often suggested that the biggest problem in the 1980s and 1990s could be the old, because both demographic and economic factors were causing the whole situation to worsen from year to year. The 1970s had been the decade of the problem of youth; the 1980s and 1990s might be decades of the problems of the old.

Did Professor Södersten look at the case of the old in terms of their attitude to work? And was it possible that changes in industrialisation might either cause more of the old to retire or to stay in the labour market? In an OECD discussion in which he had participated it was suggested that people were starting to think that early retirement was no solution because the later one worked, the more power one had. Did Professor Södersten think it possible that such problems would be important in future?

Professor Odaka said the attitude to work might have changed, but he was not convinced that the idea that work had disutility was wrong. It might be changes in independent variables that led to a change in attitudes. What did Professor Södersten think?

To Dr Gordon and Professor Södersten he pointed out that the former had spoken of differences between the USA and Sweden, for example, in the rise in the female participation rate in Sweden. She had also spoken of different unions. Was there a big difference between the USA and Europe in attitudes to work and in the independent variables affecting work?

He wondered whether he had understood correctly that the view that the increase in female participation rates at the professional level had increased unemployment. He wondered whether women really did become unemployed because of this?

Professor Holt was surprised there was no comment on the role of technology in the household. It was a mistake not to give credit to this, and to the consequent rise in the standard of living, for freeing women for the labour market. It was not simply that there had been a change in attitudes. He thought there was a correlation between an increase in the demand for labour and economic development. For example, the movement of women into the labour market since 1945 had been a result of economic conditions. In Italy, perhaps the Phillips curve had moved to the left, giving unemployment a strong anti-inflationary effect. Perhaps there had also been a shift from an urban to a rural economy with women taking up work when they moved to the city. One then had to remember that migration was cyclical, and that some non-reversible factors were at work here.

Professor Kolm had spoken about industrial democracy, but this was not a prominent concept in the USA. However, there was a book on the 'invisible revolution' emphasising that union and company funds now accounted for as astonishing proportion – perhaps 40 per cent – of corporate shares. At some point, the trade unions would be able to elect the whole board of directors. This was called a quiet revolution because it had so far been largely unnoticed by the public.

Professor Rehn thought that in a way the paper stressed the interrelation between full employment in developed countries – and even now employment was higher than the 1930s – and a change in attitudes. When full employment was approached there was a rapid increase in labour turnover as an expression of the need for freedom in work. We should note the counteraction of employers: laws on job security, etc. This had not been strongly resisted by employers because they saw it as a counter to high labour mobility which locked in the worker. The difference between those who stayed and those who did not was increased, and we should perhaps be aware of the lack of freedom for workers even under full employment. There were those with tenure, but the numbers in the secondary labour market might increase.

He would also like to mention flexi-time. Once again, he saw workers as taking freedom and employers as responding by organising it. His point was simply that over the whole field the attitudes of both workers and employers were changing.

Professor Bergmann noted that one reason for the change in female participation rates was that while women were moving away from their traditional role, men were refusing to play another role in the family. As for new attitudes to work, sociologists and anthropologists always looked at the position of work in life and status. It was not so much that attitudes had changed, or that economists were recognising the importance of such issues, especially the problems of educated youth. People expected money, status and an interesting job and the social and political implications of denying these expectations were severe. It was not just a question of low output and low income, but of the whole basis for self-esteem.

Professor Södersten suggested that people in jobs might be disadvantaged in their access to training opportunities. This had been found in a study of Chicago where firms taking on whites gave them training, but did not do the same for blacks.

We should reduce the segmentation of the labour market caused by discrimination and should contribute to the restructuring of jobs to make them more interesting. It was not true that the dirtiest jobs paid well. They often paid least because of the segmentation of the labour market. So we needed more education and less prejudice to give a better attitude to work.

Professor Timofeev pointed to the necessity for an interdisciplinary approach to these problems. He thought it a mistake to suggest, as many did, that the problem of female participation rates was only a question of demography or of pure economics. There were social implications, and he was glad that Professor Bergmann had related social and economic factors.

In the USSR there was no discrimination in work for women but there were still social problems. In many industries, like textiles, there were social problems, for example, because nurseries were needed. Professor Södersten was close to an interdisciplinary approach. As he understood it, Professor Södersten said we needed a new approach to work, and were not simply to see it as a way of earning a living, though there were still those who thought that work was only to do with the standard of living. If we looked at the problem in sociological terms, we saw that there were very important problems here, and that we could understand the trend if we looked at social movements. For example, in Italy there was a strong labour movement, and an interesting and recently controversial book had shown how labour was exploited by producers. This confirmed the ideas put forward by Professor Södersten.

M. Salais said that many factors had been put forward to explain female employment. He would add the fall in the birth rate, which was a matter of choice. There was a link between female employment and the decentralisation of employment. There had been changes in the location of jobs, with movement to less-developed regions which had reserves of female labour and where incomes were also lower. The result had been a strong fall in the difference between female participation rates in urban and agricultural regions. There was a continuous call for female labour which led to more stable increase of female activity rates. The role of this reserve labour force of women was less important now.

M. Salais agreed on the need for interdisciplinary studies, but if the growth of the employment of women came to an end, then what would be the causes? Would it be a real change of attitude or would it be because of high unemployment which discouraged activity and job search on the labour market?

Professor Eastman was glad that it had been recognised that man was not condemned to live by the sweat of his brow. However, he thought one could overdo this idea. The question was how much work should be done, and this depended on rewards. So economic theory did have something to say, and one did not need to be totally interdisciplinary in one's approach.

Professor Onitiri wanted to ask about one factor. What was the effect of the new style of life on the family? The need for all the gadgets was now seen as a minimum, families wanted more holidays and he thought it was this that forced women to go out to work. We were looking at a new level of expectations by the household. Perhaps one needed a more balanced view of participation by women in the labour market than that.

Professor Södersten replied to the discussion. Dr Gordon had said that well-educated women obtained a sense of achievement from their jobs, but this understated the importance of pecuniary rewards. The real question was how these interacted with non-economic factors. Professor Hines had a pseudo-Marxian view of women as forming a reserve army of labour. He did not fully accept this. In Sweden there had been a big increase in female participation in the labour force. The overt unemployment rate was constant, so there was no support in Sweden for this reserve army argument. He was not sure what had happened in other countries.

Professor Södersten said he had not suggested that the female labour force was totally homogeneous. A corollary was that, in future, perhaps some women would have more children, and others not. There was evidence for this view because there was a conflict between those who wanted big subsidies in order to support their children and those who were calling for day-care facilities. Upper-class women wanted the latter, and the implications were important.

In general, he agreed with what Professor Kolm had said. Professor Kolm wanted greater worker influence, and he sympathised with this. However, it might well be that management of enterprises by labour could come only after a hard social struggle. The real reasons lay in property rights, as Professor Holt said. Perhaps people would say they were entitled to increased participation in running their firms. In Sweden, the argument about the role of the pension funds was certainly used, and a combined scheme had been suggested, where some wages went to the capital of the firm and some profits to the workers. Perhaps in this way socialism in Sweden was being postponed. There was, however, a big difference between Professor Holt's argument and what happens in Sweden. One would not get control directly through the pension funds, but needed more militant moves.

As for what Professor Frey had said about the old, he would not disagree, but this was a difficult issue, and it did not naturally arise from the discussion in his own paper. He agreed that work was power, and that the docility of the old had been astonishing. Perhaps they might now react.

Professor Odaka had not been persuaded of the change in attitudes about employment. His own paper had begun from the economic argument, and had tried to build in changes in preferences and attitudes. He had taken a Wicksellian line, seeing the problem as a cumulative process. Professor Odaka also wondered whether there was a big difference in attitudes between the USA and Europe. He thought there was, because there had been big developments in Western Europe.

Professor Holt's point on household technology was a well-known one, and he had therefore not thought it necessary to make it explicit in his paper.

To Professor Bergmann, he would say that he was glad for her point of view, because perhaps the original point of the paper was assertions about discrimination in the provision of on-the-job training. One needed a direct subsidy to the firm, and he had not seen this stated in the literature. However, if this point was now accepted, something useful had come from his paper.

He agreed that there was a need for an interdisciplinary approach, but economists must start from economic issues.

M. Salais had wondered whether the rise in female participation rates was irreversible. Professor Södersten thought it was. What was important was the trend rather than the cycle, but the issue needed looking at more closely.

Professor Onitiri had stressed the new style of life. Any discussion of attitudes of this kind was bound to sound vague, but he had discussed the effects of the new situation on income distribution. The difference between households where there were two workers and those where there was only one would be important.

Dr Gordon noted that Professor Odaka had said that an increase in unemployment resulted in part from an increase in female participation. It was often asserted that this was so, and she had followed the OECD paper by looking at the employment of women and teenagers. She had taken decennial data and asked if women took jobs from young people. In fact, the changes in occupational employment were similar for both. Many women were employed in low-level services and so were young people. There was a clear switch only in jobs involving driving, which were given to women rather than to teenagers.

14 Income Distribution and Labour Supply

Luigi Frey
UNIVERSITY OF PARMA, ITALY

I LABOUR SUPPLY AND ITS CALCULATION

Italian interest in an income distribution/labour supply analysis has developed out of dissatisfaction with the apparent implications of the labour supply surveys made by the official Statistics Bureau (ISTAT). Moreover, conflicting estimates and characteristics of supply and demand have made it difficult to make reliable future labour supply calculations.[1]

Up to 1976, quarterly investigations on labour supply gave barely credible data on the dimensions of labour supply and its behaviour over time. Just how far off the mark this data was is illustrated by research over the last ten years, which has shown that the effective labour supply has not (contrary to what the data mentioned above have led one to believe) diminished in absolute terms, nor probably even in relation to population.

Research indicates a distinction[2] between components of the labour supply; the potential labour supply and the effective labour supply should be defined as explicit or implicit. Over the course of a year, a distinction between potential supply and effective supply is necessary in order to include those who did not work on a continuous basis and were consequently excluded from a particular survey period, but who at the same time needed to work to earn an income, given the living conditions within the system.

The effective supply is part of the potential supply. These two components should coincide on a yearly basis. But, during any given period, people who (for various reasons) only supply labour in particular periods during the year may remain outside the survey at the time it is taken. Part of the effective supply is quantifiable and may be analysed on the basis of official statistics. We refer here to the explicit supply. But a large part of the

---

[1] The difficulties mentioned have been emphasised in a series of articles listed in *Quaderni di Economia del Lavoro* (ed. Angeli), Milan, No. 1 (1975).

[2] Many have been mentioned and commented upon in articles in *Quaderni di Economia del Lavoro* (ed. Angeli), Milan (1975, 1976, 1977).

supply eludes official surveys because it involves evasion of contracts and regulations. This is the implicit supply. Quarterly ISTAT survey results have normally been the primary base for quantification and analysis of the explicit labour supply. Corrections to this base served to provide more satisfactory information. Most of the corrections were based on population census data.

Since investigations on the labour supply were made on a sample family basis, two types of problem had to be taken into account:

(a) the representativeness of the sample with respect to the whole Italian population, or with respect to a population with particular characteristics in terms of sex, age and geographical area;

(b) the reliability of the replies from those asked about their position as regards labour-supply or non-labour-supply.

The first problem lies within the more general realm of the significance of sample employment surveys at the statistical level. The sharp defects which emerged from overall surveys, effected through a population census of the whole nation, and their enormous costs, have obviously discouraged frequent repetition. The alternative indicated was the continuation of quarterly surveys, even though their results demand very cautious analysis and interpretation. The surveys would then be integrated with the census material so as to provide an analytical integration.

However, even a census presents the second type of problem. The last population census in 1971 used a form (to be compiled by the head of the family) with a separate sheet for each family member, requiring profession (by type of activity, position, whether or not a main occupation, current professional activity, the name of the plant, office, ente, etc. where the family member worked) as well as their non-professional status, whether pupil/ student, in search of first job, housewife, retired or other status. Even though the interviewer had theoretical control over the replies, it was the head of the family who gave the answers. The answers may have been influenced by objective or subjective considerations that may have encouraged the interviewee to rank himself, or one of the family members, in a position other than as labour supply. In the case of student-workers, pensioner-workers or housewives working under irregular conditions, the family head's wishes may have outweighed fact.

This naturally leads to substantial underestimation of the number of persons in employment and a consequent overestimate of the number of persons not part of the explicit labour supply. The census of economic activity, directed at those responsible for production units (rather than the head of the family), are even worse.

In this case, the motives that induce concealment of part of the effective employment (if not the existence of the employment unit itself) are an impediment to inclusion of such employment among the workers covered in the census. Such proportions does this phenomenon assume that it has been suggested[1] that the difference between census data on the population and the industrial and commercial census in Italy represents underemployment or precarious employment and should be considered as labour supply, even though the production unit does not list it as employment.

The 1976 labour force surveys underestimated the labour supply in Italy to a greater extent than the census results. This was true to such an extent that the census was considered one of the means of correcting the explicit labour supply (or in current employment, apart from unemployment, as such) from 1951 on.[2]

In calculating labour supply figures and characteristics, the classification, or lack of it, of persons in search of first jobs is just as important as the inclusion, or otherwise, of persons with an existing occupation.

The conceptual problem here is very important. It involves the so-called active search for work. One must define willingness to supply work in terms of both time and content. This includes those who do not declare that they are employed at the time of the survey. The limitations of certain features of the ISTAT labour force surveys were partly revealed after 1971 in special ISTAT investigations on the non-labour-force that followed the example of analogous American investigations.[3] The special surveys revealed the existence of persons available for remunerative work who were not classified in the labour supply – either because they said they were 'in search of a job' without appearing in the 'active' search in the sense defined in the quarterly investigations of the work force, or because they said they were 'able to carry out work under certain conditions'.

Labour supply surveys undertaken in Italy have sought to determine how many of the persons above mentioned ought to be included in the effective labour supply as implicit supply, or at least as still unspecified potential (for lack of sufficiently reliable analytical information) in the effective supply. Availability of data on the characteristics of the non-labour force and their behavioural motivations is a basic starting point in assembling the qualitative

[1] P. Sylos Labini, 'Osservazioni sull'evoluzione economica del Mezzogiorno' in *Studi di economia e statistica in memoria di A. Molinari* (Giuffre, Milan, 1963) pp. 656–7.

[2] Cf. ISTAT data for the period 1951–72.

[3] As far as the Italian investigations are concerned cf. the definitive results in *Annuari di statistiche del lavoro* (1972, p. 130 for the February 1971 survey; 1975 p. 109 for the April 1973 survey; 1976 p. 103 for the April 1975 survey). From 1973 on, the survey was carried out in conjunction with that on the labour force and was called 'Indagine speciale sull'atteggiamento della popolazione nei confronti del mercato del lavoro'.

information on implicit underemployment gathered in field surveys into a complete, coherent quantitative frame-work.[1]

Until 1976, the link between the special ISTAT surveys on the non-labour force and the normal quarterly investigations on the non-labour force was made by those who did the research mentioned. It was done with obvious margins of uncertainty and of judgement relative to the underlying labour supply concept.

After lengthy discussions, ISTAT was persuaded to consider a new survey model at the beginning of 1976. This new system improves the credibility of replies to interview questions and permits formation of an official homogeneous link between the special and the regular surveys.

From the point of view of explicit labour supply measurement, the new model is more refined and complete. In particular it permits a better look at the concept of active search for work, using the lessons acquired from the special surveys. It puts the accent on various possibilities (the question 'active search for work' has seven possible replies), on the search action, on the period of the last action, and on the causes behind the lack of a search.

It also greatly improves the description of occupational status, or lack of it, within the family groups surveyed. Among other things, it distinguishes between principal and secondary activities and attempts to ascertain whether persons in the family have worked any hours under whatever conditions, as well as questioning (in the interest of information on the work of minors) mixed worker/student situations in the case of students or pupils between 10 and 15 years of age. Finally, there is also a question that makes possible reference to broader labour supply definitions than that adopted for explicit supply.

In fact, there is a question asking if the members of the family contribute in any way to family income through their own work. The question is designed as a check; it goes beyond the link between labour supply measurement and the interviewee's opinion on labour supply. *Aggregate economic analysis of labour supply is aimed at better comprehension of employment problems so that strategies to correct and overcome them may gradually be adopted. Thus the subjective elements in the definition and quantification of the labour supply must be reduced to a minimum.*

The new model for ISTAT labour supply surveys adopted in 1977 has

---

[1] The writer has made ample use of the above mentioned data for this purpose since the first special survey in 1971, e.g. in an unpublished article sent to the Ministry of Labour and Social Services, and in research on 'Lavoro a Domicilio in Lombardia' published in July 1972 under the auspices of the Lombardy Regional Council's Department of Labour and Demographic Problems. The results of the special labour survey in April 1975 formed the starting point for estimates on 'Potenziale di Lavoro in Italia' which the writer calculated and published in Documento Isvet No. 50/19 (Rome, August 1976).

reduced these subjective aspects in the measurement of the explicit labour supply. In fact, (cf. Table 14.1) a substantial number of persons of both sexes who did not say that they were employed but stated that they had had some working hours during the week (911,000 units of both sexes in 1977, or 4.5 per cent of the total employment figure of 20 million employed, with an 8 per cent figure in the case of women), were included with those who declared initially that they had employment.

Moreover, in addition to those who declared themselves as underemployed or in search of a first job, there were numerous other persons (641,000 in 1977, equal to 41.5 per cent of total unemployment and to 3 per cent of the revised labour force total of 21,607,000 and with percentages that are above 50 per cent and 6 per cent respectively in the case of women), who declared a non-occupational status but who later in the same interview declared they were looking for work. The resultant explicit labour supply is 1.5 million higher than that registered in previous surveys. And participation rates rise slightly under 3 percentage points for both sexes and a little over 3 per cent in the case of women.

At the same time, the new model for ISTAT labour supply surveys, which blends the previous labour-force surveys with the special non-labour-force surveys, shows a considerable number of persons among the latter group who are willing to work under certain conditions (990,000 persons, 775,000 of them women).

Should they also not be considered part of the labour supply to correspond with the potential supply concept, or in terms of the number of persons willing to work under the living conditions currently existing under the present system?

Field research made in Italy over the past ten years suggests an affirmative reply to the question. At the same time, one must take into account an implicit labour supply in excess of the 990,000 supply figure for 1977.

A recent implicit underemployment estimate which the writer made on the basis of ISTAT information and qualitative data from field research[1] indicated an implicit 1977 underemployment figure additional to the surveyed labour force (the 21,607,000 workers, including 6,943,000 women show in Table 14.1) equivalent to 3,250,000 persons, of whom a little less than 70 per cent, or 2,250,000 are women.

This considerable underemployment total was calculated with the inclusion of young people between the ages of 14 and 29 years of age, persons over 50 years of age, and women of intermediate years, all of whom (on the basis of data available and information gathered during research) can reasonably be assumed to be labour supply, at least for part of the year 1977.

With respect to young people, we paid particular attention to those who were neither classified in the explicit labour force nor among those enrolled

---

[1] See 'Il lavoro nero nel 1977 in Italia' in *Tendenze dell'occupazione* anno III, No. 6 (June 1978).

TABLE 14.1 THE 1977 POPULATION OF ITALY SHOWING STATUS, TERRITORY AND SEX (thousands of persons)

	Employed			In search of employment				Total labour force	Non-labour force		Total population
	Those who declared themselves employed	Those who worked some hours during the week	Total	Proportion underemployed	Unemployed and seeking employment	Others[a]	Total		Number	Willing to work under specific conditions	
MEN											
Northern Italy	6609	196	6805	89	139	78	217	7022	5339	82	12,361
Northeast	2630	89	2719	44	48	32	80	2799	2177	37	4976
Northwest	3979	107	4086	45	91	46	137	4223	3162	45	7385
Central Italy	2642	74	2716	31	109	41	150	2866	2319	51	5185
Southern Italy and Islands	4318	151	4469	81	224	83	307	4776	4782	84	9558
Total Italy	13,569	421	13,990	201	472	202	674	14,664	12,440	217	27,104
WOMEN											
Northern Italy	3043	258	3301	101	161	162	323	3624	9429	302	12,053
Northeast	1199	129	1328	53	66	63	129	1457	3777	144	5234
Northwest	1844	129	1973	48	95	99	194	2167	5652	158	7819
Central Italy	1068	101	1169	34	95	76	171	1340	4096	169	5436
Southern Italy and Islands	1471	131	1602	100	176	201	377	1979	8001	302	9980
Total Italy	5582	490	6072	235	432	439	871	9943	21,526	775	28,469
MEN AND WOMEN											
Northern Italy	9652	454	10,106	190	300	240	540	10,646	14,768	384	25,414
Northeast	3829	218	4047	97	114	95	209	4256	5954	181	10,210
Northwest	5823	236	6059	93	186	145	331	6390	8814	203	15,204
Central Italy	3710	175	3885	65	204	117	321	4206	6415	220	10,621
Southern Italy and Islands	5789	282	6071	181	400	284	684	6755	12,783	386	19,538
Total Italy	19,151	911	20,062	436	904	641	1545	21,607	33,966	990	55,573

a Persons who declared they were not engaged but who during the same interview declared they were looking for work.

in training courses. Research on youth employment,[1] excluding the numbers in military service, showed an implicit underemployment figure of 120,000 young men between 14 and 29 years of age and almost 650,000 women. We thus looked at young students employed in non-occasional work in precarious, non-continuous conditions.

Research shows that diffusion of mass education and the widening gaps in income distribution and social structure have stimulated an increased number of young worker/students. As a result, calculations for 1977 show at least 15 per cent of the young students between the ages of 14 and 29 enrolled in various types of courses should be classified among the implicit underemployed. They number 400,000 young men and at least 240,000 young women. Thus, total implicit youth underemployment is slightly over 1,400,000 persons (17.5 per cent of the effective supply, i.e. of the explicit supply + the estimated implicit underemployment), made up of 520,000 young men and a little less than 890,000 young women (almost 25 per cent of the relative effective supply). Student/workers form a majority of the young male underemployed. But in the total of young underemployed women, it is those classified in official data as housewives who predominate.

As far as older persons are concerned, it is apparent that the number of workers over 50 years of age classified as in the labour force is too low as compared with the present population of that age group. While the difference in the male population can be almost totally explained by pensions, there is a margin of 3 million units in the female population over 50 years of age that is neither explicitly labour nor in receipt of pensions. Moveover, some of the older people officially classified as retired continue to supply labour because the transfer income obtained is insufficient, or for other reasons.[2]

Once again research has shown underemployed estimated at 1,250,000 persons over the age of 50 not included in the ISTAT 1977 labour supply. These include 500,000 men (350,000 officially retired from work) and 750,000 women (300,000 officially retired). Of this figure 650,000 persons were between the ages of 50 and 59 and 600,000 60 years of age and over. This implicit underemployment represents 21 per cent of the effective labour supply over 50 years of age. The percentage goes up to 33 per cent in the case of workers of 60 years of age and above. It is a phenomenon with radical consquences at the economic and social level.

In the 30 to 50 age group we focused our attention on the women with family ties. A reasonable hypothesis in the light of information gathered in the field would be to assume the possibility of extending the average participation rate (a little over 50 per cent) for women between the ages of 20 and 29 to higher age levels, up to 45 years. Using this hypothesis as a

[1] Cf. a synthesis of that research may be found in *Quaderni di Economia del Lavoro* (ed. Angeli), Milan, No. 1 (1977).

[2] Cf. the analysis in *Economia del Lavoro* (Ceres, Rome) No. 2 (1978), 'Politiche del lavoro e persone avanti nell'eta'.

departure point, we calculated an implicit 1977 female underemployment for this 30 to 49 age group of 600,000 units.

These 600,000 units, added to youth underemployment (1,400,000 units) and the underemployment of older persons (1,250,000 units), produces the figure given above of 3,250,000 units. It represents 13 per cent of the effective labour supply (an explicit supply of 21,600,000 + an implicit underemployment supply of 3,250,000 totalling 24,850,000 units) for both sexes and 24 per cent of the effective female supply (an explicit supply of 6,950,000 + an implicit underemployment supply of 2,250,000 totalling 9,200,000).

Thus implicit underemployment assumes considerable importance in labour supply estimates and characteristics. The participation rate climbs to almost 45 per cent. The female rate goes up to a much more logical rate of almost 32 per cent and becomes comparable with that in other countries.

This underemployment picture also modifies the age distribution in the labour supply structure, accentuating the young and the oldest workers. The young between the ages of 14 and 29 thus move from 30.5 per cent of the explicit labour supply to 32.2 per cent of the effective supply, while those of 50 and over rise from 16.3 per cent of the supply to 19.2 per cent.

However, these estimates do no more than provide an account of the labour supply stock existing in Italy in 1977. To calculate data for past periods, one would have to make an analogous series of estimates based on comparable official data and on similar field research. Some efforts have been made in this direction for the years 1971, 1973 and 1975. They are based on reconstruction of comparable ISTAT data for the labour force in line with the new series,[1] and results of 1975–76 supplementary research on the labour potential in Italy.[2]

These efforts reveal a considerable increase in effective labour supply in absolute terms from 1971 on, and probably also in relation to population. Particularly marked increases are evident in youth labour supply, in female labour supply in general, and in that of older persons.

However, the increase is limited to explicit supply. This is apparent for female supply, in part in connection with the expansion of tertiary employment, and to a lesser extent for youth labour supply. On the other hand there is a very evident increase in implicit supply.

Thus the economist is principally faced by these questions: Why does the effective labour supply continue to increase? And in particular, why does the female, youth, and older generation supply increase? Why is the implicit component of this supply particularly increasing?

The answers to these questions are extremely important in the search for a better understanding of the problem and a future policy for it. They can

---

[1] This reconstruction has not yet been released.

[2] Cf. the summary *Il potenziale di lavoro in Italia – Domanda ed offerta di lavoro in Italia* ISVET document No. 50/19, (Rome, August, 1976).

be used to help to design strategies to prevent the problem getting worse and to move towards its gradual solution.

In answering the first question we initially tried to focus attention on the potential labour supply (defined as the number of persons willing to supply labour given the living conditions current in the system) rather than on the effective supply. On the basis of qualitative information gathered in field research, we reasoned that the potential labour supply essentially depended not only on the population present in the system (and therefore on the demographic trends and the migration within it as well as on its structural composition) but also on the living conditions current in it.

The starting point best indicating living conditions as they affect potential labour supply seemed to be the distribution of income. This assumption was based on the conviction that persons present in the system would tend to evaluate living conditions not so much at the absolute level (even at constant prices) of individual income as in terms of purchasing power differentials between various spending units or families – as they are defined statistically.

The difference in income distribution between various families is a strong incentive to members of a family to join the labour supply in order to fill, or at least reduce, the immediately perceptible gap.

II ITALIAN INCOME DISTRIBUTION AND LABOUR SUPPLY

Introduction of such an assumption in reference to the functional relationship between personal income distribution and potential labour supply brings our analysis close to some of those made both for industrialised countries, notably the US, and for developing countries. There have been investigations into US underemployment[1] that concentrated on youth of working-age not engaged in any full-time educational activity. Since they were members of families with lower than average incomes as calculated for the previous year, the assumption was that they were suffering from underemployment or that they represented potential underemployment. Moreover, recent investigations show a considerable increase from 1970 onwards in the number of women who head families. The fact that they have steadily increasing income lags compared with the average is a major influence on the female participation rate, and consquently on labour supply in general.[2]

As far as developing countries are concerned, the International Labour Organisation has been investigating underemployment for some time. The ILO's analyses reveal underemployment to be merely unemployment hidden beneath a system, without adequate social security, that actually induces a

[1] Cf. T. Vietorisz, R. Mier and J. Giblin, 'Subemployment: exclusion and inadequacy indexes' in *Monthly Labour Review* (May 1977), pp. 13ff.

[2] Cf. B. L. Johnson, 'Women who head families: their member income lags', in *Monthly Labour Review* (February 1978), pp. 32ff.

search for any employment whatever ('. . . much underemployment is merely a
manifestation of unemployment in a country where the absence of social
security systems forces a worker to obtain income somehow . . . ').[1]

The link between income distribution and labour supply is also
underlined, inasmuch as the distinction between employment and
unemployment is obscured by considerable, more or less visible, margins
of underemployment.

Although the increasing tendency toward in-depth analyses is somewhat
handicapped by lack of satisfactory income distribution data, nonetheless
there is a growing conviction that persons of working age, in family nuclei with
below-average incomes, that do not figure in explicit labour supply are largely
in this condition, either apparently, or temporarily, or even involuntarily,
through given socio-cultural and institutional obstacles.

This conviction leads to the assumption that a large number of the
working-age persons who belong to family nuclei with below-average incomes
should be included in the potential labour supply, in the realm of implicit
supply, or at least in that element of potential supply which is unable to
translate itself into effective supply because of exclusion from it.

Unfortunately, data on personal income distribution in Italy are
particularly unsatisfactory. The only source with any continuity in time,
though its findings are limited and its inquiries include figures and movements
of figures that are open to challenge, is the series of Bank of Italy surveys on
Italian families from 1967 on.[2] Tables 14.2 and 14.3 show the results of
selected surveys. In 1976, this survey covered only 3000 families, although
in preceding years (1972 for instance) it took in close to 6000 families.

In this survey, families and family incomes were divided into deciles.
From 1972 on, the average family income lay between the sixth and seventh
decile in the grouping. Although families below the sixth group represented
60 per cent of the total, they cumulatively received less than a third of the
total income (with a minimum of 30 per cent in 1973 and 31 per cent in
1974, see Table 14.2) which wage equalisation and cost-of-living policies
brought up to 33 per cent in 1975 and 34 per cent in 1976.

The same Bank of Italy survey analysed data on individual income
distribution (see Table 14.3) which showed that 60 to 65 per cent of
individuals (with a maximum number in the years 1973 and 1974 and in the
current decade) had below-average individual incomes. They received little
more than 30 per cent (or even less in 1973) of the total income (33 per cent
in 1976). Moreover, even in 1976, there was a 1 to 12 ratio between the

---

[1] Cf. *Concepts of Labour Force Underutilization* (ILO Geneva, 1971), p. 50.
[2] Methodology was widely commented upon in the book published by G.
Campa and L. Visco, *La Distribuzione dei redditi — Problemi teorici e analisi
della situazione in Italia* (Angeli, Milan, 1973), as well as in a recent article by
G. Bianchi in *Economia del Lavoro* (Ceres, Rome), No. 4 (1977)—No. 1
(1978).

TABLE 14.2 AVERAGE INCOME AND INCOME LEVELS IN ITALY FROM 1967 TO 1976 PER FAMILY GROUP CLASSIFIED IN DECILES (thousands of lire and percentage)

Income groups	Average income (thousands of lire)					Shares of total income (percentage)					Annual average increases (%)	
	1972	1973	1974	1975	1976	1972	1973	1974	1975	1976	from 1972 to 1976	from 1967 to 1976
Up to 1° decile	410	569	743	949	1.434	2	2	2	2	2	+30.2	+18.3
From 1° to 2° decile	769	1.081	1.358	1.736	2.478	3	3	3	4	4	+28.1	+17.2
From 2° to 3° decile	1.103	1.573	1.911	2.295	3.202	5	4	5	5	5	+25.1	+16.0
From 3° to 4° decile	1.429	1.991	2.233	2.835	3.817	6	6	6	6	6	+23.2	+15.3
From 4° to 5° decile	1.720	2.367	2.875	3.431	4.468	8	7	7	7	8	+22.8	+15.1
From 5° to 6° decile	2.011	2.789	3.413	4.019	5.200	9	8	8	9	9	+22.7	+15.0
From 6° to 7° decile	2.376	3.413	4.119	4.721	6.203	10	10	10	10	11	+22.4	+15.7
From 7° to 8° decile	2.880	3.976	4.922	5.664	7.333	13	12	12	12	12	+22.2	+15.4
From 8° to 9° decile	3.647	5.052	6.091	7.183	9.360	16	15	15	15	16	+22.4	+14.9
Over 9° decile	6.468	11.099	12.593	14.101	15.978	28	33	32	30	27	+20.5	+15.2
All incomes	2.282	3.380	4.070	4.680	6.000	100	100	100	100	100	+22.6	+15.5

SOURCE Bank of Italy, 'Reddito, Risparmio e patrimonio immobiliare delle famiglie italiane nell'anno 1976', in the *Bollettino*, October–December 1977.

TABLE 14.3   INCOME DISTRIBUTION FOR A SAMPLE GROUP IN ITALY FROM 1972 TO 1976 (percentage)

Income group (thousands of lire)	Number of individuals per income group					Levels of total income				
	1972	1973	1974	1975	1976	1972	1973	1974	1975	1976
Up to 500	24	20	10	4	3	6	3	1	1	—
From 500 to 1.000	20	18	19	20	14	10	6	6	5	3
From 1.000 to 1.500	18	13	11	11	11	15	8	6	5	4
From 1.500 to 2.000	17	13	12	10	8	20	11	9	6	4
From 2.000 to 2.500	9	12	13	12	9	15	13	12	9	6
From 2.500 to 3.000	5	8	10	12	11	9	11	11	11	9
From 3.000 to 3.500	2	5	6	7	7	4	8	8	8	7
From 3.500 to 4.000	1	3	5	7	9	4	6	7	9	10
From 4.000 to 4.500	1	2	3	4	6	3	4	5	6	7
From 4.500 to 5.000	1	1	3	3	5	2	3	5	6	8
From 5.000 to 6.000	1	1	2	4	6	2	4	5	8	10
From 6.000 to 8.000	1	2	3	3	5	3	6	8	8	10
From 8.000 to 10.000	—	1	1	1	3	2	3	4	4	6
Over 10.000	—	1	2	2	3	5	14	13	14	16
Total	100	100	100	100	100	100	100	100	100	100
Average income	10.241	9.284	7.924	7.557	5.128	—	—	—	—	—
Sample base (units)	1.443	2.040	2.438	2.827	3.537	—	—	—	—	—

SOURCE Cf. Table 14.2.

average family income in the lowest decile and that in the top decile. This reinforces the impression that a remarkably unequal income distribution exists, despite some movement towards more equality after 1975.

Statistics on the job qualifications of heads of families (see Table 14.4) show that a considerable proportion of families with below-average incomes (6 million lire per year in 1976) are headed by blue-collar workers and unskilled workers. Out of the total 64 per cent of families with an annual income below 6 million lire, 22.4 per cent are headed by workers in industry and wage earners in tertiary activities, 2.7 per cent by agricultural wage earners and 20.3 per cent by unskilled workers mainly dependent on transfer incomes. On this basis one may assume that about 70 per cent of the families of blue-collar workers or wage earners in other activities and 80 per cent in the non-occupational category show a 1976 income which at best reaches the national average. If, along with blue-collar families, we include all the heads of families that figure in the employee category, the number of families with an average income under 6 million annually would drop very little – to about 60 per cent.

Thus, if we assume that there is a strong impulse to offer labour supply to round out earnings in families with below-average income, we could deduce that working-age persons in 60 per cent of the families headed by employees (excluding management levels) and 80 per cent of the families headed by unskilled workers may largely be classified as potential labour supply for 1976.

If we combine available information on the population and its behaviour in the labour supply market with the income distribution data,[1] we can estimate the number of working-age persons in family nuclei with similar income characteristics who should be classified among the labour force and the number of persons outside the labour force. In this case, the potential labour supply, including all working-age members of those family nuclei, may be estimated at 29 million persons for 1977, a difference of 7,500,000 persons as compared with ISTAT's explicit supply figures. There would be a particularly sharp jump in the female labour supply figure (absorbing slightly under 80 per cent of the difference) which would then rise to 13 million persons, while the male labour supply would rise to 16 million persons, an increase of only 1.5 million as compared with the explicit supply.

It should, however, be observed that the incentive generated by differences in income distribution to supply labour to round out the family income does not exclusively concern families with below-average incomes. There may be factors other than the desire to supplement income that determine labour supply. Otherwise there would be no explanation why many members of families headed by managers, entrepreneurs, professionals and the self-

[1] Further indirect evidence on the Italian situation may be obtained from an ISTAT family consumption survey of 31,545 families and 104,025 individuals in 1976.

TABLE 14.4 INCOME DISTRIBUTION PER FAMILY IN ITALY IN 1976 BY TYPE OF EMPLOYMENT PER FAMILY HEAD (percentage)

Type of employment of family head	Annual income levels (thousands of lire)							Total	Average income
	Up to 2.000	From 2.000 to 3.000	From 3.000 to 4.000	From 4.000 to 6.000	From 6.000 to 8.000	From 8.000 to 10.000	Over 10.000		
No. of families									
Manager	–	–	–	0.2	0.3	0.2	1.1	1.8	12.650
White-collar	0.2	0.5	1.9	4.8	4.1	3.2	4.1	18.8	8.010
Agricultural wage farmers	0.6	1.2	0.5	0.4	0.4	0.1	–	3.2	3.670
Wage earners in other sectors	0.8	3.0	7.3	1.3	5.4	2.2	2.3	32.3	5.660
Self-employed in agriculture	0.9	1.0	1.5	1.1	0.7	0.6	0.4	6.2	5.320
Self-employed in other sectors	0.5	1.3	1.7	2.6	1.9	1.0	1.4	10.4	6.460
Entrepreneur, professional	–	–	0.2	0.3	0.6	0.3	1.2	2.6	11.350
Not employed with incomes	6.5	5.3	3.9	4.6	1.9	1.2	1.3	24.7	4.160
Total	9.5	12.3	17.0	25.3	15.3	8.8	11.8	100.0	6.000
Income levels									
Manager	–	–	–	0.2	0.4	0.4	2.9	3.9	–
White-collar	–	0.3	1.2	4.1	4.8	4.7	9.9	25.0	–
Agricultural wage farmers	0.1	0.5	0.4	0.3	0.5	0.1	–	1.9	–
Wage earners in other sectors	0.3	1.3	4.3	9.3	6.2	3.3	5.8	2.3	–
Self-employed in agriculture	0.2	0.4	0.8	1.0	0.9	1.0	1.2	0.4	–
Self-employed in other sectors	0.2	0.6	1.0	2.1	2.2	1.4	3.7	11.2	–
Entrepreneur, professional	–	–	0.2	0.2	0.6	0.5	3.3	4.8	–
Not employed with incomes	1.5	2.2	2.3	3.8	2.2	1.8	3.4	17.2	–
Total	2.3	5.3	10.2	21.0	17.8	13.2	30.2	100.0	–

SOURCE cf. Table 14.2.

employed, or by employees (particularly white-collar workers) or by unskilled persons with a considerably above-average income, are led nonetheless to supply labour.

Thus the assumption previously outlined merely serves to indicate some of the reserve of labour potential that is excluded from the explicit supply. Nonetheless, it provides a substantial contribution to the better understanding of the relationship between socio-economic structures and labour supply. It paves the way for sensible schemes that take sufficiently into account the labour supply functions in place of those based on unrealistic assumptions (i.e. using wage variables) or on simplistic assumptions derived solely from demographic data.

Acceptance of this assumption, like acceptance of the more complex relationship between income distribution and labour supply, has radical consequences at the analytical level as well as a serious impact on forecasting the effects of economic policy measures.

III ANALYTICAL CONSEQUENCES

If we assume that potential labour supply depends upon population and differences in income distribution (i.e. on the number of family nuclei with below average-incomes) and the width of the income distribution gap among families, (identifiable with Gini and Theil indexes), then the greater are these the greater is the potential labour supply. The first analytical consequence worthy of note is that there is no effect on potential labour supply from variations in income earned by individuals or families (either in monetary or real terms) while there is an effect from state action and variations in the relative income positions of families in comparison with others.

This removes the aggregate functions of labour supply from traditional neo-classic positions in which attention is concentrated on the family income effects provoked by wage changes. The function of the assumed supply is quite rigid in terms of wages, although it may be influenced by modifications in the wage structure that have repercussions on income distribution between families.

A second analytical consequence worthy of attention is supply measurement. This is important from the point of view of the overall context of economic relationships to which the supply function pertains. Where the determinant labour supply factor is the need to close the gap in family income distribution, members of the family may vary labour supply, in particular, in terms of the total number of paid hours worked by the family nucleus. The number of hours may vary along with the number of persons, whose potential (on a daily, weekly, annual basis) may be individually conditioned by institutional or socio-cultural restraints (evident in different proportions on worker/students, pensioner/workers, and housewife/workers

taking account of a woman's social function as wife-mother-daughter) as well
as with the number of hours worked by each family member.

So-called second jobs become relevant at this point. This represents labour
supply in terms of extra hours worked (usually in implicit circumstances, i.e.
uncovered by contract rules and regulations) and refers to persons who are
already officially counted as employed in a particular capacity in a given
sector. In Italy, this forms a substantial component of the labour supply.
Research is currently under way in Italy to quantify the phenomenon and to
discover some of its qualitative characteristics. Several universities, financed
by the National Research Council, are working toward this end. Results are
not yet sufficient, however, to produce a total picture of the phenomenon.
Only two sources of data, which probably somewhat underestimate the
extent of second jobs, are available. The first, produced by Oensis-Isfol-Doxa,
indicated 1,008,000 workers in Italy with two or more jobs in 1974. Some
226,000 of them are classified as employed (161,000 blue-collar and 65,000
white-collar workers) and 782,000 were classified as self-employed (mainly
agriculture).[1] The second source is a Bank of Italy survey on income
distribution for 1976. On the basis of the results of this survey one may
calculate that 963,000 employed workers have second jobs. The greatest
proportion (even in the case of high-income earners) concern the areas of
self-employment in general, the civil service, agriculture, and tertiary
activities. These same results lead to the conclusion (cf. Table 14.5) that
labour supply available for second jobs is directed mainly at tertiary activities,
self-employment in agriculture, and to a lesser extent at the white-collar
level (10 per cent of cases), blue-collar level or similar (15 per cent of cases),
or agricultural employment (6 per cent of cases).

The nature of jobs leads inevitably to measurement of supply in terms of
hours rather than of persons and makes the link between income distribution
and supply even more complex than that assumed with lower-than-average-
income families (there is no doubt that the prevailing motivation is still the
impulse to fill the standard-of-living gap from family to family, although it
includes numerous families with medium-to-high incomes). It also switches
attention from potential labour supply to effective supply.

Population trends and the existence of radical pre-existing differences in
income distribution (on the increase up to 1973) explain the reason why
potential labour supply in Italy has grown at least as fast as population over
the medium term (the last 10—15 years).

Women, young people and older persons are all considered as secondary
labour supply components compared to the head of a family in any industrial
society. It is this group that is particularly subject to the impulse to
supplement family income through additional work, in that those already
employed who resort to a second job have not achieved the kind of income

[1] Cf. Censis, *Aspetti quantitative e qualitativi dell'occupazione non
istituzionale in Italia* (Rome, 1975), pp. 1/65 etc.

TABLE 14.5 MAIN AND SECONDARY ACTIVITIES IN ITALY IN 1976 – BANK OF ITALY SURVEY ON FAMILY INCOME AND SAVINGS (percentage)

Professional status	With a secondary activity	Secondary activity										
		Professional status							Sectors			
		Entrepreneurs, professional	Manager	White-collar employees	Agricultural employees	Employed in other sectors	Self-employed agricultural	Self-employed in other sectors	Agriculture	Industry artisan sectors	Public administration	Other activities
Professional status												
Entrepreneur, professional	11.2	−	−	76.9	−	7.7	7.7	7.7	7.7	−	15.4	76.9
Manager	8.8	60.0	−	20.0	−	−	−	20.0	−	20.0	20.0	60.0
White-collar employees	5.5	50.1	−	12.5	−	7.1	7.1	23.2	8.9	7.1	1.8	82.2
Agricultural employees	6.6	−	−	−	10.0	−	90.0	−	100.0	−	−	−
Employed in other sectors	3.7	11.3	−	1.6	3.2	24.2	35.5	24.2	37.2	30.6	6.4	25.8
Self-employed in agriculture	5.8	−	−	−	58.3	16.7	8.3	16.7	66.6	16.7	−	16.7
Self-employed in other sectors	4.2	−	−	−	5.6	16.7	55.5	22.2	61.1	11.1	−	27.8
Sectors												
Agriculture	6.0	−	−	−	36.4	9.1	45.4	9.1	81.8	9.1	−	9.1
Industry, artisan sectors	3.8	18.2	−	1.8	1.8	14.6	30.9	32.7	32.7	36.4	1.8	29.1
Public administration	7.4	37.7	−	13.2	1.9	13.2	13.2	20.8	17.0	7.5	5.7	69.8
Other activities	4.1	19.6	−	21.7	2.2	19.6	28.2	8.7	30.4	2.2	8.7	58.7
Total	4.8	22.3	−	10.3	6.4	14.9	26.2	19.9	33.1	15.4	4.6	46.9

SOURCE cf Table. 7. p. 6.

that accords with the standard of living believed necessary. It should be added that where institutional or socio-cultural motives render female labour normal, the increase in potential supply includes a marked involvement among young people and older persons.

This growing potential labour supply, with its qualitative structure, tends to translate into effective labour supply. It becomes effective when the worker is able to obtain an income, or at least hopes to obtain an income, within a relatively brief period. Opportunities to obtain income may derive from work or from substitutes in the form of subventions granted to those workers who figure in the search for gainful employment, but who are unable to obtain it because of a variety of circumstances which are not apparently dependent upon their will to work. Subvention substitutes are not easily obtainable. Nor are they high or permanent. As a result, they are not a substitute for gainful employment, and the effective supply remains normal in the face of a corresponding effective demand. In a country like Italy, where gaps in the social security system as far as unemployment is concerned mean largely unsatisfactory subventions, supply and effective demand generally tend to coincide. With considerable increasing pressure from labour supply, effective labour demand (i.e. the production system in its various forms) may select and dictate conditions to a large part of the supply, to the point where it may evade conditions imposed by contracts and regulations. Thus, effective demand is separated into two components: one absorbs supply under the usual conditions imposed at the contract and regulation level and this, therefore, corresponds to demand/supply (included in official statistics because it is explicit) distinguished by the qualitative characteristics of workers and their particular strengths within the productive structure; the other absorbs workers under conditions (monetary or non-monetary) that are below normal at the contract and regulation level and that therefore correspond to supply/demand that may be classified as more or less explicit underemployment. Naturally, implicit underemployment, not included in official statistics, is part of this component. It covers the weaker workers. This weakness may be traced to their qualitative characteristics or to their impotence in the face of those within the productive structure who hold power. Thus on the one hand implicit underemployment is increased by the pressure of a growing labour supply in search of income, while on the other it is increased because of the opportunity the productive system has to select its supply and to apply conditions that favour the objectives of the production unit at the expense of the unfavourable consequences in the form of the underemployed labour supply and the social system in general.[1]
Women, young people and older persons not only form a considerable

---

[1] Research into underemployment published in various editions of *Quaderni di Economia del Lavoro* (ed. Angeli), Milan, clearly outlined these consequences.

proportion of this implicit underemployment total but their numbers are growing. They figure in this total because they show qualitative characteristics (such as rigidity in respect of terms of labour, particularly important in any system in which labour shows a growing tendency to be almost a fixed factor) that are less acceptable to the productive system in its selection from the total supply. They may also create some difficulties in the selection process from the supply point of view or they may be particularly weak in contrast to those already within the productive system who hold decision-making powers.

In an economic system like Italy's where there is a considerable labour potential that is constantly expanding so far as explicit employment is concerned, and where the social security system offers only inadaquate income guarantees for unemployed workers, underemployment is by far the most important aspect in the analysis of unemployment problems. Concentration on unemployment, defined as the quantified labour supply unemployed at the time of quantification or during a reference period, would make no sense, for the following reasons:

(a) the lack of transfer-type income-flows for unemployed workers, and/or unsatisfactory government employment mechanisms, discourage numerous potential supply units from registering on the unemployment lists or defining themselves as such during surveys or research;

(b) little or no transfer of income induces the majority of supply units without regular jobs to accept any opportunity that comes up, whether or not they are registered with the unemployment lists or classified as job seekers, just to make the money they require and in the process they expand underemployment.

Unemployment data offer only partial information (from the point of view of the qualitative structure on the employment problem).

The dimensions and characteristics of underemployment emphasise the need to concentrate on underemployment, eventually combining it with available unemployment figures, once the risk of duplication (due to the fact that the unemployed do not regard themselves as excluded from contributing to family income) has been carefully avoided.

Thus, underemployment is an essential component in the effective labour supply. Neglecting it in analysing such a system as Italy's (and international seminars have shown some evidence that this is true of other industrialised systems that have a substantial immigration of foreign labour or massive domestic migratory movements) would be vastly misleading and affect the explanatory significance of the analysis as well as the development of principles affecting economic policy.

But underemployment also neglects one of the components of labour supply potential: that potential, often termed 'non-employment', which does not translate into effective supply. The extent of this phenomenon may be seen in the importance of institutional or socio-cultural obstacles which force the potential supply units, given the standard of living within the system, to withdraw from the effective supply. Any complete analysis of labour supply must also consider this component of potential supply. Its impact on the dimensions and characteristics of the employment problem are anything but negligible.

Despite the difficulties arising from the qualitative and quantitative structure of underemployment, it is still possible to make enormous strides toward improved understanding of the employment problem. Attempts at analysis made in Italy[1] show, for a series of demand/supply periods, how the underemployment component of the effective labour supply may be profoundly affected by income distribution and income distribution trends, given the pressure of potential labour supply on effective demand. This requires reconsideration of other aspects of the analysis which are particularly significant for arriving at a forecast of the possible effects of economic policies aimed at containing and gradually resolving the employment problem.

IV SIGNIFICANT ASPECTS FOR ECONOMIC POLICY

Our earlier discussion emphasising changes in the income distribution structure, rather than income or wage variations, as the principal factor affecting employment, thus switching attention from demand to supply, leads the scepticism (already underlined by considerations of labour rigidity and the complementarity between labour and capital) regarding the efficacy of economic policy designed to expand employment by restricting or even reducing, real wages.[2] Moreover, an analysis of the relationship linking income distribution, potential labour supply and effective supply-demand, carries us well beyond this point by changing the order of magnitude of the role of containment (or even reduction) of labour costs as an efficacious economic policy line in meeting employment problems.

Even if one uses the Keynesian employment function as a starting point, making employment dependent upon production trends, and assuming 'expansion effects' are linked to restriction over a period or reduction of unit labour costs per product, one must still clarify three points.

(1) How restriction or reduction of labour costs is accomplished; if it is obtained by acting upon monetary wages and thus has made the income distribution situation worse (which would happen in Italy if it were

---

[1] Cf. the article in 'L'Offerta di Lavoro in Italia' ('Struttura produttiva, distribuzione dei redditi ed offerta di lavoro') in *Quaderni di Economia del Lavoro* (ed. Angeli), Milan, No. 1 (1976).

[2] More extensive estimates, already partially presented in a paper discussed at an OCSE meeting in Paris in the Spring of 1977, will be made in Rome in November 1978 when the Italian Economists Society meets.

accomplished through suspension of the 'scala mobile' or indexed cost of living rises, as agreed in 1973, which have had a substantially equalising effect in recent years), any possible positive effects on effective labour demand may be accomplished through greater stimulus to expand potential labour supply and a possible deterioration, rather than an improvement, of the employment problem; the situation would be different if lower unit product costs were the result of an increase in product per labour unit, which would not directly influence income distribution.

(2) What type of labour demand is involved in the expansion of production; the fact that implicit underemployment has a much lower unit labour cost than regular employment (in Italy it is often less than half) and that it is, in particular, much more flexible in terms of increase and reduction, may stimulate production to expand that component of effective labour demand rather than to expand explicit employment fully covered by contracts and regulations; once again, the employment situation would deteriorate, rather than improve – unless production expansion were accompanied by economic policy measures designed to discourage recourse to so-called black labour.[1]

(3) If the productive structures are such as to provide substantial complementarity between capital and labour, and thus if there is a possibility that growth of capital investment will have production expansion effects on employment; it appears less and less certain that increased profits automatically stimulate investment to expand production inasmuch as the degree of utilisation of plant capacity, the cost of short-term credit and the prospects and levels of profits (and therefore the effects on income distribution and the consequent social structures) in the medium/long term appear to play a more important part in a company's investment decisions.

Given the difficulties of obtaining satisfactory expansion of explicit employment from more or less 'endogenous' production increases, there has recently been some discussion of opening up new employment possibilities by reducing the average number of working hours per worker. In this case, the daily-monthly-annual wages remain the same so that there will be no negative effect on production demand, provided the system is extended to a number of industrialised countries so as to avoid a fall in international competitiveness in the country that has recourse to it.

On the basis of research under way in Italy, it is evident that there is some danger that reduced working hours stimulate implicit underemployment (given the enormous potential that is not regularly employed and the extreme inequality of distribution) rather than stimulate employment governed by norms and contracts, since it is more convenient for production to take this form (given greater labour rigidity), and the need for increased family income

---

[1] In Italy this means measures to exercise greater control over fiscal and social benefits evasion, progressive fiscalisation of social benefits and a radical selective revision of the productive system.

is likely to encourage workers to use their free hours as a source of income, possibly expanding a second job. Research suggests that this kind of phenomenon can be avoided by making reduced working hours part of an overall strategy that would include:

(i) an economic policy directed at rather substantial production increase stimulated by a special investment policy;
(ii) a careful revision of some important aspects of work organisation;
(iii) a different organisation of work time, on an annual or possibly longer basis, of which reduced weekly or annual working hours would be only one aspect.[1]

To reduce the incentive to use free hours in further labour supply (thus maintaining labour potential in terms of hours unchanged), it would be necessary to improve income distribution so that there would be less movation to seek the better standards of living enjoyed by other families.

Thus, intervention at the income distribution level is an essential part of any economic policy effectively aiming at a positive impact on the employment problems in systems where there are extreme distribution inequalities alongside enormous differences between potential labour supply and employment fully protected by norms and contracts. Without this intervention, it is illusory to think it possible to resolve employment problems merely by using Keynesian or similar employment policies at the labour-demand level. In a sense, underlining the importance of income distribution from the labour supply point of view turns to account some ideas deriving from neo-Richardian theoretical analysis.[2]

It has been suggested that one effective distribution-type intervention might be the introduction of a guaranteed minimum wage extended to all potential labour supply (at least up to given family income levels). This form of income transfer would have a sharp effect on the stimulus to supplement income at any cost that is assumed to be the fundamental labour supply motivation, particularly where there are family members with below average incomes. At this point it should be observed that:

(a) extending this kind of institution is not an easy solution since it puts an enormous load on the public budget (already burdened in all industrialised countries by growing difficulties), and presents difficulties in identifying potential labour supply. For example, housewives might be included in labour supply to an extent well beyond that recorded in official statistics; up to

---

[1] The problems here have been thoroughly discussed in *Tendenze dell'occupazione*, no. 3 (1978) and in *Economia del Lavoro*, nos. 3–4 (1978) (Ceres, Rome) dedicated to 'Gestione del Tempo di Lavoro'.
[2] These ideas were developed by Italian economists at Cambridge, England, starting with the work of P. Sraffa.

what point should a minimum guaranteed wage be extended to the housewife group? (b) Such a scheme should obviously not be made additional to other transfers like pensions; but where this did not occur, the pensioner would still be motivated to supply labour to supplement inadequate pensions unless the pension were substantially raised to coincide with the income the supply unit believed necessary. (c) Within the inflationary context predicted for Italy and other industrialised countries for the near future, the minimum guaranteed wage would have to be indexed with a 'scala mobile' type of mechanism to prevent the distributive consequences of inflation from creating even more powerful incentives to add to labour supply in order to supplement inadequate incomes. (d) The solution of adopting assistance-type income transfers might provoke widespread indifference, with enormous social repercussions leading to greater alienation and less participation of the individual in control over the power structure within the system and over its changes over a period of time; it might also have limited effect on the size and character of labour supply since individuals might be motivated more and more by the need to acquire and consolidate active participation in the social system, with its attendant social roles, than by the sole need to supplement inadequate family incomes. This final observation turns the focus from the field of economic analysis to other social sciences. At the economic level, however, the observations made on the general extension of a minimum guaranteed wage reveal that none of these policies can *per se* decisively provide the solution of the employment problem, given its complexity and innumerable aspects. To obtain any appreciable results, it would be necessary to aim at an articulated economic policy that would make an all-inclusive attack on the whole complex, acting both on the factors that determine the trends, and on the structural modifications of labour demand and the structural modifications of supply. The considerations outlined in this paper are aimed at contributing, or forming a starting point, in however limited a way, to focusing attention on factors from the supply perspective which have seldom been adequately considered by economists.

Discussion of Professor Frey's Paper

Professor Eastman said the paper was interesting, not only for the light that it threw on what was happening in Italy but also for its analysis of the statistical problems. Italian statistics seemed to have understated the number of job vacancies. New information now available allowed the labour force to be described in a better way. It seemed that 3 million out of the Italian labour force of 21 million worked either temporarily, or were effectively outside the wage system. Professor Frey called these the underemployed and they worked in less favourable situations.

The second part of the paper was more theoretical, and began by asking why participation rates were still increasing in Italy. There seemed to be no evidence as to the fact. However, the theory was that the share of income going to less-advantaged families pushed them into more-active participation in the labour market. They took two jobs, or sent their children out to work, in order to get what they thought they needed compared with others. This was not a question of sociology but of the impact of income distribution on family decisions. There certainly seemed to be societies where this did not happen.

When one passed to the statistics in the text, one could see that the incidence of the second or other member of the family who worked was stronger for the higher income groups. This might be attributable to other causes than the distribution of income and the author said that there were other reasons for the lowest-paid becoming more active. This raised a question about the consistency between the facts and the thesis about income distribution. One could say that participation by a second worker in better-off households resulted from the fact that the possibilities for work for them were greater. One then had the 'discouraged unemployed' in an unfavourable position relative to the better-off. There was also the possibility that those in work were paid less because they worked in black/grey labour markets. This was not easily seen from the paper. If one accepted the thesis, however, one would observe that those who did not get jobs were being affected by factors other than income. Examples might be the birth rate, social insurance, social attitudes etc. These factors, and changes in them, gave a better explanation of the fact and a richer theory.

As for the black market, it seemed that, in Italy, the labour market was regulated in a radical way. A result was that conditions of work differed greatly between official and black markets, which posed problems for the interpretation of the statistics. It would be interesting to study this but perhaps better to do so with a more inclusive system. Black market labour might not be directly paid but given benefits in kind. In each market one would then have a wage benefit. Work in a parallel market would have some kind of relationship with the more visible market.

Professor Eastman thought the problem that really interested Professor Frey was how one could adjust the supply and demand for labour in the official market, to increase the demand for such labour and reduce the supply. An increase in the demand for labour required increased productivity, which was not easy to achieve. It called for structural/industrial policy. Alternatively, the increase in the quantity of labour demanded on the official market could be obtained by reduced real wages in Italy, which would equalise opportunities to work and so equalise the incomes of the groups which benefited from the more favourable régime. There might also be a decline in the standard of living of labour which would bring a better balance between demand and supply.

Professor Bergmann reported that when she asked undergraduates why there were now more women in the labour market, they suggested, first, Professor Frey's point: people below wanted to catch up. Second, they said that inflation made people feel worse off, and so caused them to cancel this out through taking two jobs. She was tempted to say that there had always been a problem of income distribution and that there was no evidence of any recent change. Why did something which was always true therefore lead to a change?

As for inflation, she would here say that real income had increased, so this argument could not be true. One could not, of course, rule out the possibility that people felt worse off because of 'false consciousness' or money illusion, but it was still not clear why the lower paid felt a stronger need to catch up now than in the past. Was it to do with trade unions?

The other reason might be sociological. There used to be low wages for women, depending on the fact that they did not have children before they were married. Once married they had children and a husband. If the latter died, provision was made for the children. However, in the USA this was now a poor basis for a lifelong decision. There was divorce; the sexual revolution; and more one-parent families. It was possible to argue that security was now less. Perhaps one needed a new application of the theory of uncertainty. Perhaps some American women felt it was now less desirable than formerly to be a housewife.

Dr Kaufman wanted to ask Professor Frey what was the latter's evidence for his rejection of the neo-classical conclusion that changes in wage rates led to changes in the labour supply. Why did he prefer the conclusion that the change in the labour supply was a result of changes in the distribution of income?

Professor Timofeev noted that while the paper was based on Italy some international comparisons were possible, and this had been recognised by Italians. Professor Frey wanted an increase in the incomes of the lower paid, but what was the implication of this for Europe in general? Many said that this would be acceptable in Italy, but was that not equally true for all Western Europe?

Dr Kaufman noted that some economists maintained that enhanced job security arrangements and high social security contributions in Italy (and elsewhere) had greatly discouraged firms in the private sector from officially

hiring new employees. As a result, unemployment had risen and the unofficial
or 'black' labour market had grown substantially. While he himself was
sceptical about the importance of these factors in explaining unemployment
in the USA and most of Western Europe, he wondered how important
Professor Frey thought they were in Italy.

Professor Bergmann wondered why an unofficial market should be called
'black'. She felt it should be 'white', particularly since taxes there were
lower.

Professor Frey began his reply to the discussion by commenting on the
remarks by Professor Timofeev. When issues like this were discussed in OECD
meetings, he often asked his colleagues whether there were similar problems
in their countries. The answer was always that they did not know. They never
denied their existence outright.

When one looked at employment problems of young people and the old,
it was hard to find any researcher who was studying these issues. He
remembered, in 1972, a discussion on the unemployment of young people in
the USA. Someone had asked whether the problem was the same in Italy and
no-one knew the answer. Later research had shown that youth unemployment
was a big problem in Italy, but its existence had been learned from America,
where there was research.

At a seminar in Florence in 1977, it had been said that underemployment
in Italy continued. This was like the problem of looking for a black cat in a
dark hole. One could not see the cat, but if it was important, one needed to
try to find it, or at least its dimensions. In Italy, the unemployment of the
old and the young was a large and increasing problem. It was not a question
of primary and secondary labour markets. The American situation could not
apply because the market was more fragmented. The cause could be demand
deficiency, not high wages in the primary sector.

The question of the standard of living in the secondary sector had been
raised. For young people, the cause of unemployment was not inadequate
wage rates but other factors. A hypothetical income distribution gave an index
of social structure. Unfortunately, income distribution data were bad for Italy,
but he had found that one could explain a lot in this way.

The reason one referred to 'black' work was that this was a direct
translation from the Italian. One simply meant irregular work. However, the
difference in labour costs was very big, perhaps 10:4. If one asked students in
workers' schools why women, young people and old age pensioners were
being forced out to work again, they said the cause was inflation. However, it
appeared to be more a result of the effects of inflation on income distribution
than its direct impact. People were trying to keep up the standard of living of
their own families relative to those of others and there was a chain of reaction
from poorer to richer families. This might be very important in terms of the
standard of living, and had political consequences. If one accepted the
hypothesis, one could follow a strategy which looked at the effects on
standards of living as positive. In 1971–75, underemployment had not been

important. There had been indexation of wages to offset price increases. After 1975, the problem had been linked to inflation with a worsening of the situation, especially outside the industrial sector where indexation continued.

In 1976, one knew that unemployment was high, and yet the published rates were quite low. He therefore got his ideas about the 'black market' from American experience.

Enquiries into the labour market situation had begun in 1971. It had been found that part of the labour force could be shifted. Questions had been asked of heads of families about active labour market participation. Now different questions were being asked, and it was found that there was an increase in participation. It was therefore more possible now to make international comparisons with Italian data.

There was a link between job security, primary labour markets, unemployment, etc. A superficial analysis showed that 1965 saw the beginning of mass unemployment in Italy. The causes were structural, were linked to economic development over 30 years, and arose on both the demand and supply side. Studies were now being made of industrialisation, taxation, and changes in agriculture. On the supply side there was the effect of migration. Three million people had moved from the South to the North in 20 years.

15 Employment Sharing in Japan*

Konosuke Odaka
HITOTSUBASHI UNIVERSITY, TOKYO, JAPAN

I INTRODUCTION

Except for several years immediately following the Second World War, unemployment has seldom posed a serious threat to the economic policy-makers in Japan. The annual rate of unemployment has consistently registered a markedly low, 'super-full-employment' figure. The published unemployment statistics have never exceeded 3 per cent; if anything, they were kept below 1 percentage point during the phase of rapid economic growth in the 1960s (Table 15.1). The rising unemployment in the 1974 recession, eventually exceeding the 3 per cent level, may therefore mark the beginning of a new era in the Japanese economy.

The low level of unemployment is indeed remarkable in view of the widely-accepted notion that the economy had been endowed with a relatively abundant supply of labour. Only after 1965 – so the argument goes – did the economy emerge from the phase of unlimited supplies of labour (Minami, 1973).[1] But how can this view be reconciled with the official statistics quoted? One might suspect that the Japanese unemployment is under-reported by the western standard, and that it is not comparable with the figures for other countries. Perhaps it needs to be multiplied by some factor in order to match its counterparts.

The first part of the present paper examines this question and comes to the conclusion that the concept and the definition of the Japanese unemployment statistics are roughly equivalent to those adopted in the United States of America and that, even after making appropriate adjustments, the Japanese figure needs to be raised by only a small margin.

Having established that the published statistics reflect economic reality, the next, more substantial task will be to examine the working of the Japanese labour market that manages to keep unemployment low. Does the

*The work embodied in this paper has been supported in part by a research grant from the Ministry of Labour. Views expressed in it are not necessarily those of the Ministry, and the author alone is responsible for them.

[1] In fact, the rapid growth was greatly facilitated by the abundant labour supply Cf. Galenson-Odaka (1976).

TABLE 15.1 JAPANESE UNEMPLOYMENT AND RELATED STATISTICS (In thousands except where otherwise indicated)

Year	(L) Labour force[a]	(U) Unemployed[a]	Not in labour force	Unemployment rate (%)	(A) Employable population above age 15[b]	(B) National defence force[c]	(D) Unpaid family workers Total	Of whom working 14 hours or less per week	Number of college students[e]	Recipients of unemployment insurance (%)[f]	Vacancy/applicant ratios[g] (ratio)
1950	36,347	722	19,234	1.99	1116	105	12,250	1388[d]	419	6.22	0.20[h]
1955	40,027	765	19,450	1.91	1068	155	11,894	1348[d]	610	5.43	0.27
1960	44,028	337	21,313	0.76	684	211	10,478	1187	712	2.94	0.59
1965	48,269	659	24,818	1.37	672	224	9284	1150	938	3.25	0.64
1970	52,948	713	25,944	1.35	396	233	8536	594	1407	2.36	1.41
1975	54,390	1249	30,283	2.30	178	238	6945	499	2088	3.69	0.61

SOURCES

[a] The series L and U have been derived from Bureau of Statistics, Office of the Prime Minister, *Population Census of Japan*, various issues.

[b] The series A has been estimated as: the total population of age 15 and above, *less* the total number of senior high-school students, excluding night-school enrolments; the number of students has been obtained from the Ministry of Education's *Gakkō kyōiku kihon tōkei chōsa hōkoku* (Report on Basic Educational Statistics), various issues.

[c] The series B has been obtained from the Population Census, except that the figure for 1950 has been estimated by applying the 1955 ratio of the number of policemen to that of the defence force personnel.

[d] Estimated by applying the 1960 ratio of series D to the total number of unpaid family workers.

[e] Taken from the same source cited in note[b] above.

[f] Bureau of Employment Security, Ministry of Labour, *Shitsugyō hoken jigyō hōkoku* (Report on Unemployment Insurance Activities), various issues.

[g] Bureau of Employment Security, Ministry of Labour, *Shokugyō antei gyōmu tōkei* (Report on Employment Securities), various issues, and ditto, *Rōdō shijō nempō* (Annual Report on the Labor Market), various issues.

[h] The figure for 1951.

economy operate some system of employment sharing? Are the practices of the Japanese management significantly different from those in other countries? Section III through V of the paper present preliminary attempts at answering these questions. Concluding observations will be made in Section VI.

II UNEMPLOYMENT IN JAPAN

There are two major statistical sources for measuring Japanese unemployment: the Population Census (*kokusei chōsa*) which is taken every five years and covers the entire population, and the monthly labour force survey (*rōdoryoku chōsa*) which is a sample survey of about 76,000 adults drawn from all over the country.[1]

Essentially the Japanese definition of unemployment conforms to that of the Current Population Survey (CPS for short), which is administered by the Bureau of Labor Statistics in the United States. As will be seen in Table 15.2 below, major distinctions between the two systems are: first, the Japanese labour force includes the youngsters of fifteen years of age, while they are excluded from the American survey; second, military personnel are excluded in the American definition while the defence forces are treated as part of the Japanese labour force; third, whereas in the United States unpaid family workers cannot be counted as part of the labour force unless they worked fifteen hours or more during the survey week, the Japanese definition in this regard is more lenient (i.e. one hour or longer); and fourth, workers laid-off as well as those who have already found jobs and are expecting to be at work within thirty days are regarded as unemployed by the CPS, but are classified as 'employed' or as 'not in labour force', respectively, in the Japanese survey.

There is an additional complication arising from a peculiar practice of Japanese personnel management, which is especially noticeable among the larger corporations: a system of 'stand by' (*ichiji kikyū*). During the 1974–75 recession, for instance, a large number of workers were temporarily put into reserve while maintaining their formal ties with their employers; the employees did not lose their employment status but their salaries and wages might be reduced substantially. The precise figure of 'stand-bys' is not available. However, it may be estimated by referring to the cumulative totals of the firms and the employees that become eligible for the provision of wage subsidies under the newly-enacted Employment Insurance Act of 1975 (*Koyō Hoken Hō*): on the monthly average, to give an illustration, 237,332

---

[1] Approximately 33,000 households are covered by the labour force survey. The corresponding size of the sample in the Current Population Survey in the United States is 52,500 households (increased from the previous level of 35,000 beginning in January 1967). See Stein (1967), p.5.

TABLE 15.2 MAJOR DEFINITIONAL DIFFERENCES IN LABOUR FORCE SURVEYS IN JAPAN AND THE USA

Category	Japan	USA
Labour force	A Lower age limit is *15*	A Lower age limit is *16*[a] B Excludes military personnel
The employed	C Persons who were engaged in paid occupations for *1 hour or longer* during the survey week, inclusive of those who had jobs but were temporarily absent from work, irrespective of whether or not looking for other jobs D Unpaid family workers who worked for *1 hour or longer* during the survey week E Persons waiting to be recalled from 'stand by'	C Persons who did *any work* at all during the survey week, inclusive of those who had jobs but were temporarily absent from work, irrespective of whether or not looking for other jobs.[b] D Unpaid family workers who worked for *15 hours or longer* during the survey week
The unemployed	F Persons who did no work at all during the survey week and had engaged in some specific job-seeking activity (time period of job search unspecified)	E Persons who were currently available for work and were waiting to be recalled from lay-off F Persons who did not work during the survey week and had engaged in some specific job-seeking activity *within the past 4 weeks*
Not in labour force	G Persons waiting to start a new job.[c]	G Persons who were currently available for work and were waiting to start a new job in 30 days, excepting new school graduates.[c]

[a] Lower age limit was 14 up to December 1966.

[b] Up to December 1966, persons who were absent from their jobs the entire survey week, because of vacations, illness, strikes, bad weather, etc., and who were looking for other jobs were classified as unemployed.

[c] Not engaged in job search by definition.

SOURCES

Japan: Bureau of Statistics, Office of the Prime Minister, *Annual Report on the Labour Force Survey 1976*, pp. 142–87; Ministry of Labour, *Shōwa 52 nen rōdō keizai no bunseki* (The 1977 White Paper on the Labor Economy) (Tokyo, 1978), supplement, p. 9. *USA*: President's Committee to Appraise Employment and Unemployment Statistics (The Gordon Committee), *Measuring Employment and Unemployment* (Washington, DC, 1962), pp. 42–62, 242–44; Stein (1967), pp. 3–27; *Employment and Training Report of the President 1977*, pp. 30–3, 127–78.

workers received assistance during the fiscal year 1975.[1] Presumably the
figure underestimates the true incidence of the workers who were ordered to
'stand-by'. Nonetheless, they are useful to indicate the extent of the excess
manpower; the employees concerned might have been discharged and become
unemployed had there been no provision under the Act.

Table 15.3 presents an attempt to adjust the Japanese Census statistics to
suit the CPS format.[2] The change in the lower age limit (item A in Table
15.2) hardly affects the unemployment rate.[3] With regard to items B and G,
there is no reason to believe that the exclusion of defence personnel and of a
portion of the unpaid family workers will influence the numerator;
consequently, they will make the unemployment rate somewhat smaller
than the officially reported figure.

There is room for ambiguity concerning the true magnitudes of items E
and G. Taking the item G first, note that a special labour force survey in
March 1975 has yielded the information that 830,000 out of 31,360,000
persons in the 'not-in-labour-force' category had already committed
themselves to job offers, and that 670,000 of the 830,000 were expecting to
start their new jobs within 30 days. Eliminating further the number of new
school graduates (280,000), the estimated item G figure for 1975 comes
down finally to 390,000. The ratio of 390 to 31,360 (i.e. 0.0124) was
subsequently applied uniformly to the 'not-in-labour-force' figures in other

---

[1] The old Unemployment Insurance Act of 1947 was revised and enlarged in
1975 in such a way that the 'depressed industries' are entitled to apply for
financial support from the government insurance fund to supplement as much
as 50 per cent (75 per cent in the case of smaller firms with 300 employees or
less) of the stipends of their 'stand-bys' up to a maximum period of three
months, provided that the 'stand-bys' amount to more than 1/3 (1/4 in the
case of smaller firms) of total monthly manhours. The 'depressed industries'
are to be officially designated by the Labour Minister when the following
four indices have declined by more than 10 per cent (computed on the three-
month average basis) over the corresponding levels in the same period of the
preceding year: output, overtime work, the number of unfilled vacancies and
the number of new entrants.
The cumulative totals of the firms and the employees receiving the
provision were: January—March 1975, 5887 firms (355,005 employees);
April 1975—March 1976, 59,418 (2,847,978); April 1976—March 1977, 4081
(254,301); and April 1977—March 1978, 162 (12,524). It is estimated (*The
Japan Economic Journal* (in Japanese), 2 April 1976, p. 3) that about 54.5
billion yen was expended during the calendar year 1975.

[2] I have judged that the Population Census is more suitable than the labour
force survey for the purpose of the computation simply because the former
covered the entire population.

[3] This adjustment makes the unemployment rate slightly overstated, as a
portion of the population of age 15 is in fact unemployed (but is ignored in
the computation).

TABLE 15.3 HYPOTHETICAL JAPANESE UNEMPLOYMENT RATES ACCORDING TO THE CPS DEFINITION

Year	(I) L – A + B – D + G	(II) U + G	(III) U + E + G	(IV) U + E + G + 0.1S	(V) (II)/(I)	(VI) (III)/(I)	(V) (IV)/(I)	Official unemployment rate
		(thousands)			(Percentages)			
1950	34,187	961	1161[a]	1203[a]	2.81	(3.40)	(3.52)	1.99
1955	38,007	1006	1206[a]	1267[a]	2.65	(3.17)	(3.33)	1.91
1960	42,632	601	801[a]	872[a]	1.41	(1.88)	(2.05)	0.76
1965	46,979	967	1167[a]	1261[a]	2.06	(2.48)	(2.68)	1.37
1970	52,513	1035	1235[a]	1376[a]	1.97	(2.35)	(2.62)	1.35
1975	54,341	1639	1995	2204	3.02	3.67	4.06	2.30

For variable names, see Table 15.1.

[a] A figure of 200,000 is assumed for item E; the adjusted rates in columns (V), (VI) and (V), which were derived by use of this assumed figure, are enclosed in parentheses to indicate the somewhat speculative nature of these estimates.

years to yield similar estimates.[1] These estimates were then added on to the officially reported unemployment (see columns I and II of Table 15.3).

No information exists to help one guess the magnitude of item E. The closest one can get to it is perhaps by using the number of 'stand-bys', as mentioned before. The writer has ventured to adopt an inflated version of the figure by multiplying it by the factor of 1.5 to obtain an estimate of 356,000.[2] In reality, however, the 'stand-by' workers can hardly be classified as unemployed, since they receive part of their remuneration. The rate of unemployment based on this estimate (column VI in Table 15.3) is thus no more than a mere conjecture.

It is sometimes claimed that in the United States a large number of self-supporting college students, inclusive of those enrolled in junior colleges, undergraduate as well as graduate students of universities, are partly responsible for raising the unemployment rate. In order to entertain this view, the present writer has made the hypothesis that as many as 10 per cent of Japanese college students are 'unemployed' during the survey week (column VII in Table 15.3). This, however, is a most questionable procedure, for they seldom consider themselves to be 'unemployed' so long as they keep their status of regular students.

Of the three adjusted versions of the Japanese unemployment rates in Table 15.3, the first version (column V) seems most acceptable. If one agrees to settle on this version, it follows that even after the disturbed years of 1972–73, the unemployment rate never reached as high a level as the American rate.

To provide an additional frame of reference to the above estimates, one may take the ratio of the recipients of unemployment insurance to the total number of the insured labour force: 3.7 per cent for the calendar year 1975 (see Table 15.1). Similarly, the monthly average of active job searchers, as registered at the government's Employment Security Office, was 1,536,000 in 1975, excluding new school graduates. It seems that these figures do not differ as widely from the corrected unemployment statistics as they used to do some 15 or 20 years ago (cf. the last two columns of Table 15.1).

When one turns one's attention from the absolute level to the movements of the unemployment rate over a period of years, a striking picture emerges. Umemura (1963) once observed that the ups and downs of the unemployment rate, after having been adjusted for seasonal variations, match perfectly with

[1] The resulting estimates are:

1950	239,000	1965	308,000
1955	241,000	1970	322,000
1960	264,000	1975	390,000

These figures probably overestimate the true picture in the labour market, for people are particularly mobile in the spring time, March being the closing month of the Japanese fiscal year.

[2] The latter figure (31,360) does not agree with the number reported in Table 15.1, as it is a result of a sample survey.

the opposite movements of the net outflows of labour from the farm households. In the same sense, simple correlation coefficients between the unemployment rates and the gross national expenditure in real terms, as measured between corresponding quarters over some 22 years (1954 I–1976 IV), indicate mild and yet significant correspondence:

–0.54, with no lag introduced,
–0.59, with unemployment lagged by one quarter,
–0.56, with unemployment lagged by two quarters,
–0.51, with unemployment lagged by three quarters, and
–0.41, with unemployment lagged by four quarters.[1]

It is hard to believe that both the Population Census and the official labour force survey have similar procedural defects. Despite minor definitional problems, one may in principle accept the published statistics as they are. The low level and small amplititude ought to be explained by the inherent mechanisms of the labour market itself.

III THE INCIDENCE OF UNEMPLOYMENT IN JAPAN

In the remainder of the paper, I shall revert to the official unemployment statistics as the basis of discussion. To continue first with the Japan–US comparison, it is easy to see, from Tables 15.4 to 15.6,

(1) that the great majority of the unemployed may be regarded as 'voluntary unemployment', and that its level is much higher in Japan;
(2) that the issue of long-term unemployment seems to be less serious in Japan;[2] and

[1] The following data sources have been employed in the computation: the monthly unemployment rate (seasonally adjusted) as found in *Annual Report on the Labour Force Survey 1976*, p. 137 and GNE published by Economic Planning Agency, *Annual Report on National Income Statistics 1978*, pp. 251–67.
[2] Subsequently, however, the Japanese situation got worse; in the year 1977, the composition of unemployment by duration was reported as follows (male only):

Duration	Japan	U.S.A.
	%	%
Less than 3 mos.	50.0	73.4
3–6 mos.	19.5	11.0
Over 6 mos.	30.5	15.6
Total	100.0	100.0

(*Showa 52 nen rōdō keizai no bunseki* [The 1977 White Paper on the Labor Economy] (Tokyo, 1978), supplement, p. 12.)

(3) that the burden of unemployment falls relatively heavily on the young people in the United States, whereas it falls on the middle-aged and older in Japan.

The findings of (1) and (2), taken together with the low level of Japanese unemployment, lead to the conclusion that the incidence of unemployment has been relatively lighter in the case of Japan as compared with that in the United States. The point (3), on the other hand, reflects clearly the prominent characteristic of the Japanese labour market: the system of employment tenure, whereby the middle-aged and older are at a disadvantage in securing new employment opportunities, even if they want them. This is particularly serious not only because the compulsory retirement age limit continues to be in the neighbourhood of 55, but also because the distribution of the Japanese population in the forthcoming years will increasingly be lop-sided, with heavier weights in the relatively aged.

TABLE 15.4 THE RELATIVE SIZE OF VOLUNTARY UNEMPLOYMENT IN JAPAN AND THE USA (Percentages)

Reasons for unemployment	Japan		USA	
	1975	*1976*	*1975*	*1976*
Have lost last job	33.6[a]	37.8[a]	55.4	49.8
Have left last job	32.7	28.3	10.4	12.2
Have joined labour force[b]	33.6	33.9	34.2	38.1
Total	99.9	100.0	100.0	100.1

[a] Of whom 7.1 per cent (1975) and 6.3 per cent (1976) of the total lost their jobs due to compulsory retirement.
[b] Comprised of those who re-entered the labour market and those who have never worked previously.

SOURCES

Japan: Bureau of Statistics, Office of the Prime Minister, *Report on the Special Survey of the Labour Force Survey*, March 1975, p. 20 and March 1976, p. 18.
USA: Employment and Training Report of the President, 1977, p. 174.

TABLE 15.5 THE DURATION OF UNEMPLOYMENT IN
JAPAN AND THE USA (In per cent)

Year	Sex	Duration	Japan[a]	USA
	Male	Less than 3 months	86.6	65.2
		3–6 months	9.0	17.7
		Over 6 months	4.5	17.1
		Total	100.0[b]	100.0
1975	Female	Less than 3 months	84.2	72.2
		3–6 months	7.9	14.9
		Over 6 months	7.9	12.9
		Total	100.0	100.0
	Total	Less than 3 months	84.8	68.3
		3–6 months	8.6	16.5
		Over 6 months	6.7	15.2
		Total	100.0[b]	100.0
	Male	Less than 3 months	80.7	64.3
		3–6 months	13.3	15.0
		Over 6 months	6.0	20.7
		Total	100.0	100.0
1976	Female	Less than 3 months	81.1	72.2
		3–6 months	13.5	12.3
		Over 6 months	5.4	15.5
		Total	100.0	100.0
	Total	Less than 3 months	81.5	67.9
		3–6 months	12.6	13.8
		Over 6 months	5.9	18.3
		Total	100.0	100.0

[a] Excluding from the total those who failed to report the duration.
[b] Omitting rounding errors.

SOURCES

Japan: Bureau of Statistics, Office of the Prime Minister, *Report on the Special Survey of the Labour Force Survey*, March 1975, p. 24 and March 1976, p. 22.
USA: Employment and Training Report of the President, 1977, pp. 178–9.

TABLE 15.6 COMPOSITION OF UNEMPLOYMENT BY AGE GROUP IN
JAPAN AND THE USA (In per cent)

Sex	Age group	1975		1976	
		Japan	USA	Japan	USA
Male	16–19[a]	6.1	21.8	5.4	23.4
	20–34	40.9	46.1	40.5	45.7
	35–54	31.8	22.9	31.1	21.2
	55–64	16.7	6.8	17.6	7.4
	65–	4.5	2.3	5.4	2.4
	Total	100.0	100.0[b]	100.0	100.0[b]
Female	16–19[a]	5.7	23.1	5.9	23.3
	20–34	51.4	44.8	55.9	45.8
	35–54	34.3	24.4	32.4	23.0
	55–64	8.6	6.3	5.9	6.4
	65–	0.0	1.5	0.0	1.6
	Total	100.0	100.0[b]	100.1	100.0[b]
Total	16–19[a]	6.1	22.4	5.7	23.3
	20–34	45.9	45.5	44.8	45.7
	35–54	31.6	13.2	31.4	22.0
	55–64	13.3	6.6	14.3	6.9
	65–	3.1	2.0	3.8	2.0
	Total	100.0	100.0	100.0	100.0[b]

[a] 15–19 in the case of the Japanese data.
[b] Omitting rounding errors.

SOURCES

Japan: Bureau of Statistics, Office of the Prime Minister, *Annual Report on the Labour Force Survey*, 1975 and 1976.
USA: Employment and Training Report of the President, 1977, p. 167.

IV THE CO-EXISTENCE OF LOW EMPLOYMENT AND ABUNDANT LABOUR SUPPLY[1]

A traditional argument to explain the paradox of the co-existence of low unemployment and the overall abundant labour supplies has been to recognise the characteristic nature of the non-wage employment sector, where work effort per head can vary while output level is kept unchanged.[1] According

[1] See, for example, Ishikawa (1967), Ch. 3, Sen (1975), Ch. 4.

to this school of thought, the low unemployment level in itself is nothing to be amazed at. Even in an underdeveloped economy, people must find some income-generating activities if only to survive. The case is reinforced in a country that has little accumulated wealth. Moreover, the current systems of labour force survey pay attention primarily to the income-generating aspects of employment and unemployment and, as such, are bound to yield low estimates of unemployment. Take, for instance, the case of India, where Census unemployment figures constitute only a fraction of her labour force (3.2 per cent of males and 1.4 per cent of females in the urban areas in 1961; Sen (1975), p. 124). However, this does not necessarily mean that all the gainfully occupied contribute equally to the growth of output.

In reference to the Japanese economy, observers have noted that a relatively large proportion of its labour force has been engaged in unpaid family-work (see Table 15.1). This category presumably represents a small, family-owned unit of production, whose percentage in the entire work force has kept declining at a phenomenal speed due basically to the sharp decline in the number of persons engaged in the primary sector (see Table 15.7 below). By contrast, note in the same Table that the relative share of all manufacturing has stayed at a fairly constant level, and that of the service industries has increased rapidly.

It is reasonable to suppose, for the sake of discussion, that the modern, capitalistic system of production is represented by mining and manufacturing (sector M), the traditional mode of production by agriculture, forestry and fishing (sector A), and a mixture of the two by the service industries (sector S).[1] Given that the unemployment level was maintained at an extremely low level at least until the 1974–75 recession, it follows that a relative reduction in employment in one sector must have been absorbed either by a counter-balancing increase in other sectors, or by a decline in the labour force participation rate, or both.[2] Figure 15.1 depicts the annual rates of employment changes in the three major industrial sectors as suggested above.

Looking first at the Panel I of Figure 15.1, one may note that the rate of change in manufacturing employment shows a declining trend, eventually crossing the zero-growth line (1.0 on the vertical axis) in around 1974. Second, the rates of change in sectors A and S correspond roughly to the equipment cycles;[3] that is, they absorb a large number of persons in

---

[1] Sector S includes the following activities: retail and wholesale trades, financial and real estate transactions, money and banking, professional and other services.

[2] Actually, the labour force continued to increase during the entire period under observation. An absolute decline in employment in a certain sector has, *a fortiori*, increased the burden of other sectors to absorb the redundant.

[3] The peak (P) and trough (T) of equipment cycles are marked on the tops of Figures 15.1 and 15.2. I have adopted the reference dating of the cycles suggested by Shinohara (1978), p. 86.

TABLE 15.7 CHANGES AND DISTRIBUTIVE SHARES IN EMPLOYMENT BY INDUSTRIAL SECTOR (Percentages)

	Growth rates of		Employment in				
	Population of age 15 and over	Labour force participation rate	Agriculture, forestry and fishery	Construction	Manufacturing and mining	Service industries[a]	Public utilities and government
Average annual growth rates, 1966–75							
Male	1.4	0.0	−5.3	4.1	1.4	3.0	2.0
Female	1.4	−1.0	−5.2	3.0	1.3	2.5	3.0
Distributive shares of employment							
Male 1960			26.7	7.8	25.3	28.1	12.1
1965			20.2	9.4	27.7	29.2	13.5
1970			14.1	11.0	28.4	32.1	14.4
1975			10.1	12.9	27.2	35.0	14.8
Female 1960			41.0	1.5	18.3	36.3	2.8
1965			33.7	2.1	21.2	39.7	3.2
1970			22.6	2.6	26.0	45.2	3.5
1975			16.9	3.0	24.4	51.7	3.9

a Inclusive of retail and wholesale trades, insurance, money and banking, real estate, professional and other services.

SOURCE

Computed from Bureau of Statistics, Office of the Prime Minister, *Annual Report on the Labour Force Survey*, various issues.

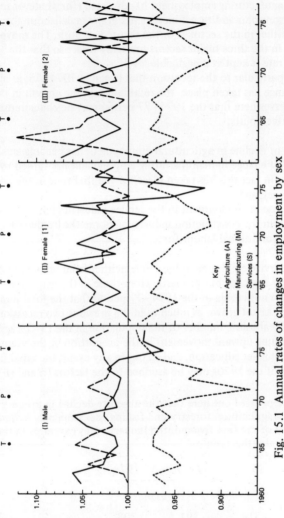

Fig. 15.1 Annual rates of changes in employment by sex

SOURCE Computed from Bureau of Statistics, Office of the Prime Minister, *Annual Report on the Labour Force Survey*, 1970 and 1976 and ditto, *Monthly Report on the Labour Force Survey*, January–December 1977.

downswings and release them during upswings – functioning, in essence, as a reservoir of labour. Third, cyclical correspondence is not as clear in the M sector, but this is understandable because the manufacturing industries have been subject to a continued advancement in labour productivity through labour-augmenting technological progress (Watanabe, 1968). Nonetheless, whenever the manufacturing employment has declined (for whatever reasons), the released persons plus additional increments in the male labour force have been absorbed either in the sector A or the sector S or both. The movements of employment in the three major sectors mutually offset so that the unemployment rate is kept at a negligible level.

Referring in particular to the recession that began in 1974–75, a pronounced change has taken place: the retardation in the growth in the M sector. One observes here that the 1974–77 period may be characterised by the following three points:

(i)   the rate of decline in agricultural employment has become smaller;[1]
(ii) the rate of change in manufacturing employment has turned to negative (in fact this has taken place for the first time in the post-war experience); and
(iii) the increase in employment in the service industries has – together with that in the construction industry – borne the burden of absorbing additional labour force.

The increase in service employment has come neither from self-employment nor unpaid family workers, but primarily from those in the employee category. It is also noticeable in the 1974–77 period that the total number in the labour force has not grown as much as in the previous two recessions, due to a decline in the absolute number of the population in the 15–19 age bracket, a continuing upward movement in the proportion of the young persons receiving higher education, and so on. In any event, the rapid increase in the latter half of the 1970s may be ascribed to the factors (i) and (ii)

[1] It should be pointed out here that the absolute decline in primary employment (i.e. agriculture, forestry and fishing) has seemingly *halted* in 1978. The record of the first five-month (January–May) averages in the past three years illustrates this point:

Sex	1976	1977	1978
	(numbers in thousands)		
Male	314	301	308
Female	278	269	278

(Computed from *Annual Report on the Labour Force Survey*, 1976 and *Monthly Report on the Labour Force Survey*, January 1977–May 1978.)

above, in spite of the decline in the growth rate of the labour force itself and of the expanded employment in the service sector and in the construction industry.

The counterbalancing actions in female employment are not so distinct as in the male work force (see Panel II of Figure 15.1). In the female labour market, however, one must remember that the labour force participation rate fluctuates visibly; the so-called marginal-worker hypothesis seems to be most applicable to this portion of the labour market.[1] Therefore, if one eliminates artificially the ups and downs of the female labour force participation rate by assuming that it has declined at a *constant* rate of −1.0 per cent per annum over the entire period of observation (1960–77), one obtains the size of redundant female labour that would have had to be absorbed by the market in order to keep the unemployment level unchanged. Panel III of Figure 15.1 displays the same picture as shown in Panel II of the same figure, except that the redundancy thus calculated has been added to the employment in the sector S. The result indicates clearly that here again the counterbalancing has been at work.

In regard to manufacturing employment, it is interesting to see that changes in female employment have recorded wider amplititudes than those of male employment, and that on several occasions the movement of the former preceded that of the latter (Figure 15.2). This implies that the female labour force acts as a buffer to employment fluctuations: when a sign of recession comes into sight, for instance, the employer first discharges female workers in so far as choice is permissible. During an upswing, by contrast, women are rehired prior to men.[2]

So far the discussion has tacitly assumed that the wage employment section of the economy forms a homogeneous market. However, there is good reason to expect some duality in the market, reflecting the size of the enterprise. In fact, while the labour force as a whole has grown at a slower rate in the years following 1974, the smaller firms have actually recorded a gain in their share of employment. In other words, there has been a reshuffling of the employment distribution in favour of the smaller firms. In terms of annual rates of changes in employment, computed over three four-year periods, the small firms have shown a contrasting performance as

---

[1] Absolute differences (declines) in the female labour force participation rate, calculated over successive five-year periods, are shown below:

	%
1955–60	−2.4
1960–65	−3.9
1965–70	−0.8
1970–75	−4.0.

Note that the timing corresponds roughly to upswings (1955–60 and 1965–70) and downswings (1960–65 and 1970–75) of equipment cycles.

[2] Cf. Nakamura (1978).

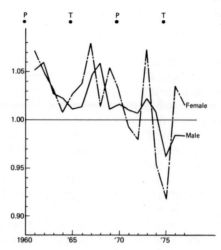

Fig. 15.2 Annual rates of changes in manufacturing employment by sex[a]

[a] Inclusive of mining.

SOURCE   Computed from Bureau of Statistics, Office of the Prime Minister, *Annual Report on the Labour Force Survey*, 1970 and 1976 and ditto, *Monthly Report on the Labour Force Survey*, January–December 1977.

against the larger ones (see Table 15.8). It seems as if the degree of labour redundancy in the cyclical downswings has been more pronounced, the larger the size of the organisation.

V HIDDEN OVEREMPLOYMENT IN MANUFACTURING

During the 1974–75 recession, it was frequently argued that under the Japanese employment system large corporations in particular were prevented from discharging redundant employees. According to the proponents of the view, this was due mostly to the practice of permanent employment whereby employees and trade unions would strongly resist any attempt at reducing the size of the work force; from the management's point of view, too, it was considered not the best policy to release well-trained, capable employees, since it would be extremely hard either to replace or rehire them when the economy recovered.

Taking account of this line of argument, several estimates were attempted to determine the magnitude of hidden 'overemployment' in manufacturing. The actual figures varied widely even though they dealt with the same year (1975): a minimum of 400,000 to a maximum of 1.5 million (see Table 15.9). However, most of such estimates were highly suspect, because it was not always made explicit what was meant by 'overemployment'.

Japanese corporations, having faced the severe recession, typically took the following steps in alleviating the mounting labour cost: firstly, the

TABLE 15.8 CHANGES AND SHARES OF EMPLOYMENT BY SIZE OF FIRMS

Period[a]	*Average annual growth rates*		*Distributive shares of employment*	
	Firms with 29 employees or less	*Firms with over 500 employees*	*Firms with 29 employees or less*	*Firms with over 500 employees*
		(*Percentages*)		
1964–67	4.2	3.1	36.9	30.5
1971–74	2.4	1.1	37.1	29.8
1974–77	3.3	–1.2	38.3	28.4

[a] All the three periods surround cyclical troughs.

SOURCE

Computed from Bureau of Statistics, *Annual Report on the Labour Force Survey*, various issues and ditto, *Monthly Report on the Labour Force Survey*, January–December 1977.

TABLE 15.9 ESTIMATES OF OVEREMPLOYMENT, 1975

Estimated by	As of	Manufacturing	All industries	Methods of estimation
		(In thousands)		
Ministry of Labour	Oct/Dec	400	–	Comparison of actual with 'optimum' work hours
Economic Planning Agency	June	603	–	Production index is related to vacancy ratio
Nikkei Business Magazine	July	859	1567	
Sanwa Bank	April/June	1070	–	Comparison of actual with peak-value indices of labour productivity, and its variations
Kansai Employers' Association	May	1410	2170[a]	
Sumitomo Bank	June	1455	–	

[a] Manufacturing and service sectors.

SOURCES

The estimate by the Ministry of Labour is taken from Statistics and Information Department, *Monthly Labour Statistics and Research Bulletin*, Vol. 28, No. 4 (April 1976), p. 22; all others are quoted from Ministry of Labour, *Shōwa 50 nen rōdō keizai no bunseki* (The 1975 White Paper on Labour Economy), pp. 213–16.

recruitment at mid-year was suspended; secondly overtime work was either judiciously reduced or prohibited; thirdly, the redundant workers were transferred to other sections of the same company or to related firms where manpower demand was relatively stronger; fourthly, temporary employees and/or subcontracting firms were either discharged or reduced; and, finally, when all these measures proved inadequate, last resort would be the reduction of the regular work force (Tables 15.10 and 15.11). Even at this final stage, the management normally preferred to employ the system of 'stand by', as described previously, and to encourage those prepared to retire of their own will.

Such practice of Japanese personnel management is reflected in the magnitudes of employment elasticities with respect to output variations. According to an international comparative study by Shinozuka (1978), the Japanese economy has been just as sensitive as the US economy in absorbing the excess labour created by the 1974–75 recession; however, the speed of employment adjustment in Japan has been significantly slower than that in the United States.

Knowing these characteristics of Japanese management practices, one might make a case for utilising the movement of work hours as an indicator of excess employment, if any. Ever since the 1960s the total hours worked in

TABLE 15.10 PROPORTION OF
RESPONDING COMPANIES WHICH HAVE
ADOPTED SOME METHODS OF EXCESS-
MANPOWER ADJUSTMENTS

Period	Proportion (*Percentages*)
Jan–June 1974	16
July–Sept 1974	37
Oct–Dec 1974	58
Jan–March 1975	67
April–June 1975	64
July–Sept 1975	61
Oct–Dec 1975	54
Jan–March 1976	47
April–June 1976	29
July–Sept 1976	31
Oct–Dec 1976	28
Jan–March 1977	28

SOURCE

Ministry of Labour, *Rōdō keizai dōkō chōsa hōkoku* (Survey Report on the Labour Economy), various issues.

TABLE 15.11 RANK ORDERING OF PREFERENCE ON ALTERNATIVE
METHODS OF REDUCING EXCESS MANPOWER,
October 1973–March 1977[a]

	Methods	Average rank[b]		Methods	Average rank[b]
(1)	Curtailment of new recruits other than new school graduates	1.2	(6)	Introduction of five-day week	5.7
			(7)	Temporarily closing down	5.8
(2)	Restriction of overtime work	1.8	(8)	Enlisting voluntary quits and/or discharging regular employees	5.9
(3)	Transfer of personnel to other departments or companies	3.0			
			(9)	Advancing paid holidays	6.6
(4)	Discharge of non-regular (temporary and day) employees	3.9	(10)	Others	6.8
(5)	Extending summer vacation and/or New Year holidays	5.6			

[a] Based on a sample survey of corporations with 30 or more regular employees; the size of responded sample is approximately 2800.

[b] Does not come down to an integral number because of tied observations.

SOURCE

Derived from the data given in Ministry of Labour, *Rōdō keizai dōkō chōsak hōkoku* (Survey Report on the Labour Economy), various issues.

manufacturing have demonstrated a clear downward trend. Probably one can assume a similar tendency for the entire wage-employment sector of the economy. If it is taken to represent the long-run natural direction, an especially deep dip in the total work hours observable in the few years around 1974–75 may be ascribed to short-run disturbances (see Figure 15.3). If so, one might use the dip to measure the extent to which the reduction of work hours substituted for the discharge of regular employees.

The procedure has been very crude. By drawing a straight line to join both ends of the 'total work hours' curve in Figure 15.3 and measuring its vertical distance from the horizontal axis at June 1975, one reads a value of 178.5, which is about 6.5 hours longer than the actual record (i.e. 172.0). Assume for the sake of discussion that the former stands for the *optimum* level of total monthly work hours at that time. Since the total number of employees

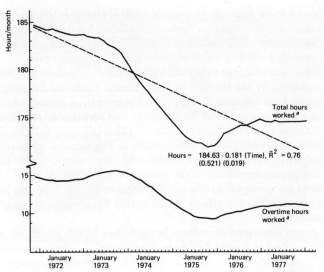

Fig. 15.3 Statistics on work hours, 1971–77 (Average per employee)

a Seasonally adjusted; inclusive of service industries, covering enterprises with 30 or more regular employees.

SOURCE   Original data taken from Ministry of Labour, *Maitsuki kinrō tōkei chōsa sōgō hōkoku sho* [Annual Report on the Monthly Labour Statistical Survey], various issues.

was 36,280,000 in June 1975, the above figures would imply that about 1,320,000 people were 'redundant', or about 3.6 per cent of the total employees (i.e. 36,280 × 6.5/178.5).[1]

If one adds the above 1,320,000 to the adjusted unemployment figure that was hypothesised in Table 15.3 above (i.e. U + G = 1,639,000) and divides the total by the corresponding labour force, the unemployment rate for the month of June in 1975, corrected for the CPS definition, would be approximately 5.4 per cent.[2]

VI THE EFFECTS ON FEMALE EMPLOYMENT

Economic modernisation is likely to result in a relative decline in family-operated economic activities. Inasmuch as the roots of the disguised

[1] On the other hand, if one extrapolates a straight line going through January 1972 and January 1973, the *optimum* work hours for June 1975 would be 181.2, yielding a redundancy of about 1,840,000, or 5.1 per cent of the total employed. In any case, the redundancy would hardly reach as high a level as implied by most of the figures reported in Table 15.9.

[2] Adopting the procedure suggested in the last footnote, the result would of course be a higher unemployment rate: 6.4 per cent.

unemployment are traceable to the existence of family enterprises, workers on own account, etc., one may foresee a declining trend in the employment-absorbing capacity of the system as economic development proceeds, and, as a consequence, a levelling up of the general unemployment rate.

In this connection, one may positively evaluate the role of industrial policies adopted by the Ministry of International Trade and Industry, which, for example, have consistently supported the growth of medium- and small-scale firms — a sector of the economy that presumably contributes to the creation of added employment opportunities (all other things being equal) since the average labour productivity of this sector is relatively lower compared with that of the larger, modernised corporations. By the same token, the protective policies of the government, starting from the agricultural price support to non-tariff barriers to import, may also have had the employment creation effects, which in turn have 'beggar-my-neighbour' implications.

The strong downward movement in the female labour participation rate has been ascribed to a rapid decline in the primary sector as a place for women's employment (Galenson-Odaka, 1976). Naturally, however, it has also been influenced by other factors as well; to mention a few of them: the number of infants per household (X_1); the vacancy/application ratio in the government's Employment Security Bureau (X_2); the proportion of self-employed and unpaid family workers in the total working population (both sexes) (X_3), etc. Clearly, X_1 has a negative effect on the participation rate (Y), whereas X_2 and X_3 have positive influence on Y. As a simple exercise to illustrate this, a multiple regression equation has been estimated to yield the following result:[1]

$$Y = 33.10 - 25.32\,X_1 + 1.41\,X_2 + 0.66\,X_3, \quad \bar{R}^2 = 0.995, \quad (1)$$

$$(3.89) \quad (0.30) \quad (0.03) \quad\quad D.W. = 1.6$$

The time period of observation is 1955–75. By using this equation, the changes in the female labour participation rate may be accounted for by the respective changes in the independent variables. Note that the influence of X_3 is relatively larger than that of others; needless to say, this variable (X_3) reflects the relatively declining trend in the primary sector (Table 15.12).

At the same time, however, there is a possibility that the participation rate may start increasing, at least in a portion of the female labour force, as it becomes more and more susceptible to the substitution (price) effect, so that

[1] Income level of the head of household, the use of labour-saving household appliances, and female wage levels are all among the more important variables in explaining the behaviour of Y. They have not been incorporated in equation (1) above simply due to technical difficulties (i.e. a high degree of multicollinearity).

TABLE 15.12 FACTORS CONTRIBUTING TO THE DECLINE IN FEMALE LABOUR PARTICIPATION RATE[a]

Period	Absolute difference in five years				Errors
	Y	X_2	X_2	X_3	
	Percentages				
1955–60	−2.4	3.3	0.5	−6.4	0.2
1960–65	−3.9	1.1	0.1	−4.9	−0.2
1965–70	−0.8	0.6	1.1	−2.4	−0.1
1970–75	−4.0	0.3	−1.1	−3.3	0.1

[a] Calculation based on the regression equation (1) in the text.

it will eventually follow a U-shape locus suggested by Durand (1975).[1]

A noticeable change in management practice during the recent decade is that more and more women are actively engaged either as part of the regular work force or as supplementary workers. In the automobile-parts manufacturing industry, for instance, quite a few married women are employed on semi-flex time basis. In essence they are regular workers but with the status of secondary citizens in terms of compensations, promotion, fringe benefits, union membership, and the like. They can easily be discharged or rehired at will so the management judges that it pays to rely on them instead of employing male regular workers, who must at one time or another be given employment tenure. It is not uncommon for companies, in an attempt to attract such female workers, to run their own day-care centres to look after children while their mothers are at work. The burden of labour market adjustment thus falls in part on the shoulders of female labour.

The possibility of the upward movement in the female labour participation rate foreshadows a future likely event in the labour market – that an increasing number of women will be discontented with being secondary or marginal workers and refuse to retire from the market during cyclical downswings. If such becomes a reality, there is another important reason to anticipate an upward drift in the official unemployment rate.[2]

Japanese labour issues in the future will centre around two major problems: female labour for one and workers of middle-age or older for the other. With regard to the latter, the rapidly increasing proportion of middle-aged male workers has already created a headache for the management, if only because of the mounting sums of severance payments. From the

[1] According to Durand, the female labour participation rate will be reduced first and then move up again as the economy undergoes the process of economic development.

[2] This seems to have already been taking place in the United States.

workers' point of view, the middle-aged are clearly at a disadvantage in the market unless their capacities are somehow upgraded and become marketable. It is likely therefore that the incidence of unemployment will be particularly heavy for the relatively mature, experienced workers. It is the present writer's opinion that there will be an ample part for an active manpower policy to play in the years to come.

REFERENCES

Durand, John D. (1975), *Labor Force in Economic Development, A Comparison of International Census Data, 1946–1966* (Princeton: Princeton University Press).

Galenson, Walter, with the collaboration of Konosuke Odaka (1976), 'The Japanese Labor Market', in Hugh Patrick and Henry Rosovsky, (eds), *Asia's New Giant, How the Japanese Economy Works* (Washington, DC: Brookings Institution).

Ishikawa, Shiegeru (1967), *Economic Development in Asian Perspective* (Tokyo: Kinokuniya Bookstore).

Minami, Ryoshin (1973), *Turning Point in Economic Development, Japan's Experience* (Tokyo: Kinokuniya Bookstore).

Nakamura, Takafusa (1978), 'Koyō fuan no genjō to mitōshi' (The Insecurity of Employment: Current Condition and Future Prospect), *ESP* (Economy, Society, Policy), No. 72 (April), pp. 17–21.

Sen, Amartya (1975), *Employment, Technology and Development* (Oxford: Clarendon Press).

Shinohara, Miyohei (1978), *Gendai keizaigaku sai nyūmon, keizaigaku vs. reality* (Relearning Modern Economics, Economics vs. Reality) (Tokyo: Kunimoto Shobō).

Shinozuka, Eiko (1978), 'Koyō chōsei no mondai ten, riron to keisoku no gap' (Notes on Employment Adjustment, How to Fill the Gap between Theory and Reality), *ESP* (Economy, Society, Policy), No. 72 (April), pp. 22–26.

Umemura, Mataji (1963), 'Keiki hendō ka no rōdō shijō ni okeru kanshō sayō' (Cushioning Function in the Labor Market during Business Cycles), *Keizai kenkyū* (The Economic Review), Vol. 14, No. 1 (January 1963), pp. 69–71 (reprinted in his *Rōdōryoku no kōzo to kōyō mondai* (The Structure of the Labor Force and the Problems of Employment) (Tokyo: Iwanami Shoten, 1971), pp. 114–20).

Watanabe, Tsunehiko (1968), 'Industrialization, Technological Progress and Dual Structure', in L. R. Klein and Kazushi Ohkawa (eds), *Economic Growth: Japanese Experience since the Meiji Era* (Homewood, Ill.,: Richard D. Irwin), pp. 110–34.

Discussion of Professor Odaka's Paper

Professor Khachaturov said this paper contained interesting statistical data
and made important comparisons and conclusions. The history of the rise
of the Japanese economy since the war was well-known. This rise was connected
with: first, the increase in the productivity of labour and, at the same time,
rather low wages; second, the borrowing of foreign technology on a large scale;
third, low military expenditure, and other factors which led to a significant
accumulation of capital. Later there was the development of Japan's own
science and technology, and a further rise in productivity, higher wages and
economic progress. This had to be taken into account in examining Professor
Odaka's paper which covered only one of the issues mentioned earlier,
namely, employment in Japan.

The author underlined what he described as a paradoxical situation,
namely, that there was both a low level of unemployment and a relatively
abundant supply of labour. The author asked why this was. A possibility was
that Japanese unemployment was under reported by western standards so
that Japanese data could not be compared with that of other countries.
Professor Khachaturov did not find any paradox here. In fact, there was
a redistribution of the labour force between the broadest sectors of the
economy, as was shown in Table 15.7. There had been a reduction of the
labour force in agriculture which had been similar in extent to the growth
of the labour force in industry, construction and services. Professor Odaka
referred to Umemora, who observed that increases and decreases in the
unemployment rate matched perfectly the counter movements represented
by net outflows of labour from farm households.

As to the comparability of Japanese data with that from other countries,
Professor Odaka showed with great accuracy that in official Japanese data
there was some underestimation of the number of unemployed. He came to
this conclusion by comparing the particular features of labour statistics
in Japan and the USA. This comparison showed that there *was* some
underestimation of unemployment in Japan. This was particularly due to
including in the labour force, and in the number employed, such categories
as those in the defence forces of Japan, unpaid family workers who worked
for one hour or more during the survey week, etc. These differences were
shown in Table 15.2. The data given by the author showed that the actual
number of unemployed was higher than official sources suggested. The rate
of unemployment was also higher, though it was substantially smaller than
in other developed countries – for example, the USA, the UK etc.

The paper gave more detailed comparisons of unemployment in Japan
and the USA, using classifications according to age and sex. Professor Odaka
concluded that in the USA the burden of unemployment fell relatively
heavily on the young, and in Japan on the middle-aged and old. It was
important to notice that there were many people engaged in unpaid family
work in Japan, though Table 15.1 showed that, as a percentage of the whole
labour force, they were declining rapidly.

As for the distribution of the labour force between the broad sectors of the economy, the share of agriculture in the total labour force had declined systematically, the share of industry and the public sector was stable, and the share of construction and service industries had increased. There had also been changes in the numbers employed in enterprises of different size. The proportion of the total labour force employed in small- and medium-sized firms had increased as the economy had developed. The author explained this by the low level of productivity in such firms, but Professor Khachaturov did not find this convincing. Large firms discharged fewer of their redundant employees by comparison with other businesses. This depended not only on the resistance from trade unions but also, as the paper explained, on the management policy of the larger firms which would not release well-trained, capable employees because it would be difficult to replace or rehire them when the economy recovered. The author set out the measures which corporations took typically to overcome the undesirable consequences of discharging redundant employees. In Table 15.9 there were estimates of overemployment for 1975, showing that the total exceeded 2 million. By a very simple method, the author made estimates comparing the optimal number of hours worked by monthly workers and actual hours. He came to the conclusion that the total number of redundant workers was about 1.3 million. However, perhaps the method of estimation was oversimplified. The calculation would have been more reliable if carried out with the use of data on the productivity of labour. If one divided the amount of production by the achieved productivity of labour before the recession, one could calculate the necessary numbers of workers and compare this with the actual number.

In the final part of his paper Professor Odaka listed measures which had been taken, mainly by large enterprises, to engage more women and, in particular, the way they had organised their own day nurseries to look after children while their mothers were at work. This not only showed a very good attitude to workers but also the strength of the demand for labour, resulting from the rapid economic growth.

It was understandable that even such a good and stimulating paper had some deficiencies, and Professor Khachaturov thought it might be helpful to give Professor Odaka some ideas about possible further development of his work. These suggestions were mainly connected the desirability of including in the paper an analysis of factors which could influence employment and unemployment. By this, Professor Khachaturov meant not only economic growth but other factors which influenced employment, such as the creation of new jobs, which was necessarily connected with investment; technological progress, which was also connected with investment; wages and employment policy, and so on. In other words, it would have been helpful to have included in the paper a discussion of causes of fluctuations in employment.

Professor Khachaturov understood that it was very difficult to find new and effective ways of solving problems of unemployment in a market economy. His opinion was that new investment provided the best way to increase employment. Certainly there could be other opinions on this, but it was possible to hope that an analysis of the causes of unemployment could show us how this complicated problem could be solved.

Professor Odaka said that Professor Georgescu-Roegen's paper earlier in the conference had made him happy in one way, but had also suggested modifications for his own paper. He wondered whether he should have taken account of working hours in the production function. These were not actually fixed, and he was glad that Professor Malinvaud had agreed earlier with his own view. He thought that one should perhaps adopt a downward exponential rather than a linear relationship because in the end the latter would lead to negative hours.

Professor Holt noted that the paper referred to the relationship between the wealth of the family and unemployment. This was a new idea, but if the family depended on the worker's income, it was harder to resist taking *any* job. This seemed to be a useful research area.

He wanted to raise a point. At the end of Section II of the paper, Professor Odaka said it was hard to believe that both the population census and the official labour force survey had procedural defects. On the contrary, he found it very easy!

Dr Kaufman thought it important to emphasise that several of Professor Odaka's estimates were maximum adjustment. Professor Odaka himself stated that the smaller adjusted unemployed rates in column V on Table 15.3 seemed to be the most plausible. Recent data obtained by the US Department of Labor indicated that even these figures were too high because over 40 per cent of the Japanese respondents reported as unemployed might not have actively searched for a job within the past four weeks. In addition, more recent estimates of those laid off for the entire week were less than one-third of the estimate of those laid off during the week, which was the figure used by Professor Odaka. Finally, Professor Odaka estimated that about 1.2 per cent of the Japanese labour force should be classified as unemployed because they had a job which they were waiting to begin within 30 days. This estimate seemed to be rather high inasmuch as the comparable figures for the US, Canada, and France were about 0.14, 0.24 and 0.15 per cent, respectively.

In his alternative adjusted data Professor Odaka assumed that 10 per cent of Japanese college students were unemployed. Whereas in the United States a high percentage of students were in the labour force, he thought the percentage was much lower in Western Europe and Japan.

Nevertheless, this paper provided some very interesting insights into the Japanese labour market. He had always found the role of temporary and day workers especially intriguing. Japanese corporations seemed to use these workers as a buffer stock. How often were these people actually 'laid-off' and what happened to them during these lay-offs?

Finally, the Japanese system of wage payments might also provide a key to their low unemployment rates. Wage inflexibility, as we saw it in Western Europe and North America, would result in involuntary unemployment following a decline in aggregate demand. In Japan, 30 to 50 per cent of the annual wage payment was usually given in the form of semi-annual bonuses, which seemed to be linked to profits and/or sales. This added flexibility might allow the Japanese economy to weather difficult recessionary periods without experiencing large increases in unemployment. It would be interesting to test the actual flexibility of bonuses in the 1973–78 period.

Professor Malinvaud thought Professor Odaka's results showed a flexibility in the active population and in employment greater than in Western Europe. The falls in hours of work were smaller and transfers of population between sectors were more important. Flexibility of activity within the cycle seemed to be greater, and the labour market in Japan very different.

How could this be explained? Was this flexibility a trait of a society that was more traditional, with a bigger role for the family?

Professor Odaka noted that Professor Khachaturov did not find it a paradox that there was low unemployment in Japan and so much labour. However, it remained a paradox to him, and this was the reason why he had written the paper. Of course, if the abundant labour was not to be unemployed, it must go somewhere, and the paper had tried to explain what happened.

There had been a reference to small- and medium-sized firms. He had not intended to suggest that as the economy developed the share of small and medium firms increased, but he was simply trying to say that they had a big role in absorbing the labour force. Professor Khachaturov was right about the policy of large firms in manufacturing and service industries. He recognised that he had used an oversimple explanation but he had done so purposely on finding that, especially in large manufacturing businesses, Japan had adjusted the labour supply by changing working hours rather than the number employed. He therefore felt it was legitimate to use this crude method though he agreed that he should look at it again.

Professor Khachaturov suggested the need for more analysis rather than description. He agreed with this, but one could not do everything in a short paper. He had wanted to give the salient features of the situation, and especially to emphasise to the co-existence of low unemployment and abundant labour. He would take this view into account in future.

Perhaps the Japanese government had aggravated the employment situation by not responding to the 1974–75 recession through demand management.

He thought Professor Georgescu-Roegen was right. He had used the exponential as well, and for this purpose he got the same results.

He was pleased that Professor Holt found his ideas on the wealth of the family useful. There were two points he would like to argue in this respect. First, if one took the official statistics, he wondered why, with a serious recession, the rate of unemployment was so low. He had come to the provisional conclusion that the only mechanism for reducing unemployment was through family-oriented organisations like small firms, agriculture, or even self-employment. Perhaps a developing country could not afford a high unemployment rate — and certainly Japan had been less developed ten years ago. Since Japan had become a developed nation in terms of GNP, however, there might be a modification in the future in the percentage of family organisations. It was likely that the Japanese unemployment in future might be greater than it was now.

He found Professor Malinvaud's comments interesting in that perhaps Japan was in a position which was at the other extreme to that in Western Europe. In Japan, the retirement age in the large corporations was usually 55 or 57, though some progressive ones had increased the retirement age to 60. Certainly the general tendency was for the retirement age to rise at a time when many in the West were arguing for a fall. Professor Malinvaud had praised this system, but it was not clear who was following whom.

Professor Holt had not been clear what he meant in what he said about Japanese survey results. The point was that some in Japan argued that the official statistics were wrong, took the definition of unemployment statistics too strictly and so led to unbelievable results. In fact, Japanese statistics were correlated systematically. They were not artificially biased or adjusted to make them unusable to economists.

He would agree with Dr Kaufman that he had made the maximum adjustments. He did not think that 10 per cent of Japanese college students were unemployed and had gone on to say that stand-by workers could not be called unemployed because they received part of their pay.

Regular, temporary and day-workers were included in labour force surveys. However, it was not clear quite how far temporary and day-workers were covered by the Japanese Ministry of Labour. He would argue that in the 1960s, when there were cyclical fluctuations in the Japanese economy, it was the temporary or day-workers who usually took the main brunt. Now, perhaps, the brunt fell more on women.

He felt that annual bonuses did make wages more flexible. Even government employees received an annual bonus equal to about four months' wages. This, in theory, could lead to adjustment to the cycle. In practice it did not, because firms had to negotiate with trade unions.

Professor Khachaturov wondered whether one could measure unemployment in agriculture. For example, in the 1960s, a poor farmer working in agriculture might have wanted to go to the city. He was not unemployed but supplied labour.

Professor Odaka said one answer was that there was virtually no unemployment in Japanese agriculture. A negligible percentage of workers were agricultural employees, and this was why there was little unemployment. One could also view the problem from the production side which would give a measure of disguised unemployment if one could work through marginal productivity.

Dr Gordon saw no necessary paradox between an abundant labour supply and a low unemployment rate. The crucial thing was the rate of growth of both employment and labour supply. There was a high rate of growth of employment in Japan, so that labour was perhaps easy to absorb. In the early post-war period, agriculture had been mainly a household activity so that overall unemployment there could be low.

Dr Gordon had done a good deal of work on the retirement age, and had found a clear relationship between average life expectancy and the normal retirement age. In less developed countries the retirement age was low because average life expectancy was also low. She agreed that a pensionable age of 55 was an anachronism in Japan, and was a hangover from a period of lower life expectancy. But, she did not think it strange that there was pressure now to increase the Japanese retirement age even though it was being reduced elsewhere.

Dr Kaufman believed that few Japanese workers stopped working at the 'official' retirement age of 55 for women and 60–2 for men. Instead, they often worked on successive 1-year contracts in a subsidiary of the firm which had previously employed them.

In the USA economists often pointed to the desirability of perfect competition, citing its relation to Pareto efficiency. Yet the Japanese economy, which had been extraordinarily successful since the Second World War, was highly cartelised. Similarly, many neo-classical economists would deplore job security arrangements because they created market imperfections. Nevertheless, they might have beneficial effects on productivity, and they might have been instrumental in Japan's economic success. The Japanese unemployment rate would probably be significantly higher were it not for the country's job security provisions. Economists had not adequately assessed the role of job security in Japan or elsewhere, not even in the USSR. Why was there so much job security in some countries and so little in others? What effects did this have on output, employment, productivity, and the natural rate of unemployment?

Professor Malinvaud explained that the case of Japan had been included in the conference programme because of the lower employment rate. As he understood the paper, Professor Odaka showed that the low employment rate was due to factors that one would not expect to meet in Western Europe.

Professor Odaka had stressed the importance of bonuses. These existed elsewhere, though in France they were very rigid, and including them led to small modifications. He wondered how much bonuses varied in Japan.

Sir Austin Robinson was interested by what Dr Kaufman had said and wondered whether the problem of rational expectations was limited to the expectations of future prices. If one thought of Europe of the 1950s and 1960s, one's expectations of future demand were framed in terms of the effect on the individual firm and the limits on its capacity to expand. He had said, in discussing Professor Malinvaud's paper, that the limiting factor was often skilled labour. In those earlier circumstances, a firm hoarded labour through small fluctuations because it knew that retaining it was very important to its future expansion. Japan had been in a world of rapid expansion, but it was doubtful if this would go on for ever and ever, and now perhaps the situation might be much more difficult if Japan moved in a world more like that of Europe.

Professor Tsuru took the view that the high rate of growth era ended in 1973. One was now looking to a rate of growth in GNP of 4–5 per cent as a maximum. Some Japanese economists said that 6 or 7 per cent was possible or, at least, that it was necessary if the potential labour force was to be employed. If one took that position, one might have to admit that there was a need to increase the size of the armament industry and some Japanese businessmen certainly advocated the export of arms. He thought this was dangerous if one thought it important to get 6 per cent growth in order to absorb the labour force.

Sir Austin Robinson said that the individual firm made its own employment decisions. What Professor Tsuru had said was true for the economy, but what did the entrepreneur think?

Professor Tsuru replied that this depended on the industry. Some industries where growth was still rapid were steel, vehicles and electronics. Rapid growth in shipbuilding had ended earlier, and now Korea was strong in that market. Even in the growing industries one did not expect similar expansion to that of the 1950s and 1960s. It was now up to the government to regulate aggregate demand through public works or investment in energy. So, there was a big problem of absorbing employment, and it might be necessary to look to a fall in working hours.

Professor Modigliani was amazed to keep hearing presentations referring to a different world from the one which had learned the lessons of Keynesianism. We had learned that increasing activity was possible, even if people insisted on saving a great deal. Only a year or two ago it had been said that there was enormous need for capital investment because of energy, and that there was a real problem if one could not get adequate energy at a reasonable cost. Why should one be pessimistic in a fundamental sense? One could not say that we had both insufficient demand and insufficient energy supplies, as long as energy could be produced with labour and capital.

Professor Giersch recalled that Keynes had said that, if full employment policies were pursed, then the marginal efficiency of capital could be reduced to zero in one generation. Nowadays, one might even more oppose this view because of poverty and capital shortage in less-developed countries. But the real rate of interest was now often negative. The fact that the marginal efficiency of capital was declining even in the face of poverty and capital shortage suggested that relative prices were wrong. We must remember that J. M. Clark, in the first full employment report to the United Nations, had stressed the importance of relative prices, wages, profits, etc. for a satisfactory level of investment. The changes that were taking place in the newly industrialising countries were leading to increasing competition, and to structural change of a kind not known in the 1960s when all countries were keen to buy American goods in exchange for dollars. There was also uncertainty today because of inflation, and the fact that generally-acceptable methods of inflation accounting had not been developed. In addition, there were environmental pressures.

This meant that we needed lower real wages than otherwise to keep investment increasing. The cost of uncertainty and of environmental pressures had to be borne somewhere. If the real rate of return was now zero, then perhaps this was at the expense of work opportunities. If the working of the labour market meant that one could not reduce real wages, this would lead to job rationing.

Professor Modigliani responded that he was not arguing that there was no problem. He agreed with much of what Professor Giersch had said, but he thought that the reason for the apparent lack of profit was that businessmen (and equity holders) did not account properly for inflation. There was no evidence in the USA that total return to capital − profits before interest and tax − had fallen inappropriately relative to the capital stock. They were possibly a little low but then the American economy was still far from working at capacity levels. To be sure, the composition of total returns appeared to have shifted from profits to interest. But this appearance had hardly any substance and merely reflected interest rates swollen by the inflation premium and a failure to take properly into account the gains and losses from changes in real debt resulting from inflation.

Professor Kolm pointed out that a negative rate of interest did not mean that profits were negative. A negative rate of interest helped to increase output and investment, and so profitability. He thought it was important at present to look at the relationship between the firm and its bankers.

Professor Kolm argued that one could not get investment by transferring the income of capitalists, and if one wanted to work through the public authorities, one would not solve Keynesian problems. The simple point we had to consider was that if the average Japanese worker wanted the standard of living of the average American, there was plenty of room for an increase in economic activity.

Professor Odaka said he had no disagreement with Dr Gordon. On the role of job security, it was hard to say whether its effects were good or bad, but it did seem to have helped work morale, reduced job conflicts, etc. We might go on to say that this would reduce labour turnover, because it caused the worker to stay with his firm. This might be good for productivity, but was not necessarily good for the worker's own welfare; and small firms could offer less security, so that in the past they had represented the mechanism for varying employment. Overall, it was not clear whether job security had good or bad effects. It was important to separate security of employment from the seniority wage system. The latter was eroding but the former not as yet. Japan had been able to maintain security of employment with a high rate of growth, and it would be very interesting to see what would happen in future.

Replying to Professor Malinvaud, Professor Odaka said that the job security practices of large firms absorbed some of the labour force and reduced unemployment, but it was not clear to him what the lessons of this were.

16 Summing up the Conference

Professor Hague was asked to attempt to summarise the work of the conference. He said there had been four kinds of paper. First, there were macroeconomic papers like those of Malinvaud, Georgescu-Roegen, Fitoussi, Parkin and Kaldor. Second, there were labour-market papers both macro-economic and microeconomic, by Holt and Bergmann. There were papers dealing with broader aspects of society and the future, namely, those of Emmerij and Södersten. Finally, there were country papers on Italy, Japan and the USA.

At the beginning of the conference he had suggested that the papers spent too much time on symptoms and too little on causes. He would now say that there was perhaps too much macroeconomics and too much reinterpre-tation of Keynes relative to microeconomics. Not that he should complain too much over this since he enjoyed the re-interpretation of Keynes.

On the causes of the present unemployment there seemed to be general agreement on four points. First, the resource constraint became important during 1973–74 when oil was only a special and extreme case. Second, there had been greater international synchronisation in the cycle, which was one disadvantage of freer trade and of economic integration, like that in the EEC. He was less certain that Professor Timofeev was right in saying that the short-run and longer-run cycles had now synchronised, though he did want Professor Timofeev to know that he had a sneaking feeling for the Kondratieff. Third, the shock of the early 1970s, including the commodity price boom, had been very severe. It was important to remember that the inflation of 1973–74 had been just as important and serious as the later recession. Perhaps the shift to flexible exchange rates and the commodity price boom were the main causes of inflation at that stage. One had to remember that once raw materials were in short supply, speculation and stock-piling drove up prices. They could do so quite dramatically, and had done so in 1973–74. The shock to the world economy at that time had been severe and this was why recovery was slow.

Professor Hague did not think that the oil problem had been so much one of prices as of the large amount of spending power transferred to OPEC. The problem of the developed countries in the last few years had been that they were paying a rate of interest to others to borrow what used to be their own money. And they were borrowing from those whose savings ratio was very high, like Saudi Arabia, so that there had been a big switch in the world from consumption to savings. In these circumstances he did not think it surprising that the marginal efficiency of capital in developed countries was currently low. So far as this particular element in the situation was concerned, he thought one had pure Keynesian underconsumption.

Professor Hague was gratified that he had pointed to these three elements during the first half-hour of the conference, but he had only implicitly mentioned the fourth. This was an omission which was dealt with in the Georgescu-Roegen–Fitoussi paper. All agreed that innovation led to unemployment, with the consequent need for adjustment. There was, however, little agreement with Georgescu-Roegen–Fitoussi that there had been less employment as a result of innovation since 1945. It had nevertheless been valuable to be reminded of Schumpeter's major contribution to modern economics. The conclusion was that we needed a dynamic society with a great deal of labour mobility, but that trade unions preferred immobility. This led to difficult problems, though these were more serious in some countries than in others.

On the theoretical papers, Professor Hague thought it was best to draw a veil over the discussion on Professor Hines' paper. He thought the conference had made very heavy weather of the distinctions between involuntary unemployment, frictional unemployment and voluntary unemployment. As Sir Austin Robinson had said, the session had repeated almost every fallacy put forward in those Keynesian, Cambridge days of forty-five years ago. What was interesting to him was Professor Modigliani's idea that perhaps Hines should concentrate on equilibrium unemployment and on identifying and analysing fluctuations from that equilibrium.

A good deal of time had been spent on disequilibrium models, but he was not sure that he agreed with Professor Bergmann that economics could deal only with equilibrium. He did admit that doing so was very much easier!

Professor Malinvaud's paper had rightly been acclaimed as systematic, precise and concise. There had, however, been some uncertainty over what precisely Malinvaud's adjustment process was. We had returned to the old, Keynesian problem that one could not generalise the conclusions of partial equilibrium analysis to the whole economy. A reduction of wage rates in one industry might reduce unemployment, but would not necessarily do so in the economy as a whole. There had been much discussion on the adjustment process and the length of the time period, but what *was* the adjustment process? Professor Malinvaud concentrated on quantities rather than prices and Professor Hague wondered if it might be helpful to introduce the distinction made by Sir John Hicks between fixprice and flexprice markets. In the latter, price quickly adjusted to changes in supply and demand, whereas in fixprice markets there was much more reliance on adjustments in supply. Perhaps this might make Malinvaud's model more elegant, always a French ambition!

In his role as a company director of a fixprice firm, Professor Hague said he saw the firm as almost always in disequilibrium. This was partly because the firm was a conglomerate and it was hard to control diversity. It was partly due to lack of data. The directors did not know when the firm was in an optimal position because there was simply not enough information to tell. It was therefore perhaps right that economists were concentrating on information and on expectations. Professor Hague said he thought he had worried Professor Parkin in the Saltsjöbaden conference by suggesting he should learn sociology. Perhaps he would worry Professor Parkin again by suggesting that he might now have to become a cybernetician. It was possible that Professor Malinvaud should introduce a resource (raw material) constraint as well as a capacity constraint.

There was also what Sir John Hicks called Real Wage Resistance, where workers resisted, usually by wage claims, a fall in real wages. There had been two very stimulating contributions on this. One had come from Professor Modigliani, who had pointed to the fact that in Italy, with indexation of wages, there had been too little investment because there was too little profit at the margin of the business. Professor Modigliani had also pointed to LDCs and the co-existence of a high-wage, modern sector with a low-wage traditional sector.

Lord Kaldor had suggested that Professor Malinvaud should clarify what kind of economy his was. One had to point here to the fact that disequilibrium was less in the world economy than in an individual country because of imports and exports. This fact had led Professor Giersch to recall having written a paper on the acceleration principle and the propensity to import in the early 1950s. Professor Hague had been very interested in what Professor Giersch had said about the UK, pointing out that bottlenecks led to imports, which led to a balance of payments deficit. The solution was to increase investment, but that required profit. The situation was much the same as that noted by Professor Modigliani for Italy, and Professor Hague confessed he noted with some alarm that whenever one looked at comparative statistics within the OECD, Italy and the UK always seemed to be bracketed together.

Professor Hague said he had already noted that profits were bound to be low with underconsumption but perhaps Professor Giersch had been over-persuaded by German businessmen about the need for higher inflation-adjusted profits. He thought that too much of the discussion of inflation by businessmen tended to overlook the fact that a balance sheet had two sides! He always thought that the British Treasury had not yet recognised this. It certainly seemed to make rational discussion with the Treasury on the pricing policies of nationalised industries quite impossible. It was important to remember that a nationalised industry which financed itself entirely by borrowing on fixed-interest debt would make a gain in inflationary periods, but that such a gearing adjustment did not automatically represent part of cash flow. Professor Giersch also pointed to the satisficing behaviour of managers and the effect of the shocks of 1973–75 on expectations and on the marginal efficiency of capital.

A solution was to be found only through increased profits and/or productivity. However, this meant a politically acceptable shift to profit and brought us back to real wage resistance. Perhaps this was why Lord Kaldor suggested that income elasticities mattered more than price elasticities. He had expected that to be a controversial point but no-one had challenged it.

Professor Hague thought Professor Parkin's performance had shown honesty and integrity. For example, Parkin would not say that the world would be a perfect one if there were no governments and if the money supply were held constant. Professor Parkin's contribution was therefore impressive, even if one did not agree with him on all points. For example, there was the question of whether trade unions could cause inflation. He thought that, in general, there was now much less dispute between monetarists and others. For example, during the conference the Phillips curve had frequently been referred to, and with much less disdain than three years earlier. He thought the Phillips curve was alive, convalescent, and probably living in Chicago!

The main doubts in the discussion of Professor Parkin's paper were concentrated on the idea of rational expectations. Professor Georgescu-Roegen had made the important point that expectations represented a state of mind and therefore had to be looked at in terms of probability. The issue was an important one, and perhaps Professor Modigliani was right in wanting to talk simply of non-irrational expectations. Similarly Professor Parkin was right that one *could* control the money supply; that fluctuations in it were often too large; and that what was needed was a stronger political will. And Professor Kolm was right that price changes in free market economies put pressure on consumers and alienated them.

A basic problem was that we still found it hard to know how an increase in aggregate demand would divide itself between an increase in output and an increase in prices. If one looked back at the *General Theory*, one found that Keynes himself was very exercised on this point even in the 1930s. Because of their 'black box' approach, monetarists had little to say on the issue. Research was needed. As Professor Modigliani had said, much of our thinking on this went back to Sylos-Labini and Bain. Professor Holt had made a significant point. If the price mechanism did not determine what happened, but rationing did, who was it who decided then?

Perhaps the monetarists had also paid too little attention to the dispersion of prices and wage rates. Professor Holt's paper had something to say on this issue and had been seen as a major contribution, doing something to fill the gap between market equilibrium and the economics of search. Professor Holt began from the simple, elegant and rigorous neo-classical model and moved to one where there was segmentation of the labour market and dispersion of wage rates. The conference had found the paper difficult to deal with, perhaps because, since it used two regulatory variables, wage rates and the relationships between vacancies and unemployment, one was faced with multiple equilibrium.

There had been some worry over whether it was necessary to distinguish, in Professor Modigliani's terms, between quits and drop-outs and some argument over whether Professor Holt's equations were under- or overdetermined. Another important issue was how far the adjustment would be in prices or quantities, with Professor Holt saying that most short-run adjustment was through quantities. One conclusion was that we could not look at the labour market simply in terms of wage rates. We must also consider it in terms of tightness, and so the probability of obtaining a job. For example, one could choose a higher wage rate and a lower probability of job, or *vice versa.* Professor Holt pointed to evidence that in less-developed countries both wage rates and the rate of unemployment affected migration.

If one had different wage rates in different cities, one would traditionally say that this would lead to movements which caused equalisation. Professor Holt argued that this was not necessarily so. Each city had its own equilibrium (or should he say, disequilibrium?) but there was no necessary convergence between these, and the wage rate could rise when the demand for labour fell.

There had been a good deal of agreement that Professor Holt was doing valuable work at the microeconomic level, but doubts on whether one could extend it to the macroeconomic level.

Professor Bergmann's paper represented an interesting analysis of what Professor Holt called the 'sorting process'. There was some feeling that more division was needed between quits, fires and drop-outs, but Professor Bergmann would be working on this. There was also some uncertainty on how the parameters were established. One conclusion was that most women were in a segment of the market where there were few very attractive jobs so that there was high labour turnover, but a reduction of barriers in the labour market might reduce turnover and make the situation worse. Professor Bergmann would no doubt add that the revolution in the position of women in society would in any case lead to a change in the roles of men and women in work.

The discussion had pointed to some difference in the response of labour turn-over in different countries. In Sweden, the 'captive worker effect' had resulted from the fear that if one left a firm one would have no job. This seemed to have reduced turnover. In France, however, there had been a steady increase in turnover during fifteen years, and it had been little affected by the recent recession. The conference did, however, seem to agree that labour market segmentation was important. Professor Hines had even gone so far as to suggest that women and blacks represented a reserve army of labour.

On the future, Professor Emmerij had raised two important questions. First, what kind of future would we have? Second, how would we adjust to it? Differences of view about how things might develop over the next twenty years had not been reconciled. He himself agreed with Professor Eastman and Lord Kaldor that there was much to do, for example, in developing new sources of energy. He also thought that many current problems would turn out to be temporary. The issues were unresolved, but he would make three points. First, he had been interested that others had repeated what he said at the beginning. Economists were consistently surprised when the future turned out to be different from the past. For example, there had been astonishment in the 1950s when the depression of the 1930s had not returned. Second, we had to remember Professor Modigliani's point that when we thought a problem was unbeatable it often disappeared, so that a minimum of good luck would work wonders! Third, Professor Georgescu-Roegen had asked us to remember that in the physical world there was no stationary state. There were likely to be continuing developments, many of which we did not anticipate. As a student in 1946, he and his colleagues had spent a good deal of time asking when the next great depression would come, but never whether it would arrive. As Professor Georgescu-Roegen said, the stationary state might have surprisingly dynamic shocks, and, at present, even in developed countries, people insisted on increasing real living standards and would work for these. One must remember another quotation about physical science. On the title page of Marshall's *Principles of Economics* there was the phase 'Nature does not make a leap'. There were some discontinuities but the underlying trends were the important element. He would emphasise that the only things one could change overnight were expectations and prices, an important point to remember in analysing what had happened in 1973–74.

Professor Emmerij had also looked at whether there would in future be constant or rising real incomes, and whether the active labour force would increase or decrease. His impression was that during the conference many participants had been thrown because they saw themselves faced by an entirely new situation, and one which they found difficult to discuss. As John Stuart Mill had said in the quotation recalled by Professor Tsuru, it would mean that we had to learn the art of living.

Yet the conference had clung to old ideas. Both Professor Tsuru and Professor Khachaturov seemed to be slaves to the protestant work ethic, which Professor Hague had not realised they even espoused! Moreover, it seemed that participants from socialist countries felt cheated at the suggestion that the crisis of capitalism might not be terminal. Greater wealth might lead to greater choice, and there might be no need for planning. Even so, it was clear that choice would be difficult because, as Professor Tsuru had said, if Professor Emmerij was correct, society would have to be revolutionised, one had to hope that this was possible peacefully.

Professor Hague noted that 1984 was now only six years away and, for him, too many participants had called for national planning in the future. He was therefore glad that Professor Kolm was worried about the increasing power of the bureaucracy. With Professor Emmerij he would, however, be happy if the bureaucrats were called upon only for a framework into which they could fit free choice by the individual.

Others went further, especially those from socialist countries, calling for planning to ensure that the individual did what was required of him. Why could one not give human beings the choice to work out their own response to living in a wealthy society? It was ridiculous to suppose that people would not be able to choose sensibly between work, education, retirement and other things. At least, they might, as Professor Kolm had pointed out, choose circuses, or their modern equivalent, football matches.

He was worried that some participants were behaving as the equivalent of Professor Samuelson's favourite soap-box orator. They seemed to be saying, 'When the revolution comes, my friends, you will eat your strawberries and cream, or take your retirement, or your period of training, and like it'.

If increasing wealth did give us greater choice in future about whether to work or not, he would himself leave the organisation of the new situation to individuals and small groups rather than see it imposed by the state. However, there was first the question of whether we were, or were likely to see ourselves as being, rich enough for such change. We in developed countries might be, but did we not have a duty first to less-developed countries? Perhaps we should spend a period reducing unemployment in the richer countries by working to produce goods which we then gave to less-developed countries. The issue had been mentioned during the conference, and he would be worried if it was simply cast aside without, first, a good deal of heart searching.

Professor Modigliani said his feelings about the conference took him back to what he had been told during a bus trip during the conference. He learned that Alsace had been created by the erosion of a mountain into a plain with little hills. He felt the conference had failed to discuss the core of its own mountain. There had simply been a reconnaissance on the periphery which had not looked at the basic structure. He was not sure how far others would agree, but he would like to find out.

He felt that at the core of unemployment today there was a conscious political decision, perhaps helped by confusion, that we must fight inflation by increased slack. He agreed that development had happened in real terms, but felt there was a gap between where we were and where we could have been. In particular, there was the fact that we had underconsumption resulting from saving caused by the action of OPEC. He agreed that this had generated an increase in savings, but that did not necessarily justify calls for an increase in consumption spending. One could have offset the shift. The most intelligent thing would have been to increase investment, but we had not done that and part of the reason was the determination to fight inflation. Most governments were convinced that more aggressive monetary expense would simply lead to price increases. Perhaps, instead, they had ended by using the extra savings of those with a low propensity to consume to finance increasing government deficits and unemployment. There was some underconsumption and some pure waste. But there was also underinvestment.

He agreed that one would choose football matches or circuses. Herbert Simon had said that the circus of the modern world was not the football match but the space programme. Perhaps the USA now needed an expanded space programme.

On Professor Holt's paper, he would like to get back to the basic issue.

At the core of the mountain, a fundamental question was whether what lay behind inflation was a modified Phillips curve or rational expectations. In the medium term there was a correlation between accelerated inflation and the level of employment. If there were too few vacancies, firms would increase wages. If increased demand led to enough jobs, vacancies would persist and acceleration would continue. This was what he meant by equilibrium unemployment. He thought there was enough stability for some kind of Phillips curve to be used. With an equilibrium rate of unemployment, one got a constant rate of inflation, not a zero rate. However, a reduction in the rate of inflation led to more slack. The trade-off was modest, and American experience was inconsistent. The mechanism was slow and hit by random shocks. This was especially so if one had, for example, an increase in the minimum wage, social security payments, agricultural protection etc.

If one looked at Professor Holt's paper, he thought much of the objection to it in the conference had been over Professor Holt's remark that there were two costs to the firm. First, there was the wage rate; second, there were other variables, or the difficulty of filling vacancies. One could construct an indifference curve relating them. Given the wage rate and the number of vacancies, one could have another set with the same cost to the firm. It was quite possible to have the same equilibrium, in principle, with two different combinations of wages and vacancies. However, if one went to the macroeconomic level, he doubted if this held true. Wages were set by firms in the labour market, and the wage rate did depend on Professor Holt's factors, but not through the wage bargain. However, there was an equilibrium situation. The cause of unemployment was not a new factor which arose in 1974, but the consequence of the price shock.

Professor Holt pointed out that macroeconomic and microeconomic issues reacted in very complicated ways. At the macroeconomic level, the traditional, static Phillips curve analysis looked at the trade-off between inflation and unemployment. We now saw that the situation was dynamic and that the trade-off in the short run was with unemployment, and in the medium run with inflation. This led to the question of the level of aggregate demand. One could not deal adequately with this question by looking at a closed economy, but needed to look at the international trade balance and the open economy. This led one on to trade issues and structural questions. How could one adjust easily and at low cost to lubricate the employment process and minimise the aggregate response of wages and prices? One had to remove friction, not to movements of relative prices and wages but at the aggregate level.

These were short- to medium-run issues. Long-run issues had to do with agriculture, technology, population, life-styles, and the development of the third world. There had been concern in the conference with Europe, where unemployment problems seemed to be short-run and medium-run. Perhaps one should stick to issues of macroeconomic demand, international trade and structure.

In response to points made about his own model, Professor Holt said Professor Modigliani had asked whether the model of allocation by wages and availability was more applicable to sectors. He thought now, having examined aggregation, that it did apply at the macroeconomic level. It had long been recognised that the classical model posed problems if the wage rate were too high. In his own model he was looking at recent processes. Where firms had a slack labour market, the internal operation of the firm could be damaged as increasing demand led to increasing employment. Each firm had fewer potential employees, and of lower quality, to take on. So productivity fell. If one had very aggressive trade unions and high wage rates, then to pay those high wage rates might not be acceptable unless the firm faced slack in the labour market. There was a conflict between efficiency in the firm and in society. One could get this at the aggregate as well as at the sectoral level.

Professor Kolm noted contradictions in what Professor Modigliani had said. He said that the transfer to OPEC had increased savings. He also said that these savings could have been used for investment, but that would have led to inflation. Professor Kolm objected a little to discussion of the 'OPEC crisis'. This was not simply a question of increased savings or the behaviour of the oil countries. It was partly a result of operational research, diplomatic history, etc. It was due to the fact that because the oil industry was an oligopoly, it behaved as if it were a monopolist faced with customers. One knew what happened then. If an oil company asked an operational researcher what to do about long-run profits he would suggest that high prices should be charged to reap monopoly profits which could then be invested in the development of alternative energy sources. The price increase was therefore suggested to OPEC by the US oil companies with the support of the US government. He thought these were very important points.

As for the Phillips curve, he thought this took too simple a view. It looked for the point where the rate of inflation was zero, but an inflationary régime was more complex than that.

The crisis had been used to stop inflation, but another solution would have been to push the rules of the game to the limit; for example, through price control. This might be politically difficult, but it was certainly possible. Professor Kolm did not want the sovietisation of the western economies, but one could modify the whole system, and especially the relation of unemployment to society. The crisis was a case for research.

Professor Bergmann said Professor Modigliani's contribution caused her to remember 1961–62. There had been little inflation in the USA, but widespread resistance to increasing aggregate demand in order to reduce unemployment. This was not because it would lead to inflation but because it might. It was said that an increase in employment was impossible because round pegs would not move into square holes. She was forced to the conclusion that there must be somebody there who did not love full employment. Perhaps it was a result of the attitudes of those who wanted the labour force to show proper respect for their jobs. She thought it significant that fear of inflation did not stop governments increasing agricultural prices, reducing imports etc. There was resistance to increasing aggregate demand even where opinion was averse to fighting inflation directly and then dealing with the demand problem.

On the problem of the employment of young people, six or seven years ago Professor Feldstein, noting high unemployment rates for them, had said that one difficulty was that young people had no good way of achieving an acceptable position for themselves in the labour force. Feldstein said that what the USA needed was a European system of pointing youth in the direction of jobs, and that there would then be a smooth transition between school and the labour market. Now, the Europeans were also finding the employment of young people difficult, and a new solution was necessary. Perhaps for a person in an unhealthy environment the weakest part of the organism sickened. If so, it meant that the development of a healthy environment was necessary. If we could, we should move back to a state of healthy demand for labour.

She wanted to remind the conference that in the USA in 1940–44 the labour market was nearly all made up of the low-quality labour, which was now alleged to cause trouble. These were people not in the Army, but the labour market worked well and unemployment was low. This was done under wage and price control.

Professor Henin said one point leading to problems was whether the cost of labour relative to capital was too high. The conference had looked much at Keynesian unemployment, where high wages did not mean more unemployment. Perhaps insufficient attention had been paid to other aspects of the question. When one looked at the supply side, the neo-classical approach said that everything depended on the scale of substitution. Professor Henin did not think the problem could be solved outside the context of vintage models.

In a putty-clay model, a high elasticity of substitution had two opposite effects on the number of jobs. First, the higher the degree of technical substitution was, the more an increase in wages would reduce the number of jobs in new capital vintages. But more substitution would also mean that labour-augmenting technical progress would generate less labour-saving bias. According to some earlier personal work in this field, the second effect could well dominate the first, the traditional neo-classical substitution. In that case more substitution would mean more jobs on new vintages.

He found that putty-clay models gave a consistent account of aspects of recent economic experience. In one of his own studies, he had found that wages corresponded quite well to their predicted level, namely, average productivity on the last vintage in use. One way of reading the story was in terms of classical unemployment, increasing wages reducing the number of profitable vintages and then employment. But the story was not inconsistent with a Keynesian demand-constrained situation. The same situation came then from invested causality. When union pressure was strong, and aggregate demand was falling, old vintages were put out of use but wages could continue to rise until they reached the average productivity level for the other vintage in use, which depended on aggregate demand. So we had a pure Keynesian unemployment; not general excess supply but a situation on the boundary between Keynesian (in the wide sense) and classical unemployment.

On economic policy, Professor Modigliani had suggested that the conference had been inconsistent on many points, but perhaps one had to go further. One had to recognise some inconsistency in both Keynes' and the 'Keynesian's' position on economic policy. One could agree with Modigliani on the deficiency of market system in regulating aggregate investment and income. One could agree with him on the efficiency of the market system in allocating resources between goods. But one could not agree with both propositions because it was much harder for the market system to allocate resources than to guess the correct level of aggregate investment. So we could not correct any deficiency in regulation at the macro level without improving allocation at the micro level. This was the common error of Keynes, the Keynesians and the monetarists.

This 'non-separation theorem' between macro stabilisation and micro allocation policies implied some inconsistency in the separating of the short-term stabilisation objectives from longer term allocation ones. Some kind of indicative and flexible planning was the proper locus of an employment policy.

Sir Austin Robinson was less happy than some participants. He had been worried by things that had not been fully discussed, or even discussed at all.

There were two kinds of problem. First, there was the question of how much unemployment there should be. Second, there was the question of who should be unemployed. He shared the worries of Dr Gordon and Professor Bergmann over the unemployment of the young and the underprivileged, but he thought this was a symptom of a wider issue. One obtained economic progress by releasing resources as industry became more efficient and absorbing these resources into new expanding activities.

Since 1974 expansion had broken down, with the adjustment taking place by a reduction in the number of old and of young people taken into work. The effects of the breakdown had fallen heavily on youth. This was deplorable, but perhaps a symptom rather than a cause. It made it necessary to come back to the question, not of who was unemployed, but of how much employment there was. The question was, why were things going reasonably well until 1973, and so badly since? To answer that question would be to get to the root of the problem. Why could we handle expansion well in the 1950s and 1960s? Why was it more difficult now?

Perhaps one had to start by asking what were the constraints. Why was economic activity not growing faster? He thought the first question to be asked was how important inflation was in inhibiting growth. Had it become more important? Had we suddenly recognised its importance? Did we now value price stability more? He was not sure that this was the change.

Perhaps the change had been a more dangerous one – a change of the whole process of wage bargaining. He had shared in the general admiration for the skill of presentation in Professor Parkin's paper, but thought that Professor Parkin's concern with a particular 'patent medicine' prevented him from looking at how the way we handled inflation reacted on our handling of employment. If we asked different people whether inflation was today more dangerous, we should get different answers. He would himself say that it was more dangerous for the balance of payments.

If one looked at the world in general, it was true that we were now trying to run a more open world economy. The success in the 1950s and 1960s had come because countries had managed to expand in step. Expansion now was not very rapid because if one country expanded too quickly this would lead to balance of payments problems. Economies were now more open and thus more sensitive, and the emphasis on inflation was, in part, due to the impact of inflation on the balance of payments. This was, he suggested, more important than the effect on internal issues.

Another constraint was the limitation of supply. Again, one should ask why economies were more sensitive than they used to be. Perhaps, again, the point was that the remedy for a shortage was to import, and this led to balance of payments difficulties. Even more, there had been a reluctance to invest, and balance increased demand with increased capacity. This led back to the level of profit. However, there was also in the UK now a different concept of prudent management. In the 1950s and 1960s prudent business management meant expansion to seize opportunities. More recently, there had been concentration on maintaining liquidity and in taking care that overexpansion should not lead to vulnerability and difficulties. There was therefore now a condemnation of managers for behaving in ways that would earlier have been seen as showing that they were competent.

Sir Austin said he would like, in conclusion, to emphasise a point made earlier. There was currently a need to adjust to major changes. It was not just OPEC that had affected commodity prices. The increase in the price of wheat had begun through the agricultural problems of the USSR. Adjustment was also needed to the creation of the EEC and the uncertainty to which that led in deciding where comparative advantage now lay. So more structural change was required than in the 1950s and 1960s.

He would therefore like to ask Professor Malinvaud a political question. If one looked at the processes and instruments influencing adjustment to structural change within a country, one found that all countries had some form of regional policy to deal with declining regions. Such policies were used to control and steer and mitigate the rate of change. He wondered whether some policy instruments, used to deal with regional problems within countries, were left out when one was working on a world scale? We paid lip-service to free international trade, but failed to take account of possible speeds of transition. Perhaps the policies of the EEC for dealing with backward areas were not able to deal with the scale of the problem presenting

itself in Europe. The magnitude of adjustment required had grown, and with
it the difficulty of structural adjustment of the speed that was required.

Professor Malinvaud recalled that Professor Hague had mentioned the
constraints imposed by raw materials, seeming to suggest that constraints
on raw materials were general, and that oil was simply a special case. He
did not want to let this pass because he had a personal interest in the question.
He was convinced that energy was the only case of exceptional shortage. Of
course, there might in the future be shortages of food, which might become
important. He did not think it was necessary at present to engage in much
rethinking to deal with other supposed scarcities.

It had been suggested that there had been too much concentration in
the conference on macroeconomic issues. He would agree with this, even
though that was the field of his own work. He had come to the conference
with no knowledge of labour markets etc. and wanted more information on
microeconomic problems. Professor Bergmann had suggested that, to solve
the problem of youth unemployment, one would have to suppress
underemployment. He wondered whether she was saying that this was the
only way of doing it, or perhaps the best way? If it were the only way, then
he was depressed, because this meant that only macroeconomics had
anything to say.

Perhaps macroeconomic distortions led to unemployment. He thought
there had not been enough discussion of this. We had the habit, at the
macroeconomic level, of describing prices, in relation to output, labour and
capital, by two indicators: the rate of pure profit and the cost of labour
relative to capital. The question we should face was whether there had been
disturbances or not, because of the cost of labour relative to capital, or
because the rate of pure profit was too low. By and large, he thought most
economists would agree that the cost of labour relative to capital was too
high. He thought that acceptance of Professor Rehn's proposal of special
labour subsidies would then lead to some reduction in the marginal cost of
labour.

There was less agreement on the idea that the rate of pure profit was too
low. Lord Kaldor would probably protest that this was because global demand
was low, and so the conclusions were not quite what they might seem.
Perhaps one should refer to the full employment rate of profit. Then there
might be differences between countries. There probably were before 1973, and
these might still be there. A serious study by Feldstein on the rate of profit
in the USA showed that this was not exceptionally low. Professor Giersch
had reminded us of the increased uncertainty faced today when taking
decisions to invest. This was due in part to inflation, but in part to low
growth and to increasing competition from newly-industrialising countries.
This increased uncertainty might require, other things being equal, an
increase in the rate of profit. Assuming that, recently, the cost of labour relative
to capital had been too high, and the rate of profit too low, this might no

longer be quite true in his own country, now that price control had been removed.

If what he had said was correct, operation on relative prices was difficult, not least because of the interdependence of relative prices and aggregate demand. The first effect of an increase in prices was to reduce aggregate demand. This feature made the policy problem particularly difficult.

He thought one had moreover to distinguish two factors. The first was the re-equilibration of aggregate demand within the country. The second was the distribution of aggregate demand at the international level, where past development had produced some distortions. If there was a lack of adjustment in aggregate demand or relative prices, and if growth was slow, one would need marked sectoral adjustments. The Georgescu-Roegen–Fitoussi paper had shown that there could be serious problems at the sectoral and regional level. Structural policies, not only those appropriate to the labour market, were needed.

To Professor Robinson, he would say that the question was whether France should make a bigger effort to develop the poorest sectors of the EEC. This depended on the degree of solidarity in Europe, and he did not seem an enthusiastic member of the EEC, and it was therefore hard to persuade French voters to be helpful.

Sir Austin Robinson pointed out that he had not been asking for charity, but simply wanted to know how far the EEC saw itself as an organisation committed to achieving full employment.

Professor Kolm noted that Professor Malinvaud saw two sources of difficulty. One was deficient demand; the other was relative prices, especially the relationship between wages and the cost of capital. With inflation, the cost of capital was negative, so that one could say that wages were high if the cost of capital was not low. He wondered what the conclusion was.

Professor Malinvaud replied that the cost of labour was made up, not only of wages and social cost, but also of taxation and other elements.

Professor Kolm said the question was still whether one should reduce wages or the cost of capital.

Professor Malinvaud replied that a reduction in wages would reduce the cost of labour relative to capital and raise the profit margin. However, he wanted to insist that he did not have any ready-made solution.

Professor Odaka said that problems might arise from a lack of political leadership on economic policy. The Japanese were not yet monetarists. The budget had always been in surplus so that there had been tax reductions. Now the budget was in deficit, and the Finance Ministry found it difficult to know what to do. Perhaps economic behaviour had changed since the oil shock. One could once explain the level of consumption in Japan by the Duesenberry hypothesis. This seemed no longer possible because the propensity to save was high despite recession in recent years. Perhaps attitudes had changed.

Professor Odaka was pleased that Professor Modigliani said that the labour market determined money and not real wages, though real wages were clearly related to them. He would hate to be on the side of those who said that Japan was different, but there were noticeable differences on unemployment. Japan also had a labour market where wages, even real wages, were more flexible.

Professor Emmerij wanted to look at four points needing discussion, all of which were long-run issues. He wanted to start from the point that the developed countries were not alone on an island, but operated in a sea of less-developed countries. First, there was the question of what rate of growth among developed countries would lead to full employment, given the problems discussed by Sir Austin Robinson. On technology, discussion in developed countries ignored the question of what was an appropriate technology for less-developed countries. If, as he did, one assumed a slower rate of growth, then the capital/labour ratio became important.

Second, there was the role of the public sector. There had been little systematic discussion of this, or of the socialisation of demand. If one agreed that the private sector found it hard to preserve jobs, one had to look at what the public sector could do. There was less international competition here and so more scope in adapting technology. The question was how to stimulate demand, and to make a useful contribution to the situation.

Third, there was the internationalisation of demand — the worldwide Marshall Plan. This could boost industrialisation in the less-developed countries, and by the same token boost demand in developed countries. It was necessary to discuss this in relation to the international division of labour, and perhaps the accelerator impact on industry in developed countries. Could we look at this in terms of the relative costs of capital and labour, or should we even welcome it?

Finally, there was intervention on the supply side. There had been mention of this in discussion of his paper, but we needed to look at more effective ways of organising its 'presentation' to the labour market. One had to remember that there were other objectives as well as unemployment.

Professor Bergmann answered Professor Malinvaud on the problem of participatory groups. She was saying that one should not do nothing because one feared that this was a zero-sum game. One could spread unemployment between groups. The difficulty was that young people had to bear so much of the burden. This was not so true of blacks, because their need for integration had been accepted. She thought one had to look at the problem in terms of a hierarchy of groups.

Index

Entries in the index in bold type under the names of participants in the Conference indicate their Papers or Discussions of their Papers. Entries in italic type indicate contributions by participants to the Discussions.